100 Voices
~
An Oral History of Ayn Rand

Scott McConnell

NEW AMERICAN LIBRARY

New American Library
Published by New American Library, a division of
Penguin Group (USA) Inc., 375 Hudson Street,
New York, New York 10014, USA
Penguin Group (Canada), 90 Eglinton Avenue East, Suite 700, Toronto,
Ontario M4P 2Y3, Canada (a division of Pearson Penguin Canada Inc.)
Penguin Books Ltd., 80 Strand, London WC2R 0RL, England
Penguin Ireland, 25 St. Stephen's Green, Dublin 2,
Ireland (a division of Penguin Books Ltd.)
Penguin Group (Australia), 250 Camberwell Road, Camberwell, Victoria 3124,
Australia (a division of Pearson Australia Group Pty. Ltd.)
Penguin Books India Pvt. Ltd., 11 Community Centre, Panchsheel Park,
New Delhi - 110 017, India
Penguin Group (NZ), 67 Apollo Drive, Rosedale, North Shore 0632,
New Zealand (a division of Pearson New Zealand Ltd.)
Penguin Books (South Africa) (Pty.) Ltd., 24 Sturdee Avenue,
Rosebank, Johannesburg 2196, South Africa

Penguin Books Ltd., Registered Offices:
80 Strand, London WC2R 0RL, England

Published by New American Library,
a division of Penguin Group (USA) Inc.

First Printing, November 2010
10   9   8   7   6   5   4   3   2   1

NAL REGISTERED TRADEMARK—MARCA REGISTRADA

LIBRARY OF CONGRESS CATALOGING-IN-PUBLICATION DATA:

McConnell, Scott, 1958–
  100 voices: an oral history of Ayn Rand/Scott McConnell.
      p. cm.
  Interviews conducted between 1996 and 2003 with Ayn Rand's family members, friends, and
associates.
  "The Ayn Rand Oral History Program began in April 1996 as a project of the Ayn Rand
Archives, a department of the Ayn Rand Institute"—Pref.
  Includes index.
  ISBN 978-0-451-23130-7
  1.   Rand, Ayn. 2.   Novelists, American—20th century—Biography. 3.   Philosophers—
United States—Biography. 4.   Rand, Ayn—Family—Interviews. 5.   Rand, Ayn—Friends and
associates—Interviews. I. Ayn Rand Archives. II. Title. III. Title: One hundred voices.
  PS3535.A547Z79 2010
  813'.52—dc22   2010028772
  [B]

Printed in the United States of America

Contents

1950s

1960s

1970s

1980s

Preface

The Ayn Rand Oral History Program began in April 1996 as a project of the Ayn Rand Archives, a department of the Ayn Rand Institute. The purpose of the program was to gather and preserve knowledge about Ayn Rand's life. It supplements the Archives' collections of Ayn Rand's personal papers and related materials in all media.

From 1996 to 2003, I tracked down and interviewed family members, friends and associates of Ayn Rand's and edited their interviews. The first interview I conducted was of the woman who inspired the character Peter Keating in *The Fountainhead*. (See the 1930s chapter.) I conducted more than one hundred and sixty interviews, for a total of more than three hundred hours and approximately five thousand pages of raw transcript. Nearly all of the interviews were taped, with the vast majority being conducted over the phone. The shortest interview was three minutes; the longest was fifty-two hours (twenty-five phone meetings over a two-year period). Interviewee locations ranged across the globe, from Saint Petersburg, Russia, to Geneva, Switzerland; from New York to Los Angeles to Hawaii and Australia. All but two of the interviews were conducted by me, the exceptions being the interviews of Ayn Rand's sister in Saint Petersburg and Ayn Rand's French-speaking cousin in Switzerland, who were interviewed in their native languages, with questions I supplied.

I selected the interviews in this collection to cover a broad range of years, contexts, relationships and observations, and to supplement the limited number of reliable biographical sources available elsewhere. Not all the interviewees are fans; nor did they all admire Ayn Rand or agree with her ideas. Those interviewed provide new and valuable perspectives on Ayn Rand, and no interview has been previously published. The reader will "hear" Ayn Rand's family, friends, fans, associates, doctor, dentist, lawyer and secretaries. Discussing her will be a former prime minister, a rock guitarist, Hollywood stars, TV celebrities, university professors, fiction writers and philosophers.

And while some interviewees discuss her ideas, this book focuses, not on philosophical issues or literature, but rather on Ayn Rand's personal and business life. It focuses on the private Ayn Rand—the

Ayn Rand whom most people did not know—Ayn Rand in her living room or study, at work, at a party, with her nieces, at the theater, or in her doctor's or lawyer's office. Covering almost seventy years from the mid-1910s to her death in 1982, topics and contexts discussed include Ayn Rand as employee, employer, friend, host, houseguest, portrait model, mentor, editor, lecturer, fiction writer, client, godmother and Playboy Club "tour guide." The interviews reveal Ayn Rand angry, happy, betrayed, in love, fighting for her values, triumphant. They also show many aspects of her personality and the wide range of her values and life experiences.

I have organized the interviews in chronological order, and in order to better show Ayn Rand's relationships and life and to support the storytelling drama of the remembrances, I did not break up the interviews into separate themes and topics.

The interviews in *100 Voices: An Oral History of Ayn Rand* are edited extracts of the original oral interviews. From these I have cut many repeated stories and observations, but some repetition of content remains, in order to keep true to the person's relationship with Miss Rand, or due to the interviewee's request. I edited these published transcripts to eliminate lack of clarity, wordiness or confusing grammatical slips and in many cases reorganized them for logic and/or drama. But I have kept the oral, conversational tone of interviews that reflect the individual voices of the interviewees and the content of their communication. It should be emphasized that every interviewee (or heir) approved his or her interview as published in this volume.

Because remembrances can be faulty, all statements of fact have (where possible) been checked for consistency with other interviews and material in Ayn Rand's papers or in other document collections. But not every recollection can be affirmed and consistency does not guarantee accuracy. These are the thoughts and recollections of the interviewees. Neither I nor the Ayn Rand Institute necessarily agree with all the interviewees' factual claims; inconsistencies have been identified and corrections of facts have been provided in footnotes where necessary. Other footnotes provide the historical background needed to understand an interviewee's comment.

A project of this size and duration demands important thank-yous. First, to transcriptionists Larry Salzman, Marc Baer and Robert Benz, and to archivist Jeff Britting. To Simon Federman for his layout/production contributions. To Donna Montrezza for her proofreading, copyediting and design contributions. To Alexander Lebedev and Irina Chabatayeva, whose research work in Russia made the interviews of Ayn Rand's sister possible. And especially to Michael S. Berliner, not only for his editorial assistance, but, as the Ayn Rand Institute's then executive director and now senior archives adviser, for his much valuable—and appreciated—advice and support over the full length of this project.

Of course, the greatest thanks belong to the interviewees themselves. They have given generously, often enthusiastically, of their time and memories of Ayn Rand, and allowed their anecdotes and observations to be recorded and published. They have often donated to the Ayn Rand Archives historically significant material such as photographs and copies of Ayn Rand book dedications and letters. The Archives and I wish to express our most grateful thanks to the interviewees in this book and to the dozens of others whose words reside permanently in our tape collection. These individuals have enriched our knowledge of Ayn Rand and provided the opportunity for an adventure that enriched my life.

What emerges from this collection is the picture of a larger-than-life, truly unique and fascinating individual, Ayn Rand. I hope that readers of this book are as fascinated by these recollections as I was when first hearing them.

—Scott McConnell
Los Angeles

While at the Ayn Rand Institute, Scott McConnell established the Media Department, as well as the Oral History Program. He has lectured in the United States, Europe and Australia on Ayn Rand's life and has appeared on radio and television discussing Rand's life and thought. His writings have been published in The Intellectual Activist *and in* Essays on Ayn Rand's "We the Living." *Mr. McConnell is now a documentary producer living in Los Angeles.*

Chronology of Ayn Rand's Life

1897   *September 22: Frank O'Connor (Ayn Rand's husband) born in Lorain, Ohio*

1904   *May 3: Parents married*

1905   *February 2 (January 20 on Julian calendar): Born in St. Petersburg*

1907   *June 28: Sister Natasha born in St. Petersburg*

1910   *September 4: Sister Nora born in St. Petersburg*

1918   *Fall: Family moves to Ukraine*

1919   *Spring: Family moves to Yevpatoria, in Crimea*

1921   *Family returns to Petrograd*

       August 24 (circa): Enters Petrograd State University

1926   *January 16: Departs Leningrad*

       January 20: Departs Soviet Union

       February 10: Departs Le Havre on the S.S. De Grasse *for America*

       February 19: Arrives in New York

       February to August: Resides in Chicago

       August (circa): Hollywood: American Movie City *published in Soviet Union*

September 3: Arrives in Hollywood

September 4: Meets Cecil B. DeMille

1927 *January 11 (circa): Hired by DeMille as a junior screen writer*

1929 *April 15: Marries Frank O'Connor in Los Angeles*

May (circa): Begins work in the RKO wardrobe department

June 29: Obtains a green card upon return from Mexico

1931 *March 13: Becomes a U.S. citizen*

1932 *September 2: Sells "Red Pawn"; hired by Universal Pictures*

1933 *July 12: Hired by Metro-Goldwyn-Mayer for eight weeks*

1934 *April 9: Makes first entry in philosophic journal*

June 25: Hired by Paramount Pictures

October 22: Woman on Trial *opens at Hollywood Playhouse*

November 24: Moves to New York City

1935 *September 16:* Night of January 16th *opens on Broadway*

December 4: Makes first notes for The Fountainhead

1936 *April 18:* We the Living *published*

1938 *May 7 (circa):* Anthem *published in England*

June 26: Begins writing The Fountainhead

1939 *Early January: Receives last communication from parents in Soviet Union*

1940   *February 13:* The Unconquered *opens on Broadway*

1942   *December 31: Delivers* The Fountainhead *manuscript to Bobbs-Merrill*

1943   *May 8: Official publication of* The Fountainhead

August 18: Writes outline for "The Moral Basis of Individualism"

October 12: Sells The Fountainhead *to Warner Bros.*

November 25: Travels by train to California

1944   *July 1944 to October 1951: Resides at 10,000 Tampa Ave., Chatsworth, California*

June/July: Hired as a screenwriter by Hal Wallis

September: Writes screenplay for Love Letters

1945   *January 1: First notes for* Atlas Shrugged

December 24: First episode of the illustrated newspaper serial of The Fountainhead *appears in newspapers*

1946   *January 19: Writes outline for screenplay about the atomic bomb*

February 2: Begins writing Atlas Shrugged

February 18: Attends her first meeting of the Motion Picture Alliance.

July: Anthem *(revised edition) published by Pamphleteers*

1947   *October 20: Testifies before House Un-American Activities Committee*

1948   *March 23: Begins work on* The Fountainhead *film at Warner Bros.*

1949   *June 23:* The Fountainhead *movie opens at Warner's Hollywood Theater*

1951   *October 17: Leaves for New York City*

October 23: Arrives in New York City

1953   *First American hardcover edition of* Anthem, *published by Caxton*

1955   *October 13: Finishes Galt's speech*

1957   *March 20: Finishes* Atlas Shrugged

October 10: Atlas Shrugged *published*

November 30: First notes for unpublished novel, tentatively titled "To Lorne Dieterling"

1958   *January 18: Begins fiction-writing class*

March 6: Gives first campus talk (Queens College)

1960   *February 17: Delivers "Faith and Force" talk at Yale*

1961   *March 24:* For the New Intellectual *published by Random House*

March 26: Delivers first Ford Hall Forum talk: "The Intellectual Bankruptcy of Our Age"

May 14: Delivers "Esthetic Vacuum" talk at U. of Michigan Arts Festival

1962   *January: First issue of* The Objectivist Newsletter*; Nathaniel Branden Institute (NBI) opens*

June 17: First Los Angeles Times *column printed*

October 2: First radio show appearance, WKCR (Columbia University)

1963 *February 2: Delivers "How Not to Fight Against Socialized Medicine" talk in Ocean County, New Jersey*

September 29: Delivers "America's Persecuted Minority: Big Business" talk at McCormick Place in Chicago

October 2: Receives honorary doctorate from Lewis and Clark University

1964 *December:* The Virtue of Selfishness *published by New American Library*

1966 *April: First installment of* Introduction to Objectivist Epistemology *appears in* The Objectivist

November 23: Capitalism: The Unknown Ideal *published by New American Library*

1967 *August 16: First appearance on the* Tonight Show Starring Johnny Carson

1968 *May: NBI closes*

1969 *March 8: Begins nonfiction-writing class*

July 16: Witnesses Apollo 11 *launch at Cape Canaveral*

October 11: Gives first workshop on Objectivist epistemology

November: The Romantic Manifesto *published by World Publishing*

1971 *October 11: First issue of* The Ayn Rand Letter *published*

September: The New Left: The Anti-Industrial Revolution *published by New American Library*

1974   *March 6: Gives talk at West Point ("Philosophy: Who Needs It")*

September 4: Attends White House swearing-in of Alan Greenspan as chairman of the Council of Economic Advisers

1976   *January to February: Publishes last issue of* The Ayn Rand Letter

July 27: Attends White House dinner for Malcolm Fraser

1977   *April 10: Ford Hall Forum luncheon honors Ayn Rand*

September 6 to 18: Outlines script for Atlas Shrugged *miniseries*

1979   *April:* Introduction to Objectivist Epistemology *published by New American Library*

May 1: Appears on the Phil Donahue Show

November 9: Frank O'Connor dies

1981   *June 10: Writes first page of* Atlas Shrugged *miniseries*

April 26: Delivers last Ford Hall Forum talk: "The Age of Mediocrity"

November 21: Delivers last lecture, "The Sanction of the Victims," in New Orleans

1982   *January 1: Final writing for script of* Atlas Shrugged *miniseries*

March 6: Dies in New York City

100 Voices
~
An Oral History of Ayn Rand

The Interviews

Eleanora Drobysheva

Eleanora "Nora" (Rosenbaum) Drobysheva was Ayn Rand's youngest sister. Mrs. Drobysheva died on March 12, 1999, at the age of eighty-eight. Ayn Rand (born Alisa Rosenbaum) was closer to Mrs. Drobysheva than to any other relative, as attested to in Ayn Rand's biographical interviews in 1960–61[1] and by Mrs. Drobysheva's letters to Ayn Rand between 1926 and 1936. Separated for forty-seven years until 1973, when Miss Rand learned that Mrs. Drobysheva was still alive, they were reunited in New York City. However, their values had diverged over the years, and their relationship ended unhappily.

Mrs. Drobysheva was interviewed numerous times between February 1997 and May 1998. The interviews were prepared and managed by Scott McConnell and conducted and organized by ARI's St. Petersburg researchers, Alexander Lebedev (who supplied most of the later footnote material), Irina Chabatayeva and Sergei Bernadskiy. Suspicious of strangers, even in those post-Soviet days, Mrs. Drobysheva was reluctant to speak about her family and declined to have the interviews tape recorded. The following (edited) transcript, mostly in chronological interview order, is from interview notes and summaries of answers. Using questions prepared by Scott McConnell, all interviews were conducted in Russian and translated into English by Dina Schein Federman. The ARI interviews of Eleanora Drobysheva are the only extensive interviews ever conducted with Ayn Rand's sister.

Report by Alexander Lebedev of first telephone interview with Mrs. Drobysheva, February 15, 1997

Mrs. Drobysheva could not clearly remember whether, in 1974, Ayn Rand had made her a definite offer to stay in the United States—"presumably it had been implied." Soviet officials had also implied the same thing: when Mrs. Drobysheva received her documents to visit the United States, officials told her: "If you would like to stay there for

---

1 In 1960–61 Ayn Rand gave approximately thirty-five hours of biographical interviews in preparation for Barbara Branden's biographical essay in *Who Is Ayn Rand?* (New York: Random House, 1962). Audiotapes and a transcript of the interviews reside in the Ayn Rand Archives.

good, just let the Soviet embassy know." Mrs. Drobysheva reported that "My husband and I decided to return—they lead a completely different life, which did not suit us."

Mrs. Drobysheva liked her sister's husband, Frank O'Connor—"so handsome and controlled." She was surprised that, although he had been an actor, he hadn't made a career in acting.

Mrs. Drobysheva does not think much of her sister's literary talent. She was genuinely surprised at the interest in the person, the literary work, and the philosophy of her sister. She believes that there are people who are more worthy of attention. When the issue of individualism came up several times, Mrs. Drobysheva kept talking about the unfortunate and the poor and the need of compassion for them. "Individualism must have a limit" is Mrs. Drobysheva's view.

Second telephone interview by Alexander Lebedev, April 1997

Alexander Lebedev: *Nora Zinovyevna, have you read* We the Living?

Eleanora Drobysheva: Yes, I have read it. Its heroine is in love with a Red and a White at the same time. You know, this is all contrived, don't you think? It's from the time of my childhood and I see how unnatural the whole thing is.

But it's written very well.

I have read many good books in my life—and many not so good, of course—but I can't admire this falsehood. Go ahead, judge me! And the novel doesn't resemble an autobiography either. She had just artificially constructed the whole thing while living in America, that's all. She had made up all of our lives, do you understand?[2]

Third telephone interview by Alexander Lebedev, April 15, 1997

Eleanora Zinovyevna Rosenbaum was born in 1910 in Sestroretsk, where the family often rented a summer house. She is a theatrical artist by pro-

---

2 For the relationship between characters in *We the Living* and Ayn Rand's family, see Scott McConnell, "Parallel Lives: Models and Inspirations for Characters in *We the Living*," in *Essays on Ayn Rand's "We the Living,"* ed. Robert Mayhew (Lanham, MD: Lexington Books, 2004).

fession, but after World War II she worked in display design and graphics.

She has a modest one-room apartment. The walls are decorated with antique plates, and a glass-walled cabinet contains several china figurines. Her narrow bookcase is crammed full of books. Among them are Carl Sandburg's biography of Abraham Lincoln, and books by Faulkner, Hemingway, Poe and Irwin Shaw. She has a summer house in Sosnovo, seventy kilometers from St. Petersburg. Mrs. Drobysheva does not like to complain about her life. She is tense around people she does not know and distrusts them. She is interested in politics. Among Russian politicians the one she likes best is Grigory Yavlinsky, the leader of the "Apple" [political] movement.

By the time the Rosenbaum family settled in St. Petersburg, the city already had a religious Jewish community, a synagogue, a Jewish cemetery, and several Jewish educational organizations. Boris Kaplan—Nora and Alisa's [Ayn Rand] grandfather—a tailor, had the right to live in St. Petersburg.[3] Zinovy Rosenbaum [Ayn Rand's father], a pharmacist, had a Warsaw university diploma; therefore, he too had the opportunity to settle in St. Petersburg.

Nora has mixed feelings about Alisa. Reminiscing about the years when they lived together, she calls her tenderly "Aliska," but she is critical of Ayn Rand, rejects her philosophy, considers her writing to be fake and lacking in talent. She considers only bits of her writing to be valuable. However, she treasures a short article with Ayn Rand's photograph from *The Columbia Encyclopedia*, which her friends printed off the Internet and gave to her.

The family also on occasion used to rent a summer house in Terijoki[4]—this is what they called Finland—as well as in Sestroretsk.

It was at the summer resort in Sestroretsk that the sisters listened to the marching band.[5]

In her childhood and during the 1920s Nora was close friends with Alisa. The sisters loved going to the movies. Mrs. Drobysheva remembered that in the 1920s they saw *The Cabinet of Dr. Caligari*, *Song of the Nibelungs*, *The Indian Tomb* and American movies. Alisa

---

3 Under the tsars, St. Petersburg was closed to most Jews.

4 Terijoki was a resort town on the gulf of Finland, thirty-five miles from St. Petersburg. After 1918 it belonged to independent Finland. After the Finnish war of 1939–40, it became part of the USSR. In 1948 it was renamed Zelenogorsk.

5 In her 1960–61 biographical interviews, Ayn Rand discusses being introduced at age six to music played by a military band in a park.

liked worldly movies, where Nora liked cowboy movies ("probably Alisa wanted to have a worldly life").[6]

Alisa liked Conrad Veidt, while Nora liked William Hart and Hans Albers. They both liked operettas. They would attend performances of [Emmerich Kálmán's] *Countess Maritza* and [Franz Lehár's] *Where the Lark Sings* in the smaller operatic theater. Both liked the tenor Stepan Balashov.

At that time among Alisa's circle of acquaintances was a Leo. Mrs. Drobysheva could not remember his last name.[7] He was hook-nosed and dark-haired, but Nora liked blonds, so she did not like him. Mrs. Drobysheva does not know what happened to him. Alisa had a boyfriend at the movie institute, but Mrs. Drobysheva could not remember anything about him.

When the Rosenbaums rented a summer house in Lisiy Nos, near St. Petersburg, Alisa's "fiancé" was a certain Seriozha, a blond. But Mrs. Drobysheva does not know his last name or what happened to him.

According to Mrs. Drobysheva, there were no major conflicts among the Rosenbaums, nor did Alisa and her mother clash.[8]

Mrs. Drobysheva remembers no evidence of any rebellion of Alisa against her parents. Alisa was the favorite of the whole family—and that says it all.

Alisa was close friends with her cousin Nina [Guzarchik], who was a daughter of her mother's sister Elizabeth.

Their middle sister, Natalia [aka Natasha], liked French novels and worked to get admitted to the conservatory. Her practicing the piano did not get on anybody's nerves—as Barbara Branden's book alleges. Mrs. Drobysheva called that book "dirty and slanderous." Natasha graduated from the conservatory and was married twice. Her first husband was named Isidor; they got married in 1920.[9]

In the Crimea the Rosenbaums lived in Yevpatoria in a two-storied house with a terrace. The girls attended the Yevpatoria gymnasium, whose windows faced the harbor. Natasha had tuberculosis. Natasha married for the second time in 1929.[10]

---

6 In a later interview, Mrs. Drobysheva described "worldly" as referring to "high society: romance, tuxedos, décolletés, floor-length ball gowns, diamonds."

7 His name was Lev Bekkerman and he was the model for Leo Kovalensky in *We the Living*.

8 This differs from what Rand said about her mother in a biographical interview.

9 They actually married in 1929.

10 She actually remarried in 1939.

Her second husband's name was Volodya. Their mother's brother, also named Volodya, was a lawyer and helped the Rosenbaums after they returned from the Crimea in the 1920s.

Zinovy Zacharovich Rosenbaum, Alisa and Nora's father, died in 1939 of heart disease. Their mother, Anna Borisovna, died in November 1941 at the beginning of the blockade, presumably of cancer.[11] They are both buried at the Jewish cemetery.[12]

Natasha died in June 1942 in Leningrad during an air raid, as she was taking a walk in the Mikhailovsky Park near the Church of the Savior's Blood [Church of the Savior on the Spilled Blood].

Cousin Nina died in the summer or fall of 1944, when a ship she was sailing on was bombed at Astrakhan.[13]

Alisa talked about her relations with their Chicago relatives in her letters to Nora. She wrote that they did a great deal for her, and that she would try to repay them for bringing her to America. From all those relatives Mrs. Drobysheva remembers only Sarah Lipton, but she says Sarah was not a close relative, but a relative of her grandfather. Sarah left for the United States as far back as the end of the nineteenth century, and in gratitude or out of family feeling she sent an invitation for one of the Russian relatives to visit her in Chicago. Naturally, Alisa was chosen because she was the family's favorite. Everyone approved of her departure. Everyone pooled their money to pay her expenses.

Alisa first went to Moscow, because that was where all the necessary documents were; then she went to Riga, and from there to America.

Alisa wrote to them from Chicago that it would be impossible for her to make her career there, so she was moving to Hollywood. Even before she left Russia, Alisa thought of becoming a scenario writer in Hollywood.

The Rosenbaums got a letter from Alisa in 1928, in which she told them of her bad financial situation during the Great Depression. She also sent photographs, which their mother and Natasha took to the bank in order to get permission to send money periodically to Alisa in the United States. They were permitted to send $25 a month, which they did for a while.

Nora got married in 1931. She met her husband in a rest home in Luga, where she was staying under the supervision of her aunt,

---

11 The 900-day siege of Leningrad by the Nazis started in September 1941.

12 Their Jewish names were Zelman-Wolf and Hannah Berkovna.

13 Astrakhan is 900 miles SE of Moscow, on the Caspian Sea.

her mother's sister Doba Borisovna [Konheim]. In 1931 Nora got an invitation from Alisa to visit the United States. Because her wedding took place right around that time, Nora did not take her up on the invitation. Nora's husband, Feodor Andreyevich Drobyshev, worked at a military factory, Pyrometer, making electronic equipment for the navy. The Drobyshevs lived in the blockaded Leningrad until June of 1942, after which her husband's factory was evacuated, so they moved to a town near Moscow called Ramenskoye. They returned to Leningrad after the war ended. In 1970 the Drobyshevs were assigned an apartment in a good, cooperatively owned building on the Petrograd side; Mrs. Drobysheva still lives there. She and her husband never had children. Her husband died fifteen years ago.

When Alisa sent the Rosenbaums her play *Night of January 16th*—Mrs. Drobysheva calls it by its original title, *Penthouse Legend*—Natasha's husband gave it to a famous producer, N. Akimov, but Akimov doubted that he would be able to produce it. Akimov's production of the American play *Dangerous Turn* is known. Mrs. Drobysheva thinks that *Dangerous Turn* is much more accusatory and critical than Ayn Rand's work. However she liked her sister's play; she remembered that its plot was connected to the suicide of the Swedish match king Ivar Kreuger; she recalled the characters of the secretary and the gangster who was in love with her. Mrs. Drobysheva considers the gangster to be Al Capone. She does not regard *Night of January 16th* to be on a par with her sister's novels, or her philosophy, which she does not like.

The correspondence between the Rosenbaums and Alisa stopped in 1937. Alisa told Nora later that there were warnings posted in American post offices saying that a letter to Russia can serve as cause for arrest of its recipient.

In 1945–46, Mrs. Drobysheva and her husband Feodor received a package from the Unites States from a relative of their mother's sister Deborah Borisovna. This relative lived in Germany for some time, but with Hitler's rise to power emigrated to America.[14]

When Mrs. Drobysheva came to the United States in 1974, Alisa told her that she had sent them a package back then. Mrs. Drobysheva remembered that package—it contained, according to Mrs. Drobysheva, something inedible, like dog food. However, they did use the broth concentrate cubes. After she arrived in America, Alisa also used to send them books, such as Dreiser's *An American Tragedy*. Anna Borisovna

---

14 This refers to her cousin Volodya Konheim.

and Natasha used to translate these books for publication at the Gosizdat, among others.[15]

While in New York, Mrs. Drobysheva's husband suffered a heart attack. Mrs. Drobysheva called 911: "I was terrified and kept crying 'help, help, help!' but I was able to give them our address." Mrs. Drobysheva also called Alisa. An ambulance arrived with a black doctor and two assistants. Her sister never came. She also never got the medication that Mrs. Drobysheva asked her to get for Feodor, a medication that is impossible to get in Russia. Feodor was taken to a hospital for the poor, Bellevue, where he stayed for two weeks. He was in a big room with other patients, but each bed was in its own niche and separated off by its own curtain. Nurses took care of Feodor, and they refused Mrs. Drobysheva's help in caring for the patient.[16]

They told Mrs. Drobysheva, "This is our job." Mrs. Drobysheva asked hospital staff to call Alisa again, to tell her what happened.

Shortly after Feodor got better, Alisa suggested that they leave, even though their three-month visiting period was not yet over. This was caused by constant arguments between Nora and Alisa about Alisa's philosophy. The most heated debates were on the subject of altruism. "It is the altruism of our entire family that enabled Alisa to get out to the States in the first place," says Mrs. Drobysheva. When Mrs. Drobysheva discussed with her sister Alexander Solzhenitsyn, one of whose stories was published in Russia in the magazine *Noviy Mir* [*The New World*], they disagreed. Leonard Peikoff brought in a three-volume set of Solzhenitsyn's writings. Mrs. Drobysheva was glad and was much more interested in those books than in Ayn Rand's novels. According to Mrs. Drobysheva, this irritated Alisa very much. On the last day before her departure, the sisters fought about Solzhenitsyn's "Letter to the Leaders." At the end of the fight, Alisa threw the book down on the floor and said, "Take this disgusting person with you!" Mrs. Drobysheva says that Alisa did not like Solzhenitsyn because he was for the restoration of "self-rule." Before Mrs. Drobysheva left, Alisa demanded that Mrs. Drobysheva return all the books Ayn Rand had given her earlier as a gift, and did not even go with Mrs. Drobysheva and her husband to the airport to see them off.

Neither Nora nor Alisa had thought that it would come to this. "Yes,

---

15 Gosizdat is the state publishing house.

16 In Russia it is standard practice for the relatives, not the medical personnel, to care for the patient in a hospital.

Alisa was disappointed that we were different from what she expected," says Mrs. Drobysheva. "She always wanted adoring fans. First I filled that role, then it was some boy in Chicago."

Mrs. Drobysheva does not consider herself to be anti-American and pro-Soviet. She liked certain buildings in New York City and its people. She did not like that Central Park was dirty, that there was an Easter Parade in Rockefeller Center, and that the salespeople at the store did not help her choose a toothpaste. Among Alisa's circle Mrs. Drobysheva remembers Leonard Peikoff and his wife. Mrs. Drobysheva does not understand why Frank [O'Connor] wanted to learn to draw so late in life.

Mrs. Drobysheva expected that her sister would be a rich noble lady with a three-story house, and was very surprised to find out that she lived in a regular apartment building—although in a good neighborhood—and considered herself middle class.

Transcript notes from this interview by Alexander Lebedev

Alexander Lebedev: *What philosophical issues did Alisa and you discuss in Russia?*

Eleanora Drobysheva: We did not philosophize at that time.

What were Alisa's childhood hobbies?

She did not have time for hobbies. She was interested in prehistoric animals. We also went to the movies.

Which of your relatives worked for the czar?

Our grandfather, Boris Kaplan. He was a tailor and sewed uniforms for the czar's guards.

When did Alisa start smoking?

In America.

Does the novel We the Living *describe events that really happened?*

The novel's plot has nothing to do with real life.[17] The only thing

---

17 Letters (1926–1936) to Ayn Rand from her family indicate that actual living conditions in Leningrad mirrored living conditions as described in *We the Living*. Those letters (nearly nine hundred of them) are housed in the Ayn Rand Archives.

that is autobiographical in it are the ideas. Also the city and certain small details of daily life.

What happened to Alisa's letters from America?

The entire correspondence was lost during the blockade and after Leningrad was evacuated.

Edited transcript of three interviews conducted by Sergei Bernadskiy in 1997 and 1998

Sergei Bernadskiy: *Describe your parents and Natasha. What did they value? What hobbies did they have?*

Eleanora Drobysheva: Papa was tall and handsome, but not energetic. He was broken by the Revolution. Figuratively speaking, Mama was the one who wore the pants in the family. Mama was short, not very good-looking, but she ran the household. Natasha was cute, a good person with a heart. Alisa and I were goal-oriented—we were career-ambitious—but Natasha wasn't. She was married twice. What hobbies are you talking about?! We simply struggled to stay alive.

Were you close to your parents?

I was afraid of Mama, even after I got married. She was a tyrant in the house.

What was your mother's profession from 1931 to 1941?

She was a teacher. She taught first at a factory vocational school, then at institutes. She knew French, German and English.

Your mother used to translate foreign books into Russian. Who were these translations made for?

For Gosizdat [the state publishing house].

What were your mother's views? What was her goal in life?

She didn't have time for views. Her goal was to raise us, her children. Actually, she was a "pink"—she would occasionally talk about "beautiful ideas."

What were your father's views? How did he change from 1926 to 1939?

Everything was taken away from us. And Papa was unable to

withstand the tragedy.

What were your father's final words?

I didn't hear them. He was sitting on the couch and talking with Mama as usual, and suddenly he did not respond to a question she asked him. She rushed to him, but he was already dead. It was an easy death; they call such a death "the kiss of God."

What relations did your family have with your father's relatives? What happened to them?

We kept in contact with Mama's side of the family more than with Papa's. Papa's relatives didn't like Mama much. She was energetic and was the boss in our family.

What did Natasha do from 1936 to 1942?

She was married, but she continued her studies in piano.[18]

Did your grandfather, Boris Kaplan, ever work for the czar? What stories did he tell?

Count Ignatiev graduated from the Page Corps, became an officer, got an appointment to serve in the Guards, and went to my grandfather to have grandfather make him his uniform. The officers of the Guard would go to Kaplan to have their uniforms made, because everybody saw how good Kaplan's workmanship was, not because the czar commanded to have uniforms made at the czar's tailor.

What other names did you have for Alisa?

Alisa and I had nicknames taken from Conan Doyle's *The Lost World*. We derived our nicknames from the bird-reptile pterodactyl: she was "Dact One," and I was "Dact Two." I was Alisa's constant shadow.

Were you Alisa's favorite?

I might have been. More exactly, I was her shadow and yes-man.

What didn't you like about Alisa in childhood?

---

18 Natasha studied at the conservatory, in the Department of Performers, in the piano class of professor Nadezhda Golubovskaya from 1922 until 1929. Golubovskaya considered her to be a very talented pianist. There was a "cleansing" at the conservatory in 1925. Natasha was allowed to continue her studies because she was very talented, but on the condition that she become "socially active."

Childhood was the period when I liked everything about her.

Did your family observe the Jewish holidays?

We observed Passover, its first Seder. I loved matzoh; my father used to make it. All our relatives from my mother's side would come over. Actually, I need to go get matzoh now at the synagogue.

What happened to the Guzarchiks and the Konheims?

Guzarchik was mother's sister. Her husband was a gynecologist. They all died in the blockade. The Konheims were the family of my mother's eldest sister. They also died in the blockade.

How did Volodya Konheim leave Russia? What happened to him?

He married a Russian governess, was disowned by his parents, and they left. What happened to him afterwards, I do not know at all.[19]

Could you describe your family's vacation in Finland?

We lived in an ordinary dacha in Terijoki. There were the three of us and the three Guzarchiks. I also remember that we ate magnificent cottage cheese and sour cream.

In which Swiss city did you spend the summer of 1914?

Montreux.

What do you remember of your trip to Switzerland?

I remember only the Chillon dungeon. There was a long staircase going down. I ran down the staircase, but it ended at a blank wall with a pile of refuse.[20]

What were the consequences of World War I on your family?

None, if you mean the war itself. I remember only that we were returning [from England] to Russia on a Swedish ship. They said later that the ship before ours and the ship after ours were sunk. We were over there on vacation. But everything we had was here: the pharmacy and our house. No one had any idea that there would be a revolution.

Did Alisa have any fears or weaknesses in childhood?

---

19 For more information, see *Letters of Ayn Rand*, ed. Michael S. Berliner (New York: Penguin, 1995), pp. 279, 399, 358, 420, 434, 480.

20 The Castle of Chillon is near Montreux.

No one paid attention to such things. We were living through the war and the revolution.

Which foods did Alisa like?

Simply obtaining food was a problem in those years. We ate peas often. Any food was a favorite food.

Which plays did Alisa like from 1915 to 1936?

She liked operettas and dragged me with her to the Mikhailovsky Theater. I remember, we saw [Carl Millöcker's] *The Beggar Student* and [Franz Lehár's] *Where the Lark Sings*. At the operetta, we sat in the so-called paradise—a side balcony, in the cheapest seats.[21]

Did Alisa have any publications in Russia besides what was reprinted in her Russian Writings on Hollywood? *Any biographies of movie stars? Plays? Scenarios? Had she tried to publish anything?*

No. *Pola Negri*, I remember. Yes, this very book you are showing me. But *Pola Negri* was published without her name on it, because she simply needed money, though the money wasn't much. That way, the book could be used by other authors.

Somebody named Zlatkin published Alisa's book about Hollywood. Who was he? What was the nature of his work with Alisa and with your mother?

Alisa called him "the crook Zlatkin." Mother translated [for Zlatkin] *An American Tragedy* by Dreiser, but that was later.[22]

Did [your cousin] *Nina and Alisa have a common circle of friends?*

Nina's father was a gynecologist, and her family was more well-off than ours. Young people gathered at her house for dances. Alisa joined that group [Uno Momento]. That was her "high society." But I couldn't join the group because I was still too young. Back then fifteen-year-olds weren't like they are now. There were no Lolitas back then.

Who saw Alisa off at the train station on January 17, 1926, on her way to America?

---

21 In her 1960–61 biographical interviews, Ayn Rand reported having seen *The Beggar Student* (*Der Bettelstudent*) eleven times.

22 The whole Rosenbaum family called Zlatkin "crook," among other pejorative terms.

I, Natasha and Mama saw her off. I can't remember if Papa was there or not.[23]

How long did Alisa plan her visit to America to be?

I think she was planning to go there for good. She wanted to get me, Papa and Mama out to the U.S.

How did Alisa change after she moved to America?

She became more egoistic and made egoism into a philosophy. Try living by such a philosophy: then you can judge whether it is rational or not.

But didn't she want to get all of you out of Russia to America?

Yes, she did, and I kept trying to persuade my parents to move over there to live with her, but they refused. Alisa would send us things. She sent Natasha a purse, some shoes for me, pajamas for me and Natasha.

Did you want to go to America in the 1930s?

Yes, I wanted to. I was even sent papers. But I got married in 1931.

Alisa sent you a college application. Which American university was it from?

It was from some local California college. The application was to the Department of Art and Drawing.[24]

What did Alisa write about in her letters?

About her life and her work.

What did she write about her meeting with Cecil B. DeMille?

She was walking through the studio. She saw a car with DeMille in it at the front gate and smiled at him. He asked her who she was, asked her to step into the car, then gave her a job.

What did Alisa and Frank think of Hollywood?

When Alisa was leaving Russia, she thought she was going to the

---

23 Based on letters to Ayn Rand from her family, many members of the family were at the station.

24 It was in March and April 1928 that Eleanora Rosenbaum wrote to and received information from this unidentified California college.

Mecca of the film industry to make her career. Her correspondence was of an impulsive nature. I recall such sentences from her letters as: "I am Cecil DeMille's scenario writer" and "I got married." I think she wanted to stun us with her successes.

The letters often mention Alisa's acquaintance Lyolya B. What was his name? What were the relations between them? What happened to him?

Lyolya [Lev Bekkerman] was a large-nosed, handsome man. She asked me about him in 1973, but I just snorted: Why does she need him, when she has the handsome Frank?

[Lev Borisovitch Bekkerman[25] was a student at the Technological Institute. Later, he worked as an engineer at a factory. He moonlighted as a secretary at the Atheneum publishing house. According to a researcher at the Technological Institute, who conducted research in the archives for his book on students and researchers persecuted by the Soviet State, Bekkerman was arrested with a large group of students and professors. However, during the search of his apartment nothing was found. He was not sent to the labor camps. KGB records reveal that Bekkerman was again arrested by the KGB in 1937 and shot by a firing squad.]

Did Alisa ever send you any of her writings from America?

She sent her play *Penthouse Legend*.[26] That is her best thing. Everyone in the family was stunned by it.

Was Alisa's play Penthouse Legend, *which she sent you in 1934, ever produced in Russia? Your mother translated the play into Russian. What happened to that translation?*

It wasn't ever produced. One of our acquaintances simply had the idea that it would be good to have the play produced. The translation was lost in the blockade.

In one of her letters of 1926, your mother wrote that The Distorted Mirror [a theatre] accepted Alisa's "Radio-Ballet," but wanted to make

---

25 See McConnell in *Essays on Ayn Rand's "We the Living,"* pp. 52–56.

26 According to Mrs. Drobysheva, the manuscript of the play was shown to the famous producer and theater designer Nicolai Pavlovitch Akimov, who was regarded as cosmopolitan for his freethinking views. Currently, the theater of comedy in which he worked bears his name.

changes to it, and your mother refused. What is The Distorted Mirror? What was "Radio-Ballet" about? Where is "Radio-Ballet" now?

The Distorted Mirror is now called "Crystal Palace." Even Utesov[27] performed there. Mother refused to give them "Radio-Ballet" because they wanted to make changes.

Alisa wrote to William S. Hart in 1926, and he sent you his photograph and autograph. What did Alisa write to Hart?

How would I know? There was a large photograph [of Hart] with the inscription "Yours faithfully, W. Hart."[28]

What did Alisa think of the actor Joseph Schildkraut?

Schildkraut played Judas in one movie. Alisa wrote that she had dinner or breakfast with him.

What did Alisa think of Charlie Chaplin?

Alisa and I didn't think much of him. We liked Buster Keaton better.

Did Alisa like Jack London?

Jack London would be more my type than Alisa's. His type is the man of physical strength, whereas Alisa was attracted more to men of high intelligence.

Which American songs did Alisa send to you? Which songs did she like?

She would send them to Natasha, because Natasha was studying to be a musician. It was the beginning of the Jazz Age. Although, one of the songs remains popular to this day. That was "Yes, Sir, That's My Baby."

Did Alisa like boxing?

Alisa wrote that [Jack] Dempsey won the championship in a fight for the title of world champion, and that they stayed up at night and listened to the fight on the radio.

What were Alisa's views on love and sex?

---

27 Leonid Utesov was a famous Russian actor and jazz musician.
28 In a May 19, 1926, letter to Ayn Rand, Nora wrote that she "cried from happiness" when she read a copy of the letter Miss Rand sent to Hart requesting an autographed photo for Nora.

As you know, there is no sex in the Soviet Union. [laughs] Alisa did not speak with me about these subjects.

Did your family ever have difficulties because of its correspondence with Alisa or because of the novel We the Living?

No. The novel probably had not attracted attention.

Why and when did your family stop writing to Alisa?

Because of the war. Nobody but me was left alive from our immediate family. Actually, she was the one who stopped writing to us. Probably because she did not have any use for us any longer.

What happened to Alisa's diaries?

They were lost in the blockade. When we evacuated, we did not plan ever to return to Leningrad. After we left, other people moved into our old apartment.

What became of the old apartment on Dmitrovsky?

Other people moved into it. We evacuated out of Leningrad and did not want to return, so we gave the apartment to other people. Incidentally, I must be fair to Alisa. When we finally met she said, "Do not ask about me, tell me about yourself."

Did you talk with Alisa on the telephone after her departure and prior to 1973?

As soon as I located her, I wrote to her. But she did not like to reply to letters. She would call on the phone. It seems that is the way they do things in America. But I wished she would write instead: once a telephone conversation is over, it's over, but letters you can reread.[29]

Why couldn't Alisa send you nitroglycerin for your husband's heart?

We had nitroglycerin in the Soviet Union. What we didn't have was Inderal. They gave us a little of it at the hospital.

Do you know English? In which language did you read novels in America?

I can read English easily, but speaking is more difficult. I did speak

---

29 Three of Ayn Rand's letters to Mrs. Drobysheva are reprinted in *Letters of Ayn Rand*, pp. 657, 660 and 662.

English while I was over there. I hardly read Alisa's novels in America.

Do you have pleasant memories about your visit to New York?

No.

How did you react to Alisa's death?

I didn't. Somebody informed me of it. At the time I was very insulted by the way she treated me during my visit to the U.S.

What did you think of Alisa from 1937 to 1973?

She didn't treat our family and me well.

What do you think of her now?

It's a pity what America had done to her. Had she had a different husband, one that would have been tougher with her, she would have been a better person.

How did your feelings towards Alisa change during the course of your life?

At first I worshipped her, then I was offended.

1920s

Fern Brown

Fern Brown (née Goldberg) is Ayn Rand's cousin and a novelist with thirty-two children's novels published. Miss Rand stayed with the Goldberg family for several months in 1926, soon after her arrival in America.

Interview dates: July 2, 1996; March 13 and 18, 1997; April 14 and June 8, 1998

Scott McConnell: *Could you give me information about Ayn Rand's family tree?*

Fern Brown: I can tell you about the aunts and uncles that brought her over. My grandfather, Harry Portnoy, lived with us. She called him "Uncle," but I think he was her great-uncle. Ayn was the granddaughter of Harry's sister.

Harry had five girls and three boys. His eldest son was Ike Portnoy, and there was a son, Jack, who died on a train during the First World War. The last son was Mandel.

The five girls were Anna, who married another Mandel, Mandel Stone. Then there was Lillian, who married Samuel Surkin, and Gertrude, who married Maurice Hoffman. And there's Sarah who was married four times. She was our family actress and a beautiful lady. She was married first to Harry Collier, and then to Joe Lipton, then Abe Satrin and finally to Saul Lipski. When Sarah was married to Abe Satrin was when she and my aunt Ann paid for Alice—Ayn Rand—to come over here, and then live at our house, so she always felt grateful to those three sisters.

My mother's name was Miriam, but she had nicknames like "Minna," which she preferred. She was Harry Portnoy's youngest daughter and married Sam Goldberg.

The relative Ayn was really fond of was Burton Stone, who was Ann and Mandel's son. She kept up a correspondence with him and also with Aunt Sarah.

Why were Burton and Ayn Rand so close?

He was a character. A diamond in the rough. He was the kind of character that she would like, that she would want in her book, a sort of a rugged individualist.

Tell me more about your parents.

My mother was born in Chicago, and the date that she took for this was February 12, 1895. I think my mother was the only daughter born in America. She was the youngest of the whole group. They were all much older than she was. My dad was born in New York. He was in the grocery business. He had a little grocery store.

Tell me more about your grandfather Harry Portnoy.

Ayn called my grandpa "Uncle." He was a wonderful man. He was a great reader, he loved to read, and he read in Yiddish. He wanted us to talk English to him and that's how he learned it—just by us talking to him.

Was he from St. Petersburg?

I don't know. It was Poland, Russia—somewhere along the border there. He worked in a boot factory, and the Russian government was conscripting for the army and that's why his oldest son, Uncle Ike, came first, and then Ike sent for everybody else to join him. Uncle Ike told us he was about seventeen when he came, and then after he got a job here and settled here, he sent for his father and the rest of the family.

Was Harry Portnoy a boot maker?

Actually, he sewed. He was more like a tailor. The name Portnoy in Russian means tailor.

We were a very close family. We used to call those we brought over to the United States the "greenhorns." We brought over a lot of greenhorns: Joe Lipton and Abe Satrin were greenhorns. They came from Russia and Poland. They were all cousins of some kind.

Was your family rich or well-off?

We certainly weren't rich.

Was Harry Portnoy repaying debts by bringing them over?

I don't know, but I think that's what people did in those days. There was always room for more people and if they wanted to come here, then they'd get them over here. They'd want them to see the land of milk and honey. My grandpa told me America was the best country in the world and felt happy that he came here. He loved the freedom and the fact that his family was happy and growing, and that's what a father is happy about.[30]

What can you remember of Cousin Alice's visit in 1926?

I was born in 1918, so I was eight years old. My brother Harvey was five-and-a-half. She came to Chicago to stay with us for a while. Mother told me that because Alice was coming to stay with us, we had to move our beds around. We didn't even have another bedroom. There wasn't room to have people stay at our apartment. We had five of us: Grandpa, my brother and me, and my mother and dad, all sleeping in two bedrooms and a dining room.

Harvey and I always laugh because we had to give up our beds in the dining room to her. We had two little cots in the dining room, and we had to move out because she had her typewriter in the dining room and that's where she slept. I think I slept on the couch after that. The dining room was kind of a big room. It had a big round table and a long buffet with a telephone on top of it.

The apartment also had a large kitchen and a living room. One bedroom was made out of a little sleeping porch; it was a really tiny thing, not really a bedroom. That was my grandfather's room. It had a window in the front of the apartment. The kitchen was off the dining room, also off the little hall.

What music did she like?

"I'm Sitting On Top Of The World"[31]—I remember her singing that over and over again, in a kind of lilting voice. She kind of drove us crazy because she was up all night and we were up all day. She would take showers at night, as she was a night person. I don't know if they had showers in Russia, but she just loved to take a shower at night.

So she was very energetic?

Yes, she was. I think she was happy to be here.

---

30 In the Archives is a document (dated June 29, 1925) from Harry Portnoy to the U.S. government promising to look after Ayn Rand financially. He wrote that the reason he wanted to bring Ayn Rand to America was to check out the safety and security of his relatives in Russia "whom he had not seen for thirty years."

31 Written in 1925 by the team of Lewis-Young-Henderson.

How would you describe her then?

She wasn't pretty. She was very angular and she wore very short hair. She was very opinionated.

In what way?

Any of her ideas. Anything she talked about. She didn't discuss things with me when I was eight years old. I never had really intellectual talks with her.

What did she like to talk about?

She talked about the theater and about politics and her ideas. She would get very excited and strong about it.

Did she have clear political views then?

Oh, I think so. She hated, hated and hated the Bolsheviks, as she used to call them. She thought they were the worst people on earth, they were the ones who ruined all of her good living, the good life that they had before that. She was adamant about that. She had a great deal of hate for the Red Russians. She would talk about that all the time. Murderers, killers, thieves, terrible people. She hated Communism.

Did she miss her family?

She always wanted her sister to come; I know she told me that. Eleanora. She wished her whole family were here. The father, the mother and everybody, but she especially wanted that sister to come. She wanted her to see America.

Did Ayn Rand write stories there or did she have stories with her when she arrived at your home in 1926?

She wrote when she was there. The typewriter was always clacking away.

She was just a cousin, who came and could hardly speak English. We didn't know she was going to be a great writer with great ideas. She was just another one of the greenhorns that grandpa and the uncles and aunts brought in. We wanted everybody to live in the land of milk and honey.

The family used to come over every Sunday to our house, so Ayn Rand must have been part of that. They would play cards on Sunday. They would come over and the men would go out and buy what they called "farmer's chop suey": cottage cheese and vegetables and stuff.

Alice made her own way. She did everything by her sheer perseverance. I would call her a very perseverant person, who thought a lot, and some of her ideas were very cerebral.

Tell me about your mother, Minna Goldberg, and Ayn Rand.

My mother was not too crazy about her because of her habits. My mother had a lot of work to do because of Ayn being in our home and because her habits were reverse of the way my mother ran the house. Ayn was a nighttime person and we were daytime people, so it was kind of hard.

Did they read her books?

Of course, we all read her books. I liked *We the Living*, and *The Fountainhead* was excellent, but I didn't care for *Atlas Shrugged*. I think it should have been cut quite a bit. Some of her other books that I've read are interesting.

I have original first editions of her books. They were given to my parents by Ayn.

Was Miss Rand grateful to the families for bringing her over and supporting her?

Yes, I think so; especially to Aunt Sarah and Aunt Ann—you know, Burton's family.

Did Mandel and Esther and Anna have much to do with Miss Rand?

They always liked to keep in touch with her, and they would always tell us when they heard from her. Anna and Mandel owned a lumber yard and a large piece of property in Momence in Illinois. Ayn Rand once sent them a pair of peacocks as a gift. The peacocks were very beautiful and very noisy. Everybody liked Ayn as a person. I don't think any of them really got into her philosophy, except maybe Burton.

So your family did write to her after she left?

We corresponded, and I could kick myself for not keeping her letters, but I never did.

Where are they?

I just never kept them. You don't know someone is going to be famous. I don't know how many are keeping my letters and I've written thirty-two children's books. In fact, the last time I heard from her personally was about 1967 or '68, and I wrote to her that I had my first book published. I think we stopped writing to each other in the sixties.

Were the letters handwritten or typed?

She always handwrote. She had a slanted handwriting that to us was like foreign handwriting.

Did she write letters when she went to Hollywood?

Yes, and from New York. Aunt Sarah was the only one who corresponded with her, I think. And then to Aunt Ann . . . I can't say, because there's nobody left in that whole family.

How often did she write to the family?

At first we all got letters a lot. I think it was in 1965, she was in New York then, and I had written my first book—a child's book—and I sent it to her and she never acknowledged it. After that we never wrote to each other. Before that we kept up a correspondence. I wrote for my mother. Not that my mother couldn't write, but I kept up the correspondence till the '60s. But the letters are all torn apart because everyone in the family was reading them.

What was your mother's opinion of Ayn Rand later?

Oh, she was very proud. My mother liked the better things in life and she loved literature and reading and writing, and she was very happy that she had a famous relative.

Did she read Ayn Rand's books?

Oh yes, definitely. She enjoyed them very much, mostly because Ayn Rand wrote them, I would think.

What's your strongest memory of Ayn Rand?

My strongest memory is of when she lived at our home, when I was a little girl, and I helped her pick out her last name, Rand. She had this little old Remington-Rand typewriter and she had it on our dining room table. This was in Chicago at 3216 Leland Ave.

One day she said, "I'm going to change my name, but I want it to be an A and R." We called her "Alice." She said, "I picked out my first name, it's going to be 'Ayn'"; it's sort of a [Finnish] derivative, she told me. She said, "And I need an 'R.'" I was looking at the typewriter then and said, "What about 'Remington'?" She said, "No, that's too long, I want it short." So then I said, "What about 'Rand'?" And she said, "Oh, good, that's it: 'Ayn Rand.'" I think this was early on in her visit.[32]

She must have been excited to get her new name.

Oh yeah, she wanted to start new and be American.

You said you visited with Miss Rand and Mr. O'Connor in 1939. Tell me about that.

She was living in New York and I was a counselor in a camp nearby in Pennsylvania, and she invited me to come and see her, before or after the camp. Frank cooked the dinner. He was a marvelous cook. And we had a nice dinner at their lovely apartment and then they took me to see a ballet or play. So it was a lovely, lovely day spent with them.[33]

Could you describe the apartment?

All I remember is a large dining room and a long table, and it was very pretty. Nice dark wood. I think it was a lovely apartment. Frank was very good at decorating, I know, but I don't know if he was the one who did it.

Could you describe him?

I thought he was tall and, when I saw him then, rather slender. He was wearing a Japanese-like robe, and he was serving the dinner. Maybe it was a smoking jacket.

I remember that when she was writing *The Fountainhead*, she told us she wrote it for Frank. I always thought she was very, very happy with him. I really felt that she was in love with him all her life.

Frank was a gentle person, very nice, very concerned, very hospitable and was dressed to the hilt in his smoking jacket. That's the only time I really saw him, so I have no other impression.

What other stories of Miss Rand do you remember?

I remember her sitting in Burt Stone's apartment after his funeral. She promised my mother a mink coat, but she didn't come through with that one. She said when she made it big. She used to tell us that

---

32 It is unclear what Ayn Rand said or meant, because letters from her sister Nora written before Miss Rand even arrived in Chicago mention the name "Rand" and thus establish that she had chosen the name while still in Russia.

33 In 1935–37 Ayn Rand lived on Park Avenue, and in 1939 on East Eighty-ninth Street.

this Mr. Woods really rooked her, did her wrong.[34]

Tell me about the last time you saw Miss Rand.

I saw her at a lecture at the McCormick Center Theater in Chicago in 1963.[35] I went to see her backstage after the lecture, and she was sitting there, and we shook her hand and gave her a kiss and said she was wonderful.

How did she respond?

She was like a queen on a throne. She had this big gold dollar-sign on. She invited all the family that she wanted there, my mother and dad and Burt Stone. Those were the people who brought her over.

---

34 A. H. Woods was the Broadway producer of Rand's play *Night of January 16th*. In 1936 Ayn Rand won an arbitration claim against Woods for trying to take more of her royalties than their contract permitted. See also *Letters of Ayn Rand*, p. 24, regarding his doctoring of her script.

35 The date of the talk was September 29, 1963.

Harvey Goldberg

Harvey Goldberg, Fern Brown's brother, was Ayn Rand's cousin. He first met Miss Rand in Chicago in 1926, when he was five years old.

Interview dates: September 17, 1996, and December 26, 1997.

Scott McConnell: *What do you remember of Ayn Rand from 1926?*

Harvey Goldberg: As far as her habits, I remember she used to type all night, and sit in the bathtub, and let the water run at night. She worked at night and slept all day. She'd go in the bathtub and take a bath for hours at night, and then she'd type. She'd type most of the night. We all lived in cramped quarters then. I remember her sleeping in the dining room, which was right in the front of the building. She slept on a canvas cot.

Ayn said when she became famous she'd send us a Rolls Royce for taking care of her for six months, but we never got it.

What was she like in 1926?

I wouldn't say she was real friendly. She was more reserved and quiet. She wanted to get to California as fast as she could, and she wanted to become a citizen.

I believe you saw her again many years later.

Yes. She gave a lecture at the McCormick Place in Chicago [in 1963], a big theater. My wife and I, my sister and my brother-in-law, and Burt Stone and his wife went backstage and said hello to her. Burt kept in better contact with her than we did. He always kept in contact with her. We just spent a few minutes with her. She was very nice, very cordial, but we really didn't see too much of her in the intervening years. It was a very friendly meeting. She remembered all of us.

Rosalie Wilson

Rosalie Anne (FitzGerald) Wilson was Ayn Rand's goddaughter and friend. Rosalie Wilson died in 2008.

Interview dates: March 26 and April 1, 1998

Scott McConnell: *How did you come to be Ayn Rand's goddaughter?*

Rosalie Wilson: Joe O'Connor (Frank's brother) was my godfather and I knew Joe when we all lived back east. I was born in Cleveland in December of 1922, and was my mother's second child. I think she was probably married around 1920. Joe had been engaged to my mother before she met my father. I think they met in Lorain, Ohio. My mother knew Frank O'Connor from Cleveland and Lorain days.

How long did you know Miss Rand and Joe O'Connor?

My association with the O'Connors, starting from my babyhood, existed only until we moved to California in the summer of 1924 or '25. Afterwards until about 1935, with many intervals, and resuming again in the 1950s.

Your mother's name was Millie FitzGerald?

Yes. Her name before she married my dad, when she first met them, was Camille Lucas. They called her "Millie."

Tell me more about Joe O'Connor.

He always wore a beard and always looked like Christ. I think that's what drew him to California, to play Christ in the Pilgrimage play for years, year after year, at the Hollywood Pilgrimage Play Theater, which was on Highland, very close to the Hollywood Bowl entrance. I remember going to those Pilgrimage plays. There wasn't much for him to do except stand on this side of the whole theatrical stage and slowly walk up with people waving palm fronds until he got to the top of the stage.[36]

Was he crucified?

Yes.

---

36 As far as can be determined, Christ was played by Ian Maclaren during this time period. Joe O'Connor's involvement cannot be verified.

Were Ayn Rand and Frank O'Connor at the performances?

They were there one or two times with my mom and me.

What did Joe do in Los Angeles?

He and Frank worked spasmodically as extras, but Joe's main claim to fame was playing Christ for many years at the Pilgrimage play. Joe's health was very bad and his appearance emaciated.

How close was your mother to Frank O'Connor?

Both O'Connors—Joe and Frank—were like brothers to my mom.

Tell me then about this foursome.

Everything seemed very casual and closely knit. There was never any strain or I would have noticed. They just seemed like good friends of long standing.

What did you do with Ayn Rand and Frank?

Frank and Ayn took care of me one or two summers. It was probably about two to three weeks each time. I was their little girl. I have one picture I've found so far to prove that. Ayn took it of Frank and me together. I look to be about six or seven.

How were you "their little girl"?

They didn't have children and my mom worked in pictures and my dad was out of the country and they took care of me. Ayn worked at RKO and Frank didn't do much working at that point in time; I think he was an extra. She worked at the wardrobe at RKO. Frank or Ayn always had me under their wing, and I was independent anyhow.

Where was your mom?

My mom and dad were separated about that time and getting divorced, but they went away together to try to reconcile and make things up.

What was Miss Rand like at the time?

Now, this is a little girl talking to you again. I liked her, she was sweet to me, she was kind of distant, and I loved her dark hair and her big, big eyes. My mom had red hair and pretty eyes, but Ayn had big eyes. I never did anything to make her scold; she was very pleasant, mildly pleasant. She never hugged me the way Frank and Joe did, not because she didn't like me, but just because she wasn't a hugger or a kisser.

What would you and she do?

They had a big collie dog, and mostly Frank and I walked that huge dog. She took good care of me because she had me for two summers. We didn't go anywhere. We didn't do anything, except take walks with the dog. I have no other recollection of activities.

How would you describe Miss Rand and Mr. O'Connor together?

They were a good, proper substitute mommy and daddy. Again, you're talking about a six-year-old child. I was never aware of, or made embarrassed by, any physical affection. They were just nice, and soft-spoken to each other. They were discrete. I never heard an argument.

Were they poor?

They were probably borderline poor. I saw Ayn through the eyes of a young person. I just recall some of the problems they had making ends meet in those days. Those were hard days that I remember. This must have been during the so-called Depression years. Quite possibly Ayn was then into writing scripts and/or her novels.

You have a photograph of Frank from that period?

It was their patio, a patio they shared with one other unit. Frank is squatting on the other side of the camera with a dog, the collie they had, and in front of them is a fountain. In the background is one of the two entrances into their apartments, and I'm right there. There are French doors, more or less in the background, with me standing near one.

Where did you sleep?

It was a one-bedroom unit and until they went to bed, I slept in their bed, so they had the living room to themselves. When they went to bed, they pulled down what used to be called an "in-a-door bed"—it's a bed that fit away inside a closet on a frame that swung out. I slept on that.

They didn't fuss over you or control or spoil you?

No! They were very casual with me. Everyone seemed in my young life to be very casual about what I did and where I went.

What other things did you do?

When Frank was there we'd walk the dog a lot; we both liked walking because I thought that was great.

Did Mr. O'Connor hold your hand when you went for walks?

At times he did. When we walked the dog he'd hold the leash and with the other hand he'd hold mine, but I was little.

Did you have fun with him?

He danced with me. He picked me up and danced with me. They had a Victrola and whatever the music was, he would jiggle me around in the air. I thought that was great.

I liked him awfully well, and I thought he was very handsome. He kind of reminded me of my dad a bit, and I think that's why I liked him, because I saw more of him than I did my own dad.

How was Mr. O'Connor like your father?

He loved me very much. He was a very gentle, lovely man, and he always seemed a little in awe of me, as though he was kind of afraid to touch me or something. Of course, I hungered for my dad a lot, and these two men, Frank and Joe, really did a nice job.

How did he treat you?

I don't remember him ever teeter-tottering with me or swinging me or anything like that. They just treated me rather nicely, I think, as another contemporary. Frank and Ayn didn't look down to me and just were very matter of fact, and I liked it.

What do you mean "contemporary"?

They didn't think of themselves as older and me younger. I was never baby-talked to. They treated me like a person. Of course, I was a person but there's a difference in how people treat you, and children are quite sensitive to that.

Tell me more about Mr. O'Connor.

I thought he was very attractive, and for a period of time he tried to appear as Russian as he could. Frank wore these Russian Cossack shirts, high-collared, full-sleeved, Cossack-type shirts.

One birthday, Frank carried me on his shoulders, and Ayn danced around, clapping her hands. I have a crocheted doily that she made for me. It's about eight inches, and she said it was one of the few things she really crocheted in her life. It was white with red borders and I still have it.

Was it a birthday or a Christmas gift?

Christmas and birthdays in my life have always been synonymous. I was born on the 26th of December. For our Christmas, my birthday party, there was never anybody else in it but my mom and Joe, Frank and Ayn, or my dad, rarely.

What presents did they give you?

One I recall was Robert Louis Stevenson's *A Child's Garden of Verses* that was addressed to Rosalie from Ayn. Probably it was a birthday gift. "To Rosalie, Ayn."

Do you remember anything about her writing?

I knew them during the Depression, and she hadn't begun to make a name for herself. She liked writing. When I was graduating from Hollywood High School, she offered *Night of January 16th* to be performed as our senior play. But someone, a higher power than she, said they couldn't present it to us as our senior play.

What was Ayn Rand like with children?

She was nice to me. She was casual with me; she didn't try to be artificial or too sweet. She was just herself.

Which was?

Matter of fact: "Are you hungry?" or "Do you want to eat now?" That sort of thing. She didn't fuss over me and my hair was much like hers, it didn't need curling, putting up in rags or anything, it was just brushed and combed and left to itself.

What did you call Ayn Rand?

Ayn. I didn't even call her "Auntie." I called Frank "Uncle Frank" and Joe "Uncle Joe," but I never called her anything but "Ayn."

You must have been very close in ways.

Speaking very broadly, I was the only child they ever had.

Did she refer to you as being her goddaughter?

Yes. Two or three times when I was little, she said something, like, "Well, I'm your godmother." When she gave me this crocheted doily, she said this is a long overdue gift from your godmother.

Any other childhood interactions with Miss Rand and Mr. O'Connor?

I was probably seven or eight years old. It was Halloween. I was attending Grant Elementary School on Harold Way and Milton Place in Hollywood. It was a Saturday. Everyone attending this all-day affair was in some sort of costume. I didn't have one, so I elected not to attend. Ayn learned of this, and she and Frank came to my home with a harem costume from the studio wardrobe. People were apparently smaller in those days, because with only a pin-up here and a pin-up there, the costume and veils were perfect on my small frame. They drove me to the function, telling me to be very careful and not soil or tear the costume, because Ayn must return it later that very afternoon. Consequently, I sat on a bench the whole time I was there, not daring to move so much as a muscle. I was a sad little girl when they finally took me home.

Tell me about your visits to Chatsworth many years later.[37]

My mother and I would go out and spend Sunday afternoons with Ayn and Frank when they lived on Tampa in Chatsworth. I enjoyed them because I was having a rough time. I was a mother of three very small children, bringing them up alone. These visits for me were like going to Katmandu every weekend. I more or less sat in and just enjoyed the ambiance. I enjoyed the total escape from my humdrum, kind of tough life right then.

I was raising three little kids by myself and I was living in their child-world. And it was wonderful to relax contentedly with adults, so that's what it meant to me. My mom enjoyed their companionship and their discussions and I guess they enjoyed the recollections they shared with my mom. To each of us it meant something different but something worthwhile.

My children were gone for the summer and it was another world for me. My mother would pick me up around two because church was out around noon, and we'd be out there between two and three and stay until five-thirty or six. My children were with their father each summer.

---

37 The O'Connors lived at 10,000 Tampa Ave., Chatsworth, California, from July 1944 to October 1951.

I could then take on the role of adult with adult emotions and concerns and interests.

When did your Chatsworth visits begin?

I came back to Southern California in September of '51.[38] I was so happy with the change in my life each Sunday. It just changed from black to white on those occasions.

Was the purpose of the visit for you to see the O'Connors?

No, no, the three of them were very good chums. It was kind of a hair-letting-down session for all three of them. They would talk about things that I really had no interest in. I should have, but didn't. A lot of talk went on, so I excused myself. Remember, I'm a woman in my late twenties but politics had very little meaning for me. Janet Gaynor and Adrian lived in the big house on the corner, and I used to love their horses very much. I would excuse myself and wander around and go over and look at the horses.

They discussed politics a lot when we would meet with them when I was a grown woman. I wasn't part of it because I wasn't politically inclined. Of course it got into the HUAC hearings, but it would also get into what she was currently doing; she had gotten her story line all outlined for *Atlas Shrugged*. She had an office just off the living room where we always sat. Carpeted; the whole wainscoting was carpeted up to chair height, and she worked in there totally by herself. No one ever went in there but Ayn. There was a portrait of Frank.[39] The painting was done right where it hung in their house, in the living room.

Were there any other guests or servants in the house?

No. Never on Sunday. Ayn wasn't much of a cook so what we had mostly was cold sandwiches and something to drink.

Why did the Chatsworth visits stop?

Oh that was terrible. I remember it vividly. I remember my own stomach turning. I remember my heart stopping. It had been a lovely afternoon. Well into the afternoon, something like a newspaper,

---

38 The O'Connors returned to New York City in October 1951.

39 The pastel portrait was painted in 1948 by Leonebel Jacobs. It is reproduced in *Ayn Rand*, Jeff Britting (New York: Overlook Duckworth, 2004), p. 75.

sitting on a table, started the conversation about the hearings [House Un-American Activities Committee]. The conversation went on probably for a good thirty minutes before my mom threw the bomb into the middle of it.

My mother had been for some while a real bigot. She didn't like that person because he was black, or Jewish or whatever. She was very bigoted. She was particularly bigoted about Jewish people. She was a very ugly person when it came to her attitudes. She said something to the effect, "I don't think much of Hitler, but I'll have to agree with him he should have incinerated all those Jews." And we didn't know Ayn was Jewish, but it stopped me short in my tracks that anybody could say that.

What did Miss Rand and Mr. O'Connor say?

You mean after "ten hours" of total silence? It seemed like an eternity. She said in a very beautifully modulated voice, "Well, Millie, I guess you've never known, but I am Jewish." The silence was profound. I don't remember us getting up, collecting our things. I just remember Frank walking us out to the car. It seemed like the car was ten miles away, but not a word was said. He opened her door, and then he leaned through the window, and he said, "Millie, after all these years, I'm sorry it has to end this way." My mother sat behind the steering wheel looking straight ahead; I think she was crying. He reached behind my mother and squeezed my shoulder. I looked at him, and he was crying too, and that was the last of it.

It's a terribly sad ending. No relationship that's based on such a long period of time should end sadly. And if it does, it should be by death and not by hurt.

You never saw them again?

No.

Why didn't you, without your mother, stay in contact?

I felt their sense of loss and hurt. Too embarrassed—I would not have known what to say. Ayn's fame at that time was great—but her love and friendship were what I cherished. Therefore, their loss was mine also.

Your mother never apologized?

My mother never apologized in her life for anything. "I'm sorry I spilled the sugar" would be unheard of. It was not in my mother's nature to ever apologize for anything or to anyone—ever!

1930s

Dorothy Lee

Dorothy Lee (Calderini) starred in RKO comedies in the 1930s and knew Ayn Rand in the studio's wardrobe department. She died in 1999.

Interview dates: September 20 and 26, 1996

Scott McConnell: *How did you meet Ayn Rand?*

Dorothy Lee: It was at RKO studios in Hollywood. I was there for about three or four years. I was in the comedies with Burt Wheeler and Bob Woolsey. We made the first *Rio Rita* in 1929.[40]

What department did Ayn Rand work in?

She was in women's wardrobe. She was just always there in the wardrobe department, and a lot of times she took care of me and we'd have to go in there for fittings all the time.

How was she dressed?

Just very simple: a skirt and a blouse.

What did you and Ayn Rand call each other?

She called me "Miss Lee," and I called her "Ayn."

What exactly did she do in the wardrobe department?

The actresses would go for a fitting. We would go into a dressing room, and she would be behind her desk, and as you came in, she would say go to room four or five or whatever, and then we'd have fittings. Sometimes we'd be there for two or three hours trying on a dress and then they'd have to fit it, and then have it altered. She'd come in and once in a while she'd help with the fitting or would check to see that it was correct.

Doing what type of thing to fit you?

Shorten our dresses or sleeves. The clothes were all being made there. It's just like when you're making a dress: you have to keep

---

40 Ayn Rand worked in the wardrobe department from 1929 to 1932.

trying it on to see if it's too long or too short; or if you're dancing, it has to be so you can move your legs around to dance. She would pin up our skirts or shorten the sleeves or whatever needed to be done. She was very efficient.

How was she personally?

Oh, very sweet. She was very nice and a very warm lady, and I just think it's so marvelous that she wrote all those books and became so successful. She never mentioned anything about herself.

Did she work quietly or did she talk?

Oh, we'd just chatter about the picture we were making and what we were going to do tomorrow, and that's why I never knew much about her. We were talking about what we were doing next on the set. We'd discuss the weather or who we liked working with, things like that. We never discussed personal things.

Who else would Ayn Rand have done fittings for?

Ginger Rogers. Ayn Rand would know everybody, because we all had to go into the wardrobe to have our clothes done. She knew all of those people, naturally: June Clyde, Bette Davis, Irene Dunne, Thelma Todd. Katherine Hepburn, for heaven's sake. Walter Plunkett was there too. He was a famous wardrobe designer. He designed a lot of our clothes for the movies.[41]

Was he friends with Ayn Rand?

Oh, of course.

How many people were working at the wardrobe department at one time?

We had about six dressing rooms. We usually had the same ladies, like Ayn, that would fit us. Maybe two or three ladies, but I just remember Ayn, because she always took care of me.

Did she like her job?

She seemed to accept it. It wasn't that she didn't like it, and a job's

---

41 A major costume designer in Hollywood, Walter Plunkett was nominated for ten Oscars, winning for *An American in Paris* (1951). He was Ayn Rand's first boss at the RKO wardrobe department.

a job, and as I say, she couldn't have been nicer. I never saw her out of sorts or anything like that. My goodness, she was a very sweet lady.

Did you read any of Ayn Rand's books?

I loved *The Fountainhead*. That was one of the greatest books I ever read and the movie, oh, my heavens!

Marcella Rabwin

Marcella Rabwin (née Bannett) was executive assistant to movie producer David O. Selznick,[42] and Ayn Rand's next-door neighbor in the early 1930s. Marcella Rabwin died in 1998.

Interview dates: April 25 and July 24, 1996

Scott McConnell: *When did you first meet Miss Rand?*

Marcella Rabwin: I met her first in about 1930. Ayn and I were neighbors in an apartment house on Gower Street, right across from the studio. She worked at my studio, RKO. When I met her she was in the wardrobe department.

What did you do at RKO?

I was David Selznick's secretary. I was at the top for fifteen years.

Did you see Ayn Rand very often?

No. My mother, Elena Epps, did. My mother lived next door to her, and I lived with my mother. My mother was crazy about her. She just thought she was brilliant, which she was. She was extraordinarily brilliant.

Why was your mother "crazy about her"?

I don't know; maybe because my mother came from Russia and because Ayn had a peculiar personality, but she used to talk to my mother all the time and tell her how ambitious she was. I didn't know her well, but my mother did. She was interested in Ayn, who had given her a couple of stories to read. My mother said to me, "I wish you'd take an interest in this girl and try to help her."

I said, "I can't do her any good." But finally she got after me for so long that I talked to my friend Nick Carter, who was an agent for Myron Selznick.[43] I gave the stories to Nick, who said he didn't like them. He said they were very immature. I said, "Try. Try. Try some producer who's immature! Go over to Universal with them and just make the attempt, Nick." I said, "You know, this neighbor of mine has some stories and

---

42 David O. Selznick was the producer of *Gone With the Wind* and many other movies.

43 This Nick Carter was not the Nick Carter who was Frank O'Connor's brother. Myron Selznick (David O. Selznick's brother) was one of the most influential agents in Hollywood.

she's really hungry. Her husband's not working and gets a few days a year as a $7-a-day extra," but, "she's really a very up and at 'em sort of person and she wants very much to sell these stories. Would you look at them?" He said, "Oh okay, if you insist, I'll do it," and he did. He read them, and he thought they had possibilities for a studio like Universal. So I said, "Why don't you take them and see what you can get from them." He said, "What's the least she'll take?" I can't remember what I said, maybe $1,000 to 2,000 for the two of them. They were not great stories, and he was doing me a favor, not her. So he took the stories, and I don't remember how long it took him, maybe a couple or three months. He worked hard, and he sold them for her, the two stories for $3,000.00.[44] And those were days when bread was a nickel. He came back and he gave her a check. It was enough to give her the freedom to quit her job at RKO in the wardrobe department, which she loathed, and give her a little time to start working on her Russian novel, *We the Living*, that she wanted to write. From that point on you couldn't stop her. She wasn't equipped for her job in the wardrobe department. That was not her type of job. This girl was burning with ambition, just burning.

Can you give me some examples of that?

The way she kept after me. "Have you heard from Nick yet? Has he sold anything yet?" But she also talked to me about this Russian book she wanted to do. She was a zealous worker, and at home she would sit there and write all night.

Did you help her in any other way with her stories or selling her stories?

No. She sold the first two and then she wanted to work on her novel, and the next thing I knew, her novel was in print.

How long was Nick Carter an agent? What do you know about his background?

He was short and fat. That takes all the illusion out of it. He was a very good agent, obviously, because he sold these unsalable stories. Somebody at Universal recognized some talent in her. She was completely unknown. He never amounted to much, and he was not missed.

In the apartment building you shared with Miss Rand at 823 N. Gower St., which apartment was yours?

---

44 According to Ayn Rand's records, it was one story for $1,500.

I don't know its number, but I know that I was the apartment east of hers.

You were on the same side of the corridor?

Yes.

How long did you live there?

A couple of years.

Do you know how Miss Rand got her job at RKO?

She applied and they hired her as some kind of a stock girl or something in the wardrobe department.[45] Very lowly job and very low pay.

How would you describe her personality?

She always had a rough personality. She was rough. She was masculine. She was talkative, but not too talkative. Years later when she visited, she still maintained her old habit of sitting down and eating, and Frank would bring her food, and also going to bed or lying on the couch or lying on the floor, anything, willfully. She was very, very full of herself.

What was the neighborhood around Gower like when you were living there?

It was residential. Lower-middle class. Ayn and Frank couldn't have afforded anything other than something inexpensive.

They were very poor?

They really were.

What was their life like?

They didn't really have enough to eat well.

How did they survive?

They lived on her salary, which was very small. At that time the secretary got $20 a week, so she probably got $15.[46]

---

45 Rand got the job through an acquaintance, actor Ivan Lebedeff.
46 She started at $20 per week and soon was at $25 per week.

How did Ayn Rand dress?

Like a dowd. She was the worst-dressed woman I have ever known in my life. She had a terrible figure in the first place. She went around with no makeup on.

Did you meet any other of Ayn Rand's friends?

No. None. I didn't know that she even had any friends. They never did anything, never went anywhere. I never was aware of any friendships.

What did they do?

Nothing. She came home and fell asleep.

Did she have any parties or anything?

Oh no. She was a real loner in those days until she got her hands on this money and was able to quit her job and move away.

In these early days what kind of reputation did Ayn Rand have when people started to know her?

I didn't know her when people started to know her, because she moved the hell out of there in a hurry, because she wanted something better and bigger. She just wanted to get on with her life, and I made it possible for her.

Did you ever see her write?

She wrote with pen and ink on a pad, a regular eight by ten.

Did you keep in touch after she left that apartment?

No. I didn't, but I'm sure my mother did.[47]

While you were living on Gower, did Ayn Rand question you, on the philosophic level, of what you wanted out of life? What your goal was?

No. I think she knew very well what my goal was though. I didn't see her again until I had moved into an elegant house in Beverly Hills with a fairly high standard of living, and she never questioned me, because I was so busy questioning her, I guess.

---

47 Marcella Rabwin did correspond with Ayn Rand, such as the letter of February 5, 1937, which discussed *We the Living*.

What was your life goal then?

I had attained it. I wanted to be a wife and a mother. I had four children. I wanted to work until I wanted children and I did exactly that. I left Hollywood in '42 and had a family.

You were very successful in Hollywood. What was your goal there?

I got what I was after. I wanted to be an assistant to an important producer and I was.

Why did you want to be his assistant?

I think it was the one thing I thought I might be able to do. I knew I couldn't be a writer. Couldn't be an actress. I took a test and it was awful. So I knew that was about the only field I wanted to be in, production.

Did you have any strong conviction at the time about work or other things? What you were like as a person?

I was very conscientious.

Can you remember any strong convictions or opinions that Ayn Rand had?

She hated Russia. She loathed the communist system. She was dying to expose it. She thought she did in *We the Living*.

She would talk about her hatred of the communists?

Oh yes. Oh yes.

What kind of things did she say?

I don't remember. All she did was give me the impression that she loathed, absolutely despised Russia. She was so happy to get out and she didn't like the system. That's all she would say. She just wanted out of Russia, and she got out. She told me this: she was going to write *We the Living* as an exposé of what Russia was really like. It was so horrible.

In the letter that she wrote to you in 1936, she seemed very grateful to you for helping her.

Oh, she was.

How did she express her gratitude?

She thanked me. She wasn't a woman of great many words at that time. She talked like an immigrant. She had only been in this country for a while.[48]

In what way did she talk like an immigrant?

Sort of tentative. She wasn't thoroughly familiar with the language yet. And yet, I thought she had a pretty good command. She was a nice girl.

We were discussing how you helped her with selling her stories and that she seemed very grateful for that.

I don't know. She certainly didn't forget me, though she certainly didn't care for me. I mean, she didn't love and adore me. I was a very elevated person to her. She was not the kind of woman who looked up to people or looked down on people. She may have looked down, but she didn't look up to me, and she didn't forget me.

I was important in her life. I felt as though she was my protégé. I started her in the writing business.

Do you still have that or other letters?

I had one letter that was *sooo* marvelous. It was a long letter.

Was that a handwritten one?

Yes. I kept it and I kept it and I kept it and one day I was cleaning out my files. I was going to move and I was throwing everything away and I sold the letter. It broke my heart. I don't know why I did it, because by then she was very, very celebrated.

Based on material in our archives, Miss Rand was very grateful to you for giving her that break in her writing career.

You know that makes me feel good. She never told me how grateful she was, but she indicated her gratitude when she accepted the dinner invitation.

Tell me about that, the last time you saw Ayn Rand.

She and Frank came for dinner at my house in Beverly Hills about ten years after I had first met her and that's when we had the argument. When she called me, it was a startling surprise.

---

48 She had been in the United States since February 1926.

Why?

Because I hadn't heard from her in the interim. I had no idea she was going to be such a celebrity. She was a little Russian girl living next door to me.

Had she changed since you last met her?

Not one bit. We were sitting in our den. The fireplace was going and she was standing up leaning on the mantle over the fireplace and just chatting. I wanted to know what was going on with them.

I told her that I liked *The Fountainhead* and she asked what I thought about the philosophy, the theories in the novel. I said that I didn't know there was any philosophy in it, and she said, then how can you say that you liked it. I said, because I loved the story. It was fascinating. She got mad and she left, and I never heard from her after that. It was her philosophy that she was so proud of.

Did you disagree with some of her philosophy?

Oh yes, I did. I just disagreed with the fact that philosophy was the most important element. She stood there leaning on the mantelpiece giving me the evil eye. She really disliked me when I said it. She was very proud.

I disagreed with her whole philosophy of life. I don't think one lives one's life for oneself alone. Her philosophy was that you must be happy in your own self; you must do what you want to do when you want to do it. I just felt that it was so abysmal. It was more than selfish—it was really supremely selfish.

Do you remember much about Ayn Rand's politics?

No. Maybe one of the reasons we weren't friends was because we were so different in political outlook. I am a dyed-in-the-wool Democrat. I really didn't believe in the system she proposed for economics.

Did you see the movie of The Fountainhead?

Yes. I loved it. The picture was a visualization of the book. It was a good picture.

Do you remember any of the characters in The Fountainhead *that you especially loved or hated?*

I loved Dominique and I loved Roark.

What did you love about Roark?

Roark was a strong, fine, young, gallant architect. He was just a beautifully pictured man. I just thought he was wonderful.

Did you think he was like Ayn Rand?

Dominique was like Ayn Rand.

In what way?

In her strength.

What did you think of Peter Keating?

Who?

The other architect who got to the top early by using people?

Yes. Yes. Yes. I don't remember him as well. He was sort of a villain, I guess, to me.[49]

---

49 For Ayn Rand's explanation of the connection between Marcella Rabwin and Peter Keating, see Britting, *Ayn Rand*, p. 50

Marna "Docky" Wolfe

Docky Wolfe is Frank O'Connor's niece.

Interview dates: July 9 and 11, 1996; September 30, 1996; October 21, 1996; and February 21, 1997

Scott McConnell: *Sketch the O'Connor family tree for me.*

Docky Wolfe: Frank O'Connor is my maternal uncle. My mother was Agnes O'Connor Papurt, Frank's sister. She was the oldest of the O'Connor girls and was born in 1899.

Frank O'Connor was born on September 21, 1897.

Yes. Frank and his brother Joe were older than she was. Harry, or who we called "Nicky," was the only O'Connor brother that I knew through my life. He died when I was about eighteen, and Bill, the youngest of the boys, always lived near us.

My mother's younger sister was Margaret, who died before I was born in 1927. Her married name was Rhodes. The youngest sister was Elizabeth, and her married name was Donahue.

Frank's mother's name was Minerva, but they called her "Minnie." Cecil was her maiden name, and she married my grandfather Dennis O'Connor. My father was Allen Papurt. Actually his name was Aaron Moses, but he anglicized it to Allen Merle. I think my grandfather I.J. (Papurt) came from Russia. He was Jewish.

I have two sisters, Mimi, which is a nickname for Miriam, and Connie, whose real name is Elizabeth Connor. She was born in 1931. I also have a brother, Lee—four years older than I.

What was Lorain like when you lived there in the 1930s?

It was a small town, about 25,000 people. It had two major industries, a steel plant, the Thew Shovel Company, which made big commercial construction shovels, and what they called the "Stove Company." During World War II the Stove Company made airplane parts. My mother got a job there.

The town was divided by the river and there was Lorain and South Lorain; and South Lorain was the wrong side of the tracks. The O'Connors grew up on the good side.

Tell me more about the O'Connor family.

My mother can thank her brothers for raising her to believe that she was just a little bit better than everybody else, and it carried through her entire life. God forbid that she would be mistaken for shanty Irish. She'd say that the boys taught her manners, and taught her how to behave socially, and taught her that she wasn't just a little Irish brat from Lorain.

My uncle Nicky was the one that my mother said "put on airs." As a kid, I remember him saying that we were direct descendants of the last king of Ireland, Roderick O'Connor. My family would talk about the shanty Irish and the lace-curtain Irish and so on. They were definitely not shanty Irish—at least not according to my mother and my uncle Nick. My mother was a little bit of a snob.

Tell me more about Frank O'Connor's mother.

I know very little, because she died when my mother was a child, nine or ten years old. My mother told a few stories about her, and I understand from my mother that she was a beautiful woman. I have a vague memory that she was English, and my grandfather was a typical handsome Irishman. The family feeling was that she married beneath her.

Did your mother talk much about herself and her siblings?

Yes, she would always talk about them, especially the shows they put on in the backyard and that her brothers taught her to skate and ride a bike.

What exactly were the stage shows?

Skits. I think it was Joe who wrote most of the skits. I guess everyone had their hand in it, except the girls who were forced into it.

Tell me about your uncle Joe O'Connor.

I never met him. He was off being an itinerant actor, and the family didn't keep real close contact. He was with a touring Shakespearean company. When he died, we got a letter from a woman in this acting troupe. My mother got his insurance, so he apparently kept track of us. Joe died probably in the early '40s. I was under the impression that they had this troupe and that he was a manager or director, and I think he acted in it too. Nick never married, and neither did Joe, but he had a long-time lady friend.

My uncle Nick was in New York when Frank and Ayn were, and

he later died in New York. Both my uncle Joe and my uncle Nick were gassed during World War I, in France. Both of them from then on were on disability pensions due to lung damage. I have one picture of Joe in his army uniform.

When did you first meet Ayn Rand and Frank O'Connor?

The very first time was when I was in the fifth or sixth grade—nine or ten years old. That's when she gave me my first pair of ice skates. Which was a great thrill. My dad died when I was fourteen. I know my uncle Bill was at the funeral but I have the feeling that Ayn and Frank were there too. That was 1943?

Later when I was a teenager, Ayn used to send us some smashing clothes.[50] Mimi and I were the same size in those days and we used to fight over who got what. She was distant but not ever unkind.

Describe Ayn Rand and Frank O'Connor together.

Ayn was always the major personality. I remember having dinner somewhere and Frank had a couple of mixed drinks with dinner, and he wanted ice cream for dessert. She told him he couldn't have ice cream for dessert because he had had a couple of drinks and all that cold stuff was going to give him polio. He just smiled and didn't have the ice cream. I said something to the effect, if you're such a realist how can you believe these crazy wives' tales? She said: might as well be careful, maybe they're not wives' tales.

I think she mother-henned him a little bit in those days. "Button your jacket," "Don't eat too fast," that kind of thing. She said it affectionately. He seemed to be very easy going—whatever she said. I never saw him argue back with her.

Tell me about your relationship with them.

Ours was a very casual "oh there's a relative"-type relationship. I was fond of him, and I think he was of me, but we didn't live near each other. I didn't see a lot of Ayn when I was an adult. They lived in California and I lived in Ohio. So we would just see them during the regular family visits, when they would come east.

What's your strongest memory of Frank O'Connor?

That he was a very sweet man. He was one of my favorite uncles.

---

50 For details, see *Letters of Ayn Rand*, p. 391.

You can be around people and know that they like you, or at least they aren't putting you down when you're a kid. He never did that. He was very sweet and very patient.

When my son Mark [born in 1948] was little we lived in Flushing, New York, and visited Ayn and Frank when they came to New York. During that period, my son took his first steps to Ayn. She was wearing a gold dollar-sign necklace or pin, and he stepped over and grabbed it, and she got the biggest kick out of that. She said, "Now, there's my grandnephew."

Did Mark later visit Miss Rand or Mr. O'Connor?

In 1968 he was in the music business, managing recording artists, and was going to New York on business. He said he'd like to see Ayn and Frank; he hadn't seen them since he was little, and now he was twenty. So he called Mimi to get their phone number, and Mimi said, "Okay, but I'll call Ayn first, to let her know you're coming." Mimi did and called us back, laughing. Ayn wanted to know if Mark was one of those dirty, long-haired hippies. Mimi told her, "He has long hair, but it's clean."

So Mark's long hair didn't bother her?

Not at that time—all the kids had long hair then. When Mark got to New York and took care of his business, he called Ayn. She wanted to know if he was interesting enough to spend an evening with. He said he thought so. So they invited him over and he said he had a very pleasant evening with them. That was shortly after the Democratic convention here in Chicago, because I remember they talked about that.[51]

What's your strongest memory of Ayn Rand?

That she had absolutely no sense of humor.

She never laughed at your jokes or jokes generally?

No, and then when I would crack wise, as most fifteen- or seventeen-year-old kids would, she would take it seriously.

Can you remember an example?

I saw her when I was nine, and then I didn't see her until I was around fifteen when they came for a family funeral. She sat down to

---

51 The convention was held in August 1968.

start the conversation and said, "Tell me, Docky, what do you think?" I said, logically, "about what?" And she said, "Anything, I want to know how your mind works." I was a little brat, and so I spun her a tale, a fantasy. She took every bit of it seriously and discussed it with me. I was putting her on, and she wasn't getting it.

Here's a story, though, that shows she did sometimes have a sense of humor. My daughter, Marta, was a blue baby, born with congenital heart disease.[52] When she was three or four, her brother Mark was seventeen months older. Marta was crying and having an attack, and he said, "Mommy, why does Marta get sick so much?" I said, "When Marta was born God made a mistake." My mother-in-law, who was a very devout Jewish lady, heard this and said to me, "How dare you tell my grandchild that God makes mistakes." So, at a later time, when we were talking about her atheism, I passed this story on to Ayn. She just looked at me and got a little half smile on her face and said, "How dare you tell my grandnephew there's a God."

Did Ayn Rand send your family copies of her plays or novels or scripts?

She sent copies of *The Fountainhead* and *Atlas Shrugged*. When *The Fountainhead* came out I was fourteen or fifteen. I read it, and when she asked me what I thought about it, I said, "It seems to me that you wrote that whole book so you could write that courtroom speech."

What did Miss Rand reply?

"How astute of you to see that."

Any other things Miss Rand told you about the novels or any other of her stories?

During the writing of *Atlas Shrugged* she told me about how she went on the railroad, and that kind of thing. I remember her telling me she got to ride in an engine and they gave her an engineer's cap.

She was writing that book forever, and I remember asking her, "Are you ever going to finish?" She replied "Yeah, maybe next year."

When *The Fountainhead* came out, I can remember being my usual smart-aleck self, and I asked her about the sex scenes. I said, "How do you write those sex scenes, Ayn?" And she said, "You'll just have to ask your uncle Frank, dear."

---

52 She was born January 9, 1950.

What did Uncle Frank say?

He just smiled.

So she did have a sense of humor.

Yes, occasionally it popped out, but I still remember her being humorless. Of course, that could be my reaction as a child then.

I believe Miss Rand helped put you through school?

I was a high school dropout; only, I was what they called "major work." I guess they call it honors courses now.

Was it a gifted school you went to in Cleveland?

Yes. I had been in a gifted class since lower grammar school grades, fourth grade or so, and at about sixteen, like a lot of kids, I just dropped out. I was going through that adolescent pain-in-the-neck stage. So my sister Mimi was damn well going to see that I went back to school. My dad was dead then, and my mom was living on a veteran's widow's pension of $99 a month and was raising three kids, not counting Mimi. So I worked, and Mimi wanted me to go back to school. If you read the letters about this in *Letters of Ayn Rand*, you'll see that I wasn't in on any of these negotiations. Ayn, at least, did have the grace to ask me what I thought about it all. I did want to go back and finish. But I guess Mimi and Ayn were giving me more credit because I was supposedly bright. Ayn paid my expenses for a year when I went back to school and I had to finish in a year, but that deal started in April and the school year started in September. So I was supposed to make up all that work and finish in June for that semester. The next semester, when I went to the next school year I would have graduated, except that my year ended in April and Mimi pulled me out, so I didn't graduate. You'll see in one of those letters where Ayn says Docky promised to graduate and she didn't. But I did, eventually, on my own, get a GED diploma.[53]

Did you ever tell Ayn Rand that you graduated?

I think so, yes.
Ayn would say she didn't believe in charity, and I said to her, "If you don't believe in charity, why did you send me money to go to school." She said, "That was not charity; that was an investment. My return was that you did finish." Then she said, "And you didn't finish."

---

53 GED is the General Education Development Test, a high school equivalency exam.

But I had by that time.

Mimi once wrote Ayn a letter and told her that she was having me read this and read that and so on, and she wrote back that she approved of Mimi's choice. She wrote, "You should have asked me because I had a few suggestions." But they aren't in the letters, so I don't know what suggestions she had.

Tell me about your husband Fabian.

Fabian was a magician, and when we were first married I was the magician's assistant. We did a comedy magic presentation where I actually did more magic than he did. Ayn, Frank and Fabian got along famously. My husband at that time was with U.S.O. and hospital camp shows, doing his magic act. They had never met before, so he actually met them cold out in California in 1948.

Why did they get on so well?

He was very entertaining, and Ayn, as brilliant and sophisticated as she was, was very childlike about a lot of things. She got a big kick out of him being a magician and doing tricks for her.

Tell me about your husband later taking photographs of Miss Rand.

We moved to Chicago in December of 1950, so it was sometime after that, when we were at a magicians' convention in New York. We had an evening with Frank and Ayn. We went out to dinner somewhere, then we went back to their apartment and visited. Fabe had his camera with him, and I just remember him taking a picture. I think there was also a picture of me and Frank taken that same night. We mostly just talked. I believe at that time Frank had another apartment in the building, where he did his painting.

Later in New York, my husband did a photographic portrait of Ayn standing in front of that portrait of her. He was an award-winning photographer.

Did you talk with Miss Rand about specific movies that she loved?

No, but on one of her visits to New York from California, Ayn, Frank and I got together. She had a script of a movie she was writing, and she had me read a scene from it with Frank. I was about nineteen years old and reading a love scene with your aged uncle—I can remember how embarrassed I was. I don't remember the name of the story, but it was a sort of dark, brooding *Wuthering Heights-*

type tale.[54]

What was the purpose of the reading?

I think it was just for fun. She knew that I had worked in the act with my husband for a while, before Mark was born. She thought I would like to go on the stage and she was giving me a try.

Your sister Mimi had a very long relationship with Miss Rand and Mr. O'Connor.

Mimi, who was born in 1918, spent her summers, from the time she was about fifteen, with Ayn and Frank, so they were really close. In fact, Mimi was very close to both of them. I suppose that she was a surrogate child for them. I think Mimi loved Ayn and considered her a dear friend, and Frank was a beloved uncle. Mimi talked about going to the theater and going out to lunch and the things you do in New York, like going to all the museums. I guess that she and Frank did a lot of things together. Then when my uncle Nick was in New York, he was involved too.

They had a lot of fun. Mimi had a lot of stories to tell about her summers with them. She was with them when *The Unconquered*—the *We the Living* play [1939]—and *Night of January 16th* [1935] opened. She would tell me that at parties Frank would pass Ayn little notes saying, "Talk to your cousin Lotsy" or "For God's sake, talk to so and so." She was not socially outgoing. Those kinds of thing she just considered a waste of her time.

Mimi told me once that Ayn had her cat trained to hop up on the toilet seat. Instead of going to a litter box, it was trained to hop up on the toilet seat and use the toilet. I was in such awe of it when I was a kid.

Was Mimi in agreement with Ayn Rand's philosophy?

I'm not sure how much she was in agreement. After *Atlas Shrugged* came out Ayn gave a talk here in Chicago at the McCormick Place in 1963. Mimi and I went and Fern Brown and her family—all of Ayn's relatives—went. After she was through speaking and the house lights went up, Frank came out to get us. We went with them to a cocktail party and were introduced to somebody as Frank O'Connor's nieces. Mimi's husband David was a vice president of a big pharmaceutical company, and all their friends were bankers and so on—and some little

---

54 This is most probably Ayn Rand's 1947 adaptation of Maria Luisa Bombal's novel *House of Mist* (Farrar, Straus & Co., 1947).

woman asked Mimi what her friends thought about Ayn's book *Atlas Shrugged*. Mimi just looked at her and said, "Well, frankly, my friends are too busy earning money to read about it." I think that was her attitude about Ayn's philosophy: do it, don't read about it.

Mimi had a running correspondence with Ayn over the years. In later years there weren't as many letters because they talked on the phone almost every week. Toward the end of Frank's life, when he was very ill, Ayn offered to pay for Mimi to come live with her and Frank, so she could help take care of Frank.

Did Mimi go?

No. One, because she didn't want to go to New York, away from her children, family, grandchildren and so on. And, two, she wouldn't have been physically able to take care of Frank. She was very ill herself in the last couple of years of her life.[55]

When was the last time you saw Ayn Rand and Frank O'Connor?

She came to Chicago to be on the *Donahue* show in 1980. Frank was dead then. Mimi went down and had dinner with her, and then the three of us got together for a brief visit later that evening. Ayn and Mimi spent more time together. I was working.

How was she?

I watched the *Donahue* show in my office, and I remember thinking she looked pretty good. When I saw her, I said, "You look pretty good," and she said, "Pretty good compared to what?" or "How do you know I look good?" I just said, "You look pretty good to me."

When was the last time you saw Frank O'Connor?

I think the visit to New York with the magic show or a later one. Fabe and I went back to New York three or four times and we always visited them when we went there. We went to dinner or we just went to their apartment for an hour or two.

Frank was the model for a comic strip version of The Fountainhead. *Did the family read the comic strip? Were they surprised?*

No. It wouldn't have surprised us that he was the model—she always said that her heroes were based on Frank.

---

55 Mimi Sutton died in 1984.

Paul S. Nathan

Paul S. Nathan met Ayn Rand in the early 1940s when she was an "outside" reader for the Paramount story department in New York and he was an assistant play editor. Mr. Nathan wrote about *The Fountainhead* movie in his "Books into Films" column in *Publishers Weekly* (June 11, 1949). Mr. Nathan died in 2009.

Interview date: March 6, 1997

Scott McConnell: *How did you meet Ayn Rand?*

Paul S. Nathan: I came to New York from California in 1936 and I was interested in the theater, primarily. I started applying for some reading jobs at movie companies and the first chance I got was with RKO. The studio was in California but they had offices in New York City. While I was doing that, I got in touch with Paramount Pictures and they were very eager to have me come over and read for them.

Where were they?

They were in Times Square in the Paramount building. So I did some reading for them, and after a while I talked to the story editor, Richard Halliday, who later married Mary Martin. I became the assistant play editor. It was during that period that I met Ayn Rand.

Can you remember your first meeting?

No, not really, but there were readers in and out, and I got to know them by sight and to some extent personally. This would be maybe 1936 or 1937. Sometime then or shortly into the next year I did meet Ayn and the impression I got was of someone who was very driven, I would say, from her experiences. I believe she came from Russia and she must have had a terrible time and hated it.

Why do you say that?

Because she was so anti-Communist.

She was also a reader at MGM. Where in New York were they located?

They were on 7th Avenue or on Broadway, somewhere around

Times Square.

How did Ayn Rand dress when she was with you?

I remember her being kind of dramatic looking. It seemed to me she had rather sharp features. I don't know if that's true or if it's just her general air of preoccupation with something important to her and a kind of determination. But I picture sort of iron-grayish—what we used call "bobbed"—hair. It was rather short, straight hair, sort of sweeping back, and perhaps—and this may be imagination—perhaps a wrinkle between her eyebrows, sort of like a frown from intensity.

What was her manner?

It was sort of no-nonsense. I think she tended toward being a little theatrical. I never really agreed with what I understood her to represent, but I thought she was interesting.

Jack Bungay

Jack Bungay was movie producer Hal Wallis's assistant for fifteen years, and Miss Rand's secretary in 1946.

Interview dates: June 6 and 10, 1996

Scott McConnell: *How did you meet Miss Rand?*

Jack Bungay: I met Ayn when she did *The Fountainhead* at Warner Brothers Studios. I met her at the studio, when she came to do the screenplay for us. I was working for Hal Wallis, who was then the executive producer at Warner Brothers. I lived with Ayn and Frank in their house in the valley for a matter of months in 1946.

What did you do for Mr. Wallis?

I was more or less a glorified errand boy. I did a little bit of everything. I worked with the directors, with the actors, with the costumers, and I looked for talent for him, and if something would go wrong I would deal with that. I don't think he had too many writers working for him when he was working with her.

How long did you work for Hal Wallis?

I was with him for almost fifteen years. I started out from college when he was making *Casablanca* [in 1942].

Tell me about Miss Rand's relationship with Mr. Wallis.

All I can say is that as boss and writer they got along beautifully. I never heard them argue. They were very congenial. I was really surprised because I thought there might be a little friction there. They were two very dominant people, but they discussed things.

Describe Ayn Rand then.

Beautiful eyes, black hair and very beautiful lips, very prominent lips, a lovely face, not especially big, but a beautiful smile. But boy, you looked at that woman and you knew that was a dynamic personality, you could tell in her face. There was a lot of sex in her face. It was amazing. She was a very sensual woman. You could feel a sensuality about her.

What was her manner of movement? Was she high energy, high voltage?

Oh, high voltage all the time. You wondered, is this battery ever going to wear out? Just everything she did. She wasn't a relaxed person. She was thinking all of the time. This machine never turned off, never. You could feel this magnetism, this dynamo inside this lady that never shut down. It was going twenty-four hours a day and I used to wonder how she could even sleep. I adored her.

She must have felt worn out or tired at times?

I never saw it.

Why were you living with Miss Rand and Mr. O'Connor?

They just asked me to. I think she wanted me there so we could discuss things. I knew a little more about picture-making. I wasn't working for her; I had my regular studio job. I came back and forth. I was still working at the studio but I can't tell you why I even went out there, unless she asked me to come and I wanted to be with them.

Ayn had an old Royal typewriter, and I couldn't believe it. On an old, rickety, beat-up machine. I called the Royal people and told them the situation, that Ayn Rand, this famous writer, was working on an old Royal typewriter, and they sent her a brand new one. She was overwhelmed when it arrived. She was just very excited. She loved it.[56]

Describe how Miss Rand worked at the studio and at home.

She would do the scripts at home and then take them to the studio and hand them over to be transcribed. They were then sent around to the different people and all that sort of thing. I believe she handwrote them. I don't remember her typing them.

Can you describe her working method or what you observed?

No, because she'd lock herself in the room, the library, and she'd stay there. After breakfast you didn't talk to her. When she was working, Frank and I never bothered her. Never. You didn't bother her all day long.

Was she working on scripts then or was it Atlas Shrugged?

It was *Atlas*.

Did she come out for lunch or anything?

---

56 See *Letters of Ayn Rand*, p. 285, for her thank-you letter to the company.

She'd come out for lunch. Sometimes she'd talk and sometimes she wouldn't.

Would Mr. O'Connor be there for lunch?

Yes, always. You would have to leave it up to her whether or not she wanted to talk. If she didn't want to talk, you didn't—she was still thinking. But it was fascinating to see somebody work like that.

What did she do at night?

We had dinner and talk and that sort of thing. She was very sociable.

Did you talk a lot of philosophy with her?

Quite a bit.

Any special conversations?

No. I remember mostly her saying to me, "When are you going to start writing?"

Did she give you advice on that?

No. She said, you go ahead and I'll help you. And she signed in a book to me, "To the budding writer." I treasure it very, very much.

She wanted me to be a writer. That was her big thing. "You must. You must. You must."

Did you?

Not a great deal. Not enough. I should write something about studio life.

What else would she want to talk about?

She'd ask me about Hollywood, what I knew. She was always interested in Hollywood people. What they were like and what their lives were and that sort of thing. She liked music.

What would she do when listening to music?

She had a kind of cute little trick. She'd walk around with a cane and tap it on the floor and do a semi-tap dance routine. She'd come in at night with a cane and walk around swinging her cane doing a little two-step. That was a la [Marlene] Dietrich. Maybe ten or fifteen minutes. It'd be on the radio as I recall. Frank and I'd look and watch and laugh. It was quite fascinating. It was adorable.

Did she enjoy working in Hollywood?

Ayn was not too happy in Hollywood. She was happier in New York. She had a beautiful house out there in Chatsworth, but she still loved New York. Ayn was a New Yorker. That's where she was happy. She was, in a way, a displaced New Yorker. I remember later being in their apartment, looking up at the Empire State Building. She just adored it. Buildings and all. She was in heaven when she was in New York. She loved everything about New York, the buildings, everything. She told me that.

What was Ayn Rand's reputation in Hollywood?

I think she was greatly admired as a writer. Politically, it depended on what side you were on. This was a bad time for pictures as far as I was concerned. This fighting and wrangling back and forth and people's careers being ruined and all that sort of thing, it was horrible.

I was just amazed that she put up with me as much as she did, because we didn't agree politically, but we didn't discuss it.

Was she ever rude or insulting to you about this?

No, no, never. We got along without our thinking being the same.

Did you see her argue and debate her philosophy with people?

I recall her talking about it somewhat, but I don't remember her arguing about it. She was very firm in her ideas, there's no question about that. She was very much a lady that way, as far as I was concerned.

What would Mr. O'Connor do on their ranch?

Frank would look around and see that everything was taken care of in the house and then do his gardening and that sort of thing. He loved flowers and loved gardening. He had a helper or two. He grew flowers and vegetables. He did nursery work at one time.

Frank could have been a good leading man. He was handsome and he had a lot of charm. Very quiet, but a lot of charm and if that could have been captured . . .

Did you ever meet Albert Mannheimer?[57]

---

57 Mr. Mannheimer was a close friend of Miss Rand's. A playwright and screenwriter, he was nominated in 1950 for an Academy Award for his script for *Born Yesterday*.

Yes. I know she was terribly, terribly fond of him. They were very close friends. I thought he was going to be her heir then.

What did they used to do together?

They discussed politics a lot. They both seemed interested in that as well as the writing.

Did she talk about her relatives and family?

She did not talk about her family in Russia. She was terrified that they might be persecuted because of her. You were very aware that this was the whole reason, that she was afraid of that. That's why she had the name "Ayn Rand." I didn't for years know what her real name was.

Did she ever tell you where she got her name from?

She would not reveal that! We knew it was Russian. And she would not tell us her real name, ever. I asked her and we talked about it and she said there were people in Russia who might be hurt. I don't know whether it was family or friends or what. She would not tell.

Walter Seltzer

Walter Seltzer was the director of publicity and advertising for Hal Wallis Productions when Miss Rand was a screenwriter there. He later became a film producer.

Interview dates: June 24 and July 12, 1996

Scott McConnell: *How long did you work for Hal Wallis?*

Walter Seltzer: From 1945 through '54.

What was your opinion of Ayn Rand?

I thought she was a very tough, smart, definite lady who was an activist before activism among females became popular. Many of her social and economic ideas I tended to disagree with. I considered some of them extreme and philosophically selfish. I thought she was a fine writer and a very, very interesting lady. She was gifted. And she could get inside of characters and inside of people.

I can just sum up by saying she was a very serious artist. She did her work efficiently and well and as to any personal clashes or anything like that I have no recollection.

I remember her coming into the office. She did a great deal of conferring with Wallis, who was no mean judge of stories himself. And they worked together very well. I think there was mutual regard, which was really an important asset. It was a comfortable relationship. There was a lot of innocent flirtation going on.

Do you have an example?

I can't specify, but they spent long hours on story conferences. I don't mean to imply anything improper.

What did Mr. Wallis think of her?

Obviously he thought very highly of her—he kept using her. She was there for five years. That's a long time with a writer. The longevity of screenwriters wasn't normally, then or now, that long. I think he thought she was tops as a writer. Had he not, he would not have signed her to a contract or used her that much.

Can you describe the process of the scriptwriting work she did. For example, was she assigned a story to work on?

Yes. I think things were purchased to which she was assigned to write a screenplay. Then if the writer was under contract he would say, "Would you be interested in any of these?" And it would be her selection then, and then there would be a normal discussion about what direction the story would take. Then the writer would be off and running. A normal progression is a synopsis, a short treatment, a long treatment and then right into screenplay.

How often would Miss Rand come in to have meetings with Mr. Wallis?

At least weekly, sometimes more frequently.

Do you know which office Ayn Rand used on the Paramount lot?

She worked mostly at home. If she worked at the studio, she would have used one of the offices to the east of Wallis's on the second floor of the Administration building.

Did Mr. Wallis supply her with secretaries?

If she required one, it was always furnished by the employer.

Would the secretary live with Miss Rand or go out each day?

The secretary would go to work at nine o'clock or the appointed hour and work through the day, and then the secretary would go home. If she had a full-time secretary that's the way it worked. If it was just piecework, the secretary would come, take notes, take dictation and buzz off.

She started off at $500 a week, and after incremental increases stipulated in the contract, she ended up getting $1,000 a week.

That was very generous pay for a contract writer. I think that would have been above scale.

Tell me about Love Letters.

That was one that I became involved with—marketing, creating the advertising and publicity campaign, which was my job.

Was she used in the publicity?

Yes, we did some interviews with her in the local papers, the L.A. dailies—the *Times*, the *Herald-Express*, the *Examiner*, the *Daily News*.

What is the thing that really sticks in your mind about her?

A rather unique appearance. She was not your everyday picture of a Hollywood celebrity. She did not dress in the norm of the day. She dressed severely. Very dark dresses and hats.

And when she met you, how was she?

Warm and friendly.

Robert Douglas

Robert Douglas acted in many Hollywood movies and played Ellsworth Toohey in the 1949 production of *The Fountainhead*. He died in 1999.

Interview dates: August 19 and 20, 1997

Scott McConnell: *How did you get the role of Ellsworth Toohey?*

Robert Douglas: I made a test for it. I read the book and I would like to have played the Wynand part, but when they saw the test they said I'd be better playing Ellsworth Toohey.

I wanted to play the Wynand part that Raymond Massey played, and Ayn Rand didn't approve of that at all, nor did Jack Warner. Then when I saw Mr. Warner, we had a very nice conversation at lunch one day, and he said, "How about playing Toohey?" I said that he's too old, but Mr. Warner said no, don't wear a hairpiece, we'll gray you up and play you a little older.

Kent Smith [who played Peter Keating] was a lovely, wonderful person. I did my test with him, the scene where I shoved him into the chair and practically hit him and told him what a weakling he was. It was the test that Warner loved. "No question—I want Douglas to play that part."

Who else was up for the role of Ellsworth Toohey?

My main competition was a very well-known actor, Clifton Webb.

Why didn't he get the role?

He practically had it, but when I made a very good test, Mr. Warner said that he'd rather that I played the part than Clifton Webb.

Did you base your performance of Toohey on anyone real that you knew?

No, I took it purely and simply from the characterization she had conceived, and I tried to stick with it.

So how did you play him?

I thought that I should play him with strength. When I told the director, King Vidor, he and I agreed that Toohey should have a certain strength against Roark.[58]

---

58 This is in contrast to Miss Rand's view that he should be played "slippery," as she put it in her 1960–61 biographical interviews.

So you thought that strength was better than playing him as slippery and snide.

Oh yes. That would have been too easy.

Can you remember anything you did that helped you to make Toohey three-dimensional for the viewer?

Yes. Having studied the book very carefully, having studied the situation very carefully and the relationship with Roark, I decided that he should be one-dimensional: I should be very strong and resent Roark.

What did King Vidor discuss with you about the role of Toohey, and how did he direct you?

Vidor, of course, is probably one of the best directors that's ever been in Hollywood, and we got along extremely well. We saw eye to eye about a great many things. The only person who didn't quite agree with us from time to time was Ayn Rand. To read a book and sum up a character is one thing and to go along with characters is one thing, but then to portray them is another thing. It's two entirely different worlds, and Vidor and I had ideas about how it should be played, and he went along with me.

In what way did Ayn Rand disagree with you and Mr. Vidor?

It has happened many times with successful writers. They see a scene and think it should be spoken and acted the way they had written it, but sometimes it doesn't work that well. That makes for a dreadful movie, and you have to look at it from another angle. She was very short-sighted in seeing beneficial angles to various scenes and how they were played.

Can you remember any specific ones?

No, not specifically. She was always behind the camera, and there were certain scenes she'd watch and say, "Yes, that's very good. I like that." However, sometimes one improvised and used different words and she didn't like that. She wanted every single word she had written to be spoken, and that's what we disagreed upon, because to have a conversation—particularly with Gary Cooper, because dear Gary couldn't remember all the lines and all the words exactly as she had written them—so in a scene with him one would have to improvise an exchange.

What else would she be doing on the set?

She would just sit there in her chair, very close to the camera, and watch, and we would rehearse. As we would rehearse, she would then go to King Vidor, who would discuss it with her and then possibly with us. Anything that she didn't like, it was worked out.

She had that much control?

She had more control than anyone I've ever seen in Hollywood with her own book or script.

Why was that?

Those were the conditions she had in her contract.

So Mr. Vidor had to listen to her?

No, not necessarily. Up to a point he did, yes. He valued her point of view and it worked out very well between them.

How would you describe their relationship during the movie?

Very good.

Did he often consult with her?

No. He did things the way he wanted to, and then she would discuss something with him and he would give his reasons. It's very difficult for a writer like Ayn Rand to understand the effect a scene is going to have on the screen when the actors have different personalities than the characters in the book.

Were there any difficulties with the courtroom speech?

No, I think the only problem was for Gary Cooper. He was never an actor for dialogue. In all his past movies he used a minimum of dialogue, so consequently, when he was given a huge speech—now had Olivier played that speech, it would have been a magnificent speech—and that was the only time Gary came unstuck. He never had the background to be able to deliver a speech like that. The thought was that Vidor had to cut to Pat Neal and me and Raymond Massey for reactions, and poor Gary had to do it in sections and record it.

What did you think of The Fountainhead *book?*

I thought it was wonderful, a very exciting book. It was very controversial, and I think it was a book that came out of the times. It was very tough for people to be enterprising and to be original.

So you agreed with the philosophy or the ideas in the book?

Oh, absolutely.

Especially the ones on selfishness?

Yes.

Can you summarize your impression of Ayn Rand?

I didn't particularly like her. She was a very obstinate woman, and she did not exude any charm of any kind. She was down to earth about everything, even if you talked about the character or the scene, she would express a point of view, and that was the only point of view necessary.

Would you call it an intelligent or informed point of view?

Oh yes. Oh yes.

Did she convince you of her point of view?

Yes, up to a point. She made very intelligent points, and, after all, she had written the characters based on, I imagine, something she had been in contact with at sometime in her life.

When she was discussing these things with you, what was her manner?

Very simple, very direct. Very little humor. I think she was quite a difficult lady to work with. She was a very determined little woman. She wanted her own way. She felt that she had written the Bible.

Patricia Neal

Patricia Neal has starred in more than fifty movies and won an Academy Award for best actress in 1963. In 1949 she starred in *The Fountainhead*.

Interview date: August 28, 1997

Scott McConnell: *How did you get the role of Dominique Francon?*

Patricia Neal: I was walking on the Warners lot and met this man on a bicycle. He came off the bicycle and we talked and talked. Eventually, he told me his name was King Vidor, and he asked me if I would like to test for the part of Dominique. So he tested me, and apparently one test was no good, but the other was good, so I got the role.

I just adored doing the role. I met Gary Cooper when King Vidor was going to test me. Vidor had Gary come to his office and we talked and we got on well. I know that Gary was there when I did one test; it must have been the best one. I got it and then we began shooting.

Was it a scene from the script that you used in the test?

Oh yes—two scenes.

Were you playing against Gary Cooper or just a model?

Just a young boy at the studio, and Gary came in and watched the test.

I believe that there were a lot of people up for that role?

I know that one was Barbara Stanwyck. She had Warners buy the rights for her. She left Warner Brothers when she didn't get the part.

Do you remember any other famous actresses who were considered for the part?

I think Ayn Rand wanted Greta Garbo. Garbo came to see King Vidor and she said, "Do you think I'm right for that part?" And he said, "No, I don't. I think you're too old." She said, "Thank you very much," and she agreed.

That's what Vidor told you?

Yes. Getting the part was fantastic. We didn't see a lot of the writer, we really didn't. She wasn't on the set a lot. I know that when Gary didn't like something in the script and wanted to change it, King Vidor said, "Well, we'll have to send for Ayn Rand. She'll take two hours to come out."[59] And Gary would say, "Oh, well, I'll do it as written."

What did she do when she was there?

She just looked. I never saw her do any work there. She just would smile at us, that kind of thing. She'd sit in a chair or stand with her husband.

If you didn't talk to Ayn Rand about the acting, what did you talk to her about?

She said, "Oh, you'll be very good," "You're lovely." I remember her saying that sort of thing. I remember her being there about four or five times. I want to tell you that we got on well when I met her.

What do you remember about her husband?

He was good-looking. When I say good-looking, I mean I liked his looks. He seemed to be quite as interested as she was in her work.

How did King Vidor direct you?

To me, King Vidor was not the greatest director in the world. He was good and he knew the camera a lot better than he knew actors. He just was not an actor's director. He'd try to say something, but he was not very good at telling you what he wanted. I liked him though; he was a beautiful man.

Tell me about the "rape scene" in the movie.

Obviously, I wanted it. If that film was done today, you would see all sorts of things we could not do in those days. We could not do one thing that the censors wouldn't let us do. They were so powerful. Now they do not exist.

Was that the Johnston Office?

Yeah.

Were they on the set or involved with the script?

Oh yes, they were on the set a lot. They wouldn't have any curse words. I forget how many things they cut, but anything that was

---

59 Ayn Rand lived in Chatsworth, about twenty miles from Warner Bros. studios in Burbank.

shocking for people in the U.S.A.

What did you think of your performance in the movie?

I did my best, but I didn't know enough about film. If I did it now, if I were young enough, I'd be a lot better. I know a lot more about acting than I did then, and I would do a better job. But I'm a little old now.

What was Ayn Rand like?

She was very friendly.

What did you think of the script of The Fountainhead?

I thought it was good. She was a very good writer.

What did you think of the movie?

Unfortunately, it was a disappointment at the box office. I don't know why it was, but it was. I remember opening night and everybody looked the other way. Nobody looked at me except June Haver,[60] and she said, "Oh my, you were bad!" She didn't mean my performance, she meant my character.

That's why you were disappointed with the movie?

No. It just didn't do well and we wanted it to do wonders. We wanted it to be the most fabulous film ever made, but it didn't come out that way.

Was it a flop or just a mediocre hit or what?

I think it was mediocre.

Any other stories about the premiere?

I know that we went to that great nightclub on Sunset Strip, or wherever it was. I sat next to Gary, and he held my hand under the table, to make me feel better because no one was saying a word.

Did Mr. Cooper ever express to you his agreement with the ideas in the movie?

I do think he did agree more than I did.

What did he like?

---

60 June Haver was a movie actress and dancer in the 1940s and '50s.

I think being independent, being individual. I think that's what he liked best. He was sort of like that. He was his own man.

How were Gary Cooper and Ayn Rand together?

They seemed to get on very well. She wasn't around a lot, but she seemed to love him and he liked her.

Do you have any last comments about Ayn Rand or The Fountainhead *movie?*

I adored doing it. It was the greatest thing of my life when that happened.

Roy Brewer

Roy Brewer was the international representative of IATSE (International Alliance of Theatrical Stage Employees), the major Hollywood guild union, and was one of the principal opponents of the communists in Hollywood. With Ayn Rand he was a member of the Motion Picture Alliance for the Preservation of American Ideals (MPA). Mr. Brewer died in 2006.

Interview dates: September 9 and 25, 1997, and November 20, 1997

Scott McConnell: *Tell me about Ayn Rand in the MPA in the mid-1940s.*

Roy Brewer: Ayn was kind of a loner, and she was a person who lived in her own little world. Most of the conversations that we had were when we were going in and out of the meetings. We'd stop and talk, and we used to kid her. She told us union members that were in the MPA, "You shouldn't have anything to do with me," she says, "because I'm very anti-union." She was very honest and frank. We just laughed it off, because she was helping us as she could, in the immediate problem, which we were organized to try to accomplish. She was antigovernment, and so one day we said, "Well, what about the streets, Ayn? Is it all right for the government to make the streets?" We were just kidding her, that way, and she took it very seriously. And a couple of meetings later she says, "I've been giving that a lot of thought, and I kind of believe that maybe there is a place for the government to build streets."

What was she like?

She was not an attractive person, certainly. She was always studying, always thoughtful, and she believed what she believed. She was not a talkative person. I don't think she had an important impact. She didn't influence very many people. Ayn Rand was just an unusual person.

Describe Ayn Rand at one of the meetings.

The thing that stands out in my mind was that she was anti-government, everything it did, and that was an extreme position, and none of us really shared that position with her. But she joined us on the theory that the Communist movement was an evil, bad movement, and it ought to be challenged and destroyed. And she wrote our declaration of principles.

Were there any other things that she proposed or talked about at the meetings?

No, she never was a dominant person in the meetings.

Who was the dominant person?

Jim McGuinness was the spiritual leader. He made a statement once that I've never forgotten; it was that every person was a child of God, and could never be any man's slave.

Bill Johnson

Bill Johnson worked on the radio show that broadcast a dramatization of *Anthem* in 1951.

Interview date: December 8, 1996

Scott McConnell: *How did you meet Ayn Rand?*

Bill Johnson: Thad Ashby[61] was the one who made that contact, and he was working for me as a writer and associate editor on a magazine that I edited called *Faith and Freedom*. Thad knew her, and as a result, we were invited to these meetings with her. And it's probably through him that we got her to give us permission to have her on the show.

Tell me about your meetings with Ayn Rand.

We attended four or five evenings with her in her home, where we talked philosophy and theology and politics, and everything else. It was in the early 1950s. We thought she was great. Very incisive arguments. She was extremely straight-thinking on freedom issues.

Was Thad Ashby religious?

I don't believe he was. I did not attend church on a regular basis, but Thad and I were primarily interested in the freedom philosophy.

What was she like?

She was not the friendly type. We didn't want to challenge her. She was a hell of a good arguer. You could almost tell from the way she answered, that she didn't want us to debate with her. She was willing to elaborate and explain.

I was a guest in her home, and we were there primarily to talk with her about arguments and theories, and I don't recall that she revealed much beyond being a very smart woman. She was a great person.

Was the magazine Faith and Freedom *published for Dr. James Fifield Jr.?*

That's right. And he had a radio show called *The Freedom Story*.

Tell me about that.

---

61 Thaddeus Ashby was at that time a friend of Ayn Rand's and also her house sitter in the mid-1940s.

Another fellow and I wrote scripts for it. It started out where Dr. Fifield would just give a fifteen-minute talk, and then when he brought me and some others on board, we produced a show which was dramatic in nature. We would dramatize some moral or religious thinking, tied in to our belief in limited government and freedom, and then he would sew up the show with about a three-minute talk at the end.

We would work with script writers, and we would look at some of the freedom principles that we believed in, and say, "How can we dramatize this into something that would be interesting for people to listen to and think about?"

Was Dr. Fifield a preacher?

Oh yes, he had one of the largest Christian churches in Los Angeles.[62]

I guess you knew that Ayn Rand was an atheist.

Oh I knew that, yes.

Why did a religious person have Ayn Rand on his radio show, as he did for the dramatization of her novel Anthem?[63]

Myron McNamara and I controlled the radio show, and Dr. Fifield did not approve, or even look at our scripts, beforehand. We used many Hollywood or radio actors.

---

62 The church was the First Congregational Church of Los Angeles.

63 The dramatization of *Anthem* was broadcast September 3, 1950, on 475 stations across America.

Julius Shulman

Julius Shulman is a world-renowned architectural photographer. In May and July 1947 he photographed the Chatsworth home of Ayn Rand and Frank O'Connor. Mr. Shulman died in 2009.

Interview dates: August 14, 1998, and April 20, 2000.

Scott McConnell: *How did it happen that you photographed Ayn Rand?*

Julius Shulman: In 1947 I photographed the von Sternberg house, which had been designed by Richard Neutra and was then occupied by Ayn Rand in the mid-1940s.[64] The session lasted two or three days.

What was your photographic assignment?

The house had been photographed when it was first built in 1936, and the early pictures, which Neutra had in his files, showed nothing but a stark, vacant house, with no trees, no vegetation. Also, those pictures didn't show how the house was framed by the expanse of grass, the moat, trees, and by the sky. I've always ordained that this is the whole purpose of architectural photography: to show the site where the house is situated. And the original photos included no interior. But, in 1947, when Ayn Rand lived there, the house was beautifully complete. It was comfortable and there had been created a genuine lifestyle.

Why did Neutra want the house photographed in 1947?

Because von Sternberg was one of Neutra's more significant clients, with specific requirements. And the landscaping was beautiful.

What did you think was unique about the house?

Its isolation. When I came to see the house I was terribly impressed by the moat, by the aluminum wall around it. And when I was inside the house looking out, I realized, "Oh my goodness, this is wonderful. What a great lifestyle." At that time, there were vast ranches in the area. The Neutra design as requested by von Sternberg: privacy especially.

What was the lifestyle when Ayn Rand was living there, the building, the landscaping and the decoration?

The decoration was very curious, because in those days fine

---

64 Neutra designed the house in 1935 for Hollywood director Josef von Sternberg.

architecture consisted of minimal living, but not for Ayn Rand—the same for her landscaping—note my birch tree scene with Rand and O'Connor. The modern architect wanted a skeletal, thin, perfect, minimal kind of landscaping. It was called the "International Style" when it was founded in Europe—the concept was based on minimalism, not lifestyle, not what the clients want. If I were cynical and trying to be academic about the O'Connors' interior furniture, I would say it was not Neutra's preference. But it was comfortable—not too different from my own home!

How would you describe yourself as a photographer?

You could say that I like to consider the environment. That's part of the statement. It's a packaged thing in my work, that I embrace the entire thought of living in the house, the site of a house, its interior design, its landscaping—all of this comes together in one statement.

Once the composition is determined, the picture is taken. You don't do the picture until after everything else is organized—sometimes even before the camera's placed in position. Every picture, every composition we created, was done so with a premise in mind. The purpose is to show how a house breathes, how a house lives, with people occupying it. One of the biggest problems I find, as an editorial person, is that most architectural photographers don't use people in their photographs.

When we took photographs, for example, of Ayn Rand's study, she didn't realize that I was going to use her in the pictures. I got the camera set and had my assistant adjust the lights to where we wanted them. Then all of a sudden I said to Miss Rand, "You probably don't know it, but you're going to be in this picture." That loosened her up right away.

"Oh," she protested, naturally. I said, "You look fine." She had simple clothing on. So we photographed her, and then another picture with Mr. O'Connor. Then in another photograph, we have a scene in the patio behind the wall that encircles the moat, and we have a scene where we show Ayn Rand and O'Connor in one part of the picture, and Richard Neutra sitting off to the one side, as part of the composition. That picture has been used extensively all over the world. Why? Because it shows how the house works. Even on the interiors of the house, we have pictures of Ayn Rand.

I tell this to architectural photographers, architects and students. This is how you mount the peak of greatness in any kind of photography: You don't ask the architect, "What do you want me to shoot?" You just use your own rule of sense. You observe the building without your camera in your hand, walk around, study it.

It means that if I'm going to portray a statement about Ayn Rand in the house, I must find some compositions which determine how she used the house. I pride myself in saying that whenever I do a photograph I'm not taking the building alone, I'm showing where the building is: in its performance!

What other statements were you trying to make?

One of my favorite pictures, and one of my most published pictures, is the one of Ayn Rand with O'Connor walking among the birch trees. That is important because it portrays them within the confines of their acreage. They had this retreat where they could be walking right in their own private park, hand in hand, enjoying their life. She liked the idea, and I said, "I'm going to set the camera out here among the trees. Give me about five or ten minutes. Why don't you go down there at the end of the trees and walk back towards the camera and just don't pay attention to me. However, when I see you're in the right position to take the exposure, I will call you or say something," which I did—she was smiling at me, at the camera. That was it, one exposure.

I remember her walking towards me, and I snapped the picture, and then she turned around to go back, assuming that like ninety percent of other photographers that I would want one more and one more—let's do it again over and over again. I said, "I'm all through." She said, "You mean . . ." and I said, "Yes." I remember someone asking a question after one of my lectures about the fact that people joked and used to call me "One-shot Shulman." I said, "That's no joke, because I don't believe in making more than one exposure. Why waste film and the time of developing and processing?" Why not use your perceptual intuition, not the camera's eyes?

What was Ayn Rand like posing in photographs?

No problem. Once I determined what we were going to do in the patio area, I set my camera. I had chosen the time of day, and I had asked the parties involved to please come outside. I had Neutra sitting in the chair on the left with Janet Gaynor, and then I said to Ayn Rand and O'Connor, "move on the right side of the picture," where the chaise is situated. They complied with every request. When we changed to doing the photographs inside her office or the pictures of her with

O'Connor walking down their birch tree lane, she never questioned it. She was very cooperative.

Would you call Mr. O'Connor and Miss Rand photogenic?

Oh, he especially. Remember the picture of O'Connor and Janet Gaynor? In that picture O'Connor is very handsome. In every picture he looked rather nice, and so does she. There was no problem in the makeup department, which I never use! It was a very pleasant experience. I don't impose upon human subjects by doing any extreme close-ups. It's always showing the person occupying part of the space.

What did Ayn Rand think of your photographs?

She loved them. She liked the pictures of her in the office. She liked the one of her and Frank, where she was holding the cat, and she liked that because she loved the cat. Another one I took was with the stuffed animals on the couch. She particularly liked that the scenes were taken spontaneously. I set the camera and pulled the slide out of the film holder after I cocked the shutter, and I said, "Okay, now I'm making an exposure. Will you just look at the paper that you have on your desk? Will you look at me for a minute?" Click. She turned her head and before she knew what was happening I had taken her picture. I didn't say, "Now, look at me, smile." None of that. I don't work that way. I said, "Okay, why don't you tell Frank something about what you had for breakfast this morning." And of course then she smiled or laughed and I took the picture.

In the photo, the stuffed lion dolls are scattered about. She had a lion doll on the couch, which was at the other end of her office. I moved the doll over into the composition. I also moved her cat and walked back to the camera, I said, "Just a minute, the cat wants to get into the picture." That's why she was smiling in the photograph.

Were there any specific comments she made about the finished photographs?

The only thing I do remember is her statement "Oh, they're so natural." And they were.

Were there any problems while doing the photographs?

Something came up one time. We were doing an interior photograph with some flowers in the foreground, on the right side, looking through to the living room—and on the left side is a wall of glass to the outside. In that view there are some large pieces of furniture. Neutra called me, and I had made one condition with Neutra—I was not going to move furniture. Ayn Rand saw my assistant going over to her chairs, and Neutra was saying, "Move that, more," gesturing. Ayn Rand was over here on my left and she said, "Mr. Neutra, what are you doing?" "Oh, we're moving that chair away." "Why?" He said something about, I think, that it overpowers the architecture. She said to the young assistant, "No, please put it back where it was."

Why did she want it left as it was?

The chair was used that way. It was the O'Connors' seating arrangement. She liked to be very comfortable. He wanted to move her furniture out. He couldn't stand that kind of heavy, comfortable furniture—comfort is not the issue with him. He would think of his architecture. "Don't you dare hide my lines with a chair," was his attitude.

Did any other issues come up?

We spent most of our time working, even into the night, and then we had dinner there. The dinner party was fascinating. Ayn Rand and O'Connor, Neutra and assistant, and myself.

We were talking about life in general, our work and her writing. She was working on *Atlas Shrugged*, and at that time *The Fountainhead* was already a world leader; there's no question it is one of the most successful books ever. Neutra made a comment about Howard Roark blowing up one of his buildings that had been altered and wondered how an architect can blow up one of his own buildings. She said he had the right to do it: he can do what he wants; it's his building.

Likewise, she said, in the novel I'm working on now there's a matter of economic development, which she likened to a supermarket coming into a neighborhood where there's a small mom-and-pop grocery store—been there for fifty years perhaps. They weren't making much money, but they were making a living, and she said something about how A&P supermarkets could come into a neighborhood and open a store and they would see that the mom-and pop-store would be selling milk for $.15 or $.10 a quart and A&P would sell the milk for $.07 or $.08 a quart.

I used the term that this was "insidious competition," and she flared up. She said, "Of course they have a right to do it. If they

can't compete with A&P then they have no right to be in business."
I said, "That's their livelihood." When you say a person can move in
like that, I think I used the term "like a gangster with a gun at their
backs"—either you cut the milk prices down to where we are going
to cut our price down to or else you're out of business. Bang, you're
dead. She didn't like that. She was angry. She raised her voice—like
I was too naïve—and said, "Mr. Shulman, you're a young man"—I
was twenty-seven years old—"you haven't had any experience in
life, apparently. You're just a photographer shooting your camera and
taking pictures for Mr. Neutra and you haven't had any association
with the world of competition." Ayn Rand was correct when she said
I'm young and naïve. I'm still the same way today.

What do you think is the influence of The Fountainhead *on architects
and people generally?*

I think Ayn Rand brought architecture into the public's focus for
the first time. I wouldn't want to use the term too loosely, but she
was "popularizing" architecture. She wrote about certain elements
of architectural design and the rights of an architect. But more than
that: how important it was for an architect to be very specific and
demanding and disciplined in his architecture. For the first time, I think,
she conveyed to the public that the role of the architect goes beyond
putting up a building. That the architect was exercising his prerogative.
Once he's assumed and given the responsibility by the client, then the
architect carries forth in determining and creating the solution.

What's your personal opinion of The Fountainhead?

It's a very important statement about architecture. It projects to the
public how the architect's mind works, albeit it's an extreme mystery.

What did you think of Ayn Rand?

She's brilliant in her writing, her vocabulary and her concepts.
I was disappointed that such a brilliant woman would have such
a narrow concept toward society or, shall we say, be averse to my
feeling for the man on the street, the proletariat. Perhaps her Russian
experiences surfacing.

*In your personal dealings with her, besides the dinner conversation,
what was she like to deal with personally?*

She was congenial. Pleasant. Oh sure, we had no problem. The morning after our evening debate, shall we say, it was fine, congenial. We expressed, both of us at the table, our thoughts. Neutra was more concerned with the architecture than other things.

Have you met any architects motivated or inspired by Howard Roark?

Oh, more than that! You'd be surprised how many architects. Don't forget that every architect in the world read that book. It was one, first, front and center in the life of every architect who was a modern architect. And invariably, many architects would say to me, "Well, you know that Ayn Rand patterned Howard Roark after me?" Raphael Soriano said that. Richard Neutra said that. Gregory Ain. There are others. Oh, many people said that!

June (Kato) Kurisu

June Kurisu was Ayn Rand's secretary from 1947 to 1949.

Interview dates: November 5, 1996, and March 12, 1998

Scott McConnell: *How did you get your job with Ayn Rand?*

June Kurisu: My parents were working for her at the O'Connor ranch. Mom was working as a cook and housekeeper and Dad as a houseman, serving the meals. My brother was also living with them and going to school from there. My father's name was Ryoji Kato. My mother's name was Haruno, and my brother's name is Ken.

When Mom told me that Ayn Rand needed a secretary, I had just graduated from Los Angeles High School, in 1947, and Mom and Dad were working out at the O'Connors' ranch. I guess they mentioned to her that I was taking secretarial courses and wanted to go on to school to become more proficient. So I stayed there that summer and lived on the ranch.[65] And when school started, I went back to the boarding house, Evergreen Hostel. It was a church-sponsored house for people trying to resettle in California after being in the different Japanese internment camps all over the United States. I kept a bed there in the dormitory and stayed there, and went to L.A. City College from there, and then on the weekends I would take the bus and go to San Fernando [Chatsworth].

We just had the summer of '47, when our family were all there at the ranch. When they left, it turned into a Saturday and Sunday job for me.

How long did your parents live in Chatsworth?

They probably started somewhere in 1947 and they left sometime in 1949. Working on the weekends was how I came to know the two other cooks that came after my parents, the German lady and a black lady.

It was just a really hectic time for me because I was living on the East Side in a boarding house and had to take a couple of buses to get to City College. Then on the weekends, I would travel out to catch a couple of buses to get out to San Fernando where Frank O'Connor picked me up. I would stay overnight Saturday, and then on Sunday evening I would go home.

Did your parents have a good working relationship with Ayn Rand and Frank O'Connor?

---

65 June Kato started working for the O'Connors on June 30, 1947.

Yes, but it wasn't their life's work. They were just trying to accumulate money to acquire property to build their stores and get back into business. My Dad had gift shops in Laguna Beach and in Estes Park, Colorado, before the war. Being Japanese-Americans who were interned during the war, they lost both of them.

They never got any compensation?

No. If they had lived long enough there was a $20,000 reparation given to all the Japanese who were in a camp and alive at the time.

What year were the four members of your family interned?

In May 1942 all the Japanese were rounded up and put in temporary camps such as the Santa Anita race track, until we could be moved to other places. We were put on a train and taken to Parker, Arizona.

As the houseman for the O'Connors, what kind of work did your father do?

I imagine he would do some cleaning, and he served the meals, and he may have helped Frank O'Connor on the ranch, but I don't think that was where he spent the most time.

In the archives, I have a statement from your father to Frank O'Connor about the work he was doing at that time.

It says: "In reply to your request, the following is the work I did in relation to the farm when I was in your employ from February 1947 to October 1947. Picked fruits, nuts and flowers. Assisted in packing eggs, assisted in feeding chickens, took care of car. In relation to my original profession of floral arranger, I introduced you to the Pasadena Flower Show to obtain your registration there as a professional flower grower for the purpose of your later exhibiting flowers there. I also assisted you in obtaining from Sunny Slope Nurseries, who were my personal acquaintances, selected chrysanthemum cuttings. Sincerely yours, R. Kato."

I remember maybe once or twice I walked down to the end of the property to see all that was down there. I'm sure Dad did all that but when I would see him, he was more in the house.

Was your father a professional flower grower?

No, he became a flower arranger, an instructor of Japanese flower arranging, the Ikebana style. He was teaching down at Laguna Beach;

then he taught the art of flower arranging at Pasadena City College. He had his own shop again and later retired from there and bought a home.

What work did your mother do for Ayn Rand?

She cooked, and she wasn't a tremendous cook because she had previously worked mostly in the store, so the meals she cooked were very simple. I was really surprised when I heard she was the cook for Ayn Rand, but her meals were okay, probably a lot different than those of the black cook and the German cook, who were probably professional cooks and cooked for some really fine homes. I found a recipe of Ayn Rand's, for what I think she called "veal cutlets," but they were like a hamburger, except they were oval in shape and quite tasty. They probably had bread crumbs and vegetables inside, onions or celery. That was a pretty frequently served meal. Ayn Rand taught Mom to make—or gave her the recipe for—borscht. Those were the only two things I recall.

So your mother lived there and cooked breakfast, lunch and dinner?

Yes.

What was your brother Kenny's relationship with Ayn Rand?

He was very young then, born in 1937. I was working upstairs and busy all day except for meals. In fact I can't remember seeing him at all, but I know he must have been there.

What would he have been doing?

I suppose maybe playing outside or just staying in the kitchen area and the bedroom area. My folks had the use of two bedrooms back there. He was a very quiet boy anyway, so I don't think he made a lot of noise or was very rambunctious or ran around the house.

You also say in your letter [December 12, 1949] *in the archives, "Would you and Mrs. Strachova please save all the foreign stamps for Kenny?"*

He was collecting stamps at that time and we didn't know anybody in foreign countries or have any pen pals in them.

Did Ayn Rand and Frank O'Connor have a name for the ranch?

Not that I remember. I called it the "O'Connor ranch" when talking about it in general. And I never thought of her as Ayn Rand except in relation to, say, business letters that I was typing. I called her and thought of her as "Mrs. O'Connor."

What work did you do for her?

Typing. I was typing the manuscript for *Atlas Shrugged*. I remember her saying we're half way—about the time that I left, in November 1949.

What other kind of work would you have done besides typing?

I think Mom felt a little harried because she felt I was extra work being there, so I would try to help her in any way that I could. One time, Mrs. O'Connor had asked her to clean out the medicine cabinet upstairs—and that's probably the time that I saw into her bedroom, because they're adjoining. I was cleaning out the medicine cabinet, and she became really angry or upset. She told me that she didn't want me to do that kind of work, that that was work for my mother to do and not me. She had very definite ideas about what she wanted me to do. I think the cooks wanted me to eat in the kitchen with them, because I would be a companion to talk with over dinner and maybe to help with the dishes, but Mrs. O'Connor wouldn't have it. She always insisted that I eat with them.

What was your reaction to Atlas Shrugged?

I could definitely imagine Dagny Taggart as being Ayn Rand, in how strong Dagny is, and because she was in a position to want to do something and try to do something—meeting all the opposition.

I thought it was a very good story and that "Who is John Galt?" I thought was good.

I think I had a little part in its writing. She would ask what did I think of a certain episode, and once when I was typing up one of the early chapters of *Atlas Shrugged*, I think Dagny Taggart was going to be looking at a shadow, and the shadow disappeared, and it made her wonder who that was. I said, "How about having a shadow of John Galt sort of visible?" and she thought about it and said, "That's a good idea." I think she incorporated it into that chapter.[66] I was really thrilled that I could have a small part.

Is there anything else about the manuscript or your reactions to it?

No. I thought what better job could you have of typing something

---

66 See *Atlas Shrugged*, part one, chapter 8.

and reading as you go along. I would type it and I needed to be very, very accurate. I would proofread it in the typewriter and I would try to follow word by word of my typing to make sure that I had gotten it right. Every once in a while I would leave out a line and I didn't want to turn it back in to her.

Was she patient if you made a mistake?

Yes. She would always bring it to my attention, but I could always tell when she would give the rewrites back if it was a change she had made or if I had made a mistake.

How did she do it?

Cross it out and write above.

So she liked to question you about what you thought of the scenes as you were typing them up?

I think she would ask, or maybe I would just volunteer that I really liked a scene and the way the story was going. It was exciting to me to keep typing and reading and know what's going to happen. I had a lot of respect for her that she could keep the story line going to whatever conclusion it was going to come to.

How did she react when you told her this?

Very pleased.

We have in our records that she noted you as the first person who typed Atlas Shrugged.

Oh, great! I think that she just remembered that I typed the first half, and maybe she did mention that she'd send me a copy when the book was finished.

When you did your work for Ayn Rand were you upstairs in that little alcove near the bookcase on the balcony?

Yes.

Tell me more about typing for Ayn Rand.

She would give me the handwritten manuscript, maybe three pages at a time, and I would type it. She would then go over it. Sometimes I would make errors, mostly not typographical; there could be words that I couldn't read.

Did you have trouble reading her handwriting?

It really was hard to decipher. I may have said I can't read this or asked what is this word. That came up more often than I would have liked, but I would have to leave a space and fill in a word. When there was even one word that she decided that she wanted to change, it would necessitate that the whole page be retyped.

I would give her the work that I completed, and she would go over it and sometimes give it back to me the same day. If it happened on Saturday, she would give it back and I would type it on Sunday. Otherwise, it could be another week before I got to it.

Why would she give you only three pages at a time?

That's as much as she'd finished.

So, on the weekend, she would write a few pages, give them to you and then she would edit them immediately?

I think that happened. Other times, on Saturday, there would be quite a few pages to type, but ten or twelve pages at the most. I don't think there was a big bundle of pages to be typed. The writing and typing went fairly slowly.

I would also take dictation for any letters that she needed to have written, business or personal letters. The letters to Pat Paterson would go on for a whole day, into the evening.[67]

Just one letter?

Yes. There were many pages, and she would want me to read it back, and then she would change it while I was reading it. She wouldn't have me retype if I had made a mistake or she changed her mind. She would make the change in her own handwriting and send it off. They'd be very long, many pages. It took a long time, because she would think about what she would want to say. She never spoke so rapidly that I couldn't keep up.

Did she work from just memory or did she have notes in front of her?

No notes. Just off the top of her head. It was in her office. I don't remember that she paced, so I guess she was seated at her desk, and I would be seated in front of her. She was very excited,

---

67 For Ayn Rand's letters to Isabel "Pat" Paterson, see *Letters of Ayn Rand*, pp. 173–218.

very animated. When she was doing this dictating for the Pat Paterson letters, she would be very animated. Not to the point that she would be speaking very rapidly so I couldn't take it down, but she would be animated in speaking and getting her thoughts together. She used a lot of hand motions.

Tell me more about the Isabel Paterson letters.

Ayn Rand and Paterson were writing back and forth. I don't know if it was on a monthly basis, but at least every other month.[68] The letters were very long.

How was Ayn Rand when dealing with her letters to Pat Paterson?

I think she was sometimes disturbed by some of the things Pat Paterson was saying. She would remark, "I can't understand why she feels that way or why she sees it that way," or something a little more formal than that.

She would comment on the letters to you?

When she was agitated or particularly pleased. "She sees that the same way that I do."

Paterson was the letter writer that sticks out the most?

Yes. I know Mrs. O'Connor answered some fan letters. One lady wrote that she had named her newborn daughter "Ayn." Mrs. O'Connor wrote back and said she was very pleased.

Did you make a carbon copy of every letter?

Yes. They were given to her with the letters. For her correspondence, her stationery was not full size. It was either Monarch or Executive, whichever is the larger of the two.

She must have taken care of her own filing, because I didn't do any filing for her. I don't remember any filing cabinets in her office, but there were a desk and a couple of chairs, plus the chair she sat in and a couch behind her desk.

Did Miss Rand teach you any writing or grammar?

No, except she was very, very precise.

---

68 The time between letters varied from one to three weeks.

Who did her typing during the week?

I don't know. Towards the end time there, she was working on a screenplay, but I couldn't finish it. I was working on it Saturdays and Sundays, and she had to call in a studio typist to finish off the work during the week. I had worked one summer before I went back to high school, but I couldn't consider myself a really professional typist at that time. I could type, but my speed was probably not of the caliber of anyone who'd worked at Paramount typing other writers' manuscripts. I don't remember anything about the script other than the title, "House of Mist." The script would be handwritten unless it was a rewrite that was typed and changed.

Did you see her actually writing her handwritten draft? Was it from notes or an outline?

Actually, she must have been working from some notes. I know that she was very careful to be sure that everything that I typed got back to her. If I made a mistake and started a page again, she wanted those pages. I think she wanted to be sure that nothing was carried away, taken out of the house. I just got the feeling that she just wanted to be very careful with her manuscripts. I don't know if she kept all her handwritten ones or if she ever destroyed those when she got them on paper. There was just an original plus one copy.

When Ayn Rand was doing her scripts, did she ever read them aloud or did you do readings?

Yes, I remember her reading. I can't remember what it was about, but she read a script with a lot of verve and vigor. I do remember her voice and her reading from papers.

How did she dress when working?

When she was working she dressed only in slacks and a camp-type shirt. So the first time I saw her dressed up in a dressy dress, I was really stunned, because she had great legs, and I think she knew it. She was very spectacular. Her hair was always neat because it was kept in a very short style, but when she wore a dress and heels, she was stunning.

What were your pay and working conditions?

I think she paid me $24 a day or $42 a week. I thought it was quite generous. It was probably more than I deserved for my skills at the time. I remember her saying that she believed in people not being given more than they deserve; no gifts, and she didn't believe in charity. But, then, look what she did for this Russian lady and me.

Who was the lady she helped?

An old lady that came from back East and lived with them for a while was either a relative or a friend, and she lived there for maybe a year. They didn't get along philosophically, and she felt that she didn't want her to live in the house any longer and found some other place for her to live. I can't remember her name.

That sounds like Maria Strachova, Ayn Rand's English teacher when Miss Rand was a child in Russia. Her nickname was "Missis." Miss Rand got her out of an Austrian relocation camp after the war and brought her to America. Tell me more about her.[69]

She was a very sweet lady, but she was kind of like I was. I didn't know how to respond or wasn't thinking on Mrs. O'Connor's level. This lady was understanding a lot less than I was understanding. I felt sorry for her because she didn't know how to respond, and I thought, if I felt that way while I was at sea, then this lady is going under.

She was very unassuming, tried to be very agreeable, and yet she did have her own opinions, and quite a few of her opinions weren't compatible with Ayn Rand's. This woman would kind of backpedal. I think of Ayn Rand just being the way she was and all of her philosophy, and the other woman probably being much more liberal, but conservative liberal. They weren't having discussions as discussions. It was something over lunch or dinner, and I think Ayn Rand would ask her something and she would give her opinion. Ayn Rand would say, "I don't agree about that. That can't be"—because of whatever—and she would give a pretty good-sized dissertation, and the lady would back down in her opinions, trying to be very agreeable. Not that Ayn Rand would ever throw her out on the street because she disagreed with her.

To me she seemed very old. At the table Ayn Rand would talk to her, and she would answer—not excluding the rest of us—but she would direct questions to her in English because otherwise I wouldn't have been able to understand.

Let's turn to Miss Rand's work in Hollywood. Did she ever talk about script writing techniques?

---

69 See *Letters of Ayn Rand*, p. 360.

No, but she asked me if I ever thought of writing. I told her that I wrote for a newspaper when I was in the internment camp. But when I was working for her, I needed to support myself, and I needed to concentrate on the skills I would need to get a job, so I didn't write. She was very willing to help me. She really was very good to me and she offered to help me get a full-time position as a secretary at Paramount studios; I guess she knew people who might have been influential.

She was offering to help you with fiction writing?

Yes. She was very generous to me. In fact, if I hadn't had my boyfriend George in the back of my mind on this side of town, I've often wondered if I would have taken her up on that and what would have happened. I could have lived out there and worked with her on the rest of *Atlas Shrugged*. If I was single I might have even followed her to New York.

Did Miss Rand ever invite you to go to the Paramount lot with her?

She said she was going to be working at the studio and would I like to come and see. I said, "Sure, I would," but it would be on a weekday, and I would be going to school. In those days I'd never think of ditching classes to go, so I never went.

Did she ever tell you what she thought of Hollywood?

I thought she thought it was exciting, and she knew that I was excited about it. She invited me to one premiere, but I couldn't go. She was going to have a party, and she invited me to come and said— because she knew that I liked Barbara Stanwyck and Robert Taylor— "Oh, they'll be there, so come and meet them." I really wanted to, [but] because it was a weeknight, it would just have been impossible to get out there.

Was it the premiere of The Fountainhead *that you couldn't go to?*

No, I went to *The Fountainhead*, but not with her. It was another premiere.

So it wasn't one of her movies that was premiering?

I thought it was something that she had written the screenplay for, or at least worked on the screenplay for. I remember going to one at Warner's Hollywood with a girlfriend. We were roped off from the celebrities and the dignitaries. When I saw her, I called to her and she came over and talked to me a bit and met my friend. Being out in the lobby and standing behind the ropes, the velvet ropes, I called to her and she came over and said how glad she was that I was able to come.

Did you see Ayn Rand with other stars or celebrities?

I met Janet Gaynor and Adrian when they came to visit one day. It would have been sometime in '48. I knew her from movies and Adrian as a dress designer, who was very popular at that time. Janet Gaynor wasn't acting anymore, but she was still a very attractive lady.

They had come for a visit, I guess, and I was upstairs. They were on their way out and Mrs. O'Connor said something, like, "Come, June, I'd like you to meet friends of mine. This is Janet Gaynor"—and, boy, my eyes popped—"and her husband Adrian."

What did you say?

Probably blushed and said, "Pleased to meet you." They were very cordial.

Were they very close to Ayn Rand?

Yes, good friends. She would talk to either one on the phone. I'm just sorry I didn't take advantage of the times that she invited me over to parties. It's just that we lived so far away, and at the time I didn't have transportation. I could have met Barbara Stanwyck and Robert Taylor and Adrian and Janet Gaynor and Clark Gable. I talked to Louella Parsons or Hedda Hopper.

They were both friends of Ayn Rand's?

No, I think just one was. I think it was Louella Parsons. I answered the phone, and the male secretary said Louella Parsons is calling for Miss Rand. I went to call her and I said, "Louella Parsons would like to speak with you." Afterwards, I remember saying, "She had a man secretary," and Mrs. O'Connor was the one who told me that many of the female movie stars and celebrities in Hollywood have male secretaries because they also serve as escorts or accompany them when they go out.

Mrs. O'Connor was also very friendly with Ginger Rogers and her mother, Lela Rogers. When Ginger Rogers and her mother were coming over, she invited me over because she knew I really loved Ginger Rogers's dancing. She was very close to the mother, and they would talk on the phone. I knew that they were coming to visit, but

I did not see them. They were coming to dinner or to a get-together. I felt they were philosophically very close. Of the people from Hollywood, Lela Rogers was probably her closest friend.

I don't remember her going out or leaving the ranch that much. It would have to be something really special. She didn't go shopping. She was always there working and the only time they went anyplace—the only time that I can remember was when she went to get her hair cut.

Outside of the cooks and the housekeepers, I don't think I met anybody else who came to the house.

Do you remember any big current events that Ayn Rand might have talked about or that might have come up in conversation, for example, communism?

Oh, actually during the time that I was working for her, she went back to Washington, D.C., for the Un-American Activities hearings. I know that she was really upset by the communist activity in Hollywood. She was excited about going back there and testifying, and so I was off work for about a month.

Did you exchange Christmas gifts with Miss Rand?

She gave me money and lipstick and perfume by Adrian, or Chanel Nº5. It could have been Chanel Nº5, which was also a favorite of hers. I saw a really large bottle of either Adrian or Chanel perfume. I think she mentioned it was a gift from Albert Mannheimer. I remember her saying that she didn't believe in giving, that things had to be worked for. I think she told me that shortly before Christmas. That last weekend before Christmas, I got a gift and was really surprised, because I thought she wouldn't give a Christmas gift, being an atheist and all. And then I got this nice, thoughtful gift, and that was really nice. I couldn't afford much, but she played solitaire quite a bit in the evening, when she was relaxing at her desk in the evening, so one Christmas I gave her a double set of cards in a box. The cards had cat pictures on the back. It didn't cost very much, but it was more the thought. She was really pleased with it.

She didn't play cards during a break in her writing?

She could have. I know that she played quite frequently. I think she did in the middle of the day. That's the only time I would have noticed that her cards were getting pretty ratty looking, and so I mentioned to her that she needed a new set of cards. It was close to Christmas, and that's why I was thinking I knew what I could get her for Christmas.

Did Miss Rand and Mr. O'Connor take holidays or days off, such as July 4th?

Not that I know. For relaxation she enjoyed music. It really surprised me when I heard the music she liked. All I remember is that she would conduct classical music, orchestra music; like Shostakovich was one and probably other classical artists and orchestra music that I didn't know the names of. I would be upstairs typing or just reading, and she would be downstairs with the stereo on quite loud. She would have a baton and be conducting like she's conducting a full orchestra. I asked her what it was and all I can remember is that it was by Shostakovich.[70] This was a rousing . . . just the greatest piece.

Describe Miss Rand using the baton.

Since the indoor balcony area was open to the living room below, the sound just permeated the whole house. She would stand there and conduct the whole piece, just like she was the conductor in the concert hole. If you could only have a scene of that, that really would be something. She did it almost every time that music was on. That's how she would listen to it.

What do you remember about the O'Connors' house?

Upstairs was their bedroom and the bathroom. It was all glass and there was no covering on the windows. You could see houses down below but they were quite a ways away. I suppose nobody could see anything unless they deliberately got out there with a telescope. No curtains, no. Curtains would have wrecked the whole scope of it. I don't remember any curtains, even downstairs. There wouldn't be any need for privacy. It would be more to keep the sun out of the living room, to stop the fading.

Did it get very hot in Chatsworth?

Yes, it did. In fact, I can stand a lot of heat, but there were times when I just couldn't stand it anymore, and I had to ask Frank O'Connor to bring the typewriter and a table downstairs so I could type someplace cooler, even outside in the shade.

---

70 This is probably "Polka" from *The Age of Gold* ballet.

In the archives we have a letter you wrote to Miss Rand on December 29, 1949. Your then boyfriend, George Kurisu, had asked you to marry him, and you wrote to Miss Rand about it.

He lived at the boarding house. He was actually born in Hawaii. He was discharged from the service and went back to Kauai.

When you had dinner with Miss Rand, what did she say about your letter?

I hate to say it, but I really didn't understand a lot of what she was saying. My mind would wander, and I'd be thinking about whether George and I had time to go to a show if I got home early enough Sunday night.

Did Miss Rand meet George before the wedding?

Yes. A girl friend and her fiancé and George and I drove out to the ranch, and I think they all met her there. In fact, I have some pictures of our two friends by that moat.

How was Ayn Rand with strangers?

When our two friends went over and she met them, she was very cordial, very friendly and nice-to-meet-you and all. It probably took her away from her work to come out.

Was Miss Rand smoking often then?

Yes. Always with the holder.

What was her stance?

She would hold it up and out, with the holder between her first and her second finger. Other times she had another way of holding it, but I thought that was very, very elegant.

Did Ayn Rand have any other habits, gestures or ways of doing things?

She gestured with her hands a lot. She would walk with purpose. She would walk quickly to where she was going. I think this was just a natural habit of hers. And she knew what she wanted to say and she said it. She didn't seem at a loss for words.

Would you take me through a typical day at the O'Connors'?

It may have been just a casual breakfast. Maybe she just had coffee in her office. I don't know about Frank, if he actually sat down to a cooked breakfast. The dinners were always sit-down. We didn't dress— she didn't change her clothes or anything like that.

Was there a set lunch?

I think it was more like sandwiches.

How long was lunch?

Fairly brief, just eat and get on with it. Frank O'Connor went back to whatever he was doing, she went back to her office and I went back up and typed. Both of us worked until dinner time.

What time would dinner be?

About six or seven o'clock. We'd sit down, and the cook would come in and serve us all around. It was a long way from the dining room to the kitchen, so there was a cart so the server wouldn't have to go back and forth to the kitchen all the time.

What else would be happening during the meal?

She wouldn't talk about anything personal, about the ranch or anything Frank was doing. It may have been current events, or she might have asked me about school. It was never a silent meal. She would do most of the talking.

Did she have any favorite topics?

Not about her book. Maybe she would talk about something that Pat Paterson had said in her last letter, something she agreed or disagreed with.

Did you have the impression that she was trying to convince you of her views?

I don't think I ever even thought of it at that time. I think I thought she just liked to talk, and that's what she liked to talk about, and that was all right with me. She never excluded Frank O'Connor, but it didn't seem like she was expecting any responses or any comments from him. He would just continue eating his dinner. I really liked him. In fact, when I saw his images on the screen when I was watching *Ayn Rand: A Sense of Life*, it brought back really fond memories, because I thought he was a very sweet, kind, older man.

After dinner there may have been occasions when she did go back to work, but on weekends, when Albert Mannheimer was there, even when he wasn't there, Frank O'Connor and she would probably be in her office and they would be talking in there.

Why in the office?

There wasn't a den in the house, and the living room was large and more a type of place for groups of people to be together, because it was large. There wasn't a cozy, intimate area there. The couches were large and against the walls and there was a large open space in the center. I think the office was just a cozier place, because there were comfortable chairs there, and the couch. I can remember Frank lounging on the couch.

During the weekend she either chatted with Mr. Mannheimer or worked all the time?

Yes.

Can you describe her conversations with Mr. Mannheimer?

I could hear raised voices—her voice mainly—when she was in her office with the door closed. She was having these long philosophical discussions late into the night with Albert Mannheimer. It wasn't anger, but I think it was a difference of opinion. Maybe she was just asserting her views.

What was Mr. Mannheimer doing?

He never raised his voice. I'm sure it was an exchange. He wasn't at her feet listening; he was participating. The door was closed. The office was downstairs, and the room that I would stay in was down the hall and around the corner, probably back to back with the office. You could hear the sound of voices but not hear the conversation.

From your observation, was Ayn Rand's best friend Albert Mannheimer?

Yes. He was there very often. I don't know that he was writing a book—it may have just been screenplays—but she was helping him with his career. I did some typing for him. I may have brought the script home with me and typed it at home and brought it back to him the next week. I remember he gave me a tube of lipstick, maybe by Adrian, in thanks. I think Ayn Rand was actually paying me.

How was she helping his career?

I think she was advising him, helping him with his scripts. Other times I think they were just talking. He was over there about every other weekend and would stay until Monday morning.

Was Miss Rand training him, or they were equals?

I felt that she was more the helper.

Tell me more about Albert Mannheimer.

He was a good-looking man. Probably mid-30s,[71] but he could have been younger. He was well built and very pleasant. I thought they were very close.

Did Albert Mannheimer have fuzzy hair, a mop of hair, curly hair?[72]

Yes he did, but it was very nicely kept. His hair was in a standard style but it was curly. He was a very nice-looking, well-set-up-looking man. He was very even keeled. Not very emotional. I would look on him as more like a sports hunk than an intellectual. By "hunk," I mean the athletic type.

Where was Frank O'Connor when they were having these long conversations?

Sometimes he'd be in there with them, but I don't think he stayed all night. He would stay up very late, but I don't know where he was or what he was doing.

Describe Albert Mannheimer, Ayn Rand and Frank O'Connor when they were together?

Fine, cordial. Frank O'Connor didn't do a lot of talking. He would interject and reply and all of that. He didn't seem out of it or bored.

When Mr. Mannheimer was there for dinner, what did he and Ayn Rand talk about?

I don't remember, but there was plenty that they talked about. The dinners were pretty extended affairs. In fact, I think it bothered the cook because she wanted to finish with dinner, do the dishes and get out of the kitchen. They would last until pretty late. I would think sometimes until eight-thirty, nine, even. She couldn't serve the next course, dessert

---

71 Albert Mannheimer was born in 1913.
72 In some letters Ayn Rand called Mannheimer "Fuzzy."

or whatever, until someone rang for her. I think there was a push button on the wall, and I think Frank O'Connor had to get up to push it.

What kinds of things excited Ayn Rand?

Talking philosophy.

You worked for Ayn Rand for two years. What was your general impression of her?

I found her to be a very kind woman, not manipulative in any way, but assertive in what she believed and the way she wanted things done. She was totally honest in what she believed. She had very firm ideas and I can't see her changing, at all. I felt that she was a woman who knew what she wanted to do and where she wanted to go and could very well get there, who knew that she was going to achieve her aims.

I don't think she was a calm person—but confident, for sure. I think she was very volatile in her philosophy and her feelings. I don't mean explosive but I mean very full of feeling. "Passionate," that's a good word for her.

How did she treat you?

We had very good rapport. She never reprimanded me, even when I made mistakes or I didn't proofread properly, got a wrong word in because I couldn't read her writing; I didn't know the word, couldn't find it in the dictionary. But I know that the black cook and housekeeper and a German woman who were there at the time really didn't care for her. I don't know why.

Would you say that Ayn Rand was happy when you knew her?

Yes. If she wasn't happy, it didn't manifest itself in any way that I could determine. She was happy in her writing and I think her writing was going well. She wasn't alone, because Frank was there, and I think she had friends as much as she wanted, and she could talk to them by phone, so I think she was happy. That's why it surprised me that she went to New York so soon.

What was your feeling for her?

I was very fond of her. She was very, very good to me. In fact, she was my sustenance for the two years that I was going to L.A. City College, because my folks had just come back from the internment camps and did not have enough money to support me. So if I wanted to go on to school, I pretty much had to support myself, although my dad really encouraged me to go on with my education—even if to get more secretarial training. She paid me enough Saturday and Sunday to support myself the rest of the week, to be able to pay all my expenses at school.

When you get right down to it, I'm talking about extreme fondness, love. She was so good to me.

Did she influence your ideas?

At that time there wasn't the term "Objectivism." It was just "individualism" or "individualistic." That's what I really picked up from her, that the government isn't there just to support people, that people have to get out and work on their own. I know that my roommate, when I was living at Evergreen Hostel, a very nice person, a very good friend of mine, she was a very liberal Democrat. We would get into some philosophical discussions. I remember her telling me, "Oh, you're picking that up from Ayn Rand." And I thought, yeah, maybe I am.

I never felt Mrs. O'Connor was ever vicious or vengeful. She was very open, very honest. I think she had the most profound influence on my life of anyone that I can remember.

How else did Mrs. O'Connor influence you?

In the way I want to work hard for myself and become someone. I want to be honest in my dealings with people, and I don't want to knife anyone in the back. I get those feelings at times, but I just turn around and say I'm going to go with my goals, and this person's going to get his in due time, and it doesn't have to be through me because he'll get his. I really feel that.

Let's turn now to Frank O'Connor. Describe him for me.

I thought he was a really elegant, very sweet, even-tempered man. He worked very hard on the ranch.

How?

Taking care of the peacocks. They needed quite a bit of care. As I remember, there wasn't any other help. They might have had occasional help back there, but I don't remember any person coming; but I was just there on weekends.

The peacocks were in back. You'd go out the back door past the kitchen and the two bedrooms and the bath that's there. There was an open garage—a big carport. And then walk on down the roadway there and you'd come to the enormous cages that held the peacocks.

He would be dressed in jeans and just a shirt, and I can remember him carrying two buckets of meal or water, or whatever it was, for the peacocks. I imagine he had to clean the huge cages that they were in.

Was Mr. O'Connor's daily routine similar to hers?

I think so. He didn't do any housework or any maintenance work. It was strictly the yard work, or maybe driving out or doing some errands for the house. He seemed to be busy all the time.

Was he a good dresser?

When he dressed up he was stunning. He was tall and slim and so he looked great in a suit. Frank O'Connor was really elegant even though I was seeing him do ranch work. He spent a good deal of his time outside. In spite of that, he looked elegant when he was dressed up. I think Ayn Rand was very impressed with how he looked too.

He was even-tempered. I don't remember him raising his voice. He was a very calming-type person. I just felt he was there for Ayn Rand and would do whatever he could to make her happy and comfortable. He was a strong man, content with where he was and what he was doing. I had a lot of respect for him. Mr. O'Connor was a very astute man.

Can you give any example?

I can't give any specific examples, but I know that many of the comments he made in response to what Ayn Rand was talking about were apropos and very well thought out. Even at that young age—I was eighteen to twenty—I could tell that they weren't coming out of left field, that they were appropriate and good answers. He seemed very sure of himself. I never felt that he was kowtowing to Ayn Rand or that he was ever unsure of anything that he was doing.

In their relationship, did he appear to you to be equal with Ayn Rand?

I think so. It could have been vastly different. I'm sure in some cases where the woman has the career she could be very domineering, but her manner toward him was not condescending in any way. She definitely treated him as an equal and I thought that was really great.

Gary Cooper reminded her of Frank O'Connor.

What did she tell you specifically?

That she wanted Gary Cooper for *The Fountainhead* because he reminded her of Frank O'Connor.

How did she act towards Mr. O'Connor?

I wouldn't say loving in the close, touching, hugging, kissing sense, but I felt a very warm relationship both ways.

Describe them together.

I thought they had a very good relationship, that they made a very nice couple together. It was always a pleasure to see them together. I think a very warm, long, happy relationship is the way I would describe them. I know that the marriage was good.

Did you think he influenced Ayn Rand's writing?

She mentioned that her heroes were Frank O'Connor, that she patterned her heroes after him. At the time I was just thinking she meant looks. She liked tall, slim men, like Frank, but I'm sure it was more than that.

He was a strong man, within himself. He was confident in himself and what he was, and in his life and what he was doing. He always seemed like the strong one that could stand on his own and be the guard to the castle.

Why did you stop working for Ayn Rand?

It must have been about my graduation time, which would be the middle of June 1949.

Did your being a Christian come up in conversation with Miss Rand?

She was an atheist. I think she brought it up herself. She never questioned my religion, which I was mainly born into. She was interested in what I was doing, who I met, who I was marrying, and she wanted to know more about George.

She was happy for you when you were getting married?

Yes. She was pleased that that's what I wanted. I don't know that she ever complimented me, but I could tell—in thinking about it now—that she must have liked me or been satisfied with my work or didn't mind having me around.

Did you have a Christian wedding?

Yes. But it wasn't at a church. The wedding was at a YWCA residence, a three-story house for single women. It was a small wedding of very close friends. Ayn Rand came as my former employer. We were married on June 11, 1950.

Why did you invite Ayn Rand and Frank O'Connor?

I think I just sent an invitation. I probably never dreamed that she would come. It was more of an announcement that George and I were getting married. I believe she called and said that they were coming and asked for some directions. I was really pleased. I was so busy with everything else that I didn't get a chance to introduce her to people. I think that everybody knew who she was—not that she was a famous writer but that she was a famous employer. I was looking through the names of the guests, and she signed it "Ayn Rand," and he signed it "Frank O'Connor."

Do you remember what gifts she bought you?

One gift was a turquoise blue—which was one of her favorite colors—platter, about as large as if I had my hands meet and made a circle in front of me with my arms and hands, and a matching vase. Somewhere along the way the vase got broken, but I still have the platter. It may be in its original box. I don't know when she gave it to me or for what occasion, but she also gave me a toaster set.

A photographer friend of ours took a wedding picture of George and me coming towards the sidewalk. Our friend was standing on the sidewalk, and it showed the people that were our guests, standing on the porch. Frank O'Connor and Ayn Rand are in that picture.

Jack Portnoy

Jack Portnoy is a cousin of Ayn Rand's whom she met in 1926. He visited her in California on February 8, 1948.

Interview date: July 3, 1996

Scott McConnell: *Tell me about meeting Ayn Rand in 1948.*

Jack Portnoy: The next time I saw her after 1926 was when I visited her at her home in California. My cousin, Burt Stone, and I and his wife visited her, and Burt was a favorite of Ayn's. I was just an incidental. I didn't know her that well and I was young, but she looked up to him quite a bit.

She showed us the home and it was very interesting. There was a tree growing right in the center of the house.[73]

At the time she was writing *Atlas Shrugged*, and she had some very eccentric things she used to do. She used to have a needle that she wrapped around her thumb and she would press her fingers with it, and actually bring up little spurts of blood. I kept saying, "What the devil are you doing that for?" She said that would keep her thoughts alive.

Another thing she told us is that she actually wrote to music. When the music reached a crescendo, she could step up her writing to go along with it.

She was so wrapped up in some of the scenes that she had written, and she said she had cried after some of the love scenes that had reached a crescendo.

So you actually saw her writing at her desk?

I didn't actually see her writing. I saw some of the components of her writing. Actually, when she wrote this chapter of *Atlas Shrugged*, I was anxious to read it because she had been so excited when she relayed what she had written, but she said no, she wasn't interested in having me read it; she wanted my cousin to read it, but he wasn't interested in reading it.

Can you remember the music piece she was listening to when she was writing?

---

73 This was probably one of the large philodendrons that grew in the house.

No. I just know that she would play the classical music awfully loud at points, and I would say, "My gosh," and then it would go very soft.

Jean Elliott

Jean Elliott was Ayn Rand's secretary from 1949 to 1951. Ms. Elliott died in 2005.

Interview dates: September 19 and October 22, 1996

Scott McConnell: *When did you work for Ayn Rand?*

Jean Elliott: I believe I started in November 1949, and I think it lasted two years.

How did you get the job?

I lived in Chatsworth at the time and worked in a gift shop and had some good friends, the Davidsons, who lived next door to the O'Connors, on the adjoining property. They were husband and wife, and he called me one day and said that Miss Rand was looking for a secretary and asked if I would be interested. I went over to Miss Rand's, interviewed and became her secretary.

Had you heard of her?

Yes, I knew of her, that she was a novelist, and I did know that she lived there on Tampa Avenue.

How did she conduct the interview for the job?

She just asked me a few questions, and I answered her and it seemed to me that we hit it off, so it didn't take very long and she decided to hire me.

What work did you do for Miss Rand?

I was typing her manuscript for *Atlas Shrugged*. She wrote in longhand. I think there was somebody before me doing this; then I came in, and I was with her through probably the middle of the book.

That must have been exciting.

It was. She was quite a person. She was just so intelligent and certainly could put her words together like nobody else that I ever read or knew of.

What was she like as a person?

She and I got along very well. She was, of course, all business most of the time. Her whole life was focused on this manuscript, and I think she lived, ate and slept with it.

Did you ever just sit there and read the whole story through, or did you just read it as you typed it?

Both. When I first came in, she let me read what had already been typed.

Why did she do that?

I don't know, unless to acquaint me with the writing, the book, so I would have some idea what was going on with what I was typing.

What did she do with what you typed? Did she put it away somewhere?

I think that was the original that she had just the one copy of, and it was locked up.

So she had a safe?

I believe in her home, because someplace in the home it was locked up.

What was her daily schedule?

I think when I started working there my schedule was one and then two days per week. When I got there for work she was always in her den at her desk and writing. I went to her office, we chatted and so forth, and she gave me whatever she wanted me to type, whatever was done since I'd been there last time.

Were these first drafts or editing of previous drafts?

No, it was the first draft.

Did you interrupt her while she was writing her drafts?

I didn't interrupt her as a rule unless I would run out of typing, and then I would go and get some more, if she had more ready. She was in her office and at her desk most of the time that I can recall. She just wrote all the time. The only time I ever saw her she was working on the book. She was always working. She worked into the night even.

What time would she finish?

Different times. It depended if she was on a roll or if she wanted to get something done, get so far with the book, she would keep on working. I'm sure she worked way into the night many times, but I wasn't there.

Did she ever talk about her family or relatives?

Very little. I know that she had a sister in Russia. I have no idea how it came up, but I just knew that she had a sister there she hadn't seen for many years.

What was Frank O'Connor like in his personality or character?

A good character I'm sure. I would say he was a no-nonsense man.

What would Mr. O'Connor do during the day?

He was interested in flowers and he grew gladiolas on the place. There were about fifteen acres there.[74] And at one area on the acreage he grew these gladiolas. He may have grown other things too. He was always interested in flowers and was outside most of the time, interested in the grounds and keeping them up.

Was Frank O'Connor reading the draft or was it just you?

I'm sure he was. They seemed to be very close and shared the book that she was writing, and I'm sure discussed it and so on and so forth. She looked to him as, maybe, a critic.

Did Mr. O'Connor sell his produce from the farm?

He did raise these flowers and sell them. He didn't sell them out in front of his place.

Would Mr. O'Connor come back for lunch?

Yes, Ayn and Frank and I had lunch together whenever I was there working.

What did you usually have for lunch?

I can remember one thing that we had, borscht. Ayn did most of the talking and I listened.

What would she talk about?

Oh, everything under the sun. Everything, and discuss the book, and what did I think of this or that. Frank was always there, always

---

74 The O'Connor property totaled thirteen acres.

backing her up.

Always supporting her?

Yes. As I say, he didn't do a great deal of talking. It would be about an hour lunch and then back to work. I worked about eight hours all together and I had about an hour or hour and half for lunch and a break or two, one in the morning and one in the afternoon. I left usually about five o'clock.

Any last impressions of Frank O'Connor?

He was always there with her, and I think he just backed her up and was her Rock of Gibraltar.

Where was your office?

There's a balcony upstairs and it looks over the entire living room and dining area. At one end she had a desk and typewriter, and that's where I did my work.

Did you take dictation for Miss Rand?

Yes, some for business letters that she might be writing. I did very few. Usually it was people who wrote fan letters to her, and she would answer.

Did Miss Rand ever get sick or tired or have a day off work?

None when I was around at least. She was tireless. I don't think she ever got sick a day in her life.

Did you see her very happy?

Yes, she could be very happy and she could be very the other way too.

Could you give me some examples?

The happy part would be with regard to her book. If there was one particular phase that she had just finished she often would hand it to me and have me read it, not out loud. She watched my face to see my expression and reaction to what I was reading.

And she enjoyed your reaction?

Yes.

What else would make her happy?

Sometimes when Frank would come into the office. She seemed to be happy to see him.

What would she do when she was angry?

Those black eyes would dart around. She was a very forceful woman.

How?

She was very positive and she had a way with words and punctuation that nobody I ever read ever had. She could put it across where somebody else could say almost the same thing and it just wouldn't hit you.

How did she treat people?

She had to really feel that she could trust somebody before she would like a person. She didn't just instantly like or not like a person.

Did Miss Rand have anything special in the house? Furniture or paintings, anything distinctive?

She had a very large, long dining room table. You could seat twelve, at least. Otherwise, she had the ordinary things, like a davenport, chairs.

How did she dress?

Always with pants, slacks and a top of some kind, very casual. And a low-heeled sport-type of shoe.

Do you remember any movies that the O'Connors might have enjoyed or seen?

No. I don't think they really went out too much. I do know that on several occasions when they did go out or were invited to something they needed to go to, she asked me to come over and house-sit—house-sit the manuscript.

So you did know where the manuscript was?

No, I still do not know. Never, never knew.

What were you supposed to do if something happened during your house-sitting?

I don't know. I often wondered.

Did you like Ayn Rand?

Oh yes! She was straightforward, she was honest, she was no-nonsense, she was very intelligent.

Can you tell me about Christmas at the O'Connors'?

At Christmas time, Frank always had a huge Christmas tree that he brought home. A beautifully shaped fir, which would go well in that room, because of the balcony. It would be probably ten-feet tall and went up above the balcony, and it was beautifully decorated. He was rather artistic. I was there two Christmases, so I remember both of those trees—and they were just beautifully decorated.

In what way?

One time, it was all red bulbs on the tree, and I think it had ribbons coming down. It was just very professional.

Why did you stop working for Miss Rand?

I left Ayn Rand to work for J. C. Penny. They were opening a new store in Reseda, and I did the payroll and the interviewing and was personnel manager.

How was your farewell?

Very good. I told her that I had found a full-time job, which is what I needed to have and she was very good about it. She understood and said it was quite all right and don't worry about us.

Ruth Beebe Hill

Ruth Beebe Hill was a friend of Ayn Rand's who lived in the O'Connors' Chatsworth home for twenty years after they moved to Manhattan in 1951. She is a book editor and author of *Hanta Yo* (1979), a *New York Times* best-seller.

Interview dates: July 22, September 4 and 12, November 7 and 14, 1996; and June 11, 1997

Scott McConnell: *How did you meet Ayn Rand?*

Ruth Beebe Hill: I met her through a long-time friend, Jean Elliott, who became her secretary in 1949.

It was the first week in November 1949. I said to Jean, "All right, now that you've located Ayn, you have six days to get me in that house. I want to meet her." In five days, Jean called me. She said, next Thursday, eight o'clock. And, eight o'clock because Ayn quits work at eight.

Jean had never heard of Ayn Rand, but when we arrived in California, August 1949, I told her about Ayn. Two days later she heard that Ayn Rand wanted a secretary. She had an interview with Ayn and was hired. Jean thought she was to be a social secretary because of the large estate, and that probably these people had a big social life. But Ayn made her duties very clear that first morning. She showed Jean where she would be working, at the desk on the north end of the gallery. Ayn asked, "Can you read my writing?" Jean looked it over and replied that she could. Ayn said to her, "There is something you must understand. This is the rule of the job. There's just one. Do not change anything: not a comma, not a semicolon, not a period, not a word, not the spelling. Nothing." Jean said, "I understand." And so she began the typing.

Tell me about your first meeting with Ayn Rand.

That first meeting had one disaster. I made the mistake of using the word "Plato." My husband [Dr. Borroughs "Buzzy" Hill] was not invited—just myself and Jean. We were at the door at eight o'clock—that famous copper door with a bullet-proof glass inset protecting a wood carving of the Torah. Ayn opened the door, her husband standing behind her. And I said, not waiting for an introduction: "You are the most profoundly religious person I've ever known." Ayn said: "Come in."

I liked to sit on the floor. This was a terrazzo floor, so it wasn't very warm, but Frank had a fire in the fireplace. There wasn't any other source of heat in this 1,200-square-foot living room. That house was colder than the Arctic. The only heaters the O'Connors used were little portable electrical ones. No central heating, none.

Here I am, sitting on the floor, a long couch back and left. Frank is seated in the chair he always used. Ayn Rand is on the near end of the couch, Jean is on the far end. We had talked about *The Fountainhead* and Howard Roark in particular. I figured we should stay an hour and a half and then courteously leave. The question that Ayn asked at the end of an hour was my downfall. It wasn't untrue, what I said, but it was careless, faulted to the nth degree, because I was trying to impress. I was so in love with *The Fountainhead* and therefore extended that love and respect to the author. I hoped Ayn would say, I want Ruth Hill back for more conversation; I want her to come again. I know those thoughts were going through my mind.

I told her I had memorized a condensed version of *The Fountainhead*. She commented that it was quite a piece of work, memorizing that book. And I said: "Well, you'll hear it; I'm going to see that you do. Verbatim. I do not change the language, it's yours. I add nothing. I dramatize it in an hour and a half, but I like a two-hour performance better." I said that there had to be condensations, but only using Ayn Rand sentences, not mine. Her response was: that's remarkable.

Then she asked what other works I had memorized. I answer, Plato's *Republic*. But I stopped speaking, because the room became cold air, frigid, as if the room had frozen. That whole, big living room with the huge philodendron towering above us, that room froze. I knew something was wrong. I wasn't a student of Plato, and didn't know that Ayn had said, not long before in a lecture, that Plato is the grandfather of communism.

Her loathing of Plato's philosophy was intense, which Frank knew. Can you guess what he did? Instantly, he was at my side and put his arms underneath me, so that I wouldn't have to put a hand down to get up from the floor—the terrazzo floor not easy to get up from gracefully. His hands under my arms, he took me to a chair. Not a word is spoken—by anybody—and he put me in this chair. Quietly, under his breath, he's saying: "I think you'll be warmer here." And then he gets a small robe and puts this over me—from my legs up to my waist, and tucks it in. Frank O'Connor knew that something had happened. He turned to Ayn and said: "Ruth was just thinking back to college days, when she probably was required to memorize these different things." Then he added: "How about some coffee?" That was Frank O'Connor. Nothing more was said about it. Ever.

How did the relationship progress from then?

I was in touch with the O'Connors regularly, a two-year period from 1949 into August 1951. We saw Frank and Ayn frequently, even though we did not live close by. We were invited to the San Fernando Valley almost every weekend from Newport Beach, where we were living.

What was Miss Rand's relationship with your husband, Dr. Hill?

Ayn said to me once: "I like you, Ruth, and you know that, but it is your husband that I totally admire. And if you're half the woman I think you are, you'll know what I've just said." And I did, and I loved her for it. Buzzy was a scientist par excellence, the discoverer of lactic dehydrogenase, a new enzyme in blood serum. Ayn Rand picked the right one of the two of us.

My times with Ayn alone were on the telephone, but my husband and Ayn had many one-on-one in-person talks. They would walk up and down the rows of blackberries at the back of the Tampa Avenue property and eat the berries as they talked. And of course he was very close to Frank.

My husband was an ideal companion for Ayn. Being a scientist, he responded like a scientist to whatever she asked or said. I mean, there weren't any wild guesses, and he didn't have to impress anybody, wouldn't even think about doing that. He could tell her what he liked, and didn't like, and she would listen.

By the way, Ayn and Buzzy were both stamp collectors, and they did a lot of philatelic talk. They were fascinated by stamps, not commercially, but rather enjoyed the history depicted.

When you visited Ayn Rand and had these dinners, what entertainment was there?

Ayn Rand was the entertainment.

What did your husband and Ayn Rand discuss?

Well, everything. She was excited about his work in cancer research. The way he explained his work made it easy for her to understand. She seemed fascinated by talk of enzymes and how complicated the makeup of a human being is.

Do you remember any anecdotes or funny stories about your husband and Frank O'Connor?

They laughed a lot together. I remember the O'Connors coming to our house in mid-December, and Frank talked about how he loved Christmas and electric trains. So did my husband. We had an HO gauge and a Lionel, but our money had gone into the HO gauge. And this was a big thing for us at Christmas, to get out the HO gauge. Frank did the same thing. At Christmas, in that huge living room at 10,000 Tampa, Frank set up his train. These two men were very much alike, not only in their delight with toy trains but in their love of growing flowers.

What would Frank do with the train?

Play. He sat on the floor and played with the train. So my idea was, let's show Frank our train at Christmas. I invited them for dinner. I expected Ayn to wear slacks. She dressed casually when we dined at their house, so never had I seen her as when she arrived at the door. She was wearing a dress designed by Adrian. I drew in my breath. Her gown was black. Countless miniature stars and mostly crescent moons in silver tones decorated the garment. A train of at least two feet swept the floor.

What was her attitude?

A little bit girlish. She wanted to be feminine. The only time I ever kissed Ayn was when—I can't remember what it was she said, but it was so little girlish, and she was seated in a chair and I was standing. I went over and kissed the top of her head, and I knew she liked it. Her reaction was like a fifteen-year-old, and she was like that in the Adrian.

I had made a flower arrangement that evening, which I thought Frank would like. I remember saying to Frank that I hope the bouquet is Christmassy enough. I recall his response: that it was such fun to come into a house decorated for Christmas. No response from Ayn. The guys played with the HO gauge, while Ayn watched, and, in the kitchen, I fretted to myself that I was serving a casserole of pork chops to a guest who was wearing an Adrian-designed silk dress with a sweeping train!

I don't ever remember having wine at their home. Frank poured us, and himself, a martini. Ayn had 7-Up or ginger ale, or other carbonated drinks. She said she didn't dare take an alcoholic drink, that she couldn't cope with any additional stimulants.

Ayn sent Christmas cards. We received those greetings for four years. And I remember thinking that Ayn Rand did not know how to sign a Christmas card. Should she sign Ayn Rand and Frank O'Connor? Then she must have thought, well, people who don't know me—who do they think Frank is, if they don't know she is Mrs. Frank O'Connor. Most people just knew her as Ayn Rand. Three different Christmas cards have three different ways of signing. And I always had to smile when the cards came. The one from 1951 is signed "Ayn and Frank O'Connor."

I believe you arranged a talk by Miss Rand in 1950.

I had arranged for her to appear at a group called "Books and Authors" [October 8, 1950]. She refused to accept my description of the group, so I told her that I'm assistant to the founder, Helen Girvin. And I said, "Don't you want to sell some more copies?" The membership included very wealthy women. Monthly meetings were held in Beverly Hills or at the Ambassador Hotel. She said, "I have to know who I'm going to see; I have to know who's running this." All right. You shall meet the founder and president. "Shall I bring her over here? Or do you want to go to Helen Girvin's home in Hollywood?" "No, bring her here." So I brought Helen, who was right out of Boston, wearing gloves when she went out in the evening, and a hat.

Ayn didn't question; she interrogated Helen Girvin. She asked various philosophic questions and listened for what was implied in the answers. Ayn always said to watch for what's implied. She asked direct questions, and Helen gave Ayn direct answers, never hesitating for a moment. Helen was queenly. She just let Ayn know that she admired her and very much wanted her on the program. The audience would be delighted to hear her speak. At the end of a half hour, Ayn said that she'd be happy to appear on the program.

Ayn told me that after publication of *The Fountainhead*, her appearance at Books and Authors was the second time she gave such a talk. And I said, "How many people attended the salon where you originally spoke?" She answered, "It was like a small book club."

The crowd was between five and six hundred people at the Ambassador Hotel [in Los Angeles] in the Crystal Room. Laura Scudder was on the way to the hospital for minor surgery, but she had her chauffeur stop and wait for one hour, so she could listen to Ayn Rand's speech.[75] That was the big news at this gathering, that Laura Scudder was not going to miss Ayn Rand, who rarely made public appearances. And Ayn was wonderful. She spoke, I would say, less than two minutes. Each speaker, usually five at each meeting, was granted ten minutes.

What did she say?

She introduced herself as an author, made a few comments about her writing methods, and the hours that she wrote. I do not remember specifically. But suddenly, I did hear this: "Now I'm not going to give a speech. I want to hear questions. I will answer your questions."

A friend of mine asked the first question—"Miss Rand, in *The Fountainhead* there are really such wonderful love scenes between Howard Roark and Dominique, and I just wanted to know if these were—if such lovemaking is from your own experience?" And Ayn answered in two words: "Wishful thinking." That was it. And, of course, everybody loved her response.

Afterwards there was the autograph party for the various people who spoke that day. Helen put me in charge of the sale of books. I had the books arranged, at the table, for each author. When Ayn sat down to autograph, she couldn't believe the length of the line, the number of people waiting for her. But what she also couldn't believe was that I had gotten copies of *Anthem*. Because *Anthem* was now one of the books I was doing as a dramatization. I didn't buy them, but Helen had ordered copies of *Anthem*, and I can remember Ayn looking at me and saying, "What are you doing?" I said, "I'm selling *Anthem*." She said, "You located all those copies of *Anthem*?" I smiled. "Yeah, it's a good book." The admiration in her eyes was terrific. Incidentally, we sold all sixty copies. And many, many copies of *The Fountainhead*.

Ayn asked me to introduce her to a young man in the audience, whom she had noticed bore a resemblance to Frank. A week later, I invited him to a small party at our home, Ayn and Frank attending.

Did Miss Rand attend any of your dramatizations of her novels?

Ayn came to Hollywood to hear me do a dramatization of *The Fountainhead* for the AAUW, the American Association of University Women. I had invited her three or four times previously for appearances

---

75 Laura Scudder built her potato chip empire on her 1926 innovation of packaging chips in portable, disposable bags.

before other groups. But she had said: "You dare?" And I said, "What do you mean, I dare?" Her answer: "You dare to do this in front of me?" And I said, "You're damn right, and another thing, I'll make it every bit as good as you wrote it." She didn't laugh, she smiled.

I probably did a hundred and fifty dramatizations of *Anthem*. It was particularly popular with clubs because of the length. But T*he Fountainhead* was my favorite presentation.

What did Miss Rand say after she heard your recital of The Fountainhead*?*

She couldn't believe my memory. She had only one criticism, that I transposed one line, where I described how a person looked. She commented that it did not apply to where I used it.

There was a large crowd at the talk, and, at Ayn's request, nobody knew she was in the audience. The woman sitting next to her, said to Ayn, "God, I didn't even know about it, let alone read this wonderful book. Have you ever read it?" Ayn later told me that it was one of the top moments in her life, when she could say: "I wrote it!" She was very proud. And the woman turned her head away and almost fainted. She didn't know what to say or do.

So Miss Rand was happy to see the work performed?

Yes, very. I only wish she could have heard *Anthem* too.

Tell me about your conversations with her.

Ayn Rand was interested in people with ideas. Not so much ideals, but ideas, ideas, ideas. This was the context of her life, ideas. That's why conversation with her went through the night. She did listen to others—no matter what people say—she listened. I remember her listening to my husband very closely.

Did she talk about The Fountainhead*?*

She told me, "It's only a prelude. It's only a prelude, Ruth, to my new book." Of course, I didn't know the name of the new book, and my friend Jean Elliott would not tell, or even mention the words "The Strike"[76] or anything else about *Atlas Shrugged*, half-completed at that time.

When I talked with Ayn after *Atlas Shrugged* was published, I said, "I

---

76 The original title for *Atlas Shrugged*.

still love *The Fountainhead*, and the characters." And she repeated almost the same words on the phone: "Yes, but compared to *Atlas Shrugged?*"

Did Miss Rand ever edit you?

I once quoted her in the PTA bulletin [Newport Beach, California] for which I was editor. I had used this line from *Anthem*: "I will teach my child to stand on his own two feet." She criticized me because I added "two," which wasn't in the original.

What was Tampa Avenue like in 1949?

There weren't any houses, other than one on the corner of Tampa and Devonshire, and one more south on Tampa near Nordhoff. Tampa wasn't paved, just a dirt road lined on the west side with acres and acres of orange groves.

What socializing did the O'Connors do?

They told me that once they had a party with designer Adrian and actor Joseph Cotten invited. That was the night Frank made the bubble machine, and bubbles blew all over the 1,200-square-foot living room.

Any other activities at the house?

When Ayn had a writing block, she would go out to the acre field that was part of the property and pick up stones. It wasn't a rock collection. She talked about the sensuous feel of the stones. There were hundreds that she put in little boxes. She told me it was her recreation. She gathered, then sorted them by size. Because there was no meaning, she picked up any size, all the same gray color.

When we moved into that house, I found 120 little cartons filled with the stones. Each carton held stones of identical size. All of these were in the studio where she had written *Atlas Shrugged*.

Any stories about Miss Rand's writing?

One time I noticed torn up pieces of paper on the ground among the birch trees. I saw instantly that they bore writing in pen and ink, Ayn's writing, and so I said, "Oh!" and I bent to pick up the paper—I wanted them. And she said, "Don't touch. Those are just pieces of paper. That's all they are." They were discarded manuscript pages.

They just weren't good enough for her?

Correct. And then, do you remember in *The Fountainhead*, when

Dominique picked up an old sheet of newspaper that blew against her leg. A scene similar to what I witnessed appears in the book. But Ayn knew I wanted to have and to hold those pieces of her writing. And that was not what she wanted. Meaning, no, not that kind of adulation, picking up torn paper.

I think that Ayn appreciated the privacy of her studio, a room closed off from the rest of the house. Entertaining at 10,000 Tampa was primarily in the living room. Ayn wasn't big on furniture, on interior decoration.

Did the O'Connors have a name for the ranch?

It was only thirteen acres. I know occasionally it was called "ranch," even by Ayn, but it really wasn't. No, it was mostly called "10,000 Tampa."

Tell me about the plants in the house.

In the living room was a philodendron that rose up to the second level of the house. The way Frank used to polish the leaves, it would take at least an hour and a half. This plant was huge, like a tree in the middle of the room. There weren't any screens on the doors, and birds would fly in and out of the house.

He didn't mind the birds flying in?

No. And Ayn's response to that was if Frank didn't mind, it was okay.

Anything else interesting about the house?

When Ayn took my husband and me upstairs to show us the mirrored bathroom, she said, "Hollywood." The shower was separate, of course, from the tub, and the shower wall was glass on three sides, and mirror on one side. You saw yourself in perpetuity, forever on down the line. The tub was a gorgeous porcelain, very deep and long, like a bathtub for two. A bath was exciting because there was mirror on the right side (as you face the tub), and a mirror at the back, the length of the tub. A glass wall dominated one end of the tub, and the mirror as described on the other end. The toilet and the bidet were against a mirrored wall.

Did she have curtains on the windows in the bathroom?

No.

So you could look in from outside quite easily if you wanted to?

Nobody could see in. The only window coverings in the entire house were heavy old drapes at fenestration [windows] in the huge bedroom upstairs.

What plants were on the property?

Wisteria and a huge growth of bamboo on the patio that held 200 people. A dozen pomegranate trees grew beyond the birches and the row of berries. Other fruit-bearing trees and the wonderful chestnuts. There were three or four chestnut trees.

What did Mr. O'Connor grow?

Frank grew stephanotis, those fragrant, small white flowers that brides often use in their bouquets. He grew delphinium and gladiolas in quantity. And he produced hybrids. He really became a botanist, a very informed grower. But glads were his particular strength, and these he sold to hotels in Los Angeles.

Who did the selling?

He did. He picked up the telephone, and called hotels in Los Angeles. I know that it became a business, that he sold to the Beverly Hills Hotel and the Ambassador.

Acres of orange groves were on the opposite side of Tampa, not on the O'Connors' property, but the fragrance as you turned off Devonshire toward their house on Tampa was exhilarating.

Did the ranch have a watering system?

A system of sprinklers. They didn't move, but water reached so far out and so high that you thought it was raining. A similar water system was built into that big patio. During those hot days, you could open the door to the living area onto the patio and turn on the "rain" system. You could be "in the rain" whenever you wanted rain!

What fish did Frank O'Connor have in the moat that surrounded the house?

Goldfish, but I can't name the species. The moat had become choked by water hyacinths, a Japanese species. The moat was in danger of cracking. Also, many frogs inhabited the moat.

What was on the roof?

Over the large garage was a terrazzo sundeck that had nothing on it. Then there was a partition that separated what was over the large garage and the garage for two other cars. And over that section, a copper roof. From their bedroom, the O'Connors looked out through the fenestration onto a roof pool. Water covered that copper roof, eight inches deep, and there Frank grew and introduced exotic fish.

What animals were on the property besides the peafowl and caged pigeons?

Possum and many raccoons. And on one occasion, there was a cougar sighting.

Tell me about the peafowl.

Frank kept two kinds, the white ones and the type people are familiar with, the blue. Envision the path of birches that Marlene Dietrich gave Josef von Sternberg as a gift. A line of birches from the back driveway straight to the end of the property. Thirty birches, fifteen on each side, that formed a path five feet wide. At the front of those birches, envision a California water oak, twelve to fourteen feet high, with wide branches. Covering that tree was chicken wire, which enclosed the peafowl. Just a wire enclosure, but a huge area. Chicken wire over another tree provided a "cage" for thirty white pigeons.

Describe Mr. O'Connor and Miss Rand together.

Frank had the grace of the cats, and I mean the big cats, from cougars up into the lions. I'm talking about a beauty of movement, which Ayn mentioned in our conversations. Frank was tall and very slender. Ayn was not tall, but she, too, moved gracefully.

What I saw between Ayn and Frank was also what Ayn was like without Frank. He was the anchor to windward. He was the rock. On one occasion, she said to Buzzy and me, "When it gets right down to the writing and everything else in our lives, Frank is the power behind the throne." Frank comes back instantly with, "Sometimes I think I am the throne, the way I get sat on."

Frank O'Connor was a strong person, physically and mentally. Ayn was proud of those lines he contributed to her novels. Ayn had an innocence that people rarely saw. For those who knew her personally—and there weren't many—she exhibited at times a shining, childlike innocence.

Tell me about the O'Connors leaving their Chatsworth home.

Ayn said that she heard sorrow in my voice when she announced their departure plans. I didn't want her to go away, to move back to New York. I can remember when she made the phone call. We were at the exclusive Lido Trailer Park, and she said "I want you to know, Ruth, we are going to move back to New York." Oh no! Don't take away from us the stimulation that you are. Don't go. I remember feeling that. My whole body reacted—all of me, like in shock. And I remember what she said: "I will never be further from you than *The Fountainhead*." I thought it was a wonderful thing to say. And really very helpful. Ayn invited us for a last time together at Chatsworth, and the four of us made it a happy occasion, even though it was saying good-bye. And there weren't any statements like "We'll write," or "Phone us." We had martinis, then on to our favorite Chatsworth restaurant—Katchamakoffs—for dinner, then back to the O'Connors'. Actually, we spent time routing their trip through Ouray, Colorado. My husband was great with cross-country maps. We'd driven across the U.S. nine times.

How did you become the renter of their home?

Here's the telegram. "Mr. and Mrs. R. Hill, Mission Bell Motel, Ventura Blvd., Encino, CA. Date: July 12, 1952." The Tampa house had stood vacant from the time they left in October 1951 for New York. Before their departure, Ayn said, "We're not going to sell the house, because Frank doesn't want to sell it. And we're not planning to rent it. We don't want to do that. But we would rent it to you." And I remember saying we can't afford it. Frank suggested that we talk about it later. So the telegram says: "Please telephone me collect. We want to discuss the house. Ayn Rand."

When we called Ayn, she wanted us to set the price we could pay. "Just tell me, Ruth, what you will pay." I said, "$85." She said, "Fine, settled." So $85 a month to live in a million-dollar estate is pretty neat. It wasn't a million-dollar estate then, but at least I know they made a couple hundred thousand on that property, when it was finally sold in 1962. I arranged the sale with the buyer, our neighbor.

I took the house under one condition: "Ayn, I'm going to give it six weeks. I don't see how I can handle a house this big, and I know Buzzy will to try to take care of this whole property alone. We don't have the money for gardening." [Frank had employed three gardeners.]. She said, "Yes, but you will. We're going to pay for help." And so they paid.

None of us wanted a contract. We simply wanted to shake hands
on it. But I said, "I want something in writing, Ayn, because I want it
known that we will try it for six weeks." Well, that six weeks lasted
twenty years. Originally $85 per month, then $125 per month. "It's
like we're owning this together," was what Ayn said. And I said, "No,
you bought the house." Ayn answered: "We'll go half and half on the
upkeep." They'd pay a portion of the costly water bill to keep Frank's
glads blooming.

Were there any problems with the ranch?

No. We were not going to be selling the flowers. All Frank said was:
"As long as you can, keep the glads alive." I told him how we sat in the
garage with those glad pips, thousands of them, which we sorted, then
took to his field house, to store in huge drawers. Doing this for Frank,
because he hoped to return one day to live on the estate. He wanted
to keep alive some of the new species of gladiolas he had created.
Especially one he called "Lipstick" and another he named "Halloween."

Did the O'Connors leave any materials in the house when they left?

Yes. One item I felt was very important to tell Ayn that she had left
behind. It was a first edition of *The Fountainhead*. First edition, first
printing, that she had autographed to Nick, Frank's older brother. And
this is in her writing, bottom of the page: "May 5, 1943." At the top of
the page, first page, "To Nick—My technical adviser—the editor-in-
chief of the New York Banner—for all the evenings when you listened
to the reading of this book. Ayn." She told me to keep it for our son
Reid, who was nine years old.

I was amazed at the amount of furniture that they left. The dining
room table—I think they left the table because it was too big for their
New York apartment; on the large patio they left a round metal table
and outdoor chairs and those eight furry dining table chairs. In the living
room there were four other chairs.

Upstairs one bed had been left on the gallery, and a cat-clawed
chair on that same upper level. In the greenhouse, where Frank grew the
stephanotis, were unwanted boxes of photos, with no identifying labels.

Ayn left railroad magazines. One magazine was called *Reading
Railroad*, stacks of these, absolutely stacks. I saved and brought some,
dated 1946, to [my home in] Friday Harbor [Washington]. I asked Ayn
if she wanted any copies, and she said no.

In the late 1950s there was an eminent domain issue involving the property. How did Ayn Rand react to that?

You mean relative to the school, Nobel Junior High, as it is called?[77] They wanted to buy portions of the O'Connor property. Not a lot of pressure. I telephoned the O'Connors and handled the business as directed.

So Miss Rand wasn't upset or didn't fight it?

No, no. There wasn't any problem there. Ayn cared less and less about Tampa. It was Frank who really believed, for awhile anyway, that they would come back. Here was the life he loved.

What happened to the house in 1971?

The house was then owned by Katherine Houchin, who is now deceased. I arranged that sale; nobody had to pay any commission, and my husband and I continued to live there. We moved out in August 1971, after twenty years residency. And as we drove out of the driveway, the tenth of August, the bulldozers had already come in and knocked down the house where Frank grew the stephanotis. The bulldozer's next move would be to raze the house. I did not want to see that happen. I did not look back as we turned off Tampa—10,000 Tampa—onto Devonshire and headed north to our new home on forty-five wooded acres in Puget Sound.

---

77 The City of Los Angeles bought 1.663 of the thirteen acres for $15,000 in 1959.

1950s

Ake and Jane Sandler

Ake Sandler was a professor of political science at Los Angeles State College in the early 1950s when he knew Miss Rand. He and his wife Jane visited Miss Rand's home in Chatsworth. Dr. Sandler died in 2008.

Interview dates: May 24 and June 4, 2002

Scott McConnell: *How did you first meet Ayn Rand?*

Ake Sandler: That was back in 1950, when I was active as a foreign correspondent in Hollywood, and she was present at some of those parties that the Hollywood Foreign Correspondents Association gave. I introduced myself and told her who I was and that I would like her to give my students a lecture.

What do you remember about that meeting?

Nothing, except I had read *The Fountainhead,* and I was generally interested in her philosophy and invited her to speak to one of my classes at L.A. State. I had a class at the time in American political thought, and she thought that would fit her interest, and so she accepted. The first time she spoke to my class was in May 1950.

I also had a class on the history of political theory, beginning with Plato.[78] She was interested in that. It started with some early philosophers, Plato, Aristotle and so forth, and went all the way up to Marx. From what I recall, she was very well versed with the theories of Plato, Aristotle and Socrates and so forth, and the Socratic method. I have an impression that she was very well educated in the field.

Tell me about Ayn Rand coming to this class.

I wanted to respect her privacy, so I didn't invite anybody besides my students to attend. She gave a lecture on her own political philosophy. I can't remember exactly what she said, but I know that the students were immensely interested because she was a very intense

---

78 At this time, Dr. Sandler taught three classes: History of Political Theory, American Political Thought, and International Relations.

lecturer and very sharp. After the lecture, the students asked her if they could get to know her better, and she invited some of them to her home. She had one stipulation: she was not interested in anyone going to her home who was a communist. That was an absolute. I think a dozen students accepted her invitation. My wife and I and some of the students went out there a few times, and then she came back and lectured once more to my political theory class.

Mrs. Sandler, how many times did you meet Miss Rand?

Jane Sandler: About three times. The first time was at her home when we were invited out there. I remember the birds screaming all over the place. Lots of peacocks. It was weird. It was strange. There was no other place like it. Her home was quite incredible. Her furniture was huge—huge sofas, more like daybeds, with lots of pillows around. There was no such thing as sitting on a chair. You just had to kind of scooch up on these sofas as best you could, holding your legs around them. The students were sitting on the floor, many of them cross-legged.

She was just a very engaging person. Very warm. She was welcoming and all that, but there was still a certain coldness about her. It was in her personality. She had her own mind and her own opinions—and that was that. I don't think she was trying to delve into deep discussions regarding other than her own ideas, but the students loved her and were at her feet. Their discussions were animated and lasted hours and hours. I don't think anyone really wanted to leave. It was fascinating.

Ake Sandler: But it was a kind of indoctrination. I was well aware that she wanted to create followers. She wanted believers after they left her, maybe for life. She wanted to give them something that they would not forget. She wanted listeners and followers. From the beginning I had a feeling she was very anxious for her own philosophy to be accepted. I'm sure I never met a more intelligent woman. She was absolutely all brains. She was always fanatical about individualism and her philosophy and that you can know what the truth is.

She had an open house for the students, so they could come out there almost any time, but they would call her first. She had a colony of students from my classes, probably at least a dozen who were out there often, much more often than I was, so I knew she had quite a lot of converts from my students. At her home, she did a much better job of converting them. She was very good at that.

What is your philosophy of life and political theory?

I call my myself a liberal-conservative-socialist, which means that I tend to be very pragmatic. My father was a socialist, and he translated Karl Marx's *Das Kapital* into Swedish. He was Sweden's prime minister at one time as a socialist/Marxist.[79] So I was brought up in a socialist home, and my mother was a Christian. To some extent I agree with Ayn Rand, so I had no problem with her lecturing to my class.

You said she was the most intelligent woman you have ever met. Could you explain that.

First of all, the way she looked at you, like she could read your mind and know what you were thinking and talking about. I think her intelligence was so apparent, she seemed to be almost clairvoyant when she looked at something. She could see it very clearly. She was very concentrated, very focused. I have never met anybody that brilliant.

Did any of your students carry on her ideas?

Yes, I know one who wrote books and I think was very much influenced by her.

What was Miss Rand's purpose in talking so much with you?

I don't know. I told her about my father, and I think she was concerned about that. He was a socialist and she couldn't get over it, so to speak. It was wrong. It was wrong. She hated collectivism.

You didn't come to agree with that?

No, I did not. As I mentioned, I'm more pragmatic. I don't want to be talked into one particular philosophy.

Did you enjoy talking with her?

Oh yes! I liked her very much. She was very friendly, very open. My wife says she was cold. It could be that she was cold in her thinking, but she was very friendly and very open. She wasn't the hugging kind. We shook hands. I had nothing but good feelings about her.

Did she influence your thinking?

Yes, to the extent that I was willing to listen to her.

---

79 Rickard Sandler was prime minister in 1925–26.

She didn't try to "convert" you?

No, not at all, but she felt that the students were young and impressionable and that she could play a role in getting them to think differently, to give them some sort of protection. At the time there was a lot of liberalism, leftism around, especially in the academy.

Did you debate with her?

No, I didn't see that as my job. I wanted her to have a chance to really lay out her own philosophy, so the students could understand her. Of course, two lectures wasn't enough.

Were there any students in your classes who were hostile to her?

No, she had the authority to command their attention and interest, and so I don't think anybody asked hostile questions, only critical questions.

When she was at your classes, was it lectures or just discussion?

They were lectures. Believe it or not, I didn't take any notes. I must have been so fascinated I just sat and listened.

How long were the lectures?

Fifty minutes, and I had about forty to fifty students.

What was Miss Rand's second lecture about?

It was to a class on international relations, and she lectured on communism and the evils of communism, and the virtue of capitalism and free-enterprise.

Did she discuss her past in the Soviet Union?

No, except to say that she had left the Soviet Union, and that she didn't think it would last, and that it had to be fought on all fronts.

What did she tell your students about communism?

First of all she defined and discussed it the way she knew communism as a totalitarian dictatorship, where Stalin was a total dictator, and that communism sprung from Karl Marx and Engels and *The Communist Manifesto*. She regarded communism as an inhuman system.

What questions did the students ask her?

I think there were a good deal of questions about academic freedom. How did it jibe with fighting communism? I mean, on the one hand, she sounded fairly democratic and loved free speech and that sort of thing, but on the other hand, she believed there was only one basic truth and that was individualism.

Was there anything else about history or famous historical events that she discussed?

She discussed *The Communist Manifesto* and the revolutions in Europe at the time. She was very much at home in the history of Europe at the time and, of course, the principle of communism.

Was she a good teacher?

Excellent. I've had many lecturers in my class, but she was probably one of the best. Very factual. Obviously, she was a master of the subject and gave the impression that she certainly knew what she was talking about.

Did you use any of Miss Rand's material in your class?

After she had lectured, I talked about *The Fountainhead* and individualism, and there was a good deal of discussion about whether Howard Roark acted morally.

I believe you had some photographs taken while Miss Rand was at your college.

They were taken in the class by the campus photographer. I believe that there may have been an interview with her by somebody from the *College Times*, and then there was a story in the paper, with the photograph.

How did your relationship with Miss Rand end?

Very friendly. We may have said farewell in her home when she decided to leave for New York. I'm quite sure there was nothing said about keeping in touch or anything like that. That was really none of my business. We had a very professional relationship. Professional acquaintances, shall we say.

In the early 1950s, what was the general reaction of academics to Ayn Rand?

Oh, I think quite a few of them were liberal and felt that she was rather extreme, shall we say, in her views, and they certainly didn't think much of her as a political philosopher. I think they knew her primarily as a writer of fiction, like *The Fountainhead*, not as a philosopher. I talked to my colleagues about her, at lunch and so forth, and told them I was very impressed with her. They were very curious to know more about her.

Richard L. Phillips

Richard L. Phillips, a fan of *The Fountainhead*, visited Miss Rand in 1951.

Interview date: July 23, 1998

Scott McConnell: *How did you meet Miss Rand?*

Richard L. Phillips: A friend of mine had written her a letter, care of the publisher, and got a very nice reply with her home address on it in Chatsworth, California. This is 1951, and I was about to be drafted and had decided that before I went into the army, I wanted to go out to California. My first thought was that I just wanted to see the Richard Neutra house she was living in. I'd read about it, and I'd seen some pictures in an architectural magazine, so my cousin and I drove out there, found the place, and I said to my cousin, "Let's drive in the driveway so we get a closer look." Nobody was in sight, so we could just drive in the driveway, and drive out again. As we got in the driveway, a man appeared, who seemed to be the gardener, and asked what I wanted. I told him very briefly, and he said that "normally she'd be working, but she was on the phone with her friends, because President Truman had just announced that he was firing General MacArthur."[80]

The "gardener" was Frank O'Connor. He said, "Let me check and see if she can talk to you." A few minutes later, he invited us in. She came down from upstairs, and we started talking. At first, she was very guarded and was really trying to find out "Who is this guy?" and "What is his interest in *The Fountainhead*?" So she asked me why I was interested in the book. Obviously, people can have all kinds of ways of approaching it, so evidentially I could see from the things I said to her that she kind of sat back and relaxed, let her breath out, thought that I was somebody she could talk to.

What did you say to her?

I liked the ideas in the book: the idea of individuals being free and unfettered from convention and from the rules of society, and I liked the intellectualism of the book. We sat and talked for three or four hours, and it was getting late in the afternoon, and obviously my cousin who

---

80 General MacArthur was dismissed on April 11, 1951.

was just sitting there, not saying anything, but listening to everything, started getting a little fidgety, because she had kids at home to take care of. And Rand said, "Obviously you've got to go, but we haven't really finished this discussion. Can you come back?" I said, "Yes," so we made an appointment for two days later, and my cousin drove me out. And so I spent another couple of hours talking to her.

Can you remember any of the topics of conversation?

She did spend some time talking about Truman firing MacArthur, and I realized that her take on that and mine were different. I thought we had a civilian form of government, not a military form of government.[81]

What did she say about MacArthur?

She thought it was the wrong thing for Truman to do, because MacArthur knew how to win the war in Korea.

Was there anything else Ayn Rand said about MacArthur?

Oh, that he was a great man, the usual stuff.

Tell me your impressions of Mr. O'Connor?

Very quiet, but a very strong presence. He gave off a lot of electricity, and some of her descriptions of Howard Roark were absolutely perfect descriptions of O'Connor—of being absolutely relaxed, but coiled like a cat. He would lie back and be in total relaxation, but all the coils were poised, like if something happened, he'd spring up in less than an instant and be in physical action. That was my feeling about him. He was a very handsome man. Very contained. In the whole two visits, I don't think he said more than a dozen words.

Why?

I think she said everything for both of them. She was incredibly verbal.

Do you have any observations about the decorations or inside of the house?

---

81 Ayn Rand wrote to California Sen. William Knowland about the firing and sent MacArthur a personally signed copy of *Anthem*: "From an author who voted for him for President of the United States in 1952—with profound respect and admiration."

The one thing I remember was a little brass carousel sitting on one of the tables. It was driven by candlepower, where if you light the candles, the heat going up would hit little blades and turn the carousel around. The whole thing was maybe eight or ten inches across. It may have had some special meaning to her. I thought it was a tacky little thing, and I was surprised to see it in her house, because the house was quite elegant.

Evan and Mickey Wright

Evan Wright was a friend of Miss Rand's from 1951 to 1961. Michela "Mickey" Wright is his wife.

Interview date: March 5, 1998

Scott McConnell: *How did you meet Ayn Rand?*

Evan Wright: She sent Nathan Blumenthal [Nathaniel Branden] to look for me. In late 1950 I was at UCLA in my senior year. There were communists all over the campus, including an editor on the college paper, the *Daily Bruin*. People were writing Marxist-type letters to the paper, and I wrote two or three letters denouncing their Marxist point of view, basically because I had become an Ayn Rand convert after seeing *The Fountainhead* movie and reading the book afterwards. What happened was that I eventually called Nathan, who also was a UCLA student and who had clipped out my letters and showed them to Ayn. Ayn was mystified by them, because I was saying things in them that she was just then writing in *Atlas Shrugged*, and there was no way that I could have known what she was saying in her novel; it was still in manuscript form. So she asked Nathan to find me and bring me over to meet her. She called me the "mystery man," because there was no way I could know what she was doing.

How did Mr. Blumenthal track you down?

He looked me up in the school register and sent me a telegram and asked me to call him. I was so busy at school, reading a book a day and trying to study for my English comprehensive at the same time, that I didn't have time to call him. I didn't know anybody named Nathan Blumenthal, so I threw the telegram into a drawer and didn't answer it. The next year, I think June or so, I graduated and I had a little more time, so when I ran across this old yellow telegram, I called the number. Nathan said he was leaving for NYU the next day, but would I like to meet Ayn Rand? I said, certainly. I guess he must have given me her phone number and directions to her place in Chatsworth. I called her, went out there and we got to be good friends.

Tell me about your first meeting with Ayn Rand.

When I knocked on her door, Frank answered and brought me to the living room. Ayn came in, and my manners were a little lacking;

I remained seated, and of course Frank was unhappy that I was still sitting, so I had to stand up. We talked a lot after that.

What was your first impression of Miss Rand?

I was very impressed, and awestruck by this very successful, wonderful writer. I was delighted to be there.

Was she in person what you expected?

Pretty much. I quickly got the impression that if I wasn't an atheist I wasn't going to be her friend. In fact, she once asked me to describe what causes a waterfall. I had just taken geology, so I knew all about how a waterfall is created; I described it blow by blow. If I recall correctly, the waterfall is caused by the flow of water over a layer of hard rock, which itself overlies softer layers of rock. When I finished my detailed explanation of how her waterfall was created, she said, "What did God have to do with that?" That stopped me.

But she was so impressive. Over our scotch and soda we had many conversations until three o'clock in the morning—after she was through writing for the day. I could talk to her on equal terms until one conversation we had, perhaps three or four hours after we had gotten started. I quoted something to her from Schopenhauer, and she said, "Did you know that later in the same book that you must be quoting from he contradicted himself?" I was stunned—and still am. I thought, "What am I dealing with here?" She had evidently read all of the philosophers, knew their works and had her own philosophy. I began to realize I had a formidable person to talk philosophy with.

What was the value for her in talking to you?

I don't know. She seemed interested in me, and so did Frank. Frank said something about how I impressed her. We got pretty deep into philosophy and cause and effect. I was interested in philosophy at that time, and I think she learned maybe a tiny bit from me. Of course, I was learning a great deal from her.

What did Ayn Rand seem to enjoy most when you were with her?

Conversation. She loved to talk and we exchanged ideas. That seemed to make her about as happy as anything did.

What made her angry?

Being interrupted. I remember I interrupted her once and she said if I didn't stop that she was going to leave the room. That's the only time she ever chastised me. I stopped interrupting her. My wife has brought that up a hundred and fifty times—every time I interrupt her. Ayn was in a train of thought and I kept trying to put my two cents worth in. She didn't want to be interrupted. That was the only time.

I can't think of anything else that made her angry. Things were very friendly between us all the time. I didn't like *Atlas Shrugged*, but that was much later, in 1961, when I finally got around to reading the entire work. We were through with our friendship by that time.

Did she discuss World War II with you?

We had many conversations, but I don't remember any discussion of World War II. Also, she was very reluctant to talk about her time in Russia. It meant nothing to her. She said that her education in Russia was very easy, ridiculously so. She was very contemptuous of Russia and really didn't want to discuss her time before she left the Soviet Union. She wouldn't refuse to discuss it, but I didn't have any questions to ask about it particularly. I might have asked something once in a while, but she just sloughed it off as of no importance. She wanted to talk philosophy, politics and ethics and morality, things that were of most importance to her.

What political views did she have that surprised you?

She wouldn't choose the lesser evil because the lesser evil was still evil, as she would say. So she didn't mind if I chose to vote for Eisenhower, but she chose not to vote.

I once made the mistake of saying that Howard Roark was probably somebody who was based on Frank Lloyd Wright. She said, no, not Frank Lloyd Wright; if it was any architect, it would have been Sullivan.[82]

Did you talk about her early days in America?

No. Our conversations were mostly on an intellectual plane— philosophy, ethics, very high level. We didn't get into personalities, too much, to actual people. There were few other visitors. When I met Albert Mannheimer there, the conversation was lighter, more professional. Once, a group of raucous friends and/or relatives came,

---

82 Louis Sullivan, for whom Wright worked early in his career.

and over lunch argued loudly with Ayn, who did not appreciate it. They also humiliated Frank. At one tense point I interjected a paraphrase of Wordsworth: "The writer differs not in kind, but only in degree." To which Ayn replied, "I also differ in kind." Later they all went out to dinner somewhere in the Valley. I was invited but chose not to go. Ayn met with me in her writing room, where I sat at her desk. She seemed to understand why I was uninterested in her visitors, and said that she had to go. I remained alone in the house, doing some sort of writing, et cetera, at her desk until they all returned.

She gave me the book *Candide* out of her library, which was being packed up to move to New York. She recommended a book by Victor Hugo, *The Man Who Laughs*, which was one of her favorites. And we discussed Tolstoy a little bit. She said if I wanted to learn how not to be a writer, I should read Tolstoy.

Did she help your thinking?

She did a lot of straightening out of people's minds, including mine. I told her that when I had finished with my college education, which was a bachelor's degree at that time, I'd been confronted with two hundred fifty different philosophies, but it was all like a big, affixated wheel with its spokes all counterbalancing each other, and I didn't know what I thought anymore. She began removing spoke after spoke after spoke. Finally, the wheel began to turn. And I turned definitely in her direction.

Can you remember which specific ideas she changed of yours?

I gave up quoting Schopenhauer.

Do you remember any specific questions you discussed with her?

She was looking for some new power source. It would be something new and important that was to appear in *Atlas Shrugged*. I had become an electrical engineer in 1952, and she asked me about lightning. I knew about lightning, but I also asked various other engineers about it, and we came to the conclusion that although it was a tremendous amount of power, it was of too short duration. There'd be no way of harnessing it, so she would have to give that up as her fictional power source.

What else did you do besides converse?

We often listened to music on the record player in the living room.

She loved Rachmaninoff. He was her favorite composer. She did not like Shakespeare, and gave me at least five minutes' explanation, and I had no comment. I listened, but in this I failed to comprehend why she did not like him.

How did the relationship progress?

We were exactly in agreement. I agreed with everything she said, except about Shakespeare. We were on the same wavelength exactly. So we became good friends, and we were friends for about ten years.

I believe that later you became a proofreader or typist for Miss Rand?

She said to me, "You're always around here. How would you like to do a little work retyping these pages, which have too many corrections for the publisher to accept?" I took the job. She said, "What do you want for pay?" I just named a price. Fifty cents a page was ridiculously low, even then, but I didn't care about the money. So I did retype quite a few pages of *Atlas Shrugged*, but I naturally wouldn't make any significant changes. Any minor changes like typos I picked up or suggestions I made, she was always happy to know about.

Didn't she have a regular secretary at that time?

No. I hardly ever saw anybody around. It was just Ayn, Frank and me. Later on she got somebody, after I quit the job because I got very bored doing that retyping. She said she understood my boredom, and she got somebody else to type.

Frank was a tall, blondish, handsome ghost who was nearly always elsewhere. When he came inside, he was so silent he startled Ayn, so she had him wear a bell on his shoe so she could hear him coming.

What was it like reading Atlas *then? You must have been one of the first ever to read it.*

Yes. I read some of it as I was retyping its pages. I may have read a chapter or two, but I was not terribly impressed by *Atlas Shrugged*. I thought it was nothing like *The Fountainhead*. When I read the whole book later, I thought it was boring, too preachy. Your archive probably has my eleven-page letter to her, which I wrote after I finally read the entire book, in 1961. She was quite upset that I hadn't even taken the time to read her book as soon as it came out, but it was a long thousand-page book and I had no time. I was not in favor of the book, and I knew that when I told her, that would be the end of it.

Why?

Because with Ayn if you disagreed with her work you were very likely going to stop being her friend. I don't know of anybody who disagreed with her on basic principles or on something as basic as her monumental book, *Atlas Shrugged*, and continued to be her friend. And I think that if you were not an atheist, you probably weren't going to be a very close friend either. She converted me to being an atheist for quite some time.

You're not an atheist now?

I'm now an agnostic, because I am inclined to believe that in order to be an atheist you have to know everything important that exists so that you are certain what does not exist. And you can't tell a person that God does not exist unless you know everything significant that does.

I'm certainly still a capitalist, an individualist and all the other things she stood for.

Did she sign any of her books for you?

She signed my copy of *The Fountainhead* "To Evan Jon Wright, whom I discovered through this book. With my best wishes for your great future as a writer. Ayn Rand. July 15, 1951." We probably met in mid-June or late June. I probably hadn't known her more than a month by that time.

Tell me more about you wanting to become a writer, especially in relationship to Miss Rand.

I never really was dedicated enough. I finally did publish a book in 1993 called *Beltravia*, which I'd been rewriting on and off for forty years. I showed her the first draft of the manuscript in New York when I got back from Paris in October 1953. She lay flat on her back on a sofa and read with the book held up over her head, looking straight up. She read very quickly. I got a laugh out of her. I never heard her laugh before or since. It was a very deep guttural laugh. I said, "I made you laugh, Ayn." It was at some comical part of the book I wrote. She read the whole thing through and had nothing much to say about it.

Did she give you any feedback?

No comments, except she said something in French to me. In the book, I had created a language which I called "Frenglish,"

half French and half English. She said something to me in what
sounded like perfect French, but I didn't quite understand it because
I don't speak perfect French, so I didn't reply. She just went back to
reading. But the part of the book that made her laugh was the part
about parrots. The parrots were speaking Frenglish. One parrot was
named Poly Glott; others, Heidi Geaucique, Mme. Ovary and M. De
la Boue. The story was a fantasy, full of whimsy.

Needing an income, I had to go technical. I changed from research
engineering to writing or editing dozens of manuals for the old North
American Aviation, the Atlas missile and especially IBM; also many
thousands of technical reports and memos. Later I advanced to other
technical things.

When Mickey and I got married, Ayn warned me, "Don't have
any children." She was a dedicated person; she was really a writing
machine, very much dedicated to her art and craft. She knew that if we
had children it would take away from concentration on my art. But we
had children anyway, five of them.

Did you have any other business relationship with her?

Ayn asked me if I wanted to be her agent. I said to her that I didn't
think I could do her very much good, because I didn't know anything
about being an agent. She understood that and accepted it because the
only reason she would want me as an agent, rather obviously as I see it,
would be if I could be in some way effective.

She was involved with a lawsuit at that time, but she would not
discuss what was going on in the lawsuit. She would never say who it
was. I think she was being sued for something she had said, perhaps on
radio.[83] I told her I was very unhappy about it and said, "I'd like to drop
a bomb on his doorstep." She was quite impressed by that and studied
me for long moments. I think that's the first time she realized how
much I was on her side. I was quite angry that anybody should be suing
her and getting some of her money.

*In a couple of letters from you to Miss Rand in our archives, you
referred to yourself as her adopted son. What did you mean?*

This was to both signify my affection and respect for her, and
to formalize, finally, a change in her perception of a part of our

---

83 In 1947 Ayn Rand was part of a group of anti-Communists sued for libel by a
    leftist playwright, Emmett Lavery.

relationship, which was already much weakened by my marriage.

How did she look upon you?

I think it was a true understanding; I was very much in agreement with her way of thinking. She appreciated that. When we talked, we talked in the same way about the same things.

What did Mr. O'Connor do on the ranch?

He grew gladiolas and other flowers, and he had peacocks. He took me around their estate in Chatsworth and discussed his hundred white peacocks. As we went past their empty cages, I said, "Where are the peacocks?" Frank pointed up to the sky. They were all flying up there in a big flock, far up in the sky. He said, "They'll come back." It was just the way he was. He was such an individualist. Everybody does what he wants, including peacocks. We had peacock eggs for breakfast, and they were very good.

Did you know any other of her friends, besides Albert Mannheimer?

No. They were pretty much alone there in the Valley. There was very little going on. She was writing, and Frank was gardening and raising his peacocks. It was very quiet, even monotonous. There were not a lot of visitors. She had to go to court once in a while when she was being sued, but other than that, there didn't seem to be much going on, and I was around there a lot. I first met Nathan and Barbara at Ayn's apartment in New York.

I believe there's an Ayn Rand connection to how you met your wife.

I took a check signed by Ayn to a bank. It wasn't for very much money, but it had a very bold signature. I took the check to be cashed on a Friday; Mickey was the cashier. She was sprightly and vivacious and she said, "Is this *the* Ayn Rand?" I said, "Yes." She knew about Ayn Rand, having read *The Fountainhead*. She cashed the check for me, and I left. On the weekend I thought, "Oh, wait. I want to go back and meet her again." So I thought, "What excuse could I make?" I had some other check I had to cash, so I went back, waited in line and made sure I was at her window. And she didn't recognize me. I blurted ungrammatically, "I'm the one who you cashed the check from Ayn Rand for." She said, "Oh yes!" I said, "Would you like to meet Ayn Rand?" She said she would, so I said, "Would you like to have dinner there?" I didn't even ask Ayn about this, but I knew it'd be okay with her. So we made a date to go out and have dinner at Ayn Rand's. I did tell Ayn beforehand that Mickey was coming over with me. It wasn't an imposition at all to bring Mickey around. The evening went well. We all sat around and talked.

Mickey Wright: The reason I agreed to have a date with him was because I got to meet Ayn Rand. He came back after the weekend with a pretense of some kind. He didn't really have any banking to do. And he said, "Would you like to meet Ayn Rand?" I replied, "Yes, I certainly would." Our first date was on his birthday, on July 25, and it was on a Wednesday in 1951. We were married five weeks later. Obviously, we found other things besides Ayn Rand that we had in common. We got married September 1.

I remember that because when I saw her signature I was so thrilled. It was very close to the time that I had seen *The Fountainhead*. And I had just read it a couple of times. I was all involved in it. And to see her name really turned me on.

Tell me about your first meeting with Miss Rand and Mr. O'Connor.

The very first day that I met her she came over and sat near me in the living room and she asked about *The Fountainhead*, what I had liked about it. I told her that I was really unhappy at the choice of Gary Cooper to play the lead. There was a long silence and she said, "Did you know that I chose him?" I said, "No, I didn't. That surprises me." That's all we said, but I have a feeling that she thought he was a really sexy hunk and that's why she chose him.

Gary Cooper looked so much like her husband Frank. I think that that kind of person was her love interest, tall and willowy and silent.

That first meeting she brought out the thirty-page speech that John Galt made on the radio at the end of *Atlas Shrugged*, and she gave me that to read.[84] I was pleased to read it, but was not able to get all the way through it with the time we had. It seemed to me to be terribly wordy.

Evan, did your wife become friends with Ayn Rand also?

Evan Wright: To some extent. When Mickey and I got married by a judge in Santa Monica, Ayn and Frank came, and she signed the wedding certificate as a witness. Her name was on our wedding license

---

84 The first "Evan and Mickey" entry in Ayn Rand's daily calendar is on August 17, 1951, so this would have been a very early draft.

in her big, bold signature.

Did you have a reception afterwards?

No. The marriage was extremely minimal. The poor judge got only five dollars. I noticed him looking into the envelope, incredulously—but at least he got to meet Ayn Rand! They gave us a bottle of champagne and two glasses and we left immediately, just ran off from everybody. As we were driving off, Ayn Rand ran out to us and asked, "Aren't we going to have a drink or something?" I just gave her a look and drove off—sorry to say—for our wedding night in Malibu, where the ocean evened the score by thundering against our pilings all night long.

Mickey Wright: She brought a bottle of champagne and a couple of glasses with ribbons on them. She also gave us a lead crystal candy dish.

How did Miss Rand react when you asked her to be witness at your wedding?

Evan Wright: I don't think I did. It was just sort of understood, but I might have asked her casually, "Would you like to be there?" She said yes, she would. She and Frank drove over to Santa Monica. It was quite a thing for her to take off time from writing her book. She always said, humorously, that she was "with novel"—and that novel was *Atlas Shrugged*.

Tell me more about the O'Connors at your wedding.

Mickey Wright: My best friend, Hsi-Yen Hsu, who was there from New York, and Ayn signed as the two witnesses. Van and I had made no plans to have any kind of a function because I had eight dollars and he had sixty-eight dollars. And so we were going off on our honeymoon. We did not invite my family and Frank and Ayn to stop in at a bar for a drink or anything. Ayn gave us the gift and she chuckled. That's the only time I ever heard her chuckle. She said, "They're not even going to ask us for drinks?" And she seemed to understand and think it was all right. She thought it was amusing. We just said, "Thank you for coming. Good-bye." And we got in our car and drove off to our honeymoon.

Did she seem very happy to be there?

I thought she was. I had a feeling she felt a little bit of sentimentality that she didn't show very often, or else why would she have come to our marriage?—because she was responsible for us getting together. I think she got a kick out of that.

Ayn did ask Van and me if we wanted to take care of her place when she moved to New York until such time as it was sold. We turned her down. The house was too far away from our home base, and we thought utilities would be pretty high and there were an awful lot of grounds to look after. I didn't know how much of it we'd have to do and how much would be done by a gardener and so on.

When the O'Connors moved to New York, did you stay in touch?

Evan Wright: I visited her around December 1951, when she was living on 36th Street in New York. Nathan and I engaged in a goodly argument. Toward the end of that night, I called Grand Central to ask, "When's the last train to Philadelphia?" (where I was being trained as a Philco tech representative). Ayn remarked about the dramatic quality of my question. Mickey and I visited her again on our way to Europe, in March of '53, and on the way back in October that year, and perhaps one or two other times.

We mostly stayed in touch by letters and some phone calls. There was an understanding that we had: that she never answered letters. She was writing her book and didn't have time to write letters.

Was she any different in New York compared to Chatsworth?

No. I remember one conversation there, when Nathan said that compared to John Galt, Howard Roark was a humanitarian or altruist. I got upset about that and said, "He's not. Nothing is greener than green. He was not an altruist at all, so why do you say that?" We discussed this for quite a while, and Ayn said she'd never been so happy to lose an argument in her life. Nathan's point was that John Galt was so much harder and stricter than Howard Roark that he made him look like a softie.

She disagreed with that in the end?

Yes. She had to agree that Howard Roark was not a humanitarian, or whatever the word Nathan had used.

Regarding another visit, Mickey had a Chinese friend named Leonard Hsu, whose name was really Hsi-Yen Hsu. He had been in high office, probably minister of economics, for Chiang Kai-Shek. He had designed China's first five-year plan, later implemented by Mao. I took him and his wife Ruth to meet Ayn one night in New York. It was a very interesting evening. Leonard Hsu and Ayn got deep into conversation. It seemed to be on a level above all the rest of us. They were extremely intelligent genius-type people. We weren't even there, they were so deep into it.

Were they agreeing or debating?

Quite agreeable. Mickey says Leonard was a little bit uncomfortable with brilliant women and he had some points of disagreement. But basically they were locked in with each other, feeling each other out and deep in conversation to the point where we were sort of ignored.

Did Miss Rand ever mention the Empire State Building?

She took that apartment in New York because it had a view of the Empire State Building. She was very proud of that building because it was a signature of capitalism. It was a view she really enjoyed.

The last conversation I had with her was much later, long after I had written the sign-off letter about *Atlas Shrugged* to her, probably in the early '70s.

So there was no grudge or animosity?

No. She seemed quite pleased and happy to hear from me. I didn't ask to come to see her. I'm not sure I would have been welcomed if I had, because we had sort of come to a parting of ways, and I was no longer her protégé. Our friendship was kind of finished, and so I didn't make any effort to see her. I did ask her if she would like to meet Frank Cary, then CEO of IBM, and his wife Ann. I had met them both at a UCLA gathering in New York, in which Ann had expressed a wish to meet Ayn. But Ayn had no interest.

What was her reaction when you called?

She remembered me well and pictured in her mind where I must be sitting in Westchester County, in a tall building, looking out on a great landscape. She was sort of writing a picture in her mind as to where I must be calling from. She was quite friendly, even genial. She was very important in our lives and those of our children, and we have great respect for her works and her memory.

Richard Cornuelle

Richard Cornuelle is a writer who was an acquaintance of Ayn Rand's in the early 1950s.

Interview date: December 8, 1996

Scott McConnell: *How did you meet Ayn Rand?*

Richard Cornuelle: I met her through my brother Herb Cornuelle.[85] He had met her and wanted me to meet her. He did a lot of reading when he was in the Navy during the war in the Pacific. Among the books he read was *The Fountainhead* and he recommended it to me. I read it and was very excited about it, so he took me to meet Ayn. I was still in college then, so it must have been 1947 or '48, and she and Frank were living out in the San Fernando Valley.

I found her most electrifying. So alive—with a sort of piercing look. I felt like I was in the presence of an extraordinary superhuman kind of person. I was very unsure of myself and very young and naïve in a way that is now appalling to think about. She made a powerful impression on me. She was also a very welcoming, cordial person— forbidding in a certain way because I felt I was in the presence of an extraordinary intellect.

What did you do when you visited?

We just sat around and talked. That's all I ever did with Ayn—sit around and talk.

How often did you see her?

I don't imagine I saw her more than once or twice when she was in California. Then when she moved to 36 East 36th in New York, and I visited her there. I came to New York in 1948.

I was in the [Ludwig von] Mises seminar and casually knew Henry Hazlitt and Leonard Read. My brother was by then working at the Foundation for Economic Education, a sort of safe house for libertarians at the time. It was our main gathering place. Ayn was very much in touch with that crowd in those days. There was a social circle of the

---

85 Herb Cornuelle was a businessman and the director of the Foundation for Economic Education.

151

older and wiser and more experienced than I. I wasn't part of that.

I also know she knew Hazlitt socially. She had worked for Frances Hazlitt when Frances was working in the script department at Paramount. Ayn was a reader there.

I used to go see Ayn by myself, with Murray Rothbard and with Herb. We just sat around and talked. We talked about everything, but mainly listened to her. I lived in terror that she was going to ask me a question to which I didn't have the right answer. I was mainly just sitting at her feet and asking her questions.

Describe her physical presence and her personality.

When I think about Ayn, what comes to mind is her sitting with her legs tucked under her on a big sort of ottoman in her 36th Street apartment, smoking cigarettes with a long holder and with that very characteristic, rather severe hairdo. There was an intensity in the way she looked at you when she was talking to you, which I found fascinating and almost frightening.

Were there any specific issues you were interested in?

I was interested in learning about Objectivism. I came out of college with a piece of paper that said I knew something, but I didn't feel I knew anything. It was a tremendous relief for me to find a point of view that suddenly gave me an answer for everything. I suppose I was questioning her about what we called "the hard cases." I had been conditioned to believe in the brotherhood of man and open-ended social responsibility and so forth, and how libertarians dealt with those issues must have been on my mind.

How was she personally during those meetings?

She was great to me. She was always very cordial until we had a little spat.

What was that about?

I was then in Mises's seminar, and she knew Mises. I was home in California and she called me one day, which was the last contact I had with her. She said that she'd been at a party at Hazlitt's with Mises and "We had the following argument." It was an argument about the draft. She was opposed to it and it didn't surprise me in the least that Mises disagreed. These Austrians that we thought of as our gurus and main theorists on economic matters weren't really libertarians by our stern definition. We'd read *The Road to Serfdom*, and the concessions that Hayek was willing to make for state authority, for social security and all sorts of other activities, were absolutely anathema to us. Somehow we overlooked that and thought of Hayek as one of our most important gurus. I can understand Mises thinking the draft essential under certain circumstances.

What did Ayn Rand want in making this phone call?

I was in the Mises seminar at that time and she said, in effect, "Here's his position and here's my position. Whose side are you on? You have to choose. You have to make a decision." I said, "Well, I'd rather duck." She said, "You can't," and that was it. I never spoke to her again after that.

So you stayed with von Mises?

Yes, and I stayed with him for a long time. His wife was godmother to one of my kids, and I've got a picture of him on my desk as we talk. I don't have a picture of Ayn, but I have a picture of him.

Did you ever make a decision on the draft issue?

I never had any doubt about it. I always thought it was out of the question and still do.

Why didn't you tell Ayn Rand that?

It wasn't the argument that mattered. She didn't want me to agree with her. She wanted me to discontinue my relations with Lu [Ludwig] as a way of showing I was on her side.

I don't think everybody was in the position I was in. I was close enough to the inner circle at that moment that I had to go one way or the other. I don't think that was a choice very many people had to make. The dispute probably led to a freeze between Ayn and Mises.

I remember Ayn's belief that people were your adversaries in almost inverse proportion to their proximity to your position. She thought that people—like Taft[86]—who seemed very much on our side but were willing to make exceptions, because of their apparent popularity, were worse than people who were utterly and elementally opposed to what we stood for.

---

86 Robert Taft was a conservative Republican senator from Ohio.

Do you remember anything else happening at her apartment when you visited?

One time, either because the weather was very hot or the air conditioning wasn't working—we went to the roof to talk. There was a wall around the edge of the roof that was at least four-feet high. The idea that you could fall off unless you were really trying to was impossible, but when Frank got within a couple of feet of the wall, Ayn got almost hysterical. That's something of an exaggeration, but she was very, very agitated that he might be in danger of falling off the roof. And there was no possible way he could have unless he had a ladder.

Did he move away from the edge?

Oh, yeah.

Did you ever see her lose her temper?

The only time I saw her somewhat out of control was when she thought Frank was in danger on the roof. She would talk very angrily when she was talking about Taft. When he had caved in on the issue of federal aid to education, she talked heatedly about what a disappointing defection this was.

How did she treat people generally?

I thought she treated people with respect and cordiality. She was never rude—she was emphatic without being unpleasant.

Did she recommend any books to you?

She always told us to read a certain textbook on the history of political thought. Sabine was the author. What was striking about it was that it was very widely used in the universities, but Ayn still thought it was a very accurate and reliable book.[87]

There was a book that she thought neglected—*The Builders of the Bridge*. She admired it and thought it was a great American book. It was about John Roebling, a Roark-type guy who overcame great difficulties to get a job done with integrity.[88]

---

87 The textbook was George H. Sabine's *A History of Political Theory* (New York: Henry Holt, 1937).

88 *The Builders of the Bridge: The Story of John Roebling and His Son* by David B. Steinman (New York: G. P. Putnam's Sons, 1941). The book recounts the story of the building of the Brooklyn Bridge.

Mike Wallace

Mike Wallace is one of America's most celebrated TV journalists and interviewers. He interviewed Miss Rand several times between 1957 and 1961.

Interview date: March 3, 1998

Scott McConnell: *How did you first come across Ayn Rand or her novels?*

Mike Wallace: *Atlas Shrugged* was the first novel of hers that I read. Various people[89] in my shop were devoted to her and said that I should be more aware of her than I was, so they booked her on a telecast named *Nightbeat*, back in 1957. I found her fascinating.

What was your reaction to Atlas Shrugged*?*

I found it an interesting book. It didn't change my life, but I found it a fascinating book. It made me want to know more about her.

You brought her onto Nightbeat *and what happened?*

One on one, I found her a fascinating woman, as simple as that. She was, in effect, fresh to a lot of New Yorkers. She had an interestingly assertive and offbeat—as far as conventional wisdom is concerned—take on life and on morality and altruism, and so she got me to thinking more about the kind of thing she was talking about. And she did the same to the audience on *Nightbeat*.

So there was a strong audience reaction?

Yes, there was.

In the Mike Wallace Interview *program* [February 25, 1959] *with Ayn Rand, you seem to focus on the issues of morality, altruism, service to others. Why?*

I was looking to go a little deeper. What I was looking to do was to focus to some degree on the kind of controversy that she had generated when we did that first piece and then in the years intervening.

What was the reaction of the other media to your having this celebrity

---

89 They were Edith Efron, Al Ramrus and Ted Yates.

of the political right on your show?

They knew me by then for trying to get on my broadcast people who were not run of the mill. It's hard perhaps to understand it, but forty years ago the ordinary interview was fairly pallid stuff; it was pabulum. It was "and then I wrote," "and then I sang," "then I appeared in." Ideas—particularly irreverent or abrasive questioning, skeptical questioning—were not a staple. So a lot of attention was paid to the broadcast for that reason, because that's the kind of thing that I did, things that had been more or less verboten, or if not verboten then at least not practiced widely. She was, from that point of view, a perfect guest because she got people who were up at eleven o'clock at night, thinking.

How did she react to that give and take?

She loved it. She made it quite apparent. She couldn't have been more forthcoming in her reactions to me. She wanted to be friends, and I went to her home, met her husband, and her cat.

Did Ayn Rand have any influence on your thinking or your values?

In a subliminal way, of course. When you do the kind of journalism that I do, and particularly when you do the kind of interviews that I did, she was bound to. I found her fascinating. I found her good company, and I found it fascinating to listen to and weigh her notions. I found her also perhaps excessively doctrinaire.

I liked her because she was interesting to be with—she knew who she was—comfortable in her own skin. And she was good copy.

Do you have any other memories of Ayn Rand?

I remember with amusement her haircut, which is a little like the one that I wore when I was four or five years old, a Dutch cut. It was dark hair, cut straight across her forehead. It was particularly interesting to me back then because of the contrast with her skin and the sharp— the luminous eyes of Ayn Rand.

Why do you think she was interested in you specifically?

Because she liked the fact that I took her seriously, took her ideas seriously—she admired *Nightbeat* and the *Mike Wallace Interview* very much, from what I was told at the time by Al Ramrus and by Edith Efron and by Ted Yates.

Al Ramrus

Al Ramrus is a television/movie writer and producer who knew Miss Rand in the 1950s and 1960s.

Interview dates: June 6, 1997, and May 29 and June 20, 2002

Scott McConnell: *How did you first meet Miss Rand?*

Al Ramrus: I was a television journalist at the time, 1958, working with Mike Wallace. Mike also had a newspaper question-and-answer feature in the *New York Post*, and he hired Edith Efron to do the actual interviews. Edith was a very interesting woman, smart, combative and irreverent, and we became friends.

For that column, Edith interviewed Ayn Rand and—I didn't have a clue about this—she immediately responded to Objectivism, of which I had never heard. So when Edith and I went out to lunch or dinner, she began speaking in a very, very strange way about psychology, art, politics—in a way that I'd never heard before and certainly not from a New York Jewish intellectual. I thought she was going out of her mind. Soon, Ayn Rand's name and *Atlas Shrugged* came up, and I began to get a glimpse of where she was coming from.

Finally, Edith asked me, "Would you like to meet Ayn Rand?" I said, "Sure, you bet." I had never read Rand, and from everything I knew or thought I knew, she was a foolish figure with some flaky ideas. How could she be anything else, since she wasn't a liberal? I hadn't even read *The Fountainhead*, because my New York crowd considered it a best-seller read only by the lower orders on the IQ scale. But Rand was different, controversial, so I was curious. Edith took me over to Miss Rand's apartment one evening, and we spent a couple of hours there—Edith, myself, Ayn and Frank O'Connor.

What happened that night?

That was a life-transforming experience. As Mike Wallace's writer, I was always dealing with national and international figures: politicians, Nobel Prize winners, writers such as Norman Mailer, Tennessee Williams, Aldous Huxley; Frank Lloyd Wright and Salvador Dali; Sidney Poitier, Bette Davis. Just to name a few. I mean, we're talking about some of the most important figures in American culture at the time. But I had never met anybody like Ayn Rand. She was so brilliant and so perceptive, and her comments were so fresh and original. You know, most prominent writers, political commentators, TV anchors and celebrities sound more or less like echoes of the *New York Times* editorial page. But there was no similarity between anything Ayn Rand said and the *New York Times*. I mean, she really shook me to my boots and jarred my liberal assumptions.

You've got to remember, I was twenty-eight years old, from City College of New York, a left-wing boot camp. So I thought I'd flaunt my stripes at Miss Rand. We were talking about the critical reception to *Atlas Shrugged*, which was overwhelmingly negative. Without ever having read a word that she had written, I said to her—and I shudder to even think of it now—"Well, is it possible that you get these lousy reviews because you're a lousy writer?"

Miss Rand very coolly walked into the other room, returned with a copy of *Atlas* and said, "Find an example of lousy writing." I said, "Okay, sure." There were over a thousand pages to choose from, so I figured this shouldn't be too hard. I leafed through and saw this huge block of text, which is usually an indication of lousy writing in a novel or a screenplay. I said, "Well, here," and I started reading it aloud. I don't remember for sure what it was, but I think it was an analysis of Hank Rearden's psychology, the psychology of a great, productive human being who at the same time was enslaved by a mistaken morality. I must have read half a paragraph before saying, "Wow, this isn't so bad." Miss Rand just sort of smiled. I think I got off very, very lucky that night. Can you imagine pulling a thing like that on Thomas Mann?

I didn't have to read any more than that half paragraph to know there was something very special about this novel and this woman. Anyway, the evening ended on fairly good terms. I was knocked out by her, and she was very cordial to me.

So that's how I got to meet Miss Rand. And then we put her on Mike's TV interview show, and I was hooked. To a somewhat lesser extent so was Mike's producer, Ted Yates. Not too long after that, I was invited to one of the Saturday evenings at Miss Rand's or Nathaniel Branden's apartment. I wasn't an original member of the Collective, but new blood was being added: Bob Hessen, George Reisman, Edith, myself, and I think, eventually, Phil and Kay Nolte Smith.[90]

Tell me more about Miss Rand's appearance on Mike Wallace's interview show in 1959.

---

90 "The Collective" was the ironic name used by Ayn Rand to refer to a close circle of admirers in the 1950s.

She was terrific on it. Phenomenally articulate and sure of herself. This is unusual because I don't think she had had much television or radio experience. But the camera picked up those piercing black eyes behind which you sensed a powerful and unique intelligence. We got a lot of mail and created a lot of talk from that interview. And it was very exciting for me, because you don't get a chance to put on a guest like that very often. Writers like Ben Hecht, Gore Vidal and William Buckley were outstanding guests, but Ayn Rand was just in another league.

What issues were discussed?

The welfare state, altruism, egoism vs. self-sacrifice, and where the hell did Ayn Rand come off, challenging most of the sacred beliefs of Western civilization.

What was the culture's reaction to Ayn Rand in those years?

She was hated by the media, academia, the artistic community. No intellectual figure in America was more loathed than Ayn Rand in those days, because she was so formidable, uncompromising and challenging. They thought she was nuts, wacky, dangerous. And most of them had never read her. They would sort of glean an impression from what somebody else said. If you had told them that someday she was going to be honored on a U.S. postage stamp, or that *Atlas Shrugged* would continue to be a best-seller, considered by many people the most influential book with the exception of the Bible, they would've said you were demented. They did say I was demented.

Miss Rand's greatest gift to us, along with her books, was the example she set for intellectual courage and integrity. Here was a woman who dared to stand virtually alone against ideas, political systems and cultures that were dominating the planet and had been hallowed by intellectuals for centuries. What heroism.

How did your relationship with Miss Rand affect your position in the liberal-dominated media?

I doubt whether young Objectivists today can imagine how collectivist and hostile the culture was, back in the 1950s and 1960s. During those years it was almost impossible for an avowed Objectivist or even a conservative to work in the news media. I was lucky. I got a job writing for Wallace when I was an ardent socialist, which was perfectly acceptable in the media, if not preferred. Within less than two years, I encountered Ayn Rand and *Atlas Shrugged*—and poor liberal Mike suddenly found himself with a fire-breathing Objectivist on his hands.

I didn't hide it from anybody, in fact regarded it as a badge of honor. So I got into lots of arguments and fights with people I worked with, including Mike. But he also has a maverick streak and appreciates other mavericks. In addition, I knew my job and could deal with his, shall we say, difficult personality. It was the same later, when I worked with Hollywood producer David Wolper. They needed me, and there's an old saying in show biz: "I'll never deal with that bastard again, until I need him."

Did you or Edith Efron try to influence Mr. Wallace regarding Miss Rand's philosophy?

Mike and I became good friends, so you couldn't help but discuss ideas outside the office. It was in the nature of the kind of animals we were. So we'd get into heated discussions. Whether it made a dent or not, I don't know.

What were Mr. Wallace's personal reactions to his interviews with Miss Rand?

Well, you have to understand Mike. He may be a liberal, but he was unique in television back then because he loved drama, controversy and excitement. The worst crime to Mike was an hour of dull talk. So he was intrigued by Ayn Rand. He thought she was a valuable guest, great for the show. He also got off on interviewing unusual characters, which was far more interesting than interviewing an Adlai Stevenson or Hubert Humphrey, who'd bore you to death before even opening their mouths. So where other TV personalities or interviewers might blacklist Miss Rand because they regarded her philosophy as the work of the devil, Mike disagreed with her but he also found her interesting as hell.

As a writer, did you ever collaborate with Miss Rand on anything?

At the time, I was primarily a television journalist. Then I came to L.A. to write documentaries for David Wolper.[91] Lots of Hollywood and historical documentaries. But I always wanted to move into writing feature films. Miss Rand knew that and said, "How would you like to write the screenplay to 'Red Pawn'?" Which was quite an honor, particularly for somebody who had never written a movie

---

91 David L. Wolper produced dozens of television shows, including *Roots* and *The Thorn Birds*

before. I think she felt that at least I understood her sense of life and philosophy perhaps better than any writer in town. Still, I asked her why she didn't write the screenplay herself; but for whatever personal reason, she just wasn't motivated to do it.

This was 1963. She admired Robert Stack's portrayal of Eliot Ness on *The Untouchables*, and thought that he'd be a strong, romantic lead as the commandant of the prison camp. I phoned Stack at home, said Miss Rand and I had a project for him. He immediately said, "Come on over," which I did, and I gave him Rand's synopsis of the story. He read it on the spot and said, "I'm interested."

Now we had to interest Paramount, which owned the rights to the story. I met with an executive in Paramount's story department, an old-timer, fleshy and jowly, waiting, I'm afraid, to be put out to pasture. Later, I described his eyes to Miss Rand and she complimented me, writer to writer, on the simile. I said, "His eyes looked like old marbles that had lain in the gutter too long."

He knew about Miss Rand, and I said she'd like to see "Red Pawn" produced, and that if Paramount wanted to do it she'd help me by supervising the writing in an editorial capacity.

So why didn't it get off the ground?

Paramount just didn't have sufficient interest. Too bad.[92]

Did Miss Rand ever talk to you about fiction-writing techniques?

She gave me some invaluable advice on how to be critically objective about your own writing. How can you be objective about your material once you've written a draft? I said, "If I see flaws in somebody else's writing, I know instantly what's wrong. But frequently I can't see it in my own writing." She said don't commit yourself by putting something down on paper prematurely, because once you do that, seeing it in print, it takes on a reality and a sort of permanence in your mind and you can't see the flaws. She advised me to think about the material, the scene, the chapter, whatever, and get it as clear as I could in my mind first. Get an objective overview first, then write.

Did she mean you should do that before writing even rough notes?

She meant you could write all the notes and rough ideas you

---

92 For Ayn Rand's synopsis of "Red Pawn," see *The Early Ayn Rand*, ed. Leonard Peikoff, rev. ed. (New York: Signet, 2005).

wanted, because they're provisional. But take your time before you chisel in rock your dialogue, scenes, chapters.

Did you spend much personal time alone with her?

Unfortunately, only a couple of times. In 1967 I came to her with an idea for a television project, and we met in her study where she wrote. Not a very big room but a big old desk, and over the desk hung several photographs, one of them of Frank as a young man. After about an hour, I said, "Forgive me, but what a beautiful photograph. Frank makes John Barrymore look like an office boy." And he did. It was a professional publicity shot, I think, posed, dramatically lit, of Frank in the late 1920s or early 1930s. He looked what John Galt might've looked like. Ayn said, "Thank you very much." You know, that was the way she was when you praised something that was personally important to her. Just a very nice "Thank you very much."

Did you ever talk to Mr. O'Connor about his acting work in Hollywood?

No. I do remember Ayn telling me a story about the first time she ever saw him, on the trolley going to a studio; and then later in a toga as an extra in one of those Biblical epics [*The King of Kings*]. She said, "I liked his legs."

Did you discuss with Miss Rand the movies she liked?

Some of Fritz Lang's silent German films. The first James Bond film but not, I think, the later special-effects orgies. Also, Alfred Hitchcock's *Notorious*, a great thriller and love story written by Ben Hecht, who she thought had betrayed his own talents.

Did she ever meet Ben Hecht?

Once, on a radio talk show in Chicago. They clashed immediately. Ben was a very cynical guy who revered anarchic freedom while Ayn Rand revered ideas, heroes and the human spirit. When I was with Mike, we produced a late-night TV show with Hecht telling stories and delivering outrageous opinions, and he liked to invite other writers as guests. We invited Miss Rand and she refused. She said she didn't want to appear on the same screen as Ben Hecht, whom she regarded as nihilistic and anti-intellectual.

Tell me about the Collective during those Saturday evening gatherings.

Ayn would usually arrive after most of the others, and all the men would rise to their feet as a gesture of respect. There was a lot of reverence and hero-worship directed primarily at Miss Rand and much of it was reflected off her to Nathaniel Branden. Sometimes it was like being in a room with two people treated as demigods. Miss Rand never asked for that openly, but she had to be aware of it, and perhaps she could've changed it, but she didn't.

The evenings were primarily very serious. Stimulating discussions about art, philosophy, politics. Hardly ever light conversation, very little laughter or casual socializing. And lots of cigarette smoking. I was one of the few nonsmokers. So to sit there and see—particularly the girls with their cigarette holders trying to look like Ayn Rand and Dagny Taggart—it was very sad. Talk about social metaphysics.[93]

Tell me more about the people around Ayn Rand.

You had people in their twenties, in formative stages of their lives, sitting at the feet of a genius. Not only that, but many of them had no other life except Objectivism and Ayn Rand. Alan Greenspan was one exception in terms of having an independent career. Now what do you expect to happen in that kind of relationship? They were immature, they were overawed, easily swayed, influenced, intimidated. It was overwhelming and, in some cases, psychologically and creatively stunting and paralyzing. I'm afraid for some it was a mixed blessing.

Did you have much interaction with Mr. O'Connor at those gatherings?

I didn't, and I don't think anyone else did either. He'd sit in an armchair, usually in a corner, and say almost nothing all evening. Sometimes I'd go over and try to engage him in conversation because I felt uncomfortable for him sitting there with a thin smile on his face for three or four hours while his wife held court. He was always very pleasant, but remote.

Mickey Spillane came to an Objectivist party with, as I recall, an alarmingly ancient ex-burlesque queen; it was either Sally Rand or Georgia Southern. Ayn greatly admired Spillane's novels in those days, thought he wrote in essentials and dealt with characters clearly representing good and evil. That night, Mickey did something I never

---

93 "Social metaphysics" is Ayn Rand's term for the belief that "the consciousness of other men is superior to [one's] own and to the facts of reality."

saw any male do with Ayn Rand. Right in front of everybody, in an innocent, breezy way, he flirted with her, and I think she got a big kick out of it. He said something, like, "Ayn, if you weren't married, I'd be after you like a shot." They both enjoyed it, and I don't think she got that very often from men.

Any last words about Miss Rand?

There was something very sweet about seeing her lying on her couch, and her cat, Frisco, would jump up and lie on her chest, and she'd be discussing high-powered philosophical or political issues while petting her little kitty.

Sylvester Petro

Sylvester Petro was a writer and a law professor specializing in trade unions. He attended meetings in Miss Rand's apartment in the late 1950s and early 1960s. He died in 2007.

Interview date: August 22, 1996

Scott McConnell: *How did you meet Ayn Rand?*

Sylvester Petro: I met her for the first time just after I had a book—*Labor Policy of the Free Society*—published. All my writings have been pretty much scholarly and no one reads them, but she read it and invited me to come to one of her lectures at the Roosevelt Hotel. It was 1957 or '58, because it was about the same year that *Atlas Shrugged* came out.

Did you know Miss Rand's work?

Ludwig von Mises used to hold a weekly, sometimes monthly, seminar, which we called the "Mises Circle," maybe in emulation of the Vienna Circle. She was there more than once. So I had met her before her lecture, but it was just an introduction, I had never talked to her. I read *Atlas Shrugged* and was fascinated by it. Whether I read it before she invited me to her meeting or afterwards I just can't tell you now.

Is your background in economics?

No, I'm a lawyer, but my main interest was law, economics and politics and how to keep the government from sucking the blood out of the economy.

New York in the late '50s and early '60s was a great place to live. It wasn't just Ayn Rand living there, but maybe even more significant, in the long run, was that Ludwig von Mises was centered there. Of course, if you don't know Mises, let me just say to you that I, as a scholar myself, think him the most important economist of the century—maybe of every century. He had a tremendous intellectual influence on Ayn Rand.

You witnessed that?

Yes. She said to me, "I don't agree with him epistemologically but as far as my economics and political economy are concerned, Ludwig

von Mises is the most important thing that's ever happened to me."
She was an excellent economist, by the way. She was a brilliant human
being and a very warm-hearted one too.

Can you give me some examples of that?

She was always very loving toward her husband. I never saw
anything but sort of a loving, kind relationship between them.

What did you see?

Just that. It's an expression of Somerset Maugham's: "Loving
kindness is being about as good as a human relationship can get."
She used to have meetings at her apartment at East 36th Street.
She always had a crowd there and was always the reigning princess.
She loved to sit on the back of a couch so that her eyes were above
everybody, except those of us who didn't sit. She was queenly. She
was the regal type of human being as well as being very brilliant, witty,
quick as could be. Like most literary people she loved words and played
on words a fair amount. She was tough.

In what way?

She never gave an inch on anything that she believed in. No
compromises, no qualifications, no "on the one hand," no "on the
other."

Were there areas that she didn't talk about?

She'd talk about anything, including Renaissance art. I remember I
was a great admirer of Michelangelo and she thought he was a god.

Why?

He played on the heroic, the way she did. All of his figures are
heroic figures and she loved that. She didn't have any pretensions. She
said, "That's what art's all about—the heroic."

Were there any specific statues or paintings that she discussed?

The *David* and the *Moses*. The *David* especially.

What did she say?

Man as man should be. I'm not sure I'm quoting her but that was
the general idea.

What other topics would you discuss at these meetings?

Everything, including money and banking and the gold standard.

Describe Ayn Rand and Ludwig von Mises together.

You'd have to know the kind of really exquisite person Mises was. Mises was about as cool as they come. I knew him intimately, he was the dearest friend I had for many years, and I never saw him get excited about anything, ever. He was laconic.

Was he passionate when talking about economics?

No. Cool as he could be. He never raised his voice, but he had a really coruscating wit.

What did Mises tell you about Ayn Rand or her philosophy? He must have had disagreements with her philosophy?

This is something we talked a lot about, but I'm so far away from it now. Philosophically, Ayn Rand thought a lot more of the conflict between her and Mises than Mises thought about it.

Tell me more about Miss Rand and Mises together?

I don't remember them engaging in anything more than pleasantries. One time we had a dinner party for another person who was very important in this circle—Henry Hazlitt. Henry Hazlitt was an old, old friend of Ayn Rand's. He knew her long before Mises got involved in any relationship with Ayn.

His wife Frances Hazlitt was the one who got Ayn Rand a job in Hollywood.[94] Frances did many things herself. She wasn't a sit-at-home housewife. She wrote and did a lot of work with Henry and his writing, and she was an excellent hostess too. We had a circle whirling around in an orbit adjacent to Ayn Rand's orbit in New York. It was composed of Leonard Read of the Foundation for Economic Education, Mises, Lawrence Fertig, Henry Hazlitt and myself. We'd trade off dinners and all of us knew Rand and admired her, but she was not a member of anyone's circle. She was a dominating, independent, strong, vigorous person. Christ! She had eyes that would drill holes in you—really!

Did you ever debate with her?

---

94 It was Richard Mealand, a story editor at Paramount, who got Ayn Rand a job as a reader at the Manhattan office of Paramount, where she met Frances Hazlitt.

I never really had a debate with her, but I used to kid her because she took herself awfully seriously. Just to irritate her, I would ask her why she couldn't sit down at a regular level like everybody else.

What did she say?

She'd kid back. Like, I told her that she reminded me of Jesus Christ, which I knew would get her back up because she was so proud of her atheism. But she was a Christ-like figure. I told her, "Hell, you're so Christian, it's not funny." I don't remember what she said, if anything.

It must have been a very exciting time in your life to know all these people.

It was a good time. It was a time I was glad to be a part of. Coming off those Roosevelt years and into a period when you had people like Rand and Hazlitt and Mises productive and active in New York. This wasn't happening anywhere else in the world, people speaking of freedom, free enterprise and laissez-faire. Hell, it damn near died in those '30s and '40s.

Was there a set time to arrive for Ayn Rand's meetings?

When I was there it was always after one of their Objectivist lectures.

So people would go back to the O'Connors' apartment?

That's right. Half a dozen of us, maybe as many as a dozen.

How many times did you attend Ayn Rand's meetings?

Maybe half a dozen. Ayn Rand's meetings were not Ayn Rand's meetings, at least not the ones I went to. Nathaniel Branden would do most of the talking and she would come in toward the end and trade some artillery shots with him. I don't know whether it was a joke or part of the theater. She was a theatrical person. She was on stage all the time. She was a performer. One didn't really carry on a conversation with her—or at least I didn't.

What did happen?

She had a way of collecting about her some truly gone people, mostly young kids who regarded her as a goddess. I was about thirty-five then, and I'm not a venerating type. These kids who adored her, Christ, a good number of them were my students in law school.

Who else do you remember from the meetings in Miss Rand's apartment?

There was a guy named Peikoff who was there very often. He was an able, good economist. Ayn thought well of him. She was always very friendly and kind and forthcoming when she was around him.

Can you remember examples of this friendliness or kindness?

She would refer to him and say, "Isn't that so, Leonush?" I think it's a typical Russian, amiable diminutive.

Did Ayn Rand disagree with any positions in your books?

I don't remember anything. She thought it was a good thing that someone was around who wasn't an apologist for trade unions. That was my specialty. I thought unions were a disgrace to mankind.

What else did she like in your writing?

I think she thought it was clear and good. She said somebody needs to say something correct about unions, instead of everyone thinking they were the friend of the working man. My position was a straight Austrian position: that productivity is everything, and if workers are not productive they're not going to improve their lives, and that unions are not about making workers productive.

Any other comments on Ayn Rand?

She was the most articulate person I think I've ever encountered. Her conversation came out in chapters, paragraphs and sentences.

Would she listen?

She did listen, but only to allow someone to have a part in the discussion. She was one hell of an expositor, let me put it that way. She knew how to express herself.

I love her for her indomitable spirit.

You saw examples of that?

Well, shoot, I heard her speak. I saw her debate. I saw her on TV and God damn it, she was a humdinger.

Whom did you see her debate?

Actually, it might have been me debating [John Kenneth] Galbraith, and she was there, at NYU, in the audience. She says to Galbraith: "Why don't you ever meet what Mr. Petro is asking you or confronting you with?"

What did he say?

He stuttered around. He was the biggest faker on the face of the earth. He never meets anything that you confront him with. He told me, "I wouldn't say such a thing about your books," as I had said about *The Affluent Society*, that it was a trashy distortion of reality.

Describe Ayn Rand with Galbraith?

You know, you have to see her. She was a tiger. Her big black eyes would snap, as they say. It was a question-and-answer session. Galbraith and I had been having a series of debates on various current subjects at the time at different places in New York. I think she was in one. It's possible that on this occasion it was one of those panel situations, where about half a dozen people are sitting up at a desk, each with a microphone, and she said something like "It gets very tiresome if you never, never meet what Petro presents to you."

What did he say?

I don't remember what he said, except that it went off on something else, which is what always happens.

Rosemary Torigian

Rosemary Torigian was Miss Rand's typist in the late 1950s and early 1960s. Ms. Torigian died in 2010.

Interview dates: January 21 and 22, 1998

Scott McConnell: *I believe you attended the very early Nathaniel Branden Lectures* [NBL] *in New York City.*

Rosemary Torigian: It was so great to be there in the beginning and see those lecture series growing. The first one I attended was the second one that was given—the first was given for what we called "The Inner Circle," which was Alan Greenspan and Leonard Peikoff and others.

That was the first series of public lectures on Objectivism, except at the time we didn't call it "Objectivism." Miss Rand objected to that. She didn't want it called "Objectivism," so we referred to it as "the philosophy of Ayn Rand," and it wasn't until about the third or fourth series that she just finally gave up because there was just no stopping people using that name.

This was in 1958, right after *Atlas Shrugged* was published. Everybody who came to the lectures had a copy of *Atlas* on their arm, and she was very kind to sign them. In the back of the first edition was a notice that said that if you wanted to know more about Ayn Rand's ideas, you could contact this organization. I contacted them and was told that there was a series of ten lectures that was going to be given and that I could attend it by paying—it was some ridiculously small amount of money—like, twenty dollars.

It was in a small hotel room that Nathan had rented, and only about twenty people attended. The first series of lectures was greatly expanded as time went on. I attended the first and second series.

Did Miss Rand attend the lectures?

All of them. As I say here in this excerpt from my memoir, "Ayn Rand was present for the lectures and answered questions from the floor. Her presence awed and utterly mesmerized me, the cape swirling about her straight, proud shoulders as she swept into the hall and took a seat, smoke curling up from the long cigarette holder, head held high, her great, dark deeply intelligent eyes fastened upon the speaker." And that is true. She would come and she would sit up on the little stage, and just sit there with that cape wrapped around her and her legs crossed, with her cigarette holder in her hand. Her hair was always very sleekly groomed and would come around in one single curl on her cheek, and she would just listen. She never moved her eyes off of whoever was speaking. She was just utterly interested in what was going on.

After the lecture was over, Nathan would make a little speech, like "Miss Rand is not here to defend her philosophy or anything that was stated here tonight. She's here only to answer questions from people who want to learn more." Then she would get up and we would ask questions from the floor.

One night, [comedian] Mort Sahl came to the lecture and wanted to poke fun at it. In the question period, he asked a question in an extremely sarcastic way. Miss Rand wiped the floor with him. She let him know that she knew he wasn't serious, that he was here trying to be funny and that she didn't appreciate it. I could just see him shrivel. She utterly backed him down so that he didn't know what to say.

Did any other celebrities come to lectures?

Mickey Spillane came one time, and he walked up to the microphone and said something that meant he was very pleased to be there with everybody, and we all applauded him, and he talked to us for a little while about how pleased he was to know Miss Rand and pleased that she appreciated his books. It wasn't a very astounding kind of speech, but Ayn Rand was very pleased that he was there.

Tell me about your newsletter.

Myself and a friend, Ellen Runge, published the first Objectivist newsletter. When the lecture series had really taken off, we realized that there were so many things going on, so many lectures, so many radio programs and events, that somebody needed to give this news to the Objectivists, so we started the newsletter.

We put it out with the intention of being informative, and Miss Rand asked us to write "This is our private enterprise" and "At our request, Mr. Branden has consented to give us his mailing list but neither Mr. Branden, Miss Rand, nor the associate lectures of Nathaniel Branden Lectures are in any way connected with this project. We have created this service because there is a need for it. If you are one of the people who can use it, send in a dollar."

Our first issue was March 1960 and in it we listed some upcoming speeches and a sample of how the newsletter would be run. Miss Rand had made it very clear to us that we were to say that she and Nathan were not connected with us, but by the second issue, they had already endorsed us as an information page. She didn't want us to do the magazine, but we insisted we were going to do it because she didn't have a way of controlling us. Then we were told not to write anything about her, so we didn't.

She didn't want you misrepresenting her ideas?

That's right. She was extremely careful about things like that. We didn't do any kind of editorializing at all. It was just notices like, in the second issue, "Coming out in May of 1960, the Signet pocketbook edition of *We the Living*. The exact date to follow soon." By the third issue, we were publishing once a month, and Miss Rand asked me to come by each time before we published and she would go over the newsletter and check it to make sure everything was right and give us any information we didn't have. So by then we were endorsed.

By the sixth issue, we got really classy and started doing it on mimeograph, and we actually had a name: *The Runge-Torigian Newsletter*. In it we wrote, "Beginning in the next issue, Nathaniel Branden will, at regular intervals, make recommendations of books that are of interest to students of Objectivism." By that time Miss Rand and Nathaniel Branden started to make plans for the actual *Objectivist Newsletter*. Our publication was like a proving ground, and it was shortly after this that her newsletter came out.

What was your first meeting with Ayn Rand?

The time she asked me to type something for her. I had already been working for Nathan. She came into the office one day and asked if I would be interested in typing a speech for her. She said that it was in handwriting, so it would be more difficult. I said that was okay, so she handed it over to me and I typed it up for her. From then on I typed many of her speeches.

Were you nervous or tense with her?

Yes. I worked for her for quite a while on an extremely impersonal basis. It was only, "How are you? How are you doing?" And that was it. But the following incident on the day we were coming back from Yale University was the first time she ever spoke with me personally and asked me questions about myself.

We had gone up to Yale University to listen to her speak,[95] and we were on our way back, and I was in the car with her; I was in the back and she was in the front. It was dark, and we were headed back to Manhattan when she just suddenly turned around and started chatting with me.

She asked me all about myself. I also told her that I had at one time wanted to be a writer, but I'd given up the idea. I said I was now working as a bookkeeper with the Paul Tishman Construction Company, and she just gave me a very sharp look like "Why did you give up writing?" and she said, "You gave up so easily without trying?" And then I remember that I really was uncomfortable because she was just staring at me in the dimness of this car. Staring at me with those great big eyes. And I said, "Well, I'm happy enough." And she said, "Happy enough? Why don't you get work that's in some way connected to writing and not so completely distant? Why don't you at least get a job in publishing?" I sort of stammered and said, "I just can't run out and get a job in publishing." She answered, "You can't? Why not?" And I said, "I don't think I could do something like that. I don't write anymore. I just dream about it. I don't have the kind of courage that you have to lay my soul out on the written page." Then she just reached over the back of the seat, touched my hand and she said, "My dear, there are no guarantees in life. You must risk. The only way to know you can do something is to do it." And then she turned around, leaned her head back and closed her eyes, lost in her own thoughts.

She changed my life that night because I went in to work the next day, quit my job, pulled myself together, opened up the classifieds, turned to publishing, found an ad that said "editorial assistant wanted, will teach," went there, had the interview, got the job immediately, started work with them and I just never looked back.

Did you tell Miss Rand?

Oh yes! She was pleased. It was like she was saying, "Well, of course you did. Of course you got the job and you're working at that." It was wonderful. She changed my life.

Why did you stop working for her?

I didn't do much work for her after about '63. After we started *Verdict* magazine. And sometime later I moved overseas to Italy.

---

95 Ayn Rand gave two talks at Yale in 1960: February 17 and November 16.

Do you have any Ayn Rand material?

The only thing I have of hers that is personal is a copy of the very first paycheck she gave me. I photocopied it because I was so thrilled that I was working for her. It says, "My first paycheck from Ayn Rand in payment for typing the speech 'Faith and Force: The Destroyers of the Modern World,' given at Yale University on February 17, 1960." The check is for seven dollars and it's signed "A. Rand," but it's not signed the way she usually signed, because when they published *Atlas Shrugged*, they published her signature in the book, and her bank called her and told her—she told me this herself—that she had to now change her signature that she wrote on checks. So on this check she just has "A. Rand" and it's not written the way she writes "Rand." From the time the bank called her, she always had to sign her name differently. Except for her autographs, which she signed in her usual way, but any kind of financial things she signed this way.

Tell me about Ayn Rand and Frank O'Connor together.

Oh, they were wonderful together. If they sat together they held hands. She was always with Frank O'Connor holding hands. She was very sweet with him. This is also a little excerpt from my notes: "I went over to deliver a speech to her one day that I had typed for her and she answered the door in an apron, and I just stared at her like I was aghast. She said, "What's wrong?" I said, "Miss Rand, you're wearing an apron. I can't believe you're wearing an apron." She just looked at me and she said, "Why not? I cook and I do it well." So I went in and O'Connor was there. She was cooking dinner for him. I mean it was just so inconceivable to me that she would be cooking, in an apron, dinner for anyone.

Frederick Feingersh

Frederick Feingersh was an NBI student in the 1960s.

Interview date: August 17, 1999

Scott McConnell: *How did you meet Ayn Rand and Frank O'Connor?*

Frederick Feingersh: I met her when I was going to Brooklyn College in 1958 and there was an Ayn Rand club there, which had invited her to speak, and I knew I had to hear her. I was just awed by the amount of people that showed up and the power of what she had to say.[96] I don't remember specifically what she spoke about, but the audience was very hostile. She fielded the questions and didn't take anything personally; she was completely devoted to her principles.

What happened after that, regarding your meetings with Miss Rand or Mr. O'Connor?

Whenever I could, I spoke with her. "Acquaintance" might be a little too strong, but she certainly knew who I was; and at her lectures we always spoke. I always asked her questions like, "Who is your favorite poet?"

What were some questions and answers?

Regarding favorite poetry, let me put it the way she did: Kipling was like a triumphant march, and that to her knowledge—she would qualify it by saying she didn't have extensive knowledge of poetry— Swinburne was the best with structuring language, and that she loved his skill.

She was asked about popular music and specifically The Beatles. She said that she did not particularly like popular music, but at least The Beatles were well-dressed.

One night at an opening lecture—at a hotel on 34th Street and Seventh Avenue—she came in at the end to join Nathan answering questions. I was helping set up the chairs, and before the lecture I noticed that Ayn and Nathan were talking alone in the kitchen area. Then Nathan gave the lecture, and Ayn was sitting behind me in the back, and she said, "I hate doing this. Every time I walk down that long aisle, I feel like a bride getting married." But she walked down that aisle.

---

96 The talk, an introduction to Objectivism, was given on April 23, 1958.

Then after the lecture Ayn and Nathan were back in the kitchen again for a brief time. She was sitting down and he was standing over her and they were sort of comforting each other. They both seemed to have tears in their eyes. And when walking home, because I lived in that direction also, I saw Ayn walking with Nathan, and Frank was walking behind them, and I was walking behind Frank. It seemed extraordinarily sad. This was June or July 1968, a month or two before their break.

Did you ever hear Miss Rand discuss Martin Luther King?

She called him a "racist" because he made a definite separation between blacks and whites, rather than looking at people as being equal and individuals. This must have been the mid-60s when his peace marches were something that she considered violent, especially at one point when he stopped traffic on the Belt Parkway, in Brooklyn. Amongst the autos that were stopped was an ambulance that was carrying somebody who consequently died. It was very upsetting to her.

On the day President Kennedy died, that evening I was at a lecture that she gave. In the question-and-answer period, somebody said something like "You never liked President Kennedy so his death is nothing to grieve about." She got terribly upset about that remark and said, "This is America. This is not the way we do away with Presidents. We do away with them in a very civilized manner. We vote. We do not kill people."

What other meetings did you have with her?

In the late '60s she started inviting me to the Ford Hall Forum in Boston. As a matter of fact, she used to save me tickets to insure that I got in instead of having to wait in line and possibly not get tickets. One year Miss Rand saved two seats for myself and a friend, and I didn't know that she had saved me the seats that year, so my friend and I stood on line and we couldn't get in. It was jam-packed.

After we came back to New York, I saw her right afterwards and walked over to her. She sort of wagged her finger at me and said, "I saved two seats for you. What happened?" I said, "I didn't know you saved two seats for us. I was outside." What came out of her mouth astonished me, because I looked up to this woman as the epitome of just pure intellect, and she said, "I'm so sorry you missed it. I enjoyed myself so much! I had so much fun there!"

Along those lines, at one of the NBI lectures, Miss Rand walked in with another woman about the same age as she, and I was sitting right behind them. I thought, "Oh, well, they're going to talk about ideas or books." But they were just gossiping, kibitzing and talking about shopping and clothes.

What is your opinion of Ayn Rand?

Ayn Rand had a searing intelligence. I was always ready to hear the unexpected coming from her. That's what I miss these days. Whatever I thought the response to a question would be, Ayn always had something else or something more to add. She always kept me on the edge of my seat. She was like a walking novel being resolved in ways I hadn't even thought of.

Sunny Abarbanell

Sunny (Barron/Trachman) Abarbanell was a student of Objectivism who met Ayn Rand in the late 1950s.

Interview date: April 2, 1999

Scott McConnell: *Tell me about meeting Ayn Rand for the first time.*

Sunny Abarbanell: I had just finished hearing Nathaniel Branden read the play *Ideal* at an NBL event, and my fiancé introduced me to Ayn Rand. I was crying because I was so overwhelmed by the play, and her. I was almost afraid to meet her, because she was so intense, her eyes could see so much, and I wasn't sure if I would measure up, but she touched me very deeply. *Ideal* really touched my soul, and she knew it. She said, "Don't be afraid." It was like, "Don't give up on your dreams," "Hold fast to searching for the truth, and for your ideals."

What was she like during the lecture Q&As?

She was a real teacher. There was always someone in the audience who would challenge her. She always understood the premises behind their questions, so she never took it as a personal attack or felt threatened, and she patiently explained the concepts. She was strong.

You had something to tell me about Ayn Rand and your daughter.

I told Ayn Rand that we were naming our daughter after her—Lee Ayn Trachman, and any time after that when I would see her, she would refer to herself as my daughter's "fairy godmother."

Kathleen and Richard Nickerson

Kathleen Nickerson (née Morris) was in Ayn Rand's 1957–58 fiction-writing seminars and was a friend of Miss Rand's from 1955 on. Richard Nickerson, MD, also attended lectures and was an acquaintance of Miss Rand's.

Interview dates: October 14 and November 2, 1999

Scott McConnell: *How did you meet Miss Rand?*

Kathleen Nickerson: First I met Nathan in about September of 1955, and after a suitable period had passed, he decided I was a serious admirer of Ayn Rand and I was introduced to her.

After I had been in a group with Ayn a few times, Nathan told me I should be specific about why I was committed to her philosophy. That caused me to write a letter to her, and I believe the letter pleased her. I was then included in many events that included Ayn.

Since the older members were known as "the Collective," myself and about five others were known as "the Junior Collective," or the "juniors," who were younger and less advanced in their knowledge. We heard informal lectures by Nathan and Leonard, before they were formalized and put into official form. We were on various levels and did our best to keep up with Nathan and Leonard.

We wrote papers as a result of what we heard. For example, I wrote one on my understanding of rights, which Nathan said was really very good and said he would show it to Ayn.

In 1956 and '57 I attended NYU and managed to challenge every professor with my newfound knowledge. When I had a query I couldn't handle, I would ask Ayn or Nathan for suggestions.

Was it easy to ask Miss Rand's advice or questions?

In the appropriate setting, sure, such as if she was in the apartment and before we all sat down to discuss whatever we were there for. I could say, "There's something I really want to ask you about.".

How did you have an unpublished copy of Atlas Shrugged?

All the Collective and the Junior Collective got one before publication day. Ayn had arranged to get all those copies.

My copy said "To Kathy—to help you discover how a benevolent universe is real, possible and achievable—Ayn. August 20, 1957." When

I read *Atlas*, my reaction was very strong. I called Ayn and told her that I thought it was a great book, but that I was worried that people would come storm her apartment and try to do violence of some sort. I really was afraid that some people would see themselves in the book and react with hatred. She calmed me down, and at the end of the conversation, she said, "I love you, Kathy." I responded with the same sentiment.

After *Atlas* was published, reaction was very strong, and the Junior Collective were all involved in answering critical reviews of the book from *Time*, *Newsweek*, etc. *Time* had written such a bad review that we were all canceling our subscriptions and writing letters. One of the juniors agreed that this was a terrible review but did not want to cancel her subscription. It took a lot of persuading from Nathan and us to show this person that, in order to be consistent with her values, she had to cancel. She eventually did, grasping that she would be giving up a lesser value for a higher value, i.e., not a sacrifice.

And about this time Ayn's life became more harried than before and she became much more in demand as a speaker and interviewee. One request was from Mike Wallace's television interview show. She and others from the Collective came to our apartment to watch the show, to see if she thought that he did a creditable job. Television sets were not very common in homes at that time. She later appeared on the program.

About this time, Vivian Grant [another member of the Junior Collective] and I told Ayn about the showing of *The Cabinet of Dr. Caligari*, with Conrad Veidt. She very much wanted to see it after so long.[97] After seeing the movie, on the way home, Ayn said something like "I don't suppose you could see the attraction of Veidt," and I said, "Yes. I saw it in the way he looked at the woman sitting before him." She agreed with my identification and said so.

In 1957 or 1958 Vivian and I wanted to have Ayn speak at NYU, so we devised a way: The Controversy Club. We arranged debates between radically opposing views and we put up publicity signs all over NYU.[98]

At NYU, in connection with the club, I happened to be sitting next to Ayn in the back of the room, and I said to her, "It would be wonderful if you could teach us a little about your fiction-writing method." She said she would think about it and looked interested. Not too much later, a group of us were invited to attend a series of fiction-writing lectures at her apartment.[99]

---

97 Ayn Rand first saw the film on June 23, 1927.

98 This was Ayn Rand's first campus talk, March 27, 1958.

99 The course began January 18, 1958, and ended June 14, 1958.

Ayn gave me credit at the first lecture. By this time, the crowd around Ayn was getting very large. First it was just the Collective and then the Junior Collective, and then with the publication of *Atlas*, the numbers started increasing greatly. And for the lectures at her apartment there were about twenty-five people. She would sit at a table facing the inside of the rectangular shaped living room. If I could, I would sit near Frank. I always enjoyed talking to him and always felt very relaxed with him. I felt like I could say anything to him without worrying that he would take it the wrong way or think that I was too nonintellectual.

He was friendly to everybody. He smiled and he was interested and glad to see me. Just a sweet man.

Do you remember any conversations you had?

I can't remember anything specific, but he had a sense of humor, and I remember him laughing at things. But Ayn, throughout the lectures, any lectures I ever attended, always was very clear on his contributions to her works. That he had named a character and had suggested *Atlas Shrugged* as the book's title. She would also state that he had qualities that appeared in the characters—I think she mentioned Francisco—the lightness. She was just very clear and warm toward him, wanting it to be known that he was a major contributor.

Can you remember any other ways he contributed?

If something was bothering her in her writing, she would say to him, "I'm having trouble with this scene. It's just not going right. It's not falling together." Often he would just make a brief comment which steered her in the right direction. And she always appreciated it.

Toward the end of the fiction-writing series, as I was leaving one evening, Ayn took me aside and said, "Of all the people who are taking this course, I think you will be the writer." I was thrilled. I think she said it because I had written a paper on why I wanted to be a writer, and it impressed her. It also was possibly because of comments I may have made at the lectures. But I know that one play I wrote for a class assignment was quite contrived and dreadful.

Did you end up writing fiction?

No, I didn't. I found that I had no aptitude, no real interest in fiction. My interest seemed to lie in nonfiction.

Any other interesting aspects of the fiction-writing course?

There was somebody at the lectures who, no matter how well a point was explained by Ayn, would argue and then say, "I don't get it," until the rest of the class, I think, was ready to throttle him. I don't know how she remained patient with him but she did. She was unfailingly patient.

Describe a typical class and then the Q&A sessions.

They were very long evenings. We got there about eight o'clock, and Ayn would talk about different topics. One time it might be Romanticism as it was commonly construed by such as Thomas Wolfe, and she spent a great deal of time explaining why he was not a good writer, even though he could do some things well. And others were treated similarly. She would read examples of their work and give comments. This would go on for a good two, three hours.

I do remember evenings there until at least two in the morning. In the question period, people would basically ask about what they didn't understand or what she had to say about a topic. Or what did she think of this writer? She never seemed to tire.

How long would the Q&As last?

I just remember these sessions went on very late. She never cut anyone off. I never heard her say, "I'm just too tired; I've got to go get some sleep." This was what interested her most. What she was doing there and then. And it seemed she could keep going on forever. The fiction lectures were marvelous.

Was there any kind of gift or presentation at the end of the fiction-writing course?

Yes. We got together and we gave her dollar-sign-shaped bookends of some sort, as a thank you.[100]

Did your relationship with her continue after the fiction-writing course finished in 1959?

Yes. At some point, maybe in 1962, I had taken over the job as editorial coordinator at St. Martin's Press. As part of the job, I read manuscripts that were being considered for publication. One of these books had been previously published abroad, and I thought it was very well written. The author was Antoni Gronowicz, and the book was a

---

100 The bookends were made by Frank O'Connor.

biography of an early famous actress, Helena Modjeska.[101] In the cover letter, he mentioned that he also had plans to write a book about Greta Garbo. Knowing Ayn's admiration for Garbo, I decided to find out what I could about Gronowicz's relationship with Garbo. I took him to dinner and we talked about the book he was planning to write. I asked him if he thought that a meeting between Ayn Rand and Greta Garbo could occur. I don't remember what he said. But I do remember that as a result of this, I had to tell Ayn what I had done. She was very, very upset because I had compromised her by asking this author if Greta Garbo and she could meet. I had made her in some way a supplicant and she never wanted to be in that position. I apologized and assured her that I would not do this sort of thing again. She was very nice but clearly upset and I was very sorry. She didn't yell at me. She didn't cut me down. She didn't insult me. She just made it clear to me that she was unhappy with what I had done. And as nicely as anybody could, she put me in my place.

What exactly was her reason?

I had put her in an inferior position by my request. I had diminished her in the way that I put it. It was not that she would deny that she admired Greta Garbo, but that it was just not fitting for her to be in the position of asking to meet her through me. I was undercutting her in some way.

I believe that Miss Rand attended your marriage to Richard Nickerson.

Ayn and Frank did come to Richard's and my wedding on June 1, 1963, at the Americana Hotel in New York City. We planned the wedding in one week, but all the Collective, except for Alan Greenspan, who was in Washington, managed to get there. Frank said it was the best ceremony of any wedding he had ever been to. I treasure the pictures we have of that day.

On another occasion, Richard wanted to get cruise control for our car, and I wanted to pay the phone bill or something equally mundane. We didn't have a lot of money. Somehow the question came to Ayn and the message I got back was, "Of course he should get the cruise control. You need some things in life that are just fun, that are frivolous." So I thought, "Okay. Okay. I'll learn."

After 1963 Richard and I continued to attend lectures and events,

---

101 See Antoni Gronowicz, *Modjeska: Her Life and Loves* (New York: T. Yoseloff, 1956).

like the first NBI ball, but the group was now very large and my closeness to Ayn dropped off some.

Why was that?

Because she now knew so many people and had so many contacts, I didn't get invited to as many gatherings as I had. There were a lot more interesting and prominent people around, like philosophers, authors, etc. It was not that there was any break or anything, just that her circle of acquaintances grew very large.

In 1965 our son Scott was born, and about ten months later I called Ayn, with some trepidation. I didn't want to impose on her and I was afraid that it wouldn't interest her, but I called and asked her whether she and Frank would like to meet Scott. She said, "Oh yes!" What follows is the diary notes about our visit on August 28, 1966. Richard writes, "Scott met Ayn and Frank O'Connor at their apartment today. They say he'll look just like Roark when he grows up and commented on how unafraid he is, how he has a definite personality already, he seems precocious, etc. Ayn also worried about his putting things in his mouth or crawling on the floor because of germs and dirt. She paid tremendous compliments to Scott's mother." (Which he doesn't specify, and I don't remember.) Then I add to the diary, "Also, they both were very warm towards Scott. He crawled onto Ayn's lap and played with her pin and put his fingers into her mouth. Both she and Frank held his hands while he walked, etc. Ayn also said he looked like both of us. Richard mainly in the shape of his face. Also she listened to and corrected and commented on certain ideas of mine about child-raising. And she said a couple of times, 'We'll be hearing much more about him as he gets older.' A wonderful visit." That's the end of the diary.

Dr. Nickerson, do you remember any other meetings or conversations with Miss Rand?

Richard Nickerson: In the first lectures, it was relatively informal. I remember the night they announced that the name of the philosophy would be "Objectivism." It wasn't anything too spectacular. It was the first formal lecture series that Nathaniel Branden gave—every Tuesday evening in Manhattan [in 1959, at the Sheraton Russell Hotel]. And he'd given several of the lectures, and then at one of the lectures he just said that Miss Rand had decided on a name for the philosophy, and it was to be called "Objectivism." Capital "O." Everyone was pleased to hear that.

When was the last time you saw her?

Kathleen Nickerson: Probably when we took Scott to see her. I did not see her after '66. I might have, but it would have been in a group.

Did you see Ayn Rand angry?

I once saw her when she was displeased at a close friend, at a social gathering, and told him so in no uncertain terms never to do again what he had just done. What he had done was to photograph her with her glasses on. She cut him down sharply but explained at the same time the necessary motivation of someone who would want to picture her with glasses: the attempt to change her image from that of a serious philosopher to that of a bookish schoolmarm. To normalize her. To make her one of the guys. At the time he apologized and said he understood her position.

We learned the principle involved and vowed to ourselves not to make the same sort of mistake. Being with Ayn on even the most casual occasion was invariably informative but not without the element of risk-taking.

Another time at a gathering in the Brandens' apartment, Ayn was discussing, I believe, her new newspaper column and what it should be called. Sitting in a semicircle, the members of the Collective were throwing out ideas for the title of her column. The shock was severe when Ayn, after Nathan had made a half-joking suggestion that offended her, sharply said, "Do not ever tell me what to do with my work." She was evidently furious with him. He was shocked and galled by her reaction. I do remember my sense of horror at what happened. The moment passed, but I was reminded that if you had not thought out the implications of your words, you were taking a serious risk telling them to Ayn.

I have seen Ayn highly critical of almost every member of the Collective and yet I know she remained fond of and respectful of them all. For a group of intellectuals who were committed to Ayn and to reason, their only choice was to try to understand why they had been jumped on. If they had a problem with this, they were free to bring it up with her at a later date.

At lectures I witnessed some questioners being stunned by Ayn's reaction to their question or comment. But each time, on reflection, I could understand Ayn's reasoning. She never attempted to intimidate people for the hell of it, as some people do regularly. She always explained, however briefly, the implications of their question or comment. Sure, it was embarrassing for some of them. Some turned away from Objectivism forever. But some questions or comments had to be seen in the context of the implications apparent in them. Sad to say, one could not innocently say something to the effect of "Don't you think the Soviet Union was actually an improvement over the previous regime?" I don't have any record of the actual questions, so this may be a poor example. All who were lucky enough to have dealings with Ayn Rand had the chance of a lifetime to observe her intelligence in action at lectures and other venues. She was always judging the content of what was said around her and to her. But if you couldn't withstand the heat of that, you didn't belong there.

Was she in public the same as she was in private?

Yes. She was basically the same person. I think she was more formal in public. But she was always the same person. You could always count on getting a reasonable answer from her no matter where she was.

I once asked Ayn, "Is there anything wrong with wishing revenge on people?" And she looked surprised for a minute and said, "Oh, no. Nothing wrong with that at all. You are wishing for a form of justice."

Who were the people you were talking about wishing revenge on?

They were people who had written something terrible about her in print or done something bad and we wanted to wish them to hell, if that was possible.

Howard Odzer

Howard Odzer is a retired businessman who attended Ayn Rand's fiction-writing course in 1958–59.

Interview dates: April 20 and May 4, 1999

Scott McConnell: *How did you get to know Ayn Rand?*

Howard Odzer: I had attended Nathaniel Branden's initial series of lectures on Objectivism and had spent a lot of time visiting with and talking to him, especially about psychology. Being a part of that lecture series at the Sheraton Russell Hotel, probably with fifteen to twenty of us there, I had opportunity to talk with Ayn Rand. Then, friendship and interaction with Ayn and Frank O'Connor just developed.

At this time, she was starting to give lectures, and one was at NYU. I was in the audience along with my wife at that time, Debbie, and some vociferous supporters were needed in the audience, I can assure you.

Why?

The way the academic community structured these events, it was almost like a setup, loaded to attack Ayn. During a phone conversation with her, she said, "I can't tell you how nice it was seeing your face and Debbie's out there, because it was just a sea of enemies."

I went to a number of her talks, and I remember Ayn Rand as an embattled figure on the stage, attacked from all sides. The younger people were much more sensitive and responsive to her. It was a case where the young people came to listen, and the older people came to attack.

Who were the older people?

Professors. Professor-types. Smart-alecky—kind of like "I'm going to show her up."

How did she handle them?

Devastatingly. Things like "The second part of your premise contradicts the first part." She used very often what was called "Rand's Razor."[102]

---

102 Rand's Razor states: "Concepts are not to be multiplied beyond necessity"; in *Introduction to Objectivist Epistemology*, eds. Harry Binswanger and Leonard Peikoff, expanded 2nd ed. (New York: Meridian, 1990), p. 72.

Why were you invited to be in the fiction-writing class?

After a lecture question-and-answer session one night, we were talking about fiction writing. I guess she asked, because I told her I was interested in writing. She said, "Would you be interested in attending a class of lectures." I said, "Are you kidding, I'd love to."

Why was she so interested in you?

Remember, there was a group of us, and we met at her house, and we talked, and she saw some of my writings and saw what I was philosophically. She was looking to encourage students. She felt that it was a great opportunity, I believe, for young people to be able to form a spearhead for the dissemination and development of her philosophy.

Tell me about the fiction-writing lectures.

They were held at her home on 36th Street, which was way up by Morgan Library, between Park and Madison. They were held pretty much once a weekend, on a Saturday, and there were about fifteen people there.

You were on the edge of your seat, listening to what she had to say, going through the development of plot, the skeleton and the structure of the bones that tied everything together.

What was she like as a teacher?

She was very good. Sometimes she had little patience in the question-and-answer period for the seminars, but where she observed seriousness and purpose and conscientiousness, I found her to be easygoing. I didn't find her to be hostile or interrogating.

Describe a typical meeting at her apartment.

You'd come in and people would socialize, and then when she put her microphone on, everybody would hunker down. She sat at the front-door part of the living room because the room was long and narrow, with most of the people lined up on the left and right side. She'd lecture, we'd take a little bit of a break, and then she'd continue, and then we'd have a question-and-answer-period.

There were some meetings where a student would read what he or she had written for the course. Ayn and other students in the class would comment on the work.

What was her attitude or her manner during these sessions?

Constructive. She would comment about what was there, what

wasn't there, what could be done to improve it. You didn't feel—speaking for the other people as well as myself—you were being given negative commentary. It was encouraging. If faults were found in the writing, it was presented in a way so as "This is what you can do to improve it," or "This is how you can tighten it up," or "This is how you might extend it," or "This is the kind of thing you should leave out" or "This is extraneous."

Her manner was analytical. Straightforward. She would say something and concretize her reason for saying it. You learned from her comments, and you could see what she was getting at. She was like a laser in terms of looking at things and seeing through to the essence of where they were going and why they were set up the way they were, what their purpose was and how the work was being carried out.

I didn't feel like I was with a famous writer, I felt like I was with Ayn Rand. When you talked to her, it was not like an ad hominem conversation, if you were focused on the thing you were talking about, and she was focused on the thing that you were talking about, and there were no hidden agendas—no ego agendas—no personality things anybody had to get out. It was very pure in that sense.

One night I thought there was a seminar; I showed up, and lo and behold, I was wrong, that wasn't the night of a lecture, so I was the only person there. She was very gracious, and she and Frank invited me in. We sat down and we spent an hour and a half together, and she asked me to read the piece I had written. Interestingly, one thing you don't expect from Ayn in this sort of situation was that she asked me if I'd like a brandy. Then we talked about the writing.

She was very complimentary about my writing, and we talked about it for a while. She was very, very cordial and open.

Did she tell you how to improve your plotting techniques or writing premises?

She told me how she had learned a great deal about journalism in her research for *The Fountainhead* and Gail Wynand. She pointed out to me that one of the plot devices in my story, about a press breaking down, could not happen in a large newspaper organization. She said, "You'd be surprised; you've got to know 100 percent about the subject that you're going to write about, even though you'll only use 5 percent of it."

Did you call her "Ayn"?

Yes. At first it was "Miss Rand," but at the conclusion of the lecture series, she announced to everybody that we had already gotten close enough that we could now go onto a first-name basis.

Did you have interactions with her outside of the fiction-writing course?

I had occasion to be up at her apartment sometimes during the day. Debbie was giving her some private exercise in dance and such.

My wife at that time was a dancer and was giving classes in both exercise and dance movement. A number of the Objectivist students attended her classes, including Ayn. That was very interesting, to see Ayn as a student instead of the teacher, which was the unusual situation. She had such an eager face, and she was so involved with doing the exercises—just like a little girl. That was so much of her character; in so many ways she was so much like a little girl. She was just this fresh, unscrubbed person who was such a delight.

Tell me more about the exercises in the class.

There would be stretching exercises and moving-across-the-floor exercises. Stretching back muscles. Extending the spine, stretching the legs. Largely toning and getting-in-condition kind of exercises. Toward the last quarter of the class, moving in an almost dance-like stride diagonally across the floor.

Why was Miss Rand taking the class?

She was interested in exercise and in seeing what modern dance was about. The only experiences that she had had of modern dance were the Martha Graham-type things, and she had thought that a great deal of modern dance had to be ugly, earth-grounded, rather than elongated, uplifting movements.

What was her attitude during the class?

Diligent, amused, accepting; not in any way looking at it like a condescending type of behavior.

Anything else that you shared with Miss Rand?

She had a record collection. I was into classical music, and I was thumbing through her records one night and came across ones like *Countess Maritza* and *The Gypsy Princess* by Kálmán, which was my first introduction to that kind of music.

Do you know which piece of music was her inspiration for the *Halley Concerto*? It was an orchestral recording of love music from Boris Godunov, performed by Hans Kindler and the National Symphony Orchestra. That's the record she said she played over and over and over again when she finished writing *Atlas Shrugged*. I found the record at Barry Meltzer's Music Store. They had a slew of old 78 recordings from the 1910s, '20s, '30s, and I told Ayn about it, and she became a regular at Meltzer's. Her favorite song was "Get Out and Get Under."[103] They were these very, very "up" kinds of things, like the "Circus March" and the introduction in the "Circus."

What else did you discuss with her about music?

Favorite composers. Tchaikovsky was number one, and it was a toss-up between Rachmaninoff and Chopin for number two. One of her favorite pieces was the Rachmaninoff third piano concerto, with Witold Malcuzynski performing. She played that again and again. She loved that particular piece of music.

Do you have any examples of her humor?

You'd compliment her on the way she looked, and she'd say, "I have two good features: my legs are pretty good, like Dagny's were." Then she'd hold her hand up across her mouth and cover her nose so you could only see her eyes, "And my eyes, of course, are my best feature."

I remember once when Ayn sneezed, I said, "Good premises," and she cracked up.

Do you have any closing comments on Ayn Rand?

You read so much about "Ayn had a temper" or that she was sharp with people. That may have been under certain circumstances, when confronted, challenged or attacked, but the Ayn Rand that I knew was very much like a character in *Atlas Shrugged*. Very much like a young girl, open to life and to happiness, and a "face without pain or fear or guilt." She was very much an embodiment of that—very open, uncomplicated and capable of great appreciation and joy.

Once, I came over to her house with this extra work I had written, and I said, "This is good, Ayn; this is better than the other stuff," and she said, "Oooooh, that sounds good." That's part of what I mean about her ingenuousness. If you told her something—until you betrayed that—she took you at face value.

---

103 The song was written by Maurice Abrams, Grant Clark and Edgar Leslie.

Larry Abrams

Larry Abrams attended Miss Rand's 1958 fiction-writing class and became a friend. Mr. Abrams is now a venture capitalist.

Interview dates: October 30, 1997, and June 22, 1999

Scott McConnell: *When was the first time you saw Ayn Rand?*

Larry Abrams: It was at one of the first lectures given by Nathaniel Branden.[104] Miss Rand was in the audience and I was sitting next to her. I hadn't met her, but I asked a question of Branden—I have no idea what the question was. She turned to me after I asked the question and said something like "You see the question, but you don't see the full implications." It was meant to be helpful, but it devastated me at the time. I thought, "What am I not seeing here?"

After I read *Atlas Shrugged*, I wrote her a letter and asked her a question, something to the effect that she had shown me that courage was not necessary if someone had integrity.

Did she answer your letter?

No, but she indicated to me when I eventually met her that she had liked the letter and had put it aside to answer, but hadn't gotten around to it. I had already taken another step. I had seen in a newspaper article that Barbara Branden and Leonard Peikoff were teaching at some university. I called one of them, I don't remember which, and was referred to Nathaniel Branden, who set up an interview for me, in effect, with Alan Greenspan at his apartment. I came with a whole list of questions for him.

You were primarily interested in economics?

No, they were philosophical questions. They were all about *Atlas Shrugged* and apparent contradictions that I thought I had found in the novel. If this is a definition of this then how can this also be, et cetera. You have to go through that type of thinking when you're young and have no context. It's only context that allows you to understand. Based upon that interview, I then met Nathaniel Branden, and then he invited me to Miss Rand's talks on fiction writing.

Did you want to be a fiction writer or were you interested in the

---

104 Circa 1958.

philosophy?

I was thinking of being a fiction writer.

Tell me about your first meeting with Ayn Rand.

It was as part of the fiction-writing group.

Do you have a specific recollection of her at the first fiction-writing lecture?

She had an answer for everything. I had never come across anything like that before or since. People would ask her questions about everything, not just fiction. There was never a time when she couldn't answer a question, and there was never a time after thinking about it, when I thought that her answer was wrong. I would think about it and I would say, yes, that would follow, I can see how that would be. Her eyes just held you and you could see the intelligence radiating from them.

What was her attitude toward you, a relative unknown?

She was very gentle to someone she had not known before, based only on her expectations that I was interested in her ideas and was at the course for that reason. She was quite kind. If she was intimidating, it wasn't because of her manner towards me or towards anyone like me. It was because we could see how incredibly intelligent she was.

Describe the fiction-writing lectures.

After each lecture there would be a question period. She would be sitting down at a desk or table that was placed at the end of the apartment, about ten feet from the entrance, at the beginning of the living room. Around the living room there was a couch and some chairs for us to sit on. Nathaniel Branden sat at her left, really close to the table or desk, and I think Barbara Branden also sat really close by, always in the same place. The rest of us sat around the room in different places each time. At the end of the room there was a window that looked down on 36th Street.

How many people would usually be at a session?

Maybe twelve.

How long were the Q&As, and what types of questions were asked?

They were at least an hour. Often they were more open-ended than just an hour. There were always questions that came up. Miss Rand was always willing and ready and certainly able to answer any questions, and she enjoyed it. She was not particularly interested in calling a quick halt to the sessions. As a matter of fact, some of the sessions lasted quite long into the night. I would stay there until the very end. I don't think anyone left early.

Do you remember any of the questions or issues that came up during the Q&As?

All the questions were on things that were either covered by her lectures or on fiction pieces that people had written that she was critiquing. When she'd comment on some fiction piece, it would be in terms of instantiations of the principles she had been enunciating.

There was one thing she said that really surprised me. I thought that one of the best films that I had ever seen was *High Noon* and that that would have been an example of a masterful plot. Ayn Rand said, "That's not plot." I and some other people there said: "Why? How can that be?" She started her answer by saying that a plot is a purposeful progression of events.[105] I thought about the film and I said it certainly seemed to me it was a purposeful progression of events.

I think we all had the same initial reaction. One thing I learned about Ayn Rand was that no matter how strange any of her answers would sound, you had to think 3,600 times before you'd disagree with her, because when you went home and you thought it over and thought, "This time, there's no way she can be right," when you finally approached her again and said, "Miss Rand, I think the following, which is different from what you say," she would just say, "The answer to that is . . . ."

Did you actually say that to her?

I didn't say it baldly like that, but I would think things over and go back to her, sure that I was right, and she'd show me where I was wrong. She'd do it every time.

What was her manner in doing that?

Very much like a parent. Gentle and benevolent.

Did Miss Rand edit your fiction?

---

105 The answer is more fully explained in *Ayn Rand Answers: The Best of Her Q&A*, Robert Mayhew, ed. (New York: New American Library, 2005), pp. 214–215.

She didn't edit it; she would just comment on it, and talk about the good points and the bad points and things that might be helpful.

Did she discuss one of your works in class?

Yes. Mine was not good. Mine made several errors. I think everybody did one. At least everyone had the opportunity to do one. She said some good things about my work, but mainly, I had made a lot of mistakes, and she talked about those as we were going around the room, talking about everybody's.

During the course do you remember discussing Miss Rand's story "Good Copy"?[106]

Yes, absolutely. I think Nathaniel Branden read it without attribution to the author, and we were asked to comment on it, and I didn't like it. We went around the room, and everybody got to say what they thought about it, and I think there were a couple other people who thought there were problems with it, but I was the one who thought there were the most problems with it.

What kind of problems?

It was probably something like no one would do this, that such and such was unrealistic. It was then announced that Ayn Rand had written it, and I thought, "Well, there's always pumping gas."

What did Miss Rand say when you were negative?

When we were going around the room and I was being negative, she didn't say anything, just let everybody speak. But afterwards she answered all my points and showed me where she thought I was wrong.

She wasn't upset?

She seemed angry. I think she just would have liked her intent to have been better comprehended, that's all.

Any other interesting things that happened during the class?

We always had to stop a session if there was a *Perry Mason* episode on TV. Of course, she asked us all in advance, "Would it be all right if I? . . ." We all said, "Yes, it will be fine." We knew this was a favorite of hers and she didn't want to miss it, so we would all watch *Perry Mason.*

---

106 Reprinted in *The Early Ayn Rand.*

Would she make comments during the show?

Yes. It was mainly reactions like "good" and "the rotten so-and-so" made emphatically. She really loved that show.

How did the fiction-writing course close?

At the end she asked us to submit to her a title for the first book we hoped to write, and we did that. Mine was "Theirs Was the Glory." She liked it very much.

One of her favorite writers was Donald Hamilton, and she would read every one of his books as they came out. I am pretty sure that I was the one who turned her on to Donald Hamilton. She liked to relax by reading mystery stories, usually at night when she finished working. She liked Agatha Christie, and she liked the television program *Perry Mason*, but she couldn't find anybody else. That was a source of a little distress to her because she wanted more. I suggested Donald Hamilton. She read and loved him, and at one point, after she had read a few of them, and she was waiting for the next one to come out, I told her that I knew someone who worked for his publisher and that I could get the galleys of this book before it came out. She said, "Oh, could you really?!" I said, "Yes, it's not a problem." And so I did. She loved the fact that they were galleys, and she was one of the first to see it. She really loved his mystery stories. I don't know whether that held for all of his work throughout his career, but at that point in his career she did.

Did you talk about personal things with Ayn Rand?

At the Hotel Roosevelt, early on when the lectures were being given by Nathaniel Branden, I saw her smoking a cigarette. I screwed up my courage, and I said to her, "Ayn, you know that really could be dangerous." She looked at me sharply and said, "Oh, you're concerned for my health." I said, "Yes, I am." She said, "I appreciate that—I do—but there is no proof that cigarettes are dangerous."[107]

Tell me about Frank O'Connor.

He was a very quiet man, very gentlemanly. He would almost never say anything during the fiction-writing question-and-answer period. It was just one time that something happened during the course that really surprised me. The first and only time I ever saw Frank get angry. It was when it was time for *Perry Mason* to start and the TV set was

---

107 This was in the early 1960s. Miss Rand later gave up cigarettes. after lung cancer. p. 500

turned on, but you couldn't see or hear it well because the picture kept skipping quickly. Frank said, "I'll fix that." He went around to the back to fix it and five minutes passed and it wasn't getting any better and Ayn said, "Frank, the show is happening and I'm not seeing it. Can't you work a little faster?"

She was getting really impatient—she really wanted to see that show. Finally, Frank, after a few more minutes of her saying this a few more times, got up and said, "You fix it," and he walked out. I was shocked because Frank never got angry.

How did Ayn Rand react when he walked out?

I think she called after him and he didn't come back right away, but she didn't go after him. She had a whole room full of guests.

How would you describe Frank O'Connor and Ayn Rand together?

They obviously loved each other a lot. They would often hold hands. At the New Year's Eve party that I drove them to, she was sitting on the couch holding his hand. She had a unique tone of voice, difficult to describe, when she spoke to him. There was never any question that they loved each other.

Tell me about that party.

Alan Greenspan gave a New Year's Eve party.[108] I remember Robert Bleiberg, who ran *Barron's* magazine, was there, as were Leonard Peikoff and the Blumenthals. Besides that, I didn't pay much attention. I don't remember who else or what went on. All I was interested in was hanging around so if she dropped some words of wisdom, I would hear them.

Did she?

She always would say something interesting. She was the one who suggested to Alan Greenspan that he invite me. That probably would have been at the time that I was teaching her chess.[109]

So you weren't just their chauffeur?

That was only for one night. I wasn't just a chauffeur—I was a very *nervous* chauffeur. I had this great responsibility. I was carrying Ayn Rand

---

108 In 1972.
109 Ayn Rand's daily calendar notes numerous such meetings between October 1972 and June 1975.

in my car. I thought, "What if I have an accident? This is extraordinarily precious cargo. I have to make sure I don't have an accident."

How did it come about that you taught Ayn Rand chess?

She had compared something to "an intellectual chess game." She used that metaphor a lot and, at one point, I asked her if she knew that I was a pretty good chess player. She said, "No, I hadn't known that." I said, "Ayn, chess can be a lot of fun. Would you be interested in letting me show you the kind of fun that it can be? I think you might think differently of chess if you were familiar with it." She said: "Yes, that would be interesting. I'd like that." So we did it. She would tell me what time to come over and we'd sit down and I'd teach her the game. First I taught her the moves, then I would play both sides of the game and tell her why I was doing what I was doing. Then I would play a game with her and explain to her why each move was a good or bad one.

Any funny anecdotes?

There was a funny anecdote—in fact a very funny one, to me. Here's this woman who had turned philosophy on its head and who had come up with the only objective philosophy that has ever been presented to humanity and had done the world's most complex integrations. I'm showing her some chess moves, which are arbitrary moves that anybody can learn and play if they practice, and she's saying, for example, things like "How can you see all that?" She's asking me how can I see all this when she's seen things that no person in human history has seen. I said: "Ayn, any competent chess player would see this. This is not difficult." She said, "I thought this was a good move, because if I go here I'm threatening this, but then you show me that if I go here then you can go here, then you go here and it never stops!" I said, "Ayn, trust me, it stops. It stops because I'm not a grand master and I can't think beyond a certain number of moves and even grand masters can't think beyond a certain number of moves."[110] She was childlike in her reaction. The enormity of her being impressed by my ability to do that when she'd done what she'd done almost blew my mind.

What was she like as a student?

She was not terribly interested in chess, in being really good at

---

110 Larry Abrams subsequently did become the New York City Mensa chess champion and the Connecticut state chess champion.

it, and she had no one to practice with. I suggested she practice with Frank, but she said she didn't think Frank would be interested. No one can become a good student without some kind of practice.

Anything else about her attitude to chess or the intellect behind it?

I thought that I heard her be a little more lenient about chess after that and not use the phrase "intellectual chess game" so much. She really had a respect for it, as you could see from that reaction of hers.

Once she wanted to play Scrabble, which is apparently something she did play a lot with Frank. And when we played she never cared about opening up triple word letters or whatever; she would just blithely put down words for the fun of putting them down. It's not a question of being good at strategy, it's a question of caring. She obviously would have been good at anything she put her mind to.

Did you discuss stamps with Miss Rand?

I had collected stamps as a kid and I had collections of American and world stamps, and I offered these to her. She said, "No, Larry, a stamp collection—I can't. You wouldn't want to give away a stamp collection." I said, "Yes, I would. I'm not interested in stamps anymore and obviously you are. It would do me good—please take it." So she took my collection.

Did you ever talk to Miss Rand about her finances?

I think the first time was when I was teaching her chess and we were talking about other things before and after the lesson. She knew I had had some financial success and she turned to me and said, "I have $250,000 in the bank. What do you think I should do with it? Alan Greenspan is always telling me that I should invest it and make it grow. What do you think?" I said, "Why haven't you taken his advice?" She said, "I don't want to think about it. I would worry, and I don't want to worry. What I want to do is write, not worry." I said, "Did you tell Alan this?" She said, "Yes, and he said that I should do it and don't worry, he'll take care of it." I said, "Ayn, there's no way that you wouldn't worry. If you want my opinion, leave your money where it is." She said, "Thank you for understanding." I presume that's what she did.

After Miss Rand's break with the Brandens in 1968, I believe you offered Miss Rand support?

Harry Binswanger was with me at the time. We were standing outside a building, probably her apartment building, at the end of an evening. I thought she probably didn't have terribly much money and she needed financial support. I offered her access to my entire net worth. She knew that it was reasonably substantial. She said, "Oh, Larry, thank you very much but"—I said, "Miss Rand, I mean it. It's all at your disposal." She said, "Oh, Larry, you and Harry Binswanger always know exactly the right things to say."

What reason did she give for declining your offer?

I don't remember her having given a reason other than "I couldn't do that."

Any last stories about Ayn Rand?

I don't remember what the circumstances surrounding this were, but I was telling her that I was driving quickly in order to get to my apartment. I gave her some reason that I had to drive down side streets at thirty miles per hour. She really surprised me. She said, "I hope they get you." I was taken aback and it took me some time to realize that I was a kid and I assumed that my reflexes were perfect and that I could see anybody in time, no problem. She was a middle-aged lady and a very slow walker, and she was coming from a different place. She made me realize I was endangering people. I was very slow when I took her to Greenspan's New Year's Eve party. Believe me I was one of the slowest drivers on the road.

Scott Stanley

Scott Stanley is a former managing editor of the conservative magazine *Insight* (published by the *Washington Times*). He has been editor of various national conservative journals for more than four decades and knew Ayn Rand in the late 1950s and early 1960s.

Interview date: June 29, 1999

Scott McConnell: *Tell me about meeting Ayn Rand.*

Scott Stanley: I was with her a number of times and thought—and continue to think—she was one of the greatest of American literary figures and a great figure in world literature as well.

Where did you meet her?

She would go out and make speeches sometimes and I saw her at them. I met her in New York on a couple of occasions and had a memorable dinner with her and Robert Welch[111] when she was in Cambridge to give one of the Jordan [Ford Hall Forum] lectures. The young conservatives gravitated to her views then as they do now. I thought she was a very great artist, dramatic and compelling, with enormous energy. And I liked her.

What influence do you think Ayn Rand has had?

I'm sure that, without her advocacy and influence, the free-market economics of Ludwig von Mises and the Austrian School would never have gone beyond that small coterie of lower-case libertarians associated in the 1950s with the National Association of Manufacturers and the *Freeman*. What she did was to lead free-market economics out of the stuffy business community and put it into a community of artists and philosophers and intellectuals. And that was vital. They attracted to it a dimension of youthful support, which was vital as well, making it possible to raise up heroes of creativity among the business leaders who followed the age of mechanics to create electronics and high tech. The lady was a wowser.

---

111 Welch was the founder of The John Birch Society. For Ayn Rand's negative view of that organization, see *Letters of Ayn Rand*, p. 621 and p. 656.

Daniel Greene

Daniel Greene is an artist who painted Miss Rand's portrait in 1959. His portraits include many political, business and education leaders. Mr. Greene's paintings are in museums and collections around the world.

Interview date: February 5, 1999

Scott McConnell: *How did you meet Ayn Rand?*

Daniel Greene: I was in the army in 1958, stationed on Governor's Island in New York, and I read *The Fountainhead*, and became immediately enamored of it and the philosophy found therein. As chance would have it, I saw an ad in a New York newspaper for lectures that Ayn Rand and Nathaniel Branden were giving in the city, and I attended the lectures. During one of the breaks at a lecture, I met Frank O'Connor, and when Frank learned that I was an artist, he got all excited and wanted to introduce me to Ayn and show her examples of my work.

Tell me about Frank O'Connor visually.

Visually, he was a very striking, handsome man. He had finely chiseled features, was quite tall, and relatively slim, even though he must have been in his sixties when I knew him. He reminded me of John Barrymore and Gary Cooper—obviously movie-star quality in appearance.

So I met Ayn, and one thing led to another, and she agreed, at my request, to pose for various portraits. She began posing for me in my studio, which coincided with my discharge from the service, about 1959.

What did the artist in you say when you first saw her?

She had a lot of character etched in her face, and her hair, in its severe simplicity, framed the strength that she had. She had very forthright gestures; even the way she dressed was very thought out and, I think, done not really to impress people. But she had apparently thought out every aspect of her life, including the furniture in her apartment, the clothing she wore, the very minimal jewelry she wore. There was a pin, I remember, in the shape of a dollar sign that someone had given her, that she was very, very proud of.

Why did you ask to do her portrait?

Entirely on the basis of my being an admirer of Ayn Rand, and she seemed to me to be such an astonishing person that having the opportunity to do a painting of her and have some time to spend with her was very, very appealing. However, I must say that since painting Ayn, I've done hundreds, if not thousands, of portraits, and I have never had any problem of any kind, because I learned a great deal about how to conduct the interaction between sitter and painter, as a result of my sessions with Ayn.

Would you elaborate?

At that time I was quite young, and was interested in her opinion, and that opened up a whole arena of her telling me exactly how she felt about every aspect of the painting. I think I was guilty of seeking approval at the time, and I no longer do anything like that. I don't give my sitters any area in which to make any comments, and I learned that from my sessions with Ayn. Eventually she began to ask questions and set up a situation where my process was interfered with, and so I no longer do that. I was endeavoring to explain to her what I was doing, and that was a mistake, because she had her own expectations in terms of what she was looking for in painting, and it wasn't the same thing that I was looking for.

Describe a sitting with Ayn Rand.

When I left the army, I took a studio in a building on 31st Street, not far from the Empire State Building. She would come at the appointed time and pose for me, and then there would be frequent rests. That went on for weeks, if not months.

How many sittings were there?

I did three paintings of her, actually. Each one normally would take about ten or twelve sittings of three hours each. There was an oil painting that I did that took longer, and these were spread out over a period of time. I subsequently took another studio in Greenwich Village, and she came down there. Eventually, I took a permanent studio up on 67th Street. On occasion, I would get together with her for parties at her house or visit her to continue our discussions.

Could she see the Empire State Building from your first studio?

Yes. That was the only thing you could see from the skylight in the studio, and she was most interested in that.

Could you expand on that?

Apparently the visibility, through my skylight, of the tallest building in the world must have related to her knowledge of the architecture and provided a visual point relevant to her own work.

Did you always work from her as a model, or did you also work from photographs?

No, these were all done from sittings.

She could sit still?

Oh yes, she was very conscientious. She was a terrific model: she didn't move at all, and she had immense composure. She stood—it was a standing pose—for the painting that was in the *Ayn Rand: A Sense of Life* film, for hours, without complaining.[112]

Did she ever talk about her thought processes as she was standing there?

She would address particular subjects and mull things over, because it was a very quiet, contemplative time.

One of the things that she wanted to do was to bring records, so that the music we would play would keep her in the proper frame of mind, and the one that she particularly liked was [Emmerich] Kálmán's *The Gypsy Princess*, and then we listened to Rachmaninoff quite a bit. Whenever I hear this music by Kálmán, I instinctively think of Ayn, because we heard that over and over.

What was the frame of mind she was trying to get?

I can't speak for her. To me, she conveyed self-assurance, forthrightness. It was cheerful, direct, confident. All the positive attributes, that's what she personified.

What were you trying to capture or express in the painting?

It was twofold. On the one hand, the mechanics of making a painting and the aspirations to make a work of art are of paramount importance. That's the nature of the activity. And in addition, one also has to convey a sense of the salient characteristics of the sitter. So it was a two-pronged concern. I wanted to do as good a portrait of Ayn as I possibly could, given the ability that I had at that particular time, so that

---

112 The painting was first used on the back cover of the dust jacket of Miss Rand's *For the New Intellectual* (New York: Random House, 1961).

what she herself conveyed would be in evidence in the portrait. And on the other hand, I was also learning how to paint and using the sitting as a vehicle for improving my artistic abilities. That was a long time ago; I was really just starting out.

Regarding your purpose, how did you work out the combination of her stance, the lighting, the clothing and so forth?

We discussed the clothing, and I remember in her apartment one evening she, in effect, modeled clothing for me, and we both agreed on the outfit that she wore in this particular painting, so the choice of clothing was largely hers, though I had some input. As far as the pose and the lighting, I attended to that, although at one point I had started a previous picture in which she was seated, and we had a discussion about that, and she decided that she wanted to stand and to face the viewer directly, so she had something to say about that. As far as the lighting was concerned, that was not a subject we discussed. I was dealing with one of the aspects of painting, which is to paint in a north-light studio, so the light came from the skylight facing the Empire State Building.

I remember doing one portrait of her in which I had chosen a front-view pose, and I turned her body slightly to the side, to impart a feeling of more action to the picture. She took issue with that. She felt that she should be depicted in a front view of her figure and a front view of her face, because in her mind that connoted that she was facing life squarely. And it was the psychological implications of things, involving even the pose, that she was interested in.

As a matter of fact, I got to a point where I was somewhat apprehensive in bringing up various things, because she was just totally a stickler for having a very clear understanding of precisely what it was one was saying. I remember her taking issue on occasion with various words that I used. I once used the term "a priori," and she halted me, and wanted to know what my context was. Apparently, it normally has a religious connotation. We just went from A to Z in terms of covering subjects that were of interest. She was a brilliant debater, and I was about twenty-three or twenty-four years old. I couldn't in any way keep up with the rapidity of her thoughts, except in the area of painting, and in that area, she was particularly keen on having a discussion and hearing my views.

What views did she want to know about?

Just spontaneous things that came up, having to do with the

mechanics of painting, and with the thought process of being an artist. Certainly, we discussed intuition and inspiration, which were not ingredients that I held any great store with, and she agreed with me. I felt that a great deal of painting was able to be figured out, and that was the premise on which I based my technique, and that was of particular interest to her.

I had a fascinating time talking to her during the sittings, and one of the things that occurred was that during the rest periods, we would have long conversations about the process of painting, and I believe that at that time she used our discussions as information that formed the basis of some of the ideas that she subsequently had on painting and on art. We would, in effect, paint for half an hour, and then talk for about an hour and a half. At a certain point, she had an esthetician, Mary Ann Rukavina [later, Mary Ann Sures], join her, and she would, in effect, sit in on the conversations that Ayn and I had and take notes. Then, often later that evening, either I would go to Ayn's apartment, or she'd come back over to my place, and we'd sit and talk for hours and, in effect, debate every aspect of painting. I was in a unique position in that I was able to articulate what I was doing, and the other side of the coin, of course, was that she had a steel-trap mind and questioned everything in the process. She wanted to know as much as she could about the working method of creating a painting.

Can you remember some of her questions?

We discussed Degas, whom she disliked, because his work was fuzzy, and she identified fuzzy painting with fuzzy thinking, which I didn't agree with at all. She felt that Salvador Dali, except for his subject matter, exemplified the kind of artist that she most admired, in that he painted—and I remember her remark—"as though we were in a world without dust."

Frankly, I became a bit disenchanted after having a number of conversations about art, because we just were not on the same wavelength when it came to painting. She did seem to me to feel that things had to be in some way connected to her philosophy, and in painting, it was an entirely different vocabulary, and we disagreed on the purpose of painting, in a number of respects.

What was your purpose in painting?

Simply self-expression: my own personal self-confrontation.

What was she like when you had these disagreements?

Many times they were amicable, but she was an extremely intense person. She defended her views vehemently. She took everything very, very seriously, which was very much to my liking. But it was all very serious. Not hostile or rude, but she didn't mince words at all. If she disagreed and thought you were wrong in some respect, she clearly made it evident. Consequently, I sometimes had to watch what I said or be very much more careful in how I spoke, because she was attentive to every nuance, many of which escaped me until she pointed out various errors of my ways.

What is your opinion of your portrait?

I like the portrait, and I particularly like it because it's of Ayn. I would love to have had another opportunity to paint her. I'm proud of the picture.

How did your relationship develop after this?

I became quite friendly with Frank and Ayn, and the various people that they were involved with.

I was involved with both Frank and Ayn for about three or four years, and I began to do any number of corporate commissions, heads of large companies, such as IBM and DuPont. She was particularly keen on finding out if the men that I was painting were anything like the standards that she had set in *Atlas Shrugged*.

Why did your relationship with Miss Rand end?

It just petered out. I moved up to 67th Street, and we just didn't get together. I talked to her on the phone once or twice. That was about it. I still subscribe to the philosophy she proposed, and I admire very much the books that she's written and the point of view that she has, and I still hold to those views.

I think she was extraordinarily brilliant, and I am indebted to her for formulating the ideas that she presented in her philosophy. She made much more clear things that I believe in, and she put it into brilliant form. She was a very strong person, and easily one of the most memorable people that I have ever met, if not the most memorable. I am very pleased to have had the opportunity to know her.

Ilona Royce Smithkin

Ilona Royce Smithkin is an artist who painted Miss Rand's portrait and was friends with Ayn Rand and Frank O'Connor for many years. She was born in Poland and studied art at the Reimannschule in Berlin and the Royal Academy of Art in Antwerp.

Interview dates: April 15, 1998, and April 15, 1999

Scott McConnell: *How did you meet Ayn Rand?*

Ilona Royce Smithkin: Through Frank O'Connor, whom I met at the Art Student's League in New York. I gave Frank some lessons in oil painting in the late 1950s. I had a party at my house and Frank said, "This is a party with people who my wife would really like." I said, "Why don't you bring her. What does your wife do?" He said, "Oh, she's a novelist." I said, "What has she written?" He said, "Oh, you might not even know. She wrote *The Fountainhead.*" I got very excited because I was just reading *The Fountainhead.* I said, "What do you mean not know! I'd love to meet her."

Tell me about giving lessons to Mr. O'Connor.

At the Art Student's League he watched me painting and then approached me. He said, "I really think I want to speed up my learning. Would you consider teaching me?" We made an appointment and he started to work with me.

What was your first impression of Ayn Rand?

I was very impressed with her. I was very much in awe and she came through as sort of a mysterious person. She wasn't like everyone else. She dressed very interestingly and very dramatically; so did Frank. Her way was definite and absolute. For me, who at that time was still not sure of myself—I didn't know exactly who I was and where I was going—it was tremendously impressive to find someone who had found themselves, had so much knowledge, gave out so many rays of electricity. She was a personality definitely very different from anyone else.

What was your first reaction to Frank O'Connor?

Oh, he was very jolly. He had a twinkle in his eye, and a sense of humor. He was easy to be with. Usually what we did after the lessons were over, he would say, "Come on, let's get a drink at the Russian

Tea Room and relax." So we would have an hour or two, and we really would talk, talk, talk about this and that. It was delightful because he was such a charming man. He was a man who spoke his mind but he did it gently. He saw always the amusing side of life.

He never would volunteer who or what he was himself. Many people didn't even know that Ayn Rand was his wife. Which was very good, I thought, because otherwise he would be in her shadow. But he was himself a personality. He was slim and tall and elegant. I remember one thing: before anybody else wore a cape he had a cashmere navy blue cape. And before any one of the men wore these shoulder strapped bags, almost like a camera case, he would wear that. He was always dressed very chic, very elegant without overdoing it.

Tell me about teaching Frank O'Connor.

I believe he had just started painting, and he was very talented. He caught on fast and he had a good sense of composition and a good sense of color. He was always ready to learn. He was very open.

What exactly did you teach him?

Everything from the beginning—basics. Some drawing, with composition, and explaining why it's done that way. I discussed how you get such and such an effect—or if you spoil something, how you can fix it.

For how long did you teach him?

Maybe half or three-quarters of a year, because he didn't need much. I asked him in the beginning, "Why do you want to come? You are good." He said, "Yes, but this will speed it up." The lessons were two or three times each week. I had a studio next to the Russian Tea Room, down from Carnegie Hall on 57th Street, and he would come up to my place to study.

Regarding painting, what was Mr. O'Connor's style then?

Are you familiar with the furniture they had in their home? Very modern. He painted like that. He left the details out and painted more in large masses.

What was Mr. O'Connor's attitude to painting?

He was very enthusiastic and hungry for knowledge. When it didn't come out right, it was a challenge for him. He would not get angry like other people, or annoyed. He took everything with a great sense of humor. It was almost all as a game.

Did he have his own philosophy of art?

No. When you speak about philosophy, Frank was not someone who wanted to delve into philosophy. He did something because he enjoyed it and that was his philosophy. It was something which gave him something, and he felt that if he's happy when he comes home, she's happy too.

He was—not the opposite of Ayn but very different. Where she would go deep into every action—why did you do that, how did you do that, what is the purpose of it—he would never question the thing. If he enjoyed something that came along—"Great, let's do it."

What did Miss Rand say about Mr. O'Connor's painting?

She loved his work; she never criticized it. She was very proud of it.

What did she love about it?

Because he did it, he created it, and he produced it without ever having done it before—it was a creative process.

Was there any one specific aspect she liked, like the sense of life or the style?

No, she just accepted him absolutely and completely. I've rarely seen anyone so taken with their partner. He could do no wrong. She was admiring his work constantly and encouraging him. There was never a criticism as long as I know.

In our archives are some sketches you did. One was a drawing of Mr. O'Connor.

It was in sanguine Conté pencil. I did his portrait before I did Ayn's. I only remember we became friends, and we got to talking, and he said, "You know, it would be nice if you could make a drawing of me. Would you think about it?" I said, "Of course." We first started sort of playfully, and then I drew him. Then some time elapsed and Ayn came to me and said, "I like your style, that you leave half out, and yet it represents a person." Then she commissioned me to do her portrait.

What were you trying to capture in Mr. O'Connor?

All the things I liked. He had a serious face, and yet at any moment, breaking out in a smile. He was bright and cheery. He was one of the most easy people to be with.

Your drawing focuses on one side of his face. Why?

Because I am doing my portraits to bring attention to certain features, and then the rest is up to the viewer's imagination. If you tie it down too much, it becomes like glued together because nobody can represent more than a moment in a drawing. When you speak with a person, their features, everything moves; everything changes every second. Nobody's all one thing, or another; and I want to have movement in it, that's one part of it; and you capture the movement by giving enough freedom to the drawing to show that.

Do you remember Mr. O'Connor's reaction to his portrait?

He loved it. He was fascinated with it. He was into drawing, and he found that this medium interested him. He had not seen something like that; I do my portraits in a very special way.

Exactly how did you come to do Miss Rand's portrait?

Ayn Rand had seen my work before and she liked it. One day she called up and she said, "I would like you to do my portrait, which I may use for my books, if I like it. You say a minimum and express a maximum. I don't like all those fully filled out things, but you use limited lines and I like that, and I want that. I would like to commission you." Then, we set a date and she came to my studio.

You referred to yourself as doing impressionistic painting. What did you mean?

It's not precise. It's your impression of what you see. Also the technique is the interrupted line. It's not one color being pulled into the other; you get more sparkle in it because it's interrupted.

I'm looking at your portrait of Miss Rand now, and it doesn't look impressionistic to me. It looks very clear and fine.

Let me explain something. When you do a portrait—my way of doing impressionism—when you see it you will see that many of the colorations—it's done in oil by the way—but it looks like a pastel. You will see that you have many colors in order to make a shadow, not just one color. That is impressionism.

Tell me about doing the portrait.

Before I started, she said, "What if I don't like it?" I replied that if you don't like it, you don't take it and you don't pay for it. If I don't like it, I tear it up. She said, "That's fair enough."

When she posed for me, before we started, she said to me, "There are certain things I don't like and certain things I do like [physically] about me." And she proceeded to tell me them, and I stopped her and said: "Please forgive me but my first portrait has to come from me. I understand your concern, but if this isn't right it doesn't matter. I will make another one and you can tell me all the things, but my first one has to come completely unprejudiced out of my guts." She said, "Fair enough." She said one thing that surprised me: "By the way, many people—even famous people—have failed, so don't feel too bad if it doesn't come out right." She meant to be kind, but it rattled me.

I said, "Let's go to it."

Did you go through a process of really knowing her before you could capture her on the canvas?

I had seen her and spoken to her and we were kind of friendly at the time. That didn't influence me. We look at people, and you don't even know if they have blue eyes or dark ones—you don't know what their features are because they're friends. You think of what you talk about and not their features. I hadn't studied her before I sat down. She became very focused when I started the portrait. I do my portraits not only of the surface but also the personality: what they think, what they feel—I put myself in their place.

That must be very difficult.

This is why this portrait is so strong—because that's exactly, to this day, how I saw her. She was a very strong woman in her yes and no. If she didn't like something, nothing could make her. If she liked something, that was it. She was very decided. There was no wishy-washiness about her. She was really an extraordinary woman. We did the painting in one session.

So you didn't draw it first, you just started painting it?

I painted it immediately.

What did she do as you were painting her?

Occasionally we would talk about this and that, and she would ask sometimes questions about what I was doing. I would talk to her about what I felt about her—her directness, her strength. Whatever it is that I see at the moment comes out of my mouth as I'm painting.

What was her reaction when she first saw the portrait?

When I finished she got up and looked at it and took my shoulder. She hugged me and said, "This is exactly how I feel about myself."

Did she elaborate?

Yes. She said, "I like the eyes—this is how I feel, this is me." One little thing: she said, "I want you to eliminate this one little edge of my lip because I don't like sentimentality. And this is more like me without it." I changed that one little thing on her lip, and she said, "That's exactly how I want it."

Did she say what she saw in herself in your portrait?

She liked the strength in it; she liked the directness and the very strength in the eyes—the almost hypnotic strength. All you saw when you first met her was her eyes.

Do you have any comments on your painting techniques for her portrait?

Technique has very little to do with it except having the knowledge of a person who is a very, very intense, strong human being, who has faith and great beliefs, and being able to express that—that is the art in it. Not just to do a portrait because you could just have a photograph. You want to really show the personality of the person. That is, I think, what I accomplished—I know even now, after all these years when I look at it, I feel I did a good job.

I believe there was a problem when the portrait was used on Miss Rand's books?

Afterwards the portrait was on *The Virtue of Selfishness.* Also it was on *Anthem* and many of her other books. What they did is put the portrait on one of the front covers and they forgot to include credits, so I called Ayn and I told her, "You know, the portrait should include my signature." She was also very upset about it, she said, "No, that's very unfair," and she called the publisher. They apologized and afterwards put it on the back cover, [with the credit] "Portrait of Ayn Rand, by Ilona RS."

Unfortunately, at that time I was very young and very

inexperienced, because I certainly could have gotten royalties from the publishing, but I gave Ayn full rights to do anything she wanted to do with the portrait. A year later she telephoned me and said, "You know, Ilona, you signed your rights away." I said, "Yes." She said, "I think it's only fair to give you some percentage, because I found a firm to reproduce the portrait." She sent me a contract guaranteeing the percentage, which was a nice gesture of hers.

Do you have any dedications from Miss Rand?

When a friend of mine found out that I had painted Ayn Rand he became very excited and asked me if it was possible to get some books signed by her. I said, "Of course." So I called—I was a little pressed for time because I was in between travels—I said, "Could I send a friend of mine to have it signed?" She said, "No, I will be happy to sign anything you bring me, but you have to come yourself." She insisted on that. And when she did sign it she did a very interesting thing. She put little sun rays around her name. I asked her why she did that and she said that this way it cannot be imitated.

Do you have any closing comments about Ayn Rand or Frank O'Connor?

He was a very thoughtful person, really a lovely person. I must say she had good taste in marrying him. They were an exceptional couple, and I think they had a very, very positive, good relationship. She was very much in love and devoted to him. They were both individuals in their own right. For a person of her strength, she was as soft as a pussycat when she was with him.

1960s

Judy Berliner

Judy Berliner (née Block) interviewed Miss Rand at the University of Michigan in 1961 for her student newspaper. She is now a professor at the UCLA School of Medicine.

Interview date: December 14, 1999

Scott McConnell: *When did you first meet Ayn Rand?*

Judy Berliner: When she came to speak at the University of Michigan in 1961; it was one of her earliest talks. I was a reporter for the *Michigan Daily*, the college newspaper, and was one of three people the paper sent to interview her. She was at Michigan to give a talk called "The Esthetic Vacuum of Our Age."[113]

The interview was before the speech and was the main time that I had any real time with her. When I walked into that room where she and Frank O'Connor were, the first thing that struck me was that Frank O'Connor looked just like John Galt. It was absolutely overwhelming that he was the image of the description of John Galt. So my mouth almost fell open when I looked at him. He had blond hair that was brushed back like Galt's, high cheekbones just like Galt, and he had blue eyes. The pictures you see of him when he's older don't do justice to how he looked. He really looked almost like a god. It was just amazing.

For the interview, I kind of weaseled my way into being one of the interviewers, because I wasn't a major reporter for the paper, so the two main interviewers got to ask most of the questions. I only got to ask very little, but I was embarrassed at what they asked. They were highly antagonistic. I thought they should have been respectful, but they weren't.

They asked a lot of questions on two subjects. The first one was: her philosophy is leaving out the little people, and what's going to happen to people who are down on their luck? How are they ever going to achieve the kind of things you expect? She had very good answers for all that. And in that whole conversation, she never

---

113 The talk was May 14, 1961. The newspaper story was published May 16.

acted antagonistic. *They* acted antagonistic. She just gave very nice, benevolent answers. She acted like somebody's grandmother. She's this sweet little lady, sitting there, answering questions very nicely. She brought up Steven Mallory and said that she had mentioned people that had those kind of problems, but that wasn't going to dominate the book. They said that in *Atlas*, it looked like only the smartest people would have a place in her ideal society, and somebody like Eddie Willers wouldn't. She said that Eddie Willers was in the book to illustrate a number of things, and it didn't at all imply what they thought. Then they brought up questions like "How can a person who works on the assembly line ever achieve the kind of things you're writing about?" She said that nobody wants to stay on the assembly line, so we're talking about what they become after that, and they become people like Mike Donnigan. Then they would bring up people with diminishing levels of capacity, and she just said that if they work to their highest capacity, it doesn't matter what they do, that's the kind of thing that people should try to achieve, and so she explained that to them in this very patient kind of fashion.

Then they brought up a lot of modern-art-related issues, such as a lot of people like modern art, and so "You're dictating tastes when you say that modern art is not any good." This was the height of the modern-art movement. She started talking about what did they think people got out of modern art, like "Look at this painting or sculpture; what do you think they feel?" These reporters couldn't come up with anything, except they have a feeling about the world. She argued that you wanted to get more than that out of art, and she explained that to them.

During all of this questioning, Frank O'Connor went out to get some tea or something for the O'Connors' guests in the other room of the suite. I walked out and said to him, "This is embarrassing. These people haven't read the books, so they don't remember Steven Mallory, and they don't really understand what's going on. She granted this interview thinking that she'd be getting a nice, friendly interview, and instead she's being torn apart by these two reporters." He replied, "Well now, they'll find out what's true, won't they." He also said, "You don't need to worry about it; she can take care of herself," or something along those lines.

I asked Miss Rand a few things, which were much more specific than the other interviewers. I asked her why Cameron was an alcoholic. At the time, I seemed to think that was a strange thing to happen to him; how he could have been so successful when he was an alcoholic, and why that had to be such a major element of his personality. It didn't seem like somebody like that could become a great architect. She said that he became an alcoholic after he was a great architect, and that's what people would assume.

Did she say why he descended into alcoholism?

She did. I think what she said was just that there was no way out, and so that's the way he took.

I asked her what evidence she had that people couldn't get excited about modern art and don't really get a lot out of it, and she said, "You don't necessarily need that sort of evidence. You can tell from the content that there would be no way." She gave me a nice, somewhat detailed answer to that question.

Describe her during the interview.

Very animated. She was very involved in any question. She was being benevolent, and she wasn't being negative to the people, but she was just very involved in what she was saying. She always looked directly at the person, and she would give examples from her books. She gestured a lot, and her face moved around a lot. That's what I mean by animated.

How did the interview finish, and how was she at the end?

I was dressed at this interview in my usual, at the time, semi-beatnik clothing. I wore very minimalist kinds of clothes; I would wear a skirt and sweater, and usually no socks, just flat shoes. And I had long hair, sometimes back in a French roll. During the interview I told her that I admired her books and I thought they were wonderful, so as we were walking out, she said to me, "Do you consciously dress like Kira?" I said, "No." I had read *We the Living*, but I said, definitely no, this is just the style these days," and she just said, "Oh."

She said, "Thank you very much," for praising her books, and she was smiling and said, "It's nice to have someone here who's read my books and admires them." I think I told her that I was sorry there hadn't been more positive questions in the interview, and she said, "No, I enjoyed it."

How did she treat you?

Very benevolently. She treated everybody very benevolently

at this interview and at the other places I've seen her, for example, Ford Hall Forum. She always acted really, really nice to the public that were asking questions. The rest of us would say, "How does she do it? How can she take these questions that are just so stupid, and not tell the questioner, 'This is dumb; you don't know what you're talking about,' but she always could take it, and get something out of the answers.

Any other memories of Mr. O'Connor from that visit?

Miss Rand obviously wanted him to be there, and he sat right next to her during the interview, and every time she gave an answer that she thought was particularly good, she'd say, "What do you think, Frank?" and he just smiled, but he didn't say anything; he just looked at her, and smiled. I remember him being very supportive. And his making that comment to me in the other room indicated he had a lot of wisdom.

I came early to the talk and there was Frank O'Connor's sister and her husband and two girls, around twelve years old. They were all tall and very sort of stately-looking; they definitely looked like they were substantial, confident people.

Seeing them in the restroom, I asked them what it was like to have Ayn Rand as a relative, and they said, "Oh, always exciting." Something like "Oh, hey, and she was fun to have at family dinners." So I gathered she must have had a few things to say at those family dinners. They said they were very proud of her, and that's why they came up to Ann Arbor from Lorain to see her speak. They really wanted to see what she had to say, and they were positive, like they didn't disagree with her at all. And they said something like "She talks a lot, a lot more than Frank." They seemed very happy that he'd married her. After the talk was over, I saw them again, and they said that they were surprised that she could handle a lot of booing and adverse questioning.

During Miss Rand's talk, Frank O'Connor was sitting up in the front. Afterwards she was surrounded by people asking questions, and he was kind of watching out because this was an antagonistic event. When she came out onto the stage, there were about equal boos and cheers. Maybe a lot more boos.

She didn't seem to be the least surprised at all the boos. Maybe she got them at the previous talk she'd given,[114] but I was surprised. Michigan was one of the first major talks she gave, so she hadn't had a

---

114 The first of her talks at Yale, February 17, 1960.

lot of experience, but she had received a lot of objections by then to her books, from critics and the media, so I guess she kind of expected that this might happen.

How many people were in the audience?

It was a huge auditorium and it was practically full. At least four or five hundred people.

There were a lot of antagonistic questions and a lot of questions about modern art. There were sculptors there who were objecting to what she was saying, and almost everybody who asked questions was opposed to her philosophy. Almost nobody who asked questions had anything that positive to say.

Did it stay negative?

During her talk, they stopped booing and she started getting applause, and getting a lot of reactions that showed that were listening and understood what she was saying. She did swing the audience around, definitely. Not to great cheers, but to understanding somewhat.

Let's now move onto Ford Hall Forum. After 1961 you met Mike Berliner, who was working on his PhD in Boston, and you married and moved there.

We lived in Boston from 1964 to '70. We went to Ford Hall Forum every year for those years. And we went to the last Ford Hall Forum that she spoke at, when we were living in Los Angeles. We may have come another time, but every time that we went, we went afterwards to this room where she would meet with people.

How come you were invited?

Because we knew Harry Binswanger and Allan Gotthelf, and they got invited. Also, Mike was one of the few Objectivists in a philosophy graduate program.

One thing I remember about the receptions, one of the things that surprised me, was that she never seemed tired. She had just been on stage for two hours, and then gotten a lot of difficult questions. But at the reception, she liked to discuss alternative answers to the questions she'd gotten from the audience. Also, things she wished had been asked. She was still talking about the questions. That's what impressed me, that she would do that. Mainly people asked things related to the questions that she answered, and why she answered them the way she did.

Her interaction with Judge Lurie, the moderator, was really nice. He was very protective of her, in the sense of, if people got too antagonistic, he'd stop them. She had a very nice kind of rapport with him.

What about the Q&As at the Ford Hall Forum? Were they friendly or antagonistic?

I would say that, in those earlier years, most of the people were antagonistic, but I know Harry asked a lot of questions. And every time he said something, of course that was a positive. And there were other people too, who were Objectivists, and came up and asked things, and kind of balanced the negative people. As the years went on there were increasingly more Objectivists asking questions.

When was the last time you saw Ayn Rand?

At the last Ford Hall Forum in 1981,[115] where she gave the talk "The Age of Mediocrity."

Had she changed?

Seemed the same to me. There were a lot more positive Objectivist questions then. I seem to recall the crowd maybe wasn't quite as big as it had been, earlier, but there were still a lot of people there.

There was one incident that tells you a lot about how she viewed herself. Mike and I had traveled to Boston from Los Angeles to attend the lecture. When she spotted us in the lobby of the Westin Hotel, she said, in a very surprised voice, something like "What are you two doing here?" As if it never entered her mind that we would come all the way from California just to hear her give a talk. That's always meant to me that she didn't think of herself as a "star."

---

115 Ayn Rand's last appearance at the Ford Hall Forum was April 26, 1981.

Frances Smith

Frances Smith was executive director, president and chairman of the board of the Ford Hall Forum, in Boston, where Ayn Rand spoke almost every year from 1961 to 1981. The stated purpose of the Forum is "to foster an informed and effective citizenry and to promote freedom of speech through the public presentation of lectures, debates and discussions."[116] Mrs. Smith died in 2001.

Interview date: June 4, 1999

Scott McConnell: *What is the Ford Hall Forum?*

Frances Smith: It's the oldest continuous forum in the country that has an open question period. The Forum started in 1908.

What was your position at the Forum?

I had an interesting career at the Forum. I started out when I was in high school when my husband-to-be wanted to hear the speeches, so that's what we did for entertainment. It was an education hearing all those different people speak. I came up through the ranks, and I ended up being executive director for about forty years, then president and then chairman of the board, elected for life, and now I am retired.

Do you know why Miss Rand was first asked to speak at the Forum in 1961?

Yes. The program committee at the time found that as we looked over the programs for a number of years that we were really overloading the programs with left-wing people giving talks, and we felt that it wasn't a good, balanced program, which is what we wanted to present. So the committee sought somebody who was of a more conservative nature who would be interesting enough to draw an audience, and that's why we asked her.

What was the general audience reaction to Ayn Rand?

She seemed to have brought her own audience, which is part of what was unusual. People came from all over the world to hear her. They came from Africa, from the Bahamas, from all parts of the United States, so the audience was not necessarily the usual audience, but there

---

116 Taken from the 2009 Ford Hall Forum Web site: www.fordhallforum.org.

were enough people from the usual audience that peppered her with questions that were very broad in nature.

How large would an audience be?

The auditorium seated 1,300, and we would have to turn people away. For those who couldn't get seats, we would very often take a room downstairs in the YMCA and march them over to the auditorium to hear her on a loudspeaker. That room would be filled with about five hundred more people.

How were the dates and the topics for her speeches selected?

She selected them. A suggestion was made—do you want to speak on such a date—and maybe we gave her two alternatives. They were always on a Sunday night. The subjects were never approved by us. Whatever she chose to speak about, we accepted.

Can you describe Ayn Rand giving a speech?

I was very young, and I was impressed by the fact that she always wore jet black. She never wore a colored dress in all the years I knew her. I was fascinated. She was a small woman, but she seemed like a very powerful figure up there.

During the speech and the Q&A, everybody was very respectful. There were never any problems with people in the audience because they had a different opinion to hers. And there were plenty of people who did have a different opinion.

How did she take audience criticism?

She handled herself very, very well.

How was she during the question-and-answer period?

She was very good about it. She was very calm, very controlled, and it never presented a problem. I do remember as a young woman one speech that I was impressed by. She was the first speaker I ever heard speak in public being pro-abortion. I remember her saying things like "It's your body, and you're entitled to do what you want with your body."

Did you talk to Miss Rand about this issue?

No. I had very few private conversations with her. She was a very private person, and there was no time. Before her lecture she would come and talk to Leonard Peikoff and one or two others of her followers, in what we called "the Green Room"; then she would talk to the moderator if she wanted to add any information to what he already had about her. Then they would go out onto the stage. Once the meeting was over, she left with an entourage, and very often they would have a private party.

Did Miss Rand ever talk to you about your work?

The only thing she talked about was how wonderful it was that I was willing to continue along the same lines: having broad sections of the community-at-large speak at the Forum. She did praise the Forum to me very often, because she thought it was wonderful that we continued to invite her to speak. By the way, I always sat with her husband, at the back of the auditorium.

Why at the back?

It was elevated. The later auditorium we used was mostly used for music performances, and so the back of the auditorium was elevated, and that's where he sat, because you could see best. Miss Rand would often talk about him very, very kindly. She would say how devoted he was.

Who was Judge Lurie?

Judge Ruben Lurie was the president of the Ford Hall Forum at the time when she first came to the Forum, and he acted as the first moderator. It was after he became a little older, and found it difficult to do the moderation, that he had my son Jeff do it. Judge Lurie was a Republican, but he wasn't a conservative Republican by any means. He was quite liberal in his thinking, and he used to tell me that whenever they were alone, Miss Rand tried to convert him to Objectivism. He said she didn't succeed.

Did he enjoy that?

Yes. He laughed. He thought it was funny that she would try.

How would you describe her relationship with Judge Lurie?

He was very small, and she was small, and the two of them were sort of sparring, in a sense.

From the letters between them that we have in the Ayn Rand Archives, they seem to have had a warmth and respect for each other.

That's what I mean by saying that he was very, very concerned about doing a good job for her, but he wasn't going to be talked into becoming an Objectivist.

I have a note here that in 1971 at the Forum, there was a Century of Service dinner for Judge Lurie and Louis Smith.

Right. We were always looking for ways in which to commemorate people who were involved with the Forum for a long time, and certainly nobody got any money for being involved in the way they were in giving of themselves and their time. Judge Lurie and Lou Smith together had served a hundred years, and that's an excuse to run a dinner. I think I was chair of the dinner. We called it a "Century of Service" dinner, because it covered their century of service to the Forum.

What other interactions did you have with her?

At one point, when I was executive director or president of the Forum, we needed some money desperately. So I asked her if she'd be willing to come to a luncheon where she would be the guest of honor.[117] She agreed to do it. She said she wouldn't talk at the luncheon; she would only appear. We ran the luncheon for her on the Sunday prior to that evening's meeting at the Forum. We had an overflow crowd. Once we let out the word that she was going to be there, just everybody wanted to come. We had to stop selling tickets. During the luncheon, any number of people in the audience came up and brought her presents, some of them quite valuable: jewelry and things of that nature. She didn't take a single item. I was sitting beside her, so I could see. She took praise, when people said nice things to her, but she wouldn't take anything of a material nature.

What did she say to them?

She said, "No, I don't do this." I'm not sure I'm quoting her, but she was very gracious, and she wouldn't take anything, which I thought was a very interesting aspect of her life.

She did the appearance for free, to support the Forum?

That is right; and then she went to rest for a while, and she came and spoke, as usual, as if nothing had ever happened, but it had been a

---

117 The luncheon was held on April 10, 1977.

momentous occasion in the life of the Forum.

Was there an auction of one of Miss Rand's manuscripts?

Oh yes. We always needed money. We didn't pay her to speak, but we were paying many of our speakers, so we needed funds for that or for their travel and other expenses—whatever was involved in their staying here. We decided we needed to have some "gimmick" in order to get people to come, so we decided to auction off letters from famous people who had spoken at the Forum, and Ayn Rand was one of them. She gave us the speech in which she had made corrections in longhand.

What happened?

We let people know that we were going to do that, and a large number of people came. I can't tell you the exact figure, but more than would normally have come to an auction dinner that we ran. I believe we got $10,000 for her speech. There were a few people bidding for it. The rest of the items sold for reasonable amounts of money. We sold them all, and we sold pictures of some of the speakers. We sold everything in sight in order to raise some money.

Miss Rand's auction item was the biggest seller?

That is right. It was because all the notations on the typed speech were in her handwriting.

Iris Bell

Iris Bell was married to a Nathaniel Branden Institute (NBI)[118] tape-lecture representative.

Interview dates: May 11 and June 10, 1999

Scott McConnell: *How did you first meet Ayn Rand?*

Iris Bell: My then husband Ed Nash[119] was an NBI representative. In late 1962 he was being invited to Ayn Rand inner-circle events. We were invited to a New Year's party at the Blumenthals', and Ayn Rand was there.

In mid-1962, when Ed told the Brandens he was being transferred to Chicago, they asked him to run the NBI lectures there.

Tell me about the McCormick Place speech by Miss Rand in 1963.

Ed Nash came up with the idea. It was a speech that Ayn had given someplace else.[120] He talked to Ayn and Nathan about it. They agreed to it, and I took about two months off work. We rented a little office in Chicago and I managed the whole thing—designed the advertising material, stuffed the envelopes, put the labels and the stamps on them, manned the telephones and took care of all the sales.

We made a trip to New York a bit before she was to speak. We printed some very large posters promoting her speech, the size that people paste on empty buildings and hired people to do that. While I was designing them, I said to Ed that we should check with Ayn, that she should have a chance to okay them. He said no, he knew what we were doing was right, and she had given him an okay. We went to her apartment and unrolled this enormous poster and showed her that and the show cards we had done, all printed in yellow-orange, and big black type and "Rand" going the whole width, as large as it could be on these posters. When she saw it, she was shocked, and she said, "Is this fait accompli? It shouldn't be like this." Ed told her that I had said he should check with her, and she told him that next time he should listen

---

118 The Nathaniel Branden Institute opened in 1962, offering live and taped lecture courses and publishing essays on Objectivism and its application to psychology, art, economics and other areas. It closed in 1968.

119 Ed Nash was a direct marketing executive.

120 The talk was "America's Persecuted Minority: Big Business," first given at Ford Hall Forum on December 17, 1961.

to me, whatever I say.

Why did Ayn Rand object to the designs?

Because she was uncomfortable seeing her name so large. Ed said that the most important element that will attract people should be the largest.

What else did you learn working with Miss Rand?

She said something during the planning process that I've used many times since. At one point, Ed Nash was saying we don't have to put something into writing. She said, no, she believed in making a contract as if one of the parties is going to walk out the door and get hit by a truck, and you want to have everything in writing.

When she and Frank came to Chicago for the lecture, Ed and I picked them up at the airport and took them to the hotel. We were all up in the room and one of the NBI students—a high school girl who came to the tape series—showed up, and she had brought two dozen long-stem roses. Ayn said to her, "This is impertinent." It was very clear that this was inappropriate, but thank you anyway, but you shouldn't do things like this. Then she gave them to Frank and he fanned them out in a vase.

What was the girl's reaction?

At first the girl was kind of frightened and hurt, but in the end Ayn had made it okay.

Tell me about the speech that evening.

There was a bomb scare. I think Ayn was already speaking, and Ed Nash and I, and probably Ruby and Harry Newman—who were helping us—stood around and talked about the scare. We called Nathan out and decided not to do anything. We took it as just a bomb scare and we weren't going to empty the hall. And everything was fine.

I'm pretty sure we sold out—it was one of the large halls in McCormick Place.[121]

What was the audience reaction to the speech?

It was lovely. They were all fans. I don't have the sense that there was anyone in that hall that wasn't a fan.

---

121 The *Chicago Tribune* cited 2,500 in the audience.

Tell me about the photographs that were taken there.

My father took them. He was a professional photographer and used available light—so they were very soft. One picture is on the stage, and I assume it's before it began. I'm there with Ed, and Ayn is wearing her dress with the cape back.

The other picture is of the book table with Ruby Newman, and it looks like a fan talking to Ayn. Frank is there and Barbara and Nathan, and a friend of mine who was working for Ed Nash, Bob Barrons.

Tell me about the art work you did for The Objectivist. *Did you do the ads and the record covers?*

Yes. In 1965 I designed the NBI Communications logo. That's the logo on the record covers.

The Objectivist—the one with the green-blue cover and the three lines—that I designed, but Miss Rand did what's called the "copy-writer's rough." She wanted the three lines down the left side of the page. She chose the color, which I took to be the color of Rearden Metal, green-blue. Before I presented the layout to her, she had picked a typeface. I had planned a little presentation because the typeface she had chosen I considered ugly. I thought if I gave her some of the history of the typeface perhaps she wouldn't see it in the same light as she did when she chose it, because it was that Bauhaus International Style developed in Germany in the 1930s. The typeface she had chosen came out of that school of design, and there are other sans serif faces that come out of the Greek tradition of letters. I mentioned the Bauhaus group and she stopped me immediately. It was very sweet but she wasn't listening to what I was saying, and she said, "Oh, so many people think I like this German group but I really don't like them at all."

It never occurred to me that she liked them—I knew she didn't like them. She was assuming I was saying the opposite of what I was saying. If she had been listening to me, she would have understood that I was saying that I didn't think she would want that typeface. Because I couldn't get through to her about the font, she ended up using the Bauhaus font.

Did you have any other interesting conversations with Ayn Rand?

For ourselves, Ed had the idea of selling bumper stickers that said, "Who Is John Galt?" I designed that when I was living in Los Angeles. I gave her one, and she said she didn't like that. And this had been publicly stated policy for several years. She felt that it was kind of stealing her

ideas, making money off of something she created. I said there are people
living in small towns, going to college, who have no way of knowing
if there is anyone else in their area interested in the same ideas. If they
have this bumper sticker people actually meet other people this way. She
thought this was fine and then it was okay with her that we did it.

How did she treat you?

Very nicely. I went to the NBI ball, April 16, 1965, and spent a
lot of time shopping for a dress. I didn't like anything until I had my
mother sew something and it had a beautiful full skirt, dotted Swiss,
that I loved, and wide cummerbund. When I got to the ball there were
probably one hundred, two hundred people. All of the women were
wearing slinky dresses, a lot of them with just one shoulder—which is
from *The Fountainhead*, I guess—maybe *Atlas*. No one commented
on my dress. Here I was at an Objectivist function and still didn't fit
in. The only one who said something about my dress was Ayn Rand.
I went over to say hello to her, and she told me that she thought I was
lovely and I looked like a ballerina. It was so nice.

When Ed and I moved to Los Angeles, it was because he was
offered the vice presidency of Capitol Records Club. One of the things
he did there was create a very special record club for people who liked
classical music. For that, I designed a hardcover magazine that came
out every two months. It had a black cover with a very dramatic version
of the featured composer's signature. Ed hired Bob Barrons—a writer
and editor—to hire writers to do the articles he didn't write in this
hardcover magazine. We showed a copy of the first issue to Miss Rand
during a question-and-answer period in one of the lectures in New York.
She glanced through it, looked at the headlines, read a paragraph or so,
and she was very touched by it. She said, "I feel as if I'm not fighting
alone." So we called Bob Barrons over and let her compliment him. She
told him that she really appreciated what he was doing. I thought her
compliment was out of proportion.

After Ed and I were divorced, she knew who I was—I wasn't
just Ed Nash's wife, I was a person in myself. One thing I found after
my divorce from Ed was that there were a lot of people, who were
restaurant owners or people I had met at parties, to whom I was Ed
Nash's wife—they had no idea who I was if I showed up without him.
But she did and so did Frank, which was very nice.

What did she appreciate so much about the magazine?

I think seeing an Objectivist approach to the arts—fine arts, painting and music, being discussed in the series of articles about composers. One of them was Rachmaninoff, and Bob Barrons wrote Rachmaninoff's biography. Looking at the same original research you could conclude either that he had psychological problems or that he was a hero who wasn't understood—so the latter was what Bob did. We did three issues, and we sent them all on to her with the records.

Here's another story that tells you something about her. When Nathan's two nephews stayed with him for a few months and I went to a party at the Blumenthals', we were standing in line at a buffet, and the older boy—Johnny, I think—was standing beside Miss Rand. She was talking to him about his interests and things he cared about. He said he had psychological problems and would have to go into therapy. She asked him why, and he said he loved the music of Beethoven, and he had heard her say that if you like Beethoven there was something wrong. She said, "Oh, don't worry about that. We know so little—just enjoy it." He was quite relieved.

I believe you made holiday ornaments for Miss Rand and
Mr. O'Connor?

Yes. They were Christmas ornaments, and it started when I moved to New York. They were all very original things, different materials I would discover and put together. I would also create ornate gift boxes, and the boxes had almost as much thought going into them as the ornament inside.

She liked these Christmas ornaments that I gave her each year. Oh, she always enjoyed them. If she saw me she would tell me how beautiful and unusual they were or have Joan Blumenthal tell me. Or later she would ask Barbara Weiss to let me know she was enjoying them.

One year Joan told me that she had visited Ayn and the box was unopened on her coffee table. She commented to Ayn about it, and Ayn said, "Yes, isn't that wonderful? This year Iris created something that looks like a candle made out of paper." Joan argued with her for quite some time that that was just the wrapping, that the ornament was inside. Finally Ayn said okay, I'll let you open it as long as you promise there's something really inside there.

Mickey Spillane

Mickey Spillane was a best-selling writer of detective fiction and one of Ayn Rand's favorite writers. He and Miss Rand became friends in the 1960s. Mr. Spillane died in 2006.

Interview date: March 8, 2002

Scott McConnell: *When I mention the name Ayn Rand, what comes to mind?*

Mickey Spillane: We were friends. It's probably kind of hard for you to picture, but we were friends. Not only was I a fan of what she was doing, but I was a fan of hers personally. But what surprised me was she initiated our meeting, because I never would have thought that she would enjoy the kind of things I was writing. But she did. And she said she always enjoyed reading the work of Mickey Spillane because I was never gray. It was either black or white.

Anyway, she wanted to have lunch with me, and our publisher [New American Library] arranged for us to have lunch in a very fancy Belgian restaurant in New York City in September 1961. It was so hoity-toity that they only stayed open for a couple of hours a day, and they had a very high-class group of waiters—very intellectual. Lunch started at eleven, and we met then, and before we got finished, that place was jammed with reporters and people. We didn't leave there until about seven at night. By that time, all the waiters and whatnot in that restaurant had got into a circle around where we were yakking away, and they were just sitting there listening. Oh, it was incredible.

What were you talking about?

We talked about everything under the sun. We talked about people and how we developed stories, only because that's only of interest to writers. I am not an author. I am a writer. There's a big difference between an author and a writer. Eisenhower and Churchill, they were authors. They had one story to tell. That was as much as they could tell. They didn't write constantly as an income-making proposition. So I am a working writer. That's my job. I write.

Generally, what aspects of writing did you discuss?

We discussed subject matter, ways of writing a story. One of the things she always appreciated was the fact that people don't read a book to get to the middle. They read a book to get to the end and hope the ending is so great that it justifies all the time they spent in reading it. You have to get to the end of the book and "Wow!" Now that's the biggest part of the book. Anyway, we talked about things like that.

She always liked *I, the Jury* and the end of that story, because everything came to a definite conclusion. That's it. "I won." Bang! And she was like that too. She was a great writer. I refuse to call her an author. I thought she was a better writer than she was an author. She liked that attitude. And she liked *One Lonely Night*. That book impressed the heck out of her.

I was on a personal basis with her. It wasn't the case that we were professional friends. We were friend friends. There was a lot of laughing together and we had a good time talking about things. There was nothing really deeply serious about our conversations. We weren't discussing world problems. I knew she was a great economist and all that, and I loved her stuff. I hear people here today say, "Who is John Galt?"

It's just that we enjoyed each other's company. Sometimes there can be people who can be friends; you wonder, "How did they ever get together?" But here we were and we were very nice together. We had a good time talking. We never differed in our opinions. I was never political. She was quite political but in different areas.

We got along great. We were pretty close to each other in age, and we had a common background, more or less. Neither one of us came from wealthy backgrounds. I know we lived through the Depression years. We were able to discuss all that pretty well. I was a fighter pilot during World War II, and we were able to discuss things of that nature. We remembered these things. We were able to discuss things that you only discuss with friends. I don't suppose she had too many real good friends that she would open up with the way she opened up with me.

You signed your letters to her "Love, Mickey," and Miss Rand signed hers "Love, Ayn."

Yeah, I know. We were very good friends. It's hard to explain friendship.

Our conversations went from the sublime to the ridiculous. We used to talk about editorial stupidity. I remember telling her one time that I had an editor who said there's no way I could deliberately put an error into a book that he couldn't detect. I said, "Heck, I could," and we had this thousand-dollar bet on it. So I went home and wrote this book. He read the book, comes back and he said, "Oh, you didn't put one in there." I said, "Sure I did." And here is a guy who lives in New York, but he got so interested in the book that he overlooked the error. I had the tollgate on the wrong end of the George Washington Bridge.

You know something funny? She was interested in my comic books. That was kind of a low way of writing, but they made good money, and it was a job with me, just before World War II when I was writing for Funnies, Inc., in New York City. She wanted to know all about this form of writing because it was interesting to her. You know, make a good livelihood out of this. And it was writing. Whether you like it or not, the comic books taught a lot of kids how to read. I was one of the ones who used to write for Classic Comics.

Let me tell you a funny story about a book that was one of the Classic Comics. I told this to Ayn Rand one day—she thought this was hilarious. I was an only child, and I was able to read and write before I even went to school. I was a very voracious reader of everything I could get my hands on. I was in maybe the fifth grade, and the teacher pulled out a big book one day and said, "Someday, children, you'll be able to read a book like this." She held up *Moby Dick*, and I said, "Miss Fisher, I like that book." She looked at me and said, "You certainly didn't read that book." I said to her, "Call me Ishmael."

What was Miss Rand interested in regarding comic-book writing?

It was a form of writing that nobody had ever gotten involved with. It was pictorial, and she was interested in the fact that we were writing high-class stuff and we had a vast audience. You only get a vast audience when you're a good writer. Ayn was good. She had so many books left in her.

Had you read Miss Rand's work before meeting her?

I had read all of her stuff that was current on the market, but my favorite one was *Atlas Shrugged*. It was a very strange thing. I had tripped over a piece of wire and sprained my ankle, and I was stuck in the chair for a couple weeks. I read the books around me and there was a great big thick book there, *Atlas Shrugged*. I said, "Oh, I got to read something within reach." And so I said, "Oh, I'll start that." I couldn't put it down.

Why?

It was so good. I like the whole story. I like the whole thing about Rearden Steel and all that sort of stuff. And the whole book was a good piece of writing. It was something really interesting to read. I'll tell you something funny about that. New American Library told me there was a time when people were stealing copies of *Atlas Shrugged*. They'd take the covers off the book and what not. She was in the public eye, there, with that book.

What did you think of the philosophy in the book?

Her philosophy and mine were pretty much together. We like heroes. We don't like the nomads of the world.

You know what really bugged me. Ayn autographed a copy of *Atlas Shrugged* for me, and when Hurricane Hugo hit [in September 1989], he took it out. My whole library got wiped out. I had the only library in Murrell's Inlet. It was a little fishing village when I first moved here. Floor-to-ceiling books in my new library, and I haven't got Ayn Rand books. I had a whole bunch of stuff saved until Hurricane Hugo wiped me out. I lost everything. The whole house went. All of my records went. All my pictures went. I have a few things left over. Well, I lost all my old junk, and I had to go out and buy new junk.

Can you remember her dedication?

Oh, I forget it now. It was a nice one. A whole page long. It was one of my personal ones that you read, and you can remember every word when you reread it.

You probably heard about her—what they call her "disciples." When I was over at her house—I never was at her place when they weren't there, but there wasn't a whole mess of them. They were just sitting on the floor and listening to Ayn and me talking. After a while, we weren't talking about anything important and they were hanging onto every word. I ignored it real fast because that's the way I am. Probably she didn't pay any attention either. We were talking to ourselves and every time one of us would talk, all heads would follow that person, and when the other would talk, heads would follow over. It was very interesting. I never have been in a situation like this. But Ayn and I got to be friends. Sometimes we got away from the disciples.

Some of your early novels were anticommunist. Did you discuss that with Miss Rand?

Oh, she liked my attitude on it, sure.

What was your attitude?

I never liked communism. I don't like that stupidity. I never made a big thing about it. I'm not at all political. I'm one of Jehovah's Witnesses now. Politics is the thing I just never bother with. I keep it out of my life. I have to go along with it. I obey the laws. I pay my taxes. That's it.

Did you discuss the reaction of critics to your and Miss Rand's writing?

I never pay any attention to critics. They got their book for free, so shut up. They never bothered me. I had some of the worst articles ever about a writer. You know, when they pick on the audience, they say, "You're stupid if you read books by so and so." All they're doing is knocking themselves in the head. The people buy a book because they want to read it. That's why Ford sells so many cars. Nobody pays any attention to them. The more they say, "Don't read the books of Ayn Rand or Mickey Spillane," the more we sold. Let them say what they want. They never interfered with our sales concepts.

What do you remember discussing when you talked to her about the critics? She too was savaged by critics.

Oh, I know she was. We had the same feeling about critics. I don't like them. She didn't like them either. They always picked on her because she was successful. They don't pick on the poor guy who doesn't make a nickel. They pick on the guys who go up there in the limelight.

In 1960 you had seven of the top-ten best sellers in the United States in the twentieth century and were the most popular writer in America.

In the world, at that time, I had sold over two hundred million books. What was real funny was all the translations they did of my books. I was the fifth-most-widely translated writer in the world. Ahead of me were Lenin, Tolstoy, Gorky, Jules Verne and then me. I have to say, the other four were all dead. She used to like it when I'd tell her those things. She used to think that was very funny.

So here you are, the most successful living writer, and you're savaged by the critics, and then this well-known writer, Ayn Rand, makes these public statements supporting you as a great writer.

Oh, that just destroyed them. They didn't know what to say. It was very funny. I always thought those things were hilarious. The only exception among critics was Hy Gardner, who was a friend of mine and recognized all these things. He was with me one time when we met Ayn

Rand. We got along fine.

What was your reaction to Ayn Rand's public support of you?[122]

I thought it was very nice. It was always great because I always thought of her as being a great writer. I mean a writer as a novelist-type. I always thought she was way ahead of me. She was way above me in that classy type of writing.

What do you remember about reading The Fountainhead?

The Fountainhead wasn't my favorite book. My favorite book is *Atlas Shrugged.* I always liked that title too. "What would you do if you were Atlas?" "I'd shrug."

Did you shrug?

No. Ayn Rand and I, we don't have to shrug. We can carry that weight.

Did you read any of Miss Rand's nonfiction?

I read an awful lot of stuff by her, but I don't remember the titles.

One that especially relates to you is called The Romantic Manifesto.

Yes. I remember that. In fact, I had a copy of that but that got destroyed with the others. I liked it.

In her chapter "The Basic Principles of Literature," she analyzes a passage which begins "Nobody ever walked across the bridge, . . . "

". . . on a night like this."

Yes. "The rain was misty enough to be almost fog-like." From your novel One Lonely Night.

Yep. "Hardly nobody." You know, because of the ending of that, they accused me of using bad English. It said, "Nobody ever walked across the bridge on a night like this." And the end of that says "hardly nobody." Now the ending of that book is the same as the beginning because he goes back and that's where the thing winds up. He says,

---

122 On October 11, 1961, she praised Spillane during her appearance on the *Mike Wallace Interview* television show. And on September 2, 1962, she devoted her weekly *Los Angeles Times* column to him; it was reprinted in *The Ayn Rand Column,* ed. Peter Schwartz, 2nd. ed., (New Milford, CT: Second Renaissance Press, 1998), pp. 35–36.

"Nobody ever walks across the bridge on a night like this. Well, hardly nobody." It's a play on words. And the idiot editor tells me, "You can't say, 'hardly nobody.' You have to say, 'hardly anybody.'" I told them to shut up and leave my stuff alone.

Regarding this passage, did you discuss with Miss Rand the fact that she analyzed that passage in a fiction-writing class and then published a version of this discussion in The Romantic Manifesto?

Yeah, she told me about that. I said, "Gee. How can you do that? I'm just a writer. I'm not an author." I don't write great passages. I've written great things, like people at the end of *I, the Jury*, the killer says, "How could you?" And Mike Hammer says, "It was easy." See the ending is a big part of the story. She understood that. We used to discuss little things like that. It was really fun.

Did you discuss with Miss Rand the concept of the ideal man?

Oh, she had John Galt. I had Mike Hammer.

Miss Rand twice reviewed your books. The first time, she reviewed The Girl Hunters *and she was very glowing.*[123] *She wrote things like "Mickey Spillane has a brilliant literary talent. Few modern writers can approach it."*

Isn't it amazing because I always thought she was such a great writer, great intellect, and I'm not like that. But she got something out of my books I probably thought I never put in there. I used to be surprised when she'd bring these things out. I never thought about these things. You bring out these things, she'd tell me, and I'd say, "Did I write that?"

What about The Day of the Guns? *I believe that she didn't like this one.*

Well, I didn't do the Mike Hammer stuff there. That was a different type of story, Tiger Mann.

Do you remember how your relationship with Miss Rand ended?

No, we never really ended—she died. That was it.

Did Miss Rand influence you?

No. I was writing long before I ever met Ayn Rand. I was well

---

123 Ibid

established by that time. I turned pro in 1935. Right out of high school.

Are you still writing?

My last Mike Hammer is on my typewriter now.

Do you have any closing comments on Ayn Rand?

We were friends. That's the biggest thing I can say.

Friendship's important to you, isn't it?

Yeah, sure it is. I liked her. We had a good time together. I'm sorry she died. I would like to have continued our friendship.

Don Ventura

Don Ventura is a sculptor, photographer and a language teacher. He was a friend of Frank O'Connor's from 1962 to 1966.

Interview date: February 9, 1999

Scott McConnell: *How did you meet Frank O'Connor?*

    Don Ventura: I met him around 1962, when we studied at the Art Student's League together. Our friendship grew from us both being artists. I was a sculptor and Frank was a painter.

What was your first impression of Mr. O'Connor?

    We hit it off well and became very good friends. He was very warm, very generous, had a wonderful sense of humor. Everyone knew and loved him for that. He was very gentle. There was a very sweet kindness about him.

How would you describe Frank O'Connor?

    He was quite tall, maybe 6 feet 1 inch. He had graying, wavy hair. Bushy eyebrows, which he clipped. Pale blue eyes; longish, handsome nose. He was very distinguished-looking. He was soft-spoken and always had a kind of pleasant half-smile on his face. He was very, very polite. His presence was felt, but he never overwhelmed. There was something reticent about him.

What were the art lectures about that you and Mr. O'Connor were attending?

    Artistic anatomy. He studied with a painter named Robert Brackman. We also took [Robert Beverly] Hale's lectures. Joan Blumenthal was sort of Frank's guide and mentor. Joan was an artist and Ayn tried very hard to encourage Frank to study painting. She would encourage Joan to take him in hand and encourage him to come to the Art Student's League and he finally did. Joan and Frank went there together.

What was he learning from Mr. Brackman?

    Technique. Basic drawing principles, painting principles, basic technique. How to use color.

Was there anything special about the Brackman technique?

It was representational. But Frank's work didn't look like Brackman's. Most of Brackman's students, as with any other teacher, looked like Brackman's work, because they were students. Frank was very much of an individual and he listened to his own little drummer.

Can you remember some examples of the paintings?

Surrealistic themes. There was one called *Diminishing Returns* that was reproduced and was very popular with Objectivists. It was an artist's wooden figure model floating in the sky. Very surrealistic, Dali-esque kind of image. It was just humorous. I think Ayn Rand considered that her favorite of his.

Do you remember how it was conceived?

He was whimsical. I think it just came out of his whimsy, his imagination. He was very playful, and I think he approached a lot of his paintings playfully. I think he had a natural bent to do that. Frank had a lot of personality in his work. He didn't really take too well to academic training. It didn't interest him too much. He wanted to paint just for the pleasure of it. I think if it weren't for Ayn Rand pushing him to get to the League and upgrade—I think he would have just enjoyed painting.

What was it he enjoyed about painting?

Creativity, imagination—the pleasure of making something—creating something other people can enjoy. He had a very simple attitude about it: he enjoyed doing it. He didn't question it much. He was not terribly verbal about such things. He just liked to enjoy and not be terribly cerebral. He never talked about his creativity per se. He just enjoyed the process and wanted to let it go at that. There might be occasions when someone asked a probing question, and Frank would get a little bit annoyed. He would show it in a very subtle way. He didn't want to be bothered getting terribly intellectual about it. Earlier in his life he had done a lot of flower designing. He talked a little bit how much he loved doing it. It had been one of his biggest pleasures. He had done that much earlier, maybe when they were living in California.

Tell me about the Icarus painting that Mr. O'Connor wanted to do.

It was a serious idea he called "Icarus Fallen." The idea was to have a figure of Icarus lying on a rock in the middle of a lake in Central Park. He never did it, but he did get serious ideas like that. Most of the things

I saw him working on were not serious but whimsical stuff.

Did Mr. O'Connor tell you what his favorite paintings were?

One that we talked about with amusement, actually, was the Dali *Crucifixion*.[124] He enjoyed the fact that Dali had purposely painted little mysterious faces on the knees of the Christ figure. In fact, it was Miss Rand or Joan who was very annoyed when she found out about it, because she could never enjoy the painting as she had, once she knew that those faces were there. Frank and I both loved that painting and used to talk about it.

Do you know how long Mr. O'Connor was a student at the Art Students League?

A few years. He was voted vice president or president of the Art Student's League in the mid-60s.[125]

What was your first impression of Miss Rand?

I used to go to his studio on the sixth floor of the building they lived in. I would work there and he would paint, and I would sometimes bring over a piece of sculpture, or we would hire a model and draw. That's how we got to know each other. I was then about 34.

One night she came down to the studio, and Frank introduced me to her. He gave me a little bit of a build-up—you know, great sculptor. She was very cordial, gave me a warm smile. My first impression was that I was quite surprised to find her so easy to be with. We'd chat.

One time he was doing a portrait in the studio and was really into it, having a very good time. Ayn Rand came up from behind him—I was sitting nearby—and she was actually telling him that one eye was a little lower than the other—and he got furious. He just blew up and threw his arms in the air for a few minutes and said a few words about leaving him alone and went back to his work. I thought it was very funny, but she was extremely apologetic and said she was very embarrassed, and she went and sat in the corner. I gathered from that little scene that Frank just loved to enjoy what he was doing, and if he wasn't expressing himself the way he should be expressing himself, in terms of painting, it didn't matter as much to him.

What did he like to talk to you about?

---

124 *Crucifixion* (*Corpus Hypercubus*), 1954, New York Metropolitan Museum of Art.
125 Frank O'Connor became vice president in 1966.

He would just sometimes talk about his life with Miss Rand or his life in general. We would talk about other places in the world he would like to have visited, but wouldn't because Ayn Rand didn't like to fly. He was romantic and would have loved to visit anywhere in the world.

What did he say about their relationship?

He spoke warmly of her. They had a very nice, warm connection. Whenever I saw them in the street, she'd be holding onto his arm, especially in their later years. They were always close, together.

Did he say what he loved about her?

He would tell little stories about her. I remember one little anecdote. Many years ago when she heard her voice on radio for the first time—she turned to him and said, "Oh, my God! I've got an accent." She was shocked to learn she had an accent, which made him laugh. She said, "Why haven't you ever told me that I have an accent?" And he answered because he thought it was so cute he didn't want her to change her accent. He told simple, tender little stories like that.

Did he tell negative stories at all?

No. He never spoke negatively about her. And I wouldn't call it negative at all the time he blew up when he was doing that painting. He was not a negative man at all. That is one of the things that was so attractive about him. He was a very sweet person. He would express a little anger with Miss Rand over smaller issues, but not the big issues, but the smaller ones, like that incident in the studio.

They liked to make little jokes. They had a cat called "Frisco." Frank told me he used to make remarks about Frisco being out of focus and Ayn Rand would get very upset. It was a concept that didn't apply to cats—it delighted him.

He liked teasing her?

Yes. They had a wonderful relationship. They were extraordinarily different from each other.

When the three of you were in the studio, what did you talk about?

Almost anything—but general conversations, not heavy intellectual conversations. A couple of times she talked about art. One evening she talked about how she detested Picasso, and we had there a model who was a great lover of Picasso, and she was very curious to know why he liked Picasso. It was a very interesting evening—where the poor guy was worn out by the time it was over.

Describe Ayn Rand discussing the issue.

She was incredibly incisive in such a staggering, mind-boggling way. I was always totally fascinated by the way her mind worked and the way she structured questions and answers. That was always a marvelous thing to observe at her lectures and the evenings we had at Frank's studio.

How did she treat the Picasso fan?

Very well. He might not have felt that. He did get defensive toward the end of the evening.

It wasn't a problem for Miss Rand for people to disagree with her?

Not generally. She of course got angry, but she was generally so focused on content and on what she was probing for that she wasn't aware of any other issue being involved—like in this case. If this person got intimidated, she didn't mean to intimidate him. She never meant to intimidate, although it happened.

You said that one of your models was Patrecia Gullison.[126]

Yes. And she used to give Miss Rand advice on makeup, since she was working in that field. When Miss Rand went on the Johnny Carson show one time, Patrecia gave her several tips on how to make up her face.

Patrecia told her something about how to cross her legs when she sat down. Afterwards, Miss Rand had complained that she had developed a terrible cramp. Patrecia asked her why she didn't uncross her legs and change her position. And Miss Rand told her she was terrified. She had learned to cross her legs but she didn't know quite what to do, so she remained in that position and had been afraid to do anything else.

Because of shyness or decency?

The former. She was a very shy woman. She didn't consider herself to be very beautiful. There was something decidedly shy about her when you caught her off-guard; when she wasn't focused on "issues,"

---

126 She became Nathaniel Branden's second wife.

she was a decidedly charming woman. When she wasn't involved in an intellectual process she was just a very shy woman. She was very eager to make you comfortable around the apartment. She would offer me something and make sure I was comfortable. Unlike most of the other people around her, she had an uncanny ability to make things clear and simple. It was a very comforting thing. I'll always be glad I had the pleasure of seeing her in this light.

Ayn Rand was the powerful figure she was, and Frank was subordinate to that by his nature. He was a very gentle, soft-spoken man. I don't think he ever thought he had tremendously important things to say, and yet he lived with someone and loved someone who had tremendously important things to say, and he knew that. He had a tremendous faith in Miss Rand. He loved her very much.

Did Mr. O'Connor ever talk to you about his past?

He used to talk about the old days a lot. He used to love—I think he used to do it with Ayn—to take the Staten Island Ferry. It was a cherished memory of his that he used to like to ride back and forth on the Staten Island Ferry. They might have been broke at the time.

What did he say about the early days in New York?

The humble days. He was nostalgic about his early days in New York, how they used to walk around and take in the sights and marvel a great deal and ride the Staten Island Ferry.

So he loved New York?

He was fascinated with New York. He liked New York.

Did you know what he did in those "humble days" in the late 1930s?

I think there was a period where he did nothing—he didn't know what to do. How he got into floral arrangements I don't remember, but I remember him talking about that and expressing a great deal of delight and pleasure in that. There was this issue of his finding the thing in life that would make him happy, and floral arrangements seemed to be the closest he got to that before he started painting. Once he started painting, there were people who wanted to buy his paintings, and Miss Rand wouldn't let him sell any because she didn't want to part with the paintings—at least the ones they wanted to buy. He spoke about this with amusement.

Did Mr. O'Connor say anything about the people who were around Miss Rand?

He liked them all. He used to call the group "the kids." There is something he complained to me about, actually. At dinner Ayn always insisted that he be present, and he didn't like that. He would tell me how it would make him very sleepy, and he would nod at the table. They went on with intellectual discussions that he really wasn't interested in, and he would much rather have been down in the studio painting. But she always insisted that he be present, and he was, to make her happy.

Did Mr. O'Connor have problems with his hands?

Yes. He couldn't paint anymore because his hands shook a lot. This might have been around '67, '68. I ran into him at the dentist, and I remember his talking about it and, I think, about an operation. He was very sad about it that particular day. I remember we sat and talked in the waiting room a little while. He was very unhappy. He used to use a stick when he painted to steady his hand and he couldn't make that work for him anymore. He just could not keep his hands still long enough to be able to paint.

Do you have any materials related to Ayn Rand?

I have two little things. One is a matchbook cover, with her favorite colors, which was on her dining room table. The other is a figurine. Ayn Rand had this porcelain ceramic—two peacocks in battle—and he made a box to encase it. I have both the piece and the box.

Jan Schulman

Jan Schulman (formerly Crosby) ran the NBI lectures in Los Angeles with her then husband, Peter Crosby. They were instrumental in creating the tape-lecture service.

Interview date: September 26, 1997

Scott McConnell: *How did you set up the NBI tape-lecture service?*

Jan Schulman: In 1961 my then husband, Peter Crosby, and I were living in Baltimore, where he was stationed in the Army, and we read an article, in either *Time* or *Newsweek* about Miss Rand. The article mentioned that Nathan was giving lectures on Objectivism in New York, with Miss Rand there. So I quickly sent a letter off to him saying we were going to be heading back to Los Angeles soon because it was near the end of Peter's duty in the army, and had he given any thought to giving the Objectivist courses via a correspondence course, so that other people in the country could have the same advantage as the people in New York were having. We got a letter back saying, "Why don't you come on up to New York and talk to us, if you can?" So we got on our motor scooter, which is all we had—a little Lambretta—and we rode to New York from Baltimore.

In Nathan's apartment we met with him and Barbara and talked about our idea. The told us they had the lectures on tape and gave us the go-ahead to start a branch lecture series in Los Angeles. They told us that when we returned to L.A., do whatever it is we need to do, to publicize the tape-lecture series The Basic Principles of Objectivism. They said they would pay for ads, such as in the newspapers, but we would have to do all the legwork, running and promoting the course. We agreed, and when we got back to Los Angeles, I made up these little ads on the typewriter, and went around to bookstores, and stuck flyers in windows, and stuck notices up on bulletin boards in markets, and everywhere else. Then NBI ran a few small ads in the *Los Angeles Times*. We started getting phone calls, and one of the people who called had a very, very large home, and offered it, because we didn't know where we were going to hold the tape lectures or what kind of turnout we would get. The phone started ringing off the hook. I was very naïve. We were anticipating that hundreds of people were going to march on this house, and I think we only had something like twenty-five or thirty people that first night. I thought it was absolutely awful that that's all that showed up after all these phone calls that we had from people saying they would be there. I was devastated, but Nathan and Barbara thought it was fine. So that's how it started; that was the first year, when we held the courses in that house.

How did the courses progress?

They grew considerably. By the end of the third year, we had over a hundred people at each opening and were holding them in a public meeting room: the American Institute of Aeronautics and Astronautics on Beverly Boulevard. It had a wonderful atmosphere. We started out using the small rooms and graduated to the main auditorium

How many people were attending lectures at your peak?

The opening nights were the biggest. That's when Nathan would fly out to Los Angeles, but the couple of times that Miss Rand came out, of course, it was huge. We couldn't get all of the people in the building, so we didn't ask the people standing in the lobby to pay to hear her. They stood wherever they could, and we dragged loudspeakers out into the lobby. To turn somebody away would have been heartbreaking.

How many people would you guess were there in total?

In the auditorium, we could get five hundred.

How many outside?

They spilled out into the lobby, and we estimated there were well over a thousand people that first time Miss Rand lectured. We had so many people show up that the janitor, we believe, called the fire department, and when the fire chief came, he asked, "What's going on here?" I told him, "Ayn Rand is speaking here; this is the first time she's come to Los Angeles to address the group, and these people have never had a chance to see or hear her." He said, "If you do what I tell you, and you promise you will introduce me to her at the end of this, I will let everyone stay." I just took it upon myself and said, "You've got it." I didn't know if Miss Rand would be willing to meet him or not. But of course she did; she was extremely gracious.

The chief made the people create artificial aisles between the groups of people, which would have been meaningless had there been a real emergency or a crush. Afterwards, Barbara led the chief to Miss Rand, who was absolutely delighted. She was just so thrilled that he had come, that he was a fan and that he let everyone stay because of his regard for her, in exchange for being introduced.

Tell me about your meetings with Miss Rand. How many times did you meet with her?

I only met her twice. I remember when we were sitting in a restaurant in Beverly Hills, and I was wearing glasses, and she said that I should take my glasses off. I took them off, and she said, "You have very beautiful eyes. You shouldn't hide them behind glasses; get contact lenses." I remember I felt like crying. It was very motherly, and very warm, and very dear, and I did go and get contact lenses. I was always very grateful to her for that, because it never occurred to me to do that. She sort of gave me the permission to be vain.

Then we had a discussion about an artist who I happened to like at the time, and my husband was giving me a very bad time about it. The artist was Andrew Wyeth. Years before, I had come across an art book reproduction of one of his paintings, called *Christina's World*, and I related to it for reasons that go back to my own childhood. My husband felt that my relating to it really showed a very dark side of me and my psycho-epistemology, and he asked Miss Rand, "What do you think about her liking this painting?" She looked at me and said, "Why do you like the painting?" I didn't tell her the complete truth, but said, "Because I identify with the loneliness and isolation of that girl." I told her that I especially liked the clarity of the painting and its style, which was also true. And Miss Rand said, "As long as you know why you like the painting, and don't respond to its sense of life, then you don't need to explain to anybody else why you like it." I remember it was all I could do to keep from crying, because I think she was telling me things on a lot of levels, and I was not being honest with her. I also felt, that when she looked into my eyes, she looked into my soul, and I felt she saw me. When this woman turned and looked at you, you were being looked at. You were being seen. It was incredibly strong.

Can you recall any similar incidents?

I do remember that my favorite composer was Beethoven, and he was clearly not hers, and we talked about that. I certainly did not feel I was in a position to defend my appreciation of Beethoven to her.

You told her that?

Yes. That's how I felt at the time, that I had to justify it.

What did she say?

I remember her talking about his malevolent sense of life.

How did she react to you personally when you told her about your appreciation for Beethoven? Did she get angry?

No, no, no, no—she was very kind.

Did you get Miss Rand to inscribe any of her books for you?

In my first edition of *Atlas Shrugged*, she wrote, "To Jan and Peter Crosby, with my sincere appreciation of your work, and my best wishes for your future, Ayn Rand. October 8, 1963." In my first edition of *The Fountainhead*, she wrote "To Jan and Peter Crosby, with thanks, in the name of Objectivism. Ayn Rand, October 8, 1963."

John R. Howard

John R. Howard was president of Lewis and Clark College, which conferred an honorary degree of Doctor of Humane Letters on Ayn Rand in 1963.

Interview date: January 13, 1999

Scott McConnell: *How did you become interested in Ayn Rand and Objectivism?*

John R. Howard: I think my first interest in Ayn Rand dates from reading *Atlas Shrugged*. In the early 1960s I instituted what we called Reading Week. We had all the Lewis and Clark faculty and students, the entire college community, read a given book. We invited the author to the campus for two or three days. The author, Miss Rand in this case, met with different classes and with small groups, and then we had an assembly with the entire college community present. We showed *The Fountainhead* film, which we had secured from Encyclopedia Britannica of Chicago.

In her classes, and at every opportunity she had while she was on campus with us, Ayn explained her philosophy. We had some very interesting intellectual exchanges with Ayn. I don't remember specifically any of her reactions, except that she seemed very pleased that this many people were reading her book.

Why specifically was Ayn Rand invited to Lewis and Clark College?

I felt that she was an important author, that this would be a stimulating experience for the entire college community.

What in her books attracted you?

Ayn is a classical author in a tradition that stressed independent thought and free enterprise. The idea that bureaucracy and stupidity interferes with a true free enterprise system, a true capitalistic system—that was appealing to me. My own field was Soviet government and politics, so I was fascinated with her ideas. Capitalism, or free enterprise, needed to be free. You needed to accept the full consequences of freedom. As you started to inhibit that freedom, or abridge it, or compress it, you took something vital away. That very clearly came through in her writing.

How many people were in the faculty and in the community?

251

It is a college of around 3,200 now, but it was somewhat smaller then: about 1,200 students and a hundred faculty.

Tell me more about the screening of The Fountainhead.

We had the showing in the college auditorium, during which Ayn was at a microphone near the screen and giving some running commentary.

At a critical point in the film, Gary Cooper was giving his statement to the court, which is Ayn's tradition—she did it in her books. She was very explicit, telling me that she had brought her book to a climax in that courtroom presentation by Gary Cooper.

But the *Encyclopedia Britannica* had shortened Cooper's speech, because they had the film prepared for television, and they didn't think a television audience would sit still for a five-and-a-half-minute monologue. When Ayn Rand discovered the cuts while watching the film, she became quite vocal over the microphone. With the entire college community listening, she denounced all of the communist bastards who were responsible for doing this. She said that they knew what they were doing, and that this was a typical communist trick. The effect was rather dramatic, electric, on the audience. It probably excited more interest in the film and in that particular passage than if they had left it intact.

I later checked with the *Encyclopedia*, and they explained to me what I just said to you, that the reason that it was done had nothing to do with the philosophical argument; it had to do with the effectiveness of a television presentation, because presumably advertisers or others who were involved in it would not have been too pleased to have an audience walk away to the refrigerator while somebody was making such a long speech.[127]

Before this, when Ayn Rand was making her comments during the showing of the movie, was she focusing on ideas, or filmmaking or writing?

Ideas. Always. Ayn Rand is an idea woman. She's not one for small talk or for technique talk, unless it is in terms of narrative.

Describe the ceremony of Miss Rand having her degree conferred upon her.

---

127 Ayn Rand demanded and received an apology and an assurance from the college that the uncut film would be shown at Lewis and Clark.

The process is that the provost, or dean of faculty, presents the candidate to the president of the college. The ritual by which an honorary degree is presented is fairly standard throughout the academic community—"All the rights, privileges and responsibilities which pertain," and so forth. I introduced her to the audience and made note of her writings.

From the archives, I have a comment from Miss Rand that she found your remarks to be some of the most beautiful that she had heard.

She said something like that to me. Ayn Rand had experienced a lot of intellectual criticism, and it meant a lot to her to come to a place where there was a sympathetic statement—and mine was a sympathetic statement—that she was giving "an important point of view," that she was giving it in an exceptional style, that she was a unique human being.

I continue to think that while we're sort of reliving the twentieth century as we leave it, in my honest opinion, Ayn Rand is one of the more significant authors and writers in the twentieth century in the United States. In retrospect, I think anybody who would read *Atlas Shrugged* fairly, today, forty years after it was published, would find that it's probably more relevant and meaningful and proven today, even than it was then, when there was more philosophical speculation about it.

Did you find, as an academic, that inviting Ayn Rand to Lewis and Clark caused any controversy or problems?

Oh yes, yes. I was taken to task rather roundly by a number of members of my faculty people in the community, but that's not uncommon.

Did Miss Rand acknowledge to you that your taking this step to invite her had been an important or risky step?

Yes, she did say that, almost in those same words.

Describe your visit with her.

I had thought that two full days in a row of living with Ayn Rand would be difficult. I think the intensity of the woman is remarkable. And clearly, she does not brook nonsense. Ayn was not one for small talk or trivia, and I appreciate that. I don't handle small talk all that well, myself. But the truth is, I probably engage in a lot more of it—as a part of my work and a part of my lifestyle—than did she. But I did like her. I like people who are real and who are honest to their commitment. That's one of the reasons we invited her. And I found Ayn Rand as compelling in presence as she was in her writings, and I like and admire that in any person.

What was she like to deal with on a personal level?

She's strong. The strength of the woman; there's no question about Ayn Rand's strength of commitment, or ability to express herself, and she would express herself very directly. She knew who she was, and there was no question of her trying to be clever or devious in any way in presenting herself. She knew who she was, she knew what she stood for, and her books reflect that . . . and she reflected that in person.

How you would describe Ayn Rand?

I just use the phrase in the *Star Wars* trilogy, when Obi-Wan Kenobi says, "Let the force be with you." Ayn Rand was a force. Quite literally, she left a wake; she left waves when she went by, and she does with her writings and she did with her presence. She's a rather remarkable memory for me.

Gary Miller

Gary Miller was a collector of Ayn Rand memorabilia and met Miss Rand in the 1960s. He died in 2004.

Interview date: May 24, 1996

Scott McConnell: *How did you meet Ayn Rand?*

Gary Miller: In October 1963 I had dinner at a hotel with her and the Brandens in San Diego and attended her lecture there.

What happened at this dinner?

I had brought a book to be autographed by her, and what happened I think also illustrates her personality. I had a copy of *Atlas Shrugged* that was leather bound, with gold stamping, and I was going to give it to her to sign for me. When I reached for it, that's when it first occurred to me that I had changed her book. The original cover wasn't on it; it had a black leather cover and straight-back binding, with a pocket built into the book. I also had a picture, El Greco's *Toledo*, bound into the book, and the cover of the black binding said "Ayn Rand," and on the spine it said "*Atlas Shrugged.*"

So when I handed it to her, I said, "This is a little bit presumptuous, because I altered the book." She looked it over, and the people there misunderstood why I had El Greco's painting on it. They thought it was my idea of the decay of the city that paralleled the first few pages of *Atlas Shrugged*. Then she looked at the cover, and said that it looked more like a book called "Ayn Rand," by someone called Gary Miller, rather than authored by Ayn Rand. Then when I was getting the book back without an autograph, she critiqued the El Greco painting.

What did she say?

She identified it as a town about to be engulfed, and I had never noticed that about the painting. When I had looked at the painting, it was as if the spire was the lone thing left that was fighting the forces of nature. But when I looked at it later, it was as she had described. But then, very benevolently, she reached across, took the book and autographed it for me.

She was very pleasant about the whole thing. It was all benevolent, all very sweet, this very friendly discussion, with her giving me a one hundred percent benefit of any doubt that there might be.

What else did she talk about?

After dinner she was sitting on one of the coffee tables in the lobby, and I was sitting on the couch, and we got to talking about conceptualizing. I said to her, "How do you conceptualize 'red?'" and she said to me, with not even a second's hesitation, "You just did."

Did she explain herself?

She did, but I was so stunned by the quickness and ease of her response that there wasn't any way I could integrate the answer at that time.

I believe you sent Miss Rand some manuscripts?

I learned that she would be receptive to autographing books and pamphlets by mail, so I sent a box of maybe a dozen items, and she autographed all but one of them and sent them back. Then several years later I sent another box with more items, but with questionable items, like the poster of *The Fountainhead* movie, which she didn't sign. There wasn't any explanation.

Did you once send her a book galley?

It was a thick paperback called "The Unrevised Galley for 'The Romantic Manifesto,'" and it was in the first box that I sent her. She sent all the material back signed, with the exception of that book. Elayne Kalberman[128] wrote a note to me saying that the galleys would be returned to me if I signed a form saying that I wouldn't let the galleys out of my collection. I signed that, and they returned the galleys to me. I think she wanted to autograph only those things that she herself endorsed, and if something didn't have the content she approved of, she wouldn't sign it.

---

128 Elayne Kalberman was circulation manager of *The Objectivist Newsletter*.

Lisette Hassani

Lisette Hassani is the daughter of Vera Glarner (née Guzarchik), Ayn Rand's Russian cousin whose mother was the sister of Ayn Rand's mother. Mrs. Hassani grew up in France and now lives in Switzerland. This interview was conducted in French and translated into English by Helene Skantzikas, from questions prepared by Scott McConnell.

Interview dates: September 18 and October 11, 1998

Helene Skantzikas: *Tell me about Ayn Rand.*

Lisette Hassani: This lady was my mother's cousin. I first met her in New York. She was very professional. I lived on Lexington Avenue, very close to where she lived.

My father [Henri Glarner, a Frenchman] had the opportunity to visit her in 1948 in California, and he brought back a gift from her, a beautiful coat. She was very generous.[129] The coat probably wasn't very fashionable there, but here. . . . Later, I worked in dressmaking, and I could really appreciate the coat's quality. It was green, with a velvet collar and a hood. It was beautiful.

What did your father think of his visit in California?

He was enchanted. She must have been very nice to him.

How did you meet Ayn Rand?

I arrived in New York by boat, from Cherbourg.[130] I wanted to learn English. Instead of sending me to England, as I had wanted, my parents sent me to America. They told me, "You have an uncle in America; you should go there." That way, he was responsible for me. I was a student. I fell in love with New York, and I didn't want to go back! I loved the city. For me it meant freedom.

What was your relationship with Ayn Rand in New York?

We were very friendly. We had tea and cookies, things like that. She wanted me to see what she was doing there, so I attended a lecture. She was very famous, then, in America. I remember she was very much respected. I know people listened to her. I could see that,

---

129 Ayn Rand also sent food parcels to the family in France after the end of World War II.
130 Ayn Rand's daily calendar first mentions Lisette on November 30, 1961

but I couldn't understand much. She spoke English, and I was still learning English then.

She gave a lecture in a large room. I was very impressed. I thought, "What a character, my aunt!"

How would you describe your aunt?

She seemed very self-willed. A little stubborn too, in my opinion.

When you were in New York, I believe your mother visited you and Ayn Rand.

Yes, they must have seen each other then. I remember that my mother was afraid of New York. She would hold my arm all the time. She was very anxious. It was a big city and she was afraid to get lost.

Did she like America?

When we arrived at my uncle's house, I saw her kiss the earth. It was the promised land for her.[131]

Do you remember meeting Frank O'Connor?

I saw him once, maybe. She was the one I saw when I visited. He wasn't there; he was busy with his painting.

What do you remember of your visits to Ayn Rand's home?

Oh, she was very nice to me! I lived a couple of blocks away, and she would call a taxi for me, even if it wasn't very late. She didn't want me to walk back. I think she felt responsible for me. I keep a good memory of her. She gave me gifts; she was so nice.

I had very few conversations with Ayn Rand. She didn't speak to me very much. She was just kind to me, but concerning Objectivism, I don't know anything about that.

Let's turn briefly to your mother's family in Russia. What do you remember about them? For example, what did your mother's mother do?

She must have been a housewife, since she had three daughters. But I know that when my mother felt like sobbing, she could push a button, and someone would bring her a tissue! They were very rich. They lived on the main street of Leningrad [Nevsky Prospekt].

---

131 Vera Glarner left the USSR in the 1920s and lived under the Nazis in Lyon.

My mother studied in Russia and earned her diploma to be a doctor, and her father wanted to reward her by sending her on a trip to Europe. She owed everything to her father. He was a doctor. So she had come to Europe because she had gotten her diploma. First, she went to Germany, to the Institute Robert Koch in Berlin. Then, she came to Paris, to the Pasteur Institute.

I have a picture of my grandmother and grandfather. I didn't know them. I think my mother must have taken the photo in Russia.

Did your mother ever go back to Russia?

No, never. And when her father died, someone asked my father: "Do you love your wife?" and he said, "Yes," and they told him she shouldn't go to the funeral in the USSR because she would not get back out.

Roger Salamon

Roger Salamon is Ayn Rand's cousin. He is the grandson of Sarah Lipski, one of the Chicago relatives who brought Miss Rand to America in 1926.

Interview date: July 5, 1996

Scott McConnell: *Do you have any of Miss Rand's books?*

Roger Salamon: We have three signed copies of her books, and in one of them, in particular, I think the inscription is very poignant. It's in her first published book, *We the Living*. In the frontispiece, Ayn wrote, "To Sarah Satrin, With profound gratitude for saving me from the kind of hell described in this book, Ayn Rand 4/2/1936."

My grandmother, Sarah Satrin [1885–1971], received a book from Ayn every time she published. Unfortunately, I only have three.

Ayn never really forgot those who brought her over. She wasn't beholden, because that wasn't her style, but she didn't forget. In *The Fountainhead*, she wrote, "To Sarah and Saul Lipski, with love and gratitude, Ayn Rand, November 30, 1943." In *Atlas Shrugged*, she wrote, "To Sarah Lipski, affectionately and gratefully, Ayn 11/6/57."

Sarah Lipski was my grandmother. I knew her under the name Satrin, and then Lipski. She was married twice before, originally to Harry Collier, who was my grandfather, and then her second husband, Joe Lipton. Then she remarried Saul Lipski. She was good-looking and full of life and vigor and vitality, bright and talented.

My mother, Beatrice Collier, used to type Ayn's early manuscripts. She's in a big family photo, next to Burt Stone. Ayn didn't know English very well, although she had a good education. They had private tutors in Russia. My mother just said she helped Ayn out in the beginning, She once mentioned to me, "When Ayn first came over, I used to type her manuscripts."

My grandmother and Ayn used to correspond. They were pretty good friends. My mother corresponded occasionally, though I don't think they saved any letters, but they did correspond occasionally. Nobody made phone calls in those days, like they do today.

What did Sarah Lipski say about Ayn Rand?

She loved Ayn. I guess it's because, when they brought her over, they worried with her, until she learned how to speak and how to dress, and get things going. They felt a responsibility for her in some way.

My grandmother did brag about her, because she was a celebrity then, and my grandmother never necessarily said she was responsible for anything, but she always talked about Ayn as being a relative or a cousin.

When your grandmother first met Miss Rand, she was living at The Cooper Carlton Hotel, Hyde Park Boulevard, 53rd Street, in Chicago. Miss Rand stayed with her there.

It was an apartment hotel. Nothing special. Those places had in-a-door beds, and a bedroom. You open these two doors, move your furniture around, and there was a vertical bed against the wall. They called that a "Murphy bed." Her apartment had two rooms and a kitchen.

I don't think any other family members, other than Burt and Esther Stone, who were involved with my grandmother, had much to do with her one way or the other; plus my mother, of course. I think my mother and Ayn were reasonably good friends. It seemed like they got along well. Since my mother originally was involved, helping her, that formed a bond that you normally wouldn't find.

When did you meet Miss Rand?

When she was in Chicago to give a lecture at the McCormick Place on September 29, 1963, and then later on, when Burt passed away, she came in for the funeral. She was very close to Burt and Esther, with whom she remained in contact. She wasn't warm and friendly. I mean, sometimes you sit down with a person, and it's instant rapport. I just didn't find that to be the case with Ayn.

I have a pamphlet that I think was given out at that lecture, "A Letter from Ayn Rand, Author of *The Fountainhead*," with her picture on it. And it's that picture with her hair combed to one side, a very boyish bob. This is the last paragraph: "To every reader who had the intelligence to understand *The Fountainhead*, the integrity to like it, and the courage to speak about it; to everyone of you, not en masse, but personally and individually, I am here saying thank you." That's Ayn Rand, all right.

I didn't necessarily agree with her. I think she was a great capitalist, because she had to be, after what had happened in Russia. I enjoyed the lecture. It was interesting.

How did the audience react to her?

Oh, she was very well received.

Daniel Sutton

Daniel Sutton is the son of Frank O'Connor's niece Mimi Sutton.

Interview dates: August 6 and 7, 1996

Scott McConnell: *What is your strongest memory of Ayn Rand?*

Daniel Sutton: There are two. The first one was at age ten or twelve and not too long after I read *Atlas Shrugged*. The first time I met Ayn was on a train, actually. I was entranced by trains, and she got me a tour of a diesel locomotive in Union Station in Chicago. We went through the train from one end to the other, and she knew a remarkable amount of information about this, as much as probably the engineer did. She was visiting my mom and dad, and we met her for dinner. Evidently, she'd had some contacts from writing *Atlas Shrugged*, at one point, and swung a few bells for me, and it was one of the biggest thrills of my life.

What was she like?

I found her charming, and I thought she was very gracious to the engineer.

How was Ayn Rand with kids?

With me, as a kid, wonderful.

And the other strongest memory?

The second one was the lunch we had discussing the draft and the Vietnam War and the spread of communism. And the only thing I recall is that we discussed the difference between a fascist and a communist. I was probably one of the few people at that age who actually wanted to go into the service and believed in the war.

Did you talk to Ayn Rand about that?

Quite a bit. Most of that conversation revolved around my immense curiosity about communism and her experiences. We talked about that after I had read *Anthem*. I had discussed with my mom about Ayn's background, and communism, and I was extremely conservative, a right-winger. She didn't seem to believe in the war, and I was surprised. And it wasn't so much that she didn't believe in the war, as I recall, it was that she didn't believe, vehemently, in the draft. She said, "They have no right to make you go, and if you don't want to go, I'll get you any lawyer you need, or whatever expense you need." I said, number one, "Thank you, but no thanks. I don't mind."

I found in the archives a letter you wrote to Ayn Rand on April 11, 1970. "Dear Aunt Ayn, Thank you very much for the subscription to The Objectivist Newsletter.*" Is there a story there?*

I'll be darned. She was talking on the phone to my mom, and she asked for me, and she asked me to do her a favor. She said, "Do you get *The Objectivist?*" and I said, "Yes, but I have to borrow it from somebody else, because I don't have the money to buy one." She said, "I'll give you the subscription, but you do something for me. I want to put it in the wrong name, so we'll put it in the last name "Sutton," but I want to alter your first name, and then you call and tell me who else sends you mail," because she was worried about somebody else using her mailing list.

Martin Anderson

Martin Anderson was an acquaintance of Ayn Rand's during the early and mid-1960s. His book *The Federal Bulldozer* was reviewed in *The Objectivist* in 1966. He directed policy research for Richard Nixon in 1968 and Ronald Reagan in 1980, and served as economic and domestic policy adviser to President Reagan. Dr. Anderson is currently the Keith and Jan Hurlbut Senior Fellow at the Hoover Institution on War, Revolution and Peace at Stanford University. He was an adviser to presidential candidate George W. Bush in 2000.

Interview date: April 12, 1999

Scott McConnell: *How did you first learn about Ayn Rand and her works?*

Martin Anderson: I was sharing an apartment in New York City with a former classmate of mine from Dartmouth College and was teaching at Columbia University. One night he said, "I just finished reading this book and you would really like it. It's *Atlas Shrugged*." The first I heard of it was when he handed me this book, and I started to read it and got fascinated by it. This was probably 1964, '65. I remember staying up late and reading until the wee hours of the morning. I think I just read through the whole book in five or six days.

What fascinated you? Was it the story or the ideas or both?

It was a combination of them. It was a fascinating book as to what was going to happen—it had a good plot line to it. And some of the ideas are fascinating. I like things that confirm the way I already think. In a number of ways there were things that I had agreed with but never hooked together. And when she talked about them, I found myself agreeing with the flow of the whole thing. I thought it was a great book. Then at some later time, I found and read *The Fountainhead*. I liked that one too.

What did you do after reading these books?

At some point I remember reading an ad that there were lectures based on her philosophy. I went to some of the lectures, but I wouldn't call it taking a course.

Do you remember what the lectures were?

I went to the general lecture, which was a basic introduction to Objectivism. The one I remember the most—maybe this is where I met Alan Greenspan—he was giving an economics lecture. I remember, having majored in economics and studied economics, that that lecture really struck me because I thought Alan was the best economics teacher I had ever seen.

Why?

What he said made more sense. It was clear-cut, it was logical, it tied together. He was just better than the professors I'd had before. So when I went into the course with Alan Greenspan, he was applying to mathematics a value system that I agreed with.

Was the Objectivist idea of the virtue of selfishness new?

It wasn't, to the best of my recollection, new. It was that she was saying things that made a lot of good sense that I had never heard anyone else say before.

Had you said them yourself?

Not in those words or in that exact language, but when she would say something or do something it just seemed to make a lot of sense. There were some things I still don't agree with her about, but a lot of things tied together. The way I would look at it is that she would talk about metaphysics, about epistemology, about ethics—and each one separately I had looked at. But she had a way of putting it together in a conceptual way that flowed, that made sense.

She systematized it.

Yes. She took a disparate number of things and very brilliantly put them together in a clear way.

Did you ever tell her that?

I didn't talk to her personally that much. The times I spent talking to her were just small talk, so I don't think I ever did. What I found fascinating is that in all the education I had—a degree in education and going to MIT—there was a constant emphasis on the power of a theory, getting to the essence of things and showing how extraordinarily difficult it was to do that. I thought what was fascinating was that she was doing this in this area in philosophy and showing how things rolled together. She was doing much of what my professors said should be done, except could not.

Could you tell me about the first time you met Miss Rand?

It was at one of the lectures. She was very professional, very, very smart, very clear-cut. During the lectures she could be somewhat stern and dramatically different to what she was like in private.

How was she in private?

Charming, friendly. She was fun; she was nice. One night after one of the lectures, they all got together to have a cup of coffee. Someone asked me to go along, probably Alan Greenspan. I had recently broken my left arm, my left hand had a cast on it, so it was tough to move things around. We sat down to have coffee. It was brought over and I went to put the cream in. The cream was in one of these little plastic containers with the little cap on it. I was trying to do it with one hand and it wasn't working. No one else paid any attention, but of all the people there, she noticed it. She came over, reached across the table, took the container, opened it, and gave it back to me, smiling.

Do you remember other meetings with her?

I think once or twice I was invited to a meeting and, again, it was probably after one of the lectures. We went back to her apartment. We just sat around, had a drink, talked generally about a whole range of topics about what was going on—currently and politically—and other issues, nothing special or particular. It was relaxing.

What was she like at those meetings?

Same way. She was just very, very relaxed and charming, talking back and forth. In a way, I saw her quite different than she was at the lectures. In the lectures, if someone raised a question from the floor, it seemed she took it as a challenge—it often was. But in private, she wasn't on the defensive.

She was fascinating, because of what she had written and what she had accomplished. But in private, she was just very pleasant.

There was one other time we met. She came to our wedding in 1965. We had just rented a penthouse apartment on the Upper West Side, and we decided to get married on the deck of the penthouse. We must have had twenty-five or thirty people. She was one of the guests. I still have the present she gave me: a gorgeous piece of beautiful cut glass.

I believe you influenced Richard Nixon in ending the draft. What were your influences for the ideas in your proposal to Richard Nixon in 1967 and 1968?

There were a number of sources I was using. I had done a lot of reading about it; in particular, articles in the *New York Times* by Milton Friedman, and other articles I had read about the issue. I had thought about it myself, and I'm sure it came up in some of the lectures that Ayn Rand was giving where we talked about the draft. I know she was opposed to the draft. So it had come up in that context.

What were your main arguments?

I argued the twin case; one, it was the right thing to do, and two, it would make the military more effective and more powerful as a fighting force.

What was Ayn Rand's influence on you in regard to the moral argument?

I think what she did in some of the lectures, the way she discussed it, made the argument and the moral argument much tighter and clearer.

At the time, I believe you were also giving speeches for the Metropolitan Young Republican Club, with Leonard Peikoff and others.

That was probably '67. I had written about the issue and talked to a lot of people about it and had given speeches.

How did you lose touch with Ayn Rand?

I went to Washington, but I was never in touch with her in the sense of steady contact. I talked to her a couple times on the telephone. I remember she called me and asked me about Nixon.

How would you assess Miss Rand's influence on the culture today?

I'm speculating now, but I am continually surprised at the number of people I run into who have read her works. For a lot of people, reading her coalesces their ideas, and her ideas lock things in and reconfirm and make their own ideas more powerful. To that extent, the number of people she's affected is enormous.

Kathryn Eickhoff

Kathryn Eickhoff was a friend and financial adviser of Ayn Rand's. She worked for the economics consulting company Townsend-Greenspan & Co., Inc., for twenty-two years and is currently an economic consultant at her own firm, Eickhoff Economics, Inc. She is married to Jim Smith (see Jim Smith interview, page 537).

Interview date: November 29, 1999

Scott McConnell: *How did you meet Ayn Rand and Frank O'Connor?*

Kathryn Eickhoff: I was introduced by my friend Alan Greenspan, after one of NBI's Basic Principles lectures in 1962.

Tell me about the lectures, especially about Miss Rand during the Q&A.

She was very good with her answers and very clear on them. If someone was asking a question out of ignorance, that was fine. If they were asking something because they'd never read *Atlas Shrugged*, then she would be a little bit more curt, because it was understood that everybody at the lectures was to have read *Atlas Shrugged*.

Did you interact with the O'Connors after the lectures?

The Brandens, the O'Connors, myself and Alan Greenspan, if he was available, regularly went out to coffee. Occasionally the Blumenthals would join us. It was like any group of friends sitting down having coffee, talking about their work and related things.

What other interaction did you have with the O'Connors during this time?

Going out to a place that I think was in Hartsdale, New York, where there was a restaurant that had dinner and dancing and a roof that could roll back so that you could see the sky if the weather was nice. I remember going with Alan to that, and the O'Connors were there. And there would be occasions that were more parties than dinners, getting together at someone's apartment for conversation.

Describe these parties.

This would have been mostly starting in 1963. Usually Miss Rand was very nice to whoever was the newest person or someone who didn't know her very well. She usually invited that person to sit down next to her. I can remember her asking me about myself and asking me about her books and how I had been introduced to them and what I liked about them. She was very good about asking about the things that you were doing and interested in doing. At one of the early ones, Ludwig von Mises was there, and she was talking to him extensively. As I recall that was the first time that she had met him, although his books were amongst those recommended by NBI at the time, and some of the students monitored or audited courses of his at NYU. They seemed to get along fine.

What typically would happen during one of these evenings?

People would talk.

Do you mean with Miss Rand?

No, it was more the group. With Miss Rand, one on one, or more so with Frank, it wasn't a problem. But when there was a large group, then Nathan was a rather overpowering figure in the discussions. They would be on all kinds of philosophical or political issues or things people had seen happening recently.

What was the tone of the party?

Not serious. It was very congenial. A group of people who all shared major values together, enjoyed each other's company and got together regularly.

Any other specific anecdotes from those parties?

Ayn tended to be unhappy with her hair most of the time, and I had discovered some new kind of curlers that were very easy to use. I said something about it to her, and she said, "I don't have time for any of that kind of thing." I didn't bring up hair curlers again.

I think that about that same time, people were talking about when was she going to write another book or what was her next book going to be about. She was saying that it would be a mystery story, but it was going to feature a female central character who was a tap dancer. I commented that that should make for a gay and lighthearted book, because you couldn't very well be sad or downcast when you were tap dancing. She thought that was a very good observation.

At some of the parties, particularly after the Brandens and the O'Connors moved into the same apartment building on 34th Street, we would roll up the carpets and do some dancing, ballroom dancing. In fact, there was generally an enjoyment of music. Miss Rand, of course, had a lot of music that she was very fond of.

What about celebrating holidays?

Once, Jim—whom I later married—and I decided we would take the Christmas party to Ayn. On Christmas Day we called to see if she was going to be home. I asked if we could come up. Sure, she said. So we packaged up all the leftovers from our Christmas party—the punch and the eggnog and some various things that we'd had and some little presents for her—and took them over to her. She was just like a kid. Again, she didn't accept presents, but I remember her sitting there on the couch, taking the things out of the bag and unwrapping them, just thoroughly enjoying herself. She had such a good time having Christmas that she kept the gifts.

Miss Rand thought Christmas was a wonderful thing, because it had been so commercialized and that it was not a religious holiday at all. It was a joyous giving to people you were fond of, and where every place got beautifully decorated. But New Year's was actually more the big holiday for the O'Connors. And it would vary, from year to year, at whose house the party was given.

What would the O'Connors and their friends do on New Year's?

New Year's Eve would be very dressed up, and usually whoever was giving the party would have food available and play music if it was a place suitable for dancing.

What about at midnight?

There would be the traditional excitement and singing "Auld Lang Syne" and giving everybody a New Year's kiss.

Did you visit with the O'Connors at other times?

Occasionally Alan and I would. I had started working at his firm in November of 1962, but I had started dating him in late September of '62. We dated for two or three years, and I continued to work with him for twenty-three more years.

I had learned a lot from Nathan's lectures in terms of speaking and, particularly, question-answering techniques. Miss Rand did this too, repeating the question, which gave you time to think exactly what you wanted to say in answer to the question, rather than answering instantaneously in response to the question. I was very careful to do this when I gave a speech on Johnson's war on poverty, which was the first speech that I had given since I got out of high school.

It was to a political group in Queens. New York mayor [John] Lindsay was speaking on the program also. It was a great success, and after it was all over, Alan asked what I wanted to do to celebrate. I said, "You know what I'd really like is to go tell my two heroes about it." And he said, "And who would that be?" I said, "Frank and Ayn." I called them on the phone to see if it would be all right to come over, and so we went over to their apartment. I told them about the speech and gave Miss Rand a copy of it. She asked a lot of questions on the topic. Whatever I answered led to further questions on the subject, which was quite usual when talking with her. She followed a train of logic pretty much as far as it would go. We stayed there quite late talking about Johnson's war on poverty and the problems for the future that it was likely to cause. And sure enough, it has. I know we were discussing at the time that it would create problems for people on fixed incomes, that it was going to be inflationary, and that it would cost a lot more than they were estimating. It was just a horrendous program.

You called her "Ayn" from the beginning?

It very quickly moved to "Ayn," because of the relationship between Alan and her. So she was being introduced to me not as "Miss Rand" but as "Ayn Rand." It was "Ayn and Frank" from the beginning. At one point, after Alan and I had broken up, I was over at her house picking out kittens, and I called her "Miss Rand." She said, "Oh, now, Kathryn, you can't call me that. The name's 'Ayn.' We're still friends." Then I went back to "Ayn," except that I tried to remember to call her "Miss Rand" in front of people who were not personal friends of hers.

Once I stopped dating Alan, to the Brandens it was like I didn't exist anymore, which was very upsetting to me because I had been with them every week, two or three times a week, for the prior two and a half years. With Frank and Ayn, the relationship didn't change in any fundamental way. She made clear early on that she'd mostly be seeing and talking to me at social occasions or at the lectures or things of that sort. But she was very clear on what she was able to give to me in terms of her time, which was very valuable. And I understood that.

What was her manner of dealing with you and treating you?

She was always very lovely to me, and very friendly. I never had any surprise. She was always very kind. All things considered, she was very generous with her time to me.

Would you describe Miss Rand's relationship with Mr. Greenspan at that time?

Mr. Greenspan had provided a significant amount of the steel industry research for *Atlas Shrugged*. Alan's specialty in economics had begun in the steel industry when he worked at the National Industrial Conference Board, and it had continued after he founded Townsend-Greenspan.

What did she think of him?

She had very high expectations of him from a very early period. To me, the best summation of it was the dedication that she gave to him in his hardback copy of *Atlas Shrugged*, "To My Sleeping Giant." They had a good relationship through the years. He'd call and take her and Frank out for dinner whenever he had a chance to. He traveled a lot, so he wasn't necessarily always available.

When Alan was going down to Washington, initially with the Nixon administration, but of course, it turned into the Ford administration, she was very concerned that Alan might be making a sacrifice in doing it. She was also very clear that as long as it wasn't a sacrifice on his part, she was very supportive of his doing it. That was true throughout the period that he was down there.

We also talked similarly when I was being asked to come down to Washington in 1981. She warned me about being careful that I didn't find myself in a position where I had to compromise values and make sacrifices. Otherwise, here, too, she was very supportive. She was generally very patriotic, so working in Washington appealed to her from that standpoint. But she couldn't see herself doing it because her field would have put her in total conflict with anyone in government if she were down there. In Alan's case, it was somewhat different, and in my case it certainly was. Economics was a little bit further removed from the direct problems, although one can argue about that. In both our cases, we were able to work for less regulation and a reduction in the redistribution of income. However, there are three questions regarding high-level positions in Washington. Do you want to let the whole system collapse or do you want to try and make it work as efficiently as you can, until such time as you can get it fixed right? If you answer the first question "no" and the second "yes," as Miss Rand clearly would have done, are you sacrificing your values when you go along with a compromise in a battle you cannot win? I never asked her this question, so I do not know her answer. She did encourage me to go on down, but to be very careful that it didn't become a sacrifice and if it did, to come home.

What was Miss Rand's influence upon Mr. Greenspan?

Very profound. Of course, by the time I knew him he had been an avowed Objectivist for quite a number of years, but I think her views gave a foundation to his own views on economics and broadened those views, giving him a philosophical underpinning that they didn't have. And Objectivism gave him, I think, a better appreciation of people and their motivations. Also, it certainly provided him with a methodology for thinking. In fact, that's the thing that Jim and I personally find the greatest benefit of Objectivism: it gives you a way of coming at problems that is rather different from that followed by other philosophies.

Ayn was very thrilled to be asked by Alan to come to his swearing-in and to meet President Ford and to go into the Oval Office.

Do you remember any of her comments about that?

No. I know that she was pleased. Again, she always reminded me of a proud parent in her feelings toward Alan.

What was his feeling for her?

Much the reverse.

A proud son?

Yes. And there has been no change in that view since Ayn passed away. I think Miss Rand would be very pleased with what he's accomplished and done for the United States.[132]

What was Mr. Greenspan's relationship with Mr. O'Connor?

Other than generally friendly, I don't know that they had any real independent relationship. I felt close to Frank because we spent a lot of time together at the lectures. He took me to see his studio and showed me what he had painted and what he was working on, so we had a closer relationship.

---

132 "This statement was true in 1999 when I gave this interview. Ayn probably would have been concerned Alan was sacrificing his values as chairman of the Federal Reserve in the later years. Furthermore, if she had read his book [*The Age of Turbulence*, 2007], published after he left the Fed, I imagine she would have been very disappointed. I know I was."—M. Kathryn Eickhoff-Smith, 2009

Tell me about those visits to the studio.

The studio was relatively small. It was over on 28th Street then, between Park and Lexington. It was at the time that he was working on the painting *Diminishing Returns*, which had his self-portrait in the colored balls. And he showed me some cityscapes that he had done or was working on.

Tell me about the O'Connors and their cat Thunderbird.

This is the story of the O'Connors getting Thunderbird. Two NBI students, after one of the lectures, came up with this kitten in a little hat and wanted to give it to Miss Rand. And, as was Miss Rand's custom, she said, "Oh, no." She didn't accept gifts, but there were exceptions; after a few minutes, she did accept the gift, and she and Frank took the kitten home.

Quite some months later, I was visiting with the O'Connors, and Ayn was commenting on how wonderful it was that Frisco and Thunderbird were so fond of each other and that fortunately Frisco was too old to have kittens. Alan Blumenthal, having later heard a similar comment, looked at Thunderbird and said, "I think you're wrong about Frisco. Thunderbird is going to have kittens in about a week." And she did. She had four of them. And one looked like Frisco and the other three looked like Thunderbird. Alan asked them if I could have one and they said "certainly." So I got mine and named it "Dominic." Actually, I named him "Dominique," but then he turned out to be a him instead of the her I had been told he was. Ayn referred to herself as "Dominic's grandmother," and I gave her regular reports on how and what he was doing.

They kept Frisco Jr. And after Frisco died, it was Frisco Jr. and Thunderbird that lived with the O'Connors.

Do you have any other cat stories?

She never had her cats declawed and she never had the males neutered.

Why was that?

Because of her views on sex. Sex is a very important, pleasurable aspect of life, and Miss Rand thought it was probably equally pleasurable to cats. If you neutered them it was the same thing as castrating a man, so she'd never do it.

Did you give stamps to Miss Rand?

We had an Objectivist friend who had a business that received a lot of letters from overseas. He would save all the pretty stamps and give them to Jim and me, and we'd take them over to Miss Rand on our next visit. She was always happy to see stamps. She didn't accept gifts, but she would always accept stamps.

What about Miss Rand and beards?

She did not like beards. She thought men in beards looked like they were trying to hide something. Jim had a beard back in the early '70s, and Miss Rand always said she'd never kiss a man with a beard. But she would kiss Jim, even though he had a beard.

Didn't it bother her?

No. She would say something like "You know, I don't kiss men with beards." She and Jim would have just kissed. It was funny.

You knew Miss Rand after her lung cancer operation in 1975.

We tried and failed to talk her into exercising more and taking vitamins to help her get more strength. She said that she couldn't do exercise because she had no energy. We tried to explain to her that that was because she didn't do any exercising, that if she would exercise she would have more energy. She wouldn't do anything with vitamins, because she would have to do a lot of research to find out which vitamins did what and which ones were of questionable value. She had one doctor that she trusted, and if he didn't say do something, then she didn't do it.

Did you talk to her about any of her projects?

She talked to me on the telephone and told me about *Atlas Shrugged* being made into a movie and being very excited about the agreement that she had been able to reach with a producer. That never came to pass.

Later, she was going to write the script herself. Jim and I asked her, "Would we be able to invest in it?" She was very averse to our doing so, because she thought we would be doing it because it was her, not for true investment purposes. But we said, "No, to us it seems like a good investment." So she said okay, we could.

Did you ever have any girl-talk with Ayn Rand? Hair, makeup, shopping, that kind of thing?

I wouldn't say we ever discussed girl topics except perhaps the problems of her height and therefore needing, she felt, to wear extraordinarily high heels in order to look taller. But, because she wore such high heels, she couldn't walk very far in them. This always annoyed her. We occasionally talked about confidential things.

Can you tell me about one of these private conversations?

I became her financial adviser in the last few years of her life, so we talked about her finances. She was very pleased and proud of what she had accumulated, and we talked about the royalties and what she'd gotten on *Atlas* and what was still coming in on *The Fountainhead* and other books. I asked what did she have, how did she have this invested. She had it across the street at a savings bank. I guess the utter horror that I felt was apparent just looking at me. She had always expressed the view she didn't want to be in government bonds, because of it being government. I said, "You know the savings banks, the only thing that's keeping them afloat is the government." They were probably the riskiest place to have money over the minimum that the FSLDIC insured, because they were borrowing short and lending long. After that conversation, we started changing what her investment holdings were.

I introduced her to Chuck Brunie of Oppenheimer Capital. Chuck was an Objectivist and a big fan of Miss Rand's. I remember taking him over to her apartment and her saying, "How am I going to compensate you for this?" And he replied, "Oh, Miss Rand, you've more than compensated me. This is little enough for all you've given me through the years." She was very pleased by the expression of admiration and respect that he was indicating. He took on her account and it was invested in very safe securities. As I recall, money market funds probably yielded as much as you could get from a safe return without per se being in government bonds. And at the time, she did say she didn't want to invest in equities because then she would have to investigate the company and the people who ran the company and whether they were taking government subsidies or things of that sort. She didn't have time to do that.

She didn't want to invest in the stock market. To me, it was somewhat like not taking vitamins: that she'd have to do too much research herself to feel comfortable doing it. I'm sure Chuck took that into consideration in choosing what he put her in. I didn't make any effort to find out exactly what he had her in. The one thing we did buy was "flower" bonds. These were a specific series of government bonds, which, while they were at the time selling at a discount from par because interest rates were high, in case of death they could be used at face value to settle estate taxes and they could be purchased quite close to the date of death.

Never in all the years that I knew her did I ever see her be anything other than kind and very generous with her time to Jim and me. I don't think we were necessarily the most stimulating intellectual companions for her. Maybe we weren't worth getting upset with, but I certainly never saw her exhibit any negative, or angry, behavior in her relationship with Alan or with us.

What illnesses did Mr. O'Connor have?

I talked to him about the problem he had with his hands kind of shriveling up, the muscles contracting, and about the surgery he had on them. After that, he had to exercise a lot with a little ball, as physical therapy for the hand. I can recall him explaining to me how he had to do this off and on all day long, trying to strengthen and control those fingers. The illness was very devastating for Frank, because it meant he couldn't hold a paintbrush anymore. I took them some extra pillows so he could rest his hand better and fixed a "pot roast" dinner for them. I think they particularly enjoyed that. I had the sense that they mostly ate TV dinners in the evenings.

Frank also had a heart attack and was hospitalized for some time. Ayn commented this was the first time she had ever been away from Frank overnight. Mary Ann Sures stayed with her until Frank got out of the hospital.

Did Miss Rand's character or personality or sense of life change over the twenty years you knew her?

Not that I saw, particularly if you mean in any sort of negative way. If anything, I would say it changed more positively over the years. At least from my standpoint, it became easier and easier for me to talk to her. In part that may have been her becoming more personal with me, and it may have been my becoming more confident with myself.

Earl, Della and Anna Lively

Earl and Della Lively were acquaintances of Ayn Rand's; Anna Lively, Earl and Della's daughter, is a cabaret singer and is Miss Rand's goddaughter. Earl Lively was a newspaper and radio columnist at the time he knew Miss Rand.

Interview date: August 9 and October 15, 1999.

Scott McConnell: *How did you meet Miss Rand?*

Earl Lively: I was doing radio commentary and a newspaper column in the early 1960s and became the rep in Dallas for Nathaniel Branden Lectures. Della and I took all the courses from NBI with Branden, and sometimes with Leonard Peikoff as a guest lecturer. I got to know Nathaniel Branden fairly well, because he came to Dallas a couple of times to kick off the lectures. I got to know Miss Rand when she was doing *The Objectivist*, and people were saying, "Miss Rand, we want to see what you have to say about current affairs." But she was too busy putting her philosophy together, and getting it all down, organized on paper.

Branden told me they were thinking about getting someone else to write articles for *The Objectivist*. In the end, they decided not to do that, but he suggested I send some of my articles to her. She was taken with one of the articles, and she quoted it in *The Objectivist Newsletter* in October 1965, and then I corresponded with her. Then in 1966, I was in Washington, D.C., for a couple of months in the summer, and we went to New York and some mutual friends introduced us.

It was arranged for us to have dinner with Miss Rand and Mr. O'Connor at a friend's apartment on August 26, 1966. So we went to New York, although my wife then was very, very pregnant with Anna. In fact, she gave birth to her two weeks later. So we talked. And we talked and we talked and we talked. And at three o'clock in the morning, I drove her and her husband back to their apartment.

What did you talk about?

A lot of things. We discussed the article of mine she had quoted. She told me, when we first were talking, "You may be pleased to know that the quote I took from you in the newsletter is going to be in my new book, *Capitalism: The Unknown Ideal.*" I said, "Well, I am very pleased." And I said, "Miss Rand, I will tell you a story about how I knew which one of the articles I sent you, you were going to use."

The article was where I wrote in my column, "Lively Comments," April 28, 1965: "Afraid to stand alone, even on his knees, [George] Romney then tells the rest of us that we do not know the definition of Capitalism; we do not understand our economic principles, and we'd be better off if we'd quit going around defending such an unpopular concept as capitalism." He wanted the world to know we had moved on to a higher concept called "Consumerism." "Afraid to stand alone, even on his knees"—I thought that sounded like a line that Ayn Rand would have written. I told her so and said, "I knew that must have been what appealed to you." And she looked at me admiringly, and said, "It is the kind of line I would like to have written."

I replied, "Well, Miss Rand, then you trumped me, because in your article you said, 'Mr. Lively is admirably precise in his description of the posture involved,' of Romney being on his knees, and then you went on to analyze it brilliantly, so you trumped me by playing on what I said." She replied, "No, my dear, you played the trump, I merely followed suit." She was so absolutely gracious that it was overwhelming.

What else did you discuss with Miss Rand that night?

We had some questions about Objectivism, and she was very interested in Della and asked about her. Miss Rand didn't want her to be left out of the conversation, and she asked her about her ideas, and she was very interested to hear them. It wasn't that she was just trapped into something. David Dawson (at whose apartment we were meeting) was doing anti-draft work then, and he started to ask her something, and she said, "Now, David, I can talk to you anytime. I'm here to listen to Mr. Lively's ideas," and dismissed him. One of the things we talked about—I was writing some articles then for *American Opinion* magazine, some on military strategy, and some on political economy, and I had sent her a copy of an article that I had written, and I showed her the contents in the front, where the editors' comments were, and there was also an article by E. Merrill Root, who had written an article about her in *National Review* after *Atlas* came out. Professor Root loved Ayn Rand's work, and constantly defended her to other religion-based conservatives by rationalizing that she really wasn't an atheist.

The editor had commented about my article and also written

that "Professor E. Merrill Root will shock Ayn Rand's friends and foes alike," or something to that effect, by showing that she's really religious. Of course, that's the worst insult. I circled that with a red pen, and I put an exclamation point at the end of it, thinking, "Isn't this preposterous?" So toward the end of our conversation, she mentioned this to me, and I said, "If you're telling the truth, you can't get printed many places. That's one of the reasons I write for *American Opinion*." She said "Oh, no, that's perfectly right, and that's true. But, to be in there, and keep company with someone that wrote that. . . ," and I said, "I put a red exclamation point to indicate how preposterous," and she said, "I expect my friends to defend me." And I said, "That's right, I probably should have told them that I didn't agree with that." She winked at me, and kind of squeezed my hand, and said, "But that's all right, I still like you."

Tell me about your impression of Ayn Rand from that evening.

Of course, the eyes; it's always the eyes. When you see her, they are so intense and so deep, and she was so gracious, and we were talking about serious things, but I felt a warmth, and certainly she didn't talk down to you, or anything like that. She was interested in what I had to say. And she told me, "You know, a lot of people who write things from the Objectivist standpoint try to write like I do, but you have the Objectivist ideas in your own words, without using my terms, or anything like that. You analyze in the same manner."

After we took them home late that first night, the next day Della and I took the boat cruise around Manhattan Island. When we got back to her hotel, our friends were there, waiting to contact us because Miss Rand was trying to get in touch with me. They gave me her unlisted phone number and said she wanted me to call her. I called, and this is another thing about how Ayn Rand was: she said she'd been thinking about the fact that I was having trouble getting syndicated, because you know how the syndication market is—you make a name, you write a book, either intelligent or stupid and get famous, and then people want you to write a column. They don't want to take it on the basis of what you have to say. She asked me if it would be all right for her to intervene with the L.A. Times Syndicate, and try to get them to carry my column. And her publisher, then, was owned by the same company that owned L.A. Times Syndicate—she had those connections. She asked me for my permission, so she wasn't at all presumptuous, and I said, "Why, of course."

We went back to Texas. Anna was born the day after we got back and we named her Anna Rand Lively.

Did you tell Miss Rand about that?

Oh yes! We had planned, if it was a girl, to name her Anna, but hadn't thought of a middle name. Della, just out of the delivery room and not in full focus, was asked for a name. My mother's name was Jeannie and Della's middle name was Jeanne, so she told the hospital registrar, "Anna Jeanne." And when the certificate came out, I said, "We can't do this. We've got to name her for Miss Rand." It kept bothering us that we had botched it, so I got a lawyer to draw up the papers for me, and I officially changed her name.

It happened that the day we went to court to finalize the change, it was the tenth anniversary of *Atlas Shrugged*. So I wrote Miss Rand a letter, and I think I sent her a copy of the document, and I wrote, "Happy 10th Anniversary of *Atlas Shrugged*. Here's what I did on this day. I changed my daughter's name to Anna Rand." So one of Anna's real treasures is that they had a special-bound tenth-anniversary edition of *Atlas Shrugged*, boxed, and they were all numbered and signed by her. I wrote Miss Rand right after that, and I said, "would you please write in one of them, 'to Anna'?" And I sent her the money, but she never cashed the check, and she wrote a little special message at the top of the page, and put her initials.

Did Miss Rand ever make a comment about you giving Anna that name?

Oh yes. She was very happy about it. And then later I took Anna to meet her in 1978, just before Anna's twelfth birthday. We met with her and her husband in their apartment, and we sat and talked. I had called Miss Rand to see if she would be available, and that I wanted to bring Anna to visit with her and meet her. Miss Rand said, "I am very, very busy"; that's when she was doing the screenplay for an *Atlas Shrugged* miniseries on NBC.[133] And she said, "Now, I have to swear you to secrecy about this, because the producer should be able to announce it, and I shouldn't tell anyone about it, but I have to tell you that one of the reasons I am so busy and have very little time, is because I am now working on this script." She said, "However, I must make time to visit with you and your daughter, for after all, I am her godmother." And I said, "If you'll pardon the

---

133 NBC later cancelled the miniseries, terming it "controversial."

stolen concept." And she said, "It's a lovely concept, and if we want to borrow it for a little while, we will."

So she was the first one to refer to Anna as her "goddaughter"?

Oh yes, she said it to me.

Earl Lively: *Anna, what do you remember of that visit?*

Anna Lively: It's a weird combination, because the vision that I have is that if she hadn't been so dear, you would have been, like, a little frightened, because she was so powerful. But she was so little, and she looked like somebody's little grandmother, but very tailored and very striking. She was so warm and sweet, but those eyes were unbelievable, because you couldn't take your eyes off her. She had like a glow, and at that young age I was overwhelmed. And I felt totally at ease; she didn't make me nervous, because she was so friendly, and so loving and sweet. It was like being in the presence of real greatness. I've never felt that way being in the room with any other celebrity I've met. It was real strength.

Scott McConnell: *What did you talk about?*

It's funny. The one thing I really remember is that I said something about hating algebra, that it doesn't make any sense, and she went into this talk about algebra, and why we need it. By the time I left there, I thought algebra was the greatest thing on earth. I can't remember what she said, but I just remember thinking, "That's the best explanation I ever could imagine hearing. Now I get why we have it."

Earl Lively: *Anna, do you remember she said that you're a little young but do you have any idea of what you might want to be? Anna had just seen a big King Tut archeological exhibit that had come through.*

Anna Lively: I wanted to be an archeologist. And she said, "and go to all those awful countries."

Earl Lively: Anna said she'd thought some about archeology, and Miss Rand kind of looked like she was eating a lemon, and she said, "But Anna, you'd have to work and live in those awful countries." You got the impression that Ayn Rand was no Third-Worlder. And that's the thing that got me—is that nobody ever loved this country, and the concept of this country, like she did. This was the most important country and the most important thing that ever happened.

Anna Lively: She was very, very friendly, and she was very warm, and like Dad said, not at all what people think.

Earl Lively: I knew that she didn't like Ronald Reagan. She had spoken about his being a compromiser, but in 1976 I had created an organization called "Pilots for Reagan," and I got a list of all the pilots in the United States, and we gave out little wings and supported Reagan against the Ford primary campaign. I asked Miss Rand, "What are we going to do for a candidate in 1980? There's nobody out there." I said, "I know you don't like Ronald Reagan, because he's a compromiser. I know exactly why you said that, but I don't see anybody else out there." And she mentioned William Simon, who was probably the best man around. She said she thought he might be pretty good, but he'd been off on a Catholic religious kick, getting that involved in his politics. She said that Alan Greenspan liked Reagan, and "That's okay, but I could never support him." I asked her reasons for that, and she mentioned his compromising in fighting the Reds in Hollywood.

How did he compromise in Hollywood?

She explained that she and others, including some of the big studio heads, were determined to get the communists out of the industry, and they were standing their ground and expecting to defeat the pro-Reds. Then another group, with Reagan in the leadership, started working for compromise between the two sides, and this middle group kept the anti-communist group from expelling the Reds. I said, "That's terrible," and she said, "That's not the worst of it." I asked, "What could be worse than that?" And she answered, "The Reagan group called themselves 'the extreme middle.'" I said, "That's one of the most contemptible things I ever heard of!" And I never voted for Reagan again, not in 1980 or 1984.

Any other anecdotes about Miss Rand?

I asked her about Alexander Solzhenitsyn, and I said I had noticed that Solzhenitsyn was always bad-mouthing the United States, and the tenor of most of it was that we weren't religious enough. In so many words, that our country's no good because we're just not obsessed with religion. I said I saw his recent speech at the U.N., and that as usual, he displayed a strong bias against American society. Miss Rand told me that she had obtained the original transcript in Russian from the U.N., and translated it herself, so there wouldn't be anything misquoted and said that it was worse than the interpreter reported.

She reached down on her coffee table and picked up a Pat Oliphant cartoon she had clipped out of the paper, and said it was the best comment that had been made about Solzhenitsyn's speech. In the cartoon, there's an old Russian woman with a heavy black dress, and a scarf over her head, with a doctor, coming into this completely bare room. Solzhenitsyn is sitting on the floor in the far corner with a little cloud and thunderstorm above him, and there's one of these little American desk flags on the floor in front of him. He's sitting there glaring at it, with eyes just like saucers, and this thunderstorm over his head. And the woman says, "He's like this around every July Fourth, Doctor: all those people enjoying themselves. All that fun, all that pursuit of happiness. Oh, it's a very bad time for Mr. Solzhenitsyn." And there are two bugs in the corner and one of them says to the other, "Get the whip, that'll cheer him up a bit." Miss Rand said that was the best comment in the country.

What she didn't know was that I knew Pat Oliphant. So, when I got back to Dallas, I called him and told him the story and about what she had said about him. I asked him if he possibly had the original full-size drawing, and without hesitating, he said, "Do you want me to send it to her, or do you want to?" So he obviously was an admirer of Ayn Rand. And I said, "Why don't you autograph the original, and send it to me, and I'll have it framed, and send it on to her." Which I did. Across the bottom, it says, "For Ayn Rand, with my best wishes, Pat Oliphant."

There's one other little thing I might tell you about Ayn Rand—that she always liked good ideas from anybody. I had a friend named Harry Knickerbocker Jr., who encouraged me to read her works.

She said that philosophy and the curriculum in all the colleges are bad, some are just worse than the others. And I said, "My friend Harry Knickerbocker said that what the colleges do for our children is give them non-surgical lobotomies." And she said, "He said that?" Oh, she thought that was great. Then I mentioned that he noted that people say about capitalism: "It's the best economic system, or the fairest economic system," but, he says, "It's the *only* economic system. The rest of them are not economic systems—they are just systems of dividing up the spoils. Capitalism is the only *economic* system." She thought that was brilliant.

Mrs. Lively, you must have been excited when you got to meet Miss Rand?

Della Lively: Oh yes, I was thrilled! In those days Earl was a political writer and quite popular. I knew that Miss Rand wanted to meet him and was interested in his ideas. I knew that I would be there to listen, and believe me, I was excited. I was going to be in the same room with the woman who had changed my life by writing *Atlas Shrugged*! She and her husband arrived, and although she and Earl did have a grand time talking to each other, she took time to show interest in me. She knew I was pregnant—she didn't know that night that we would later name our little girl Anna Rand Lively—and she asked me personal questions about how I felt, and was I excited about having my first baby. She was as nice and as wonderful to me as she could possibly be. Later, when I heard people say she must be a cold person, caught up with herself, I would always correct them by telling them how very, very nice she had been to me on that summer night in New York in 1966. I'll never ever forget that evening.

Miss Rand was fun too. We drove Mr. O'Connor and Miss Rand back to their apartment; we all had stayed at our friends' home until three o'clock in the morning. Earl was excited and wanted to talk to Miss Rand all the way—he drove but turned his head around a lot—she was in the right rear seat—anyway, she laughed and said, as she tapped him on the shoulder in a friendly way, "Earl, I really am very interested in what you are saying but please don't look back at me—you're in New York—please watch the road and get me home safe!"

Miss Rand called Earl at our hotel the next day and told him how much she had enjoyed meeting us and talking to him especially. They remained telephone friends until she passed away.

Robert Stack

Robert Stack began his acting career in 1939 in Hollywood. From 1959 to 1963 he was the star of the hit television series *The Untouchables*, playing renowned Chicago FBI agent Eliot Ness, for which he won the Emmy for best actor in 1960. Mr. Stack died in 2003.

Interview date: February 23, 1999

Scott McConnell: *What is your strongest memory of Ayn Rand?*

Robert Stack: The article she wrote for the *Los Angeles Times* about *The Untouchables*.[134] This article is very special. I have it framed on my wall. It's a wonderful article that is very comprehensive and tells pretty much the way I feel and the way she does about the show. The article was in direct response to critiques of *The Untouchables*, which created quite a stir in many areas. The show was quite simply a morality play—good versus evil—and I made sure the hoods were exactly what they were—a bunch of crumb-bums. You didn't qualify them, make them terribly sensitive, mixed up people. We just made them the bastards that they were.

I was criticized in doing *The Untouchables* because of the violence. I said, you cannot show evil unless you show good—you cannot show good unless you show evil. Unless we show these bums doing the terrible things they did, Ness has absolutely no value. And towards that end, Ness was an individual. The reason he did this, and maybe it's apocryphal, but this again gets back to Ayn in the sense that Ness did it for a reason that was important to him. He got six guys and went in there and fought, not only city hall, but Capone and the rest of them. That's the reason that Ayn hewed to the show and was sympathetic to the concept.

What struck me about this article is that in the last part Ayn says, "If moral influence on children is your concern, ask yourself which will help to shape a child's moral character: the conviction that justice, values, struggles and victories are possible, and that there are heroes that he can live up to—or the conviction that nothing is possible and anything is permissible, that the good he desperately longs for is an illusion, but the evil that tempts him will bring him loving sympathy, that nobody can help what he does and there is no way out of the

---

134 Ayn Rand's *Los Angeles Times* column of July 8, 1962, is reprinted in *The Ayn Rand Column*, pp. 12–14.

incomprehensible terror with which life seems to confront him. Which will shape his soul? Which made you, perhaps, renounce yours?"

In response, I wrote her a note, which I've got here. It says, "Dear Miss Rand, I'd like to thank you for your wonderful article regarding TV and in particular *The Untouchables*. The moments of real gratification in our profession are rare indeed. I remember what I was told by an old character actor, when I first started in the business. He said the first thing an actor could hope for was to command the respect of the very few whose opinions he respected. I think even this dour old Scot would have been impressed by such an article on the editorial page written by Ayn Rand."

I felt so honored by her article. This is such beautifully written use of the English language, which is something people have forgotten how to do. Reading her article, you say to yourself, talk about a shining intellectual—whether you agree or disagree—this is something that is very special. So I've got it framed.

What was the effect on you of getting that review, especially in the period you were being attacked?

It was a validation. As I told the producers early on: if you glamorize or excuse the behavior of these crumbs, you're talking about the lowest form of life. To take them and somehow humanize them, I'm not going to do it. Eliot Ness was a guy who went in there with six other guys and he declared war, which is second cousin to suicide, against these animals who controlled and owned Chicago. This is true, even if it's not Roark in *The Fountainhead*; it's certainly an individual who went out there against the odds, against the corruption of that particular city.

The one thing that sealed everything was this article. It's really an outstanding piece of writing and to me it struck to the core of the individual and the good guy versus the bad guy. And that goes all the way back to World War II, Iwo Jima, Guadalcanal, the people who risked their lives for their country, who salute the flag, who're quite simply heroes. That's where my heart lies.

I felt so close to her when I read this. Many times you do something as a performer and you just hope and pray somebody will understand what you're trying to do. You spend your life throwing what you do out to people and hoping someone is on the other end. Someone once said it's like blowing into a barrel hoping someone can hear you on the other end. In the case of Miss Rand, this article is such that it makes you feel that not only is it worth it, but the things that you try so desperately hard to communicate have been received on the other end completely and have manifested themselves in the written word in a way that is even more than you'd ever hope for. When I read it, I felt like adopting her.

You mentioned the name Howard Roark. Was he a hero of yours?

He was. There are areas that you can get into if you take her philosophy to its logical extension; you can take it to a degree whereby you're antigovernment entirely and the individual has a right to everything but yell "Fire, fire!" But I understood Roark and I understood where she was coming from. I think there must be a couple of qualifiers to *The Fountainhead*, but I think that, by and large, individualism is what made this country great, what made this country function from its very inception. I remember one young lady who wrote an article decrying the heroes, saying we should pay more attention to the bravery of the common man who has to get up in the morning and all the rest of it, which I think is hoo-hah.

What was it specifically about Howard Roark that you admired or enjoyed?

Those of us who try to be creative, do it and march to our own drummer. And Roark did this to fulfill his own creative dream while he was being bastardized on all fronts.

Was there a particular scene in the novel or the movie of The Fountainhead *that inspired you or that you especially enjoyed?*

As a so-called artist, I think I just plain empathized with Roark's indomitable marching towards a given goal and letting nothing stand in his way, to a degree whereby he might be called an "extremist." The creative juices, I guess, whether you're a concert pianist or an architect or whatever, in theory, should be unqualified and pure and true and toward that end that's what the art, if it is an art form, is all about. I give you Frank Lloyd Wright. I give you the ones who have done it their way without having to qualify it. What struck me most of all is that it's a continual battle between the artist and, on the other side, the pragmatist who wants it to succeed for other reasons.

When did you first read The Fountainhead?

When it first came out. It was a best-seller and of course everybody wanted to play Roark.

Did you?

Oh, of course!

Did you try for it or get a chance?

When you've got Gary Cooper or Clark Gable going for the role, you don't have much of a prayer.

Is The Fountainhead *one of your favorite books?*

Yes, it's one of my favorites.

Arnold Newman

Arnold Newman was a world-celebrated portrait photographer, whose portraits include every American president and Israeli prime minister of the last fifty years. He photographed Miss Rand in 1964. Mr. Newman died in 2006.

Interview date: April 5, 1999

Scott McConnell: *How did you come to photograph Ayn Rand?*

Arnold Newman: At that time I was asked, I believe by her publisher, New American Library, to photograph her. With my photographs I mostly work on location. When I asked to see where she worked, she said, "At the apartment," and she invited me over. When I went over there, she was with her husband—and I think she was somewhat cautious—and I looked around and I was sort of startled. Everything was covered with heavy plastic: the rugs, the chairs, the sofa, the lamps, everything—I was absolutely stunned. Of course, I said nothing about it at all. Then we said we would call each other to make a final date and time so that I could do the photograph. I don't know whether it was then or later, she told me she preferred to do it at my studio—she would not want to be photographed at home.

Had you read her work?

I did read some of it. Not that I disliked her work—what I mean is, I just didn't agree with her, so I didn't read much of it.

Later she did come to my studio, and she wore her favorite pin—a dollar sign. I don't know whether you've seen those photographs I took, but on them she wore a black dress with a dollar sign. I just made some head shots, things like that, and I don't particularly remember any unusual exchange or anything like that.

Was there anything unique or interesting about her face or her stance?

As far as her face was concerned, she was not, in the Hollywood sense, a great beauty. But that sort of thing doesn't worry me or concern me when I photograph people. I photograph people, I don't photograph faces, but she had a rugged face, and I photographed her as she was. I didn't try to make her beautiful, nor did I try to make her ugly. I deal

---

with reality. Particularly when dealing with women, I avoid anything that is unpleasant about them and their looks or personality. For one of the photographs, she just closed her eyes, sort of like she was meditating or something, so I took the picture. Although that isn't the one that was used, the others are very similar, but her eyes were open.[135]

What was the purpose of the photo? Was it for a book cover?[136]

I think so, or a part of the back jacket.

What were you trying to capture in her?

I don't try to "capture." To some degree, I try to obtain the individual's common denominator as best I can. No. People generally pretty well present themselves as themselves. I don't have any trouble with that—I'm not looking to capture the soul. The hell with it. If priests, psychiatrists and rabbis can't figure out what the soul is and define it, how the hell can I? I'm just a photographer. I look for that common denominator; I try to get them to relax, so for the moment they're not uptight—they're not overly aware they are having a picture made of them. I just try to find something that they themselves present when they're relaxed.

Have you ever been on a bus or subway or some public conveyance where people have to sit for a while? I notice that their expressions are very neutral, and that's very often what I go for. Sometimes some people will be a little bit towards the humorous side, or the depressed side or the arrogant side, and that comes out.

What do you think came out with Ayn Rand?

I think, particularly in the picture with her eyes closed, pretty much of the dreamer, the person who is trying to put over her version of what life in the world and business and everything else should be about.

What was she like as a model?

She's not a model. A model is somebody without character. She was a person, a personality that I was photographing. She was willing enough—I mean there was no objection that I can recall or any demands that she made or anything else. She came in one dress and I photographed her in that one dress.

---

135 It has since been published in *Arnold Newman* (Taschen, 2001), p. 162.

136 The photograph appeared on the back cover of the first edition of *The Virtue of Selfishness* (New York: Signet, 1964).

She has a scarf wrapped around her neck in several of the photographs. It's a very interesting touch.

Yes, on some of them she had the scarf, but on most of them it seems she didn't.

You seem to have focused a lot on a half-light across her face.

Oh, when she's standing. I don't know why the hell I did it that way. It's a terrible photograph. She has her hands on her hips in one of them. She's rather intense, and then sometimes she has sort of a smile. She had a variety of expressions; I think she was trying to look intense and very serious.

You've certainly captured that.

They pretty well give themselves away—let's put it that way.

How long did the shoot take?

Oh, I don't know; maybe up to an hour or so. There was nothing unusual happening that would make me remember the sitting as anything special. Now that I look at them, I realize that we did quite a bit, and she was very cooperative.

How many do you have?

I see one of them marked "48." That's quite a bit, even for this kind of sitting.

From your dealings with Ayn Rand, what was your opinion of her as a person?

She was a pretty straightforward, no-nonsense kind of a gal. And she was bright. I purposely did not talk to her about her books, because I didn't agree with all her writing, and so it must have been a light conversation, whatever we had.

What did you think of the photographs?

They're in several of my books. I think the one used by NAL was a very good portrait, and I think I did a very good job in showing Ayn Rand.

Alvin Toffler

Alvin Toffler, author of *Future Shock* and *The Third Wave*, interviewed Ayn Rand for *Playboy* magazine's March 1964 issue.

Interview date: February 17, 1999

Scott McConnell: *Why were you chosen by* Playboy *to interview Miss Rand in December 1963?*

Alvin Toffler: Simply that I had done interviews and they liked them. I was competent and a good journalist. I don't think there was any special reason.

Did you have a strong ideology then?

I was shaking off ideologies rather than adopting them. By that time it was well shook, but I started on the far left and migrated. I thought that Ayn Rand's views were extreme, but that she was a very sharp lady, very smart. I frankly didn't know a lot about her until somebody said, "Pay attention."

What did you know about her?

I knew that she was controversial. I had probably read some of the reviews of *Atlas Shrugged*. The really funny story is that when I got the assignment I made it my business to read everything I could get my hands on except *Atlas Shrugged*, which was eleven hundred formidable pages. I went to see her, dragging—in those days—my huge tape recorder. I spent quite a bit of time, perhaps an hour or two, with her. At one point, she sat up, bolt upright, and in a truly prosecutorial tone said, "You didn't read *Atlas Shrugged*!" I tremblingly responded that she had, in fact, got me. I had read everything else but hadn't read *Atlas Shrugged*. She said, "Go out and leave and don't come back until you've read it." Which I did. It was really funny.

Did she later quiz you to see if you actually had read Atlas Shrugged*?*

Listen, we authors can spot that from ten miles away.

When you met her, what was your impression?

Surprise. I hadn't known that she spoke with an accent, and she made me think of a nice Jewish grandmother.

Describe the interview process.

The first session was probably a couple of hours in her apartment in Manhattan. Then I came back, and I don't recall how long that interview lasted. I didn't challenge her views. My job as an interviewer was to elicit them, and I think that's what I did. She was a very striking personality. You didn't forget an encounter with her, particularly one in which she threw you out and invited you back.

Why did you choose the questions and topics that you did?

I'm sure they did reflect my interests. My interests have always been sociological, in terms of social analysis and economics, and philosophical as well. The interview was long, so you had an opportunity to develop ideas and that's why I liked those.

Can you remember who decided which questions would be published?

Playboy would say, "Do an interview with X, Y, Z," and they might suggest a few lines of interest, but I would work up a set of proposed questions and probably send it back to them.

I do remember that she had been burned by the press so much that she was absolutely fierce in her demand to control every aspect of this project, including—and this goes beyond the usual by a long shot—the captions under the photographs. That's not a standard thing at all to allow an interviewee. I never encountered anything like that before in a person that I was interviewing.

Did she have editing control?

I believe she had some sort of control. She would not have done it without some sort of advance read. I don't recall any great controversy or any great difficulties.

What did you think of her answers?

Sharp! She was extremely intelligent and very, very sharp. Because she was working from a philosophical system, she probably could anticipate the direction of any of the questions, and had very well-formulated answers.

What was your general opinion of your interview of her?

I thought it was a good interview, but then again I was a prejudiced observer. This was a woman with whom you didn't have to agree in order to recognize the scintillation.

As an interviewer, what is the key to a good interview?

The irony, especially in light of what I've told you, is do your homework before you get there—and read all of it—read *Atlas Shrugged*.

As a writer and a journalist, I've had many wonderful encounters and adventures with all kinds of people—from presidents and prime ministers to Nobel Prize winners, and I'd rate her highly in that company. She never disappeared into the background. She sparkled.

Tania Grossinger

In 1964 Tania Grossinger was a publicist for *Playboy* magazine.
Interview date: February 11, 1997

Scott McConnell: *How did you meet Ayn Rand?*

Tania Grossinger: I was Director of Broadcast Promotion for
Playboy magazine, here in New York. My job at that time was to place
people who were the subjects of *Playboy* interviews on radio and
television talk shows.

I would get the galleys of the interviews about two months before
they were published. So when I got Ayn Rand's, along with a contact
number to reach her, I called her up and asked her if she would be
willing to cooperate for this. She said absolutely and gave me her
address. We made a date for me to come over so we could just meet
each other. I liked the fact that she invited me to her home the first time.
Some people don't want to do that until they get to know you or don't
want to have a stranger in their home.

So this is my first meeting with Ayn Rand. After knocking on
the door, she opens it and she's wearing an apron. She's waiting for
someone to come to fix the refrigerator. And Frank was there with the
cats, and she says to me, "Behold Ayn Rand, eminent philosopher who
can't get the refrigerator to work." So I make a decision at this point
that even though I was categorically opposed to her philosophy that this
woman was terrific.

Tell me about the interviews you set up.

I had placed her on a radio talk show with Barry Farber on WOR
radio. My modus operandi was to pick up the writers and take them
with me to the station. On this particular day was the St. Patrick's Day
parade, but because of our responsibilities, it wasn't going to work the
usual way. She says it's not a problem, that she'd take a cab and meet me
at the radio station, which was at Broadway and 41st Street in New York.

I got there first and she's not there and the show was supposed to
go on at 7 PM. It's 6:30, 6:45, 6:50, 6:55. Barry Farber is not happy. I am
not happy. We had no idea where Ayn Rand was and if she's happy or
not.

Why was she late for the interview?

It was the St. Patrick's Day traffic; she couldn't get through. Finally, Barry says to me, "We have no choice, you're going to have to go on. You're going to have to be Ayn Rand." I said this is not going to work because not only am I not Ayn Rand, but I really categorically disagree with everything that she has to say. He said, "Then do that on the air." Well, we do an hour broadcast of me talking about Ayn Rand. I kept saying what a wonderful woman she was and how much I admired her personally but disagreed with her philosophy. It just so happens that Ayn and I had never talked about how I felt about what she had to say, because it was totally irrelevant to our relationship. The show goes off the air and the phone rings in the studio. Barry Farber says, "Tania, it's for you."

I pick up the phone and say, "Hello," and Ayn Rand says, "I never knew that's how you felt about my work." I said, "Well, it's about your philosophy. It's not about your work. I'm sorry about that." She was very calm and said, "Okay. Now you owe me one. You were Ayn Rand for an evening, and the next time you have media people at the Playboy Club that you are going to show around, I'm going to be Tania Grossinger." Well, it was hard to say no to that, so I said, "Okay you're on."

After I had done the show, I realized I had really misspoken. My job was not to get on the air and talk about what I think about Objectivism. My job was to promote her, not to disagree with her. She just took it in the finest of humors. She was laughing, although she could have been upset. Not only wasn't she upset, again, she just said, "I'm going to get you." But with such charm. It was a wonderful experience.

It sounds like you really hit it off.

Yes, I just approached her as an interesting writer. I read her books and told her that I disagreed with her. She honored my disagreement. There was never any harshness. She never tried to change my opinion. Once, she said to me, "You know, maybe you ought to read it again. I'm not sure you really understand what I'm saying." I said, "I think that's a very valid request." Then she sent me all of her books and said, "Read." It was done nicely.

Did you take Ayn Rand to the Playboy Club?

At that point, I had a Scottish boyfriend, a physician, and the four of us—Andrew and myself, Ayn and Frank—were planning on having dinner at the Playboy Club in the VIP room, which is a very lovely place.

I said to her, "Do you realize we're double dating?" And she just laughed. She was really fun to be around.

At the dinner my beeper goes off; there are some German journalists who need a tour. Ayn Rand looks at me and says, "Okay." I follow her downstairs to meet the journalists. They had never met me, of course, and she says, "Hi, I'm Tania Grossinger, let me show you around the club. Do you know that Hugh Hefner goes to bed with all of the bunnies?"

I was totally mortified, I mean, people are looking at her like, "This is someone who does public relations for *Playboy*?" She kept talking about the bunnies: "You have to be very careful, they'll spill coffee on you. This club looks like it's very nice and the bunnies are supposed to be trained, but they come in off the street and just pull on these ears." It was slapstick more than anything.

She did this for about ten minutes and they're taking notes, and they have television cameras. This is real trouble. So at one point, she bursts out laughing and says, "Excuse me, I'm not really Tania Grossinger. The woman behind me who's ready to drop dead is Tania Grossinger." So I introduced myself, and I said, "Now let me tell you who was showing you around the club." And she said, "Don't you dare." And I said, "Of course I will. Ladies and gentleman, Ayn Rand." Well, they got themselves some interviews, and we had them join us for dinner. It was just terrific.

What was Frank O'Connor doing during all of this?

He and my date were having dinner. Neither one of them wanted to be a part of this because they knew what was going to happen. But the point was that Ayn had this deadly sense of humor. She was a delight, but in everything I read about her—I became a fan of hers personally if not philosophically—she came across as a real hard-nosed person. No one ever caught the sense of humor this woman had. I really treasure the memory because I've never heard of anybody refer to her as other than a tough lady.

And we would keep in touch. If she didn't hear from me, I would get a phone call, "You forgot me already." We genuinely liked each other. We had dinners together, and we never spoke about her business or mine, but we just talked like real people. I just found her astonishing and I absolutely adored her.

I'm curious about her attitude to nudity; did she ever discuss that?

No, but she was very comfortable being at the Playboy Club. I remember asking her once, before she did an interview, if she would like to join me at the Club or if there is some other place she'd like to go. She said, "No, the Club's fine."

She went a few times, usually with Frank. I once said to her, "Look, we don't really have to go to the Club tonight, we can go somewhere else." She said, "No, I like it."

What did you talk about with Ayn Rand?

Everything. I grew up in a resort hotel called Grossinger's in the Catskill mountains.[137] She asked what it was like to grow up in a hotel. She was very curious about that.

About what specifically?

The celebrities and what were they really like and what was it like for a child to grow up in that kind of atmosphere. She took a genuine interest in my life. During that *Playboy* period, I was dealing with a lot of prominent personalities and some were interested and some were not—but she really was.

Tell me about Frank O'Connor.

Frank was quite quiet. But he was really nice, and she seemed devoted to him. I remember the first time I met him with all the cats. He was very warm to me and thanked me for coming over to his house and that it was nice that I was going to do all these things for Ayn, setting up these interviews.

Can you make a judgment about Ayn Rand's personality?

My estimation goes against the stereotype. Her stereotype was cold and I didn't see cold. I spent enough time with her, and I didn't meet her through her work, through Objectivism. She wasn't trying to impress me. I wasn't trying to impress her. She wasn't trying to convert me.

---

137 Grossinger's was the most famous resort in the so-called Borscht Belt.

Wesley Halpert

Wesley Halpert was Ayn Rand's dentist.

Interview date: January 21, 1999

Scott McConnell: *When did Ayn Rand become your patient?*

Wesley Halpert: In 1960, and she was referred to me by one of the people in her circle, Alan Greenspan.

Why did he recommend you to her?

I was his dentist. He thought that I was a good dentist.

Ayn didn't like to go to the dentist, but nobody does. But being a rational person and seeing what I could do for her, she accepted it.

Did she interview you before she became your patient?

No. I was so highly recommended by so many people that she came in trusting me—and I suppose my personality, my appearance, were such that she saw fit to become my patient. It was a very happy relationship. She even came up to my house one time, when I lived in Westchester. A lot of this happened before 1965. I used to go to the lectures, and we generally had a very nice relationship. I had a great deal of admiration for her.

What did she say about your work?

Oh, she loved it. She recommended patients to me, so I know she liked it.

Did Miss Rand say anything else about dental care?

No, she put herself into my hands. Of course, I explained everything and that's what impressed her.

She wanted to know everything?

She sure did. I explained the whys and wherefores, because I don't do anything if I don't have a reason for it.

Ayn would come in on Friday afternoons, and we would work and then we would talk. I devoted the whole afternoon to her. I had wonderful times there discussing various issues of the time—and of all time. We talked about the problems of drug addiction and about capital punishment. She clarified many points in her philosophy, such as understanding one's psycho-epistemology, and we talked about how children are so damaged by their parents' irrational behavior. This was an upsetting thing for her. She thought that only people who are prepared to have children and can bring them up rationally should have children.

I used to drive her home in a little sports car. She used to love that. She lived down on 36th Street.

Did you discuss dating or romance or marriage?

Yes, she always expressed the great admiration she had for her husband, Frank. In fact, he became my patient as well. She said that when she first saw him, she said, "That's my ideal." I think she even intimated that she knew right away that he was the man she wanted to marry. She loved him very much.

Did she tell you anything else about their relationship or her love for him?

No, but it was always there. It showed by the way her face lit up when we talked about him.

Can you describe Mr. O'Connor?

He was a very handsome man and he dressed in a very flamboyant way. He wore a big hat like Frank Lloyd Wright used to wear.

During these post-work discussions, she gave you a lot of time, why?

She liked me as a person and also as a professional. She thought I was very rational in my work. She told me something interesting. She said to me, "When you are working your face lights up, and you're really an alive person, and you're enjoying so much and functioning so well. Then, when you finish working you settle down and you become much less the person you were when you were doing the work." Today it's the same thing. I get so turned on when I work. She noticed that. She noticed things that a lot of people don't notice.

I'll tell you one important thing she told me: she didn't want a coterie of followers. She said unless they can see the concepts themselves, she wasn't interested. She didn't want people like that. She wanted to be close to people who understood her ideas from their own intelligence.

You were reading Atlas Shrugged *at this time?*

Oh yes, *Atlas* was wonderful. First of all, it's a great suspense novel. More than that, I saw the things that she predicted coming true. She predicted that when the Chinese communists broke up the farms and everybody was going to have a steel mill in their backyard, it would fail. She ridiculed that, and it failed, and the Chinese had a famine because of that.

She told me that this country was overly fearful of the Russians. She said with their kind of irrational thinking they can't and don't have a society that can really produce the weapons and that sort of thing that will make them a danger to the U.S. Sure enough, Gorbachev came along and what she said was confirmed. And at the time the Egyptians were building the Aswan Dam, the materials they got from the Soviet Union were so defective that they had to get rid of them and buy them from France, I think. She predicted all those things. I said to my wife, "She predicted this, and look what's happening now." She predicted it in *Atlas Shrugged*.

Anything else about the Soviets or the communists?

A very important principle: If something is philosophically wrong, it's not going to work. It may seem to work in the beginning because you prop it up in various ways, but eventually it doesn't. That was her attitude toward the Soviets—it's not rational and it's not going to work.

I also remember that when the slogan "Better Red than Dead" came up, she said, "Better Dead than Red."

Did you discuss with Miss Rand the political/economic situation that you experienced as a dentist in the '60s, with government encroachments on the medical professions, such as Medicare?

Sure. Ayn saw it as the impending death of the medical profession. She was very upset about that.

John Higgins

John Higgins was the primary veterinarian for Ayn Rand's cats.

Interview date: June 9, 1999

Scott McConnell: *How did you become the veterinarian for Ayn Rand's cats?*

John Higgins: Around the mid-1960s someone she knew recommended me. She had a cat by the name of Frisco. It's amazing that I would even remember a cat's name or even close to it. It did impress me.

What do you remember about Frisco?

The cat was old. It was a nice cat, but it was old and had kidney disease. In fact, it was an intractable kidney disease called "chronic interstitial nephritis." It happens when the kidneys age. I think the cat was twelve or thirteen years of age, and at that time that was pretty old for a cat. Now cats live a little longer because of medical science.

Ayn Rand and Frank O'Connor brought in this cat, and we diagnosed it through laboratory tests. It was pretty obvious, clinically, that the cat did have kidney failure. One night I tried to explain this to her because she was very, very intelligent but very humble in a strange sense. She was very attentive—her husband stood a little bit behind her—and they were very concerned. They knew the cat was extremely ill. I tried to explain to her that over a period of time your kidney tissue wears out, because you don't get reproduction of kidney tissue, so on a yearly basis you lose more and more kidney cells, and you don't detox enough—the toxins remain in your system. Sooner or later there is a downward spiral.

We were treating the problem, and I think we did some intensive treatment. I had to tell her after a while that the cat wasn't doing well—it was losing weight and nauseous, and that you had to look at it from the standpoint of the quality of life of the cat. I was astounded by the fact that, even though I seemed to sense she was a very caring woman—very cat-like in her attitude—very dignified, and I'm saying this in kind of a positive sense, she didn't understand one thing. She said to me, "Doctor, why my cat?" And I went back and explained again—that the kidneys through wear and tear lose tissue and the cat's quality of life is affected. Then she'd say, "But why Frisco? Why my

303

cat?" It was almost like a little child trying to understand why her pet—her beloved animal—was failing.

Some people will ask why is this happening and then you explain to them and they sort of acknowledge it, but some people do have a defense mechanism; they don't want to believe it. But it was almost a childlike thing, for a woman who was very intellectual and very spiritual; it seemed a little strange that she had trouble understanding it—almost like denial. I know her husband was standing by. He was a very sweet, sensitive man, an artist. He was just very attentive and very supportive. I could look in his eyes and could see he understood what I was saying.

I remember that vividly, because I remember the man's face. It was a beautiful face, a very sympathetic face. He was sort of perplexed that this great woman, who was known worldwide, had a little trouble conceiving this one thing. That stood out in my mind. It's not a criticism, it's more like she had a childlike disbelief that something could happen like that, when she was so spiritual and believed so much that animals can survive and repair and get through a bad situation.

I think she really understood what the feline personality was. I think that she and her cat had a bond that was so, so close that it was very natural to have denial. It just happened to be that the denial expressed itself as subjective, rather than objective. It was an innocent thing.

I was more impressed, not by her reputation, but by the woman herself—how she had this gentle, kind, loving, nurturing feeling about a cat, which always appeals to me. This cat was really very special to her.

You said that Ayn Rand was "cat-like"?

What I meant was that she seemed to understand the personality of a cat. She seemed to have that resiliency. For instance, a lioness is much more difficult to deal with in the wild because she protects the young, and the male sort of goes out and does his thing, but the lioness is much more tenacious. Ayn Rand seemed to be a very tenacious person without being brutal or hard-edged. It's a compliment when you're like a feline and you're very strong. I think she revered cats and I think she revered their spirit.

Mr. and Mrs. O'Connor always came together to the surgery?

Yes. He never came alone with the cat; she never came alone. They always came together, like parents. It seemed like it was a different part of her career, where she wasn't so much a celebrity, she was just a cat-lover and a mom.

Perry Knowlton

Perry Knowlton was Ayn Rand's literary agent at Curtis Brown Agency from 1957 to her death in 1982. He was owner and president of the agency until his retirement in 1996. Mr. Knowlton died in 2007.

Interview date: March 26, 1999

Scott McConnell: *How did you first learn about Ayn Rand and her work?*

Perry Knowlton: I think the first I ever heard of it was when I read *The Fountainhead* as a young man. The next thing I saw was the movie, which she hated. I thought it was pretty good.

What did you think of The Fountainhead *book when you read it?*

I thought it was an interesting story. I didn't really think of it as being political at all. It was published in 1943, and people were talking about the book even then.

Do you remember any stories about Miss Rand before you became her agent?

I do know stories about Ayn Rand, from before I went to work at Curtis Brown in 1957. When I began in the publishing business, I started out as a college traveler and moved into the editorial trade department for Scribner's and even was sent by Scribner's to London to scout over there for them for a six-week junket.

I had run into Archie Ogden[138] through friends of mine, and he said that when I come to London be sure to call on him. I'm talking about 1959 or 1960. I think he was then the 20th Century Fox story editor for Europe and England. Of course, I had heard the story of Archie Ogden and *The Fountainhead*, which was one of the major stories of publishing in those days: that he told his bosses at Bobbs-Merrill that if you don't publish *The Fountainhead* he would quit and take Ayn Rand someplace else. He got his way.

What did Mr. Ogden say to you about Miss Rand and The Fountainhead*?*

He was nuts about Ayn Rand and thought she was a wonderful storyteller and had a philosophy that was fascinating, was a real

---

138 Archie Ogden was the editor of *The Fountainhead*.

thinker, and in that sense, she was sort of his hero.

What did you think of Atlas Shrugged*?*

I read it before I got to Curtis Brown. It was published in the fall of 1957, and December is when I left Scribner's and went to Curtis Brown. I was reading it because I was not only going to be involved with Curtis Brown, but I also wanted to see what the book was like. It was good. It was a powerful book.

Even for a liberal like yourself?

Yes, even for a liberal. Because she's such a good storyteller. She knows character; she knows story line. This is one of her attributes that helped her in her film writing. She knew how to dramatize things.

Did you work with Alan Collins [Ayn Rand's agent] *while he was representing Miss Rand?*

At that time, I hadn't worked directly with her. I was very much involved in advising Alan. Alan seemed to have a real admiration for my judging the market for how much to ask a publisher for a book. The biggest advance Curtis Brown ever had up to that point was $75,000. Then when Alan came to me and said would I read Ayn Rand's proposal for her novel after *Atlas Shrugged*, I said, "Okay, what's it about?" He said, "She hasn't really written a proposal, she's just got an idea in her head, and we're calling it the John Doe novel." I said, "You're going to go out to sell the next book of Ayn Rand's?" And he said, "Yes, how much do you think we could get for it? Do you think we'd get $50,000?"

I said, "No, you shouldn't ask for any less than a quarter of a million." That blew his stack. I then said, "If I were you, I'd go to Victor Weybright at NAL. She's really an admirer of Victor Weybright, and she's sick and tired of Bennett Cerf at Random House—she thinks he's a chicken and unloyal to her and doesn't want to be there anymore." Cerf had already told me this. And so Alan did try and Victor said, "Sure, go ahead. We'll go to contracts right away." The contract was drawn up very quickly. NAL never paid the whole advance, for some reason I can't now remember. I think Alan took some money up front and then paid it back later when Ayn never delivered the book.

That was too bad, because everybody was waiting for the John Doe book, and it and the contract with NAL were actually the only things that Ayn Rand and I, when Alan and Victor Weybright were dead, were able to use to make NAL stay and try to do their best, to do what we wanted them to do: sell Ayn Rand's books, not just rely on her existing market but instead do actual advertising, promotion and publicity. They'd say, "Oh yes, yes, we will, we will." One editor in chief after another would lie about it and not deliver.

The one reason we were able to get anything out of them was mainly because of that one promised novel and the earlier history, of course, because Ayn had been really a tough, tough author when it came to her demands on contracts. So it was a delight for me and Alan working on her behalf, because she would just as soon walk away unless she could get exactly what she thought she deserved and what all authors should get.

Of course, it didn't work with all authors, but it certainly worked with her. She got very straight-backed and said to the publisher, you either want me or you don't, and if you do want me you're going to have to go along with these conditions. It was a long list of things. This came to haunt her, because she carried on the same sort of attitude towards film companies on account of her dislike of *The Fountainhead* film and that it was badly handled. She said she's never going to sell anything to a film company that doesn't allow her the right to pick the director, the screenwriter and to edit in the editing room. And, of course, a lot of people make contracts thinking they can get this type of deal from the backers, but never could. It became one of the problems that she never got over, but she refused to give up her way of doing it because she felt she was right, which she was. She didn't like what was done with *The Fountainhead*, and therefore, she was trying to make sure it wouldn't happen again.

What was the "John Doe" novel about?[139]

It never had any subject, not written down anyway. She never discussed with me what she had intended. I asked her a couple of times and she said she'd really never been able to come up with a subject that competed with *The Fountainhead* and *Atlas Shrugged*. That's why she told me, near the end, that she wasn't going to write it: she just didn't have a story that would be equal to the other two.

Do you remember any other conditions that she had in her contracts with publishers?

---

139 For her working notes, see *Journals of Ayn Rand*, ed. David Harriman (New York: Plume, 1997), pp. 704–16.

Certainly. They couldn't make any deals at all without her absolute approval. It wasn't "approval not to be unreasonably withheld"; it was just out-and-out flat approval. If she wanted to, she could renegotiate the deals. She could up things and get people. She was the backbone behind a lot of chicken publishers who didn't think they could get as much for the reprint rights or the book club rights as she did. So she would say then we're not going to sell them. Finally they would come through and pay what she would agree to.

Do you remember any specific examples of books or publishers that she went through this kind of thing with?

New American Library, time and time again. There were only two publishers. We were not involved with Bobbs-Merrill regarding *The Fountainhead*. I think she may have done that work on her own without an agent.

Did she have only bad relationships with her publishers?

No. She was very happy with Bennett Cerf for a while. Then when *Atlas Shrugged* was released, she said that he was really behaving badly and wasn't getting behind the book. There were a lot of people knocking Ayn Rand as a thinker and saying she's nothing, she's hollow, and Bennett Cerf would not fight for her. So she said the hell with Bennett, I'll stick with Victor Weybright. Victor Weybright had been in on the paperback reprint end of the publishing of *Atlas Shrugged*. He started up NAL and was one of the original reprint publishers. He also was the first publisher to go for both hard- and softcover deals.

What did Bennett Cerf say about Ayn Rand?

He would sort of smile and giggle about it a little. Bennett Cerf was a fairly shallow person, and Ayn was not. She really had depth and a lot of convictions that she stood up for. It took a while to get to know her before you could find out that she wasn't the bad person that everybody had spread rumors about.

What were the rumors?

That she was a Nazi, that she was as far right as Hitler. Of course she wasn't. She hated any kind of totalitarian government. She was for freedom.

Were there any of your other clients who were upset that you had

Ayn Rand as a client? I can imagine a lot of your other clients were very liberal, and it must have raised their eyebrows that you were representing Ayn Rand.

Oh yes, but we had a standard reaction for that one. We had represented Lenin, we had represented Churchill, we had represented Hitler, we had represented every side of every coin you have ever heard of over the years, and our U.S. office started in 1914. We were very proud of the fact that we wouldn't allow anybody to tell us who we should represent and who we shouldn't represent. I think that's what got Ayn really happy with us. We felt strongly about this, and we thought anybody who had a book to be read, that was an important book, we would try our best to get it published. That was also true for *Mein Kampf.*

Has her reputation changed in the literary world in the last forty years?

Oh, I think so. I think she's gained a lot of respectability, and there are a lot of people who feel she makes a lot of sense and have come and joined her side.

Anyone famous that I should know about?

I keep running into people, I'm not sure how famous they are, who tell me what fans they are of Ayn Rand. It happens a lot because they hear that I was her agent and ask questions about her to see what a wonderful person she was. A lot of people were late in life in coming to understanding her. It wasn't late in my life, but it was later than I would have liked to have had it.

How did you become Miss Rand's agent?

Alan Collins died. So Ayn and I got on the phone shortly after Alan died, and she said we ought to get together and get to know each other a little better than we did. I had never really had a personal relationship with her then, as much as I built up after Alan died.

You had met her before Mr. Collins's death?

Yes. I had met her with Alan and talked to her about the idea she wanted to do with the John Doe book. I was there in conferences with her and Alan at that point.

What did Miss Rand want you to do as her agent?

I guess whatever it was she expected, she got. I had my own idea about what an agent has to do. He has to be loyal to his authors and do the best he can to educate them about the publishing machine and get them as much money as possible. She thought that was fine.

She stayed with you a long time.

Yeah. She was with Alan a long time before Alan died. We got along very well.

What was your first impression of her?

I was somewhat amazed that she wasn't what people had told me she was. My lunch with her was really incredible. I told her straight out that I was probably not the person for her because I am a liberal. My parents were Republicans, and I was fighting the battle of shaking loose of parental pressure, because I really was a Democrat. She said, why? I explained why and she said, Okay, you have your right to think what you want to think, and I'm for that. She explained in one very easy lunch not to worry about her as someone who's going to be judging me. The only thing she insisted on in people who were working with her is that they had a philosophy which they lived by, and that they were intelligent and would listen to reason. We would always argue about things, but they were never fights, just arguments. She would laugh and I would laugh and she would say, "We're learning things from each other, Perry."

We had a disagreement on environmental issues. It is the one thing that I thought she was weak on in a serious way, because she said, "They'll fix all of this, it's not something we have to worry about." I said, "Who is going to fix all of this?" She said, "the engineers." I said, "Really? Do you have any idea of what the engineers have done so far not to fix it." But she always loved the discussion. She said, I learned things, you learned things, and that's how we learn.

What other topics did you argue about or discuss?

That was the only one we really argued about, because I did feel that she was wrong and it was my duty to try to straighten her out— even if I couldn't—because I was very active in the environmental movement, and still am.

What did you discuss with Ayn Rand at the meetings, lunches and dinners you had with her?

Everything, but what we did mostly discuss, especially after Victor Weybright's death in 1974, was how we could persuade NAL to get

behind the books in a more effective way. We tried many things. Ed
Kuhn was one of her editors, the chief at NAL, who promised all the
things we asked him to promise, and then would give up on them. So
did Ned Chase, another of her editors. He would if he could, but he
didn't have the guts and didn't have the brains that he really needed to
have to persuade the owners of NAL, which was then, I believe, Times-
Mirror in Los Angeles.

But why didn't NAL see her potential or market value?

I have no idea. I think they were all afraid of the kinds of reputation
people were assigning to her, even though it was nonsense.

*What were some of her tactics or plans to get NAL working on
promoting her books?*

The only thing we had for a while was that she had the John Doe
novel that she was hanging in front of them as a carrot. They would
listen to her and say okay, fine, but one editor in chief would be fired,
and then someone else would be put in the spot and the owners would
always say, what about this new Ayn Rand novel, when's it going to be
published? It was gradually becoming a thorn in our side, because there
was nothing we could do because she wasn't going to write it.

Did she give you other ideas or tactics for dealing with her publishers?

I was the main tactician for her in Alan's last few years and until
her own death. But there wasn't anything to do because there was
nothing to do. We were coming up with nonfiction books by her, but
they were not books with a large market.

So what did Ayn Rand think of publishers and agents?

She hadn't got to the point where I had since gotten to since her
death: that publishing was going to the dogs, and that it was just going
to get worse and worse. I don't think she ever felt that way. I think she
always felt there was something that could be done, but she didn't know
what, and I didn't know either.

Whom did she like in publishing?

She liked Victor Weybright and Matt Colly, who was Victor
Weybright's son-in-law, I believe.

How often did you see Ayn Rand?

We were both living in New York, and we'd have lunch every month, every two months at the most, and just go on from there.

Did you socialize with Miss Rand and Mr. O'Connor in other ways?

The only other way we did was at her apartment on 34th Street. Just every now and again she'd say, come on Perry, it's time we had dinner. She'd ask me for dinner and I'd go over and have dinner. I think that was where one of our disagreements on the environment happened, at one of those dinners there, with Frank.

They were amicable, friendly discussions?

Oh, yeah, we were kidding each other more than anything. She knew what my interests in the environment were, and I think she just kidded me on it. She didn't get angry at that. She just said, you've a right to your opinion, and I said, thank you.

She was like that all the time you knew her?

Yeah, terrific gal.

Did she change your mind on any topics?

She changed my mind on her, because I had the faulty opinion of what she was about, because I'd been listening to all the wrong rumors. She didn't try to correct me on any of that. She just said, I'm not as big an ogre as you think—all I think is that you have a right to your own ideas as long as you have a philosophy that backs those ideas up. As long as you've got that, she said, there'll be no problem, and there never was.

What was Ayn Rand like as a client?

I thought she was terrific. I wish all of my clients had been like her. I've also said that about Tony Hillerman.[140] He has been a real delight about being easy to work with, and so was she. She was very easy once I got to know her and we understood each other. We literally never had any problems. Oh yes, I did! I once grew a mustache, and she saw me when I came out to greet her in the reception area and said, "Oh Perry!" I said, "What?" She said, "That face!" "What's the matter with it? You liked it before," I said. "No, no, you've got hair on it!" I said, "Oh, that's right, you don't like people with hair on their face; I remember

---

140 Tony Hillerman was a best-selling mystery writer.

that now."

She teased you about that?

Yes.

Why was she easy to work with?

Basically, because she was a person who was intelligent. In the publishing business, if you're not intelligent, you shouldn't be in it. She was among people she liked and admired, and that's what makes things happen.

Did she change over the years?

I never knew her in any other way. I was worried in that first introduction and then that turned out to be fun and very enlightening, and it set the situation for the future.

How was she involved with publishing, in the sense of promotion, editing, covers, design?

She was very tough on design because that was one of the things that she had approval of, and NAL has always agreed to give her that.

In regard to her royalties, was there anything special?

She always wanted the highest scale of royalties that she could get, and we told her what that was. She would say, okay, get that for us, and we did. It was very simple. She always wanted to get the top of everything she was looking for, and she usually got it.

How did she go about it? What was her manner or her attitude when she wanted things like that?

She'd usually ask questions. She'd say, is it usual for such and such to happen, or is there something that we can negotiate here? And we'd say, with enough clout, and you have enough clout, we can negotiate almost anything. She'd say, "Well, let's try for it." We'd do it and we got it most of the time.

You were the agent for the film rights for Atlas Shrugged?

We represented the film rights to her books, and if someone wanted to do a screenplay, we negotiated the right to do it. I was handling it when Al Ruddy was interested in doing the movie of *Atlas Shrugged*. We had to tell him what he was going to be up against. He was really eager. He thought the property had so much strength, that he was going to be able to sell anybody on it that he wanted to bring into the production. We said, "Okay, fine, these are the conditions: she has to have right of approval of the cast, she has to approve who the director's going to be," one thing after another, all the way down, including editing in the editing room. You mention those things to any producer and he'll just laugh, and that's what Ruddy found out.

Was that the reason the NBC project fell apart?

Sure. Their lawyers would never agree to anything like that. It was so far out of the question that there was no way that the film could have been made as long as Ayn insisted on those approvals.[141]

But she did make a deal with Mr. Ruddy. They did have an agreement, and they even had a press conference to announce the film project.

Absolutely, but Ruddy had not made the deal with the people who were going to back it. Those are the people who count in the film industry. That was one of the *Atlas* movie projects that I was involved with and then there were some others too, but they fell apart faster.

Did Miss Rand have her portrait in the Curtis Brown gallery?

Yes, I've still got that picture. It was a sketch of her from her earlier days.

Did Ayn Rand change after Mr. O'Connor died?

She was quiet for about two months and we didn't see each other. Finally, I called her and I said why don't we get together for lunch. She said, "Oh yes, I've been missing you; let's have lunch." We didn't even mention Frank. I just felt she'd had her mourning period, and she was rallying.

What's your summation of Ayn Rand?

I wish she was still with us. It would be a lot of fun. She was always an exciting lady and I'd like to see her around.

Did she have integrity?

I'll say; yes, absolutely. She believed in integrity; it was one of her mainstays.

---

141 Also see producer Michael Jaffe's interview on page 513.

When did you last see her?

I didn't see her at the end. She was in the hospital and I knew she was ill. I was really shocked when she died, because I at least wanted to say goodbye to her. I didn't know she was that ill.

What would you have said to her if you'd said goodbye?

She didn't believe in God or heaven or hell. I think she thought that if there was a hell it was what you made for yourself on earth. She wasn't a religious person, so she didn't have any phony ideas about where she was going. I don't think there would have been anything to say, except goodbye.

Eugene Winick

Eugene Winick was one of Ayn Rand's lawyers, from 1962 to her death in 1982. He is the owner and CEO of McIntosh & Otis, Inc., a literary agency in New York City.

Interview date: December 15, 1999

Scott McConnell: *How did you meet Ayn Rand?*

Eugene Winick: I joined the law firm Ernst, Cane, Berner & Gitlin in November 1961 and met Ayn probably in early 1962. I became her lawyer by virtue of joining the law firm that had been representing her. Pincus Berner,[142] who was a partner in the firm, died in August of '61. I was to come in to more or less fill the empty space he left; I don't want to say "to take his place." But Ayn worked primarily with Paul Gitlin, then the lead lawyer in our firm, and I got to know her over the years and worked with her.

I don't have any specific impression of our first meeting, but most of my meetings with her included Frank. He accompanied her on virtually every get-together we had up until a couple or three years before his death.

Did Miss Rand interview you before you started working with her or was it just a fait accompli?

It was a fait accompli because the firm represented her. As a junior in the firm, I got to know her over a year or two or three. Initially it was sitting alongside Paul Gitlin, and then subsequently meeting her on matters that I dealt with. She dealt with Paul on some matters, with me on some matters, and with us jointly on some matters.

What was your work with her and what was Mr. Gitlin's?

Whenever there were any legal issues, she would consult us. That was up until the time the Branden Institute was organized in 1961. We filed its corporate papers, and then their lawyer came on the scene and represented the Institute and handled the lease at the Empire State Building and other things of that sort. So we did not get involved in that aspect of, say, the business operation very much. Most of what we dealt with, on her behalf, had to do with

---

142 Pincus Berner was Ayn Rand's lawyer from 1936 to 1961.

her publishing interests. We were copyright practitioners. If there was ever any question of libel or invasion of privacy that came up, she would consult with us. Of course, in the drafting of wills over the years, she and Frank revised their wills from time to time, as people do generally, so she consulted us on that. Then there were tax returns. We annually were involved in preparing her and Frank's joint tax return.

What matters did you personally deal with?

It could be tax returns and copyright issues. She also did speak with Mel Cane, except I think most of her dealings with Mel were more on a social level than consulting him as a lawyer.[143]

What were some of the most interesting legal problems you dealt with for her?

I remember the concern she had about being quoted in one of the Hearst/Avon books, where they were using her name to advertise a book. She did go to court on that, but we had advised against it, and she didn't like that advice and went to another law firm, did sue Hearst and her suit was dismissed.[144]

Why did you advise against it?

It was just our understanding of the law that what they did was not a violation of what's known as the right to privacy, which comes under New York State statute.

Was it a similar situation when Reason *magazine, the libertarian publication, used her name?*

Yes. She often expressed the view that she didn't like being identified as a libertarian, which some people did.

Did she explain why?

No, just the fact that it was inappropriate. She didn't like it and she didn't want it to happen, and we would write letters. There were letters that we wrote over the years on her behalf to a variety of people

---

143 Melville Cane was also an award-winning and much-published poet admired by Ayn Rand.

144 Ayn Rand won at the lower-court level, but the decision was later reversed.

or organizations who either quoted her improperly or referred to her improperly or used without permission some content from her books. For instance, people would use "John Galt" for commercial purposes.

How would she react to that?

That they were doing something larcenous.

Can you give me some examples of work you performed for Miss Rand in relation to her agents and publishers?

I think for the most part Curtis Brown represented her on book contracts. Perry Knowlton was the agent of record there.

Curtis Brown also represented her in connection with the licensing of rights to *Atlas Shrugged*, but we got involved with that in two instances at least. One was when Al Ruddy acquired an option on *Atlas Shrugged*. Ruddy was a film producer who had just produced *The Godfather* at Paramount, where he had a production unit, so he was riding pretty high. He was interested in developing *Atlas Shrugged* into a movie, but Ayn was unhappy with what had happened with *The Fountainhead*, because her own background, coming from Hollywood as a screenwriter, gave her insights that an ordinary author might not have, so she refused to release the motion picture rights of *Atlas Shrugged* without maintaining some controls. She wanted not just script approval. She negotiated and received daily-rush approval and, I believe, final editorial-cut approval, which is unusual. She also had some other proscriptions. She disliked the introduction of sound from the next scene before you actually saw it visually. That was prohibited. And as I recall, she also disliked facial hair on men and had that in as a proscription.

I do remember discussing with her other situations where the firm was involved in motion picture productions, and I used Harold Robbins as an example of the opposite approach. By the way, Ayn admired Harold Robbins as a writer because he wrote very visually. We represented Robbins, and I think Harold and Ayn met, and they did have some chats once in a while. Robbins didn't mind surrendering controls to Hollywood, because he came out of Hollywood and knew that's the way Hollywood operated and was willing to let them. Ayn came out of Hollywood and knew that's the way Hollywood operated and refused to permit them to operate that way. So she wrote in these requirements that would give her absolute, firm, unquestionable control. Well, Ruddy paid a lot of money for that option and there was a big payment down the road when they exercised the rights. But before Paramount would permit the rights to be exercised, because they were financing it, they came back and asked that Ayn relinquish those controls, possibly permitting her to keep script approval. I'm not certain that that was even permitted, but she refused, so the deal died. No picture was made. The rights were never exercised, and they reverted to Ayn.

Then, a few years later, there was another deal, at NBC with Henry Jaffe and his son Michael, who were major producers at NBC. This was to be a six-hour miniseries of *Atlas Shrugged*, and the same restrictions were written in, as a way of giving comfort that she would be able to influence the production.[145] In television there are what are called "step deals," where the network, which was financing the production, pays a certain amount at each step along the way. And before they made a major commitment they wanted Ayn to surrender control that was contained in the original agreement, because what happens is that many authors, once they go down the road pretty far and can taste the production, they're willing to surrender the rights that were originally committed to them. But it wouldn't happen with Ayn. She was absolute that she wanted to retain the control.

Did you discuss with her any questions about the philosophy of law?

Yes, from time to time, but I don't recall the substance other than that we usually punctuated our conversation with something that was happening at the time or about our system.

Do you remember her expressing outrage or joy about any legal doctrines or events that you explained to her?

I just remember that when there was something she was critical of she would have just about the same comment every time criticizing the parties who were involved. I can still hear her voice ringing in my ears, with her accent, saying, "Those Zons of Beetches." She would hit the table with her hands. That's one of my strongest recollections of her, actually. "Those Zons of Beetches."

Do you remember any example of the things that might have brought that out?

It could be someone using the name "John Galt." It could be the use of the quote in the ad for the book. Things of that sort.

---

145 Ayn Rand wrote the first two hours of the initial draft of the screenplay.

What would she do after she said that?

She would express her anger, have a bit of a release of it, and then we'd come back to regular conversation. Frank was present most of these times. Occasionally he would have a comment to make as well, if something affected him. He seemed very protective of her.

In what way?

In supporting her positions in things that were of concern and upsetting her. He didn't participate on a regular basis, but whenever he did it was very supportive of Ayn and Ayn's position. And he might have a word or two to say on his own behalf in terms of his own agreement with what was going on. He never disagreed with her.

At the time we also represented Bobbs-Merrill, publisher of *The Fountainhead*, and at the time of its twenty-fifth-anniversary edition, we were involved in arranging to have Frank's painting on the cover of the commemorative edition.[146] That was very nice.

Do you remember any of their comments about that?

They liked it very much. In fact, they both autographed a copy of the book, which I have at home.

What aspect about Miss Rand did you most appreciate?

The fact that she could always be relied upon. She was committed to what she declared she would do. It was determination.

Did you observe her applying her philosophy in her approach to business problems or to decisions?

Her integrity was always self-evident. She was very clear about what she wanted to do and when she wanted to do it. Sometimes she wasn't so clear about how to do it, and that's where she came to us in terms of legal advice.

What was she like to deal with?

I found her very responsive and appropriate.

How often would you meet?

It might be every few weeks if there was something happening. I remember being at her apartment occasionally. Certainly, no less than

---

146 The Frank O'Connor painting is called *Man Also Rises*.

once a year or twice a year just on tax matters. Ayn and Frank would come in with their records, and we would deal with the preparation of the return. Then they would come in a week or two or a month later when their return was prepared. We met on the average of three or four times a year, at a minimum.

She would call, make an appointment and then come in?

Right. She'd call about something, or we needed to get together about it, and we'd make an appointment and she would come up. It always seemed like a formal occasion. She would be pretty dressed-up. She'd be wearing very high heels and usually her mink coat, I remember. Frank would assist her taking the coat off and hanging it. She would take out her cigarette and put it in her cigarette holder. That was, as I say, her whole ritual about our getting together.

What was her attitude while paying her taxes?

Not pleased, but not unwilling.

Why would you go to her apartment?

There might be some papers to sign, so rather than pull her away from her work, I'd go there. But she seemed to enjoy coming to our office, looked forward to it.

Why was Mr. O'Connor always with her?

I don't know. It just seemed like it was something that made them both comfortable, being there together. I guess on the tax returns, particularly, since he was a joint tax payer, and he had some input. He maintained his own studio, a one-room apartment in their building. And so, as a taxpayer, he was required to give the input for the tax returns and sign the tax returns as well. They were partners as far as the tax return was concerned.

Were there any legal matters regarding his being an artist?

Yes, the matter of a gallery selling prints of some of his paintings and some original paintings. So that was a factor in the mix in terms of their tax return. He would file his own schedule C, which covers business income and expenses.

What was Miss Rand's manner during business meetings?

She was absolutely focused. No nonsense. She was very determined and very clear about what she would want. She did, however, have a sense of humor, which she displayed occasionally.

Can you remember examples?

I can't, but I know we did have a few laughs from time to time. It was always easy to work with her, although she may not have been easy in some of her objectives. I think she had a practical way of interacting with me.

Explain that.

She had an objective, and she knew what it would take to achieve her objective. I wasn't an adversary or someone who she would have to address in an adversarial way. Even that one incident where our advice to her was that the suit would create more problems for her in terms of potential publicity—which it didn't, I don't think anyone paid attention to it—than in anything she could hope to achieve in filing the suit. She didn't have any negative reaction to us because of that. I think she respected our professionalism.

You said that you disagreed with some of her objectives. Can you give examples?

That's the only one that comes to mind. Philosophically, we didn't necessarily mesh, but I think we certainly respected each other.

Did it ever become an issue that you weren't a fan or an ally of her work?

I was an ally of most of her work and her writing. I thought she did a superb job at what she did. Some aspects of what she was proposing I didn't agree with.

Did you ever discuss those with her?

We did, but I just don't recall specifics.

What was her reaction when you said, "I disagree with X"?

She would very rationally—that was one of her favorite terms—address the issue and explain to me why I was so wrong and why she was right.

Did she change your mind at all?

I don't think so, ever.

Did you ever change hers?

I don't think so, but she was tolerant enough with me.

Did she change over those twenty years that you knew her?

I don't think so. I think she was pretty consistent. I saw an occasional warm part of her. For instance, Mel Cane, a partner in our law firm and respected published poet, celebrated his hundredth birthday, and we had an open house at the office. April 15, 1979,[147] was his hundredth birthday and she came up to the office by herself. In fact, I remember a photo with Mel and Ayn, and my wife might have been in the photo with them. Ayn seemed truly enthused and pleased to be part of that social scene. Although Mel himself resented the fact that he was being celebrated for longevity and not for other reasons, he was very happy to see her.

What was Miss Rand's legal name when she signed legal documents?

She signed her tax returns "Alice O'Connor."

When Miss Rand was "retiring" from public life and running a newsletter in the mid-1970s, were you involved in advising her to apply for Social Security?

We undoubtedly discussed it and the fact that, at her option, she could apply for it, or just surrender it. I would have recommended against surrendering it.

Do you remember anything else about her "retiring"?

I don't think of her as ever having retired, technically. She was always involved in whatever she was doing until the later days when she was just unable to.

In what way?

Physically. She just didn't have the strength to do what she would normally do—write.

Did she discuss Mr. O'Connor's death with you?

Yes. She did reflect upon how difficult it was for her. I don't think she ever really got over his death, and she missed him as a companion and partner. They deferred to each other very lovingly, gracefully and

---

147 The party was April 16, 1979.

warmly whenever they were together.

What were Mr. O'Connor and Miss Rand like when they discussed their own deaths and wills?

Very clinical about it. Very easy. It wasn't a chore at all.

So you were one of the first to know of her death?

I was probably at my office, and we were called there by whoever was with Ayn to say that she had just passed away. So I went down to oversee what was happening.

As her lawyer?

Yes, and also as an executor of her estate.

To oversee what? To protect her or the property?

I didn't have any particular objective. It was just something I felt compelled to do. It was probably both protecting the property as well as making sure that things were handled properly, and in knowing that there are some technical niceties that have to be dealt with at a time like that.

Such as?

Just dealing with the police who were there. Also dealing with the coroner, and the medical examiner, and getting her body released so there could be a proper funeral. Things of that sort.

Did you attend the funeral?

When Frank died, Ayn went up to Valhalla. It's a town just north of White Plains, New York, in Westchester County. The name Valhalla is an appropriate name. Ayn went there to select a plot for Frank and for herself, where she would join him at some future time. My wife Ina and my associate Evva Pryor were with her. As Ina recalls, they went to the cemetery office, found out which plots were available, made a survey of several. Ayn selected one that was on a little hillock with a tree which would give shade, so that when you came to the grave site you could be shaded. I think Ayn had planned for a bench to be placed there, so that someone sitting on the bench would be shaded. Frank was buried there and then when we came up for Ayn's funeral three years later, we found the tree had been hit by lightening and was destroyed. We planted a new tree after her funeral, but what she had intended for this site wasn't fulfilled for her own funeral. I don't know how many people knew about that—I knew it, Evva knew it and my wife knew it—but there was a sense of something that was out of control that Ayn would not have approved.

Her funeral was at Campbell's Funeral Home. Huge numbers of people came. I remember going there the night before the actual funeral. They were receiving the public and there was a line around the block. We were approaching the home and, as an executor, as a lawyer, as "part of the family," in effect, we were directed to look for an elevator entrance that would take us up so we wouldn't have to wait in line. As we were approaching Campbell's, I saw Alan Greenspan in line with all the others who came to pay respects, and I invited him to join us and he came up the elevator with us.

It was a pretty spectacular presentation—the flowers, the adulation she was obviously held in by the people who came to pay tribute, and the loss that people felt, who were strangers, but who felt very close to her and her work. It was surely very moving.

Sylvia Bokor

Sylvia Bokor is an artist who attended Ayn Rand's talks and public appearances in New York City and Boston.

Interview date: July 1, 1999

Scott McConnell: *How did you first meet Ayn Rand?*

Sylvia Bokor: I didn't actually meet her for many years. The first time she became aware of me was at a lecture. She had ascended the podium to answer questions with the lecturer. One of the questions had to do with foreign policy. And I heard nothing. I saw nothing. I jumped up out of my chair, and I answered the question. I went on and on. I was very aware that the room had become silent. Finally, I finished answering the question, and I was shaking like a leaf, because it was mixed up with the passion I felt about answering that question. I'd just returned from abroad, and I'd seen what the question involved. At the same time, I was extremely agitated, not only because of the question, but because I knew I was standing in the front of an entire audience of some two hundred people, total strangers to me, in front of a woman that I admired tremendously, and answering a question about foreign policy.

I sat down, at last, and reached for my cigarette lighter. Dead silence. Then I heard someone clapping. I looked up and there was Miss Rand looking straight at me and smiling, clapping. And then of course everybody joined in, and it became a proper applause.

Any other NBI lecture experiences with Miss Rand?

No, not any one-on-one exchanges, except when I asked a question during a Q and A. I was always so impressed with the way she spoke to me. For example, I once asked her that if art was a "selective re-creation of reality" how did it differ from science? She asked for an example. I said, "A scientist inventing a pill." She said, "That's a re-arrangement of reality." Then she elaborated. When she finished, I said "Thank you." She looked directly at me and said, "You're welcome." She was always so polite.

What else was she like?

Miss Rand was very down to earth. Very direct and to the point. A friend of mine, Ambrose, a young man then about eighteen years old, had a great facility with languages and liked to practice whichever language he was studying at the time. One night we went to a lecture together, and he told me, "Tonight I'm going to try it on her." I said, "What?" but he didn't answer. When the lecture was over, about ten of us surrounded Miss Rand to chat with her. All of a sudden Ambrose blurted out a sentence in Russian. The look on Miss Rand's face was of the greatest surprise. She was stunned. Then she started to laugh out loud, and she said, "Your accent in Russian is worse than my accent in English." Everybody laughed. Then she asked, "Is it true that your wife is waiting for you at the railroad station?" Ambrose answered, "Oh no, it's just that that is the only sentence I know in Russian."

Miss Rand and Mr. O'Connor were friendly and gracious in other ways too. During one series of lectures, once again about a dozen of us were crowding around her. But only two or three of us actually talked to her. None of us were intellectuals or philosophers. We were all just students at the time. But we'd talk and talk with her after the lecture. I remember one time after a lecture, it was really getting late, it must have been close to midnight. But Miss Rand just kept right on talking with us. Finally, she said good night, and she and Mr. O'Connor walked almost halfway up the aisle toward the door when she stopped. She turned around and came back to us and said with simple sincerity, completely benevolent: "I really enjoy our chats."

Miss Rand was very sweet and considerate. Once, during a break in a lecture of Leonard's [Leonard Peikoff], a girl said to her, "Miss Rand, I want to give you a little present." Miss Rand said, "No, no, please don't do that. I don't like that." She said, "Oh, Miss Rand, please, I just want to give you a little something to show my appreciation. It really is the least I can do." Miss Rand said, "All right, but don't make it over three dollars."

The girl was so excited and she said to me, "Would you like to chip in?" I said, "Oh, sure." We didn't know what we were going to buy her, but with it only being three dollars there wasn't much choice. The girl bought her a really cute little lapel pin in the form of a cat. She wrapped it up and gave it to Miss Rand the following week, and Miss Rand said thank you, but didn't unwrap it, just took it. The following week Miss Rand came in with Mr. O'Connor and they sat down behind me. I turned around to chat with her, and she was wearing the cat pin.

Allan Gotthelf

Allan Gotthelf is a professor of philosophy who knew Ayn Rand when he was a student and beginning teacher. He is a distinguished Aristotle scholar and a founder of the Ayn Rand Society, a professional society affiliated with the American Philosophical Association, Eastern Division.

Interview dates January 6, 7 and 10, 2000

Scott McConnell: *How did you first learn about Ayn Rand and Objectivism?*

Allan Gotthelf: In the summer of 1961, my mother, who had read *Atlas Shrugged* on recommendation from a business friend, thought I would like it, so she passed it on to me. I loved it. It glowed with respect for the mind, which was so important to me. It showed how one could put one's own happiness first, yet respect the rights of others, without conflict. And its heroic characters were happy and the sort of person I wanted to be. That fall I went to a lecture Ayn Rand gave at Brooklyn College. I didn't take away much from it, though I was taken by her manner. She knew what she was talking about. There was a sternness and seriousness about her. It was a concern with social ideas and a precision and certainty about them that was unfamiliar to me.

When did you first meet Miss Rand?

After a second reading, I found in the back of the paperback *Atlas* the reference to the NBI lectures. I wanted to go to these lectures, but I knew I couldn't afford it. So I asked myself, "What would an Ayn Rand hero do?" And the answer was that he'd offer to work. So I wrote a letter to NBI. I was interviewed by Nathaniel Branden and was told, "Yes, you can work as an usher, but we won't need anyone for a while. Until then, if you like, you can work in the NBI office, because we need somebody there now."

After I'd been working there for a while, Ayn visited the office. She came in the door, and I jumped up and said, "Oh, Miss Rand, I'm so delighted to meet you. I really love your books." And her first immortal words to me were "Are you the accountant?" So I said no, and she went on to her meeting.

I began ushering, I think, in October 1962. I would occasionally ask a question during the question-and-answer period and sometimes afterwards. So she gradually got to know me.

Do you remember any of the questions you asked, and the answers?

One question I remember asking was really a statement in the form of a question. I had just seen at the Museum of Modern Art a painting with nine black squares, each a different shade of black. And I said something like "Would you comment on paintings like that, the corrupt artists who painted them and the fools who bought them?" Her answer was something like "Exactly."

Once, after a lecture on art, she was asked about religious art, and she observed that some of it is very appropriate and very beautiful. "In fact," she said, "my favorite painting is Dali's *Crucifixion*. Now, God knows, I'm an atheist . . ." And then she stopped and everybody laughed. And she laughed too. She mentioned that one of the reasons it was her favorite painting was that it reminded her of Galt's bearing while he was on the torture rack.

When did you first spend time with Miss Rand privately?

It was in the fall of 1963. I had done a senior undergraduate paper critical of Ernest Nagel's "Logic Without Ontology," in which I defended the view that the Law of Noncontradiction is a truth about reality and not just about language—as Nagel had argued. I asked her if I could discuss the paper with her. Ayn took a special interest in people interested in Objectivism who were good philosophically and who were going on into philosophy as a career. And Nathaniel Branden, who had already read the paper, and was there when I asked her, told her it was good. Also, as she told me later, she was interested in the topic, because she knew Nagel's paper and had thought that one day she might write a critical article about it. So she agreed to the meeting. I arrived at her apartment that evening at 9 PM. and didn't leave until 4 AM.

We sat down and we started talking about the paper. I think she had made some notes in the margin. She essentially agreed with what I had said in the paper. At one point, however, I had said that thought is prior to language. So if it's wrong to have a contradiction in language, it must be because it is wrong to have a contradiction in thought. But she said that the relationship of language and thought is very tricky, and the essential epistemological point she wanted to make was that thought can't be expressed without language beyond a certain point. So it isn't true that you can separate them in that way.

We talked about the precision of thought and of language—that language is necessary to articulate thoughts and to carry them beyond a certain point, and that it's the precision of language that makes for the precision of thought. Precise definitions are therefore necessary. And what she said about numbers, which I will always love, is that she loved that "five" means five and not four point seven or whatever—and that her goal or view was that all concepts should have the precision of "five."[148]

We got to talking about Bertrand Russell. I had made a nasty remark about him in my paper, and she laughed about that. What happened then was very typical of her and captures a big part of my sense of her. I said: "But I do think Bertrand Russell's definition of number is correct. So he's not a total loss." And the whole mood of the room changed. She got very serious and she said something like "That will be very damaging to your thinking." She explained that Russell's definition presupposes that you have already grasped the difference between one and many, and thus have already grasped the concept of "one." So you needed the concept of "one" before you could give his definition of number. And so the concept of "unit" is the fundamental concept in mathematics, not "class" or "set." This all came out of her understanding of how concepts work and we talked about that a bit. By the time it was over, I was convinced that Russell's definition was wrong, and that although we didn't have a definition of number, the way to look for it that she had described—by building it on the concept of "unit"—was the right way.

The thing that fascinated me about her manner here—and it moved me very much—was the reason for her being so serious. The expression on her face suggested that she was thinking: "Allan is making a mistake now. This is a serious mistake that is going to damage his thinking about many things. There is nothing in the world more important now than helping Allan to get right about this issue." It was as if she thought that I didn't deserve to be confused in that way. I always thought of it as an act of justice.

We discussed a second paper of mine, which was about perception. Although she had a list of points to make about my papers, and we moved through them, the discussion ranged freely across a great variety of related topics. I loved the fact that I could just sit back and relax and have that sort of conversation with Ayn Rand.

Just before leaving, I told her how much her works had meant to me and my life. She said, "They've meant that much?" and I said, "Yes." As I was leaving, there was this immense warmth as she told me

---

148 See *Introduction to Objectivist Epistemology*, p. 75.

to be careful going down the elevator and through the streets, because it was very late. One of my professors had said either about the Greek gods or the Greek heroes that they were very intense: that when they were angry they were very angry and when they were happy they were very happy, and I thought often, "Ayn Rand's like that." This intensity of warmth I'd seen was like a giant's warmth.

There are other instances of that warm, soft side of her that people often didn't see. For example, in her apartment, if you were talking about ideas, and there weren't too many people there, she would sometimes lie back or recline on the couch. And I could only think of her line in *The Fountainhead* about Roark being as relaxed as a kitten or a cat. That's how she looked. She just had this incredible relaxation.

You were one of her questioners on her radio show at Columbia University in the 1960s.

I had learned about her WKCR radio programs and that students were doing the interviews, so when I got into Columbia for my PhD, I called up the station and got to be one of the questioners. I was on maybe eight programs, and they were recorded two at a time. We would record for thirty minutes, take a little break, and then record again for thirty minutes.

I was living near Columbia and asked her if I could come down and ride back to Columbia with her in a cab. So we did. She said once or twice, "I don't understand why you come all the way down just to ride all the way back." I just made a face and said something like "Well, you know." My reason, of course, was that I got an additional opportunity to talk with her. And we had some interesting conversations in the cab.

When I got to the apartment, she was often not ready and that allowed me time with Frank O'Connor. I didn't have a lot of interaction with him, and that's probably the most time we ever spent together. Thinking of those conversations makes me smile. He was such a gentle, benevolent, gracious and graceful man. There were occasions when Frank would be going to his studio to paint and the three of us would go down in the elevator together. Then she and I would get into a cab, and she would say goodbye to him and call him "Cubbyhole."

Did anything interesting happen during the taxi rides?

Several things. For instance, if the taxi driver was driving too fast, I would put up with it. But she would say, "Driver, please don't drive so fast." This was typical Ayn Rand. She wanted it a certain way and she asked for it.

At this time I had been reading some Nietzsche. In fact, we did a radio program on Nietzsche and Objectivism—it was important to her to have her views distinguished clearly from Nietzsche's. On the way to the studio, I said to her, "I think if Nietzsche had read *Atlas Shrugged* when he was younger, he would have become an Objectivist." And she said something like "I don't think so. His attitude to reason was too antagonistic. But Aristotle, if he'd been exposed to Objectivism . . ." I said, "Yes. It's like what Andrew Stockton said in the Valley about Rearden. He'd shoot through here like a rocket." And she smiled. She had this great affection for Aristotle.

We also talked once about Dagny's relation to Galt, Francisco and Rearden. She commented that Galt was closest in sense of life to Dagny and, interestingly, that Rearden's sense of life was closer to Dagny's than Francisco's was.

What was it like interviewing her?

The host in my year was Arthur Gandolfi. The standard format was that he would introduce the program and call on the first questioner. There were anywhere from three to five of us. If you had a question that was a follow-up to a previous one, you put up two fingers. If you had a question that was new, you'd put up one finger. In a couple of cases, it was arranged for someone to do an opening—for example, in the Nietzsche program, Gandolfi asked me to give a brief summary of Nietzsche's philosophy as background. I tried to state, in about twenty seconds, Nietzsche's entire philosophy in metaphysics, epistemology, human nature and ethics, and I asked her to contrast Objectivism on each of those theses! She did so immediately, and brilliantly, in about the same amount of time.

In general, it was fun. Some of my questions were "loaded" questions. I rarely asked anything that I didn't know the basic answer to, because I had separate access to her for that. But her answers would sometimes take me in new directions, and follow-up questions would often do that. They were very relaxing sessions. She was just really so on the ball. One example is a remark she made. The program was about pragmatism. I noted on some issue that a pragmatist would say so and so. And she replied to that. Then I said, "But the pragmatist would say such and such." And she answered that. And I began, "Yes, but, the pragmatist would say—" but I forgot what point I was going to make. And there's this moment of dead air time. And she said, almost immediately, "That's right. He would have nothing to say."

Did you see her on any TV shows?

Several times. One occasion, I think, was with Les Crane, who had a local New York TV call-in and interview show. It was soon after the *Playboy* interview had come out in 1964. He began the show by saying: "Miss Rand appears in the March issue of *Playboy*. She's not the centerfold." And she laughed and said, "Thank you." The other thing I remember was someone calling up and saying: "You talk about self-reliance or something like that. But everybody gets help in his life, I mean, in his career. Who is it that helped you to get started in your writing?" And she said, "Sweetheart, nobody."

There was a TV show I didn't see, which she told me about [*Live a Borrowed Life*, on the Canadian Broadcasting Co.], where people had to guess who she was. She had chosen Aristotle as the person in history she most admired and, in the format of the TV show, had a picture of him covering her face. So there she was on the screen with her body and Aristotle's face and people trying to guess who she was.

Any other times you saw Miss Rand lecture at university?

At Brooklyn College, I founded one of the early Ayn Rand clubs, and she came to speak. There were more than a thousand people in the audience. It was spring of '63. Her lecture was titled "The Fascist New Frontier," and Ayn was in complete command of the event, capturing the audience's attention throughout. There was much discussion around the campus afterwards.

In the fall of '65, I got my first teaching job in philosophy—a part-time job at Pratt Institute in Brooklyn. It's a school for art, architecture and engineering. My course was an introductory philosophy course but I had a unit on esthetics. And I asked her if she would be willing to come and talk to the class. I proposed that we open it up to anybody at the college, and she said yes, but questions could come only from people in the class who had read "The Psycho-Epistemology of Art," which was a class assignment. I picked her up in my little Volkswagen and drove her there and back. She was a real hit with the students.

Tell me about some other philosophical discussions you had with her.

I had found in Roark's speech, in *The Fountainhead*, that ethics was based on the alternative of life or death. It was commonly

held that it was *Atlas Shrugged* that initiates the view that values
are based on the alternative of life or death. But Roark says:
"The choice is not self-sacrifice or domination. The choice is
independence or dependence. The code of the creator or the code
of the second-hander. This is the basic issue. It rests upon the
alternative of life or death. The code of the creator is built on the
needs of the reasoning mind which allows man to survive." So
there was life or death as the basis. And I said to her, "You know, I
always thought of that validation as beginning in Galt's speech. But
I found in *The Fountainhead* this passage." What I thought was that
I was showing her something about her own works that she didn't
remember. And she said, "That's true but at the time when I wrote
that, I didn't realize that even weeds have values." The idea being
that even the most grubby kind of plant has values. That was her
way of referring to the idea that the concept of value depends on the
concept of life. That important identification, she said, "didn't come
until later." I believe she worked it out while writing Galt's speech.

Around the same time, I gave an Aristotle course to friends, and
I taped the course. The last lecture was on the history of Aristotle's
influence, up to Objectivism. And I asked her, at one point, if
she'd be interested in hearing it. She was, and so we played the
tape. I had made the comment in the lecture that there was a work
attributed to Aristotle during the middle ages called *Liber de
Causis*, which actually had a Neoplatonic, theological bent to it,
and that Aquinas had realized it wasn't by Aristotle. I remember her
saying, "Yes, he would realize that." It's just a minor point—just
her admiration for Aquinas, that he would be smart enough to
recognize when something wasn't Aristotelian, when no one had
before him.

I was impressed by her ability to talk about almost anything
and to say something intelligent about it. And no matter how much
you knew about what she thought, she would surprise you with
something new. Her mind never stopped working. Not only that—it
wasn't just that she got new ideas, but that her old ideas were so full
of content that you could mine them forever. I see that now in older
writings and documents of hers that are currently being published.

Did you introduce her to any professors you knew?

I started at Columbia in 1964, and I took two classes with

Randall,[149] a general history of philosophy and a course on Aristotle. She had sent him a copy of her review, but he didn't respond. I told him about my interest in her and thought it would be great to have them meet. So we arranged a time to have lunch at Columbia. It was he, his wife, Ayn and I.

He was very shy—that is the best word to describe him. Didn't initiate very much. One of the first things she said was how much she liked his book. And she asked whether, given the respect for Aristotle and for reason he shows in the book, he felt alone in the profession. And that's interesting, because she used a very direct approach, hoping to make a connection, since if he said "Yes," then bam! they would be off. He was made uncomfortable by the question because she was very likely tapping into something which he had probably spent a lifetime denying. And he laughed this sort of defensive laugh and said, "Well, no. There's always Mr. Gotthelf to talk to."

I think she followed up on her question regarding reason. She didn't give up right away. She said something like "But isn't it true that most of the profession is really anti-reason?" He denied it in some vague way that evaporated into nothing rather than being a precise formulation. At which point, I think, she gave up on that. She also said, in the course of conversation, that she disagreed with his characterization of Aristotle as the father of the welfare state.

When it was over, she said to me, exasperated, "I can't talk to him. I can't find a way to draw anything out." I said, "It's very difficult. Once in a while I can get a little more." It was a disappointment for her because it was clear that he was very repressed, and she would have liked to make a connection.

Ayn also had some interaction with Brand Blanshard.[150] In the course of it, she and Blanshard exchanged books. She sent him *The Virtue of Selfishness*, and he sent her his book on ethics, *Reason and Goodness*.[151] She read it and she said to me, sort of smiling, "He's no friend of ours." She referred, in disgust, to the fact that he would include, in his "private gallery of heroes" of ethical philosophy, portraits of Plato

---

149 John Herman Randall, Jr., a well-known historian of philosophy and author of *Aristotle* (New York: Columbia University Press, 1960), which Ayn Rand reviewed positively in *The Objectivist Newsletter*, May 1963.

150 The distinguished Idealist philosopher, whose book *Reason and Analysis* (LaSalle, IL: Open Court, 1962) was reviewed in *The Objectivist Newsletter*, February 1963.

151 Brand Blanshard, *Reason and Goodness* (London: George Allen & Unwin, 1961), pp. 445–6.

and Hume but not of Aristotle.

I had gotten into a correspondence with Blanshard. He was reviewing for the *New York Times* on occasion, and I tried to get him to do a review of *The Virtue of Selfishness*. He said that he didn't like to review a book where he so disagreed with the fundamental thesis. Still, he said—and I think quite sincerely—that he found her a very interesting thinker.

Did you have any other discussions about professional philosophers?

One I remember was during a phone conversation with Ayn. I told her of my success in communicating a technical Objectivist position—something about concepts, I think— to a well-known young analytic philosopher of my acquaintance. I mentioned to her that I had done it not by re-expressing Objectivism in contemporary philosophical language, but by building my own Objectivist context up from ground level, with the help of reference to historical philosophers. I said that the philosopher seemed to get the idea, more or less. When I had finished the story, you could almost see Ayn smiling across the phone line. She said, "I can't do that with them. If you can, that's great."

Did Miss Rand ever talk to you about her life in Russia?

No, but one time Leonard [Peikoff], Harry [Binswanger], the Hessens and I went to Princeton with Ayn and Frank, when Lillian Gish was giving a lecture. Ayn and Frank were planning to go backstage. But in her lecture, Gish said some things about visiting Russia, and that really infuriated Ayn. She said to Frank, "Look, after that, I don't really want to go back. Do you mind going yourself?" He understood. And he went back and talked with her.

Ayn was really angered, but in a hurt sort of way, that somebody whom she had heard such good things about from Frank could still view the Soviet Union as a civilized place. She had thought better of Lillian Gish.

Earlier that evening, one of us asked her whether silent films were a separate genre and she said no. To that extent, she said, it's really like pantomime. I think she has said this elsewhere: that adding sound to movies really completed the genre rather than changed the genre; that much of a silent film amounts to pantomime, where you're limited in your communication.

What did Mr. O'Connor report about his meeting with Lillian Gish?

She remembered him from the D. W. Griffith days, and they talked a little about their lives since then. I believe that Lillian Gish knew of Ayn Rand's work, but I don't remember any evaluation.

How did you become Miss Rand's indexer?

I did the index for *The Virtue of Selfishness* in 1964 and *Capitalism: The Unknown Ideal* in 1966. Following the normal process, the publisher assigned the indexing of *VOS* to someone, but Ayn didn't like the draft index that was prepared. And they said, if you can find somebody yourself, we'll pay him. She asked me, and I agreed to do it.

We went over my draft of the index, page by page, and she confirmed that, yes, this does belong here, occasionally, no, it doesn't. We got to an item about collectivism, for example, and she said, "Wait a minute, isn't there something about collectivism in such and such an article?" She had an amazing recollection of her work, and I was impressed then at the command she had at remembering detailed pieces of information like that.

During this work, an issue came up regarding her definition of reason. In *Atlas Shrugged* reason is defined as "the faculty that perceives, identifies and integrates the material provided by [man's] senses." In "The Objectivist Ethics," which comes four years later, in '61, reason is defined as "the faculty that identifies and integrates the material provided by man's senses." The word "perceives" was taken out. I asked her why she had deleted it.

She said that Nathan [Branden] had raised the issue—that with "perceives" in the definition, it might be taken to mean that perception inherently involves reason or concepts and thus that—as the Idealists like Blanshard held—consciousness constructs the world we perceive. She deeply disbelieved that and was concerned that "perceives" might be taken that way.

During an indexing session in her study, Frank called to her and said Eloise had dinner ready. Ayn previously had said to me, "Would you like to stay for dinner because we could continue working and get it done?" Of course, my answer was yes. After a while, Frank came in and he was quite angry. He said, "Eloise spent a lot of time preparing dinner and she's going to be upset if it gets cold." Frank's tone suggested to me that this probably had happened before. He walked out, and she turned to me and smiled and said, "He's right." We put the work down and we got up. The sense I had was that she was acknowledging, in effect, "Yes. I've done this before. And yes, Frank is reasonable to get upset with me." I was impressed by her smiling and saying, "He's right." There was no strain at dinner.

Did Miss Rand ever edit you?

Yes, it had to do with *The Philosopher's Index*, which was publishing summaries, that is, abstracts, of articles that appear in philosophical journals, and indexing them by subject headings. The publishers of the *Index* got a grant to do a retrospective project for books and articles back to 1940. I was hired to do indexing for this project.

I told Richard Lineback, the editor of the *Index*, that I had a great interest in Ayn Rand and that she'd written a lot of philosophical material that people were unaware of, which should be included in the *Index*. He said something like "Yes, I too think there's probably more to her than most philosophers realize. Go ahead. Do it and I'll put it into the retrospective index." I got Ayn's approval for this.

The job, essentially, was to go through each article I considered philosophical, write a summary of it of no more than seventy-five words, and choose a number of subject headings that it would go under. I sent those to Leonard, who edited them and sent them on to Ayn, who did a final editing, and then Ayn, Leonard and I had a telephone conference.

So she did edit me—or rather, my summarizing of her. What she did was rewrite where she thought I wasn't capturing the essence. Sometimes she changed a few words. Occasionally she rewrote the whole thing. Sometimes she left it just as it was. I then typed up the final version and submitted it. And it was published in the retrospective *Index*, something like sixty-five different articles, mostly by her but also several by Leonard and a few by George Walsh. Some articles she thought weren't philosophical enough, and those were not included. And, of course, the books were included. And that was probably the first substantial listing of her philosophic writing in any academic bibliographical tool.

Did she ever tell you any stories about dealings with her publishers?

Yes. For *The Virtue of Selfishness*, the hardcover, she asked that the cloth cover be greenish-blue. She wanted the spine to be more green and the rest of the cover more blue. The publisher had originally done it the other way 'round, and she asked that the colors be reversed. This way, her favorite colors would be combined in a layout she liked.

Another story she told me was about the cover of the original paperback of *Atlas Shrugged*, which depicted the figure of a standing, nude man, with his palms turned out. After an NBI lecture she told me that the artist had drawn the figure too chunky. She had asked the artist to make him thinner. And it was still too chunky. Finally she held the artist's hand and moved it around to get the right shape.

Let's turn to Miss Rand's book Introduction to Objectivist Epistemology [ITOE].

In the spring of 1963, after a lecture of hers I'd arranged at Brooklyn College, a group of students went out to lunch with her. Later I told her about a conversation I'd had with a student in which he was insisting that definitions are subjective, and so we couldn't resolve any philosophical issue. I said, "You know, we really need that book on epistemology, on the theory of concepts and definitions and all that." She said, "Hmm."

Later, when she started writing the epistemology book, or possibly before that, she told me it was our conversation together with things Leonard had said earlier that stimulated her. So I remember her treating my remark as the precipitating remark in her decision to write the epistemology. When she autographed my book some years later, she wrote, "To Allan: the book you had asked me for many years ago. With best wishes for its full use." So it was Leonard's urging and my remark that were responsible for her finally deciding to write the book. It's a nice feeling.

Were you reading ITOE *before it was published?*

Harry and I both read the first installment before it was published. And it was a thrill. Obviously ground-breaking, and wonderful. I have a vague recollection that she had written something on mathematical infinity that I suggested to her wasn't quite right, and that she then made a change in wording. We were very impressed by the essay, to say the least.

Did you discuss it with her?

There was a time when I discussed several things with Leonard because he had been meeting with her regularly, either in preparation for his University of Denver course or in preparation for his NBI course, Objectivism's Theory of Knowledge. But I don't believe I discussed it systematically with Ayn until the *ITOE* workshop.

She also said that when she sat down to write the epistemology book, she found it very easy; it just flowed out because she had been priming her subconscious for it for years. One interesting thing is that some of the definitions, for example, of "unit," in the 1966 published version, are different from the definitions that she and Branden both had told me in 1963 or '64.[152]

How did the ITOE *workshop come about?*

Leonard told me about it and invited me to attend. I don't know exactly how it came about, but the idea, I think, was that, like the nonfiction-writing course aimed to train writers for *The Objectivist*, the workshop would train people in the Objectivist epistemology, so that they could teach it or use it in their work. I'm sure that was the primary motivation. It certainly helped. I mean, it made a world of difference to me. The work I did in preparation for it, and what I learned during it, really sharpened my understanding of the theory and my method of thinking—which has lasted to this day.

There were a lot of people at the first workshop. Leonard was there sort of as host, and he said that, because he had such access to Ayn, he wouldn't ask many questions, although he'd participate in the discussion. George Walsh and John Nelson, whom Leonard knew from Denver, were the two senior people there. Also present, in philosophy, were Harry and I and Mike Berliner. There were, in addition, some people in physics and others I don't recall.

The plan was that a designated person would be the only one to ask questions of Ayn for the first hour or so. That would give a focus to the session as well as an opportunity for that person to get his questions answered.

The first session lasted about nine hours, including dinner. So about seven hours, total. Ayn had enormous energy and could have gone on all night.

George Walsh began that session with questions about the first two chapters. In the second session, John Nelson asked questions about the third chapter, "Abstraction from Abstractions." I came third, but was asked to raise questions about the whole rest of the book because Ayn had decided that that was going to be the last session. She really didn't want to do any more. Leonard told me that she said she would continue to have sessions with a small number of people in her apartment, but the official epistemology workshop was those three meetings.

Ayn decided that the first session had gone on too long, so the second meeting was cut down to five hours. Nonetheless, she was somewhat bored, I believe, by the extent of unimportant or uninteresting

---

152 See *Journals of Ayn Rand*, p. 700.

questions, although she was certainly very engaged by the better ones and found many questions valuable.

For us, it was chock-full of new information. Anything you had ever thought about the topics, you could ask about, more or less, because it would tie in. So it was just immensely rewarding and enriching. It was an incredible intellectual experience being able to ask Ayn Rand those kinds of questions. For me, it was the equivalent of having Aristotle in the room.

How would you describe her during the seminars?

I think there was a quiet enjoyment when sensible questions were asked, answers given and the questioner then said something which indicated that he got it. I suspect there was a certain amount of strain, when people asked questions from weird contexts. But the strain, if there was any, was more intellectual than emotional, in that it mattered to her that she understand what the other person was saying, since the purpose of the event was to respond to that. My focus wasn't on her reaction, but I could see she was enjoying it much of the time. When she said, "Exactly," in response to something someone said—I felt that was an enjoyable moment for her. And she clearly enjoyed explaining things too.

In these technical discussions, there still were surprises. And she was just inexhaustible. And in what you could learn from her— "irreplaceable" isn't strong enough a word for meetings like this.

At the close of the first workshop, she told us the story about how she had arrived at the heart of her theory.[153]

Did Miss Rand give you any private advice?

I had a conversation with her once about something that was really very private, but I'd like to mention it because it's indicative of her approach. I felt I had betrayed her in a certain way. When I called to tell her, I obviously was distraught. And there was just one thing she wanted to know, and I said, "No, I didn't do that." And she said, "Oh, okay." What I want to get at was that she was very sensitive psychologically. She saw what I was doing and some mistakes that I was making, psycho-epistemologically. And she went to the philosophical principles that were relevant. It was as if she were targeting it to a place where I could understand it. She said, "You know, you've got a Hegelian

---

153 See *Introduction to Objectivist Epistemology*, p. 307.

premise. You're expecting yourself to know everything before you know anything." And I understood right away what she was referring to.

So first she wanted to know if I had done something that she would consider immoral or a betrayal. Once it was clear that I hadn't, the decks were cleared. At that point, she showed that same real concern I mentioned to you earlier—to help me see something intellectually. And that was what I needed to get through that particular thing.

Also, around the time I was doing the index, I had dinner at her apartment once or twice. There was a very attractive woman I'd been interested in who was interested in me. And then she fell for this other guy, and she proceeded to explain to me why she was no longer interested in me. One issue was that I was too overweight. I mentioned this to Ayn, and she said, in effect: "I wouldn't say that. If it was I, I'd be pushing him to lose weight, but I wouldn't give him up over that." Her perspective was that appearance matters, but there are ways of dealing with it without just walking away.

We also discussed the feeling many people have, which I felt about myself only occasionally, that they will never meet a romantic partner, someone they could love for the rest of their lives. She told me something that has stuck with me, and I've told it to others who expressed the same feeling. She said, "You're not a freak, right?" And I said, "No." "Well, then," she said, "there must be others like you. You just have to find them." Her point was that one becomes the sort of person one is by acquiring certain values and a certain character; others can acquire similar values and a similar character and a particular style that you respond to. It's like that great joke about New York City: "The thing is, in New York, even if you're one in a million, there are eight of you!" You just have to find them.

Did you witness anyone giving advice to her?

I was with her once when the 18-year-old son of a new friend was trying to explain to Ayn why he thought she should present her ideas to the world differently. If somebody had said this who wasn't the son of a new friend, she would have really let him have it. And she said, kind of sternly but still warmly, "Look, I've been doing this for a long time." It was on the order of "Why do you think that you would know better than I the best way to present my ideas?" She was quite nice about it.

What did you discuss with her regarding her novels?

We had some conversations about *Atlas Shrugged*. One was

regarding the scene at the Rearden anniversary party, where Francisco comments to Simon Pritchett that he was a pupil of Hugh Akston's. A woman had said that Pritchett was telling them that nothing is anything, and Francisco says, about Hugh Akston, that he taught that everything is something. She told me that was one of her favorite moments in the novel, and she loved that she could get these very abstract ideas— nothing is anything, everything is something—into a dramatic scene. She also said that she liked the way, in the scene where Dagny and Owen Kellogg are walking down the railroad track in the middle of the night looking for a telephone, she was able to capture the sense of a Hegelian universe of non-Identity: ". . . a space which was neither light nor dark, a soil which neither gave nor resisted, a fog which neither moved nor hung still." Those are two examples of taking very abstract philosophical ideas and creating a literary context where their meanings come across in a very dramatic way.

Another thing she was proud of was the description of the sound of the wailing siren at Rearden's mill when the furnace has the breakout. She said one of the most difficult things in writing is to communicate the idea of sound and she thought she did that really well here.

In a question period she talked about Mouch's name. It came up when someone said, "Wesley Mooch." And she said, "No. It's not Wesley Mooch. It's Wesley Mouch." She explained that she got the name by combining "mouse" and "mooch."

As to "Galt," she said, also in a question period, that she didn't remember where she got the name. And there was a question about Hank Rearden, something like "Dagny and Rearden's first relationship was a formal, business relationship, so why was Dagny calling him 'Hank'?" She said she found it was typical in American business for business executives to use nicknames or shorter names in talking to each other. And she wanted to capture that.

She also said that the young Katherine Hepburn would make an excellent Dagny—referring, I'm sure, to the Hepburn of the 1930s.

I asked her if she ever reread *Atlas Shrugged*. She said, "Very rarely. When I read it, I enter into the world of those characters and it takes weeks to get out."

Did Miss Rand ever mention to you any new fiction writing she was doing?

On one visit, she mentioned that she had just gotten an advance for her next novel. I asked her what it was about, and she replied, "Oh, I can't talk about it." She said that it was the largest advance ever gotten by a woman for a novel, and she was very proud of that. I think it was a quarter of a million dollars. Some time later the advance came up again, and she said, "Oh, I've given it back." That was after she had decided against writing the novel.

Let's now focus on some other topics. Aristotle?

It's been written that in the late '40s she bought "the complete works of Aristotle." So I asked her if that was true, and she said no, what she had bought was the McKeon *Basic Works of Aristotle*, which has most of the philosophic writings but is not the complete twelve volumes.

Eleanor Roosevelt?

She described Eleanor Roosevelt as "energy without effort." That was a concept that was used about people who hustle and bustle about but don't accomplish anything of significance. And Mrs. Roosevelt was an example of that.

Her weight?

She would sometimes be battling a weight problem, as she saw it. And she'd be proud when she lost weight. As to her height, she bought platform shoes when they were in fashion, and she seemed to like being taller.

Did you ever talk with her about how she used her mind?

Yes. There's just one thing. She said she was lucky that she had set herself on the right premise very early. I think it was the premise of asking why, of moving to the next level of abstraction, and of looking for the fundamental. This is something she had chosen to do, but it involved a discovery, so she could understand people taking much longer to reach this methodology, if at all. She felt lucky—which was not a typical response of hers—that she had found it early, and thought you really couldn't hold someone responsible if it took him longer to find his way to that good psycho-epistemology.

Were there any poets she said she liked?

She said once that she liked Swinburne.

Were there any other philosophers Miss Rand discussed with you besides Nietzsche and Aristotle?

Well, Plato, in a way. In *Atlas*, Hugh Akston says that at age sixteen John Galt asked a question about Plato's metaphysics which Plato should have had the sense to ask of himself. Leonard and I asked her what the question was, thinking it was something like the "Third Man" objection to Plato's theory of Forms—though not that precise question, since Plato had raised that one—but she said she didn't have a particular question in mind.

Kant?

Kant's ethics is based on a "universalizability" principle, the principle that you should act only on that maxim which could be made into a universal law. In the course of a conversation about Kant, she said, "I've always wanted to write an article on the universalizability principle, on what's right with it—because something important is—and what's wrong with it."

Did you have any discussions about any nonfiction she planned to work on?

During that six-hour-long meeting at her apartment in 1963, we discussed a little of what she planned to work on. At the time, I was a graduate student in math, and we talked about my view that positions in philosophy of mathematics depend on positions on universals, that the traditional twentieth-century schools of philosophy of mathematics implicitly derive from three bad schools of philosophy on universals, but that there isn't even a contemporary Aristotelian philosophy of mathematics, let alone an Objectivist one. She said, "Well, I've said to myself for years that when I'm seventy, I'm going to work on the philosophy of mathematics." That was 1963, and she'd already made some notes on the connection between concepts and mathematics.[154]

Did you talk to her about Lyndon Johnson?

I once said to her, "Johnson reminds me exactly of Mr. Thompson." And she said, "I can see that, but Mr. Thompson was modeled after Harry Truman."

Based on your observations, do you think that she practiced what she preached?

---

154 For more information, see *Journals of Ayn Rand*, pp. 700–703.

Yes. But it's more than just practicing what she preached. Her practice flowed effortlessly from what she thought. You couldn't imagine her acting against what she believed. She was a very private person, so you wouldn't get indications of any moral struggles if there were any, but my sense was that she had an absolute honesty with herself and with the world. There were no jarring elements, no inconsistencies. This was all the way through our relationship. So, yes, she was rock solid.

How did your relationship with Miss Rand end?

In the late 1970s I had a less active part in the movement and was less in touch with Ayn. But in November of '81, when Ayn was going to New Orleans to lecture, we happened to be in Penn Station at the same time. Harry was with her and saw me and came over and said, "Ayn is here and we're going down to New Orleans for her lecture." So I went to the special Amtrak VIP room to see her. We talked a bit about how we'd each been doing in the last few years. And she told me about the reason for the New Orleans trip.

I'll always be immensely grateful that I had that opportunity to see her, because it really was like closure. I had not seen her for a long time, but I could see she was declining and I was saddened by that, although you could also see that her decline was like another person's immense alertness. She didn't seem as acute as she had been, just physically weak and tired. I have really fond memories of that meeting, and I'm grateful for that opportunity because next I heard she'd gotten ill from the trip. Then I got a call from Harry that she had died. He explained that there would be a viewing and then the funeral. With my college commitments I could only go to one, and I chose to go to the funeral.

How did you say goodbye to Miss Rand at the station?

I don't know if I had a sense that it would be the last time I'd be seeing her. She told me about the private railway car the sponsors of the lecture in New Orleans had arranged for her. There was a child-like pleasure in the way she mentioned it, and I said, "That's great." I said something like "Really enjoy your trip down. I hope the lecture goes great."

In addition to what you said to Miss Rand in that first long meeting, did you ever tell her what you thought of her achievement?

Yes. It was after I played for her the tape I mentioned earlier of the lecture I gave about the subsequent influence of Aristotle's thought. We were talking and she was underscoring how great Aristotle was. And I said to her, "But you know, you've done for consciousness what Aristotle did for existence." I think I may have said Aristotle basically gave us the principle that existence has identity. She gave us the view that consciousness has identity. He brought a clarity to the world—entities, attributes, cause and effect, and so forth. She did that for consciousness with concepts, free will, art and much else. And she acknowledged that. But she would never let anybody say that she was greater than Aristotle. And I was never tempted to do that.

I miss her very much, to this day. But I'm at peace with her death. I had my time with her. How can it not be a benevolent universe if I could know Ayn Rand?

Dorothy Gotthelf

Dorothy Gotthelf is the mother of Allan Gotthelf, philosopher and Ayn Rand friend. Mrs. Gotthelf died in 2003.

Interview date: June 30, 2000

Scott McConnell: *I believe that you once talked to Miss Rand on the phone.*

Dorothy Gotthelf: Yes, I did. It might have been more than once, but the one time I remember specifically, she was very sweet. Allan had just started to be very interested in her works and spent a lot of time with Miss Rand. It was the time Allan was graduating from Brooklyn College, and she called and wanted to speak with him, but he was not at home. She then asked if this was his mother, and I said yes. She told me that Allan was one of the brightest people she had ever met, and she was so happy to have met him, and she was happy to have met me. She expressed the wish, which took me by surprise, "I really envy you. I have to tell you, I wish he was my son." And I said, "That pleasure I cannot give you." I thought it was very nice. She was so complimentary; she really made me feel very good.

Edwin A. Locke

Edwin A. Locke is Dean's Professor (Emeritus) of Leadership and Motivation at the University of Maryland at College Park (retired), and was acquainted with Ayn Rand in the 1960s and '70s.

Interview date: March 12, 1999

Scott McConnell: *Tell me about Miss Rand's 1969 nonfiction-writing course.*

Edwin A. Locke: I was trying to write things relevant to Objectivism but was pretty poor at it. The purpose of this course was to help create articles for *The Objectivist*, and I did make an abortive attempt at that. I had a paper conference with her—and I brought a terrible paper—and she said, "This paper isn't quite right," and proceeded to tell me all the things wrong with it, which were all true, and also certain things she thought were good points.

Sometimes she would be shocked at my ignorance. She would say, not condemningly, but incredulously, "Didn't you know that?" I'd say "No," very embarrassed. But she was always very objective about her comments. She was never moralistic.

Can you give me more specifics about her editing?

She'd always try to identify the essential and where you went wrong: what didn't follow from what; what you said that you didn't support properly. She would always pick out the fundamental issue, but she had the ability to pick out the fundamentals and tie it to the details, such as saying, "This doesn't lead to this" or "This sentence is unclear."

When I'd submit an article outline, she would explain why the outline should have been focused a little bit differently.

But in a way, I never could relax enough to fully appreciate her editing because I was so awestruck by just being there.

How did she treat you?

Always very objectively and fairly. Always focused on the facts. And always benevolent. We all took turns bringing refreshments to that course, and at the breaks, people would talk to her, but it was always business, always ideas. You wouldn't go up to her unless you had a comment about an idea.

I saw her get angry only once. She got mad at Frank for leaving the windows open too wide because she was afraid a cat would fall out. She said something like "You mustn't leave the windows up like that." And then when the class started, she said to everybody, "I'm sorry to get angry, but I was worried about the cats."

Sometime after the nonfiction-writing course was over, I was fortunate to be invited to attend a question-and-answer "seminar" that she was giving at her apartment. I asked her what was wrong with Henry Cameron as opposed to Roark, since Cameron had gone to pieces as his business declined and Roark did not, despite his many setbacks. She replied that Cameron was too emotional.

I was stunned by the depth of her knowledge, how she could take something as simple as an outline and talk about it for hours. It was amazing. But she was always factual and logical. Answered questions politely. She was always a totally rational person. These Q&A sessions ended after, I recall, just one meeting, due to Frank's death. I was very sorry about that, not only about Frank's death and the impact it had on her, but because I was preparing a bunch of new questions to ask her.

Did you have any private interactions with her?

I had two private sessions with her. The first was during the non-fiction-writing course described earlier. As I noted above, she wanted people to write articles, and many of us took a stab at it during the course. My effort was not successful.

My second session, sometime later, after the course was over, turned out better. I had written a paper on the concept of purpose, which she actually liked and talked about having it published in *The Objectivist*, but I think that publication ceased not long after. But I was very proud that I had produced a good piece of work. Later, Harry Binswanger completed his doctoral dissertation, which was on a related topic, and his work added important new insights on the subject.

John Ridpath

John Ridpath was an acquaintance of Miss Rand's from 1962 until her death in 1982. For thirty-four years he taught intellectual history and economics at York University in Toronto, Canada, during which time he lectured on her ideas and debated in defense of capitalism at universities across North America and in Europe.

Interview dates: July 10, 11 and 22, 1999

Scott McConnell: *How did you come to know Ayn Rand?*

John Ridpath: I was working for an air-conditioning company in the spring of 1961, having completed a bachelor's degree in engineering at the University of Toronto. A friend gave me *Atlas Shrugged*, which completely engrossed me over that summer, but only as a work of fiction. In the late fall of 1961, I returned to work in Toronto and saw a newspaper announcement that Nathaniel Branden would be giving a talk about Ayn Rand.

That lecture was pivotal in my life. I was twenty-five years old, had no exposure to the humanities, and—unable to make sense of my own life, let alone of history—I was sinking into cynicism. What mattered to me, from that lecture, was not so much Ayn Rand's philosophical ideas, but the insight that ideas are what underlie and explain lives and history. During the summer of 1962, I went back to school—to study the history of ideas.

How did you first meet her?

While I was working on my MBA at the University of Toronto, an NBI ball was held in New York City. My first meeting with her came during a break in the dancing. I noticed her alone at her table, so I introduced myself.

What did you talk about?

The happiness and gaiety of the party, the meaning of *Atlas Shrugged* to me, and my plans for graduate studies. What was more dramatic for me was not what we talked about, but how we talked—her manner. On the way across the dance floor, I was expecting to meet an intellectual Sherman tank, all focused, intent, serious, and I was geared up for this. After the first few moments, the atmosphere became one of happiness, benevolence, considerateness, even warmth. From this first

352

meeting to our last, this was the undercurrent of every occasion spent in her company.

Would she advise you on things like your teaching or life in academia?

No and yes. On my teaching, I had been successful from the outset—my first teaching was at the University of Virginia in 1965–66. On the subject of success at teaching, we did discuss the importance of both hierarchy and examples, but overall, I recall this topic being more like a report from the front lines, of battle success, than it was guidance from the commander in chief.

On life in academia, she did have advice. She helped me learn not to teach my teachers—no matter how badly they might have needed it. And she warned me about the depth of corruption in academia that went deeper than I could imagine—at least, until I became a faculty member at York University in Toronto.

Along the way, of course, she answered innumerable questions of mine, partly on economics, but mainly on intellectual history and on the ideas of history's notable philosophers.

Do you remember some answers?

Yes. For example, she commented on Aristotle's greatness, explaining it in terms of the profundity of his deepest insights; his love of scientific study; the range of issues he covered in his work; and, particularly, his independence, which allowed him to discover so much that was foreign to his culture.

I also recall one discussion on the concept of individualism, which got us into the issue of the primacy of individual entities, which got us into the issue of "what is an entity?" And if a brick can be an entity, then how can a wall be an entity? There are a lot of bricks here, so what does it refer to, one or the other? Of course, she was able to say, "It depends on the context; it refers to one or the other." The confusion was essentially from not understanding contexts. That's one of the types of conversations I had with her.

I vividly remember another example of her ability to go to fundamentals to clear up a debate. After a Ford Hall appearance, back at her hotel suite, one of us asked her if she could help with a debate many of us were involved in. The issue was: is fractional-reserve banking, because of its creation of expanded credit on a given base, implicit theft or legitimate banking business. We—several of us doctoral students, if not already PhDs in economics—were split on this issue. With characteristic focus, she asked several questions, revealing a surprising understanding, and then—bingo—the answer was evident to her. It is appropriate—it is a matter of informed, calculated risk and, in essence, not theft at all.

It was experiences like this that could keep me awake for days after the Ford Hall events. It was, without exception, always wonderful, inspiring fuel to talk to her.

Did she know the history of ideas thoroughly?

Not thoroughly in some cases, but essentially, in all cases. She said that the concept of individual rights is so prodigious a feat that few men have ever understood it to this day. She could say that, not because she knew the whole history of the concept, but because she knew the essential issues in the history of philosophy and how they would mislead people to view rights in the wrong way.

A good example of her grasp of ideas was the case of Friedrich Nietzsche. During the 1960s and '70s, it was becoming fashionable for her detractors to characterize her as a latter-day Nietzschean. In doing this, they denied her originality, made it unnecessary to openly address her ideas, and linked her to a thinker commonly believed by the culture to have been a proto-Nazi and a madman.

I had read a lot of Nietzsche and knew that—beyond the drama and passion, seemingly exhorting men to individual heroism and greatness—lay a deeper body of ideas that were totally incompatible with individualism, and which Ayn Rand had definitively refuted.

I asked Miss Rand if she thought that it would be valuable for me to write about how she was not influenced in any serious philosophical way by Nietzsche. She encouraged me to do so. I set about reading all of Nietzsche, and a lot of the secondary literature on him. In the process of doing this, I would phone her or visit her. She would help me with difficulties, and I would discuss Nietzsche with her. She had read some of Nietzsche's central works much earlier in her life, but not, I believe, his whole corpus, and not any biographies or contemporary discussion. So she was curious to hear more about different facets of his views.

What was her manner and method when she was explaining things to you?

Her manner was attentive, patient and very, very focused. It was benevolent, in the concern she exhibited that you understand, that you learn, that you overcome errors. I was constantly aware of her patience, her confidence that I would eventually understand, and her respect for the fact that I had to listen, question, learn, integrate independently, at my own pace. I never experienced her as being frustrated with me, and she was certainly never condemnatory of me—as opposed to condemnatory of the false ideas I might be holding. That I had come to agree with her was never the point; the point was—good, I am now in better touch with reality. I didn't realize at the time how generous she was being with her time.

You said that you got to know her better in the late 1970s. How and why did your relationship with her change in the last few years of her life?

First, it was just because of the passage of time, possibly getting to see each other more. And then I became her so-called bodyguard. There was a little room off the stage of Ford Hall Forum, where she would give autographs, and from which she would exit and where everybody would wait for her. When she walked out, they would be on both sides, and they'd all applaud. One year there was a young man in this room who insisted on foisting upon Ayn his treatise on epistemology, which he considered a definitive refutation of her theory. She didn't want to accept a copy of his treatise, but he was really becoming insistent on her taking it, and we got a little nervous. So someone said, "Ayn, you take John's arm. He's the biggest and meanest-looking of all of us, and then let's walk in a little group, so we'll interrupt anybody if they're going to be overly pushy." We did that, and it was a good idea. So every year—first it was at Ford Hall Forum and then at other events—if she had to walk through a crowd, she would say, "Where's John?" In that way, I became her escort to and from some of her public appearances, including her last appearance, at New Orleans, in 1981.

My relationship with her also was changing in that I had reached a point in my own learning where more interesting and complex issues would come up for discussion.

Could you tell me more about her manner?

My personal interactions with her seemed, characteristically, to combine both intellectual focus and seriousness, and lighter, joyous and very enjoyable banter.

To present her manner more completely, I'd like tell you about one other conversation, which was not on an intellectual/philosophical topic, and revealed another side of her.

One time, after a discussion we had scheduled to discuss

"business," as she called it, we were relaxing, and the subject of Victor Hugo's *The Man Who Laughs* came up. I told her that when I first read that book, in the early 1970s, it was so vivid an experience that I virtually made a movie of it in my mind. Her eyes seemed to pop open with delight, and she said, "So did I. How does your movie start?"

I told her: with undulating black water, and sounds of human scuffling and waves lapping, while the credits rolled. She said, puzzled, "Black water, why?" And as I told her she became delighted, energized, almost childlike with enthusiasm, as she enjoyed my explanation. In fact, she rewrote her own mental movie to incorporate this.

Did you have any discussions with her about art?

Not in any detail. Although we talked about various works of art, and my reaction to them. Other than Hugo, I can recall talking about Beethoven, Rachmaninoff, the kinds of jazz I liked, *Cyrano de Bergerac*, Nietzsche as a poet and the horrors of the contemporary art world.

Tell me about Beethoven.

We talked about him because I'd been very moved by Beethoven, and she hadn't; she observed that he had a malevolent-universe premise.[155] I told her that I'd gone to a symphony to listen to Beethoven, and I found it very deeply involving, and we talked a bit, because she was interested in that.

Did she ask questions to find out specifically what it was that you liked?

In every case, the common thread—as I recall—was what images, moods, responses I had, in connection with works of art.

Did you discuss current affairs with her?

I don't recall any lengthy discussions about current affairs. One thing I do remember is her disbelief at things we would report to her. A good example would be "Jesus Freaks" on the sidewalks of America. She just could not conceive of depravity at such a deep level, and so she used to think we were joking with her.

Tell me about attending the epistemology workshops.

---

155 The theory that "man, by his very nature, is helpless and doomed" (*The Virtue of Selfishness*, p. 56)

I was not living in New York, so I attended only one or two of the writing courses, and some—but not all—of the epistemology workshops.

The epistemology workshop was held in a small seminar room at a hotel. There were about fifteen active participants who were in philosophy, and they sat around the outside of an oval ring of tables. The non-philosophers sat behind the group, and were not allowed to participate. I was one of these auditors.

Describe her teaching manner.

She would arrive, unceremoniously, expecting everyone to be present and ready to go. Other than a friendly hello, there was no chit-chat. She would sit down and take her cigarettes and lighter out of her purse and place them on the table. No notes. No paper. No pen. No *ITOE*. She would take on a "this is serious, no-nonsense business" demeanor, and we would begin.

She was organized, directive, very powerful—and yet patient in her explanations, and attentive to people's questions. One soon realized the incredible power and organization of her mind, including her ability to keep track of everything that was occurring, and its connection to what had been covered earlier in the workshops.

Tell me about what happened during the workshops.

The sessions, as I recall, went on for three or more hours. One of the participants would have been given a topic in advance, and an hour to discuss it one-on-one with her at the workshop. Some portion of *ITOE*, perhaps, a given chapter—I'm not sure. This took up an hour, and then the rest of the session was a general Q and A on the assigned material. Any misquote from *ITOE* would immediately be corrected by her. She knew every word, every comma and why they were there.

As questions and comments were put to her, she was focused, inquisitive and considerate. The more significant the question, the more enlivened she became, and the more intense was her focus. Her patience in being sure the question itself, plus attendant implications of the question, had been sufficiently answered was remarkable, especially in view of the fact that some of the participants did not understand Objectivism well, or even necessarily agree with it and were captives of deeply wrong ideas and under-cut psycho-epistemologies.

It was the most remarkable demonstration, in all of my experiences with her, of the power of her mind and her benevolence. She had available at her mental fingertips a huge integrated body of knowledge. Once she understood any question put to her clearly, she would have no difficulty in answering it completely, including bringing her questioner to see other implications of the question, and even to answering, in advance, ramifications of the discussion she knew the questioner would arrive at later. And all this transpired in a considerate and unthreatening manner, even when—in my own opinion—a questioner had overstepped the boundary of precision and respectfulness.

Let's turn now to other aspects of Miss Rand and her life. Do you remember any examples of her humor?

She certainly did have a sense of humor, which was easily triggered. My most vivid memory of this occurred during an after-the-talk gathering at her hotel suite. I can still see her, lying back on the sofa or bed, telling us about an occasion with Isabel Paterson, when they tried to portray what life inside the mind of a beaver would have been like. She was laughing—heartily—at the whole memory, and I was struck at how unencumbered her pleasure was, as she relived the memory.

Do you remember any examples of her anger?

Only in public, not in small gatherings or any private occasions at which I was present. In public, however, there were occasions where her anger was on display, prompted by hostile and malicious treatment by questioners and others who were using the platform and audience she had created to treat her with disdain and sneer at her. A dramatic example of this occurred during a public debate, where Albert Ellis was misrepresenting and laughing at her fictional heroes.[156] She stood up, and in a loud and firm voice put him in his place.

If a questioner was polite and showed a serious concern about something, she would be polite, serious and even caring in response. But, if someone's manner was inappropriate, she would cut them off quickly and either insist they ask their question directly, or sit down. Such instances evaporated as quickly as they arose, and she was never distracted in any significant way from her manner and her purpose by these occasions.

I experienced her as being very loving, very easy. People who tell you, "Ayn Rand was the hardest person to be with"—that's a reflection of their own tension, because they couldn't be at ease with her. I never

---

156 Albert Ellis is the originator of rational-emotive psychotherapy.

worried about her judging me. Sometimes I'd just sit there and watch her interact with other people. I was well aware of the tension she "created" in other people, which I felt was very sad, because she wasn't the source of that.

Tell me about Mr. O'Connor.

I did not have a lot of exposure to him, but when I did he was always the same. He hovered lovingly in the background, watching, without being present. It was easy to see how he adored her, as she was enjoying her company, after talks. And yet, he exuded an "I'm in charge here" aura, and when he thought she was tiring, he would gently but firmly come to the fore, and join her in wishing us well and saying good-night.

Were you at Miss Rand's final speech, at a financial conference in New Orleans in November 1981?

Yes, I was. I flew down from Toronto for the speech and to be her escort to and from the talk. It was a memorable event. When our limousine arrived at the site, we went in some inconspicuous entrance. And inside, there was a huge crowd waiting with an electric anticipation.

The crowd was so large that the conference used a large projection screen, so people further back could see her. After it was over, when I caught up with her backstage, she was pretty tired, and faced with a line-up of VIPs waiting to see her and give her their cards and offer her seemingly unlimited funds for the movie of *Atlas*, which she had just announced. Afterwards, in the car on the way to a luncheon, she commented to me that the demonstration of seemingly limitless funds was likely empty, that few corporations would actually identify themselves with such a controversial message.

What was the last time you saw her?

It was after this talk, when she, Eloise and a few others were traveling in a private railroad car, courtesy of an admirer. She had decided that she wanted to sleep on the car the night of her talk, so after she saw people at her hotel, and signed autographs, Leonard and I accompanied the two of them to the train station. When we got to the car, she was tired, but she delighted in showing us how luxurious the car was. The last time I saw her was when we left them and she and Eloise waved good-by. Only a few months after that I was caught unprepared by a phone call, telling me she had died.

Did you go to her funeral?

Yes. My wife Ginny and I flew to New York, and I was present at both the funeral itself and the day before at the funeral home.

At the funeral home, her friends and associates were given an hour or more in the room where her body lay in an open coffin. It was part of the process of paying our respects, supporting each other and separating from her. Each of us—or most—at some point went to the side of her coffin by ourselves to say good-by.

Her favorite music was playing while the public was waiting in a line that went around the block. Then they were admitted—hundreds of people, most of them unknown to us, and they quietly and respectfully filed by. At the last moment, I was asked to join the security people at the entranceway to identify anyone that we didn't want present, so they could be turned away. No such people turned up.

When this public time was over, Leonard remained in the viewing room alone for a while, and then we all left.

The next day was gray and tranquil. When we got to the burial site in Valhalla, there were hundreds of people already there. There was no wind, and large snowflakes were falling. A flock of Canada geese flew over the site—like it was a symbolic fly-over.

At the graveside there was a small shelter for us, and the coffin was surrounded by yellow flowers. Kipling's poem *If* was read, and then the coffin and its yellow blanket of flowers was slowly lowered.

Do you have any closing remarks about Ayn Rand?

I have two remarks. First: those who seek to diminish her, to characterize her negatively, are—to paraphrase Nietzsche's condemnation of Christianity—a rebellion of everything that crawls on the ground, against that which has height. Their characterizations cannot change the fact of the intellectual and personal heights achieved by heroes such as Ayn Rand.

And, second: I miss her sense of life. In addition to all she taught me, and prompted me to think about, and in addition to the direction she helped me find for my life, she also showed me, through her sense of life, what our work and our battles are for. They are for living and for achieving happiness.

M. Northrup Buechner

M. Northrup Buechner was an NBI student in the 1960s and is an economics professor at St. John's University in New York City.

Interview date: December 14, 1999

Scott McConnell: *How did you meet Ayn Rand?*

M. Northrup Buechner: The first time I saw her in person was the summer of 1965 at NBI lectures. I saw her being angry, which was very interesting, and then I saw her being sweet, sympathetic, open and supportive to other people.

Regarding the anger, what happened?

I was standing at the front of the room waiting to speak to her, and she was sitting next to Nathaniel Branden, and somebody came up and said, "What do you think of subjectivism, in essence?" She kind of drew herself up and said, "Have you read anything I've written?" He said, "Yeah, I was just interested in what you would say." She said, "Well, now you know!"

I asked a question and got a very different kind of answer. At that point, I was struggling with a claim made by Mises that everything in economics is deducible from a priori categories, and particularly from the concept of human action. I was also struggling with the claim of the Chicago school that you had to project hypotheses, and then go out and collect data to prove them true or false. I couldn't see how to put those two claims together, and neither one of them seemed correct.

The answer I got from her and Branden was that it was really too big a question to answer casually standing around after a lecture, and that, in fact, neither was right: you couldn't deduce from anything a priori, because everything was derived from experience, and even starting with things you derive from experience, you couldn't just deduce things; you had to constantly refer to reality to check on your deductions to be sure they were correct. You couldn't deduce in a vacuum without checking on reality.

I think they also said something about statistics not being an appropriate means to prove or disprove economic laws. I walked out of that high as a kite, because it was a whole new perspective on this problem. The right track was: you had to integrate deduction and experience. Neither apart from the other was valid, and that was a

361

whole new idea.

Did you spend much time with her?

Yes. I spent the summer of 1965 working in a bank in New York as a summer intern. I attended all the lectures and functions going on at the time and did get to talk to her occasionally after lectures—to ask her questions. Then Dr. Peikoff had a seminar where a group of graduate students got together to discuss her ideas. As a result, we were all invited to a meeting with Ayn Rand. I think the purpose was to disabuse us of wrong ways of trying to understand Objectivism.

It was after that meeting that I got a chance to speak to her, and to thank her, and to tell her how much her works had meant to me, and that I was in a debt I knew I could never repay. And to ask if there was anything I could do for her. I expected her to say, thanks, that's very nice, but she didn't react that way. She said, "There is something you can do. You can maintain your loyalty to reason. You can keep your loyalty to reason in your life, and that will act to repay me." I was stunned and said, "I will do that." And I did.

Did you attend the debate between Albert Ellis and Nathaniel Branden?

A lot of people thought that there was something significant in common between the ideas Ellis was promoting and Branden's ideas on psychology, so a debate had been organized. Ellis's comments were not directed at Branden's ideas in psychology, hardly at all. They were directed at Objectivism, and toward the end of his comments, he was ridiculing and sneering at her heroes, particularly Galt and Roark.

Now, this was a big audience, and I think everybody was shocked. She stood up in the middle of his comments, and called out, "I am not the one under attack here," and stopped that whole thing cold. She was furious, and then Branden supported her and said, "Yes, we're supposed to be debating psychology, and you're attacking *Atlas Shrugged*." He said that he didn't think it's appropriate to attack somebody who, by the rules of debate, is unable to defend himself.

I don't know what Ellis said, but then there was an intermission, and during it a girl who I was very friendly with at the time took a photograph of Ayn Rand. There was an immediate explosion. She wasn't in a good mood to begin with, and she jumped up and said, "Give me that camera. You cannot take my picture." My girlfriend was utterly mortified and horrified that she'd done something to make Ayn Rand angry, which is the last thing in the world she wanted to do.

Miss Rand said, "Give the film to my lawyer. You cannot have that photograph." And so there was a little negotiation, and they agreed that the lawyer would develop the pictures, and send her the pictures on the roll, excepting the one of Ayn Rand. And that indeed was what was done. This experience totally traumatized this girl. I think that probably was the beginning of the end for her with Objectivism.

The principle regarding the photograph—and I don't know who enunciated it—was that Miss Rand's image belonged to her, and that you did not have the right to take a photograph of her without her permission.

Duane Eddy

Duane Eddy is a Grammy Award-winning guitarist and member of the Rock and Roll Hall of Fame. His many hit records during the 1950s and early 1960s established him as the most successful and influential instrumentalist of the Rock and Roll era. His most famous recordings include "Rebel Rouser," "Because They're Young," "Forty Miles of Bad Road," and the themes for the hit television shows *Have Gun Will Travel* and *Peter Gunn*. He met Ayn Rand in February 1967.

Co-interviewer is Harry Binswanger (friend of Ayn Rand, Objectivist philosopher and fan of Duane Eddy).

Interview date: March 9, 1999

Scott McConnell: *How were you introduced to Ayn Rand's works?*

Duane Eddy: I picked up *The Fountainhead* in a bookstore when I was about twenty-three years old. I had read it once before, but I read it again and really got interested. I then bought and read *Anthem, We the Living* and *Atlas Shrugged*.

Were there any issues regarding art or being an artist that specifically interested you in The Fountainhead?

Yes. I'm a great admirer of Howard Roark blowing up Cortlandt Homes, and would love to do that to some of the records I've made that have been re-released and ruined in the process. The record companies repackage my old material for box sets or new CDs and to do this, the recordings must be remastered. This is a process that can change the mix and the entire concept originally intended when creating the record. Young know-it-alls who work for the record companies today say, "They didn't know how to make records way back then" and proceed to change the original recordings to the way they think they should sound. I would love to have the opportunity to destroy these versions, or at least correct them. I was able to participate in the remastering of one box set for Rhino Records, *Twang Thang: The Duane Eddy Anthology*, and that is the only definitive package of my music around today. I can't imagine anyone saying, "They didn't know how to make paintings in the old days," and go about changing classic paintings by brightening colors or clearing up shadowy parts that don't stand out. But that's essentially what they are doing with older recordings these days.

In Atlas Shrugged, *and the other novels, were there specific issues or aspects of the book that especially interested you?*

Everything about *Atlas Shrugged* interested me. It clarified life. The entire book stunned me. I still read it again at least once a year, and *The Fountainhead* every two years or so. When I first read *Atlas Shrugged*, I loved it so much that when I saw a notice for the Objectivist meetings, I started attending them in California, where I was living at the time. This was in 1963 or 1964. When Nathaniel Branden came out to give a lecture in person, I went and met him.

Did the scenes with Richard Halley, the composer in Atlas Shrugged, *influence your attitude toward your music?*

I could certainly relate to them. I believe I identify with his attitude more now that I've reached his age than I did when I first read those scenes.

How did you meet Ayn Rand?

It was in February 1967. I would have been twenty-eight at that time. I mentioned to Nathan that I was coming through New York to do some business on my way to London, and he said, "Great, we'll have dinner." So I went to dinner at his apartment, and he was living in the same building on 34th Street as Miss Rand.

Nathan asked me to arrive early and as dinnertime approached, there was a knock on the door. When we opened it, there stood Miss Rand and Frank O'Connor. This was an exciting surprise for me! Soon after that, several other guests began arriving.

What was your first impression of Miss Rand?

I've met a lot of stars in my life, including Frank Sinatra and Elvis Presley, and she had the same quality—a presence, a sparkle, a self-assurance and warmth that was immediately apparent.

Mr. O'Connor struck me as a very quiet, Gary Cooper-type. It wasn't too long before he wandered over, found a chair and sat quietly. He was very friendly but just very quiet. He looked pleased that everyone was so aware of Miss Rand, and he seemed to enjoy watching her and seeing everyone's reaction to her. She was much more outgoing and came over and began talking to me. I told her, "I wish you'd move to California and we could see more of you out there." She said, "I've thought of that, but I'll never leave New York." I started trying to sell her on the idea, saying, "My own experience is that when I cross the

Mississippi heading west, it's like coming out from under a blanket; everything kind of opens up." She said, "That's funny, because it's the same way with me when I come back this way. Everything here is like living in a big garden." Then she laughed and said, "I don't know what philosophical significance that has!" That's the way she was. She was often joking and she laughed very easily. When it came time for dinner, she asked me where I was sitting and explained, "I want to sit next to the guest of honor," which certainly made me feel special, and I felt very comfortable around her.

After a while she took us all up to her apartment. She wanted to show us her new paintings by Capuletti and play me her favorite song.

She said it was a song that most profoundly illustrated her conception of how music should be. She told me that she thought—correctly—that as a musician, I would be interested in hearing it. As she was putting the record on the turntable, she explained that this song was one of her favorites of all time and that to her, "this recording expressed human joy—musically."

The song was an upbeat, very happy-sounding piano instrumental from the 1930s called the "Will O' The Wisp" by Otto Dobrindt and composed by Herbert Küster. She played it and I listened carefully, then turned to her as it finished and asked, "Could that possibly be the 'Song of Broken Glass' in *We the Living*?" She was startled for a moment and then she called out, "Frank, Nathan! Come here! Come here! You won't believe this—Duane just guessed after hearing it once, what this music is." She turned back to me, smiled warmly and said "Of all the millions of people who read my books, I've always believed that I've got," she paused, thought quickly and then continued, "approximately a hundred thousand readers out there who really understand what I'm saying." That was so like her, to be so specific. I remember briefly thinking that I wasn't sure that it was all that complimentary, to be included with a hundred thousand other people. But I realized that she was being totally honest with her estimate, and it was a great compliment when you considered all the millions who have read her work. She was very excited and happy that I had been correct about "Will O' The Wisp" being the song which best represented "Song of Broken Glass."

She apologized for the quality of the recording because it was so scratchy. She explained that even though she cherished it and kept the record as protected as possible, it was very worn from being played so often over the years. I told her I would keep a lookout for it in my travels, and she informed me that she had been unable to replace it because it was out of print. I copied down the information about the song anyway, because I had an idea. I had heard that BBC Radio in London had a copy of nearly everything ever recorded, in their archives. So when I went on to London a few days later, I called a friend of mine at the BBC, gave him the information and asked if he would try to find it for me. He found the recording and loaned it to me. I took it back to the recording studio in California and had my engineer clean it up and take out as much of the noise as he could—the pressing noise, any scratching or hissing and all that sort of thing. The BBC copy was better than Miss Rand's copy, but was still old and a little noisy. We cut a couple of fresh acetate copies and sent them to her and I sent the original back to my friend at the BBC.

That's when she wrote me the thank you letter that's in *Letters of Ayn Rand*. She was extremely delighted. I had sent the recording to her with a little note saying this was very easy to do, and that my engineer friend was responsible for making it sound so good. At the bottom of her letter to me there was a handwritten note which said, "P.S. Please give my thanks to your friend the engineer who processed the record. A.R."

Do you remember any other discussions with Miss Rand during that first meeting?

After seeing the paintings and listening to the song—and meeting her cats—we went back down to Nathan's apartment, and Miss Rand, Nathan and Leonard Peikoff got into an advanced philosophical discussion about a subject that I've since forgotten. I could follow it intellectually, and to me it was like watching a "philosophical jam session." Nathan or Leonard would begin a thought and run with it for awhile. Then the other would jump in and say, "Yes, but . . . " Ayn would listen while Leonard and Nathan expanded their ideas and then she'd speak up and clarify it to where it all made sense and the idea was resolved and complete. Then one of them would ask, "But what if . . . ?" And they'd be off and running again. It was quite an intense conversation. Suddenly, someone looked up and noticed it was 2:30 in the morning. Miss Rand smiled and said, "Well, . . . to be continued."

Harry Binswanger: *Did you find that she had heard your music and, if so, did she have any opinion of it?*

Not that I knew of. After dinner, Nathan played her a couple of cuts from what I call my "string albums"—recorded with a big orchestra. One album was *Twangy Guitar, Silky Strings*; the other was called *Lonely Guitar*. I don't remember which tracks he selected. She commented that she thought they were beautiful. Nathan wouldn't play her "Rebel Rouser" or any of the rock and roll songs. He said he didn't think she'd like those. She didn't like rock and roll particularly.

I've always regretted that I didn't just insist that Nathan play her a couple of my hits, even if she would have thrown me out. Well, I wouldn't have liked that, but she was too gracious to have done that anyway. I think she might have enjoyed the happy and carefree sounds of those recordings or simply said it wasn't her taste in music.

Did you talk to Miss Rand about rock and roll generally or about people such as Elvis Presley and other stars?

We had a short conversation about that, and she said something to the effect that she supposed they were nice people and everything, but she didn't care for most of rock and roll music. She didn't say all of it. I know she's written things about Elvis, and though she didn't care for his music, I don't recall her saying anything against him personally.[157] Nathan mentioned to Ayn about my friendship with actor Richard Boone, and she was curious and asked me what he was like. I related what a great personality and intellect Mr. Boone had, why I enjoyed his company so much and how he would often seem "larger than life" to those around him. She was very interested in hearing about him, and I described some of the qualities he possessed that in some instances were similar to those of some of her heroic characters. She told me she was delighted to hear that, because she loved his work, and she said she would like to meet him someday.

Did she mention anything about the phenomenon surrounding Elvis and all of the adulation?

She mentioned the fact that the same thing had happened before that for Frank Sinatra and Rudy Vallee.

HB: *She obviously didn't despise Elvis, but she meant what she said, that she doesn't get rock and roll herself.*

She thought it was a bit on the mindless side, which in a way it was. Even though I was into doing rock and roll music, I've heard some of it that *is* mindless. At the same time there was an

---

157 See "What Is Capitalism?" in *Capitalism: The Unknown Ideal*, p. 27.

attitude about most of it—though I never discussed this with her. I hadn't thought it through enough in those days to have successfully presented my side of it to her. But in rock and roll there was an attitude of happiness and fun. It wasn't necessarily mindless any more than dancing to the big bands would have been mindless.

SM: *Did you have later meetings with Miss Rand?*

After that I went to one of her lectures in New York, watched her work and gave her a ride back to her apartment in a taxi. At one point she said an interesting thing. I was attempting to tell her how much I thought of her, and I ended with the words, "You're so great." She said, "I'm not, but the philosophy is." I thought about that for a moment, but before I could question her about it further, we had arrived at our destination and it was time to say goodbye.

Did you have any more interactions with Mr. O'Connor?

Nothing beyond small talk. If I had to describe him in one word, it would be "benevolent." From what she said, he was sometimes wiser than she was. You have to remember how completely she loved him, but I could see why she would think that. When he commented on something, it made complete sense. He quietly enjoyed being there and was very aware of everything that was being said, but he just didn't participate all that much.

She actually said that he was wiser than she was?

She said "sometimes." She also said that, at times, she bounced ideas off him. She would discuss things with him and he would point things out to her that she hadn't thought of yet.

You commented earlier on Mr. O'Connor being the Gary Cooper-type.

Oh, he definitely was. He had huge inner strength and confidence. I thought he even looked a bit like Gary Cooper.

From your interactions could you describe her personally?

She laughed easily and heartily. She was very down-to-earth. I was expecting somebody not necessarily condescending or affected, but perhaps a bit aloof and overly serious. She turned out to be the opposite. She was genuinely warm, gracious and kind, and immediately made me feel very comfortable and relaxed.

I think she's the most coherent, most logical, most far-reaching thinker that I have ever been able to discover. I had my own little title for what I considered the adventure of meeting her and spending time with her: I called it my "real miracle on 34th Street."

Shelly Reuben

Shelly Reuben, a popular mystery novelist, was Miss Rand's typist from 1964 to 1965. She is the author of *Julian Solo*, *Origin and Cause*, *Spent Matches*, *Weeping* and *Tabula Rasa*.

Interview date: March 2, 2000

Scott McConnell: *How did you become Miss Rand's typist?*

Shelly Reuben: It must have been '64 or '65, when I was eighteen years old and just back from Israel. I had dropped out of college, because I hated it. I figured you can't become a writer by going to college. I took a course in typing, moved to New Rochelle, New York, and worked for the Conservative Book Club for a while, but it was so easy I couldn't stand it.

I called up The Objectivist [Inc.] and said, "Hi, this is Shelly Reuben; I'm working in New Rochelle, and I like Miss Rand's ideas. I'm wondering if you need a typist." Elayne Kalberman, who was very kind to me, was the person who answered the phone, and she said, "Why don't you come down and talk to me." We had an interview and she hired me. Basically, I worked for *The Objectivist Newsletter*. Every once in a while they would lend me to the Nathaniel Branden Institute, but I worked for The Objectivist, Inc., and I typed Miss Rand's articles, which she wrote longhand.

I don't know if anybody told you her technique. When she was ready for me to type, I would go up to her apartment. The first time I got there must have been the first time we met, and she introduced herself; then she introduced me to her cat. This made me think that she really loved cats, and that they were like little people to her. And she showed me one whole room filled with file cabinets, which, being a writer, now I understand. There may have been a desk in there, but boy, were there a lot of file cabinets. I remember the living room, and that I was disappointed that the furniture was tatty, but now I understand it was because of the cats.

We'd go in and sit down on the sofa together, and she would ask me if I wanted a glass of water; she was always very considerate. Then I read the handwritten manuscript aloud to her, and she could tell whether or not there was anything that confused me. She was

---

considerate of minutiae, in the sense that she might say, "Okay, here's one line where there are two of the same words, one directly under the other, so be careful." Also, if I couldn't read her handwriting, she would tell me what the word was. After I read the whole article, I'd go back and type it.

So you'd go downstairs and type, and then bring it back?

No worry, no pressure, no nothing. And then I gave it back to her.

Miss Rand was so sensitive. One time I was sitting next to her, and a key started to wiggle in the lock of her apartment door. I looked towards the door, and she said, "Oh, it's just my husband. Don't worry, let him struggle." I must have had a horrified expression on my face, because she looked at me as if she wanted to reassure me that she hadn't really meant that. She said, "His key's already in the lock, and if I get up now and try to open it for him, it would just confuse him." I thought, "My God, she's insightful. She knew I was thinking 'Oh, you can't really be mean to this man, can you?'" And she explained it to my satisfaction, so I didn't try to go out and defend Mr. O'Connor with my life.

What was your first impression of Miss Rand when you went up to the apartment?

I was surprised how short and dowdy she was. That was my instantaneous response. Then as I got to spend time there, I thought, "My God, how can anyone be so naïve?" I also thought that half the time, she was surrounded by vipers. But I didn't think I had the right to say anything about it. I don't know if that's because I could have been wrong, or just because I was so aware of the intellectual gap between the two of us.

How was she naïve?

She didn't realize that even though most of the people who surrounded her always agreed with her, normal people can't agree with anybody that much, ever, ever, ever, unless they are trying to put something forth that is not true. And even if you don't disagree, you are not going to understand a concept in all of its ramifications that fast.

It's not a flaw in her I was perceiving; it's an isolation. I thought there was an element of sycophancy in the in-group around her. I felt she was surrounded by many people who gave her back what was essentially herself, and that she thought it was coming from them, which led to more isolation and more loneliness.

One example of this is when they all bought the same dining room table. It was like an Objectivist Dining Room Table. Miss Rand bought one, and then two more couples got the same dining room table. There was a level of conformity where people seemed to be doing what everybody else was doing.

What was Miss Rand like to work for?

She was kind. She was the exact opposite of somebody who was born with a silver spoon in her mouth. She may never have been a secretary, but she had the ability to know what a secretary's problem would be, or what a typist's problem would be. And that's pretty smart. I thought she was very nice.

I was an outsider, and I was not in the in-group. I was never warm and fuzzy with her. It wasn't like, "Let me sit down and tell you about my latest boyfriend." I'll tell you one story that said so much to me about her. I had done her typing for the whole time I'd been there, and once, on my way to work, I saw her getting out of or into a taxi. She was standing by the taxi door, and I yelled, "Hi, Miss Rand!" She turned to me with this unfriendly look on her face, and she said sternly, "Yes." When I responded, "I just wanted to say hello," she broke out into the most beautiful smile I remember her having in all the time I'd worked with her. My head went "click," and I thought, "Wow, she thinks people always want something from her." When it turned out that I didn't, she looked like the sun had just burst out.

As to Mr. O'Connor, I loved him. He was like somebody with the lyrical soul of an elf. A magical character . . . like a muse. I thought he was the gentlest, kindest man in the world. Whenever I met him at the elevator, he'd greet me, and if we were walking in the same direction, he would always take my briefcase and carry it. And he didn't really even know me. He was a gentleman of the old school. Beautiful. His soul was beautiful.

Has Ayn Rand influenced your fiction writing?

The answer is Yes, and the answer is No. The No is that as a fiction writer, I was so conscious of the strength of her style that I knew I had to be very, very careful not to copy her. I'm sure that the earliest things I tried to write sounded too much like her writing, which is why I threw them out. I worked very hard not to be influenced by her style. I haven't reread her as often as I'd like to, because she is so powerful, I am afraid that I'll inadvertently pick right up on it and start imitating her.

The Yes is that she influenced me as a human being in so many ways. Her books are responsible for many of my values, the direction that I've gone and the fights that I've fought.

Kerry O'Quinn

Kerry O'Quinn was an NBI student and artist who was an acquaintance of Ayn Rand and Frank O'Connor's in the 1960s. Today he is a writer and publisher.

Interview dates: October 20, 1999, and November 1, 1999

Scott McConnell: *I believe you worked for NBI.*

Kerry O'Quinn: There were certain events that I got very involved with at NBI. I started doing most of their design work once they moved to the Empire State Building in 1967. And when NBI Press started, I worked with Miss Rand extensively on the covers for *Calumet K* and *The Man Who Laughs.*[158]

It was an eye-opening experience. I had a very different relationship with Miss Rand than with Frank O'Connor. I felt very much at ease with him, while she was very intimidating to me. I respected her tremendously and was thrilled to be able to work with her on something like those book cover designs, but it was made very clear to me right up front that whatever she wanted, from the typeface to the particular shade of the color, she got it, and even as a designer of some years experience, I really had one purpose: to do what she wanted.

What did she want and what were her principles?

I'll give you an example. She had very particular ideas on typefaces, and I came in with a number of designs. I designed the first cover, for instance, for her booklet *Introduction to Objectivist Epistemology.* She told me exactly what she wanted for the design of that cover. She didn't know the names of typefaces or the names of colors, exactly, but she would describe it to me. I would bring back one after another until she said that's the one.

I brought in several samples of typefaces, and she said, "I don't like those squat, fat typefaces." What she meant by that was what we call "extended typefaces," typefaces that have a very strong horizontal line to it. She thought they were fat-looking. What she wanted was what we call "condensed typefaces," which have a very vertical line to them. That's all she liked: there was no other category that was an acceptable typeface.

---

158 *Calumet K* (Merwin-Webster) and *The Man Who Laughs* (Victor Hugo) were published by NBI Press in 1967.

Can you remember if there was a specific font that she liked?

Yes, it was a sans serif, like a Helvetica condensed. She didn't want it too thin or too thick or too bold. She wanted a medium.

Did she give any other indication of what else in design she liked?

She liked a kind of a blue-green, mainly a blue kind of a blue-green. That was her favorite color to use for things. She didn't like bright colors like reds and oranges and things like that.

At NBI you helped organize their film series, The Romantic Screen. Did Miss Rand discuss Errol Flynn, who had a movie in this series?

Yes. We showed *The Adventures of Robin Hood*. I cannot tell you any specific comments that she made, but I know she liked him. I can't say I heard her recommend the movie, but I remember her approval of him as a screen hero.

Did Miss Rand attend any of the screenings?

Oh yes. I think she attended several, just like she attended the NBI fashion show and all kind of strange little activities that we ran in those days. I was in the NBI fashion show with Frank and Leonard and everybody else. Everybody was there that night. It was the first time NBI had done a fashion show. We all put on clothes of the day and paraded. She was in the audience. I had designed the program that night. We made it an elegant affair. Sue Ludel was in it. Patrecia Gullison appeared as a bride at the end. I think Frank presented her. It was quite an amazing evening.

There were even some NBI dance nights and things like that. NBI got into all kinds of activities near the end.

Tell me about Mr. O'Connor in the fashion show.

Well, he was quite a dapper lad. He went through several changes of costume.

Did you talk to Miss Rand about the movie Siegfried?

She came over and watched it at my apartment, as a matter of fact. That was the first time I got hold of a print, and I did a special screening just for her. I think Frank came with her and a few other people. She had said it was one of her favorites. I was able to get a few still pictures from the Museum of Modern Art that we could use in the NBI brochure, and she loved those because she said every frame of that movie was like a painting, like a work of art. She said the reason she loved that movie is because you could stop the movie at any single frame and it was perfectly composed, perfectly lighted. She said that, to her, was what made a motion picture a work of art, and that's what Fritz Lang created and especially in that movie. She liked him as a director in general, and she liked some of his other movies, also, but this is the one that had struck her particularly.

Describe Miss Rand watching that movie.

Needless to say, she was always intense. No matter what she was doing she was intense. And she was delighted. She was happy about it and she was kind of in awe of it too. She was kind of amazed by that sort of thing because although she had an appreciation for painting and movies and sculpture and visual things of that sort, I don't think it's anything she ever felt was her forte. So she kind of admired people like Dali and Capuletti and artists of that sort who could create paintings. Fritz Lang was in that same category for her. So she became like a fan. Like those of us who surrounded her were her fans. It was nice to see her sometimes see someone that she kind of adored in the same way.

Tell me about your art associations with Frank O'Connor.

I remember one day I was at his studio and I saw a painting. It was just some snow-covered mountains, and he had some power lines running right across the canvas right through the middle of it. I said, "Frank, that's a very unusual thing. Most people would leave out power lines because that's just sort of a naturalistic detail of something that happened to be in the way of the painting." He replied, "No, but you see, that's civilization out there in the midst of all this. Otherwise it's just mountains, and that's the hand of man coming through there." I said, "Oh, I see, of course." It wasn't one of his extraordinary works, but it sort of represented the kind of thing that fascinated him: just beautiful snow-covered mountains and some power lines going right through it.

What did fascinate him?

He had a young kind of spirit and attitude about him that I saw and that I enjoyed and that I related to. There was a painting he had called *Diminishing Returns*, on the wall, and in it he had a mannequin that artists use sometimes to put into different positions, and some Christmas tree ornaments. He was fascinated with little toys and little silly things.

The kinds of subject matter that often interested Frank in terms of his artwork were similar to the tiddlywink music that Miss Rand liked, which was a silly little music of no particular heaviness, but that was something that caught something in her spirit that was very deep. I think little shiny Christmas tree ornaments had the same kind of role in Frank O'Connor's life in a visual way.

Describe Mr. O'Connor.

He was a tall, gaunt man who had a kind of a lanky, lopey manner to him. He didn't walk tall and command the scene. He was unintimidating, and he put me, and everyone I ever saw him around, at ease. If somebody came up to him and said, "Mr. O'Connor, it's an honor to meet you." He would say, "Frank. Call me Frank." He brought people down to where they weren't nervous to be around him. And he smiled easily.

He didn't talk about the state of the world, and once in a while we would make sarcastic remarks about some current event, but then we laughed and then we passed onto the next thing. When Miss Rand would get onto something that she didn't like that was going on in the world, she didn't leave it at that, she wrestled with it a bit, but Frank would toss it away and go on to the next thing.

Would you describe him as happy?

As far as I knew, he was. He was a witty man, and he was funny with me. He had funny little things that he would say, and he was easy to joke with. He was a punster too. You'd toss them off and then you kind of groan with everybody else. I heard Frank do that sort of thing, too, but he was delightful and witty and funny and happy-seeming to me.

One of the interesting things about Frank, to me, was he never burdened me—and it may have just been because I was young—with problems or complaints or anything. When I was around him, he was nothing but the most positive person in the world. He talked about things he was interested in, and he expressed an interest in who he was with.

Describe Ayn Rand and Frank O'Connor together.

They seemed like cute kids. She always wore the fur that Frank had given her. She loved it. She treasured it. She luxuriated in it. And when they would come into a party or an event, they were like a teenage couple, and they were quite delightful. I thought they made each other young. There was an obvious effect that they had on each other. It was very youthifying. I enjoyed seeing them together. Now, very often when they got to a party, they would separate and Miss Rand would go and talk with some people, and Frank would go and talk with people. They didn't stick together the whole evening, but it was fun to watch them come and go, because they were a cute couple.

Doug Messenger

Doug Messenger met Ayn Rand at public lectures. He was a studio musician, a guitarist and musical director for Van Morrison, and is now a recording engineer/producer.

Interview date: October 22, 1996

Scott McConnell: *How did you come to talk with Miss Rand?*

Doug Messenger: On December 8, 1968, my wife and I went to the Ford Hall Forum to hear Miss Rand's lecture "Of Living Death." After the lecture and question-and-answer period, we hung around outside the hall. It was a cold night, probably ten or twenty degrees Fahrenheit, and when Miss Rand came out, she walked toward us. I was bold enough to ask her a question, and she decided that she liked my query, so she gave me a little talk.

What was the question?

It concerned the relationship between her concepts of psycho-epistemology and sense of life.[159] She talked to me for awhile, and her companions kept saying, "Come on, Ayn, come, let's go." She said, "No, I like his question."

Can you remember what she said?

It was basically that someone in contact with reality, someone who has a good agreement between reality and his thoughts, would tend to have a good sense of life and a psycho-epistemology that followed suit. This isn't necessarily the case, however, because many confusions are possible in a given life.

During the discussion, she was far more specific, but I don't remember the details now. It was clear that she was always willing to look at the facts, always willing to examine reality, and that rationalism[160] was not her way, as opposed to rationality, which was.

By telling me that I had raised a complex subject that requires

---

159 Psycho-epistemology is one's characteristic method of thinking. A sense of life is "a preconceptual equivalent of metaphysics, an emotional, subconsciously integrated appraisal of man and of existence" (*The Romantic Manifesto*, p. 25).

160 Rationalism is "the view that man obtains his knowledge of the world by deducing it exclusively from concepts, which come from inside his head and are not derived from the perception of physical facts" (*For the New Intellectual*, p. 30).

a good deal of thought, she indicated that my question was not as simple as it appeared to be. Nonetheless, she went on for five to ten minutes. It seemed like an hour to me, and it was absolutely freezing out there. I remember looking down at a small woman with intense eyes. It was an amazing, exhilarating experience.

What was she like while talking to you?

I remember her accent, timing and focus, as well as a glee in talking about the topic. She loved a question, and you could also see that during the question-and-answer period.

Here's an interesting sidelight to that meeting. At the time I had longish hair, cut just above my shoulders, a sort of "Rubber Soul"-era Beatle-ish haircut. It was something I always had liked, and Miss Rand understood the reason without even asking me. She looked at me and said, "Your hair looks nice on you; you look like a musketeer."

Did you see her again?

The morning after the Ford Hall Forum talk, we went to Harvard and sneaked into the breakfast room where Miss Rand was speaking to the Harvard Business School.[161]

She was wonderful. They came and they were as rude as can be to her for the first ten or fifteen minutes, but at the end of the question-and-answer period, she received a standing ovation. She had won them over.

One particularly troublesome man had tried to take her on, so to speak, and she demolished his argument—elegantly, nicely. I remember that a reviewer of the proceedings wrote, "They came to jeer, but they stayed to cheer."

---

161 She was invited to an informal breakfast discussion (December 9, 1968) that covered a wide range of topics in philosophy, including the "social obligations of businessmen."

Jackie Gillam

Jackie Gillam attended an Ayn Rand speech in 1971.

Interview date: September 5, 1998

Scott McConnell: *How did you meet Ayn Rand?*

Jackie Gillam: It was in the winter of 1971. My sister and I were living in Cleveland and we were big fans of Ayn Rand. We had an old Volkswagen car, and we decided to drive from Cleveland to Boston, because we knew that she was going to be giving a talk there. We drove nonstop from Cleveland to Boston. We got to the place where the talk was going to be held, and we were sitting on the stone steps of this big old stone building with twelve to fifteen other people, and we realized we hadn't purchased tickets. We're sitting there not knowing what we're going to do, when a big limousine pulls up, and this little tiny person gets out, wearing a black full-length cape, and she starts coming up the steps. It was Ayn Rand. She obviously summed the situation up very quickly: that none of us had tickets. So she lifts her arms and spreads her cape, like Bishop Sheen used to do, and says, "Oh, my children, follow me in." So we all went in the stage door, and she said, "I want you all to sit with me." So we all sat on the floor of the stage near her as she gave her talk.

Susan Ludel

Susan Ludel, a TV news-feature producer and writer for *TV Guide*, wrote several articles for *The Objectivist*. She was married to Leonard Peikoff from 1968 to 1978 and was a friend of Miss Rand's from 1968 to 1982. Ms. Ludel died in 1999.

Interview dates: October 8 and 28, and November 4, 6 and 25, 1997, and February 26, 1999

Scott McConnell: *What is your strongest memory of Ayn Rand?*

Susan Ludel: There are two. There would be her serious, intense side. I think of her sitting on her couch and having an intellectual conversation with someone, or me or Leonard. She could have been writing all day and been exhausted, but as soon as anything interested her intellectually, she would become completely transformed. She would be energetic, alive, passionate, completely focused, as though she were like her eyes, brilliant and penetrating. It would just be her eyes that you would be aware of, and her mind. That's exaggerating, of course; she was a person. She could go on for hours. Until one or two in the morning was nothing to her.

So the first memory is of her passion for ideas, where she would give a talk and give explanations. If you were serious about ideas, and honest, she would answer anything you asked in the most extensive way. She would give her reasons, and it was a full explanation. I never met anyone like that.

She always explained everything she said. If you were at all baffled or didn't understand something or even if there was a quizzical look in your eye, she would always give reasons for everything, fully, concisely. The two characteristics in her judging people—which she says in her essay "What Can One Do?"—are: are they honest and serious about ideas, intellectual? That's how she dealt with people and that's how she dealt with me.

What's your other strongest memory?

Her soft, gentle, feminine and delightful side. I picture her dressed up in a specific black dress. She was very stylized when she got dressed up. It was a simple black dress, and she would have around her neck what I would call a chandelier necklace of little globes of crystal that went down toward her waist. There was just a softness about her that

I don't think most people saw, and a very feminine part of her, which she'd be aware of—how she looked and walked. She had terrific legs.

The feminine side came out when she was dressed up and going out. I especially remember New Year's Eve. There used to be a big party. She had the custom that at midnight, no matter where they were, she and Frank would leave the main living room where the party was and go into the bedroom so they could be alone at midnight.

What would they do?

I think, kiss and hug. It was a secret.

There was also this kind, nice, gentle aspect of her, gracious. The kind of person who, when you would leave her apartment, no matter what time it was, she and Frank would stand at the door and wait until the elevator came, and then they'd go in.

What do you put that down to?

The old world and a time when manners were taught. It shows respect for people. There was something elegant and gracious about her. I'd say it's old world, only because Americans don't do it anymore. Frank, particularly, was gentlemanly towards women. He would hold open doors for you, and when you sat down at the table, he'd hold your chair for you.

Give me the general background about your relationship with her.

I met her in 1968, which was the year I started going out with Leonard. As a student of Objectivism I had seen her at the Basic Principles of Objectivism lectures, which I took in 1966. She would come and give answers in the question-and-answer periods. So I had seen her, but I hadn't met her personally.

For how long did you know Miss Rand?

I knew her until she died in 1982. In '81 I left New York and was in Atlanta and Washington, but I kept in touch with her by phone. I separated from Leonard in 1978.

When you first saw Miss Rand what was your first impression?

Like she came out of her novels. She was like the serious Ayn that I just described.

In 1968 Leonard took me to her apartment to introduce me to her. I remember this gracious, pleasant, well-mannered woman, a lady, in the best sense of the term. She asked me if I wanted to see her lion collection. She had three live cats at that time, and I loved cats, but she also had a collection, in a little Lucite shelf unit, of cats made of semiprecious stone and ivory—all different little sizes. In the same shelving were semiprecious rocks that she had collected over the years—from little tiny ones to big ones. The whole shelf was so uniquely her, because it held things that mattered to her.

What was her attitude when she was showing you all this?

I think she just had me go into her office and look. She was delighted that I liked it. She always was delighted if people liked what she liked. If someone had an honest reaction that was similar to hers in any respect, in positive things, she would be delighted by that.

Did you meet Mr. O'Connor then?

Yes, he was elegant and genteel, a gentleman, soft-spoken, and both of them were really "there" in the way that most people aren't. Most people are sort of half-focused on what they're doing, and they're focused inward, or their minds run to something else, but both Ayn and Frank were present in a way that was unique. They were solid, like the world is.

Could you explain that more?

The part in *Atlas* where Cherryl talks about giving up, and everything is unreal and murky because things aren't what they are— Ayn, in person, was the absolute antithesis of that. Cherryl needed to see Ayn, because she was real and unchangeable. She was absolutely, thoroughly intelligible. She was, in person, like her writing was: black and white, clear, straightforward. No matter what she was talking about, she was clear.

She was always the same and predictable, which was one of her most glorious traits, and most unusual ones. She was consistent. She wouldn't throw you by expressing an idea out of context or one that didn't make sense. Everything always made sense.

One of the most important things about her as a person is that she was always the same no matter where she was—whether it was at the '21' Club or at a street fair—no matter who was there or what the subject was. She was the only person I have ever met in my life whom you could count on in that way. There wasn't some quirky, schizophrenic, neurotic thing that would come over her and she'd be different one day. She was always the same, whether she was going to some fancy place or cooking dinner or walking around in a housecoat or in the presence of celebrities.

Anything else?

Her eyes. That to me is Ayn because they were so intelligent and penetrating and they could be so perceptive—they saw everything. Then they could be twinkly or gay or cheerful, like the tiddlywink music.[162]

What else did you do that first evening?

Just talked. Through the years, the usual thing was conversation or dinner and conversation.

Conversation about what sorts of topics?

Philosophical ones. Leonard and Ayn's interest in philosophy coincided. He was so active intellectually that it was predominantly intellectual discussions, but there were conversations on all different levels. It would be from abstract philosophy to topics I would be more interested in, such as why the Left was running the network news operations. There would be political discussions, but she wouldn't be interested for long in politics; it would always lead to something more abstract.

Do you remember any issues that she was especially aggrieved or excited by?

I lived through the campus riots with her, and that was a big, big thing at the time. There were even people rioting in the streets near where we lived. During that period she wrote about these issues.[163] She was outraged at what was going on and extremely pleased with the union people who were responding against the students.

The thing I remember most was her reaction to the *Apollo 11* space shot, because it was so positive—a really big event to her. Everything from the look of the ship standing before lift-off, to the lift-off itself. She was thrilled by the *Apollo* launch. That was her universe, but given the events and the state of the culture, I wouldn't often see her reaction

---

162 "Tiddlywink" is Ayn Rand's term for turn-of-the-[nineteenth]-century, popular, joyful music with fast rhythms.

163 See "The Cashing-In: The Student 'Rebellion'" in *Capitalism: The Unknown Ideal.*

to positive things, because they were such a rare occurrence.[164]

I want to emphasize that not everything was a serious philosophical discussion with her. Although ideas and philosophy were the most important things to Ayn, she didn't live her whole life sitting in her living room talking about philosophy.

Would she discuss intimate problems or issues?

Yes, she certainly would. I discussed personal problems with her for a long time, as did other people. She would call it psycho-epistemology or psychology. Her focus would be on getting you to articulate what basic premises you had that you weren't aware of. She was interested in getting at the idea that the subconscious held conflicts and ideas and premises that could be brought into consciousness—because of her interest in the mind and thinking.

What type of personal issues did you discuss with her?

I would discuss personal relationships, difficulties with people, difficulties at work.

I want to clarify one thing, and that is that she would say, explicitly, all the time, that she was not a psychologist and that psychology was a science as yet undiscovered and not worked out. She would not hold herself out in these personal discussions as someone who knew psychology. She had views about what she called "psycho-epistemology" [see footnote, p. 380], which is how the mind works, and that you hold subconscious ideas. Her view was that you should try to get at subconscious views that you were not yet aware of.

What was her manner and method during these conversations?

Her manner was very serious. It was like any other intellectual discussion. No moral judgment was allowed, because it was psychology; it was about the subconscious and therefore out of your control. She was very serious about having that view. Her method was to discuss it intellectually.

Did she talk about intimate things about herself?

No, she did not talk about herself. I was really surprised when the *Letters* book came out, because I learned things about her that I never really heard from her. I fault myself a great deal because for some

---

164 See "Apollo 11" in *The Voice of Reason* (New York: New American Library, 1988).

reason, I think fear, I didn't ask her many personal questions. I would now ask her things I wouldn't have dreamed of then because I was a young, scared kid.

You were afraid of her?

I felt very comfortable and confident in her presence, more so than in anyone else's, except Leonard's. But intellectually I was dealing with a genius. I hadn't dealt on that level ever before and didn't know how to, so there was fear. There was fear about her anger, which would come up and not be intelligible to me.

Did she offer any advice about how to handle romantic problems?

Yes, but not practical advice. It was an intellectual approach. It wasn't: "If you have a romantic problem, go out three times a week and have sex once." It wasn't on that level. It was: "Understand intellectually what your conflicts are." And if you really understand it, you will act correctly.

People who appeared to be or who were very close to Ayn Rand never seemed to ask her personal questions or questions about her history.

No, they didn't. I don't know why. Everyone was on a more "intellectual" plane. The more commonsense things you would ask people, you just didn't. I think mostly because people were afraid of her, and she didn't particularly like talking about personal things.

So you never asked her about her past or her family?

Her family, yes. She would talk about that, but very surreptitiously, because of the Soviet connection. She didn't, for example, want people to know what was going on or to contact her sister Nora.

Did you ever discuss fashion or feminine things with her?

Yes, she'd talk about Adrian and why she liked him as a designer. She didn't wear them in New York by the time I knew her, but she had saved several dresses, which she showed me. I knew his work from the movies and I was delighted to see [the dresses].

What did she say about them?

That they were unique and flattered the person who wore them. They were very tailored, but there was always something unique, unusual, offbeat about them, which you could see. They were very flamboyant. You'd notice an Adrian creation.

She was very big on jewelry, from costume jewelry to good jewelry. She always went for unique, unusual things that would just be Ayn, like the crystal necklace I mentioned. She'd see lion pins and rings at a street fair and she'd be delighted as much as if it were fine jewelry.

What other sides to Ayn Rand were there?

She had a cook, Eloise. When Eloise wasn't there, Ayn would cook. There was a seriousness about daily undertakings that was uniquely hers. It wasn't serious in the sense of a philosophical discussion, but she was so purposeful and so focused on what she was doing; she couldn't be interrupted if she was concentrating on something. That's another side to her.

Eloise would put together the food, and Ayn would have to warm it up. She would focus on stirring at the stove, and that was her purpose at the time. She wouldn't talk to anyone or do anything else—that's what she was doing. The same thing if she were writing a check. She would write the check and proofread it, and nothing was done sloppily.

She liked to be on one track?

Yes. Interruptions, particularly if she had to go out for appointments, like the doctor or hairdresser, would last for days. She would have to recover and not be able to write.

There's also the moralistic side of her, where she wouldn't compromise. That came through to me most regarding making *Atlas* into a movie. I lived through I don't know how many writers or producers who were interested. They always, at the end, didn't know what they were doing. If they didn't come through in the sense of understanding and being able to apply their knowledge to a script, it didn't matter to her who they were. It was just a dead issue. No one could flatter her. The thought of making money, a financial killing, on *Atlas*, wouldn't even occur to her. It had to be a certain way and she knew how. It was going to be that way or nothing.

She was moralistic in the proper sense of the word—not pseudo-moralistic. She was completely consistent on that level. There was a meeting on some local neighborhood controversy, and the Peikoffs and the O'Connors went to it. I think the meeting was connected to the rioting kids in some way. It was during the campus riots, that whole liberal, Left-wing era. Someone at the meeting took the leftist position and she was on her feet as though she were denouncing Kant.

She was very outspoken in a funny way sometimes, because she was so innocent about how people would react to her. She hated beards, for instance, because she thought a person's face was the most important part about them, and she thought if men had beards, they were hiding behind hair, and they didn't look like modern men. Someone she hadn't seen him for sometime walked into her apartment, and he had grown a beard. She said, "Oh, my God, how could you have that thing on!" She'd be so outspoken—not having a clue that you don't say that to someone.

She had the same view of bangs on a woman, in that they hid her forehead, which is where your intelligence and your eyes showed. She thought it was silly for women to hide their foreheads.

Anything else about hairstyles?

Dagny had Ayn's hairstyle. Ayn had her own hairdresser [Lawrence Kazan], who she went to for years in New York. When she was going someplace she would always go there first. She had a very slick, stylized, dramatic haircut, short.

What about long hair on men?

She didn't care for it. She had a very big commitment to the modern times, and she thought of short hair as being modern.

What other aspects of Miss Rand did you see?

She was intense and brilliant—that all-seeing Ayn. Then the twinkly, gay Ayn, the one dancing around listening to her tiddlywink music. She would play it and march around the living room of the apartment, waving a cane in time to the music. And the way she responded to cats. She had three at that time.

Who looked after the cats?

Both of them, but Frank more than she. Frank was the one who took care of them physically. One of them was Tommy, and another was Junior. Tommy was Thomas Aquinas and Junior was Frisco Junior. They were just always around. I can't remember if she locked them out of the office or not, but one would inevitably land on her desk.

She liked Persians the best, without any question. She loved the way they looked. She loved their coats, and their eyes, which are very big, and their intelligence and independence.

How would she play with the cats?

She would just have them come and sit next to her, and pet them.

Do you have any stories about their cat Frisco?

She hated when people changed the words of a song, because it's taking away some authorship, so she would tell you this story very discreetly: When they were driving home from the West Coast to New York in 1951, she made up new lyrics to the song "It's a Long Way to Tipperary." It was something like "Hello to 36th Street, We're Almost Home." It was the two of them and Frisco in the car. It was for Frisco. They'd sing it to him in the car as they were nearing 36th Street, because she loved New York so much. She would get a little shy and little-girlish and say, "Would you like to hear the song?"

Tell me about some of Miss Rand's friends.

I'll just mention a couple of people I saw her with. I have my own firsthand view of what her attitude was toward them. Alan Greenspan was one. She was extremely fond of him. She respected him intellectually. She thought he was extremely intelligent. She was very proud of what he was doing in Washington and thought the major contribution he was making concerned things that people would never hear about or see because it was evils he was preventing.

She projected a kindliness toward Alan and an understanding that was different, for instance, than what she projected toward Leonard. Toward Alan, she was not motherly but treated him as a colleague.

Her attitude to Leonard was really motherly. I think she regarded him as a son. I don't think she would have said so, but she certainly acted that way. Leonard was like a son, and I think Frank loved him in that way too. She and Leonard were always in touch. They spoke almost daily. They always could speak for hours about philosophy. They shared their own world.

Any others?

There was a group of people who came into her life over stamps, whom she really liked, such as Jacques Minkus and Leonard's father and Mary Ann Sures' husband Charles, who was a stamp collector at the time. They would take her to stamp shows. Ayn became very friendly with Mr. Minkus, who was in the stamp business. She became passionate about stamps, and he used to bring her stamps, and they would go to shows together periodically. Dr. Holman, her surgeon, was also interested in stamps. She admired Dr. Holman because he was a very good doctor. She became friendly with Leonard's father, Dr. Sam Peikoff, because he collected stamps. They would exchange letters and stamps. There was also a little girl, Tammy [Vaught], in Florida, whom she got to know while seeing the *Apollo 11* space shot. She maintained a pen pal relationship with her over stamps and would send her stamps.

What was Miss Rand's attitude toward Tammy?

She liked her so much. She thought she was so cute, and she loved her interest in stamps. She would send her new stamps and discoveries.

Tell me about Eloise Huggins, Miss Rand's cook. First, what was Eloise like as a person?

I liked her a great deal. She was extremely good at what she did. She was extremely warm, serious, kind. I liked her attitude with Mr. O'Connor—she appreciated him and treated him well. She seemed to be very fond of him.

I think Ayn and Eloise were very close. My impression was that Eloise certainly cared for her and I think she cared for Eloise. I don't know how open Ayn was about it, but toward the end, when Frank had died, Eloise was there all the time.

She talked to Eloise openly and trusted her. Eloise was a very decent, hard-working woman, very loyal to Ayn. As more and more people disappeared from Ayn's life, I think Eloise became more important, as a steady presence. She was not intellectual by any means, but she was a good person and very kind toward Ayn.

In what way?

She took care of Ayn. She took pride in taking care of the things she was supposed to take care of, whether it was shopping for groceries or cooking a meal.

How close did they become?

She wasn't close in the sense that Ayn was close to Leonard, but Ayn liked Eloise and they were friendly.

Did Ayn Rand have a sense of humor?

It was not an overt personality characteristic that you would mention about her, but she would get a kick out of Frank's puns or

Oscar and Oswald[165] or a cat doing something funny. She was not the type of person people would tell jokes to.

I have one joke Ayn Rand told. She would get cute and shy when she would tell this joke. The idea was the following: In a crossword puzzle it was asked, "What is a four-letter word ending in 'I-T' that is like Eleanor Roosevelt and is found on the bottom of a birdcage?" She'd start to giggle and say, "I hope this isn't too dirty," and then she would say the answer was "G-R-I-T."

You knew Ayn Rand the person and Ayn Rand the writer. How did they integrate?

There's absolutely no difference between Ayn the novelist and Ayn the person. That passion for ideas and the moralist and the person who sees and is aware of everything around her is the novelist too. That penetrating commitment to understanding and explaining is the same voice that you hear in *Atlas*.

I want to tell you one thing about the fishwife character in *Atlas*: Ayn told me she wrote it as herself. It was her Alfred Hitchcock-type appearance in *Atlas*. The love for Galt that was projected by the fishwife was Ayn's. Read the passage and you get a flavor of what her attitude toward Galt was.

Let me ask you about some of Ayn Rand's favorites. First, did she have any favorite restaurants?

Her favorite restaurant at that time was the Russian Tea Room. She loved the borscht and the piroshki. She also liked a restaurant next door to her called Jungle Jim's, a sort of neighborhood burger and steak place. Her other favorite restaurant was a combination French-Japanese one called La Maison Japonaise.

Favorite food?

She loved Sara Lee frozen desserts. And there was a commercial, "Nobody doesn't like Sara Lee," and she loved the commercial and bought Sara Lee all the time. She loved Russian nut cake and cheese sandwiches on black bread with mayonnaise.

What did she drink?

She didn't really drink liquor. She did sip champagne on New

---

165 The O'Connors' stuffed toy lions. See *Letters of Ayn Rand*, p. 27.

Year's. When she went to Boston for Ford Hall speeches, we would stay at the main hotel, where they had a Polynesian restaurant called Trader Vic's. She would love the drink with the little umbrella and fruit. It didn't have liquor in it, just that concoction that made it look like it was from the South Seas.

Favorite chocolate?

She loved Godiva chocolates, which she referred to as Lady Godiva chocolates. She loved the boxes, which were gold—and still are—and the whole way they were presented, and the taste of the chocolate.

When would she have them?

If there was a special occasion where she wanted to celebrate having written something or completed something, or friends would bring them, or if it was a holiday. It was a special occasion just by virtue of eating them. She spent her whole life fighting to remain thin and to be on a diet, so she wouldn't allow herself to have them often.

Music favorites?

She loved Rachmaninoff and the Romantics, and she loved Arthur Rubinstein and Vladimir Horowitz, but I heard her talk about them more than I ever had the experience of seeing her enjoy them. I saw firsthand her reaction to the popular tiddlywink music and American patriotic songs like "Over There" and the George M. Cohan-type of music. She also liked marches.

What was it about Horowitz's style that she liked?

It was dramatic, and he took chances. She thought he was exceptionally good and bold and passionate in his playing. Rubinstein was beautiful and lyrical but self-contained. Horowitz would just sort of leap.

Any other patriotic songs that she liked?

Sousa-type marches such as "The Washington Post March." She always thought that "America the Beautiful" should be the national anthem, not "The Star-Spangled Banner." Frank loved the song "Down South."[166] He would just beam and beat his hand to the music.

---

166 A 1901 song written by W. H. Myddleton.

Any movies that you know she liked?

One movie she liked a lot was *Fallen Idol*, with Ralph Richardson and Bobby Henrey. She thought Bobby Henrey was terrific, and she liked the hero-worship aspect and thought it was a very good mystery. It was intricate; it wasn't obvious. She liked Terence Rattigan's movies for the same reasons.

What actors did she like?

She thought Alec Guinness was a spectacular actor. He could play any part and was capable of doing any role, and you wouldn't even recognize him in these different roles.

What about Ruggles of Red Gap?

That too was one of my favorites, and I remember when I discovered it and told her, and that she thought highly of it. She thought highly of Charles Laughton as an actor.

What about Greta Garbo?

Ayn thought Garbo was the best. She thought she was an absolutely amazing actress; that she could communicate a great deal in just her facial reactions. She also thought Garbo looked dramatic and elegant.

Do you know what she thought of the movie Born Free?

I remember her loving *Born Free*. She loved the cubs, of course. They were rambunctious and bright and clever and cute. She liked the story, but I remember her reaction to the cubs more. Those cubs she just died over.

Also, there was a movie we went to—I can't recall the name—and it had some sell-out to Russia, and she was just outraged and exclaimed aloud, in the middle of the theater while everyone else was watching it, and made loud comments about the propaganda as she was exiting.

Did you see The Godfather *with her?*

I remember her discussing the film, which she thought was very well done from a dramatic point of view. She thought it was well-characterized and the action was good.

Favorite TV shows?

I remember her liking *Charlie's Angels*, because of Farrah Fawcett. She thought she was delightful, innocent, feminine and pretty. She loved Farrah Fawcett's looks, and she thought there was an innocent benevolence about her. I think she even considered her for a role in *Atlas*. Raymond Burr in *Perry Mason* was another favorite. She liked his seriousness and the story lines. There was another man, Hans Gudegast [now Eric Braeden], an adventure hero, in *Rat Patrol*. She was crazy about him and would watch him all the time. This was near the end of her life. She would comment always on his looks, how much she liked him, that he was her type of hero.

Her favorite painting?

Frank's.

Her favorite opera?

La Traviata. We went to see it at the Met. She loved the drinking song, but she was almost like a child—disappointed, because in Russia it had been staged in an absolutely grand way with beautiful scenery and costumes, and here she thought it was shabby in comparison. She was so disappointed.

What did she think of rock and roll music?

She hated it. She thought it was loud and unmelodic.

Her favorite poem?

If [by Rudyard Kipling]. She also liked *Invictus* [by William Ernest Henley].

What did she like about Invictus?

Where it says: "I am the captain of my soul."

Why did she like Agatha Christie?

She thought she was very clever and liked her mysteries. She referred to her as "Agatha." She loved the plots and tried to guess them.

Did she ever figure out the mysteries?

I don't think so. She read every single one of her books, but she liked Poirot, not Miss Marple.

Favorite ballets?

She liked the idea of ballet more than any given one. She thought it was a very abstract art and that the meaning itself was beauty or grace—characteristics like that.

Favorite color?

Blue-green.

Do you know the exact shade of that?

I have a small ashtray of hers. It's in a shell shape that's in that blue-green color. It's an aqua color, which is more green than blue. It's bright and cheerful.

Any other pleasures or entertainments she enjoyed?

She thought Nureyev was a great dancer, because he was unique, and he came across as a Romantic hero. Ayn liked him very much. Not with the passion that I did, but she certainly admired him, his artistry.

Leonard and I went with two couples to see him dance once. I think he was doing *Don Quixote*, which was just spectacular, the way he played this bravura role. Afterwards, when we were discussing him, one of the couples we were with mentioned that Nureyev was a homosexual. I got really upset and I told Ayn, who agreed with me that it's improper to raise a negative when you're talking about this great experience that you've had of seeing him. That is not the time to bring up clay feet. She was very big on that.

It hurts your emotional moment?

Yes. He was such a rarity. Regardless, you don't say he has a cold sore when you admire him.

Did Ayn Rand ever see Nureyev perform live?

Oh yes. I recall once or twice she went to see him. It's like saying would you hear Ayn Rand give a talk? If there's a great artist, you go.

Who were her heroes? Who was she intrigued by in the public arena?

There was no one in politics. She thought it was much too early in politics, and she meant it. There was no one she found intriguing. She had great admiration for the astronauts, and seeing the *Apollo 11* space shot was a major event for her.

What other public figures?

Aristotle because of the greatness of his mind and the ideas he originated. She really admired Aristotle as you would admire a living hero.

Capuletti was a living painter whom she greatly admired. She wouldn't put him in the same category as Aristotle or Michelangelo, but she greatly admired him. She loved the way he painted.

Do you remember her talking about any specific world leaders?

No. She wrote that most people don't focus on ideas, but on men. She didn't. She would regard ideas, not people, as the significant things. If there were contemporary people to admire, great people to admire, she would have, but there weren't. A figure like Aristotle, or to a lesser degree, Hugo, those are the people she would admire. She didn't admire them in an abstract way, as though they were people from the past who taught us great lessons. They were extremely real to her, as real as though she had known them—the way people would say Jackie Robinson is my hero, she would say Aristotle is hers.

Was she interested in, would she study, the lives of these people, like Aristotle?

She knew about all of them.

What about sporting figures?

Muhammad Ali. And she liked gymnastics but that was, again, a response to a person, Olga Korbut. She liked her very much and thought she was unique and artistic in her approach and that she stood out from everyone else.

There was the cat Morris who was the spokescat for 9Lives cat food. In his ads he was a big alley cat, sort of orangey red with a great deal of personality. He had a voice and a distinct form of aggressive personality. Morris the Cat was her hero. She loved him. There was Morris and another commercial with a beautiful white Persian, a lady. Ayn would always stop to talk about them. I think she bought a book on Morris; his autobiography had come out. He had a little "M"—you know, how they have little frown lines on their foreheads? His was in the shape of an "M" for "Morris."

She admired Bobby Fischer. She thought he was very intelligent, and she liked the fact that he defeated Boris Spassky.[167] But she didn't believe in those arranged Russian-American competitions, so it was not a major thing to her.

---

167 See "An Open Letter to Boris Spassky" in *The Ayn Rand Letter*, September 11, 1972.

What scientists or adventurers did she like?

I think ones like Leonardo da Vinci, but it wasn't in the same category. She would put people in levels in her mind. After Aristotle and Michelangelo and Hugo, there would be everyone else.

Why did she love Michelangelo?

Because she thought he was a great painter, particularly in the way he characterized man in the *Creation of Adam*, with man as the center of the universe.

The point of many of the things I have noted is that she had values in every single part of her life. There was no area where she didn't have favorites. There were her profound values that are well known, but in everyday kinds of things, she would always know what she liked. It was definite and absolute. There was nothing wishy-washy about it.

Did you ever ask Miss Rand about her meetings with Gary Cooper?

She would talk about her experiences with him on the set and trying to teach him his lines, and how she loved his face. He had the face of one of her heroes, that high-cheekbone look. Ayn loved a man's face that looked like that. But he wasn't very intellectual, and he didn't really understand the courtroom speech in *The Fountainhead* film.

Tell me about Ayn Rand's study.

In her study, where she spent the most time, were her desk and bookshelves. I told you about her shelf unit with all her precious collection of lions and rocks. The room was always a mess. She didn't want it to be messy, but she never got around to straightening it out, because she was always writing something.

Tell me about other social activities with Ayn Rand.

We would periodically take the ferry—called the Circle Line— around New York. It goes around the whole of Manhattan, and she and Frank would go on it. We would generally go when the Sureses came in from Washington. She loved that and would make comments about the buildings and the architecture as we passed and point out buildings like the Chrysler Building and the Empire State Building. She would comment about the changes from the old skyscrapers, which have character, compared to the new, meaningless boxes, which have nothing. During the trip, she wasn't in her working mood. She would be on the premise of thoroughly taking in the view and enjoying it.

Which was her favorite building?

The Woolworth Building.

Was she very generous with her money?

With her friends, or with her sister Nora, obviously. She wouldn't even think twice about what it would cost her to deck out a whole apartment and pay for everything, even medical treatment. Or if a person she cared about needed a loan, she would be there. Her attitude was generous. It's funny, because people who were as poor as she had been—and she talked about that a couple of times, when they were in New York just starting out and only had soup for meals—you would think that they would attach a great significance to being comfortable when they became financially successful. Ayn lived well and spent money, but it was not important to her. She would be as happy with a piece of costume jewelry as with fine jewelry. She was not ostentatious.

Did she give gifts?

No, she didn't. She was in constant conflict getting gifts. She would always say, when you gave her one, "Oh, you shouldn't give me anything," and then she'd be delighted at whatever it was. She didn't want people spending the money on her.

Did you get gifts for her?

I had found for Ayn, as a surprise gift, a still from one of Frank's movies called *Three on a Match*. I was working at Channel 5 in New York, an independent TV station, that had the movie. I had an editor friend who got the movie and took out the shot. She wasn't in a very happy state at that time in her life, but she was very pleased about having it.

Tell me about Ayn Rand and holidays.

They celebrated Thanksgiving and Christmas. It was a full-fledged American Thanksgiving dinner, with turkey and all the fixings. Every year, Leonard and I would go and have it with them. It was very festive, and Eloise would set the table in a special way. And on Christmas the two lion cubs, Oscar and Oswald, would appear with Christmas hats and bows. They always attributed Frank's bad puns to Oscar and Oswald—"that was Oscar speaking."

Ayn had a Russian tradition that she kept on New Year's Day: what you wanted to be doing for the rest of the year, you had to do during that day, so she would always take time out on New Year's Day to write.

Did she play games?

Yes, at parties. One game played at Ayn's apartment was that people had to bring an excerpt of music that they thought was their happiest music and everyone would have to match the person with the music. At the time I picked for myself *London Suite* [by Eric Coates], which turned out to be one of Frank's favorites also. It's a very gay marching music. Frank's was "Down South," which was so adorable, with banjos. Ayn had her one piece of tiddlywink music, something from a Viennese operetta. Alan Greenspan had something from a symphony. You just put it with him. The game was very interesting.

Then at another party, again in Ayn's apartment, everyone had to bring a picture of when they were very young, and the game was to figure out who the person was, which is very hard. I think you had to have titles for the photos and Leonard's was "Tabula Rasa," and I think Ayn guessed who it was. Those were the kinds of games. Then there were regular, more charade-type of games, but they always had a twist.

Was there a game about Atlas Shrugged?

Yes. In those old days the Collective would always do that and play "casting *Atlas*."

Whom did Miss Rand want?

She never had a Galt.

Who did she want as Francisco?

A French actor by the name of Alain Delon, when he was younger. She like his face—it had that sharp-cheekbone look—and there was something dashing about him.

And for Dagny?

She named Raquel Welch once. She liked her face. Ayn placed a great deal of stock in the way people, particularly actors, looked. Not only that, but she did it initially in the way Frank looked, for that matter. She had a definite image in her mind of what her characters looked like and what her kind of people looked like in her universe. She had a definite view of the type of faces that represented the kinds of souls she loved. In men particularly, it was chiseled, high cheekbone, piercing, light eyes, very American-looking. Frank was very American-looking.

That sort of tall, lanky American. That high-cheekbone, chiseled and yet cheerful face. It's intense and American, benevolent.

What did she say about Frank's face when they first met?

That she knew immediately that he was her type of man from his face.

Any other actresses she liked?

She thought Faye Dunaway was very feminine, but career-woman-looking. She looked intelligent and feminine.

Can you remember any specific outrages of the liberal media bias that Miss Rand felt or saw?

The *New York Times* was a major outrage. She read it, marked it and always answered it, when she felt obliged to.

What was her response to your work as a news producer?

There were two stories in particular that I produced when I was at NBC that she would always comment on. I think she and Leonard would watch my stories together, and they would both phone me. Ayn was very big on people deserving compliments, particularly regarding work.

One story was on Nureyev. I produced a profile of him for NBC News. I remember her just being delighted by what I had done. She said, "You know how much dancing you were able to get in? No one ever is able to get in that much dancing." So she congratulated me on that and on how his personality came through and his role as a Romantic hero in ballet. Those three things she responded to and commented on.

There was another story I did on Tom Hayden and Jane Fonda. I followed them on and off for months. They had this organization called "Campaign for Economic Democracy." That was a battle for me at NBC. Ideologically, they loved Jane Fonda. In the story I got in every piece of propaganda that I wanted. I got in that footage of Fonda in Hanoi, speaking to the North Vietnamese troops when we were fighting against them. I got in footage of veterans protesting against her. I did interviews with her where she just came across as a complete zero. I did it in a way that the people who liked her thought it was fair to her. Ayn thought it painted a devastating picture. So Fonda came across, to people who were objective, as completely evil and dumb. And she is very stupid. One of the points that I made is that she was programmed by the man she was with. She didn't have a thought of her own in her head. So I obviously won on that. Ayn was very complimentary of how much I achieved on that story.

What did Ayn Rand think of Spiro Agnew?

She liked him. He seemed very moral, and his stance toward the press was very good. He denounced them as "nattering nabobs of negativism." He was excellent in his attacks on the left-wing press.

Did you have any trouble at NBC or with any other employer with people saying, "There's Ayn Rand's friend" or "She's an Objectivist"?

Not about Ayn, because I wouldn't make that known. I wouldn't go around preaching Objectivism. They knew I had "strange" ideas, but they didn't know I was an Objectivist. Ayn counseled me not to make a big deal about Objectivism, because I was in enemy territory. She gave me some hints about how to suggest ideas in terms that the people with whom I worked wouldn't get hostile.

Did she give you other advice about your work?

When I went to NBC, I think in 1968, working for the news division, you had to be a member of the union, NABET,[168] which was for broadcast engineers and technicians. How news writers and producers ever got into this union, I don't know. It's a very hard-line teamster-type union. I didn't want to be in that union—they took an enormous amount of your salary for dues, and did nothing for you, as far as I could tell. About a week after I arrived at NBC, the union went out on strike, for contract reasons. It was some typical labor dispute. I was angered that I had to be in a union, let alone go out and picket. I was just going to ignore the whole thing. Anyway, I was mentioning it to Ayn, and she said adamantly that I had to go out and picket, and do whatever the union required of me, because it could be held against me at the end of the strike, and for all I knew, I could be docked an enormous amount of money or there could be repercussions as far as my job was concerned. She also said that I had no choice about joining the union, and I certainly had no choice about picketing and being part of the union, once those were the terms

---

168 National Association of Broadcast Employees and Technicians

of getting the job. I took her word for it, because she knew more about this than I did, and I found myself outside of the Empire State Building, one summer day, picketing, which she approved. Ayn was just as much against the whole thing as I was, and sure enough when the union went back to work, there were people who were fined heavily for not having picketed. Ayn turned out to be absolutely right.

Did Ayn Rand say anything about Israel?

She admired Israel in principle. She hated what it is politically, being to the Left, socialist, but she thought they were the only people in the world who took moral stands and had the courage of their convictions, like the Entebbe raid. She would say that the United States should learn a lesson from Israel.

Tell me about Miss Rand and Mr. O'Connor at your wedding to Leonard Peikoff in 1968.

I remember we had a mini-rehearsal in Leonard's apartment, which she and Frank came to, with everyone sort of chitchatting meaninglessly, and Ayn blurted out, "Can we get to the business at hand." She said, "Don't we have a purpose for being here?"—or something to that effect.

At the wedding, Ayn was the matron of honor and Frank stood up too. I wanted them to wear black. I think at that time it wasn't always done. Ayn thought it was a good idea because it was a dramatic picture of all of the men and Ayn in black, and I was in the white wedding gown. She and Frank looked elegant that day.

Did you ever see Ayn Rand cry?

Yes, when one of her cats died. The Sureses and Peikoffs arrived at her apartment on one of the days we were going on the Circle Line, and Tommy had just died that preceding night. We asked her what had happened, and she started to cry about Tommy's death, and she was embarrassed and didn't know if she had the right to cry.

Tell me about Ayn Rand and buying your cat Frisco.

It was 1981. I had a Himalayan named Ritzy, for Countess Maritza, and she was beautiful, but she was struck with feline enteritis and died. I realized at a certain time that I was not getting another cat because I was afraid that it would die also. Once I named that, I wanted to get one instantaneously. I said to Ayn that I wanted to go and look at cats and told her about what my reaction had been. It was not too long after her cat Tommy had died. She wanted to go with me when I went to look at cats, and I leaped at the opportunity. There were cat stores at that time named Fabulous Felines that specialized in cats and had beautiful cats, so we went there.

There were two absolutely adorable Himalayan kittens, brothers. I fell in love with them immediately, as did Ayn, and the question was, which one. I couldn't stand the idea of splitting them up. I was thinking to myself, "Maybe she would be tempted to buy one for herself," but that never happened.

She never wanted another cat?

She was somewhat depressed. It was soon after Frank had died, I think, so she wasn't in the most cheerful mood, although going out to look for cats definitely cheered her up. She wasn't cheered up in the sense of wanting another cat, though. Anyway, of the two cats, I went for the one that jumped around and was more active. Ayn said she'd like to offer to buy it for me as a going-away present, as I was then going out of town, for the first time, to live in Atlanta, because I had gotten a job at CNN. I sheepishly said, "Ayn, I have a serious question to ask you. Would you mind very much if I named him Francisco after Francisco d'Anconia? I need your approval to use that name." She said, "Oh, absolutely." He was Frisco from then on, and I would show her pictures of him as he grew. She thought he was beautiful. He was so active and energetic and seemingly bright.

What was her reaction when she was being applauded or cheered?

She took it in as though she deserved it, but she got somewhat embarrassed if the applause went on too long. She didn't like people fawning over her at all. If she was speaking and there was applause, she would acknowledge that it was right to be applauded and then she would communicate that now it's on to business.

A time that was very meaningful to her was her West Point appearance. The fact that a place like West Point, which has a historic place in America's history, recognized her and wanted her to speak to them meant a great deal to her personally.

Tell me about her visit to West Point.

I remember all these wonderful-looking cadets in their uniforms listening attentively to every single word she said. There's a very austere, dignified look that West Point has, which she took in and acknowledged as something worth being a part of.

Ford Hall Forum also meant something to her. We would go up with her on the train, where she would be finishing the speech, writing all the way to Boston. She would read the speech from her handwritten notes.

Why did she like speaking at Ford Hall Forum?

It was a yearly appearance that she looked forward to because she thought it was an intellectual forum that honestly presented different viewpoints. She greatly admired Judge Lurie, who was the emcee, in effect. He was very distinguished, and he respected her. He never gave any hint of his own views, but treated her in a dignified way. Even the train ride to Boston—although she was always writing—was part of a whole adventure: eating in the dining room at the hotel and having one of those funny drinks with the fruit and the umbrella, and then having a post-mortem party, where friends discussed the audience's response and what she had said, and asking her questions.

Did she give you Christmas cards?

No. The only thing I have is a copy of *Atlas*, which she autographed. It says, "To Sue and Frisco: Wishing you both a great future. Francisco d'Anconia through his secretary, Ayn. 9/7/81."

Why did she do that?

Because she knew how much Francisco d'Anconia meant to me, and she was just doing it as his professional secretary. It was he signing it. I adored that character, I still do. I would tell her that I didn't have the same reaction to Galt. I would try to explain to her why I liked Francisco the best.

Did she agree?

No. She liked Galt the best, but she could understand. She said it was perfectly understandable, because Galt was so much more abstract, and Francisco's whole character and childhood were dramatized.

Ayn had marvelous reactions to my reactions when I would talk to her about what I loved about her books as literature. I would tell her about the characters I liked most and the scenes I liked most, and she would listen, be very interested and sort of beam and ask why.

There were two things I got dispensation from: I confessed to her that when I first read *Atlas*, I skipped Galt's speech because I couldn't stand not knowing what happened in the story. She said that was fully understandable, although I shouldn't broadcast it.

The other thing was when she was giving an epistemology seminar. I sheepishly confessed that I couldn't get interested in epistemology. She said there was no reason why I should be, that it's an area of knowledge for professional intellectuals, philosophers, and I wasn't one and that was the end of the story. But I always felt guilty about this and she thought that was ridiculous.

What was her attitude to reading Atlas *herself?*

She was afraid to read it because, no matter what she was doing, if she just wanted to look something up or find something for an article, she would be completely drawn right into the book, as a reader. She would lose herself and put away everything else and want to finish the novel.

With regard to one article of hers, I remember her making a big deal about what I had told her in reaction to it. She wrote an article, called "The Comprachicos,"[169] on how young minds are destroyed. It was an important issue to her: what happens in early childhood to minds that are grasping to know and how teachers in schools can devastate them. I had gone to a Progressive nursery school, which I was terrified of, which she had known. When she wrote the article, she said, "You know, that's what happened in your nursery school." She felt very bad about it, and from time to time over the years, she would refer to what had happened to me in my school.

Tell me about the visit of Ayn Rand's sister Nora.

Ayn was so excited about Nora's coming and rented an apartment for her in her apartment house, which she then set up for Nora and her husband, Fedya. Ayn got her a television set and had one memento from Russia: a drawing of a woman that Nora had made as a young girl. Ayn loved it because it was a very stylized drawing. She put it in a very noticeable place, but Nora didn't care about it.

How did Ayn and Nora interact?

As the days wore on, it was obvious that Nora and Fedya did not

---

169 Reprinted in Ayn Rand's *Return of the Primitive: The Anti-Industrial Revolution*, ed. Peter Schwartz, expanded ed. (New York: Meridian, 1990).

fit in here and did not particularly like what they were seeing. They looked dismal. After the shock of learning Nora's attitude toward Russia, which was not very negative, Ayn would tell Leonard and me about it. Nora liked the idea that she was well taken care of in Russia, meaning they had pensions and all the government-given things. When it was clear that Nora preferred the Soviet state to the freedom of this country, Ayn was outraged. It was a mixture of profound sorrow—she viewed it as having lost her sister—but once she knew how Nora felt and thought, Ayn wanted to have nothing further to do with her.

Nora and Fedya wanted to go back. They didn't like having to pay for things here that the Soviet state "provided." They didn't like the choices open to them here, that they would have to choose. They wanted the security of a dictatorship. Nora's husband wasn't very well, he had some heart problems, and I think he had a medical checkup. Of course, Ayn paid for everything. She was a very generous woman.

What about good things Ayn Rand and Nora shared? Was it a loving meeting at first?

No, I don't think so, because Nora wasn't a valuer or a thinker, and those are the two things that Ayn valued in people. When, for instance, Nora had no reaction to what Ayn considered the best of Nora—her little drawing—Ayn reacted negatively.

As someone who wrote for Ayn Rand's magazine The Objectivist, *tell me about your editing sessions with her.*

I remember Leonard's much more than I remember mine. But I do remember her general attitude in editing, which was as a saint— very patient and purposeful and businesslike. She wouldn't edit; she'd have suggestions, but the writer would come up with them too. First of all, she was endlessly patient, on the premise that every single detail had to be discussed and explained. And I mean everything from periods and punctuation to meaning were discussed and changed. Nothing was changed without the writer's approval. She explained everything. Editing sessions could run hours.

Regarding Miss Rand getting angry, did she apologize to friends at whom she got angry during philosophic discussions?

Yes, whenever she lost her temper, she would say, "Please understand it's not directed at you. It's the idea that I'm responding to." She would say she was getting angry at the idea, not at the person. Ayn was on the premise that every single thing, from writing to personal dealings, was eminently straighten-outable, and discussion was the way of doing it. Everything was always discussed, endlessly.

What did you learn from Ayn Rand as an editor?

The biggest contribution she made was helping me tie abstractions to concretes. I was good at telling a concrete story, for instance, my Marchenko article.[170] I could tell that story very well. I knew Objectivism enough to know the abstractions, but they stood somewhat as floating abstractions, at that point. So the difficulty in writing, as in thinking, was tying the two together. There was no split in her between abstractions versus concretes. She was excellent—that is an understatement—at this particular thing. Her editing was teaching me more, specifically about how to think, even more than about translating it into writing, which is still yet another step.

Also, I noticed when I recently read over my articles—and this had to have been from Ayn—my writing was very, very specific and concrete. Very rarely do you see an adjective. That's her lesson that concretes give rise to abstractions. Don't just say everything was "wonderful." If you're writing, "wonderful" means nothing without the concretes that support it. You have to give the specifics that add up to the exclamation. And that's what I saw in my writing. I was so specific that you could picture things, and that's definitely Ayn's influence.

When writing for her, did you have to submit a plan or an outline first?

No. We discussed it. Then I would go ahead and submit many drafts. Ayn's view about writing was that you took time in doing everything about it. There was no such thing as rushing through anything. If there was a word in question, you would sit there for two hours, if necessary, debating which word to use. That's the source of my irritation when anyone says they don't have time to do something regarding writing.

As editor she'd okay a contributor, then she would review the article for as long as it took to convince the writer of some point. It was a rational discussion and someone would win and lose. There was no such thing as just taking her word or, on the other hand, saying, "Well, that's me." Her view was that it was an objective enterprise with rights and

---

170 A review of Anatoly Marchenko's *My Testimony* in *The Objectivist,* July 1970.

wrongs and goods and bads. If the article was very bad, it would have been killed initially. Her premise was that this is good enough to run but it needs work. And "work" meant work.

What about discussion during the pre-writing stage?

We would talk about the main idea and the points you wanted to make, and then you'd have to go away and see what was logical or not. Since I was there in her apartment all the time, it wasn't a formal session when I discussed an idea.

How many drafts would you do?

Four, maybe as many as six. It would depend. For the Marchenko one, I remember it was probably two, which was nothing. Some other ones—the more concrete ones, like the book reviews, were less. But for the more abstract pieces, there were many.

Why did you do an article on Marchenko and not on other dissidents?

Because he wrote *My Testimony*, which I had read. He was astounding in the sense that he was a laborer who was supposed to be the typical communist man. The Soviets should have been able to point to him and say, "A laborer—he believes everything." Here he was, a crusading dissident who became an intellectual in the prisons. He was very different because of the background he came from. He eventually was looked up to by other dissidents, like Sakharov and Daniel. They all knew each other, and they thought very highly of him. He was very first-handed.

What did Ayn Rand think of these other dissidents?

She hated Alexander Solzhenitsyn.

Tell me about Miss Rand and Victor Reisel.

Victor Reisel was an old-time labor newsman, who was enormously courageous as a fighter against the mob and labor and the communists, particularly during the attempted Hollywood takeover by the communists. He was practically the only newsman who was writing about the communist takeover. He was eventually blinded by mob gangsters who threw acid in his face, because they didn't like what he had been writing. He never stopped saying what he thought was the truth.

I had met him at Channel 5 in New York, where he was doing guest commentary. He would come across as a sort of irascible conservative, but a liberal conservative. When I met him, I started chatting with him and found him very interesting, and I mentioned to Ayn that I had met him, and she then filled me in about him. It was from her that I learned that he had been one of the only newsmen who spoke out against the Hollywood Ten and all that was going on at that time.

I don't remember how it happened, but I asked her if she'd be interested in getting together with him just to talk about that time, and she said "certainly," and he said "certainly." His wife, Eleanor, was a wonderful woman who took him around everywhere. I don't remember if the O'Connors and the Peikoffs and the Reisels went to dinner first, but I do remember that we ended up at the O'Connors' apartment. I don't remember the details of the conversation, but they did talk about what had gone on then, and why newsmen weren't speaking out, and how even today the Left had taken over the media, and there was no more courage. Both of them enjoyed the meeting, as much as that kind of meeting is enjoyable, because Ayn liked philosophy more than politics, but she thought very highly of him, very much admired him.

You knew Ayn Rand when she was ill in 1975.

She had lung cancer. She went to the doctor and they discovered something on her lung. She had been coughing a great deal, but she wasn't in pain. They immediately put her in the hospital and did surgery. I don't know if she ever fully recovered. The lethargy was overwhelming for a long time.

Why did she smoke?

Her view all the time had been that there was no scientific evidence against smoking.[171]

She regarded hospitals as purgatory, as not fully life, something you got through. It was a place where none of your values existed. It was a place to take care of medical problems and get out and get back to your world.

Did you ever see Ayn Rand when she was nervous or afraid?

No. Before a speech, she would be enthusiastic, not nervous. She was frightened about certain physical things but those are absolutely minor. I think she was almost run over by a car in Hollywood[172] and

---

171 But, when presented with evidence of her own illness, she quit immediately.
172 This was reported on the front page of the *Hollywood News*, November 26, 1926.

she was somewhat tentative about crossing streets. If you would call that fear, that's the only thing I could think of.

What other activities did you do together?

We voted together. Since we lived in the same building or a few blocks away, we invariably went to the same voting place, and we would make a date to go together. The only ritual was seeing what the *New York Times* came out for and voting for the opposite.

There were always amendments to turn down and people to vote against.

She took it very seriously?

Oh yes.

Did she tell you stories about her time in Hollywood?

She told the story of going to an elegant dinner party in Hollywood at Joan Crawford's house. It was butlers and nineteen courses and everyone was well-dressed and beautiful. At the end of the dinner, Joan Crawford stood up and said, "All right, everyone can go to the bathroom now." Ayn repeated that as an example of how crude and inelegant Joan Crawford was, in contrast to her image.

Did she say anything to you about the actor Adolph Menjou?

Ayn always referred to him as the one actor in Hollywood who was a clear-cut victim of the Hollywood Ten. In other words, he was an anticommunist who was blackballed from working. I don't know for how long, but in a much more serious way than the Hollywood Ten claimed to have been.

What did Ayn Rand think of Joseph McCarthy?

She thought he was a coward who didn't live up to his promotion, that he was right to be doing what he was doing, but he knew much more. He only focused on the lesser names of the communists in the government.

Did Ayn Rand ever meet him?

She said she met with him and tried to convince him to be as courageous as his PR was, and that he just was not up to it intellectually.[173]

Was she bitter about that period or about him?

Oh, no. "Bitter" is not a word to use with her. She thought he was a fool, and she was disappointed that he didn't have the courage of his own convictions.

Do you have a favorite story about Ayn Rand?

Mary Ann [Sures] and I loved Frank Sinatra beyond belief. We had once been at Ayn's and we both had been talking about him, and later Mary Ann was in town and we decided we had to bring Ayn Frank Sinatra records to get her response to them. So we came to her apartment with about a dozen long-playing records. We were crazy on the subject—still are. We put on one record after another trying to get her response, and she would say she saw how seriously he took the lyrics and that's very nice and that she likes his voice. She was trying so hard to like it and be nice about it, because it was not her kind of music. On the other hand it wasn't offensive to her. She was trying too hard to be nice to us and we were just gushing. Then she said to us in this little sort of apologetic, soft voice, "Do you mind turning it down a little?" So we didn't continue to play all twelve records; she was being so gracious.

From your observations and discussions, was Ayn Rand happy?

Yes. She achieved everything she set out to do.

What did Ayn Rand think of herself?

She would never characterize herself. She would never talk about her early life. She didn't talk about herself in any way. She talked about her ideas but not her person.

How did she see herself historically?

She would always say she didn't have that view of herself, that there was no way a person could view themselves in historical terms or even as a great figure. That was not how she walked around thinking of herself. You take yourself for granted in a certain way. Leonard would say to her that she had the greatest mind in the universe, and she would say, "No, I'm just honest and intelligent." And she was not aware of her fame.

---

173 The Archives has no record of Ayn Rand meeting McCarthy.

Earl, Jane, Tammy and Tommy Vaught

The Vaught family hosted Ayn Rand and Frank O'Connor in their home when they visited Cape Kennedy in July 1969 to watch the *Apollo 11* launch. The Vaught family consisted of Earl, who worked at NASA, and Jane and their children Tammy and Tommy, who at that time were twelve and nine, respectively. Mr. Vaught died in 2001.

Interview dates:

Tammy Vaught Lyons—September 29 and October 20, 1998
Jane Vaught—September 29, 1998
Earl Vaught—October 2, 1998
Tommy Vaught—October 2, 1998

Scott McConnell: *When I mention the name Ayn Rand or Mrs. O'Connor, what comes to mind?*

Tammy Vaught Lyons: A space launch a long time ago, a couple that came in to see a space launch, and that we were just young children. We didn't know who they were; we never knew who the people were that would stay with us. I think my parents had different couples come stay four times.

Mrs. O'Connor came to stay at our house during that weekend *Apollo 11* was launching, and I also got to know her through her stamps. She was just a nice lady.

The reason my parents did this was at the beginning, if you wanted to come to see a space shot, there were few motels where you could stay, and everything booked up immediately. So people at NASA opened their homes as hospitality. It was like being a bed and breakfast.

Earl Vaught: Titusville is not a very big town. It's only 40,000 people.

Jane Vaught: They made reservations through the Titusville Chamber of Commerce to stay with us in our home. They came by train, because she was quite concerned that if she flew, the plane might be hijacked to Cuba,[174] and she could be taken and end up in Russia, and that they would never let her go if she was taken back there.

Earl: We had told the Titusville Chamber of Commerce that we

---

174 There were many hijackings at the time.

would keep one bedroom for visitors, and she contacted the Chamber of Commerce and worked it out with them. Her secretary called and confirmed it, and then she called back later. I guess she thought we probably didn't know who Mrs. Frank O'Connor was, and then she told us it was Ayn Rand, and of course, I knew who that was.

Tammy: She wanted to keep her identity secret.

Jane: I really wasn't aware of who she was. If it hadn't been for my friend . . . She nearly went into orbit when I told her on the phone who was coming, and it still didn't mean anything to me, because I hadn't earlier read her books, but I went and got several, and she autographed all of them. It was nice to have them autographed by her with a little inscription.[175]

Earl: When she arrived, she went to the Chamber of Commerce in Orlando, and they had a special vehicle to bring her over, and they came and picked her up and took her back. I thought, you've got to have a little status before the Chamber of Commerce does that.

How long did the O'Connors stay with you?

Jane: About two or three nights.[176]

Do you remember your first meeting with Ayn Rand?

Tammy: Yes, they came that morning, and we all went out to breakfast. I was in awe that she traveled around the world. That, to me as a child, was really neat. I was only eleven or twelve at the time. We were told, as children, to be quiet, because people were coming for the weekend, and they needed a personal life, so we were not to interfere. But Big Mouth me never listened. I was a very independent child. I was outgoing. I never was quiet.

Jane: Tammy is a very vivacious, talkative person. She's always been that way.

What did you call her?

Tammy: Mrs. O'Connor.

---

175 Miss Rand signed book dedications to members of the Vaught family. One in *Atlas Shrugged* reads, "To Mr. and Mrs. Earl W. Vaught—with many thanks for your gracious courtesy 'above and beyond the call of duty'—Cordially, Ayn Rand 8/20/69."

176 The O'Connors stayed with the Vaughts July 14 and 15.

What did you talk to her about?

Tammy: We mainly talked about stamps, and things I'd done at school, and my friends. She was interested in the stamps that I collected from different people. She thought it was odd that I actually collected them in an album. She had always kept hers in a great big box. She wanted to know how did I get a book to put the stamps in.

Jane: She was excited about starting to do that when she went back to New York.

Tammy, why did you start collecting stamps and when was it?

Tammy: I started collecting when I was about four or five. My grandmother had given me some really old, old stamps that were in a drawer. I just thought it was neat that they looked different from the stamps I saw as a child, and so I collected them. Later, somebody gave me an album for my birthday. The stamps were organized by year, and I tried to get as many as I could to match up to the different countries. And that's how I began to learn where the different countries were, as I was growing up.

Mrs. O'Connor thought it was neat that I wanted the stamps from around the world. At that age, it's hard to believe that the world's so big.

How long did you collect stamps?

Till I was about seventeen.

Why did you stop?

Because I got married, had a son and just got busy, but I did keep them all. I have all of the stamps that Ayn Rand gave me, and I have all of my first-day of issues from the space shots.

Do you remember her sending you a key ring of the British Guiana one-cent stamp as a gift?

What she actually sent me were the stamps that she would tear off the letters from people who wrote to her.

How would you describe the nature of your relationship?

I know this may sound very odd, and I don't want it to be a put-down, but I was so young, I didn't know her as an artist; I knew her as a friend, through the stamps, and things like that. It was more of a grandmother, or an older person, that just took an interest in you, and just kept in touch. I don't think as a child I had any idea of how famous she was. She didn't act like a famous person. At that age, I didn't know of her work.

What was it like having a relationship with a famous person?

I thought that was neat. They would take the time to talk to you. But, of course, at that time, you have to realize, an eleven-year-old doesn't realize how famous a person really is, other than what the adults have told them.

Mr. Vaught, what did you think of Tammy having a friendship with a famous author?

Earl: We were impressed, of course. I was really surprised that somebody of Ayn Rand's status would utilize her time writing to my daughter.

What was the later relationship between Tammy and Miss Rand?

She corresponded with Tammy a long time, but Jane and I weren't really that involved in it. Tammy is a very independent person, so she wrote and corresponded back.

Did you ever see her again after that visit?

Tammy: We wrote and she talked to me on the phone, but not real often. She called me, probably three times. She called me to see if I got my stamps and if we were doing okay. Once she sent me a magazine that had stamps in it, and I think she called to see if the package arrived.

Earl: She later sent Tammy a package of stamps. She had her secretary cut them out of correspondence she got from foreign countries. The secretary would send an envelopeful at a time, to us. Miss Rand didn't have to do it, and it was nice of her to do it.

Tammy, do you remember sending Mrs. O'Connor some astronaut stamps?

Tammy: Yes. I have the same ones. I had a first-day of issue of each of the shots that went up. Any of the NASA first-day of issues she had, from probably that year for the next five years, were from me. I made sure I sent her a copy when I got mine.

Why did your correspondence with Miss Rand stop?

Just that as a kid I got busy, and I never was a letter-writer.

Do you remember reading Miss Rand's article in the Minkus Stamp Journal *called "Why I Like Stamp Collecting"?*

Yes. I thought it was neat that somebody had written about that topic and put it in the magazine. I was just fascinated for it to be in print.

How did Miss Rand and Mr. O'Connor act toward your children?

Earl: I was surprised about her not having children, because she seemed to be so good with them.

What about Mr. O'Connor?

Earl: He was good with the children. He was nice.

Jane: She seemed to enjoy the children so much. They were swimming in our pool, and she just enjoyed listening to them laughing. She gave Tammy a small gift, a small key ring.

Tammy: Mother had taken it as a key ring and turned it into a necklace for me. Mom said I wore it as a necklace for a long time.

Mr. Vaught, did Miss Rand talk with you about your work for NASA?

Earl: We discussed a little bit what my job was. At that time I was an engineer on the ground-support equipment, which is the swing arms and the hold-down arms.

Tell me about their visit to NASA for the liftoff of Apollo 11.

Jane took them in the motor home down to get the bus to go out to the space center. To get out to the Cape, NASA ran a special bus from here in town.

Do you remember anything about their reaction to the liftoff of Apollo 11?

Tammy: They were just fascinated; all of us were. I believe they had VIP passes, and went over to a special viewing area.

Earl: Mr. O'Connor was very impressed by it all. They were both very impressed.

What else do you remember about Ayn Rand?

Tommy: She was a very interesting person to talk to, with her background and her experiences.

What did she tell you?

How life was in Russia prior to her getting out, which was quite different than what you had read in the history books . . . the difficulties of life in the country at that time.

What did she tell you about her life?

Jane: About the oppression in Russia.

Earl: She talked some about the railroads and other problems, and I'm very conservative, particularly with the problems of the railroad, because at about that time, what she wrote in *Atlas Shrugged* about what happened to the railroad, where it was just flat broke, was sort of what she predicted. So it was interesting.

She was really opposed to welfare. We discussed that some, because over here in the South, we have a lot of people on welfare. We more or less agreed that we can't keep the world. I was very impressed by her. I'm a conservative myself, so I fit into her ideas fairly well.

She told us she was a Russian Jew and that she came to this country as a young girl, went to work for Cecil DeMille, and that's where she met her husband.

How was she when she talked to you?

Earl: A real nice, easy-going, down-to-my-level person.

What did you talk to Mr. O'Connor about? What was your impression of him?

Jane: He didn't talk a lot. He just was there when she was talking, and he was just sort of quiet. Frank was thin, tall. He was a little bit frail. He always spoke to the children. He seemed to like them.

Earl: I'll tell you what we did have here that impressed her: a series of books by Victor Hugo. I guess that was one of her favorite authors.

What else did the O'Connors do while staying at your home?

Jane: She didn't meet anybody, especially the press. She said that after she left, we would be more than welcome to tell the press she had been here, but she didn't want them to know at the time she was here.

Did she say why?

Yes, she just didn't want the publicity; she just wanted to be left alone while she was here. One of my friends was quite a fan of hers and had read all of her books, so my friend wanted to meet her, and I told her that Miss Rand didn't want to. She begged me to ask her. Miss Rand said, "I'll meet two or three of your friends, but it has to be just very private." My friend brought a friend with her and we could ask Ayn Rand questions, and she talked with us quite some time that night.

What did you and your friends talk with Miss Rand about that night?

Jane: They asked her a lot of questions. They were mostly interested in her philosophy, and she did not believe at all in the welfare programs, and she explained why, which was very logical. It seemed selfish, at first, but it's not, the way she explained it.

I remember that she had on a ring that had several rubies in it, and some diamonds, and it was for, I think, her fortieth wedding anniversary. Her husband had given her this ring, and each ruby signified a year. They were very devoted. You could tell that they were very close, and that they meant so much to each other.

Were there any photographs taken of Miss Rand with your family?

No, we didn't even think of it. I have an article out of the paper. After she left, I told the reporter of our small local paper, and she wrote a column about them being here.[177]

What was Ayn Rand like as a guest?

They were very quiet, except when we talked to them. She liked to have her coffee the first thing in the morning. My mother was visiting with us that weekend, and I frankly was terrified, because Ayn Rand was such a celebrity, and I just didn't know what to say half the time, so my mother, who could just talk to anybody and wasn't at all nervous, took her coffee in every morning.

After I found out who she was, I was so impressed I was scared to death of her, because I hadn't been around that many people who had written books, and I just was in awe of her, but she put you at ease. She was a very, very easy person to talk to, actually. She made you feel comfortable. She was a fascinating person.

In what way?

She told us a lot about her beliefs and her life, and her husband also

---

177 There were two small articles in late July 1969.

was fascinating. He was an artist and had illustrated the front of one of her books.[178]

Tommy: She was very polite, a very comfortable person. I felt she was very approachable, when I'd be talking to her. She and her husband were very easy to talk to.

Earl: We felt she was really a nice person. You stop and think about it—somebody that's opposed to welfare, you might think she'd be sort of harsh, but she wasn't. We didn't think that and were pleased with everything she did. We were real pleased with them. They were nice house guests. They were just easy. Didn't ask for a whole lot of things, didn't complain about anything, and my house probably did not compare to theirs.

Tammy: A quiet couple that had come to visit, and were friendly. They were very nice to us, and wrote back to us, and as children, would talk to us. They were just a nice friendly, elderly couple. To me, as an eleven-year-old child, she would be an elderly person. She was just very quiet and soft-spoken, but she answered any questions very openly. She would sit down and talk to you.

She would hold a conversation with us, whereas, some of the people who stayed with us just came as guests, and you were there just as children. They didn't hold a conversation or anything with you. Mrs. O'Connor talked to me, and we sat down and she would go through things, and she would come to see my bedroom, and walk through the house with us, and watch us swim in the pool, and things like that. She was like a friend.

---

178 It was the 1968 twenty-fifth-anniversary edition of *The Fountainhead*.

Duncan Scott

Duncan Scott is a film director and producer who edited the restored version of the 1942 Italian film of *We the Living* (in two parts, titled *Noi Vivi* and *Addio Kira*).

Interview dates: August 18, 1997; July 19 and December 16, 1999

Scott McConnell: *When did Miss Rand start working on the* We the Living *movie?*

    Duncan Scott: In 1969. I had two or three work sessions with her.

How did you become associated with her in the first place?

    I had never heard of her until I saw her on *The Tonight Show* with Johnny Carson in 1967. I responded so immediately to everything she was saying, even though it was a lightweight sort of talk show. It was like fireworks went off in my mind, responding to her ideas. "Revelation" is not too strong a word to use. I ran out the next morning and bought my first Ayn Rand book, *The Virtue of Selfishness*.

    I was subscribing to *The Objectivist Newsletter* when, in the June 1968 issue, on the back page, there was a brief announcement that Henry Mark Holzer and Erika Holzer [then Ayn Rand's attorneys] had found the long-thought-to-be-lost Italian film of *We the Living*, and were bringing it back to the United States to be re-edited and released in America for the first time. The Holzers were the people who made the decision to find the film, and went ahead, investing their time and resources, searching for the film. It was quite an involved process and took them about two years, I think.

    I was a 21-year-old assistant film editor at the time the announcement came out, I wrote the Holzers a letter and I got a response that the arrangement Henry Holzer had with someone to re-edit *We the Living* had fallen through, and he was looking for help with the re-editing of the film, and that he'd like to meet me.

    We had a meeting in his offices in the Empire State Building. He had an arrangement with Ayn Rand that the film would be re-edited and that certain changes would be made. I got hired to do the editorial changes to the film. My involvement in the film over the years grew quite a bit, as my own career grew.

How did you meet Miss Rand?

After I was hired, a meeting was set up to run the film and discuss, in a general sense, the changes that were to be made. When the film was first made, the fascist authorities, who controlled the film industry in Italy, forced the studio to add some propaganda here and there into the story line, and that stuff had to come out. I made an arrangement with the company I was working for, Thomas Craven Films, to use their equipment in the evening so that we could run the film there. There were six or eight people in addition to Ayn Rand and the Holzers and myself. Chairs were arranged in a semicircle in front of a television monitor. We had this big, bulky black-and-white camera pointed at the tiny screen of a Moviola, which is a professional editing machine, that was running the 35-millimeter film. It was kind of a crude setup.

We had to run the film in order to discuss it, and we had to run it on a Moviola, which has a screen that's only about five inches diagonally; it's designed primarily for a single film editor to use. Obviously, for a group as large as we were, there was no way we could all look at a screen that small. And everyone thought: wouldn't it be a great idea to get this film on this newfangled video—new for home use anyway.

So we videotaped the Moviola screen and used the larger television monitor as the way for this group to look at it. Of course, every twenty minutes we had to take a reel off and put a new reel on.

Another thing that made the screening quite unusual was that there were no subtitles on the film; it was entirely in Italian. There was a very rough translation on paper, and Erika Holzer read the dialogue as the movie went along. This was pretty challenging for Erika, because she also had to have a pretty good sense of what the actor was saying in Italian.

As you can imagine, it was quite a long evening; the original running time of the entire film was close to four hours.

Was this the first time you met Ayn Rand?

That's right. I was a pretty young guy and the thought of meeting my hero totally filled me with awe. As soon as I met her, though, I felt completely at ease. It's not that she made any particular attempt to put me at ease. It was just that when somebody is extremely straightforward and obviously has no agenda or anything like that, they are what they appear to be, and that's something that puts me at ease. She was clearly there for a definite purpose and was happy to be there. She had a lot of energy and enthusiasm and optimism about this project, and that was conveyed very quickly upon meeting her.

She didn't care that you were only twenty-one?

I didn't get any sense of her reacting to my age. The perception
was that I was really going to be carrying out instructions that were
being worked out. The reality is—and I have no idea if she was aware
of this or not—the editorial process is a lot more than just "Okay, go do
this." It's figuring out how to make certain editorial changes work once
you say, "Oh, I want this scene to be changed." So, in a certain way,
there is a remarkable amount of creativity in how you go about making
those changes. If you were to give the same challenge to ten different
editors, they would very likely solve it in ten different ways. There were
things that had to be changed in the film, and they were the crux of the
discussions at these work sessions with Miss Rand and the Holzers.

One thing I was quite struck with is how immediately Ayn Rand
grasped editing principles and how little explaining I had to do. I know
she wrote screenplays and so forth, but that's not the same. A lot of
people in the film industry don't understand film editing. It's a very
difficult craft to understand unless you've actually done it.

This was all happening while you were viewing the film?

I don't think we went into the actual creative discussion that first
night, because just getting through the entire film was such a long
process. Primarily, it was a viewing. Ayn Rand had not seen it, I believe,
in many years.[179]

What was Miss Rand's reaction on seeing the movie?

Mainly, she was very happy with it, but there were reactions to
the horrendous and obvious additional things that had been forced
into the film by the fascist authorities in Italy. Even someone who was
not familiar with Ayn Rand would have winced at these things. They
were completely misfit into the script. I mean, characters completely
contradicted themselves. The fascists decided that the heroic figure
of Andrei must make a speech in support of the Collective. Actually,
there was dialogue something to the effect of bashing America, and so
forth, that was added into the script in Andrei's climactic speech. It was
ludicrous.

These insertions were so crude, it was clear that they had to come
out, and it was obvious that she just thought they were awful. It was
more like how one might react to a child acting up. There was no real

179 In 1948 Miss Rand saw a print of the film and tried to get it remade in Hollywood.

anger or anything like that on her part. It was silly, actually, ludicrous and silly, the things that had been put in there.

We all felt that most of these changes would not be that difficult to make. Some would, of course, but there was a confidence that there was a beautiful film in there and it was a matter of getting these sections out—restoring the film to more truly represent the book.

Tell me more about the meetings with Miss Rand where you discussed editing the film.

Those were much more intimate work sessions. Only Miss Rand and the Holzers and I were there. At those sessions we actually huddled around the Moviola with the five-inch diagonal screen. We ran it backwards and forwards and discussed what needed to be done to various scenes. In many cases it was simply a matter of cutting the bad scene out in its entirety. And with other scenes it was cutting out certain dialogue. And then there were a few cases where it was more complex than that.

Another form of editing we used was to rerecord certain dialogue for characters in Italian to match the original recording. So I went back to Italy, and we cast actors whose voices were as close as we could get, particularly to the character of Andrei. New dialogue was written by Erika Holzer. We got started on the work and we did a lot of the straightforward editorial work, but in the early '70s the work stopped when Miss Rand was not available to work with us. She assured the Holzers that she would return to the project eventually. Hank Holzer didn't want to proceed without her involvement. The movie had been originally produced without her involvement, and Hank wasn't going to let that happen a second time. But she died before ever coming back to finish it.

How much had been completed by then?

Most of the serious work had been done. Going to Italy and recording an actor doing new dialogue for Andrei's critical speech was done after her death, after we resumed the restoration process. The other thing done after her death was the adding of the subtitles to the film, which was no small task. We frequently went back to the novel and, wherever possible, made the subtitles reflect the actual dialogue or, at least, the spirit of the novel.

Did Miss Rand ever tell you what she thought of the movie?

She was extremely happy with the way Andrei was portrayed, although the actor portraying him was much older than she had envisioned. And she was very happy with the way Alida Valli portrayed Kira. I think she had mixed feelings about Rossano Brazzi.

Why?

He was too damn pretty! At the original screening, a few people commented—or joked—about how pretty Brazzi looked in the film and, as I recall, she concurred. But, I got the sense that she was satisfied with his acting.

What was Miss Rand like to work with?

Oh, a delight. I started out, as I told you, as a somewhat intimidated young guy meeting this heroic figure. I found it very stimulating. She was very decisive about what she wanted to do, and that made it easy for me, because there was a lot of clarity about what we were going to do in each scene. She was just very pleasant, very quick to understand, like when I would explain what could be done with editing and how certain shots could be juxtaposed and how we could remove sound from one scene and add it to another.

In the original version of the film, Andrei does not commit suicide, as he does in the book. He is heartbroken: he realizes what his life has meant and not meant and he's lost Kira and he's staring into the fireplace. Then the authorities are sent to Andrei's home. They bust down his door and shoot him.

Miss Rand said, "How do you undo this? I really want him to have committed suicide as it was in my book." I made a suggestion. In the scene where Andrei is staring into the fireplace, he actually takes out the nightgown he was going to give to Kira and he tosses it on the fire, and he's throwing other things on the fire, and he looks down at his gun. Now all of that is certainly a very good set-up: that he's considering committing suicide. The filmmakers obviously wanted you to think he was considering suicide. I suggested that we juxtapose a few shots and remove some others. We had him looking at his gun, going back to the fireplace; then we added the sound of a gun shot. And, as you continue to see the nightgown burning in the fire, you realize that he's killed himself. Then we eliminated the scene where the authorities break down the door and shoot him.

Explaining that to her was a very easy process, because she understood, right away, this shot will go here, that shot will go there, that will achieve the desired change. She understood all this quickly and approved it quickly. The work sessions went extremely fast compared to what I thought might happen. I couldn't actually do the changes while she was there. It's too time-consuming a process.

Now, the movie had been shot in a fairly haphazard way. They had thrown the script out just before filming, and new script pages were being written the day before filming. As a result of that style of production, scenes were not tight; pieces of dialogue that served no purpose were slowing down the story. It was just sloppy screenwriting. As Miss Rand, the Holzers and I went through the movie, we discussed this, scene by scene, line by line.

Many years later, after Ayn Rand's death, Leonard Peikoff reviewed everything in great detail, and approved all the subtitles and the speeches.

Did she have any other important changes—in addition to Andrei's suicide scene?

Yes, Andrei's speech to the tribunal. It was crucial that that scene be in there, but it had to have different dialogue. It had to be restored. The scene exists in the book, but in the movie the dialogue was badly twisted and distorted to fit fascist goals. In the original film, an official complains that Andrei "doesn't have the courage to face reality." And then Andrei says—and this is one speech that she very much objected to—"Which reality? Yours? We shed blood along a road we thought straight and luminous, so that everyone could walk with pride and their head held high. Instead, on that same road, you have cast a shadow, and all our efforts in the mud, so as to sell it one day to our masters, the middle classes. This is what your ideal amounts to. Your aims, the servitude of the Russian people to foreign capitalism."

In order to fix that dialogue, I went to Rome, hired an actor who sounded like Andrei, and recorded new Italian dialogue that reflected the original dialogue from her novel. We had to write it so that it would roughly match the original lip movements. So it was dubbed into the movie and replaced the objectionable dialogue.

Other important editing included the removal of the original ending to the film. As shot, it was a very literal rendering of her escape attempt in the snow, across the border, and unlike the book, it evoked nothing; really, it was so clumsy. In a long shot, you see somebody in a very fake-looking snow scene walking along; you hear a shot ring out—boom!—this body topples over, and that's it. No dialogue, none of the inner thoughts, as the book has it, of what was going on in her mind, what it meant to be trying for freedom, whether she made it or not—none of that was conveyed. You never saw a guard, you never saw anything; you just saw the figure walking in the snow; a shot rings out, the figure falls over, "The End" fades in. So we ended the film where Kira pauses by a tree and remembers when she first met Leo. She then walks out of frame, and we know she is on her way to the border.

Another change was made in the beginning of the film, where a number of characters had been established as part of a subplot, and it was decided that these subplots were not handled very well—in contrast to the main story line with Kira, Leo and Andrei. Plus, the subplots added to a very long running time to the film, so it was decided that they should be cut out.

Can you remember some of the subplots that were cut?

Yes. One was the Sasha and Irina story. It was not well executed in the movie. Also, inexplicably, some important parts of their story line were never filmed at all. One example is the very poignant scene in the book when they are put on separate trains and sent to the labor camps.

There was also the scene where Leo and Kira are trying to escape, in which guards who stormed the ship are kicking a bunch of nuns on the ground. Gratuitous things like that, presumably to show what monsters the Soviets were, because that's what the Italian propaganda machine wanted to show at that point, and so they would add things that were outside the context of the book.

And of course, in most cases, it actually wasn't too hard to cut these things out, because they were so clumsily dropped in. The film actually just kept getting better and better as we cut these things out.

Miss Rand was pleased that there were other ways to deal with these problems. I recall her saying that she was concerned about the integrity of the story, if we cut out scenes with the objectionable dialogue. I remember telling her that, in my opinion, we could maintain the integrity of the story, or even restore it, not by just cutting scenes, but also by restoring dialogue within scenes. She seemed pleased with that.

The restored *We the Living* finally had its premiere at the Telluride Film Festival in Colorado in 1986—the first public showing of the film in the U.S.A. Soon after, it was released in theaters throughout the U.S., Canada and overseas. By and large, the film received terrific reviews. Looking back, my only regret is that Ayn Rand didn't live to see how beautifully the film turned out.

Eloise Huggins

Eloise Huggins supervised the O'Connor home and planned and cooked their meals from 1965 to 1982. Mrs. Huggins died in 1997.

Interview dates: September 4, 6, 10, 17, 1996, and February 19, 1997

Scott McConnell: *How did you meet Ayn Rand?*

Eloise Huggins: It was a strange thing. I had come from British Guiana in South America, where my father was a headmaster of his own school, a Christian school. I came to the U.S. with the purpose of working in a hospital. I had worked in a hospital in South America and had a certificate as a dietician. I went into the food business and caring for sick people. I came to the U.S. about thirty years ago. When you come to the U.S., it's hard at first, but you have to live, because in this country, no one gives you anything. And I looked after two little girls for a while. One day I went down to the laundry and met this woman who was doing laundry, and we started to talk. She did cleaning for Ayn Rand and said that Miss Rand wanted somebody to supervise her house and plan her meals and so on. She gave me Ayn Rand's phone number and I called her. I had some good references, and she interviewed me.

What year was that?

It must have been 1965.[180]

What was your first impression of Ayn Rand?

She was just a person. She had a heavy Russian accent and wasn't somebody you looked at and liked right away. You had to know her. Quite different from her husband, Frank O'Connor. You looked at him and he's such a likeable guy. He made you feel at home right away. But there was something about her that was stiff. She seemed to shut out the world while concentrating on her writings.

So you were hired. What was your position?

I did the cooking, and she and I would get together, and we would plan menus for a week. I would order groceries or sometimes buy them myself. I liked walking and shopping around Third Avenue and

---

180 On August 2, 1965, Ayn Rand noted on her calendar, "Eloise starting."

Lexington, and so I went out myself. They liked an Italian market, called Verdi's, a very exclusive market that had a lot of unusual things. We did a lot of shopping there. Frank and I sometimes went there.

What was he like to shop with?

He liked really to shop by himself, but when I went out with him, which was very seldom, I was able to save him from himself. He would pick up things that we really didn't need. And I said "We really don't need that," and he said, "Yes, you're right." Things like gourmet food and bottled stuff. He would buy something and then wouldn't use it.

Were you happy with your work conditions?

Yes. In the first years I was not, because this is not what I wanted to do, but eventually when I realized that I just couldn't leave them like that, I sort of made myself comfortable. I had opportunities to leave them, but I'm not that type of person. I cannot do this. They would have survived, but I would not have survived in my memory to have done that.

I got really hooked with these people. I didn't think that I would be working so long in the type of job that I didn't plan to do in the first place, but I got involved with them and that was it.

Did the O'Connors seem to appreciate you?

Yes. She would say things like, "I don't know what I would do without you."

What exactly was your relationship with Miss Rand? You sound like much more than a housekeeper.

We were friends, actually, which was why I felt so disappointed that she didn't leave me anything in her will. I was with her seventeen years, and during the first five years, it was just being a housekeeper and planning meals and doing some shopping and ordering stuff, and all of that. After she had cancer surgery [January 1975], that sort of broke her, and we became close. From then, her nurse went away. I took over and I did very personal things for her and our whole relationship changed. She became more gentle, more understanding, she seemed more human, like a woman. She started to tell me things; she'd talk to me about her feelings, and we would go for walks together, like at six o'clock in the afternoon. I'd get her dressed and we'd go out and walk several blocks in the neighborhood and come back home. She looked forward to that. She depended on me; we went everywhere together after that illness. When she went out, I went with her.

In some ways you probably knew Ayn Rand better than anyone did.

I think so. Because I was so closely connected to her in very personal ways, especially after she became ill, she depended on me. She leaned on me a lot. I sort of saw her as a person, not famous, not as Ayn Rand. I saw her as just a regular human being who had feelings and needs just like everybody else.

How would you describe her personality?

She was really a very private person and she never gave out that much. You know there are people who talk a lot. From the time they come in, they are this personality. She was not one of those. She was quiet, intense, but more on the quiet side.

She was a very stable person—dependable. She was honest. I don't think she would indulge in deceptions. She was a very straightforward person.

Did she have a sense of humor?

Oh yes, she did. She and Frank saw jokes where other people wouldn't, and then you could really see with them and could laugh together. Both of them had that kind of humor.

Did Ayn Rand change over the years?

She changed in that she toned down her life in some of the things that she was lecturing about. She cut it down a lot, to almost nil.

Did her personality or character change at all?

No. No.

What about her clothing or dressing? Did she have any interesting or different ways of doing things?

No, but she never liked to buy new stuff. She had some old things in good condition, but she seemed to be quite content, not want to buy new things. She never really liked shopping. She was not one of those women that liked to run around going to stores. Very seldom would she want to go into a store and look around. If it was something that she really had to have. But a woman's hobby of shopping around or window shopping, she never did that. She was not one of these people who thought about herself; she didn't think much about personal things. Not that she didn't like to wear something good, but the time that it takes to get yourself something good, she couldn't spare.

What about makeup and things like that?

Makeup, just a little, not much. She never really paid much attention to herself in that way. No, but she saw her hair dresser regularly.

The times that I was there she started putting on weight. It was a constant battle with her. She really struggled to lose weight, but it wasn't happening and she always wore oversized clothing—more or less protective—because of weight.

Did she say anything about you both being immigrants and coming to America?

She told me about her coming to America. She did talk about the difference between America compared to Russia and what a change of life it was for her. She really did enjoy living in America. The change, the freedoms, the very fact that you can eat everything. She really did like fine dining. It was really a big change for her.

What did she tell you about her life in Russia?

Her life in Russia was one of yearning to get out of Russia. She spoke mainly about details, little things. The shortages of foods. It was a starvation kind of life. Those were things she kept talking about. She always made comparisons between America and Russia, the oppression of the communist life. The grandeur, not really money-wise but the things the most ordinary person could get, the comfort. She never got over the freedoms and comforts of America.

Did she talk about her family?

No. I didn't even know that she had a sister until they corresponded. In lots of ways she was a very, very private person. But there were times when she would get into a mood where she wanted to reminisce. Then suddenly she would be aware of what she was saying; I could be wrong, but this is the impression I got. And there were times when she let herself go and other times that she clammed up and she didn't really want to talk. When she started to write her last book, I was with her when she had lot of paper and just wrote; she said to me, "This may very well be the last book that I write." And I didn't know what to say to something like that.

She's not a person that you could just tell her what she wanted to hear. About "not suffering fools gladly"? I would have applied that statement to her. She would prefer you to be honest before you be foolish.

After she had her illness, she'd never really get into any long conversations. She would be short but precise, and I remember that she had to lecture in New Orleans, and I went with her, and we sort of got close there. She never liked flying; she always thought she would be hijacked. She always said that if she got hijacked to Russia, she would never come out again. She felt that the very anti-Russia things she wrote about would make her a marked woman. A very wealthy man got a special railroad car put on a train for her, and we went to New Orleans by this special car, which was very exciting for me. I've never done anything like that in my life, and during that time we talked a lot.

Did you ever watch Ayn Rand when she was on the talk shows, such as Phil Donahue?

She was always very much herself on TV and very on top of what she was saying. Nobody could put one over on her.

So she was the same on TV as she was in her living room?

Yes.

Who would be her most constant visitor?

Leonard, of course. She saw him a lot. I think if she would have had a son, it would've been Leonard.

Who after Leonard was closest to Miss Rand?

I think he was the last person. I can't really remember anybody else. She was not a person that really got very close to people. I know one of her good friends was Alan Greenspan, because many nights he came to dinner. He was a very nice person too.

Did she convince you to read her books?

No, she didn't have to, but when I went there, I didn't even know about her writing. But I have always read; that is a part of my life. So when I realized who she was, she gave me a hardcover of

The Fountainhead, and I read it and I realized what a great writer she was. Then I read everything she wrote. She gave me copies of her books and autographed them.

Take me through your normal day with Miss Rand.

She always slept late. She sometimes wouldn't get up until 10, 11 AM. Frank got up early, not when he was sick and really couldn't take care of himself, but when he was well. He always let me in. I didn't get there until noon. They were not breakfast people, who would have a meal in the morning. She would always have a pot of coffee going and that's all she needed, and he would have a cup of coffee. He didn't have anything either. I was really there to prepare their main meal, and eventually I found myself doing all the housekeeping. They wrote checks, but I more or less decided what was needed for the house, in addition to preparing meals. Apart from meals there were other things that had to be bought, cleaning stuff, different things. So I was in charge of that.

Once we entertained fourteen people. I think it was connected with publishing, people that she was involved with, and there was a big spread. I prepared for days, and it was a buffet. Everybody ate, talked and had a good time; then I cleared up and left them.

How was Miss Rand during all this?

She was very hospitable to them and very nice. She really could let herself go and get into things when she wanted to.

And Mr. O'Connor?

He always tried to enjoy himself until the end of his life. He always lived life fully.

How would your typical day conclude? You'd talk, you'd prepare meals, and what else?

I'd make the dinner, and really she and I didn't have much to talk about because there was Frank and I. We would talk. He too told me a lot about his earlier days. He would talk about when he was young, about his family and California.

She would tell me things about Russia and about her first coming to America and living in California—what a different life. She never could stop comparing what it was to be here to what it was there.

I always paid attention, and I read a lot, and she and I would talk about places and things that I've read about, and I've been a couple places. My daughter in England lived in Singapore for a while, so I've been there. And Brazil.

And you would tell Miss Rand about that?

Yes. But, she really never got into it. She would listen and we'd talk about it for a little while, but her work and what she was doing were what really held her attention.

I remember the last thing before she took really ill. She started to write a screenplay, and she'd written about ten pages.[181] I don't know what the name of the book was, but what I can say is that when she got ideas and wanted to write, she would sit down there and write sheet after sheet and pages of ideas.

I don't know what the book was about, but she was very enthusiastic about what she was writing, because the ideas came to her and she just wrote. She wrote rapidly. And then a couple days passed, and that was it. And she really got ill; that was the end of it. When she got into that, it was like she was completely unaware of anyone else or anything.

When she wrote lectures, she would sometimes write something and then just discard it and write again because she was very meticulous about what she did. So even if it was just a small speaking engagement she put a lot into it. She always had a certain standard, and she always liked to keep to that standard.

She was a very private person and shy in lots of ways—unless she was talking about something that she was really interested in. She couldn't just get into a next-door neighbor or even Eloise's family. But she wasn't the type of person to really get involved with too many people in depth. Just on the surface, because of her work.

How would the day close?

They never had dinner until seven o'clock, so by the time I was finished, I often didn't leave until 9 o'clock PM.

What were the O'Connors' favorite foods?

She brought a lot of recipes from Russia. I'm not flattering myself, but I'm a very good cook. I took a lot of her recipes that she brought from Russia and modified them. When I saw the recipe and saw what

---

181 Ayn Rand was working on the script for a miniseries of *Atlas Shrugged*; she did her last writing for it on January 1, 1982.

it called for, I invented a little bit and she would say to me, "You know, this tastes so much nicer."

When I first went to work for her, she had liked a Russian soup called borscht, but I improved on the recipe. It was kind of tasteless to me, and you know with cooking you never have to follow a recipe.

After I started to cook other American things for them they got out of that Russian thing, because some of the recipes are so long, and so much work had to go into the preparation. There was cabbage. You'd make a special dough and roll the cabbage in or something like that. That took hours and eventually I cut down the time. I found a shorter way of doing it. That was a Russian thing she liked very much and she did compliment me on it, but, you know, in America we have so much more to work with than they had in Russia.

Did Frank O'Connor like Russian food?

Not particularly. He ate almost everything, and in the first years when he got hungry, he ate heartily whatever was presented to him. I remember he did like a steak. He liked American food, like baked potatoes and broccoli and a nice dessert. He liked pies, and I made them very good apple pie. He told me that he liked it, and I made it quite often for them.

She liked exotic fruit and chocolates. She especially liked Lady Godiva and would always take great pleasure in a box of Godiva chocolates. She bought a pound box and she would eat them sparingly, like two at a time.

Did Miss Rand regret smoking?

Not really. I can't say she regretted smoking, but what I can say is that I've never seen anybody come off of it like she did. It was in the twinkle of an eye. When she discovered that she had cancer, she didn't even say, "Let me take a last cigarette." She threw out all two and a half cartons in the garbage, and I rescued them and gave them to somebody I knew who smoked, because they were not opened.

That I admired about her. Because there are a lot of people out there who know how harmful smoking is and they cannot make the decision to give it up. And even if they give it up, they get back into it. It draws them. But she was so determined, and she never one day said, "Oh, I wish I had a cigarette." She didn't mention it again. It was as if it had never existed in her life. It was just like something she had never done.

I was told that Ayn Rand once said to you that she thought of you as her sister?

Yes, I believe so. I made a very special sacrifice, which many times I've regretted; but I don't know, maybe I should have been there to try to win her over to becoming a Christian. Maybe God had me there for a purpose.

Do you have any photographs of you with Miss Rand or Frank O'Connor?

Oh, no, we never took any pictures together. She always said as she got older she felt she wouldn't photograph well. I have never taken any pictures of myself. I have pictures of me when I was younger, but not within the last twenty years.

You also became friends with Mr. O'Connor?

Oh yes, very good friends.

What did the two of you talk about?

He talked about his work, his art. He talked about the times they lived in California, he talked about flowers, he loved cats, he found a lot of interest in little things. Just everyday things, he could make a whole conversation. It was not around big ideas, or philosophy; it was just little everyday things. I would say something about my life in South America, and he would take one hour to talk to me about one little thing that I told him about South America. He was a fascinating man. He had a lot of patience and understanding, and there isn't anything too much that I can say about Frank O'Connor.

What did he love so much about the ranch in California?

I really can't remember the details now. It's been a long time, but he loved . . . he just loved California. He was free and unhampered; he was more in touch with nature and about being free in open spaces.

He always spoke of the home in California, things he used to do, and the trees and the garden they had and all of that. So I don't think he was quite happy to be in an apartment in New York, but what was important to her was to him.

Frank O'Connor . . . I think he's the most wonderful man that I ever knew. His last days, I believe, I'm not sure, he suffered from

Alzheimer's, which affected his memory.[182] But he enjoyed his life, I think, tremendously, up to a certain time when he didn't even know who he was anymore, after he became ill.

What's your strongest memory of Frank O'Connor?

I just know overall he was kind, he was gentle, he was understanding, he was not given to strong anger. Overall he was such a comfortable person to be with. You felt good around him. He was the kindest person that I ever knew. Oh, I liked him. To me he was a wonderful guy. Really, really, wonderful. He was a real gentleman.

How did Mr. O'Connor consider your relationship? Were you like his sister, his best friend?

We were good friends. When he felt he wanted to let go or would feel unsatisfied, he would talk to me. I think he felt comfortable with me.

Tell me about Frank O'Connor and music.

Yes, he was a music lover. He liked good music, classical music. They had a lot of music from Russia.

Dance music or classical music?

Yes, classical. Kind of folk, Russian folk music, dance music.

How would you describe Mr. O'Connor's character?

I would say almost like his wife. I can't say Ayn Rand was a wonderful woman, but I can say Frank O'Connor was a wonderful man. I can say that she was an unusual person, but I wouldn't say "wonderful."

Was Mr. O'Connor a fancy dresser?

He was always well dressed. He wore simple things, always. He reminded me of an Englishman. English way of dressing. He was always well-dressed, even when he went out during the day. He never dressed casually.

He looked like a movie star. He always looked imposing, significant, somebody you gave a second look. I think he stood out in that kind of way. He wasn't someone that you just looked at casually. It was always

---

182 Frank O'Connor suffered from arteriosclerosis, which has symptoms similar to Alzheimer's.

that second look. He had that way about him.

Did Miss Rand like to look at him?

She'd talk about how he looked, how good-looking he was. She always talked about that. It would seem that she was fascinated by him. I remember pictures of her when she was younger, but apart from her eyes, I don't think she stood out like he did. She always said that she was lucky to be involved with him. She always felt that she was fortunate to meet a man that she could live with.

Did he want children?

I don't think so. Both of them said that they wouldn't have wanted children.

Did he love movies?

Yes. And they played card games a lot at night after I left. They played dominoes. Scrabble.

Did he read or watch TV?

He looked at TV once in a while, not in the day. In the day he would go for walks and then he would go to his studio and paint. He spent a lot of time there.

What other interesting little habits did Mr. O'Connor have?

He was funny. He would always see something funny where no one else would, and then suddenly you'd realize that this is funny. But you would not have seen the funny side of it if he didn't draw your attention to it.

What type of humor was it?

Just everyday, casual things. Maybe something about the cats, but he would laugh. Just even walking the street, he would find someone that was odd and he would be amused. Just ordinary things. He could find humor in them.

Would you call Mr. O'Connor confident?

Yes, he was. He was a confident man. He was always sure of himself.

Any stories about Mr. O'Connor and cats?

He was very devoted to them, and at first, it was three, and then two. And the cats liked them. It was just a mutual thing between the cats and between them. I got into the act because I cleaned the litter box. Frank liked to feed them and that was it. We never had a smell in there.

What did he do with them?

They would sit and jump on him and climb all over him. She liked them too, but she didn't have time to play with them. But there was one cat that would be in her room with her for hours until she let her out and the cat went to the litter box.

Did Miss Rand have a favorite cat?

Morris the Cat. That was a TV favorite, and he used to be on television a lot. She liked that cat.

What did she like about him?

He was a very famous cat and almost human. He didn't stand for any nonsense and he was very assertive, knew what he wanted and she adored that cat.

Did Mr. O'Connor have any special games he played with the cats?

No, it was just loving them. He just liked to play with them, be close to them and pet them and all of that, and the cats liked that too.

Tell me about Frank O'Connor and painting.

He never talked about it much, but he was very intense in his work. He had the studio upstairs and he did his work up there.

How long would he be there?

Sometimes from twelve or one o'clock in the afternoon until their dinner time. He'd come down around six, and they'd eat around seven o'clock.

How was he when he came down from painting?

Very relaxed.

What did Frank O'Connor love about painting?

It was something that he could do. I think he liked what he was doing. It was something that involved him alone. It had nothing to do with writing or other people, it was just a part of Frank O'Connor.

Was he very much involved in his art?

Yes. He did very good work. I have one painting of his, a simple thing, but he put so much of himself into it.

What was Miss Rand's attitude to his paintings?

She always was very enthusiastic over anything that he did. Very. She really cared for her husband and there was no time in all those years that I can say that she was really angry. If there was anything, it was not for long; it wasn't prolonged.

Can you give an example?

When he went out and he did not come back for a long time, and she didn't know where he was, she got a little anxious and fretted a little about it. It was nothing that lasted for any length of time.

They were a loving couple. Very fond of each other, very concerned about each other. They took care of each other in lots of ways. He in his own way and she in her own way. He was always careful that we didn't disturb her, and he knew when she wouldn't want to be disturbed.

How was he with Miss Rand in his last days?

Sometimes he was aware, and sometimes he wasn't. I always had the impression she was not quite sure he was in that last stage. She didn't believe he was going to die, but she spent a lot of time alone with him in those last days.

How was Miss Rand during this period?

She was upset, but she was never one of these people who would show their feelings very actively. But I know she was upset because she sensed that his death was impending.

It must have been a terrible time for you all.

Yes, it was. I loved him a lot. He was a very nice man and one of the best people I've known in my life. It really amazes me that there could be anybody who could have said anything that was compromising about him, because he was such a gentle person and kind.

How did Miss Rand try to help him during this period?

She tried to be extra loving and talk with him, and that's how you would be with someone you love, try to comfort them.

How was Miss Rand after Mr. O'Connor died?

Her life went down rather quickly, because she didn't even realize how much she depended on him, until he died. And suddenly, it was downhill with her. She didn't see much left to live for and suddenly, I guess, she realized that death is so final. Whereas for me, it isn't.

Did you attend Mr. O'Connor's funeral?

Yes. For me, it was very sad. At the funeral, she was not emotional. She was very calm and composed, but I will never forget him lying there in that coffin and he looked so majestically dead. And it was a sad occasion. We went up to the place where they are both now buried, Valhalla. It was a long drive out of New York. I went with her. She was not overly emotional, but she was not that type of person anyway to break down and cry, but I think she felt it a lot. It was really like a tearing apart of the relationship—she really was very affected. That was a time too when she really began to think seriously, she would say things like "What is life? Life holds nothing much for me." She went down a lot in her way of thinking, living. I wouldn't say depressed, but she really got no joy anymore out of living.

Did she say anything to you about Mr. O'Connor after he died?

We would sit and talk about the things he used to do. She would say, "Frank said that" or "Frank did that" and "Do you remember this and that." Little things I can't ever remember, but the little casual things we would reminisce about. I encouraged her to talk about him, because it took her out of this depressed state of mind that she was in.

How was her attitude when she talked about those memories?

She sort of became herself, enthusiastic. It was just like he was still alive. We would talk about him like he had just gone somewhere; we never thought, "Oh, he's dead." We didn't focus on that. Although I tried to tell her that death is not the end of everything. I know that she thought that when you die that was it. You're dead and your mind is gone and your brain and everything and you cease to exist mentally and physically, but I don't believe that.

Did she say anything about your saying things like that?

No. I don't know how she would have been with anybody else, but our relationship had gotten to the stage where I would tell her what I believe and she would say, "It sounds good, I wish I could think so, but I don't believe that."

Besides talking to you, do you know other things that she used to do to comfort herself after Mr. O'Connor's death?

I really can't remember, but this lady did not have much besides her writing. I think that was the time when we started to walk. She and I were often together. She would always take a cab and would never walk the streets alone. After he died, we went for walks a lot, in the neighborhood—not far. Or sometimes I would go with her if she was going anyplace, like to the stores or if she wanted to do any shopping, which she didn't do much of anyway, but she would invite me to go along with her and help her. She liked the Bergdorf Goodman store.

What did she talk about when you went for your walks or shopping?

Not anything intense, just ordinary things. Believe it, she would talk sometimes about food.

Were there any other ways in which she changed after Mr. O'Connor died?

She didn't take much joy in anything afterwards. She wouldn't get into details about meals the way we used to. She would enjoy her food but, more or less, I made the decisions. She really didn't care, but I said, "Well you have to eat, you know," and she said, "Whatever you want to do" or "I like your cooking anyway." Maybe not in those exact words, but she would eat anything that I prepared. She wasn't enthusiastic about anything anymore.

Did she like to look at Mr. O'Connor's photographs or go through his belongings? Did she keep his belongings?

She kept them up to a certain point, and then I think she sent them to one of those places that you give things to. There were personal things that she kept. Little things. He really did not collect much. Like little things of his that she had given him. Any gold tie pin or things like that, she kept those things, but there wasn't much apart from his paintings that she kept.

Did Miss Rand know how much you cared for Mr. O'Connor?

Oh, she knew that. She knew that down through the years and she appreciated it. She felt that she could trust me to look after him even when she was not there. She knew that I cared for him.

Who was his best friend besides Ayn Rand?

I don't think that he had a best friend. He knew all the people that came to see her, and he was comfortable with them. There was none that he really selected. I think he liked Leonard, but the relationship between Leonard and him was not like the one between Leonard and Ayn. I think he was a loner. If you can call anyone a loner, I think he was. He didn't need people.

I think he was quite satisfied with the way they lived and with the life that he lived. They both had liked living in California. I think he missed California more than she did, but he tried to accommodate himself. He knew New York more than she did, but she just liked remaining at home and doing what she wanted to do. She liked the thought that she was in New York, but he liked walking around.

Did he go anywhere special on his walks?

No. I think he just walked blocks and blocks. Walked over to the West Side or over to the East Side, because we were more or less centrally located.[183]

When you were with Miss Rand, did you play any games, listen to music, watch TV?

Watched TV a little bit, but the things that she liked, I didn't like. She liked mystery, detective shows—that was not my thing, murders and solving. We didn't do much together, except the walking, and she would walk very quietly. She liked to walk without talking.

Did she have a special route, or building that she had to go near?

She loved Manhattan. She liked the progress of the building. It's true Manhattan is kind of futuristic, but to me, it is not holy. You can get lost in those apartment buildings, and they are so impersonal. But she loved everything about Manhattan and the building and everything. When we went on walks, she just would hold my arm, and she would walk very slow her last days, and we walked very quietly without speaking. When we got to the building and went upstairs, that was it.

When did you first call Miss Rand by her first name?

After her illness, she got better, and we really got a little closer, and she asked me to call her "Ayn."

---

183 The address was 120 E. 34th Street.

Was that a surprise to you?

Yes and no. Because two women, especially in the things I had to do for her, can get to that stage. I never called her "Ayn" in front of other people.

What did you call Mr. O'Connor?

Always Frank.

What influence do you think Mr. O'Connor had on Ayn Rand?

I don't know how I could answer that, but I can say that he was a comfort to her. He was a part of her life that she turned to when she was finished with writing. He was a part of her life, and she could turn to him and shut out the outside world, and they could be comfortable together.

This is why I think she went down so rapidly and got so depressed after he died. Because she was so used to being a pair, a couple, that she couldn't really survive without him. They were two people not into much apart from each other. Despite some of the things that have been written about them, I can't see these two people being anything else but what they were, what they appeared to me for all those years.

Describe Ayn Rand and Frank O'Connor together.

They were good for each other; they were good together. This is not describing them together, this is just an observation: they were not Christians. They were unbelievers, but as husband and wife, they were better together than some Christians I know. As atheists, they put more into their marriage than Christians do. They were very happy and right together. I look at marriages as they are today: the two people that did not really believe in anything hereafter, they had a good marriage.

Did Mr. O'Connor and Miss Rand ever fight, have arguments or disputes?

Not before me, not that I know of.

Did she ever tell you private, personal things about Frank O'Connor?

Yes; that he was the great love of her life. And they really cared much about each other. One thing I know, she didn't like children. Not that she would look at children and dislike them, but she didn't want that to be part of her life.

And her whole life, I think, her object was to do the things she wanted to do. She wanted to write. And she wanted to put all her feelings on paper. I can't remember how they met, but I think she thought that it was the best thing that could have happened to her.

There was no friction between them, and that's good when two people are happily married and you don't see any friction. There's none of this finding fault and picking and things like that. There was always a calm composure between them. But then again, I think he was a very thoughtful man, and he showed his love for her in many ways. I don't know if she quite understood him to that point. Even if he was angry. He never spoke about that, but I could see when he was not pleased about something. I saw the expression on his face.

Did you exchange gifts with the O'Connors over Christmas?

No. I made cakes. I volunteered to do things that I really didn't have to do, but they always gave me a gift.

How did they celebrate their birthdays?

Not really in any spectacular way. They sometimes might go someplace to eat, but in most cases, I would just make something nice for them and that was it. I didn't see too much of an exchange of cards or gifts given or anything.

What do you remember as some of the big events in Miss Rand's life when you were with her?

Believe it or not, not very much. You see, her life was pretty quiet because, as I said, all her time and energy was for writing. So after she spent the day in her office writing, there wasn't too much that she wanted to do. She'd just have dinner, and I left them and she relaxed, listened to music or, very seldom, they would look at the television in her room. There was a nice, big TV in her room. She liked *Perry Mason* and stories like that.

You said that Ayn Rand influenced you? Could explain how?

She was very straightforward, and I sort of patterned myself after that. She was very honest in giving answers. She never hedged. She was honest in saying what she meant.

You never saw her betray her ideas?

No.

Did she understand her place in history?

I think so. She never talked about it, but she always said she hoped that she would impress future generations.

I know it means very much to you to be a Christian. What was it like debating or talking to Miss Rand about atheism?

When I did get to understand what it really meant, I was really shocked. Because just as I am deeply wed to Christianity that is how deeply she was wed to atheism. There is nothing that could have turned her. Nothing. She believed in what she believed with a passion, and there's nothing that could have turned her around. That was what impressed me. After she had her surgery, and I saw how vulnerable she was—because flesh is nothing—our flesh is the weakest part of our being, and I saw the effect on her of the cancer surgery. I really felt sorry for her. To me she started to be like a human being, like I could really care for her. She was weak and she was like a child. She had to be depending wholly and solely on me for a certain period.

When you talked to her about Christianity, what was her manner?

Although I have been disappointed in her, there are certain things I admire and one of the things was that she never pulled down Christianity. She never threw any stones. She listened to me and she respected my beliefs. But she just made me understand that there was no way that she can believe like that. "Who's God?" "He does not exist."

I talked to Ayn Rand about my religious beliefs for about ten years, and even tried to convert her. She didn't agree with me. She listened to me very carefully, but I couldn't convert her, because she was who she was. She was a born atheist.

What version of Christianity are you?

Evangelical. The church I go to is the Tabernacle. Before that I was going to what the British call Anglican. Here you call it Episcopalian.

Did you tell Miss Rand about the change?

After I became an evangelical, about twelve years later, I talked to her about God, trying to convert her. And she said: there is a difference about your talking about God; you sound more sincere.

What did she mean?

As an Anglican or an Episcopalian I was really just a churchgoer. I went to church and that was it.

I lived in Brooklyn and I went into Manhattan, and every Sunday for two years I went looking for a church. I went to several churches, couldn't find what I was looking for, and then suddenly I came to this church in Brooklyn called the "Brooklyn Gospel Tabernacle." And when I went there for the first time I felt that this is it. I'm home.

You must have been very confident in your beliefs that Miss Rand couldn't convince you out of them?

She never tried. We had a lot of discussions about it. She told me what she believed in and we debated. I tried to convert her, but she never tried to convert me.

What would she try to do?

She would tell me that she really didn't believe in God and that is what an atheist is. She believed that when you die that is the end of it and your memory dies. There is no afterlife. She was very confident of that, and I'm very confident that there's an afterlife. We spoke about it; we had lots of discussions, especially in the last few years before she died.

She was very respectful of my beliefs.

Let's now turn to Miss Rand's death. Were there any special circumstances about how she died?

It was just a slow deterioration. People do not believe that, but you actually can will yourself to die. She had no will to live, so it was a simple thing. After I came back from visiting my family in Barbados—I hadn't known how sick she was—I went to the hospital everyday. The arrangement was that I would go to work at the hospital, because I was closer to her than all those strange people. After it was discovered that she just had a short time, the doctors said that she could go home, provided she had proper attention.

Myself and Leonard Peikoff, we went back to the apartment and made arrangements for them to convert her whole big bedroom into something like a hospital. Got beds direct from the hospital and all the things that would be needed for a hospital environment. Then she came home, and I was at home when she died. The night that she died nobody expected it. She had a nurse that slept with her because I never slept there. When I left and went home, it was Friday night. Very early next morning, around 9:30, Leonard called and told me that she had died. I was really very shocked. That is something you know that must happen to each and everyone of us, but when it comes, it is always a shock.

The last time you saw her, what did she say to you?

She hardly talked. She hardly spoke anything in the last hours of her life. She just insisted that we keep the television on. But I know she was not looking at television; she was like staring into space. And she wasn't really talking.

What was her attitude to death? How did she face death?

She wasn't afraid. She was not down, because she always thought when it comes, that is the end of everything. Your brain goes and you don't know. You never wake up. And that is what she believed. She reached that state in her mind where she accepted the fact that she will be no more.

Did she ask for anyone?

I can't remember her singling out anyone. She was just quiet. It wasn't long after she came out of hospital that she died. She just existed. We fed her; we didn't have to put in any tubes. She had liquid food, but there were no tubes running in and out and all of that, and she just died.

Do you have any last memories of Ayn Rand?

Leonard Peikoff called me in Barbados, told me she was at the hospital and asked me if I could come back up. I said yes, and I got on the next plane out, which was the next day, and I came up and I went to the hospital where she was—every single day—until it was said that they couldn't do anything for her and it would be better if she died at home.

When I first got to the hospital, she said, "Oh Ellie, you're back." I said, "Yes." She says, "This is not going to be a death-bed conversion!"

Patrick O'Connor

Patrick O'Connor was Ayn Rand's editor at New American Library in the late 1960s and early 1970s.

Interview date: February 14, 1997

Scott McConnell: *What is your strongest memory of Ayn Rand?*

Patrick O'Connor: I had a lot of preconceived ideas. Before I met her, I read all her books and was trying to figure out why she sold so well.

I met someone at a party one night who said she knew Ayn Rand, and I said, "Oh, I've read all her books and I know why she sells." The woman said, "Why?" I said, "Because she writes the best children's literature in America." The woman evidently told Miss Rand this, because years later, when we met and became very close friends, she said to me, "You're the one who said I wrote children's books, aren't you?" We laughed.

What did you mean by "children's literature"?

Books for young adults—wonderful books for young adults.

Why not older adults?

It's because they're epic, Wagnerian things. The sex all takes place on the highest plane and it's wonderful, but it's basically young adult literature, and I loved it for that.

I gather you don't agree with her philosophy?

I'm a Trotskyite. I'm a Communist.

Why are you a Trotskyite?

I'm a working-class American. I'm old, seventy-one years old, and anti-Stalinist, by the way, from 1941. I'm from the old, radical, '30s left wing of the Democrat party—radical Democrat, meaning socialist. I was born into that and I never escaped.

At any rate, I loved Ayn. She was wonderful and warm-hearted and sensitive and friendly and charming. She and I became friends. We never discussed politics. We discussed our personal lives and so forth.

When you told Ayn Rand that you were a Trotskyite, what was her reaction?

It was at lunch when we first met, and it was the first thing I told her. She said, "It doesn't matter what your politics are as long as you're a good editor and do everything I say."

So you never debated with her?

No, never. That would have been inappropriate. After lunch I went back to the office and reported to my bosses, "She's just a lovable little old Jewish lady from Leningrad."

And what did they say?

"She can't be Jewish—she's a fascist!"

How important was Ayn Rand to NAL?

She paid the gas, the light, the heating bills, the rent and the Christmas bonuses. She was the moneymaker of that organization.

NAL didn't have any other name writers?

They did, but she had what I call in the article about her in my autobiography "permanent pockets."[184] During that period, the '40s, '50s and '60s, her books were always in every bookrack, and when they sold out, they got immediately refilled. That's the dream of every writer, that the pocket be permanent. There are very few writers like that.

Did her sales influence NAL's relationship with her?

I thought that they hated her. They were all left-wing Democrats. None of them had ever met her, they never courted her, they never had anything to do with her. When they told me the story of when they had been invited to her apartment for dinner and not one of them had read her books, and they had been living off her all the years, I was horrified. After dinner she had asked them which of her books they had liked best and why. The president tried to fake it. No cigar. You didn't fake it with Ayn Rand. I was only a senior editor but I said to the president, "That isn't funny. You've been living off this woman for years. She's been paying all your bills for years."

What is the general publishing-industry opinion of Ayn Rand?

---

184 Patrick O'Connor's autobiography is titled *Don't Look Back: A Memoir* (Wakefield, RI: Moyer Bell, 1993).

That she sells books. The general publishing industry is, politically left, but true publishers publish what they think will sell. There has been traditionally very little publishing from belief, as it were. They'll publish anything that will sell, and everyone respects and admires her sales.

Is she a phenomenon in any way?

I think she's one of the phenomenons of the century. In my philosophy, didactic art doesn't sell and is not supposed to sell. It certainly doesn't sell in the theater, but she's the exception to the rule about didactic art selling. She is nothing if not didactic. What she intends to do with her fiction is convert. The surprise for me, philosophically, is that it works. I think it's phenomenal in that way.

Because of her uniqueness, were her books promoted or advertised?

No, those books promoted themselves.

There wasn't a big budget for advertising or anything?

No. She was a word-of-mouth success.

Tell me more about your interactions with her.

If she was feeling blue, we would walk along the street, and she would look at jewelry stores and would say, "Oh, buying that would make me feel good." That's a specific quote.

Did she ever buy?

Yes, she did. Just small pieces of costume jewelry.

As her editor, what did you do for Ayn Rand?

I collected some pieces from *The Objectivist Newsletter* and made books out of them.

Would they have been The Romantic Manifesto *and* The New Left: The Anti-Industrial Revolution*?*

Yes. Anything that was published by NAL from about 1968 to 1971 is what I put together.

Did she make the proposals about the books or did you take them to her?

I think I went to her. We were looking for more books.

As a Communist you must have had some twinges of conscience regarding the anti-industrial revolution book.

No, no. I'm a generalist and I'm a professional editor. I pride myself on that.

So you looked at what was best for the client and picked out the best articles?

What I thought would be interesting and what I thought would sell.

What interesting things happened while working as Ayn Rand's editor?

I did everything she said.

And what did she want?

She wanted approval of copy, advertising and art. That's always a sore point, which publishers are never willing to give. I felt because of her sales and what she contributed to the company that she could have her own way, whatever she wanted to do! She should be able to put anything on the cover if she wanted to, and it was her right. I always felt that about someone who sold a lot of copies. In my heart of hearts I'm basically a capitalist—besides the romantic Trotskyite overlay. It was her ball and bat and it was her day. I fought for that. I was fierce on this subject. She had the right to demand. Writers do not usually get this. The art department is always crazy and quite fierce about keeping this control. She really hated a lot of her covers. The one thing I did for her was [that] I fought for her at the company level, and said she should get what she wants because she deserves to get what she wants.

She knew that?

She knew that. I didn't always agree with her, but I agreed that she should get her way.

Can you remember some specific things that she wanted that the company was against?

The covers. One time, all the art department could come up with was a cover that she hated a lot, sort of an artistic dismembered body. I suggested that we use instead one of her husband's paintings.[185]

Any other things she wanted?

---

185 Frank O'Connor's painting *Man Also Rises* was used for the cover of the twenty-fifth-anniversary edition of *The Fountainhead*.

She was very specific about copy and headlines and blurbs.

Did your bosses leave you alone and let you have your way?

Yes. They didn't want to have anything to do with her. They didn't talk to her, they didn't take her to lunch, they didn't take her to dinner, they didn't fête her, as it were—which she deserved to be.

You said you became good friends with Miss Rand. Can you explain what that means?

We socialized once in a while. They didn't seem to have a lot of friend friends. I used to take her and her husband to the ballet and to the theatre. I said to her there's a wonderful ballet called the Joffrey Ballet, which she had never heard of. It was a young and vigorous company, I said, and I think you would like it; they're doing the kind of things you might like, and I would be happy to take you there. And I did.

What was her reaction?

She was crazy about the evening.

What was she like when she was watching something she enjoyed?

She sort of glowed when she liked something. She reacted viscerally to that which she liked. She would sit bolt upright, and her eyes would be totally focused.

Did you do any other socializing with Miss Rand?

The thing about being with her in New York is that everyone recognized her. People often thought, because of her politics, she was on their side of certain issues. People assumed that because of the rest of her politics she would be antiabortion, but she wasn't.

People would come up to her in restaurants, unlike to other celebrities, like movie stars, with whom I would be having dinner. I remember one woman came up to her and said, "I did your chart," meaning astrology chart. Ayn was horrified, just horrified at why this woman assumed that Ayn Rand would be interested in her astrological chart.

How did she get rid of her?

I got rid of her. You know, "We're having a business luncheon here, perhaps you could write to Miss Rand." Something like that.

How was she with these people generally?

Very polite. She was an old-fashioned girl, you know. She was an old-fashioned, bourgeois Russian lady. She was from the middle class, and so she always had very good manners and was very warm and loving and sensitive. People think she was other than she was, but I tell you that in my experience she was sweet-natured. I told her about my family, and I was in psychoanalysis at the time and was having a lot of trouble—I was trying to give up drinking. I talked to her about the personal things that mattered to me at the time.

How did she treat these intimate issues?

She was a great listener.

What was her advice?

She didn't give advice, just sympathized, you know, made sympathetic noises.

Did she talk about things of a personal nature?

She talked mostly about the publishing business and the books and distribution and ads and art covers and so forth.

In another conversation with me, you used some interesting words in describing her. Could you explain them? For example, "compassionate."

Once we were riding uptown in a cab and we saw an accident and she was totally upset by the sight of this accident and concerned about the person who was hit by a car. I remember very vividly how it affected her—that she reacted very strongly to somebody's injury.

"Warm-hearted"?

Well, she was toward me. She was compassionate, warm-hearted and feeling and sympathetic to me. I talked to her about my relationship with my father and how problematic, how difficult, it was. She was sympathetic to that, to my problems, as it were.

Last one, "good companion"?

It was nice being with her, especially when it was just the two of us and she was not being bothered by fans; when we were at a table where she couldn't be seen and people didn't come up to her.

Were dinners the main occasions you had together?

They were lunches, we regularly had lunch. Perhaps monthly.

What about her clothing?

She wore that wonderful cape. As soon as you saw the cape you knew who she was.

How would you describe her manner, her personality?

She was commanding. She knew what she wanted and was a woman of great authority.

After all your dealings with her, how would you describe her character?

Strong. Honorable. Honest. No contradictions.

Would you describe her as a happy person?

No, absolutely not. She was a driven person, not happy. Driven people aren't happy. They have moments of happiness but they're not happy.

What about when you were at the ballet, for example?

Well, moments of happiness—a good time. We used to have a good time at lunch, she would laugh, I laughed.

What did she like to laugh at?

Stories of my absurd life.

What was your impression of Mr. O'Connor?

He was the great faded beauty. At one time he was one of the most beautiful men in the world, and then he faded.

Why did you stop working with Ayn Rand?

I left NAL to head up a company called Curtis Books. I continued to work in the book business for many years after that, and then I stopped and became a ski instructor.

But I'll reiterate what I say, especially to people who don't like her work: I surprise them by telling them what a gracious and nice woman she was. They expect some kind of dragon lady, and she was far from a dragon lady. One acknowledges that she could be fierce when she wanted to be, but generally in her daily dealings with people, she was a gracious lady.

1970s

Arline Mann

Arline Mann worked on a theater production of *Night of January 16th*—and was an acquaintance of Ayn Rand's starting in the late 1970s. She is a lawyer at Goldman, Sachs & Co.

Interview dates: July 28 and August 5, 1999

Scott McConnell: *How did you get to know Ayn Rand?*

Arline Mann: There were two main periods during which I came to know her. There's the *Penthouse Legend* [*Night of January 16th*] period and the period when I was dating Harry Binswanger.

My first direct contact with Ayn was while I was working on *Penthouse Legend*, when it was produced at the McAlpine in 1973. The production was produced by Phil and Kay Smith, and Gloria Alter was hired as general manager. I had a couple of jobs on the show: I did administrative work, and I also did the costumes, because I had a bit of background in theater design. I had done costumes on various smaller shows. The costumes were all going to be bought, not made.

Probably the first time I was introduced to Ayn was at one of the rehearsals, but the first time I ever spoke to her was when she came in to review some of the technical aspects of the show, which involved testing the lights and looking at the scenery and costumes.

She was sitting two-thirds of the way back in the house of the theater, and I was sitting part of the time in the row behind her, part of the time next to her, while she commented on the costumes and other technical aspects. She liked all the costumes except the one for "Guts" Regan. She did not like the fact that it made him look too much like a caricature; I had made him look like a gangster, and she wanted him to look like a businessman: very understated, elegant, well-tailored. In modern terms, she would have put him in an Armani suit.

Do you remember her explanation?

She wanted it to work against type, slightly. She thought the character was not the obvious, coarse gangster type, and she said Regan would never wear a suit like the one I had given him. She was not harsh in her comments, just definite.

Do you remember any of her comments about other aspects of the production?

I don't remember any other comments on the lighting or the scenery. I do recall that she was not fussy about it. I was surprised that she was not more critical. She was fairly accepting, I think, because she was realistic about what could be expected for that sort of small budget production. So she was very professional in that way. She knew something about the theater, and she knew what could be expected and what couldn't.

She wasn't frightening to me. She was actually very quiet, very businesslike, and extremely incisive, and always had a sense about her of not being mushy. She sat still. She didn't talk a lot. She knew right away what she wanted and didn't want. She said it without going on and on about it—very professional, I thought.

Do you remember what she thought of the performance?

She was satisfied with it. I don't think she was thrilled, but I think she felt it was okay, except for certain unauthorized script changes, which I heard occurred after the opening. Again, I think she was realistic. In my opinion, it was not a particularly good production.

Tell me about the second stage of your relationship.

I used to go to Ayn's apartment with Harry. Sometimes he would talk about whatever topic was interesting him, or she would talk, but most often when I was there, they were not discussing intellectual issues; they were playing Scrabble. At the beginning, Frank was usually there as well.

At that time Frank was not in good health, and I particularly remember one evening feeling shocked, because Ayn never behaved as if there was anything really wrong with him. She would ask him questions, and treat him as if he were there mentally, when he was not, really. I remember that I could not decide whether it was a good thing to do, or a cruel thing to do. It wasn't meant to be cruel, obviously, but he was senile at that point, and yet she would talk to him as if he could grasp what she was saying, which he couldn't, it appeared.

Once—this must have been a couple of years after Harry and I broke up romantically but were still very good friends—Harry and Ayn were playing Scrabble, and I was watching. Ayn had her head down and looked like she was puzzling out whether she should say something or not. Harry and I were always asked, at that point, because we were

such good friends: Do you think you'll ever get back together? She had
her head down and was idly moving the Scrabble tiles around, clearly
about to say something, and I think Harry and I were waiting to see
what was going to come out. We were both sitting across the table from
her. She had her eyes cast down girlishly, and she said: "May I ask
you something?" Harry and I said together, "No!" She just ignored us.
I don't even know if she heard us. And she said something like "Why
aren't you together?" We gave her some explanation, and she never
said anything about it again. But I thought it so sweet, not only that she
would think of that, but the whole way she did it, which was so shy and
not wanting to be intrusive, but still feeling that this was something she
ought to say for our sake.

Describe her and Harry's relationship.

It was definitely affectionate. Harry was very eager in his
discussions with her. Harry and Ayn used to get into philosophical
arguments, which were great fun for them. Although the discussions
could be heated, there was absolutely nothing acrimonious about
them. I remember them arguing to the last minute on something,
where we were actually out the door of her apartment, and Harry
opened up the door again and said, "I still don't agree!"

Tell me more about the interactions between the three of you.

She was always very nice to me, always gracious. When a guest
came into the apartment, she was solicitous and would offer something
to drink. But once she and Harry started discussing an intellectual
subject, then you might die before you'd get anything else. She was
not formal, so I didn't hesitate to say, "Do you mind if I get something
from the kitchen?" She was happy for me to go in her refrigerator or
that sort of thing. She was informal in that way.

In her discussions, she was very calm. She was totally involved in
what they were discussing. I never saw her get angry with Harry, no
matter what he said, no matter what he disagreed with her about. I never
saw her even as she was sometimes in question-and-answer periods—
not angry with a person, but angry about an idea.

Actually, there was an incident once in which I asked her something
about an intellectual discussion they were having, and she raised
her voice a little and seemed angry. I hadn't seen that before. I said,
"Why are you yelling at me?" She wasn't actually yelling, but she
had raised her voice. She paused and said, "Oh, I'm not. It's just this

point that makes me angry." So she was very aware of that. One thing that showed me is that she had no sense of herself as a "great person." She was certainly aware of her power and value, but that wasn't communicated on a personal level. There was absolutely no "Do you know who I am?" or "Do you know to whom you're talking?" That was simply not in her character.

Did she change after you had said that?

Yes, she did, she dropped it entirely, the anger went away.

Did she talk to you about Mr. O'Connor after he died?

I remember one conversation. She talked about herself, and she had a very dispassionate evaluation of her own reaction, and her own chances of coming out of her depression. I think she knew she couldn't predict exactly what was going to happen, but she was not optimistic about her own emotional state. She was aware that she was depressed. She did not feel there was much she could do about it, and she did not care to do much about it. She had a sense of the limitations of her life from there on; she didn't fight it a great deal, it seemed.

Did you attend the party celebrating the O'Connors' fiftieth marriage anniversary?

It was at their apartment. There were speeches. The stuffed animals were out for the party. There was tiddlywink music being played. One of the songs made me think of a cakewalk, so I started to do it, and she liked it. She wanted to know how I did it. I can't recall whether or not she tried it herself. The rest of the people there got up and we had a line in which everybody was doing the cakewalk across the living room. She got terrific pleasure out of little funny things like that.

Leonard spoke about his own learning from Ayn, his education by Ayn. And of course, everybody spoke about Ayn and Frank's marriage. Somebody spoke a little about the history of their marriage, and a bit about how they met. Alan Greenspan was there. I think Eloise was there.

Tell me about Eloise.

She was a very self-possessed lady. I thought Eloise was very beautiful; she looked rather like Lena Horne. Her demeanor was very refined and she had a terrific dignity about her. She and Ayn had a very comfortable relationship. Eloise certainly was more than an employee to Ayn. I remember them standing in the kitchen together for some reason, and they really were more like companions than employer and employee. If someone had asked you who was the employer and who was the employee, you could certainly tell, but there was a mutual respect there; Eloise was the sort of person who commanded respect. She was the sort of person you would say had a real rock-hard stable center to her. No one was going to confuse Eloise about who Eloise was.

Did you talk with her about which actors could play characters in Atlas Shrugged?

She talked about Hans Gudegast as a possibility for Francisco. Without regard to age, the name Lauren Bacall surfaced as a possibility for Dagny, and Farrah Fawcett was suggested as well. She said she liked Farrah Fawcett, partly because Fawcett's mouth turned down, which was something Ayn liked. We talked about Spencer Tracy as being very good for Midas Mulligan.

Do you have any letters or books from Miss Rand?

I have three things of hers. I have a little perfume bottle of hers. It's perfume made by Floris, the British perfume house. It's a sweet flower one, maybe gardenia. I have a scrap of paper from her desk with a to-do list. The belongings of hers which I value the most are three watercolor drawings by her sister Nora, which Ayn brought with her from Russia, in her suitcase, when she came to this country. They are creased; perhaps Ayn folded them to fit them into her suitcase. They are theatrical caricatures—very clever, gay, little drawings. They are framed and hang in my apartment.

Ken MacKenzie

Ken MacKenzie attended Ayn Rand lectures, was a lessee for Objectivist taped courses and worked on Capitol Hill. Mr. MacKenzie died in 2002.

Interview date: December 20, 1999

Scott McConnell: *Did you ever meet Miss Rand?*

Ken MacKenzie: In 1973 and '74 I was working on Capitol Hill as a legislative aide to Congress. Congressman Phil Crane, who was very free-market, introduced a bill to legalize ownership of gold, which had been outlawed. This legislation was coming up as an amendment to some other legislation, and so some aides like myself were trying to push this. I decided it would be good to put in the *Congressional Record* Alan Greenspan's article on gold and economic freedom, which had been published in *The Objectivist*.[186] So I wrote up a little introduction for the article, but it seemed that I ought to get permission, so I called Townsend-Greenspan in New Jersey and talked to Alan Greenspan. He got right on the phone and said, "Oh, that little thing? Oh, that would be fine." But he said that I should check with New York.

I called *The Objectivist*, in New York, and talked with Barbara Weiss, who was an administrative assistant there, and she recommended that I write a letter and attach a copy of the introduction, asking for approval. I explained that the legislation may come up as early as today. She said, "Oh, well, just a minute." So she goes away, comes back and says, "Okay, Miss Rand will speak to you."

I got totally caught off guard, because I didn't know that she'd be there, and all of a sudden she's right on the phone. I summoned up my most profound voice, and said something like "Gosh, is it really you?" And she said, "Oh yes, it's me." And so I said, "Would you like me to read the introduction?" "Yes, go ahead and read that," and so I did.

She listened very intently, and two or three times, she said, "oh yes, oh, good, good." And she was very supportive. When I finished, she said, "Okay," and I said, "That's all right then?" "Oh, yeah, that's fine; go ahead." She was businesslike, but she didn't suddenly say, "Okay, goodbye." She just kind of hesitated, and so I started talking with her a little bit and talked to her about the confirmation hearing for Alan

---

186 The article is "Gold and Economic Freedom," reprinted in *Capitalism: The Unknown Ideal*.

Greenspan, who had been nominated to be the chairman of the Council of Economic Advisers. I said that I'd send a copy of the hearing to her, and she appreciated that very much. So we just chatted for a minute, and then she went on. What I found interesting—and I was a total stranger to her, and it was a business conversation—but she was very pleasant and supportive in acknowledging what I'd written up. I went home beaming and said to my wife, "Boy, guess who I talked to."

That amendment got offered, and within a year or two gold ownership was legalized, and Mr. Greenspan's article was read into the *Record*.

Larry Cole

Larry Cole is an author, educator and psychotherapist and was a talk-show host in New York City when he interviewed Miss Rand on his radio show in 1973. He most recently founded and directed the Stuart Black Institute for Juvenile Justice, a child advocacy organization, in cooperation with Harvard and Columbia universities.

Interview dates: August 5 and 7, 1998

Scott McConnell: *How did you meet Ayn Rand?*

Larry Cole: I was doing a radio show in New York City called *Growing Up in New York*. My wife Michelle and I started and ran a program for street gangs on the Lower East Side called LEAP (Lower East Side Action Project). Unlike organizers of similar projects, we did not take any government funds. The program included a residence, an alternative school and a medical program, and all of the things that if we had had kids, we would have wanted to provide. I also wrote a number of books, including *Street Kids* and *Our Children's Keepers*. My work and the radio show dealt with issues of importance to young people. The radio show featured icons of social science, education and literature, whose work I thought significant to a better understanding of childhood and adolescence.

Ayn Rand was a person of major consequence to me. Although Michelle and I tended to be lumped with leftists like Abbie Hoffman and Jerry Rubin, we were not politically left. I had been influenced greatly by Miss Rand's work: initially by the movie *The Fountainhead*, then by that novel, next by *Atlas Shrugged*, and then by *The New Left: The Anti-Industrial Revolution*, where I found a treatise on education called "The Comprachicos." It was the best and most succinct analysis of the decline and fall of public education I had ever seen, and offered First Principles for what education should and could be. Of course, I wanted to interview her because I thought that her work was important, and she was a hero of mine. She said she would love to do the interview, and it was done on July 20, 1973.

It was as easy as just calling her?

I originally called her publisher and got whoever was representing her and left a message. Ayn called me back. I asked her if she would be willing to do this interview. She said she would. Her condition was that

I pick her up and take her home.

She must have trusted you, a stranger, to pick her up at home and drive her.

That was a surprise: all we had done was spoken on the phone. She seemed to be quite at ease with who I was. I had those books in print, and she may have had the opportunity to look at them; but it was clear that she knew more about me than I had told her.

I was working with street gangs, and she didn't fully understand the motives. I think she saw me as being somewhat of a challenge, and somewhat paradoxical in that I was able to communicate with her at her level.

Was she curious to find out more about your motives?

Yes, she was. We did talk about that. I think she appreciated the fact that I took time to clarify our motives: that we knew going into this work that we were not altruists and that there were many personal motives involved.

What was she like as a guest?

I don't remember using this word before to describe my first impression of anyone: she was delightful. For the first five minutes she was rather stiff and defensive, kind of wondering where I was going to come from. She turned out to just be this really lovely, warm and funny person, and that just knocked me over. It was like interviewing a film star, except she was very much more at ease. We had some call-ins, and she was feisty with people who had her wrong. I was surprised by her humor, her willingness to listen and her ease of expression.

We had almost an hour together, and it was the most memorable, wonderful fifty-four minutes and forty-eight seconds I can remember. I did some fairly objective probing, if not playing a bit of the devil's-advocate, because I wanted to get past the image distortions about her. Those were times of extremes, and public figures were typically pegged by the most provocative hyperbole, like Clint Eastwood being called a "fascist." She had that image around radical-Left types.

We had this hour together, and then I dropped her off at her apartment. We talked a bit, and she said she would send me a monograph of "The Comprachicos." I received a copy of the monograph on which she had written, "Thank you for a wonderful interview." She signed it, and I've kept it all of this time.

What was your impression when you first met her?

I must admit to being "starstruck," but managed to navigate and have some conversation while we were in the car, driving up the West Side Highway.

What was her attitude?

Friendly. I expected her to be much more diffident, much more put off by taking a morning for the interview; I expected her to be more the classic diva and she wasn't like that at all. She went out of her way to make me comfortable.

The whole relationship was a serendipitous thing: people finding commonality and a similar language; that kind of surprise discovery of something of value. I thought, when I asked her for the first interview, she would think, "Oh, God, here's another one of these counterculture types." But it didn't turn out that way. I think that our abilities and integrity were apparent, and communication was really easy. It was a relationship that began with a request for an interview, went on to the interview, to a social evening and dinner together, and to a kind of a casual telephone friendship.

After the interview, she gave me her home phone number and said, "Let's keep in touch, maybe we can get together." And I said, "I'd love to do that, and my wife would love to meet you." Maybe two or three weeks later, we were invited for dinner. We met her husband, and the four of us had a long conversation. Frank was not too much involved in the conversation at dinner, but enough to make his presence felt.

We were sitting at dinner talking about our school and a lot about education and the prevailing social decay, when Ayn said to Michelle, "What do you think is the solution to this problem that Nat Hentoff posed in his article about white kids being intimidated at American schools?" Michelle said that as long as white kids were victims, they were going to use the police to protect them. She thought that such protection would create a clear double standard leading to an even more defined underclass. Michelle said that she thought the solution was to teach white kids how to fight for themselves. Ayn laughed and said, with tongue in cheek, "You're a fascist." Michelle laughed. It was the joke of the evening, and Michelle came away with the distinct honor of having been called a "fascist" by Ayn Rand.

During the evening, we had a much more extensive conversation. There seemed to be a great question mark in her mind about why we were who we were, doing what we were doing. It was a recurring theme.

She asked us about our personal lives, why we were doing this work, and what the school was like. We had probably three or four hours together before we finally left. None of us wanted it to end. Although she never accused me of being a fascist, she did accuse me of being an activist. I accepted that from her because I was—and still am—one. When she called me an "activist," I responded with . . . "back atcha." And she said, "What do you mean by that?" I answered, "You are an advocate, you know. You advocate the primacy of reason, and you don't do it passively. So I guess you can safely be called an 'activist' as well. I'm in good company." She made a brief stage grimace . . . as if, for that moment, in some deep thought . . . and then laughed. Not only had she, in her best satirical form, called Michelle a "fascist," and less satirically called me an "activist" . . . but got an "activist" label hung on her, without any real protest. It was, after all, about the capriciousness of the labels, and even Frank laughed out loud when I stuck an unexpected one on her. It was all in good humor. All of us were exploring areas of great mutual interest. I think she was surprised that she met some intelligent people who were doing what we were doing.

Toward the end of the evening, there was some focus on specifics about the kids we were working with, and some of our experiences: the danger of being in a gang territory; the difficulties in working with adolescents who had been kicked out of the school system for violent behavior. I remember her understanding—a kind of light of acknowledgment going on—when I said that if I had been an adolescent of that social class, and was forced into New York City public schools, I would have been tossed out myself for doing something terrible, because of the accumulated rage. She said something to the effect that that wouldn't be a rational response to the situation, and getting out of there would be a better one, but she understood completely what I was saying.

Michelle said that the school system ought to just shut down, and that a kind of free market of educational institutions ought to develop on its own.

Do you remember Miss Rand's comments on closing down public schools?

She listened. She agreed with Michelle that probably that was the best thing to do. You can make an analogy to a corporation that's producing an inferior product; in a free market it would die a natural death. Ayn concurred and said she had written about progressive education being bankrupt. It follows, she said, that its adherents shouldn't be running a school system.

When she was questioning you to find out what your beliefs were, what was her attitude or manner?

It was clear and probing and persistent—occasionally a kind of friendly interrogation. It was obvious that she had an agenda; it wasn't the casual conversation that people too often make at dinner. We were wanting to get to something more fundamental. I enjoyed it thoroughly. Having someone I have so much regard for show such an interest in our philosophy, was a role reversal that I didn't expect.

What did she think of your work with street kids?

She thought it was good, and basic. I don't think that she had a frame of reference for it. It wasn't as though she admired people who did "altruistic" things. Basically, this was our family. I was trained as a psychologist, and I didn't want to be sitting behind a desk, with all that "professional" distance between me and the kids who Michelle and I thought were special.

It was obvious that she had admiration for what we were doing. When we got to talking about our experiences, she seemed to be more sympathetic, and I am particularly aware of the fact that there were some minds changed, on both sides, not on great issues, but on understanding the mechanics of how and what the education system and the juvenile justice system had become.

Did she give you her opinion on these problems and their solution?

She talked about permissiveness and expanded on some of the things that we had picked up from "The Comprachicos," such as drug use as a logical consequence of progressive education.

I read "The Comprachicos" during the time we were in the middle of a totally chaotic educational fiasco in this country, and it nearly brought me to tears. They were partly tears of recognition, especially her translation of the segment from Victor Hugo's *The Man Who Laughs*. I told Ayn that I promptly sent it to all of my radical educator friends, trying to stir up dialogue. They were all the big names in education. I sent them the article with little notes on it saying, "I think you should read this, and we should talk." It was the only time they did not respond, none of them, ever.

Why?

I think that defending a philosophy sometimes prevents people from being logical and experiencing other levels of reality. As a metaphor—each of those educators saw in it a different language that was either untranslatable or, if translatable, offensive and "incorrect."

What school of psychology influenced you?

B. F. Skinner and behaviorism.

Did you tell Ayn Rand that?

Yes.

Did she disagree with you?

No. She didn't seem to be a great fan of Skinner's,[187] which surprised me some, if for no other reason than that he didn't subscribe to the prevailing mysticism in psychology. In a world of these choices, I think that she respected the one I had made, even if she respectfully disagreed.

Anything else about Miss Rand and her conversation at dinner that night?

We touched on a lot of topics and, of course, got into our origins. Michelle discussed her own Russian Jewish origins and how she had left the religious part, once past childhood. There was nothing out of bounds. Very few people—especially people who are of her celebrity and artistic-intellectual status—have conversations as free and open as the ones she had with us.

After that evening we had other conversations, and one of the most memorable for me was while talking one day on the phone. I asked her who her favorite film director was, living or dead. She said, "Fritz Lang." She said one of the things that she would really like to do would be to meet him. I said, "I think I can do that," and within a couple of hours, I had Fritz Lang on the phone, and I was talking to him about her. He told me that he knew of her and had great admiration for her, so I called her and put the two of them together over the phone. He was in Los Angeles, and she was in New York at her apartment. I said, "I'm glad I got you two together; have a good conversation," and after a moment or so, I left them.

---

187 Rand's critique of B. F. Skinner can be found in "The Stimulus and the Response," reprinted in Rand's *Philosophy: Who Needs It* (New York: Signet, 1984).

It was two people who had never met, who had this great admiration for each other, and wanted the other to know that right up front. Right away she said that she had admired his film works throughout her life and thought he was the greatest director, and he said that he was very aware of her work and had great respect and regard for her. I don't know what became of their meeting, because soon after that he became ill and passed away.[188]

Do you know what he specifically complimented her on?

He complimented Ayn on her integrity. He said this to me, and I remember him saying it to her, that he—and I think he was talking specifically about *The Fountainhead*, probably the film—that he thought that the characters had great integrity, and he knew—from what he knew about her—that she did, and he thought of himself as a person who didn't compromise, and so they shared that characteristic.

I spoke to her a number times after that, but she never brought up her conversation with Fritz Lang because, I think, she wanted it to be hers, and I didn't want to intrude on that. She did thank me for getting them together, and she was curious about how I had made it happen. I let it remain a mystery.

She was very pleased at having had the opportunity to converse, apparently at some length, with a culture hero of hers. And at the same time, she was sorry that he was in such poor health and expressed sorrow at that. She said that if she had her druthers, *Atlas Shrugged* would be directed by Fritz Lang.

---

188 Fritz Lang died August 2, 1976.

Lilyan Courtois

Lilyan Courtois worked for the United States Information Agency in Washington, D.C. Part of her work was to respond to letters from the Soviet Union and Poland.

Interview Date: July 19, 1999

Scott McConnell: *How did you get to know Ayn Rand?*

Lilyan Courtois: I worked for the U.S. Information Agency, and I was on the staff of the magazine *Amerika* that went to the Soviet Union and Poland. The magazine was distributed in the Soviet Union under the U.S.-U.S.S.R. Cultural Exchanges Agreement, and by that agreement, the magazine *Soviet Life* was distributed in this country.

What year did you meet her?

I worked for the magazine for quite a few years. I never met her in person, but I talked to Ayn Rand on the telephone in 1973. One of my jobs was to answer letters to the editor, and one day a letter arrived from an E. Drobysheva. She wrote that she had been given a copy of *Amerika* when she went to one of our exhibits under the cultural exchanges agreement. The Bolshoi Ballet would come over here, and we'd send the New York Ballet over there, that type of thing. These exchanges went on during the time when there was an Iron Curtain.

In that issue we did an article called "On Discord." It featured photographs and biographical profiles of a number of prominent Americans from every part of the political spectrum. Among them were Benjamin Spock, Abbie Hoffman, Linus Pauling, Robert Welch, Madalyn Murray O'Hair and Ayn Rand. The article showed that in America we could think whatever we wanted to think, from the extreme right to the extreme left and anything in between. We had that freedom.

The magazines were handed out to the people who came into these exhibits. Giving them away was one of the ways we got the magazine distributed, because the Soviets had suppressed the magazine. They wouldn't let it be distributed as they should have, so the people in the embassy used to drop them off at bus stops and dental offices and everywhere, just to make sure that the Russians got them. This particular edition was handed to Mrs. Drobysheva. When she read it, she saw her sister's picture in it, got excited and wrote to the magazine. She was smart, because she sent her letter to the American Embassy in

Moscow, so it then got to me by way of the diplomatic pouch. If she had mailed it directly to Washington, we never would have received it.

What happened when you received the letter?

When I read the letter, I thought it was very important and that I had better call Ayn Rand and tell her what I have. I called the library and they gave me the telephone number for *The Ayn Rand Letter*. I talked to a woman there and told her that I wanted to talk to Ayn Rand, that I had something very important to tell her. She put her on the phone, and Ayn Rand said in her Russian accent, "Yes, this is Ayn Rand." I told her who I was and about the letter. She asked me who the letter was from, and I told her it was from an E. Drobysheva, and she said, "I don't recognize that name." But when I read the letter to her, then that's when she realized who it was from—her sister Eleanora. The "E" was for Eleanora. [See Eleanora Drobysheva interview, page 3.]

She got very emotional and I got emotional. She was in tears and I was in tears. She said that she hadn't seen her sister in forty-seven years and said, "She's alive. I thought she was dead." She was sobbing, and she was asking me questions. It was moving. She kept thanking me for telephoning her. She was so happy to hear that her sister was alive.

I was on the phone quite a while with Ayn Rand. After she got over her shock—she was kind of speechless for a while—she settled down, and I settled down. Then she wanted to know what the magazine said about her. I had to go to the files and get a copy of the English translation because I don't read Russian, and I read it to her. She said, "That's true. That's true. That's not so true, but that's all right. Go ahead." She was satisfied that what we wrote wasn't false. It was just a small piece.

She asked me to send her the letter by special delivery or in some safe way. She said that she would pay the extra postage. I said not to worry about it. Tomorrow I'll take care of it during my lunch hour. I'll go to the post office and personally mail this to you.

I sent Ayn Rand a copy of the magazine her sister had seen and two other editions: one on architecture in America that she was interested in and another on business in America. She was very appreciative. She asked me what my name and my home address were. I thought she was going to send me a little note, but she sent me a copy of *Atlas Shrugged* that was inscribed, "To Lilyan Courtois with my deepest appreciation, sincerely, Ayn Rand." She dated it April 30, 1973.

Did you write back to Mrs. Drobysheva?

Yes. What I said to her was very obscure, so that the Russians wouldn't understand. It was like "mission accomplished." My letter said, "We are pleased to comply with your request. All of us on the editorial staff of *Amerika* are delighted to know that the copy you received at the Research and Development exhibit was of particular interest to you. Good luck and best wishes." That let Nora know that the magazine had done what she had requested.

When I answered letters to the editor, I usually wrote them in English, because the language staff did not have time to translate them, but a friend of mine in the Russian language section—Natalia "Natasha" Tsonev—typed this one for me on her Cyrillic typewriter, so the letter was sent to Nora in Russian.

Was there any other United States Information Agency involvement in this situation?

The magazine wanted to do a story on this. They thought it would be a good human-interest story for the readers of *Amerika*, but Ayn Rand was reluctant to give them permission. She was afraid it would get Nora into trouble.

What was your reaction to being involved in this event?

I was excited, because I never before had had anything to do with re-uniting two people, sisters, who had been separated for forty-seven years. That was exciting.

From your brief interaction, what was your impression of Ayn Rand?

I thought she was a real lady. She was polite. Although she was emotional, of course, about the news that I gave her, she was very nice. I thought it was very nice of her to send me a copy of her book. That was her way of showing her appreciation.

Elaine Koster

Elaine Koster was editor in chief at New American Library (NAL), one of Ayn Rand's publishers.

Interview date: February 4, 1999

Scott McConnell: *How did you meet Ayn Rand?*

Elaine Koster: In 1973 NAL gave a party to which Ayn Rand was invited. First, she held court with people like Mickey Spillane, whom she was friendly with, but that evening I met her for the first time. I had relatively recently been named the editor in chief of the company, so I asked her if I could accompany her home, because I didn't want her to go home by herself. So we took a taxi together, and when we got to her address, I wanted to pay the cab driver. She was very embarrassed to see me do that, and she said that the only reason she would let me pay for it was that ordinarily her husband took care of all those kinds of things. She seemed as though she didn't even know what was involved in paying for a cab. But I was happy to pay for the cab, and then I accompanied her upstairs to her apartment, which was the most glorious apartment.

In what way?

I just saw the living room, but it had the most gorgeous art deco furniture. I don't know who the designers of the furniture and the coffee table were, but the whole look of the place was just amazingly beautiful, even to someone like me who was relatively inexperienced in deco art.

It was her husband who actually did the decorating of their apartment. What was Ayn Rand like to deal with at business meetings?

She was firm, and she knew exactly what she wanted. She was just what you'd expect, but she wasn't impossible at all. When I think of all the various other authors that I've dealt with, she was pretty reasonable.

Eleanor Friede

Eleanor Friede was a book publisher when she knew Ayn Rand in the mid-1970s. Mrs. Friede died in 2008.

Interview date: October 8, 1999

Scott McConnell: *Who were you working for in 1974?*

Eleanor Friede: I had my own company, Eleanor Friede Books, Inc., and I had an arrangement with Delacourt Press, who published my books. I worked independently for them.

How did you meet Ayn Rand?

There was a party given by her paperback publisher, NAL, at the home of her editor, and I was invited, which was rather unusual, because I didn't know either the people giving the party or Ayn Rand, but Ayn Rand had asked that I be invited. It was a big business party, and I was invited apparently because there was an interview in *Publishers Weekly* with me, which quoted me after I had recently published *Jonathan Livingston Seagull*, and everybody was amazed that this "little nothing book," as my dear friends used to call it, was doing so well and was even number one on the best-seller list. In the article, the quote that attracted Ayn Rand was when they asked me, "Where do you think we ought to put this book? It's not a children's book; it's not about flying; it's not about birds; I mean, what do we do with it?" I just simply, immediately answered, "Put it next to the cash register." That's a marvelous quote that made her laugh too, because I'm sure she agreed with it.

When she asked that I be invited to this rival's party, I know that the editor wasn't very happy, particularly because Ayn Rand and I got into a very long conversation. If she found somebody that was on her wavelength, you were sort of inseparable, and we were talking a lot at the party. When the party was coming to an end, she asked me if I would drop her home. She had come alone, so we left together. I know that the hostess was unhappy, thinking that I was trying to steal her author, which was certainly not the case. We had a lot of fun talking; she was a fabulous person to talk to and I delivered her home.

What was your impression of Ayn Rand at this stage?

I had of course been an admirer of hers and had read all her books, and that's really I guess the kind of people that they asked to this party, so it was wonderful to meet her, because she was so friendly and so articulate, and she was really a great hit with everybody who met her.

Because I'm very tall—I'm five eight-and-a-half and blonde—we were opposites, physically. And from her pictures, I thought she would be more commanding, but she just was a very sweet and open person, very friendly, I thought, for somebody with such a mind.

What was her reputation in the publishing industry in this period of the mid-1970s?

She was a star and was greatly admired.

Isn't publishing a liberal establishment?

Yes.

So would there have been some antagonism or problems the industry might have had with Ayn Rand?

Not really. They were independent people. I know she had a different view of politics, but we didn't talk about that much. She kind of stood alone. They weren't going to argue with her politics. She was accepted, except by maybe people who didn't understand the other side of her views.

Were you in sympathy with her ideas?

No. I was always pretty liberal.

Did that come up in discussion at all?

I don't remember. I doubt if I discussed politics with her. I admired her work, but I didn't share the political views.

How would you describe her?

She was this small, vivacious person who had an energy in the eyes. I remember dark eyes, and she had just kind of a pent-up energy that was very attractive. The word "vitality" comes to the fore on that. She was a wonderful conversationalist. She could talk about anything. You didn't have to talk about her stuff. I always felt that she was informed on what was happening. And so brilliant. She could meet any challenge. I have a feeling that because of that a lot of people were probably afraid of her, but not in the publishing world. I'm sure she got just what she wanted.

I'm curious how a liberal such as yourself would enjoy Atlas Shrugged.

Oh, I thought it was wonderful. It is true, though, because it's really pretty horrible politically, but she's such a doggone good storyteller. You just can't put it down. And so intelligent. I was very attracted to the story.

What other authors did she meet?

She found out that James Clavell was one of my authors, and she wanted to meet him, and of course, he wanted to meet her, so I took them to lunch at the Four Seasons to meet. First of all, he started out ordering bottles of champagne. I think they went through two bottles—that cost me $500 right there. You don't order a bottle of champagne at the Four Seasons for the cost of the champagne.

She was drinking champagne?

Not a lot. She just took a sip to be polite. They had an absolutely wonderful time getting acquainted with each other.

She had read his books?

I think so, yes. She certainly knew who he was. He was terribly popular at the time, the biggest fiction-seller. *King Rat* was his first one; then *Tai-Pan* and *Noble House*, that's the period it was. They got along famously, and I don't know if it was anything beyond that.

Why did he want to meet her?

Everybody had heard of Ayn Rand. Also, she had a reputation for being such a brilliant woman—with a man's mind. Actually, that's one of the reasons everybody wanted to meet her.

Had he read her books?

He knew her books, definitely. They talked for a long time, and they explored everything. I think he was a brilliant person, and I think he was often bored by other people who weren't quite up to that, and that's why he took so well to her, because she had a mind that could meet him, and that was the impression that I got from their meeting.

Do you remember anything else that happened at that lunch?

The check knocked me out. I didn't mind, but I was shocked because it was close to $2,000, with all that champagne.

James Day

James Day was the host of *Day at Night*, a PBS television interview program. He interviewed Ayn Rand on March 29, 1974. Mr. Day died in 2008.

Interview date: April 8, 1999

Scott McConnell: *Why was Ayn Rand invited to be a guest on your show?*

James Day: Our purpose was to interview people who had led interesting lives, and whose life might teach us something about our own lives and about the people around us, and there was just no question that Miss Rand was one of those persons. I must confess that her philosophy is not one that I subscribe to,[189] so it was not a matter of being an acolyte, but rather a matter of talking with someone who was very interesting and had led an interesting life, and certainly had a great deal to contribute to the show.

What is your philosophy of interviewing?

I try very hard to be a good listener, rather than an interrogator. I try very hard to pick up on what the interviewees themselves have said, and then follow up on that to perhaps pursue it in a little more depth, rather than challenging or arguing with them. Now, I should tell you that I have in front of me a letter from her to me about this interview, before it was actually scheduled.

What does it say?

It's dated March 25, 1974: "Dear Mr. Day: The following are the conditions under which I agree to appear on your program, 'The Jim Day Show.'"—which was not the actual title of the show. "If you find them acceptable, please sign the enclosed copy of this letter, and return it to me.

1. The program on which I appear will be a serious discussion of ideas between the host and myself.

2. There will be no debate, no engaging in personalities, no attacks on me, and no remarks of an offensive, insulting,

---

189 James Day also said: "Idealist that I am, I tend to go off in a somewhat different direction—toward altruism, for example."

or derogatory nature (that is, any disagreement is to be expressed politely and impersonally).

3. There will be no quotations from, or references to, any of my critics, or to any second-hand reports about me, my writing, or Objectivism.

4. If the program is taped, it will be broadcast exactly as recorded, without any cuts or changes of any kind. This applies to future rebroadcasts of the program, if any.

5. The exact wording of how I will be introduced and/or referred to on the program and how my appearance will be announced prior thereto will be submitted to me for my prior consent.

6. If I will be asked to sign a release, or any other documents in connection with my appearance, I will receive same from you at least a day prior thereto.

Sincerely yours,

Ayn Rand"

Now, none of these conditions were conditions that changed what our approach would have been under any circumstance, but it's interesting that this is the only interviewee that did provide us with a list of conditions and ask us to accept and agree to these conditions.

Did you ask why she had those conditions?

No, I don't recall that I did. I just assumed—and perhaps incorrectly—that she had been subjected to criticism from interviewers in the past, and wasn't willing to subject herself to that on my program.

She was a fairly controversial figure.

Oh, absolutely, and I knew that, and, in fact, it's one reason that made it interesting for me.

Was there an audience for the show's taping?

No. In fact, the interview was done in a kind of limbo in a dark studio, where the interviewee, under ideal circumstances, was conscious of no one being around them. It was just the two of us facing each other, which I felt was a very important aspect to it, because as a rule we don't talk to each other lined up side by side. The cameras were more or less out of the sight of the interviewee.

What was your audience?

It was a public-broadcasting audience. The show was on forty-five public-broadcasting stations.

What particular issues were you interested in for the program?

I can't recall, but all the shows were essentially biographical. If there was a format, it was a format that I may have stolen from the *New Yorker* magazine, in its Profiles, which began with some discussion of the work of the interviewee, and then led ultimately into "Where were you born?" and then a sort of chronological recounting of their life's experience.

Before the show, I wrote an introduction to her interview, as I did for every one of the interviewees. I see, from my file, that there are a good many cross-outs and marks on this one, which probably was my original draft. Since it's not in my handwriting, the changes were made or approved by her.

Had you met Miss Rand before the interview?

I met her maybe an hour before the program was taped, which was the format we usually followed. I never discussed beforehand the questions I was going to ask, although I may have outlined the general areas of the questioning. I am not a good enough actor, where I can respond convincingly to something, unless it is spontaneous, so I expected to respond to whatever she said at the time on the air, rather than beforehand.

Tell me about the interview.

My first impression was that she was a pretty formidable person. She was, needless to say, very serious. There was no levity about our conversation whatsoever, and she was intense, almost as though she were expecting to be challenged and was prepared for it. The thing that I most vividly remember was that at the end of our interview, because she had been so serious and so intense—in the last minute of the program I asked her how she felt about death. She said, "It doesn't concern me in the least, because I won't be here to know it. Don't you see that the worst thing about death, and what I regard as the worst human tragedy, is to lose someone you love. That is terribly hard. But your own death? If you're finished, you're finished. My purpose is not to worry about death, but to live life here on earth now." Knowing I had thirty seconds left, I said to her, "Do you find joy in that life?"

She said, "Oh yes, very much so." And I said, "What are the sources of joy? Achievement?" And she smiled, which almost startled me. She said, "Achievement and romantic love, my husband. Those are the two great values in life: career and romantic love." It was one of the most wonderful finishes for an interview, to have her change so completely, in that last moment, to a warm smile and speak of romantic love.

You said you have a full transcript of the show?

Yes. I began with my first question, "Miss Rand, you have said that your primary purpose in writing is to project the ideal man. For those who may not have read *Atlas Shrugged* and have not yet met Hank Rearden or John Galt, how would you describe the ideal man?" So it begins with some of her ideas—in this case, growing out of *Atlas Shrugged*. She also was the only interviewee I had—from over 135 interviews—that insisted I read two of her books, *Atlas Shrugged* and *Romantic Manifesto*, before I interviewed her. Now that was a perfectly reasonable request.

What did you think of the interview?

Oh, I was very pleased with it, because it not only brought out her ideas as she might wish to have them brought out, but it brought out things about her life that I think the average person does not know—her time in Hollywood, for example. These are things that one doesn't associate with Ayn Rand.

What did you think of her answers?

It was quite impressive. After all, she is an intellect and a writer, and it was not surprising to have her answer briefly, candidly and, I thought, in well-ordered sentences. I've tried to type a couple of these transcripts myself, of some famous people I interviewed, and I find it almost impossible to do the transcript. That was not so in her case; she answers in complete sentences.

What was the reaction from viewers and your colleagues?

I don't recall that I had any particular reaction at the time, but I have had reaction subsequently, particularly with young people. I've loaned the videocassette out to a number of people who are just absolutely fascinated with Ayn Rand. The reaction was mostly among people who said, "Oh, you interviewed Ayn Rand? How wonderful! Can I see it?"

Is it one of your more well-known interviews?

It is. There's no question about that. It's the only one of the interviews that I did which was actually syndicated. It says an awful lot for Ayn Rand that that's the one that was to be syndicated.[190]

---

190 Some of James Day's other interviewees between 1954 and 1974 included Muhammad Ali, Richard Rodgers, William O. Douglas and Robert F. Kennedy.

Herman Ivey

Colonel Herman Ivey was the instructor at the United States Military Academy at West Point who arranged for Ayn Rand to lecture there on March 6, 1974.

Interview date: March 15, 2000

Scott McConnell: *Tell me briefly about your military career.*

Herman Ivey: I was in the armor branch, tanks, and I learned to fly helicopters. I fought in helicopters in Vietnam, and I commanded tank units in Germany; eventually I became a little more senior and began to go into more headquarters-staff positions.

How did you move into academia?

While I was at West Point for two years flying the superintendent's airplane—this was during an interregnum between two Vietnam tours—I went to night school at Columbia University and achieved the equivalent of an undergraduate major in literature. Then I went to graduate school and got a couple of graduate degrees, and that's how I got the teaching assignment at West Point and how I came to meet Miss Rand.

Why was Ayn Rand chosen to speak at West Point?

Actually, she was first suggested to me by Kelly Weems, an officer who worked for me at West Point. When he made the suggestion, I immediately realized why it was a valuable idea: I'd read her work and knew that she could provide the kind of generalized overview of philosophy that we needed, and besides, she was a very well-known person, and it would be great to have someone like that come to my program, so we invited her.

I had read enough and seen enough of life to know the quality and the value of her ideas, and that's exactly why I went to the authorities, the two people above me, at West Point. I went to them thinking that I was going to have to sell her, because a lot of academics won't even discuss Ayn Rand, for some reason. They replied, "No trouble with us in bringing Ayn Rand." This was not because they thought they knew and agreed with her philosophy, but because they never thought I had a chance of getting her to come to West Point. And then she did accept, so she fooled them.

What was the philosophy program you were teaching?

It was a one-semester survey of philosophy for seniors. It consisted of a lot of brief primary-source readings in philosophy, religion, art and science. It was the kind of course designed to stimulate, to give some basic background in philosophical discourse, but primarily to be a vehicle for discussion, and for the cadets to come to grips with major issues in life. Of course, after her lecture, things that she had said were discussed in the classroom and applied to various philosophers and ideas. It was a very valuable experience.

Which writings by Miss Rand did you teach in class?

I did not teach her novel in the course, per se, but as part of the arrangement for her coming to lecture at West Point, she asked that as many of the cadets as possible read *Atlas Shrugged*, which obviously would be kind of a primary text for understanding her philosophy.

Ayn had told me, "I'll come and lecture to your course, but as a prerequisite, you'll have to have them all read *Atlas Shrugged*," and so I thought, "Oh, my God, we're not going to be able to get her," because we couldn't require them to read it, and we didn't have the study time available for that. If we'd been able to program it a year in advance, it would have been different. So I negotiated with her. I think this is how my visits with her began. I called her up and said, "I need to come down and talk to you," so I went down there and talked to her and said, "I've got to have you up at West Point, and I cannot require the reading of *Atlas Shrugged*, but I can make it voluntary." She said, "Okay, that's good enough."

So we had something like eighty of the about 250 students involved in the course actually agree to read the book. Now, I've got to come up with eighty copies of *Atlas Shrugged* on the spur of the moment— literally within a week. I called the big book stores in New York City. "Oh, no, we'll have to order that. We don't have that, we only have a few copies on hand, and so on." Then I got this inspiration. I had read *Atlas Shrugged* because I'd seen it in a stand in a Greyhound bus station, and I'd bought it and read it on the bus. I thought to myself, if Ayn Rand is selling in the bus stations of America, I bet I can call the shopping mall bookstores and find eighty copies.

I sent one of my guys out on a requisition trip, and in a couple of hours we had ourselves eighty copies of *Atlas Shrugged*, simply by going to the local popular outlets, instead of the New York houses. So there's a little lesson about who Ayn Rand is and who she appeals to.

How was the topic of Miss Rand's speech at West Point chosen?

I do not believe the subject came up until I had to inquire in order to meet deadlines for publicity and announcements for her lecture at West Point. Of course, I had told her that philosophy was a hard sell at the academy; cadets are action-oriented people who are not much inclined to see the relevance of philosophy to their lives. Miss Rand picked up on this, and delivered an address perfectly suited to the occasion.

She was invited and she accepted; what happened next?

She invited me down to her apartment in New York for a couple of visits. I think her purpose was to come to understand more fully and exactly what she was dealing with at my end. I think that she did her homework that way; I think she prepared herself very well for the audience, and I think that's one of the reasons her appearance was so successful.

What was your first impression when meeting Miss Rand?

A very courteous, correct and warm personality. She always treated me with great courtesy and sensitivity, and I found this noteworthy, because her thinking is so hard-boiled, that it's almost as though one needs to have known her as part of the package of reading her. She's one of those people where I think it's good to know the author.

What did you talk about during those meetings?

Basically, she talked, I listened. She would ask me questions about how we used certain philosophical figures in the curriculum. For example, we had brief readings from Plato and Aristotle, and of course, Aristotle she thought was fine, but as to Plato, she asked, "Why are you doing Plato? What is this for?" and so forth. And I said, "The allegory of the cave is useful, because it's a springboard into arts, into literature," and "Okay, so we do doubt," and that brought us into esthetics, and this conversation would go on for hours. She would go into lengthy discourses, not only on her own ideas, but the interplay of her ideas with other philosophers.

Do you remember any of her actual points?

Oh yes. Sometimes I'd frame questions beforehand. I'd be driving down to New York and I'd be thinking, "Well now, what am I going to ask her?" and the following is a question that occurred to me, because it's something I'd recently been reading and thinking about. So I asked her, "What do you think about the proposition that ambiguity is the essence of art, that art feeds on ambiguity, can't exist without ambiguity?" "Absolutely not!" she said. "Totally incorrect. There can be no ambiguity. There is an objectively correct solution to the problem of art, as there is with anything else, and ambiguity is out the window, because of the irrational aspect of it," and she then went into discussion of the irrational.

From our discussions, I realized something I later said when I introduced her at the lecture: no matter where you go in your reading in philosophy, you will usually find that she's already been there. The ideas of these philosophers, she has visited these ideas.

Meaning that she knew and understood the ideas of these philosophers?

Oh yes.

Why did she want to lecture at West Point?

She told me that she didn't do that sort of thing very often. But I think one of the reasons she spent so much time with me was that I think she saw me as somebody who might be worth her while, inasmuch as she had seen a syllabus of the course that I had organized and presented to the cadets, and she knew that if I could do that, that I probably might be worth talking to. I was flattered and honored that I got to spend a great deal of time, maybe altogether ten, fifteen, twenty hours in discussion with her; it was a wonderful experience for me.

Now, I think she felt exactly the same way about the corps of cadets, and anyone else at West Point. She saw this as a great opportunity to present her ideas in person to some of the people she held in very high esteem. I must say, and she told me this, that she had a very high esteem for the professional military officer. I'm not quite sure why that was, because, in a lot of ways, the life of a military officer is a contradiction of some of her tenets, at least in my opinion. But anyway, she did enjoy the contact a lot, and she saw it as an opportunity.

What did you especially enjoy about your conversations with her?

I got a chance to observe a first-class mind operate. And I could listen to her talk about Kant, or someone like that, and listen to her criticisms of Kant, and play them against my own conclusions. It was a wonderful educational experience for me, and that's why I did not try to talk very much, but encouraged her to talk while I listened avidly. I don't know what she was getting out of it, but I was getting a lot out of it.

Do you remember any more about the conversations in her apartment or any other anecdotes?

Oh, God, yes. Here's an impression I had that was so wonderful. There's a passage, I think it's in *Atlas Shrugged*, where she describes two people conversing in the dark, and they are both smoking cigarettes, and as they converse, they gesture, and their cigarettes trace a kind of semaphore, an accompaniment to their conversation. I always thought it was a nice image. And then we were sitting in her apartment one afternoon, and the shadows were lengthening, it was getting darker and darker, and she was sitting on a couch with her back to a window, and I could see only her silhouette and the glow of the cigarette as she gestured and talked, and in fact, I was looking at the very scene she had described in the book. I savored it, because she was solving the problems of the universe, and I was in there having a literary moment.

Did you meet her husband, Frank O'Connor?

I did. She and I and Frank O'Connor went out for dinner at '21'—and I'd never been to such a place. I mean, wow! it was great. We arrived and got out of the vehicle, and stepped up on the sidewalk and the door swung open, and, "Good evening, Miss Rand, how are you this evening?" and we were whisked upstairs to tables, and we sat down to a very enjoyable meal. Unfortunately, the table conversation doesn't return to me, but it was a wonderful opportunity, and I found him a very interesting, charming man, and I enjoyed his company.

I did see his art work. When I was in her apartment, I asked her, "Tell me about this?" and she said, "Oh, that's Frank's work," and it was beautiful—beautiful palette, beautiful colors, these greens and blues, very Mediterranean quality, and strong, hard edges. I thought it was very nice, a very evocative work, and I was impressed.

Was there anything that you learned from her that changed your life or your teaching?

No, I wouldn't say so, mostly because the points of agreement between her philosophical position and mine are such that when she's making those points to me it's like preaching to the choir. I did think that it was an important experience for me, because I was the agent of her coming to West Point. I might say, in that connection, another reason it was so important for me to have her there is that I had the wherewithal to invite only two guest lecturers from the outside to address my course each semester. I liked to go out and find a real artist, or a real scientist or a real philosopher, somebody who really did those things we were reading about in the classroom. In other words, I think the companion appearance for Ayn Rand that semester was Loren Eiseley, who was a preeminent paleontologist, and also a fine poet and prose writer, and I had him come because he combined art and science. And here was Ayn Rand. And this is one of the reasons it was so great for me, because here was a real philosopher who could talk philosophy and speak with some knowledge about many of the people who were appearing in the syllabus.

Let's move to her arrival at West Point. How did she get there?

We offered a sedan to go down for her, but she said, "No, there are several people who want to come up, and so I will drive up." She came up to the Hotel Thayer, the hotel on the military reservation, where she was staying. I met her at the hotel.

I think Leonard Peikoff and his wife, Susan, did visit West Point with her, along with some others.

We took her on a tour of the facilities, and actually I gave a couple of the officers who worked for me opportunities to meet with her, and to escort her here and there, especially Kelly Weems, because I knew it was important to him. He admired her a great deal, and it's because of him that I invited her.

Her visit with General William Knowlton, who was the commandant of West Point, was something that still brings a smile to my face. Of course, I was her primary escort at West Point, and so I got to be the horse-holder at her confab with the rich and powerful there. When General Knowlton found out that she was going to appear, he immediately put in a request for an audience, and so he was on the itinerary, and I took her up to his office. I started to remain outside, but they both said, "No, no, you come on in," and so I sat there and listened to them. General Knowlton was a great admirer of hers, and he showed up for the lecture too. He talked to her, and she talked to him, and it was a mutual admiration society, if one ever existed on this planet.

One thing I might mention. We were limited in how much moving around we could do at West Point, because at the time she was suffering from a respiratory disease[191] and had a great deal of difficulty breathing.

---

191 This was not long before Ayn Rand's lung cancer surgery.

If she had to walk more than fifty feet, she had to stop and rest. She had a shortness of breath problem, and I had a great deal of compassion for her; it was a terrible thing to see, but she was a game girl.

In what way?

She was tough. I could see she was having problems but she would not admit defeat. She would say, "No, no, I can do it. We'll just have to stop along the way."

Can you tell me more about her activities when you were taking her around the base, and what happened before the speech in the evening?

She came in to the English department, where she met with the department head, Colonel Sutherland, and the deputy head, Colonel Capps, who were tenured professors. She received a hundred dollar honorarium for this appearance. I think Colonel Capps talked her out of it, got her to sign her check over to some charity.

What happened after her visit to the English department?

I think one of the other officers might have taken her on a drive-around tour. She was not very long at West Point. It seems to me that she arrived the afternoon before the talk, and then departed the next morning.

Was there a luncheon for her?

No, there was a dinner before the lecture. We took her to the club, and wined her and dined her. At the dinner were many, if not most, of the officers and their wives from the English department. And there was a cocktail hour, where I had an opportunity to present Miss Rand to a number of people who came around to visit with her, and she enjoyed that a lot. Then we sat down and had dinner. She sat with Colonel Sutherland, and a good time was had by all. Then, after coffee and an appropriate pause, it was time to get up and make our way down to the lecture hall, which was very close by.

So her lecture wasn't just for your classes, it was open to everybody?

The lecture was for my class, but all the lectures that are delivered for courses are open to the Academy community and the public-at-large. So this lecture certainly was, and it was also advertised in the local publications and bulletins. I had a great crowd. When Loren Eiseley showed up, I had a huge crowd; people came from everywhere, but not like when she showed up. If we'd have had a larger auditorium, I think we could have probably filled it up.

Tell me about the lecture.

The whole event was recorded. The lecture began with a brief introduction by myself, because when you're dealing with someone who needs no introduction, there's no point in fooling around, and the audience wants to hear her, not me. But I did make a couple of remarks about the range of her philosophical writings and her literature, and turned it over to her. She delivered a lecture titled "Philosophy: Who Needs It."[192] It began anecdotally, with this spaceship landing on some unknown place, and you get out of your spaceship, and you don't know where you are, which way is up, and you have to figure it out. And the analogy, the metaphor, was, "This is life. Life is something you have to figure out. You can figure it out, and you have the responsibility to figure it out." It was just exactly the kind of message that I wanted professional officers—or potential professional officers—to hear.

What was the reaction of the audience during the lecture?

Very attentive. The place was packed. It was a standing-room-only crowd. We held it in the largest auditorium we had at the time, about a 1,500-seat auditorium. And there were probably a hundred or so people standing in the back.

What happened after the speech and Q and A were finished?

The question-and-answer period went on, and, like always, we were entitled only to so much of the cadets' time, so we had to cut it off. But I told the audience that she was going to the officers' club, and would be available there for questions and answers, and asked that the cadets be given priority with her.

So we made our way over to the officers' club, and we had a chair arranged there for her to sit, and places for others to sit around, room for people to stand, and so forth, and they did, and they thronged in. The place was packed with scores of young men who were there to talk to her personally, and there was a lot of philosophy talked there. It was not idle talk. I don't know that Miss Rand ever involved herself in idle talk. There were easily fifty, a hundred people—they were coming and going. Of course, the cadets only had so many minutes they could devote to this, but because of that it was very impressive to see them

---

192 The speech became the title essay in her book *Philosophy: Who Needs It.*

come over and spend additional study time talking to her, when they knew that they were going to be hurting for adequate study time when they got back to their rooms. So it was very successful that way.

What was her reaction to the speech and the Q and A?

The next morning she expressed satisfaction with the night, and appreciation, and said that it had been all that she had wanted it to be. She was very generous with me and told me that if ever she could help me in any way, to let her know. Wow! I thought that was very nice, "Thank you very much."

What was your impression of her talk?

Great. In fact, I felt it was so appropriate that I asked her if I could use a transcript of her lecture as the introduction for the course textbook for the following year. She gave her permission, and we were pleased to print the speech standing first in our textbook for the next year, to be read as the initial assignment for our cadets. Her lecture could be used, be referred to, throughout the course of instruction, so it was very valuable that way.

Any other points of conversation with Miss Rand while she was at West Point?

There were a couple things that I'd like to observe about her. We were standing in front of the Hotel Thayer waiting for transportation, talking, and one of her companions that she had brought up with her from New York City made an ethnic slur. She immediately corrected him, and apologized to me, which was, I thought, a very appropriate thing to do. I was very impressed by that, because this is a real test of people. When she did that, I saw that (a) she had the same problems a lot of us have: we attract people sometimes who are working on a different wavelength, and yet at the same time are valuable, enthusiastic supporters; and (b) there was a moral lesson. It was good for me to hear and see that, because I would not have any reason to draw a contrary conclusion from reading her philosophy. But sometimes it can be pretty harsh. For example, after the lecture there was a question-and-answer period, which I opened by observing to the audience that Miss Rand had tossed and gored a number of sacred cows that night, with which she agreed, and the audience laughed. Then there were some sympathetic questions, that is, questions from people who were on her side of things—but then there were some questions from people who were raising controversies, and one of the questions was from a cadet who asked her how she squared her conclusions of Objectivism with the kind of historical record that we had as a nation: the dispossession and extermination campaigns against the American Indians, for example. She answered, "As to the American Indians, it is always going to transpire that when a superior technological culture meets up with an inferior one, the superior one will prevail."[193] And so she wasn't yielding any ground on the question of the dispossession of the Native Americans by our culture. She was observing that, "Hey, this is the way of the world. This is what happened, you could do it gently, or you could do it roughly, but it's what happens." So you see, when you pair that position, that argument that she's making, with her refusal to countenance prejudicial remarks, you get a better picture of a well-rounded person.

Who made the ethnic slur?

It was not Leonard Peikoff. There was another man there.

Was there any other way that you taught her literature or used her work in class?

I'm sure that after her lecture it came up. In fact, one of the instructors, I think it was Jack Bergen, came to me one day and he told me that the students spent the whole class talking about her lecture. So that was a very favorable sign. I didn't teach her any other way—we did that during the course.

Do you have a general opinion of Ayn Rand?

I love her as a person. She does have the liability of repudiating the irrational, and I'm afraid that it may turn out that the thing that she is repudiating is simply a different kind of logic, and this is how she and I basically differed. She is committed to a unitary logic that what is psychological is reality, but I see biology as a different kind of logic, and what she calls "irrational" may turn out simply to be the logic of biology, rather than the logic of the psyche.

She served me so well at that time, and I found her such a good person, that I wanted to reciprocate as best I could and leave some personal memories of my contact with her. I have good personal

---

193 The main point Ayn Rand made during the Q and A was that the white settlers of America were morally right because "they represented the progress of the mind, not centuries of brute stagnation and superstition."

memories.

Is Ayn Rand influential in the American military?

I would say so. Look at the spontaneous outpouring of interest that happened at West Point when she appeared there. Of course, you've got to evaluate the source—I am a West Point graduate—but it really is true that until something happens at West Point, it really hasn't happened in the military. I saw the spontaneous support that her visit received there and could see how enthusiastically General [William A.] Knowlton—as an example; a very senior and successful general who went on to do great things—was a strong supporter of hers. I think when I was a young professional soldier, a lieutenant and a captain, the ethic of Ayn Rand, her Objectivism, was a good code to go by. It was a good guide, and it is a good guide for the active life. I'm not sure it's a good guide for the contemplative life.

How was it a good guide for the military code?

Because you must act. You must decide. You must take responsibility for your decision. You mustn't say, "I had an irrational impulse to do this." This is a very unprofessional attitude. It would not be accepted in the military, nor would it be accepted in the medical profession, nor any other profession I can think of.

Has Ayn Rand influenced you as a person or an academic?

My initial impression was "Ayn Rand, the Un-Philosopher." It was like she was tossing and goring these sacred cows left and right, and I liked this. And young people liked this, and it's good for us, and it frightens the established academic intellectuals. They don't even want to talk about Ayn Rand. It's like, "So what are you afraid of?" Afraid of a little hard-boiled logic?

Jack Capps

Brigadier General Jack Capps was the deputy head of the English department at West Point when Ayn Rand spoke there in 1974.

Interview date: March 1, 1999

Scott McConnell: *What was the purpose in having Miss Rand speak at West Point?*

Jack Capps: The course director, Colonel Ivey, and some others wanted to have her views expressed because they were different from some of the philosophy that the lads had been reading, and we were trying to be as balanced as we could. She was speaking to upperclassmen who were in a philosophy course. They were fairly early in the term and had progressed through Hume and Kant and a few others.

What was your involvement?

I was then deputy head of the department, and when we had guest lecturers, I was the one who looked after the details to make sure that things were in order—and they usually were—but, in this case there was a very practical matter: my quarters were the closest ones on the post, where she could make a stop and rest up a bit before the evening began.

As a matter of fact, that was a routine that we went through fairly frequently. By that I mean, people would come in, we would host them, fix them with a drink, and go to dinner, and so on and so forth.

And, by the way, in thanks for providing her a dressing room and, I think, maybe a drink before the dinner before we went off to the club, I received the *Ayn Rand Letter* for some years after that.

Tell me more about the cadets Miss Rand would be addressing.

The course that Miss Rand was addressing was the core course in philosophy. And the English department had two terms of composition. Then there was a literature course for one term in their sophomore year, and then a readings-in-philosophy course during their senior year. Those were all prescribed.

The majority were cadets who would graduate that spring. At the time, I was teaching an elective course in American literature, and we were doing Melville, Twain, James and others, and I had invited my seminar to attend, so they were there as well. This was an opportunity for these students to listen to a current twentieth-century novelist, whom I think most of them had read, at least to some degree. So they were rather eager to be at her talk.

There may have been some other classes, and evening lectures such as that, all cadets were permitted to attend, if they chose. Only the ones in the philosophy course were required to be there.

Was Miss Rand taught in the literature courses?

I'm sure that in this philosophy course there were some readings from her literature, and also we had a course in the modern novel, and I'm quite sure that she was taught in this course at one time or another, probably more than once.

Had you read Miss Rand's works?

I had read *The Fountainhead* and *Atlas Shrugged*, but I think that might have been my limit at that time.

Can I ask what your opinion of them was?

Certainly. I could understand the appeal, because she's a powerful and persuasive writer. I'd hesitate to make a critical judgment as to whether these are going to go down as landmarks in literature generally—I don't know. My feeling was that, to pardon the expression, they were then, and to some degree still are, rather cult pieces. That's an unkind word, I know.

What was the schedule for the day of her talk?

She arrived, I think, about 4 o'clock. These lectures were always scheduled for around 7, 7:30, in the evening, when the cadets would have finished dinner.

What happened in the afternoon? Did she visit some classes?

She might have, but I rather doubt it. I don't think she was there early enough to do that, because I believe she came straight to our quarters and changed clothes, and the outfit she put on is not something she would have worn to a classroom.

Describe the evening's events.

It was a remarkable evening. I think we went to dinner beforehand at the officers' club; that was the usual procedure. I

may have been sitting below the salt.[194] We went from there over
to the auditorium, and it was all quite decorous when the speaker
arrived. The assembled people would rise; then after the speaker was
introduced, in this case by Colonel Ivey, everyone was seated. He
made some remarks about her writing prominence, et cetera, et cetera,
then she took it from there. She wasn't a very big woman, but she was
a very forceful speaker.

Another thing to recall: at this time the Vietnam War was still
very much in the air. Of course, the war had ended by that time, but
it had some bearing on her reception there, and the cadets' reaction.
And particularly, I think, in the case of Colonel Ivey, who had two
tours in Vietnam as a pilot, and had a rather distinguished record
there. The Academy, officers and cadets alike, had been living with
some very bitter and strong criticism over the seasons. They were all
defensive about the necessary position we had maintained in sending
people off to the war and back again, so that was very much part of
our lives at that point.

I mention all that because Miss Rand then spoke to the group,
and congratulated them from the very beginning. At times, it seemed
to me almost patronizing, but nonetheless, she congratulated them on
seeing what they had to do, and then doing it with a certain amount of
enthusiasm not everyone had at the time. She expressed great admiration
for this. The cadets, and those members of the post present, were hungry
for that sort of endorsement, which they had not heard from outside, as
it were, very often. People who in the years before had come and spoken
had maintained a rather discreet silence on such matters.

*Tell me more about how the students and officers reacted to her
comments.*

They were favorably impressed. They were aching for this sort of
fulsome endorsement. At the end of her presentation, she stepped from
behind the lectern—of course, she was just barely tall enough to see
over it, but that didn't deter her at all—and giving a somewhat British-
style salute, said ". . . you men of West Point, I salute you!" And those
were her concluding words. At that point, the cadets broke into great
applause, and she got a standing ovation.

All was well up to that point. Then the questions and answers

---

194 This connotes a less desirable location, because in medieval times, salt was placed
near the king.

began. The questions were quite pointed. I only remember two or three of them.

One question that was difficult, and it rather cooled the enthusiasm, had to do with what was in fact going on at that time: the Indian demonstrations at Wounded Knee and Rosebud reservations in South Dakota.

A cadet stood up and asked Miss Rand what she thought about what these Indians were seeking and demanding. She responded that the Indians had had this country for five thousand years and had done nothing with it; that they should stand aside and let someone do something with it. And that, I suppose, was not an entirely surprising answer, but the thing that chilled the cadets was, what she didn't know, but what the members of the class knew, that it was a Native American who had asked the question. So that cooled the atmosphere considerably, and the questioning tapered off after that. It was unfortunate.

After the lecture was over, she proceeded back to the officers' club, where some of the cadets, and a number of officers, wanted to continue the discussion. Some of the people who had driven some distance were grateful for that, because the question period in the auditorium had been reserved for the cadets.

What was the faculty's reaction to Miss Rand?

I think they were grateful for her having been there, because the comparisons they could make in the classroom made for lively discussions about such things as Kant's attitudes towards phenomenal experience, which Miss Rand disagreed with. Also, the lecture filled its place in this course. It was part of the perspective we were trying to achieve. Now, how much of that the cadets took away, I don't know, but I feel sure that it was worth their while to get yet another point of view from what they had been hearing.

What was your impression of Miss Rand's talk and Q and A?

My impression was that the cadets and the faculty were very much taken with it, and I had the feeling that they were taken up with great enthusiasm for the evening, but when they had a time to sit down and think it over, that some of the things that Miss Rand advocated were things that they had gone to war against. And what the faculty were trying to do—and I think they achieved this—was to give the cadets a more balanced perspective. Though the faculty and cadets may have been persuaded by Miss Rand's presence to tip the balance in her direction, I believe it all evened out later on.

What were some of the things you thought they went to war against but that she advocated?

There was something in the principle apparent in the Indian question: that the people who serve in uniform have to show a bit more understanding of the people whom they work with and work for, than I think Miss Rand would have allowed. That's part of their business. One of the other philosophers, I think Rosenberg from Columbia, had presented to the cadets rather persuasively that they should not only understand what they were fighting for and what they had to destroy, but also what their mission would require them to destroy as they did it—that sort of insight.

Did you enjoy Miss Rand's talk?

Yes I did. I must say that as it progressed, I was more and more put off by it. She was congratulating the cadets and officers for their devotion to duty, et cetera, et cetera, but it gave me the feeling that she realized she had these people going, and she played them rather like an angler with a trout on the line, and this I didn't care for.

What was Miss Rand's reaction to the speech and the events of the day?

I think she had a great time. She was very warmly, enthusiastically, received, and then when she arrived at the club, it was interesting. It was rather like Queen Victoria on the throne. She was seated, and other people were standing around and seated on the floor around her asking questions.

Why at West Point should every student study philosophy?

Rather for the reasons that Mr. Rosenberg pointed out, and also we hope that these people will depart from the Academy and be commissioned as what we called "Enlightened Leaders." Understanding philosophical principles does a great deal to provide that enlightenment, and after three and a half years of education or courses there, it's rather important, we think, to provide them with an overarching philosophy course that might set those principles and factual matter that they've absorbed into a wiser context and some order. That's the point of it.

What is the dominant philosophy at West Point, especially in this period in which Miss Rand spoke?

I wouldn't say there was one. That was one of the reasons for this course, that it was, as I've said, to give the cadets a more balanced view in philosophical matters, and there certainly was no approved solution; the Academy had no fixed philosophy. Above all, it was not an indoctrination course at all.

Doesn't West Point have its own philosophy, such as honor?

Well, of course! Yes, yes, yes, yes. Sum it up with—and this was what Miss Rand was so taken with—the motto of the Academy, "Duty, Honor, and Country," and she saw this as honorably doing their duty in the service of the country, whenever it called upon them. This is the thing that she was complimenting them on having done, during the previous ten years.

What was your opinion of Ayn Rand?

I thought she was a very tough lady.

Murray Dworetzky

Murray Dworetzky was Ayn Rand and Frank O'Connor's internist.

Interview date: January 21, 1999

Scott McConnell: *What was Ayn Rand like as a patient?*

Murray Dworetzky: Excellent. She did what you asked her to. You had to explain in great detail anything you wanted her to do, why and where.

Tell me about Miss Rand and her lung cancer.

I was the one who made the diagnosis. It was a dramatic moment. I remember it vividly. She was a smoker, and I used to yell at her to stop smoking. She was a Russian lady, and she would hold the cigarette in the European style. The opposite of the way we do, with the back of the hand showing to you. She would say, "Give me a rational explanation for why I should stop smoking." She was big into rational. I had just gotten her X-rays, and I put them up on my viewing box. There was a nodule in her lung, and I tapped the X-ray and said, "There's a good reason right there." She quickly put her cigarette out, and I said, "I'm afraid, dear, it's too late."

I also said, "This has a very bad look to it, because your previous X-rays were normal." I X-rayed her once a year because she was a smoker. I said, "The probability is that it's not good news, and you're going to have to do this to take care of it."

I know she'd been a heavy smoker all her life. She never was without a cigarette in my office. She knew exactly what was the cause of her cancer. She never smoked another cigarette.

We talked about it, and I then immediately picked up the phone and called up the surgeon, Cranston Holman, and arranged for her to see him with the films. They did surgery, and she had treatment done; she had radiation done in addition to the surgery. I wasn't taking care of her afterwards; Dr. Holman and a pulmonologist saw her.

What was her reaction to the news?

She was a tough lady. She was very interesting. Her relationship with her husband was totally opposite to her relationship with herself. She was totally terrified of anything that happened to him. He meant too much to her. She absolutely went ape when he got sick.

Could you give me an example?

She just expressed such anxiety. If he had a cold, or anything, she would be tremendously anxious about it, like a mother hen. She made less fuss about her cancer than she did about him having a cold or bronchitis. I remember making a house call to where they lived on 34th Street. She would be absolutely bananas about him when he got sick, and with herself she was very casual about it. Rather striking. She was a totally different person in the presence of Frank O'Connor.

What was his reaction?

Oh, they got along very well, beautifully. He was very attentive, but he needed more caring than she did. He was frail. She was just unbelievable with him—not what you would expect Ayn Rand to be, because Ayn Rand wore a dollar-sign around her neck and all that business.

What was she like after the surgery?

She was quite a brick. She was a very courageous person and she showed it. She was really amazing. She lived her life and didn't let it get her down. Most of that I got from other people, her surgeon, Cranston Holman, for example.

Generally, what was her health like when she was your patient?

She was in good health, generally, except for the smoking. She always was a healthy woman. I don't ever remember her being sick. I think she came in mainly for routine checkups once a year. She was a nice, civil woman and I enjoyed talking with her about her field, and occasionally we had little talks about philosophy, but she was very serious—no joking about her philosophy.

Ayn Rand was very special in many ways. She was not big on interpersonal relationships—at least not with her doctor. I'm very much of a personal guy, but she was a cool person—really practiced her Objectivism in a personal sense. She was very intellectual. She may have been emotional—she *was* emotional—but the only time I ever saw her express emotionality was in her relationship with Frank O'Connor, where she was very emotional relating to him—but with herself she was cool, at least with me. I found her not easy to be comfortable with. She was always "philosophical" with a capital *P*—to my mind at least.

She was strictly business in my office: not a lot of humor, not very light-hearted. She came with a problem, it was taken care of and that was it. It wasn't that she was not polite—but she was straightforward and there was not a lot of nonsense, playtime—give and take. It was partly my doing because I sort of felt that was the way she wanted it and I respected that. I liked to tailor my attitude with patients toward their particular needs.

What was her attitude toward doctors?

She thought a lot of my work. She was very much into competence and efficiency. She was very fond of doctors who were good. She didn't view them as gods—she viewed them as technicians. The way that we are, really.

I knew two young teenagers, and they and their father were very enchanted by this whole business of Objectivism and *Atlas Shrugged*. I liked these kids and persuaded her to see them. She said to me, "I'll do this provided that you allow me an hour of your time sometime to talk." I said, "Okay." We never got around to it, and then she got sick and disappeared. They went down to her apartment and she spent about an hour and a half with them. They said they had a wonderful time with her.

Did you kid Miss Rand about her philosophy?

No. I just said to her, "You'll have to forgive me, Miss Rand, but I'm really not into your philosophy."

What did she say?

Something like "Just be a good doctor and you're into my philosophy."

Malcolm Fraser

John Malcolm Fraser was the prime minister of Australia from December 1975 to March 1983. He was head of CARE Australia, a foreign aid charity, from 1987 to 2002. He met Miss Rand at the White House in July 1976.

Interview date: August 17, 1999

Scott McConnell: *When and how did you first become aware of Ayn Rand and her works?*

Malcolm Fraser: It would be thirty, thirty-five years ago, through reading *Atlas Shrugged*.

What was your reaction to the book?

I thought there were some important truths in it. I read it at a time when many governments and many countries had gone too far and were spending too much money and thinking they could solve everyone's problems by so doing. I thought that *Atlas Shrugged* underlined in quite a stark way some of the problems and some of the fallacies behind such policies.

Did the book influence your thinking?

It would have influenced my thinking to an extent, but I enjoyed the book because I agreed with the policy positions that seemed to be enunciated in it. I was never one of those people who believed that you could solve all the problems facing government by throwing money at them.

You are often quoted in the media as saying that Atlas Shrugged *was your favorite book and Ayn Rand your favorite author. Tell me about that?*

It was for the reasons I just mentioned. It was a very long book, but I found it a fascinating one. And it carried a great story with it, but it wove into that story some very important messages.

Is it still your favorite book, and she your favorite author?

Oh, if not, very close to.

In 1975 you won a great landslide victory against the socialist Labor

Party and were coming into government to clean up the Australian economy. How were your policies inspired or influenced by Ayn Rand?

She obviously thought they were because when I met her, when a reception or dinner was given for me at the White House, she was there and we had a brief talk. She said to me, "You're the only head of government putting my policies into effect." We'd had in Australia a government that had spent far too much money, who had pretended all problems could be solved by governments waving some sort of a wand, and we had to draw all that back and cut expenditure and reduce government activities. This was long before Mrs. Thatcher and long before President Reagan. My government was about the first that started to turn back the tide of excess socialist expenditure or social expenditure. I don't know that these policies were directly influenced by *Atlas Shrugged*, but certainly the book and the thoughts that were in it would have reinforced my own views about what governments could or could not achieve. Also, it would have reinforced my own views about the role of individuals in society and that people must try and do for themselves.

What is that viewpoint?

To the greatest extent possible, governments should conduct policies that encourage people to do things for themselves. It's not a question of government doing things for you. It's a question of you looking after yourself. One of the worst fallacies of socialism was the idea that governments can replace your own initiative, your own energy, your own vigor.

Was it difficult to try to implement that idea in Australia?

In many respects, yes, because a lot of businesses had got used to the idea of government spending large funds, which allowed them to pick up more contracts. They came to the government and said, "Cutting expenditures is okay because the books aren't balanced, but you mustn't cut them in our area." We had to change a whole attitude of mind.

Do you feel you were successful at that?

I think so.

Did you push moral arguments or was it more the practical one of budgets and expenditure restraint?

Both. There were the practical arguments, but then there was the moral argument about what kind of society are we trying to achieve. I think that's a very important element of it.

Had you read any of her other works?

The Fountainhead I've read. I enjoyed it very much. It was a great work. Again, it was expressing some important truths. It was really about achievement. All her writing seemed to be about individuals and what they can do, what they can build, what they can create.

Did that give you a sense of personal validation or empowerment?

I certainly thought it was a very welcome change from so much of what has been written in the last thirty or forty years, which has quite a different philosophy. When you basically agree with something, it gives you a sense of enjoyment finding a great writer expressing such thoughts, such values, such views.

Is your philosophy still the same today—pro-individual?

Yes, it is, very much. Although today, I think in some respects, people have taken the ideology, which in Australia is called "economic rationalism," too far. There are certain obligations which I think governments should fulfill. I now think that governments have tended to withdraw from some things which they ought to be doing.

Do you believe in altruism?

Yes, I do.

Could you briefly explain why?

There are a large number of people in the world who are born into a condition in which they have no options, no opportunity, and where their own communities are structured in such a way that there's no real hope for them. I think that people who come from countries like America or Australia need to try and alter that situation in the Third World in a way so the people in the Third World can then advance their own interests.

On December 13, 1975, you defeated the socialist Labor government in a landslide election. I have in Miss Rand's archives a copy of a telegram of December 15, 1975, that she sent you congratulating you on your victory.[195] *Do you remember that?*

Yes, I do. It was just one of those things that was moving and touching to think that somebody so far away, in a sense, could be interested about an election in Australia.

Let's turn to your White House visit of July 27, 1976. Why did you want to meet Miss Rand?

I wanted to meet the person who had written *Atlas Shrugged*, to see what sort of person she was. I found someone who was interesting to meet, who was clearly well informed on what my government had been trying to do. She said she was delighted to meet the only head of government implementing the sorts of policies that she was advocating. I took that as a great compliment. From the nature of these events, these discussions with a lot of people around are always short, but I've always remembered that meeting.

Tell me more about the meeting.

She was sitting down. I went over to her to sit down beside her. We talked for probably five to seven minutes about ideas that we seemed to share in common and about the work that my government was trying to do.

Did she give you any advice on what you were doing?

No. She didn't give advice. She wished me good luck and said stick with it.

What was your overall impression of her?

Oh, a most impressive person. She was a very significant personality. Great character. Great strength of purpose.

What's your opinion of Ayn Rand and her works?

She is one of the most important writers of the last hundred years.

---

195 The telegram to Mr. Fraser read, "Please accept my congratulations on your great victory and my best wishes for the future. Ayn Rand."

Albert S. Ruddy

Albert S. Ruddy is a Hollywood producer whose films *The Godfather* and *Million Dollar Baby* won Academy Awards for Best Picture. In the early 1970s, he was going to produce *Atlas Shrugged*.

Interview date: October 20, 1999

Scott McConnell: *How did you become interested in* Atlas Shrugged *as a movie?*

Albert S. Ruddy: Like a hundred million other people, I had read the book in college. I had read the book three or four times before I met Ayn Rand. As a matter of fact, I had underlined hundreds of pages of lines in the book. It was like a bible to me. When I got through doing *The Godfather*, I knew *Atlas Shrugged* was a very ambitious project and I felt that it would be something that Ayn Rand might entertain— based on the quality of the film *The Godfather*. So I called up Curtis Brown, her agents, and they told me, "Look, Ayn has never given the book to anybody. Just out of respect, she'll be happy to meet you." I said, "Set me up to meet her. I would love to meet this woman."

The first time I met her was at Curtis Brown. Her representative was behind the desk in this huge office, and there were four or five empty chairs around, with Ayn in a rather small love seat. I walked in, and I squeezed right into the love seat. She just kind of looked up because I'm six-four and she much smaller than I. I had my arm around the back of the couch, and she said, "Darling, what books do you read?" I said, "Ayn, I'm not into reading a lot of novels. I'm basically someone who tries to function and get a lot of stuff done. However, I read *Atlas Shrugged*, and oh, it was fantastic."

She wanted to know in a moment what I wanted to do with the movie. I said, "Ayn, you've written one of the great thrillers, one of the great love stories—the greatest part for a woman I have read in contemporary literature." She said, "Exactly, darling. That's exactly the way I see it. That's all I ever wanted it to be."

I know I told Ayn Rand what I wanted it to be, which she agreed with. She agreed with the thriller aspect, with the love story, the sexuality of the piece. You don't have to do a paean to Objectivism, because it's there. The fact that they have to go fight to save what is theirs and then realize that Galt is turning off the motors of the world, that is implicit in the story. So I don't have to whip that. That's there. But what's in front of that? Who are the characters who you're going to fall in love with, you're going to care about, who you're going to hope live or die, who you hope are going to get what they want? What do they want? What's stopping them from getting what they want? And what happens at the end? Very simple. That's the four steps that I would look at. And it's all in the book.

Tell me more about what else you discussed at that first meeting.

She asked me about myself, how I happened to get in the movie business. I created a show called *Hogan's Heroes*. She got a big kick out of it when I told her that. She laughed.

What was your impression of her?

After five minutes of meeting her, she appeared to me much larger than she appeared to be physically, because she was dynamic, extremely incisive. The time I spent with her, even the last meeting, which proved to be not too fruitful, were moments that I'll always remember because she was fascinating. First of all, you are going to meet Ayn Rand. It's just a great honor. I was looking forward to meeting her, and it was not a disappointment.

So we had a big press conference to announce the project, and we were going to work a deal out. We worked the finances out and were working out the contract. We got to a couple of issues, and one which turned out to be the unraveling of everything: she wanted final script approval. I tried to explain to her. I said, "Ayn, in all due respect, if anyone was ever entitled to get final script approval based on how important this novel is, you would normally get it, but I can tell you right now that no one is going to give final script approval to the author of an eleven-hundred-page book. I mean, you cannot have John Galt making a speech to America at the end for sixty pages in a movie. However, you will be very involved in developing the script, but there will come a moment—and this is what frightens major authors with very valuable pieces—in this process when the director takes over the production of a film. No director is going to say, 'You have final script approval and I'll shoot what you come up with.' They want to have input, as they must, because they are the director. The same for the producer, who has other problems to consider mounting a film, and the screenwriter, who many times is a student of cinematic economy and knows how to convey what it's about without having to do it in fourteen pages. So there's a moment when you have to let go, or else. . . . I said, why don't you do this movie yourself?"

Why wasn't this issue finalized before you had the press conference? I would have assumed that at the press conference you would have announced a done-deal.

Basically, it was a done-deal as far as what I thought the crucial issues were. I have never made a deal with the author of a book having final script approval. It never entered my mind that it would be an issue here. In retrospect, it was foolish, because obviously the book was that important, but I thought I could speak to her—because basically she was a pragmatic person—and try to explain that the process itself demanded that at a point, everyone has to let go. The novelist. The screenwriter, the director, the producer, the budget, the shooting. The producer and the director have to let it go to the marketing people. That is a chain of different departments that takes a film from its inception to when it is shown on the screen at your local movie theater. And there can't be one person who has total control.

What were your plans for the movie?

It was going to be a big feature film, two and a half to three hours long. The problem you have with the material—it's not a problem, it's called an "embarrassment of riches"—is that you have got to throw out so much. The truth is that all eleven hundred pages are not going to be in the movie. That's a given before you start. So the puzzle in making a movie from the book is knowing what to abstract. We're not going to write new dialogue. Every line of dialogue that you will see in the movie is going to be Ayn's dialogue. I mean no one would have the gall to try to write new scenes with Dagny and Hank Rearden or Mouch or anybody else. But what is the abstracted essence of this novel for a motion picture? That is the question.

What did you and Miss Rand agree was the essence?

Basically, it was going to be a thriller, a love story, with the underpinnings of a man who wanted to turn off the motor of the world and to restart it again. But it was going to be a thriller and have a lot of suspense, and be a terrific love story. And it was going to be a mystery of trying to figure out who was pulling these strings. The main line was Dagny trying to save the railroad and Rearden trying to save the alloy and how they come together.

One of the humorous things that came up was that she wanted it in her contract that every time she had to go to the West Coast she had to fly in a private jet. When I asked her why, she said, "Darling, if the Russians find out I'm flying on an airliner, they'll hijack it." Which I thought was a bit extreme. But I said, "That's no problem." So most of the things she wanted I could accommodate.

What else did she want?

She wanted to meet the writer of the script before we hired him. She wanted to meet the director before we made a deal. I wanted to give her consultation rights up and down the line, because the one thing I knew instinctively was no matter what the contract said, when this movie came out, you wanted to have her approval. You didn't want to do *Atlas Shrugged* and have her do interviews saying, "This is not my movie. I hate the thing." It was just the one thing that was impractical.[196]

Did you discuss The Godfather *with Miss Rand?*

Only to the degree that she was very taken with the movie. She thought that the epic size of *The Godfather* and the time we took in telling the story paralleled what was required to put *Atlas Shrugged* on the screen.

Tell me about the Atlas Shrugged *press conference at '21', on May 10, 1972.*

It was a gala event. There must have been a hundred and fifty people crowded into '21'. Curtis Brown told me that every major director and producer both in the United States and Europe at one time or another tried to acquire the book, and she would never entertain it.

She was marvelous. She was what you would expect her to

---

196 Miss Rand clearly believed that Ruddy promised her script approval, for she wrote the following in her announcement of the project (*The Ayn Rand Letter*, June 5, 1972): "For almost fifteen years, I had refused to sell *Atlas Shrugged* except on condition that I would have the right of approval of the film script, a right which Hollywood does not grant to authors. Mr. Ruddy had the courage (and the respect for *Atlas Shrugged*) to break the precedent and agree to my condition." And in an August 18, 1972, letter to Ruddy (several months after the press conference), Ayn Rand's agent expresses concern that Ruddy does "not intend to uphold our agreement."

be. Had a great brittle sense of humor. Very charming. Incisive. Obviously, she was someone that everyone was anxious to hear and meet because—especially in New York—she was one of the great literary figures of the world.

Do you remember your casting preferences at the time?

My idea at the time was to use Faye Dunaway as Dagny Taggart, Clint Eastwood for Hank Rearden, Alain Delon for Francisco and Robert Redford for John Galt.

Did you tell Miss Rand those considerations?

Yes. She loved them.

How did the relationship end?

The last time I saw Ayn was at the time her cat had died. She had an apartment on 34th Street. I got a little Siamese kitten and drove by at about 3 o'clock, with Betty, my secretary, in the car, waiting downstairs because we were leaving for California at 6 o'clock. I brought the cat up and I tried to explain to Ayn why I couldn't give the control to her, as much as I would like to give her everything, why I couldn't give it to her. We talked until 9 or 9:30. And I said, "Ayn, can I speak to you by myself?" So we went in the bedroom, just she and I. We left Betty and Frank in the other room. I said, "Ayn, I can't make a deal with you, but I am prepared to wait as long as I have breath in me, as long as I live, to do this goddamn thing one way or another, whether you're here or not. That's how I feel," and that's what I told her straight out, which she wasn't offended by. She kind of laughed. I said, "But I'm going to be the last man standing in this contest. I'm going to get this made one day." And she laughed and that's how we ended up. I couldn't give her what she wanted, and she was adamant. She said, "Darling, if the communists buy the studio, they'll wreck my book."

What did Miss Rand say when you gave her the cat?

She was very touched. She didn't expect it. She loved it. It was a little Siamese kitten.

"Angel," I think it was called.

Her cat had died and I liked this woman a lot, I must tell you. Obviously, I would have done anything to get the book. I would have gotten an elephant and a gorilla and brought them over. But the truth is, that aside, I genuinely liked her. She was very kind to me, and at the press conference, she was deferential. She treated me very nicely, and I respected that. And I personally was very taken by the fact that she was as kind and liked me as much as she did.

She had a great sense of humor. There was nothing prim about her. There was a directness in her that I responded to. And she didn't come on like she was an important literary figure or an important anything, quite frankly. We got on a one-to-one basis. If you knew what you wanted and you had an agenda, you could hold your own. You could deal with her very, very directly. You didn't have to defer to Ayn Rand because of who she was. And I liked that about her. She didn't automatically assume a mantle. Because she could have, since she was entitled to. She didn't deal that way. She dealt straight up. I have met people of a lower caliber who tried to lord it, who tried to assume a much higher position when you started a meeting, than Ayn Rand did. She just wanted to hear the first line out of your mouth.

Michael Jaffe

Michael Jaffe is a Hollywood producer who, with his father, Henry Jaffe, worked from the late 1970s to the early '80s with Miss Rand, developing *Atlas Shrugged* into a miniseries.

Interview date: November 19, 1999

Scott McConnell: *How did you first become interested in* Atlas Shrugged *as a movie?*

    Michael Jaffe: I became interested because my father, Henry Jaffe, was very good friends with Paul Klein, who was running NBC back in the mid-70s. Klein loved the book and asked my father to see if he could get the rights. So I accompanied my father to the East Coast, where we met with Ayn and began the long process of trying to buy the rights to *Atlas Shrugged*, which we did successfully. This was around '78–'79, and it took about a year.

What was your impression of the book?

    I didn't read the book until NBC expressed an interest in it. My enduring impression of the book is its emphasis on creative vision and the right of people to market their talent as they see fit. That stayed with me for a long, long time, and Ayn and I talked about it a lot. In fact, I thought we became pretty good friends. We went out to dinner frequently and talked about a broad range of issues.

Tell me about your first meeting with Miss Rand.

    I can't tell you about the first, but I can tell you about one of the last. It was nine months into it, and, of course, Ayn had insisted on a level of control that had never been granted by any network to anybody in the past. She had achieved that, and we had worked out some very clever language in the documents to please NBC, and they were very significant, ground-breaking negotiations. When we got right near the end and needed to close the deal, we went to New York. Ayn's attorney, Paul Gitlin, and Ayn's agent, Perry Knowlton, were there. Now, Paul Gitlin had a goatee and a mustache, Perry Knowlton had the same—maybe more—and my father, and Charlie Beecker, our attorney, and I all had full beards. We got to that part of the agreement where Ayn specifically required that none of her heroes—Hank Rearden, John Galt and Francisco—could have any facial hair. She was very

513

charming about it, and we all had quite a laugh because everybody she had surrounded herself with at that table had facial hair. Bear in mind, it shows you that she was capable of making a very reasoned judgment.

I have to say that my most enduring impression of Ayn is that in person—outside the public eye in a non-confrontational environment— she was one of the most gracious, engaging conversationalists, open-minded, decisive, thoughtful, humorous. I enjoyed nothing as much as spending a half-hour or an hour at a meal alone with Ayn, which I was fortunate enough to have the occasion to do several different times when she was not around a whole slew of people or certainly not in the public eye. If it was just the two of us, or sometimes with just my father and me, she was quite a different person than the impression you got sometimes.

Were these impressions from your negotiations or those from the media?

The public, the media view of Ayn was of a very tough, monomaniacal, single-vision, exclusionary kind of dialogue person with extremely hard views about this, that or the other. I found her to be charming and engaging and very, very polite—if not formal. There would be no better dinner companion. I couldn't imagine anyone more fun to invite to your dinner party. And that's not the impression that people have of her. People say, "Ayn Rand—oh, my God! Please."

What is her reputation in Hollywood?

The reputation is that her stories are too idea-filled to make into films; if she had stayed out of it and let them just make the movies, take the best of the plot and not be whipsawed by all the philosophy, they'd be great stories. But it was the whipsawing that always killed it. It was the sense that the stories were too full of philosophy, and the people who controlled the rights to her stories would never let you just go out and make the movie.

Was it just philosophy generally or was it because it was a specific philosophy?

In the movie business it was just philosophy. I think it's a mistake to read into it that there was some deep mistrust of Ayn's philosophy. I think there was a time in our history, back in the '60s, when the general sense of Ayn was that she was uncompromising, didn't care about people, a tough guy, insensitive, not empathetic. I don't think that's the case today. Hollywood will do anything if they think they can make a buck from it. They really wouldn't care about it—maybe thirty-five, forty years ago—but not today, so I don't think it was specific to Ayn.

Tell me more about the negotiations with Miss Rand.

She was a bundle of contradictions sometimes. I remember that there was a whole section of plot that [screenwriter Stirling] Silliphant had to change to make it fit in the first two hours, and she had talked a lot about dramatic equivalents in translating from book to movie, and thought they were hard to come up with. She said that if she could have done it originally, she would have. And then there was one sentence where Silliphant added the word "just." She was apoplectic about the addition of the word "just," but the rearrangement of this entire subplot didn't bother her at all. So it wasn't always possible to focus on what was going to throw her for a loop. But as long as she felt confident that you were going to be responsive to her concerns, that seemed to be enough.

There were tons and tons of small dialogue changes, and frankly I tend to disagree with that. Every author goes out and spends however many years creating a character and having them speak in a certain way. Why would a screenwriter change the way they speak? I can understand not using *all* of the dialogue, but I can't understand changing the dialogue. The whole point is that people read the book because the dialogue is written the way it is, why change it? So she was very upset about that.

But the critical issue was control. She was not going to let the movie get made unless she approved the script and the principal cast.

Can you remember how you dealt with this issue?

We created for the NBC deal an affirmative obligation on the part of Ayn to deliver an approved script. In other words, she was free to disapprove the script, but she wasn't free to leave it there. If she couldn't find a writer to fix it to her satisfaction, then at the end of the day she was obliged to fix it.

That was a very good solution for you, wasn't it?

It was great for us, because what was critical in the marketplace was that we knew we could get a script, and she had screenwriting experience and had produced screenplays. She wasn't a foreigner to the medium, and clearly, she had the ability to do it. I think if the NBC project had gone ahead, we would have gotten the movie made at NBC, and she would not have had to write it herself. She believed in Stirling

Silliphant, but when Fred Silverman took over the network, he hated the project, so he cancelled it.

The NBC deal fell apart in '77. Afterwards, I sold *Atlas* to Turner as a six-hour miniseries with Tom Selleck, who would have played Hank Rearden. He had to shave his mustache, but he agreed to do it. Ayn was even thinking of writing the script herself. I do remember that the negotiation was: whoever we got to write the script would be assured by the fact that Ayn was prepared to write it if nobody else could get it done right.

Whom did Miss Rand have in mind for the roles?

She thought Raquel Welch was Dagny. Period. I think she was responding to the lush, flowing hair and the full, sensuous lips and the extraordinary beauty.

Did she discuss actors whom she liked?

She did talk about acting. She didn't want the DeNiro "be a cigarette" school of acting.

What did she want? The old-fashioned romantic type?

Yes. I think we also talked about Clint Eastwood, whom she loved. She would've loved him to be Hank Rearden.

How did Stirling Silliphant get involved in the project?

We put the word out in the industry that we were looking for a writer, and his name came up and she knew him from *In the Heat of the Night*, which she loved. She thought *In the Heat of the Night* was a wonderful movie.

What happened next with Mr. Silliphant?

He was in awe of the opportunity. He very much idolized her and would have done anything she said.

Was he a fan of her works?

Oh yes. He had read everything. He was very respectful of her stories, of the story construction.

Tell me more about his writing the movie and his relationship with Miss Rand.

It was an extensive and collaborative relationship. We spent

many, many, many, many, many, many, many hours talking about
what and how and so forth. He drafted his "bible" and first draft
script. He drafted the whole treatment—everything—according to
her wishes. Anytime he had a question, he'd call her and talk. We
had numerous meetings, and it was a very good working partnership
and it clearly would have worked—if NBC had stayed with it.

Tell me about those meetings.

We just went through the material in detail. Stirling would turn
work in, and they would go through that and he'd redraft it. It was a
pretty standard process. She was very much involved and we enjoyed
the process with her. She wasn't ambiguous. When she had an idea,
she was very clear about it.

Can you say more about what she was like to work with?

The thing that stands out the clearest about Ayn was that she
was just really clever. She was thoughtful. She didn't just run off
ideas without having thought them out, without having looked at the
consequences. She was a really smart person. It was a pleasure—
always a pleasure—to work ideas through with her because she did
think about things so well. Her vision was so fresh.

Did she interview Stirling Silliphant before he got the job?

Oh yes, sure she did. She asked him a lot of questions. She wanted
to determine that he was going to be respectful of the material. She did
and he was and they got along very well.

How did her relationship end with Mr. Silliphant?

Oh, very well. There were no problems there.

Do you remember what she said about constructing the story?

The principal issue was that you were not going to be able to
make a movie of *Atlas Shrugged* and include everything from the
book. There just wasn't enough time; it would take thirty hours. She,
in fact, sat down and read the entire John Galt speech and timed it.
It was four hours and twenty minutes or something, so she knew you
weren't going to take three nights on TV to read John Galt's speech.
So she said, "You have to find a dramatic equivalent for that. But I
am going to edit that speech for you, so don't worry, and I will get
that speech down to three to seven minutes. I'll have to do it; no one

else is equipped to do that."

I was always fond of talking about reducing the speech because everybody says, "Oh, everything's sacrosanct." Well, things *are* sacrosanct, but she was smart and thoughtful about what things to *make* sacrosanct.

Any other advice she had regarding writing the script, for example, on cutting characters?

I don't remember about cuts. Certainly none of the principals. We weren't going to take Francisco out or anything like that.

Trying to sell the movie, trying to get it set up at studios, and getting the script done sounds like a very arduous process. What was her attitude during all this?

It was very cooperative. She was very anxious to get it made.

How did she react when you told her that NBC had killed it?

She was very disappointed. She held her head up high and took it like a man.

So you told her personally?

That actually may have been on the phone, I'm not sure.

Did you meet her husband, Frank O'Connor?

Never did. John Galt was absolutely—and she said so repeatedly—patterned after him. Whatever it is that Dagny sees in John Galt's eyes that makes her know that he is the one and only guy for her, that's what Ayn saw in her husband's eyes.

She told you that?

Yes, sir. She did.

Can you remember the last time you met with Ayn Rand? Did you talk to her again after that meeting in New York?

Oh yes. That meeting in New York was in the '70s to conclude the NBC deal. I spoke to her hundreds of times after that, about the different developments we went through. The possibility at Turner, the possibility of doing the feature film with James Hill. We kept in active touch until right before she died.

Had she changed over the time you knew her?

No.

Did Stirling Silliphant call her "Ayn"?

Yes. He did make that part of the method of business with her. She, of course, as I told you, was a very gracious person, and to this day, I don't like people calling me Michael without asking. She was very much the same way, but on the first long meeting with Silliphant, she asked him to call her "Ayn," and he refused. He said, "Not until we solve the script. If we get the script done and get the movie made, I may then acquiesce, but until then you'll be 'Miss Rand.'" She replied, basically, that's a choice you have to make, but you're welcome to call me "Ayn."

Did you talk to Miss Rand about things like competing in the marketplace, and what you had done in business in Hollywood?

We talked about it all the time.

What did she say?

In the first place, she was very encouraging—always. In the second place, she always exhibited a tremendous respect for the competitive marketplace, and unlike her public persona, she could be very empathetic. It wouldn't overrule a reasoned judgment, but it didn't mean that she was disrespectful.

Everybody knows the books, the ideas, the controversy. I don't know her that way. I know her as the person who worked really hard with me over a long period of time. We went through so many different developments in this thing—so many different attempts to get it made. We tried features, we tried TNT, we tried NBC, we almost had CBS. But the truth of the matter, for me, is that she was a hell of a gal.

Evva Pryor

Evva Pryor, who, through Ayn Rand's law firm, Ernst, Cane, Gitlin & Winick, handled certain matters for Miss Rand, was a friend of hers from the mid-1970s until her death in 1982. Ms. Pryor died in 2008.

Interview date: July 29, 1998

Scott McConnell: *You have had some questions about doing this interview, why is that?*

Evva Pryor: Ayn Rand was famous for her theories. Most people will have known her during the time she was most active. I did not. I met her just as she was "retiring." My relationship had to do with her need and not mine. Therefore, it was different. However, above all, it must be understood that rarely have I respected someone as much as I did Ayn Rand, though we had many differences. She was intellectually the most open person, without question, I have ever met. I cherish every hour I spent with her. She was one of the very few people more interested in facts than in opinion. Each issue was discussed with an overriding respect for truth. Winning an argument was not important to her, but the truth was.

Anything I say to you must carry with it the regard I had for her intellectual curiosity and willingness to share on an equal level—given her stature, she need not have done so.

What were the differences?

My background was social work. That should tell you all you need to know about our differences.

How and when did you meet Ayn Rand?

It was around 1976 when I worked as a consultant for her attorneys, Ernst, Cane, Gitlin & Winick. My masters degree was in social work, and I had been with Mobilization for Youth and was also teaching at NYU as an adjunct [instructor] and working as a consultant to a number of other organizations. A problem came up, and her attorneys asked me if I would meet with her.

What was the problem?

She was "retiring," and Paul Gitlin and Gene Winick, her attorneys, felt she should discuss applying for Social Security and Medicare. The office asked that I go over and talk with her about it.

Tell me about your first meeting with Ayn Rand and how these matters developed.

I had read enough to know that she despised government interference, and that she felt that people should and could live independently. She was coming to a point in her life where she was going to receive the very thing she didn't like, which was Medicare and Social Security.

I remember telling her that this was going to be difficult. For me to do my job, she had to recognize that there were exceptions to her theory. So that started our political discussions. From there on—with gusto—we argued all the time. The initial argument was on greed. She had to see that there was such a thing as greed in this world. Doctors could cost an awful lot more money than books earn, and she could be totally wiped out by medical bills if she didn't watch it. Since she had worked her entire life and had paid into Social Security, she had a right to it. She didn't feel that an individual should take help.

She also changed my thinking in many ways. For example, with regard to altruism. From the day of our discussion, I was never the same. From then on whatever I did, I did because I wanted to, and I never again expected gratitude, or praise or anything else. If I wanted to do it, and felt it was important, it was my choice and no one was obligated to me. I have been so much happier.

We also discovered we both liked to play Scrabble. And did so, each time we met.

And did she agree with you about Medicare and Social Security?

After several meetings and arguments, she gave me her power of attorney to deal with all matters having to do with health and Social Security. Whether she agreed or not is not the issue, she saw the necessity for both her and Frank. She was never involved other than to sign the power of attorney; I did the rest.

What other work was there after the Social Security and Medicare issue was resolved?

Everything that came up, including taxes. Rather than asking her to go to the office, I came to her on behalf of the lawyers.

At this time were there any other changes in her that you saw because she was turning from running a newsletter to becoming a private person?

She was also still surrounded by the people who respected and shared her thinking, such as Leonard Peikoff. She was lecturing. She still had an active life.

How was she during all this debating? Is "debating" the right word?

No, debating carries with it the concept of convincing another of your being right. As I said before, truth was more important to her than being right. She was one of the most brilliant women that I have had the pleasure to know. I have been involved with others who had theories, who were, while respected, closed to new ideas. It was "their way or the highway." That was not the case with Ayn Rand. This was a woman who amazed me every time we talked.

For example, I said it was my opinion that her theory was for the middle and upper class. It had nothing to do with the super rich, nor did it have to do with the very poor, who had little chance. This led to examples of the twilight generation, whose mothers had suffered protein deficiency and they had no chance.

So there wasn't a manner of dogmatism or bullying?

None, none, none. I was very surprised. I used to say, "Why do you want to talk with me? You're Ayn Rand. People rely on what you have to say. Why do you want to discuss issues with me? She replied, "It's invigorating." I had known several people who attended the meetings at the Nathaniel Branden Institute and whose lives had been changed by an understanding of her ideas.

She was matter of fact, gave a straightforward answer. The only time she seemed upset with me, was when I asked her why she left Russia.

Why did she get upset?

She said, "Anybody who knows me knows why!" I said, "Has anyone else asked you that question?" She said, "Nobody's ever had to." I said, "How did you know what they think? You have to answer questions." So she did. I was so nervous, I don't remember that answer. I know it had to do with the killing of creativity and the soul. I was very tense. It was the only time she was ever intimidating.

How often did you see Miss Rand?

It varied. Sometimes it would be once or twice a week for a while, sometimes once a month. It was never less frequent than every month. After Frank died, it was a lot more frequent, and I would just go play Scrabble, and talk and see how she was doing.

Did she request you to come or was that your initiative?

Sometimes she'd ask, sometimes I'd just do it, and we'd decide when we were going to do it again.

Were there any other forms of entertainment when you visited Miss Rand?

We talked. We talked and we talked and we talked, and we played Scrabble. When she became interested in doing things, such as the visualizing of *Atlas Shrugged* as a film, or going somewhere, often my companion Dirck Van Sickle and I would take her to places she wanted to go.

Did Miss Rand ever talk to you explicitly about what she liked about you?

Oh, no. The only thing she ever said was that one time, when I had to go—we usually spent three hours together—and I said I'm sorry I have to go because there is something else that I have to do, and she said, "But we didn't get a chance to talk politics." We had played Scrabble, we had done our business, but we hadn't argued yet.

Let's turn to the topic of Scrabble.

She was really a good Scrabble player. I've played Scrabble with people who were defensive. If they saw you might go into a square, they might try to block you, and so on. Neither she nor I played that way. We played offensive all the way. She always played for the most points, and so did I. I really enjoyed it, and we'd have very high scores. I think 1,162 was one of them. And she'd write her highest scores in the lid of the Scrabble box. Whoever has her Scrabble set has some of our scores.

Who won and who lost?

It depended on who held what letters. She played a variation of Scrabble which was fun. You could pick up the blank and replace it with the letter it represented. In other words, if you used the blank as an *A*—there are only two blanks—then whoever held an *A* could pick it up and use the blank again as another letter.

What was her manner when she was playing?

Like always: friendly, direct, open, competitive. She was Ayn Rand.

Which is . . . ?

Whatever she was, you knew about it. There was nothing surreptitious about anything she did; everything was aboveboard and direct. You got what you saw, and that was it.

How was she in victory and how was she in defeat?

The same; it was a game! She lost as graciously as she won. Her ego was never dependant on winning a game or not winning a game, and yet she always played to win—a good competitor.

What made Ayn Rand laugh?

Lots of things did. We laughed, when we played Scrabble, at a very good word. She was just full of life.

Did you ever discuss art or music with Miss Rand?

We mostly argued politics, we played Scrabble and we did our work. We both read Agatha Christie and liked her a lot.

What did she like and why?

I told her what I liked and she agreed. Agatha Christie says in one of her books, "To only one mind is murder logical." So, in everything she wrote, she always built that logic for you. You could always figure it out.

So before the end of the novel, you could pick the killer?

Yes, and so could Ayn.

Did Miss Rand ever have a problem with you because you weren't an Objectivist?

No. She was far too open and intelligent for that. First of all, I learned a great deal from her. She knew that my background was such that I had been involved in situations involving group adherence to unexamined ideas. I really had a problem with anything that was not independent thinking. I still do. Not only had I been caught up in a psychological theory which proved problematic, she also knew that I had grown up part of my life in a religious environment and that I'd seen people who did not believe dealt with very cruelly, because thinking was not important. She knew that to the depth of my soul, I could not take this—that I did not believe in anything that would stop a person from thinking.

I'm telling you what I thought so you can see what she had to put up with in me.

Was there something unique in your conversation, in the sense that it was female talk or gossip?

No. She didn't gossip and neither do I. I cannot believe that this woman would have ever gossiped or talked about anyone. I don't think she would know how, number one, and I don't think she was that indirect, number two. She was far too honest and far too open. If she ever thought anything about something, you'd know about it.

How did she react when you were somewhat negative about The Fountainhead?

I was absolutely not negative about the overall premise. I just thought the relationship between Roark and Dominique wasn't the kind of thing that would ever work. Ayn didn't mind anything that anybody said or did. She was a self-assured, self-contained person.

I once asked her who Dominique was based on, and she said, "Me, on a bad day."

What about stamp collecting?

One time at the office, one of the older partners had died and left Paul Gitlin his large stamp collection. He turned it over to Ayn and she was delighted.

Did you ever observe her working on her collection?

She spread it out, and once we talked while she was putting stamps in albums. She showed me how she did it and what you had to do, the cellophane wrappers and the boxes she had stamps in. That was it.

What was her attitude to stamp collecting?

She enjoyed it. I couldn't believe it, but she really enjoyed it. She had a real child's glee when she opened up those stamps. She was ecstatic. She really loved them.

Now another important topic: cats.

She had two cats. I don't remember their names. I just remember their pretty little cat beds. One was wicker with a pillow in it, and it was in her bedroom.

So the two cats slept there?

Yes.

Did Ayn Rand ever discuss smoking?

Yeah, I smoked. She had had cancer. When I found that out, I said, "Look, I'm not going to smoke in your home." She said, "Please do, it's the only time I get to smell it. I didn't quit because I wanted to, I quit because I had to."

Did she discuss with you her sister Nora?

I didn't meet Nora, but Ayn talked a lot about her visit. That she had offered her and her husband sanctuary in America and that she would set them up here. And her sister said she'd think about it and then went back to the Soviet Union. Ayn became furious and disinherited her.

So she actually changed her will?

She made it known that nothing was to go into Russia, period. She felt that Nora had an opportunity for freedom, and she had not taken it and she would never speak to her again.

So she was very angry with Nora? Was that the attitude?

No, anger is not exactly how I would describe her emotion. It was too theoretical. Nora had the opportunity to leave an oppressive state, and she did not do it.

Did you meet Miss Rand's cook, Eloise Huggins?

Oh yes. She was sweet and strong.

Why strong and why sweet?

Because she could tolerate some things that Ayn said and because she was there for her. It was strength all the way.

What kind of things did Miss Rand say?

Eloise believed that Ayn's theory could not apply to the low-income black. It had been illegal for them to read, they had no pattern of marriage, there were just so many things. And what Ayn's theory was really about was people who had at least the information to know what to go for. So, when we'd argue, I'd see Eloise's face. She liked Ayn very much. Both women liked each other. Eloise was a very strong woman, and they had a very good relationship, and it was very equal.

Explain that.

They had a lot of respect for each other. Eloise's relationship with Ayn was a relationship that had nothing to do with the theories of Objectivism and everything to do with the two women.

So they were very close friends?

Yes. I know Ayn liked her a lot because she told me.

Did she say why?

No, just that she liked her an awful lot. And I could see it in the way they interacted.

Could you give me some examples of their relationship and of their closeness?

Eloise took care of Ayn. That was what her job was, but beyond that, the relationship was a friendship.

What things, as friends, did they share?

They talked all day, especially after Frank died.

How was Mrs. Huggins after Mr. O'Connor died?

Very, very helpful to Ayn. Eloise really kept her together. She was with her day in and day out. Every day. Eloise was very good to Ayn. It was when Eloise was gone that Ayn didn't eat.

Did you discuss with Mr. O'Connor his past, his childhood?

Ohio. He talked very openly about it, about his brothers. He talked about his family, talked about his growing up. They were fond reminiscences, emotional. You know, when you talk about your past.

Describe Mr. O'Connor before he became ill.

He was shy, retiring, happy, satisfied, and he was Ayn's intellectual companion.

Did he discuss how he felt about his life?

Both he and Ayn were more interested in the present. The past was used to explain something in the present.

Do you remember what you discussed with him?

I would talk about what I saw in his artwork. I liked it a lot. He was glad that I liked his art. He had one painting of the back of a woman looking out a window. It reminded me, as I told him, of Degas.

Describe Mr. O'Connor's personality and his character.

Above all, he was a gentleman. He was tall and he reminded me of a gentrified Gary Cooper. He was intelligent, kind, courteous and proud of Ayn.

You also told me, "he had a certainty." What did you mean?

He was very much in control of his own emotions, of his own world, of his own ideas.

In my opinion, when describing Roark in *The Fountainhead*, she used the things she loved most about Frank. It was the whole sense of his being a man of few words, his strength.

I think it would be wrong to minimize his contribution to her work. At least, Ayn told me it was so, and he agreed.

What were these contributions?

She would say, "See, Frank got there before me, and it was Frank who taught me this." She was very open that hers was a real friendship with Frank, besides loving him. They agreed theoretically, and she said he had been a part of her growth in that direction.

They were really companions, a couple, they were in this together. It was she who would do all the talking, but he really supported it 100 percent of the way. He would talk with her endlessly about philosophy.

Do you remember any other mentions about his past or about their early romance?

Just that she had seen him and fallen in love with him. In my opinion, she was deeply in love with Frank. All through my relationship with her, that was evident.

In what way?

The way she looked to him for advice, the way they talked and when he died.

Closing The Ayn Rand Letter *must have brought some changes in her relationships?*

I think it did. It was also a consolidation of her relationship with Frank, at least for the years until he started to get sick, due to his arteriosclerosis.

He died in November 1979. Was it long before that?

Not long. Initially, when we started to argue, it was Ayn, Frank and myself. But with him, it was mostly listening; but generally when he said something, he was right. He was a very interesting man. Ayn would tell me that he was more intelligent than she was. She was quick to tell me that he had named *Atlas Shrugged*.

Can you give me more examples of his intelligence?

In our conversations, I was always amazed with his insights.

How would you summarize what Ayn Rand thought of Frank O'Connor?

She loved him, and she respected him and thought he was a talented painter.

Did she say specifically what the love was based on, what she specifically loved and admired?

Yes, his intelligence. She was very clear about that. She was very clear that Frank was the man who had taught her a good deal.

Did Mr. O'Connor tell you what he loved about Ayn Rand?

No. I never asked him. I just know the way he looked at her and the way they talked. They had a wonderful relationship when I knew them. They were very friendly together, very considerate of one another. They would go out in the daytime, they walked, and they did things together.

Tell me about her opinion of Frank O'Connor's paintings.

I once asked them why they didn't sell them, and she said she never would let anyone have them; they were all for her.

What did Mr. O'Connor say?

He just smiled. She did have them.

Tell me about the death of Mr. O'Connor.

It seemed to happen very suddenly. She called me when he became sick, and I went over. He seemed to be fine, a little more dependent on her, and she didn't want him to be alone. She wanted to be with him.

Because he had been in the house with her, they hadn't really been aware that he was becoming disoriented. And then when they were in Boston for a few days to do a lecture, he became disoriented—possibly a small stroke—and this persisted even when he came back to their apartment. He was frightened, terribly frightened. I went over to try to calm him down. I think Leonard came. I thought Leonard was a doctor, and I left. Ayn called me, and I spoke with Frank by phone.

How did you calm him, and what did you talk about?

We talked about all the things he was afraid of that night. I talked to him about the fact that he had been away and that it was frightening to be there, not knowing where you were, that everything had changed, and that nobody had done it deliberately to him. I talked to him until he fell asleep. That was the start and he never got better.

What was the effect of this on Miss Rand?

Terrible, devastating. She had loved him very much. She respected him, and she relied on him, and suddenly he was not there. He was no longer able to be the type of intellectual companion that he had been.

Tell me about the funeral arrangements.

Ayn Rand was not sentimental. When Frank died, she asked if I would go and get his burial plot. She did not cremate him; she said she could not do that. So she asked me to choose a burial plot, to make the arrangements, and to choose the coffin, to do everything. She didn't want to be involved. In my heart of hearts, I knew she couldn't let anyone else do that planning.

Did she say why?

She couldn't, she was so bereaved. She said she really wanted no part of it. I had suggested Campbell's funeral home because I had been there; it was nice. She chose Valhalla cemetery, because Rachmaninoff was buried there, and that was where the burial was to be. I was to go there and make the arrangements. Ina Winick [Eugene Winick's wife] was to meet me there, and we'd choose the plot. Before I went, I called Ayn and said I had a car and that I'm going to go up, but I won't leave unless you tell me to go alone. And she said, "I don't want you to go alone. I want to go with you." I picked her up, we went, and she chose her burial spot along with his. She chose the spot that had a tree, and when the tree was, after her death, destroyed by lightning, it was Leonard who made certain that a new tree was planted. She had wanted the shade of the tree.

Then Ayn and I went to the funeral home. She set up her own funeral arrangements at the same time as his. I had asked the funeral home not to embalm the body until I told them to do so. They kept their word. After all the arrangements had been made, she said she was sorry not to have seen the body before it was embalmed. I told her it was still possible. She was in the room alone with the body and then we left.

She said that I was the only person in her adult life who had ever seen her cry.

What happened?

It was in the car after choosing the burial plot. Her loss was enormous. He was her life. She just cried.

How was she after Mr. O'Connor's death?

She didn't walk or exercise. In a way, she let herself die. Not doing all the healthy things. Her will to live began to diminish.

Did she discuss this with you?

No, no, except that I would say, "You've got to go out and walk because your circulation depends on it." I think she said, "So what?" After Frank died, I called her one day to see how she was feeling. Eloise was on vacation, and she hadn't eaten. I went over to the grocery store and brought food back and fixed it for her. I asked her why she hadn't told me she was out of food, and she said she just forgot.

Not long after that, she went into the hospital. Since I had power of attorney over health matters, I was the only one who could make decisions. I knew the terms of the will: Leonard Peikoff was her heir and her friend. I did not make a decision without discussing it with him. She had all of the care that medicine could offer at that time, and he made each decision with me.

Finally, she asked to be taken home to die. She knew nothing more could be done. I signed her out of the hospital.

And her death?

When I took her home from the hospital in the ambulance, she squeezed my hand, smiled at me and said, "Thank you." I knew that I was bringing her home to die, and she knew she was coming home to die. The doctor told both of us, if she goes home, she will die.

If she stayed in the hospital, she would have lived longer, was that the implication?

That's what I asked the doctor, how much longer, and he didn't know. But definitely if she went home, she would die within a few weeks. If she stayed in the hospital, it was a matter of weeks or perhaps months, but she would not recover.

And what was her reaction to that?

She wanted to go home and die. And she asked if I would take her home. I discussed the implications with her, but she was certain. If I knew and cherished her, and if I shared one thing with Ayn Rand, it was a commitment to the right and freedom of the individual to make choices. I would not, nor could not, deprive her of that right. I said I would take her home. Leonard oversaw the preparation of the apartment, made certain that she had the best possible care.

Tell me about her funeral.

Leonard took care of any details she had not taken care of. He saw to it that her wedding rings were buried with her along with a picture of Frank. He had been buried with a picture of her.

Would you say that Ayn Rand practiced what she preached?

Yes, [laughs] that's why I had so much trouble with her.

You mean the Social Security issue and all that?

Yes.

How would you summarize your opinion of Ayn Rand?

I think she was very genuine. This was a woman who believed everything she said. She was open until the day she died. I liked who she was—full of life, intense, confident.

Dana Berliner

Dana Berliner, as a child, visited Ayn Rand on two occasions. She is now a senior attorney for the Institute for Justice, a nonprofit law firm that represents "individuals whose most basic rights are denied by the government." She is the daughter of Michael and Judy Berliner.

Interview date: November 24, 1999

Scott McConnell: *How old were you when you first met Ayn Rand?*

Dana Berliner: I was eleven when I first met her in 1978.[197] Then I had read only *Anthem.*

How did you meet her?

I was visiting Harry Binswanger in New York during the summer, and he took me to her apartment. I'd been hearing about her since I was very young and definitely wanted to meet her. I was very excited and a little bit scared, because I wasn't sure how she would deal with a child. She was almost a mythical figure to me at the time.

Tell me about that first meeting.

I remember being surprised by how nice she was. I had thought that she was going to be somewhat frightening, but she was really, really sweet, and I remember thinking initially that she was like someone's grandmother. She was very easy to talk to.

What did you talk about?

The main thing was education. She asked me a lot about what my school was like, and what I liked about it, and what the classes were like. She also asked me if my teachers expressed opinions, whether or not they refused to take stands on anything. She said she thought that teachers should express opinions and that it was good for children to have something to react to, rather than just having them discuss something without any direction.

So she wanted teachers to make evaluations and give conclusions?

Yes. When we were discussing whether teachers should express ideas and value judgments, I think we were talking about history classes.

---

197 The meeting took place on September 5, 1978.

Did Miss Rand give you any advice?

She did when we were talking about education, about questioning and—in kind of child's terms—about the importance of reason and analyzing things. I think that was when we were talking about teachers' opinions, and she was saying, "What are their premises?" "What leads them to say that?" "What was the evidence?"—things like that. So it wasn't exactly advice; it was more talking about how to think.

During the conversation about teachers, I asked her, "What if they have bad opinions?" and she said it was still better that they have opinions, and that the class be able to think about them and try to figure out what's wrong with them.

What questions did you ask her?

I asked her what she thought of children. She replied that childhood is a time when your mind is coming alive and that children are capable of understanding things and thinking about issues. I think this connected to our discussion of why it was good for teachers to express opinions, because children could judge the teachers' opinions.

Do you remember any other parts of the conversation or how Harry was involved?

Harry was there, but he didn't say a lot. We talked also about *Anthem*, and I told her what I thought about it, and I think she asked me what I understood it to be about.

Did you get over your nervousness?

Almost immediately, because she was so warm, and so welcoming and engaging to talk to.

She looked at me really directly when she was talking, and she seemed interested, and smiled. She listened to what I was saying and reacted to it.

The main impressions that I got of her were that she was very warm and very intellectual, because we had—for me at the time—very intense, challenging conversations, about school, books and *Anthem*. I think she asked me about what other books I read, and we talked about what book of hers I should read next.

So how did you feel when you left?

I remember walking, crossing the street and talking to Harry nonstop about what she said. I really enjoyed it, and I was very excited about it.

How did the second meeting come about?

I was going to visit Harry again, and I wanted to meet her again. I was fourteen this time.[198] That meeting was sort of unfortunate, because I had a good friend, who also had wanted to meet her, and who was in New York at the same time, so we both went. The conversation went awry to some extent. I didn't realize that my friend was not as friendly towards Objectivism as I had thought, so the conversation was not as genial as I remember the first one being.

Did Miss Rand remember you?

Yes, and she was friendlier, like, "Welcome back."

Had she changed?

She seemed a little more frail, but she was still very nice and very warm. I told her about my reaction to *We the Living*, and I think I asked her if Russia had really been like that, and she said yes. I told her about my reaction to the book, which is that I didn't understand how human beings could act that way to each other. She may have tried to explain it to me, although I'm not sure I really I understood it at that age.

What did you discuss?

At that point, I hadn't read *Atlas*, but I had read *The Fountainhead* and *We the Living*, and we talked about those. The main discussion we had was actually about my friend, who was very interested in Judaism, not the religion, but the culture, and with needing to be a part of the group, or connecting with one's roots; and my friend was trying to defend that. Miss Rand was explaining why wanting to be a part of something like that was collectivist. She said that it was one thing to enjoy a shared activity, but another thing to want to be with others—not to share an activity, but just because you are part of the same group. We were kids, and she was still very friendly, but it was much more her kind of correcting this belief, and explaining why it was wrong, and I was a little alarmed that the meeting had taken this turn, and didn't really know how to reduce the level of conflict.

Miss Rand talked about how needing something like that to believe in showed a lack of independent spirit, and how instead you should not judge people based upon their group membership, like being Jewish, or upon what their parents did. Those things are really not about who you

198 This meeting took place on August 18, 1981.

are, or what you do. It was very educational and was reinforcing *The Fountainhead*, but on a personal level.

The meeting was genial, but it was not as fun as I remembered the first one being, because of this.

Jim Smith

Jim Smith was an acquaintance of Ayn Rand's in the 1970s and early '80s. He is the former owner of a jazz club in New York City and is married to Kathryn Eickhoff (see Kathryn Eickhoff interview, page 268).

Interview date: November 30, 1999

Scott McConnell: *How did you meet Ayn Rand and Frank O'Connor?*

Jim Smith: I met them personally for the first time at our wedding party that Alan Greenspan gave Kathryn and me after we came back from our honeymoon in the spring of 1973. Kathryn had known them both for quite a while. Ayn was seated next to me at the reception. They gave us as a wedding gift a set of ice tea spoons to go with our pattern, which was very nice, and which we still have.

I was flattered, sitting next to her. We talked about a lot of different things. The only part of the conversation that stands out in my mind was I had recently read a book called *Rally Round the Flag, Boys!* [by Max Shulman], which dealt with the issue of conservatives in the Republican party. The writer was taking a position which in a lot of ways was very similar to Ayn's and Objectivism, and so I mentioned to her that it looked like he was using some of the Objectivist ideas. I thought that she would be pleased. She wasn't at all.

What did she say?

It wasn't so much that she wasn't pleased about him having done it, but that she thought it was not a good thing for somebody to tell an author that somebody was using part of their ideas, and I hadn't noted whether he'd used them with attribution or not. So I said to myself, "Uh oh, I've finally met this woman who I have all this admiration for and the first chance I get, I offend her." But she saw my confusion or mortification and immediately went on to make it clear that she wasn't accusing me of being disrespectful or anything. She realized that it was something that I had done in ignorance, not being aware of the issues that were involved.

What I later came to realize was that Ayn would take everybody at face value, and she would assume that they know what they're talking about or they wouldn't be talking, and so she responds at that level.

What was your impression of Frank O'Connor?

Also, I had seen but not met Frank.

Frank didn't seem to have any problem with the fact that for a lot of people, Ayn was the reason that people were in their presence. He was the husband of the queen, her consort. He just accepted the fact that people were much more interested in what Ayn had to say than what he had to say, and in my case, that was certainly true.

What was Miss Rand like to deal with?

I found her very easy. I never experienced any of the kinds of demanding harshness and, quote, "toeing the party line." I was never looking for anything from Ayn. I enjoyed her company. I was pleased that we got along, because she was a fun person in that regard and easy to talk to. You could turn from a light subject to a heavy subject at the drop of a question, so to speak. I never got the idea from her that you had to do certain things or you had to behave in a certain way.

Did you tell her jokes?

Yes. The first time I did this to her, I said, "This funny thing happened yesterday at the bar. There were two fellows sitting down at the end of the bar. And one said, 'My God, you see those two women coming across the street? One's my wife and the other is my mistress.' The other guy said, 'You took the words right out of my mouth.'" Initially, Ayn thought I was recounting something that really happened, and her first reaction was literally a "how unlikely," "what an extraordinary coincidence" kind of reaction. But then she realized I was joking. She laughed. She didn't feel like I had duped her or anything like that.

I believe you had a beard for part of the time you knew Miss Rand.

I had a beard when we got married and for a number of years. One time, we were going over to Ayn's apartment, and Kathryn went in and they hugged, and I kind of hugged and kissed her on the cheek, and she said, "Oh, that's the first time I've ever been kissed by a man with a beard." I didn't have any sense that she was pulling back from me when I kissed her. There was nothing in her tone of voice that was disapprobation of any kind.

Did you discuss stamp collecting with Miss Rand?

A friend of ours did a lot of international business, and after he found out about Ayn's stamp collecting, he would save the stamps and give them to us to give to her. She would sort of apologize for the fact that she couldn't wait till we left to look at them. She'd open up the envelope that they came in; then she would look at them, but with an apology for this breech of etiquette, if you will.

What did you observe of the relationship between Mr. Greenspan and Miss Rand?

They were friends up until she died. I was at a party, I think at Alan's place in New York, and it was shortly after he had gone down to Washington, and Ayn was asking him questions about his job.

I remember him being asked—at a presentation he was making— about things that had to do with which way the government was moving—toward greater or lesser economic freedom. He likened it to a big ship and with a tugboat pushing against it, and that, initially, the changes are almost imperceptible, but that the tugboat does alter the course of the great big liner.

Did you ever discuss Hollywood with Ayn Rand?

I asked her about Walt Disney. It might have been around the holidays, and I mentioned something about liking one of his cartoons and remembering it fondly. She said, "He's just too cutesy for me. I don't like that kind of animation style." But she made it very clear that it was a matter of personal taste, and nothing more than that. It didn't mean that she didn't approve of Walt Disney, it was just that what she called "cutesy" was not her cup of tea.

You ran a jazz club in Greenwich Village. Did she ask you about that?

Yes, but she never questioned why I was doing it. At one point she told me that she hadn't been in bars, and she asked me if the play by Clifford Odets, *Waiting for Lefty*, which is set in a New York City bar, was typical of the way things were in a bar. I told her that it was hard to say because my main focus was providing jazz.

I believe you had a discussion with Miss Rand about a woman's legs.

No. What ended up happening was that Ayn asked me how tall I was, and I told her, "five-foot-seventeen." She got a big kick out of that. She liked the unexpected. I think that she was five-one,[199] and I said, "We could call you 'four-foot-thirteen,'" and she said, "Oh, no." She

---

199 According to her Russian passport of 1925, Ayn Rand was 5 feet 4 inches.

didn't want to do that, because four-foot anything would make her sound even shorter, and she just didn't want to sound shorter than she was.

But in one of the NBI question periods someone asked her about why her heroines had the physical attributes she gave them, such as long legs. She said she had to give them long legs because they are very useful sexually, almost saying it somewhat abashedly. I don't want to say that she turned red; it was like she wasn't comfortable saying it in a public forum.

Did you see Miss Rand near the time of her death?

Kathryn and I went to see her while she was in the hospital. She was aware that she wouldn't recover, and she was glad we came to see her. It was sort of like "Oh, you shouldn't have. You didn't need to." It was sort of like when you tried to give her a present: "I don't want you to put yourself out for me." I also remember her telling us to be sure to look after Leonard—Kathryn being her financial adviser and Leonard her sole heir.

Theo Westenberger

Theo Westenberger was an internationally respected photographer, who photographed Ayn Rand in 1979 for *Look* magazine. The article was published in the April 14 edition and focused on the proposed *Atlas Shrugged* movie. The photographs were some of the last taken of Ayn Rand. Ms. Westenberger died in 2008.

Interview date: September 30, 2002

Scott McConnell: *Why did you photograph Ayn Rand?*

Theo Westenberger: I was assigned to photograph her for *Look* magazine, in January 1979. I was working at *Look* as a contract photographer. It was one of my first assignments.[200]

Had you heard of Miss Rand?

Oh, of course. I had read *The Fountainhead* and *Atlas Shrugged*. I expected a very imposing woman. She did not seem that way to me. She was very amenable to doing something difficult for a woman of her age—it was hard for her go down in Grand Central to the platform, where it is very cold. It was January. And she did it. I wanted to photograph her there with the trains going in and out. Some people I photograph don't do what you request that they do, so that Ayn Rand doing what I asked her was actually very positive.

At Grand Central, she put her arms out in quite a striking pose with the station in back of her. That's the picture that ran in the magazine. Then we went to her apartment, and we did more shots there, which didn't run, but she did everything that I requested of her.

What were you trying to capture in the photographs?

Basically, it was just the idea that the location is what inspired her, or was a partial inspiration for *Atlas Shrugged*. Her pose implied that this is where *Atlas Shrugged* was sort of inspired.

And she enjoyed that?

Yes. She seemed to be fine with that.

Did you also have a purpose in what you wanted to capture in Ayn Rand, the person?

---

200 It was Theo Westenberger's first celebrity shoot.

I did that in the apartment. I did a more sort of stark image; it was all a matter of a very spare composition. Both shoots were architectural in the sense that she certainly was into architecture. And the scope of her books is huge, and that's sort of what Grand Central evokes in me too, and her gesture as well.

Where were those shots taken in her apartment?

It was the living room.

What was she like as a model there?

She was rather uncomfortable, but at the same time, I'm used to people being uncomfortable, so it didn't strike me that she was any more uncomfortable than some people.

Why was she uncomfortable?

I guess there was nothing for her to do. Also, I had more dramatic lighting there, so we had to position the lights, and all that kind of thing. This means that the subject just has to stand there, and it's not very comfortable. It's not like you're uncomfortable in a weird position, it just means that you can't leave and go get a cup of coffee, because then the light will be all messed up.

Were the apartment shots very thought-out poses?

Yeah, I think I was trying to do something that was more what I thought Ayn Rand was. I don't know if "severe" is the word, but just dignified and powerful.

How long were the shoots?

I think it was probably two different days. At her apartment, we probably would have been there for several hours. And at Grand Central, we probably would have been there for several hours. I believe she was alone.

Do you have a philosophy of photography?

A lot of people these days are just doing more of a fashion statement with their portraiture, rather than a statement of character. I try to suggest character, not just an interesting composition, or trying to make someone as beautiful as possible. So I'm just really trying to see what the person is, and show that, and, to me, that's what I was trying to do with Ayn Rand, evoke her books, and at the same time, her.

Did you think you captured her character?

I thought I definitely brought something out in her, and she seemed to be willing to give.

What was it that you brought out?

Both the power of her language and of her self, and then also the more natural side, or the less commanding side.

Was there anything unique or dramatic about her?

I think the unique thing was that I was surprised that she was amenable as she was.

Are you a fan of her books?

Yes, but I read them years ago! I have to read them again. I certainly remember Howard Roark.

As a great literary example of the man of integrity, an artist of integrity, has Howard Roark inspired you?

I certainly think I'm a person of integrity, but definitely, he was such a huge figure in literature, I mean, definitely. I think he certainly inspired a lot of architects, that's for sure. Every architect has read that book. And there's always Peter Keating. Everybody knows the Peter Keating in their life or if they're a Peter Keating or not.

It was a thrill to be able to meet her and to take such an important picture of someone who I'd always looked up to. And also a woman who had been such a powerhouse. Back then few women were CEOs or famous writers; there are more women out there today than there were then, and she was definitely one of the most intriguing and powerful.

Cynthia Peikoff

Cynthia Peikoff (née Pastor) was Miss Rand's secretary and friend from 1978 to 1982.

Interview date: January 13, 2000

Scott McConnell: *How did you first meet Ayn Rand?*

Cynthia Peikoff: In 1976 Leonard Peikoff gave a live course at the Statler Hotel in New York, on the philosophy of Objectivism. Ayn Rand participated in the question-and-answer period, so I got to meet her and see what he was like too.

Tell me about meeting Miss Rand and your first impression.

I knew she was going to be there, so I brought my copy of *Atlas Shrugged*. I went up to her at intermission as she was talking to some people. Her husband was with her. I asked her whether she would autograph my book, and she seemed a little surprised but she was gracious, and she said, "Do you have a pen?" And I said, "No." She got out a pen from her purse, and I asked her to autograph the last page instead of the first. She said, "Why?" and I said, "So whenever I come to the end, I can see your signature. It's special to me." So she wrote something fun. "To Cynthia Pastor, I hope you have enjoyed reading this book. Sincerely, Ayn Rand." That was thrilling. She was a very gracious woman.

And what was your impression of her before that?

I had seen her previously at the Ford Hall Forum. That was my first impression of her. She was on a darkened stage. She came out and sat with her purse next to her. I was impressed with the luminescence of her eyes and how directly she looked out at the world. I know it was popular in those days to describe auras around people. "Oh, I can see your aura and tell what kind of person you are." But she really did have an aura—in the sense that it was like a crown of benevolence around her, around her face. I had never seen anyone look that way in my life.

What surprised me was that she read her speech in a way that was not overly emotional. It was a very, not exactly matter of fact, but direct presentation. The other thing was that her accent threw me. When you read her books you don't think of a Russian accent, but she had a thick one.

After that first meeting at Leonard's course, how did your relationship with Miss Rand progress?

Leonard and I were going out when Miss Rand became ill and was hospitalized with pneumonia. He wanted me to see her, so I went up to the hospital with him. When I met her, I said something like "I wanted to come to New York to do two things: to meet a man like Howard Roark and to meet you, and now I've done both." She smiled in a charming kind of way. Of course, saying anything good about Leonard made her happy.

Did you then start seeing her socially or had you become her secretary?

No. I wasn't her secretary quite then, so I would see her at Leonard's house. Leonard had her over to dinner one night. I know I went to her fiftieth wedding anniversary party in April '79. [April 15.] So I saw her there, but I don't think I talked to her at all.

What do you remember of the occasion?

She sat on the couch holding Frank's hand. He was very fragile. He couldn't at that point in his life carry on a conversation, but he was smiling. I remember her looking very radiant and happy.

So after that you would socialize with her?

Yes. I would go over there with Leonard and talk to her or listen to them talk. I always found her answers to questions of the day—political or ethical questions, or any commentary—to be unexpectedly original. If Leonard and I discussed questions of that sort, he would have very brilliant insights. Sometimes we would ask her the same questions; she would have a deeper, more integrated approach to looking at the problem. That was delightful.

Could you describe a conversation between Leonard and Miss Rand.

They would both be kind of half reclining on the sofa or the chair. She would always be on the sofa. He'd be in the chair. That always surprised me—the way they slouched when they talked philosophy. When her heroes in her books talked philosophy, they sat up straight, but actually Ayn and Leonard were in that relaxed pose. They would have animated intellectual conversation in which he would ask questions and she would answer them, or they would simply discuss something.

Besides this relaxed pose, what was her manner during all this?

Intensely interested. Never relaxed in an intellectual manner. I wouldn't say patient with Leonard, but affectionate. She would call him "Darling." She always held a tremendous affection for him.

How would you describe their relationship?

It was complicated. She was his intellectual mentor and also his friend. He was the closest person she had in her life, especially after Frank died. Sometimes she'd get mad at him if she thought that he wasn't understanding something; she couldn't understand why he didn't understand it; she thought that perhaps it was volitional, so she'd get mad. I know she and Leonard talked about this. But I will tell you one thing about her. Leonard tried to explain to her that what was obvious to her, what she called "honesty," was not obvious to other people. She had a problem of often taking people the wrong way, because they would say things that she thought were obviously outrageous and dishonest. She couldn't grasp that other people didn't see what was obvious to her. That's why she would get mad.

Their discussions were very intellectual, more than personal, although they had many, many personal conversations throughout the years.

Miss Rand would give advice on personal topics or explain certain personal issues?

They would just discuss their lives, and he would turn to her if he had a problem. She did that for all the people she knew.

Did you have intellectual discussions with her?

No. You know how you feel when you're talking to a friend or family member you've known a long time? And you don't necessarily talk about anything very deep? Sometimes we'd talk about deeper issues or what I was doing in school, because I had gone back to college at Columbia University. Sometimes we'd just talk about fashion or sales at B. Altman's or the cat.

How did you become Miss Rand's secretary?

Barbara Weiss was her longtime secretary. I knew Barbara from when she was running Leonard's lecture courses. At one point, she decided she wanted to go into the work world, so she gave Ayn notice and then Ayn had to look for a secretary. I was working part time as a secretary for another firm while I was attending Columbia full time.

Leonard suggested I visit her, and she was very resistant to hiring anybody. For her to make a change of secretary, to bring a new person into her life, was difficult.

Ayn had been betrayed by many people who were her friends. So when it came time to hire me as a secretary, she wasn't welcoming many new people in her life. She went for weeks without anybody doing her work. Finally, she took me on, and Barbara instructed me. She gave me a wonderful notebook of form letters, and Ayn gave me instructions. Little by little, I learned how to do the work with her. I would go over to her house on Saturday morning and work with her, pay the bills, open the fan mail. I would pick up her P.O. box mail and take some of her letters home from her box to open and categorize them. She would later give me dictation; then I would type up letters for her to sign or for me to sign. I helped her go through her contracts and deal with her lawyers, and deal with the media, who would frequently ask her to do appearances or interviews. Because I ended up being her secretary, I had the leisure to sit with her for hours doing something she hated so much, which was writing her bills—she was only too eager to change the subject. It was interesting and fun.

And here's a funny story: I asked for a raise because I had received a raise at my other secretarial job. I asked her for one in the name of capitalism and free trade, but she wouldn't give it to me. So I said, "That's it, then. I'm not going to work for you at this wage. I deserve more." So I stopped working for her. She changed her mind.

I didn't quit as a ploy. I quit because it just wasn't worth it to me. The work was too hard. It was difficult to work with her, because she hated it. I didn't need this.

Did she say why she didn't want to give you the raise?

She thought it was too much money. Ayn was very thrifty.

When exactly did you work for her?

It probably went from 1980 to 1982. It ended when she died.

Describe for me a typical workday with Miss Rand.

I would come in, not too early, on Saturday morning. She would greet me at the door, unlocking both bolts, the inside and the outside. She was not a very fast person, at least in her old age. She would greet me slowly and graciously. "Hello. How are you?" and we would walk over to the dining room table where we did our work together. She would offer me something to drink, which would always be put on a coaster. I think we would start with the bills, and I would write her checks, and she would sign them. She would open the letters herself with her letter opener and then hand them to me. She looked over all the checks. She had a particular way she liked her checks to be filled out, and I had to do it that way.

What was different about it?

You'd have forty-four dollars and she would want you to write two little zeros and then a division sign and then "xx" underneath. This was safer. She was very cautious about money. After we finished the dreaded bills, I would balance her checkbook. Then we would start with the fan mail. She always had two stacks: fan mail that she liked and fan mail that she didn't like. We would go through the stuff she didn't like first.

Why did she start with the bad stuff?

To answer it.

Why answer it?

Because it required answers. These people asked her questions or told her things that were incorrect or irrational or untrue. Or asked her philosophical questions that implied they didn't know what they were talking about. She had to correct it.

But why not focus on writing to the people who either applauded her or thanked her?

I asked her that. "So why are you doing this? Why are you doing any of it?" It was so exhausting for her. I said, "You didn't write *Atlas Shrugged* just so you could answer fan mail." She liked the good letters, the nice letters. She would sometimes be very charmed by simple things that people would say. There are some lovely fan letters that were written to her; in essence, it was the same old thing, but this time from somebody in Iowa who said it in their own way.

How did she answer your earlier question about "why do you do this?"

She had no answer. She shrugged. She would get so mad. She'd tear up some of those letters into little pieces, and she didn't have a whole lot of energy at this time. She would walk slowly, and her breathing would become slightly labored once in a while. She'd always sit back after doing the bills and say, "I'm so tired." She flopped her hands down on the side of her chair and said, "I can't stand this. I can't take any more of it." Then we'd get to some bad letters. Suddenly, this incredibly weak, "can't take it anymore" person turned into a volcano, tearing thick paper into pieces. Another thing about her, she would pile the pieces up neatly or put them neatly in the trash next to her. That always amused me.

Do any letters particularly stick in your mind, positive or negative?

One thing I remember is that when I first started working for her, an old friend of hers from Hollywood wrote her a letter. She gave it to me as a test. She said, "What do you think of this letter?" I read it and she said, "How would you respond? Would you show me this letter or would you just respond? Miss Rand thanks you but she can't answer all her letters personally." It turned out to be a famous Hollywood costume designer who did a lot of movies.

Not Walter Plunkett?

Yes. That was it. Oh, it was a lovely, friendly letter, and she was very happy to hear from him.

He was a major costume designer who worked on such movies as Gone With the Wind. *He was from the days when she worked in the RKO wardrobe department between 1929 and 1932.*

So that was my test. She said, "What would you have done with that had I not been here to tell you to look at this?" So that taught me a lesson: when somebody who's very old writes her a letter like that or if somebody implies that they really did have a friendship, show it to her.

Her reaction to that letter was different from any other letter that she got. It seemed to bring back a look in her eyes that was warm and beautiful.

Did she tell you any stories about her time working with Mr. Plunkett or in the wardrobe department?

Probably, but I don't remember. She wasn't the kind of person to elaborate on "my friend." She was not a boastful person. She didn't over-elaborate about people she knew to impress you at all. She was completely unaffected and did not need to impress people. I loved working for her in some ways, but in some others, like the writing the bills part, it was really onerous because she just hated it.

Here's one of the things that endeared her to me: when you worked for somebody as a secretary in those pre-computer days, you usually had to retype an entire letter if you made a typo. Well, when I started working for her, if I made a mistake, she would cross it out, correct it in her handwriting and send it off. I thought that was the height of having made it in life. She didn't have to impress a soul. That taught me an important lesson about life and about impressing other people. When I see people who need to make everything so perfect in order to impress the world, when they're in business or whatever, I always think back to Ayn Rand and how it really doesn't matter. I loved working for her, because I made lots of typos.

She never chastised you?

Never! Even when I typed the script for the *Atlas Shrugged* miniseries. You can see how many mistakes I made, and she was so kind about it. I don't even know if "kind" is the right word. It just wasn't that important. I'll bet you when she was younger it was important though, because if you look over her manuscripts and correspondence, you'll see that they are perfect.

Anything else about her work methods?

She was the slowest reader I've ever seen. She saved her copy of the *New York Times* on a daily basis, so she could go back and reread it. That's how she got her information for her speeches and cultural or political articles. She would read articles, underline the important ideas, highlight them in ways that were meaningful to her so she could go back and use them. She had piles of papers next to her on the dining room table, so if she was waiting for me to finish doing something, she might pick up the newspaper and look at it. She went one word, one line at a time. The most profound thinker that I will ever meet was the slowest reader I have ever seen!

Did she explain if there was some psychological process going on? Was she breaking it down into every phrase or clause and analyzing it?

I never said a word to her about it. For instance, if she was going over a contract, she would read each word for its exact meaning in the context and put question marks for her lawyer. She never ever read a contract that she didn't go over word by word. She was extremely careful in that way.

What other things did you do during a typical Saturday work meeting?

We would look at catalogs when we got sick of the routine work. Altman's department store was closest to her house. Lord & Taylor's and Gump's of San Francisco. Gump's had an unusual catalog. We liked to look at clothes. I'd say to her, "Do you like that?" We could have been looking at house dresses or slippers. I'd tell her what I liked. She told me what she liked. I had a game that I played, which was to pick out my favorite thing on the page. So we would go through it and each pick out favorite things.

What was her attitude to these?

Always cheerful. She was much more pleasant than when she was doing bills or negative fan mail.

What about when doing the media requests?

Yes. She was very careful with them. I remember that the *Christian Science Monitor* wanted to interview her. She wanted complete copy control, so they turned her down.

Any other media stories?

At the time she died, there was a new cable TV station that was interviewing celebrities for a program called *Biography*. They wanted to interview her. We were working on that when she died. She had been going to do that. It was scheduled, I think, in March.

Did you go over anything with Miss Rand about her life story?

Not that I can remember. She did not discuss her past. My impression was that it didn't interest her.

Tell me about the Donahue *interviews.*

She was pleased to be asked. The producers were very nice to deal with, especially since she was making her first foray out into the world after her husband died. And it was kind of exciting to go and be on the *Donahue* show. She had a keen sense of publicizing herself to keep her books selling well.

What did she think of the interviews?

She liked them. She liked Phil Donahue. She said something like "he's a very nice man." He treated her with respect and affection; took her hand and was warm. He seemed sincere. He understood that her husband had just died, so he was being very sympathetic, at least what I saw before the Madison Square Garden show.

Was that the show where there was a conflict when the woman got up and insulted Miss Rand?

Yes.

What was Miss Rand's reaction to this later?

I was upset because Donahue didn't stand up for her, and he was supposed to, by contract, not allow that kind of hostility. I don't remember any big deal about it afterwards. It surprised me that she came out with a positive impression after that. I was angry, but I don't think she was.

Any other major interviews?

She was interviewed by Louis Rukeyser. I was there for that one. She went on the last trip of her life down to New Orleans to a big gold-conference business expo. She was the main speaker. One evening Louis Rukeyser was doing his show from New Orleans and invited her to be the guest. He was a very nice man, very gracious, and he admired and respected her. Just the right kind of treatment that she deserved, and so it went very well.

What about Tom Snyder?

Oh, I think she liked him too. That was a nice interview. What I saw in the last interviews was different than my impression of the earlier part of her life, in that the interviewers weren't out to get her, to ridicule her or to provoke her or put her down. So you came away with a good impression of the interviewer. You can learn a lot about Ayn Rand from watching the interviews. She wasn't in the position of having to defend herself. I don't think she wanted to do that anymore. Contractually, she demanded that there wouldn't be hostile interchanges during the interview.

At this time Miss Rand attended a party for Mike Wallace.

Yes. It surprised me that she went, and it surprised me that she was treated with such respect by him. My impression was that he liked her very much. And she liked him. The party was a celebration of his career. So he invited people he had interviewed for his biography series way back in the '60s.

Were there any other interesting episodes or anecdotes regarding the secretarial work?

Yes, there was a funny one. She would dictate angry responses to negative fan mail. And she would ask me, "Do you think that's too strong?" "Am I too angry?" Sometimes I said, "Yes, I think you are, and I don't want to put my name on it." She'd have me sign some of those nasty ones. She'd say, "Miss Rand does not have time to answer all your questions" or "Miss Rand has asked me to tell you," blah, blah, blah. But she didn't want to put her name on the letter, because signing the name means that person will now have Ayn Rand's signature, which gives the letter value. I was amused that Ayn Rand asked me if she was too angry. And I would say, "Yes, I think you should tone it down." And she would do it.

What was her office like?

It was very crowded with bags of unanswered fan mail filling the room. So we did not work in there together.

I believe you were the person who organized Miss Rand's papers, and so forth, after she died.

Me and Leonard, yes.

What material is there regarding the Brandens?

The most relevant was a long journal that she kept in the days and weeks and months before the final break with them, during which they would come individually to her home to discuss what was going on, to explain to her their behavior and rationalize the things they were doing that were incomprehensible to her. They would lie from week to week to week, and she didn't know they were lying. After they left, she would go and sit down at her desk and write on her unlined blue paper pages and pages, trying to understand what they told her. She would repeat the entire conversation and then analyze it sentence by sentence: what it really means about them, or maybe she needs to consider this, or maybe she needs to ask this question, because this doesn't make sense. She was trying to make reason and sense out of what they were fabricating.

So she was trying to salvage the relationship and understand them?

Oh yes. She wanted to keep her relationship with them but this was becoming more impossible because of their behavior. By the end, she finally figured out through enormous intellectual effort on her own part that they were lying to her.

It was both of them?

Oh yes, but more so Nathan. To know the seriousness with which she took what people said to her—and for them to lie to her continually and make up new lies for the purpose of deceiving her so they could keep the money and the prestige and power that they had through her relationship with them and sanction of them—to do that to her is a crime of such magnitude. It's a moral crime to do it to her of all people. It cost her a lot of emotional grief. All I can say is if anybody is a fan of hers and can grasp the depth of her mind and power of her thought and the depth of her feeling for the people that were in her life who she loved or liked and trusted, then you can just imagine the impact that had on her.

I hope in the name of truth and justice, someday, when this stuff comes out, that the world will know that they're all pathological liars.

Did she ever discuss the Brandens with you?

Around 1981 Barbara Branden, out of the blue, sent Ayn a friendly letter stating that after all those years she'd like to see her. Ayn said to me, "Well, I wonder what this is about now. I think I'll meet her and see what's on her mind. See what she's like." So she had her up to her apartment. I believe they were alone for lunch or discussion and then Barbara left. I went over to her apartment the next day and was anxious to know how it went. Ayn said, "Not much. There's nothing special here. And there was not anything special that she wanted." I don't remember the words exactly, but the feeling was that Barbara was a disappointment. She didn't turn out to be much of anything.

A day or two later, I brought up the mail from Ayn's box downstairs, and there was a letter from Barbara neatly written and formulated with one intention. It stated that she was writing a biography of Ayn and that the past was past. Would she consider contributing to it? And that Barbara was going to go ahead with it anyway. She put in the sentence that it was very good to have met with her on that day and put the exact date. Ayn read the letter and she looked up at me and she said, "That's what this is about." When you're writing a book about someone, there's an old trick in which you meet the person, and then you write them the letter, "I'm glad we met on such a date," so that in your book, you can state that you actually met the person, and it looks as though the person gave you their sanction to meet with them. It gives legitimacy to the meeting and the book, and so that's what this meeting was all about.

Did Miss Rand say anything else about that?

She was disgusted with it. She didn't care about this forthcoming biography at all. She just shrugged. Believe it or not, it didn't pass through her consciousness for very long. When Barbara Branden's book came out, I looked at the index to find the reference to that meeting, and Branden had made up a story that hadn't happened. If you look at her book and listen to what I just told you, they're two separate and opposite accounts. When she met with her, Barbara did not mention to Ayn that she was writing a biography.

At this time, what was the situation with the Atlas *movie script?*

The Jaffes were involved. Stirling Silliphant had done a treatment, but it was unsatisfactory to her. It was too naturalistic and undramatic at certain points for her. He was a good writer—one that she had admired. She was editing what he had written and at some point the deal with the network fell through. So this project was in limbo when she saw, on television, an actor who she thought would make an excellent Francisco, and she decided that she would write the miniseries herself.

Tell me about any writing problems that you observed.

She didn't have any problems. Many years ago she had done the outline for an eight-hour miniseries. She had also outlined a four-hour, two-part feature film and a shorter miniseries.

Tell me about her working on the teleplay.

She got out her copy of *Atlas Shrugged*, underlined the dialogue she wanted to keep, scene by scene. Then she sat down and in longhand on her blue paper, in screenplay form, with the proper formatting, wrote everything down. She got all the way through the first third, and I typed it up for her.

Did you discuss her writing of the teleplay with her?

We discussed a little bit about how you condense characters. She would explain why she conflated two characters into one or why she left out Cherryl Taggart.

What other characters did she conflate? Any of the major ones?

Oh, no. Never. They were all in there, but she was going to get rid of Cherryl Taggart, and in one of the versions, she got rid of the Wet Nurse. It was so tightly constructed.

The cutting had to do with subplots that weren't really critical to the theme of the book, to advancing the action. Cherryl was not central; it stood without her, and there just wasn't time. What fascinated me was how quickly she did it, because the thinking had already been done a long time ago on how she would do it, as evidenced by this outline.

Which actors did Miss Rand want in the Atlas Shrugged *miniseries?*

I know in the '60s she liked Lee Remick for Lillian Rearden. She also liked a young Catherine Deneuve for Dagny. You have to understand that Ayn had an unbending view of who she wanted, what she wanted. If Gary Cooper couldn't act the way that she hoped he could, she still wanted him because of his looks.

Did you ever discuss We the Living *with Miss Rand?*

Once. I reread *We the Living* while I was working for her, and I couldn't bring myself to read the last part where Kira dies. I said to her one day, "Ayn"—I just said it kind of wistfully—"Why does Kira have to die? It's just too sad." She explained to me that given totalitarian dictatorship and the nature of life there and the theme and the plot of the story, she had to die. There was no way out. Remember the original title was "Airtight." And I said to her, "I can't stand reading these sad stories anymore, these Romeo and Juliet endings where the person has to die." She was not offended at all by that. She was very sweet.

Did you ask her questions about any other of her fiction?

I once asked her, "How do you come up with your visual descriptions of scenes?" She said that when she is walking out and about or wherever, she sees an image, describes it to herself and stores it in her memory.

Did you ever discuss falling in love?

Yes, we had one conversation. We were saying goodbye one night and got on the subject of being in love. I know that she was in love with that fellow from *The Rat Patrol*. I said to her, "I've never understood this, but I've been in love with somebody since I was six years old." And she said, "Well, so have I been." And I said, "Really? You mean all your life you've been in love with someone?"

And she said, "Yes."

Did you talk about femininity?

No, I never had a conversation with her about femininity, but I did have a conversation with her about feminism. I asked her once if women had it harder getting into professions in her day or before her time, and she thought I was a feminist and got mad at me. Launched into a tirade. I corrected her when she was done, and I told her that I wasn't a feminist. Just asking a question. So that was my one opportunity of being the object of her jumping to the conclusion that I was committing a basic form of dishonesty.

Had Ayn Rand changed over those few years that you knew her?

Yes. She was pretty sad after Frank died, and she also became very tired. Her heart was failing. She had congestive heart failure, so she didn't have the strength that she used to have. She wasn't about to go out to parties.

What else was she occupying herself with at this time?

She was reading Agatha Christie—book by book.

That was after Mr. O'Connor died?

Yes. I think so.

Why Agatha Christie?

She liked Agatha Christie for the plots. In fact, I have some of her copies of Agatha Christie books. She would write her initials in ink on the first page of the book to indicate she'd read it. Then she would put a pencil check mark over it after she read it again.

Did she ever figure out the endings?

Yes, in *The Murder of Roger Ackroyd*. But her favorite one was *The Mysterious Mr. Quin*.

Was there anything else she was reading besides Agatha Christie?

She would be given novels by famous authors. I think, James Clavell, Richard Bach. She received lots of books that were signed by authors.

Did they send them to her or did she meet them? Do you know anything about those relationships?

I know Clavell came to her apartment with his daughter. He wanted to meet her. He was a great admirer of hers. Do you want me to tell you the inscription he wrote to her in his book *Noble House*?—"This is for Ayn Rand one of the real true talents," which he underscored twice, "on this earth for which many, many thanks." And there are many other popular authors whose dedications we have. Richard Bach, the author of *Jonathan Livingston Seagull*, wrote, "For Ayn Rand! With highest thanks for giving us men who matter and for returning to language its word 'consent.'"

What else was she doing with her time?

She was working with Leonard on his book *The Ominous Parallels*. He would bring her each chapter and they would go over it. He was in the final stages of editing, chapter by chapter, when I met him, and she was thrilled with what he had done. I remember when she wrote the introduction to the book—"If you like my works, you will like this book." She had never introduced anybody's book before, except for Victor Hugo.

Did you play Scrabble with Miss Rand?

I think so.

Did you beat her?

You have to understand: she was the most noncompetitive person you'd ever want to meet, because she would help you. She was so nice. She just didn't have any sense of needing to win. She really enjoyed Scrabble, but it would be a slow game. She took her time, and she was generous. If you were going to try to make a fifty-point word, she'd want you to try your best and get one.

What other activities did Miss Rand have?

She would have people over to talk ideas with. She allowed us to set up an interview with our friend Steve Jolivette, who was studying history and wanted to ask her questions. She agreed, and he went over one night with us, and he sat and asked her history questions. I remember her saying, "I don't know much about history. I don't know what I could really tell you."

He wanted to know about the French Revolution and I can't remember what else. You have to remember she studied history in college. When she says she doesn't know much about something, that doesn't mean she doesn't know anything. What she had was a sweep of history in her mind.

Tell me about Eloise Huggins's relationship with Miss Rand and Mr. O'Connor.

At first Eloise was more fond of Frank than of Ayn. She got very close to Ayn after Ayn's lung surgery. She would buy their food and prepare the meals, and do some of their housekeeping. Eloise was a very conscientious person. She didn't like the way the housekeeper cleaned the house, so she would do some little things. She would set the table for dinner and probably would wash the dishes when she came back the next morning.

How did Miss Rand react to Eloise proselytizing about becoming a born-again Christian?

Oh, she didn't mind. They would discuss it at length because she didn't see Eloise being an Objectivist. She wasn't trying to change her mind. But Eloise had a fine mind. She was born in British Guiana, where her father was the principal of a school under the British Empire. Their schools were excellent. Eloise was raised by her father, who made his children read a newspaper every day, starting when they were eight years old, and summarize the news stories. We're talking about a finely educated individual, not a cook. Due to the socialist takeover of Guiana, the family escaped to Barbados and, eventually, she emigrated to New York and took a menial job. But what Eloise really wanted was to go into nursing, but because she liked Frank so much, she stayed as the O'Connors' cook. After Ayn died I think she regretted that—that she hadn't gone into nursing.

You sound like you knew her very well.

I did. Eloise and I were close. We developed a friendship because we were both working for Ayn. We would be there together as her employees. And given that, I had a peer relationship with Eloise. Eloise was somebody who was down-to-earth, so we could talk easily with each other about what we saw and what was going on.

How would you describe her relationship with Miss Rand?

When Ayn was dying, she called Eloise her sister. Eloise went to visit her one day in the hospital, and she told Eloise, "You are my sister, and I'm dying." She's the only one she told that to, "I'm dying." Because you see, Ayn had a special relationship with her. She was like family. They were just that close. It was kind of an unconditional-type relationship, not one where Eloise was an Objectivist whose disagreement would be extremely important to Ayn. Ayn accepted Eloise with their differences.

What other differences were there?

They had a lot in common. They both witnessed, firsthand, the results of the takeover of their countries by communists. They were both raised to be intellectual and ambitious. They both loved the same man. Eloise loved Frank. They were both protective of Frank, worried over him. And they developed their own friendship. But they differed when it came to religion. Another difference was that Eloise had children. Ayn didn't.

What was Eloise's opinion of Miss Rand at the end?

She was very sad about her death, but she was pretty shocked that Ayn didn't leave her any money in her will.

Why?

After all those years, one would think that Ayn would have left a small sum for her. I was shocked. But then you have to understand Ayn Rand. She was very concerned about her property and about her copyrights and the uses to which they would be put after she died. I do not think she wanted any question about her will after she died. She wanted it to go to Leonard, because she trusted him. When she didn't remember Eloise, Eloise and I were both upset. I remember walking down the street, telling her what had happened. She stopped in her tracks. That really caused her a lot of grief, but in the meantime, I talked it over with Leonard, and he decided to give her a gift of $10,000, which she deserved.

She stayed and helped me pack up some of the apartment. We were pretty close and would have long discussions about Ayn and Frank and Leonard and what she'd seen through the years about the Brandens and all those people, what her view of them was. She said, "They were all a bunch of phonies." The one she really liked was Leonard, I think.

Do you have any cat stories about Miss Rand or Mr. O'Connor?

She had lion bedsheets and cat jewelry. She tore out pictures of cats from *TV Guide*. She liked Morris the Cat commercials on TV. When she died she had stacks of pictures of cats. She would cut out pictures that gave her pleasure. She had a tremendous number of things in her life that she derived pleasure from, like collecting rocks and stamps, pictures of cats. She would cut stamps off letters. She had one wonderful cat. One day, when at the vet's, she adopted another male cat that nobody wanted. She named him "Tommy," a gray alley cat, very sweet and fluffy. That was her last cat.

We said to her, "How are you going to do it?" Because she was concerned to have two male cats in the apartment together. She said, "I'll just keep the door closed between the back and the front of the apartment." That's what she did. They were two great cats, both extremely loving. I tried to convince her to open the door, that the worst that could happen would be that they would get in a fight. But she wasn't going to take a chance. They never met.

Whom else did Miss Rand see after Frank died?

One person she saw was her doctor, Dr. [Cranston] Holman, a prominent surgeon and a fellow stamp collector. He would pick Ayn up, and they would go to a stamp show together. I once said to her, after Frank died, "Why don't you go out on a date with Dr. Holman?" She was horrified at the thought that she would go out with any man. That wasn't in her scheme—to go and find another love. But she was fond of him. He was extremely formal and respectful to her. He was old-fashioned. Her type of person. She would see Leonard's mother from time to time and talk on the phone with her. And also the Sureses.

Anyone else?

Frank's niece, Mimi Sutton, in Chicago. All I know is they kept up relations during the years. Every Christmas, Ayn would send her money and a nice little note. They kept up a little correspondence.

Did you discuss your interest in psychology with Miss Rand?

Yes. I was going back to school and finishing my BA in psychology, and she couldn't understand why I would want to spend my time listening to people's problems on a regular basis.

Did you talk to her about your studies or school or how to survive school or the professors or anything like that?

No. We both liked French, and I was taking advanced French and enjoying it. Sometimes we tried to speak French. She had the most awful French pronunciation. Very flat.

Do you remember much more about her reaction to Frank O'Connor's death?

I know the doctor said that she took better care of him than he'd ever seen anyone take care of a patient like that. I asked her if she cried. And she said, "No. What good would that do?"

Which movies did she like or loathe?

She and Eloise went to see a movie with Hans Gudegast from *Rat Patrol*. It was a modern action movie. She was truly horrified at how awful it was.

Tell me about Miss Rand's dying.

She had taken a train trip to that businessman's conference in New Orleans and developed pneumonia on the way home. She never recovered from that, not having had much strength anyway. We had to take her to the hospital one day. Leonard had the flu, and if you had the flu, she didn't want you around, because she didn't have great immunity. So I got in the ambulance and took her to the hospital. She was really suffering but she did not remember that episode. She was delirious, and she spent about four or five weeks in the hospital while they were doing tests. She was in and out of consciousness. Her kidneys or her liver would start to fail, and then they would work again. The doctor simply couldn't understand what was happening to her.

Who was the doctor? Was it Dr. Scharer?

He was one. Of course, Dr. Holman was looking in on her. They were all at New York Hospital. She had her own private room with a TV. She recovered to the extent that she stopped being delirious and was completely lucid again, which was hopeful, but she was so depleted, weak, that she could hardly speak. She told the doctor that she wanted to go home to die. He said, "Okay, I'll let you go home, once you eat." She promised that she would. Sandra Schwartz, a friend of ours, being the cook that she is, immediately went to work making fresh chicken soup and strained broth, brought the broth over to Ayn's apartment. Ayn would try to sip at the broth just the way she promised the doctor.

Slowly that week, her strength failed. On Thursday I went to see her. She was in bed, barely able to sit up. She had around-the-clock nurses, and Eloise would come in during the day. Leonard visited every day. He had to get her to approve the copy of the jacket of her new book that was coming out, *Philosophy: Who Needs It*. She sat up and read it and gave her okay.

Then I brought in Tommy and she put her hand on him and sort of petted him. She looked at me and shrugged without speaking, as if "what could she do"—she knew she was going to die. Friday went by, Leonard visited her, and then Saturday morning we got a call from the nurse who said that she was in cardiac arrest and Leonard better rush over. He ran furiously all the way, but she was dead by the time he got there. The nurse had told him that Ayn had asked to hold her hand, and that was it.

She died with the nurse holding her hand?

I don't know if she was holding her hand, because I know the nurse ran to call Leonard, but that she had asked the nurse to hold her hand.

Any final comments?

Just that I had a special, different kind of relationship with her than other people did. I got to know her as an employee, which meant that she did not have expectations of me as an Objectivist necessarily. On the other hand, we had what was for me, I think, a very true friendship, a bond of affection. When she died, I was completely at a loss. For me, knowing Ayn Rand personally, I always felt safe in the world, because she could make sense of it for me.

1980s

Gloria Alter

Gloria Alter managed the 1973 production of *Night of January 16th* and was an acquaintance of Ayn Rand's.

Interview date February 24, 1997

Scott McConnell: *Did you have any meetings with Ayn Rand after 1973?*

Gloria Alter: Yes, at her last speech at Ford Hall Forum in 1981. A few people were always invited to come back to her hotel suite and sit around and talk after her speech. My husband Todd and I were both invited to come up. I walked into the suite and she was standing there, and I walked up to her and said, "You look so beautiful." Her eyes lit up, and she whisked me off to the bedroom and like a little girl she said, "Really!? I wasn't sure about my dress. Is this a good length for me? Is it a little too short or a little too long?" I said, "No, it's gorgeous." "And my hair was just done—is it styled well?"

And we just talked about the way she looked. She was old already, but she radiated beauty, and a childlike beauty, that was overwhelming. The interesting thing was that usually the conversation at these parties was about the speech and intellectual subjects. For five minutes it was as if that all disappeared and she was just responsive to being told how beautiful she looked.

She never lost her femininity?

Never. Part of my response to how beautiful she looked was that she radiated femininity right up until the end.

Ronald Pisaturo

Ronald Pisaturo attended lectures and classes given by Ayn Rand and met her in 1980. He is an actor, writer and teacher.

Interview date: April 6, 1999

Scott McConnell: *Tell me about meeting Ayn Rand.*

Ronald Pisaturo: I was a student in Leonard Peikoff's class on grammar. The class was given in the living room of his apartment. In the middle of one class, someone knocked on the front door. Dr. Peikoff left the room, and when he came back, Ayn Rand was with him. She came into the room in such an unobtrusive way that, for a moment, I did not know who it was, because she just walked right across the room and sat down on the side. She seemed to be trying hard not to interrupt the class.

So Dr. Peikoff went back to discussing the material, and at one moment Ayn Rand made a sound like the first half of an excited "Oh!"—like something you would hear from a schoolchild who just got an idea and was dying to say something, but who knew she first had to raise her hand and get permission. Again, she was being so careful and polite, and would not speak without permission. There was so much excitement in her wanting to say the point that had come to her mind. Dr. Peikoff recognized her and let her speak. She said she had not known explicitly the point Dr. Peikoff had just made, but that's what she had been doing in her writing. She looked so intensely interested in the subject, and she had such an expression of innocence about her.

Raquel Welch

Raquel Welch is an actress and film star. Since 1964 she has appeared in more than sixty movies and TV shows. She met Ayn Rand in 1981.

Interview date: April 1, 1998

Scott McConnell: *How did you meet Ayn Rand?*

Raquel Welch: I had been interested in *Atlas Shrugged* and had my representatives contact her people. It turned out that somebody had the rights to produce the book into a movie, and I was hoping to do it as a television miniseries.

Her representatives told me that Ayn was not interested in cutting down the book. I thought, "Oh my, at least I'll let her people know that I'm interested in her book, and that I think it's a great story with wonderful characters." I thought they were like the characters from *Gone With the Wind*—bigger than life, passionate and sexy.

When you read Atlas Shrugged, *did you see yourself playing Dagny Taggart? Is that how you got interested?*

Yes. I thought that she was wonderful because she was very modern, forthright and educated. She was also very feminine but had a lot of "masculinity" about her that would appeal to somebody of my generation. We were in a new era where, as single professional women, and in my case, show business, you had to have some entrepreneurial ability. By the time I arrived in Hollywood in the 1960s, there was no more studio system. I felt I was walking into a totally chaotic situation with no order, and people were busy wanting to tear down order. Because Ayn Rand had a very ordered, logical mind, there was a lot of what she said that appealed to me.

What was the reaction of Hollywood people when you told them about your interest in Atlas Shrugged?

When I started talking about the book, people shook their heads and said, "You're never going to get that done. It's been tried, and it's not possible. Forget about it." I'd say, "Why does everyone keep saying no? Can't we just keep going and see where it all leads?" The second level of discussion hinged on the idea that Ayn was not going to collaborate with anybody, and if she wasn't going to collaborate with anybody or compromise in any way about the length of the speeches and things like that, then there was no possible way the movie was going to get done.

How did your interest in Atlas Shrugged *progress to your meeting Miss Rand?*

I kept calling her people to try and track her down. At one point, somebody said that it would be possible to arrange a meeting in New York. I thought, "That would be great." I was also told that she had always seen me as a possibility to play one of her heroines because of my cheekbones. I thought, "Oh, well, that's good, at least she likes my cheekbones." I thought it was actually funny.

Why?

In a way it made perfect sense, because I knew she liked a certain style. You could easily picture in your mind what she was writing, because she wrote in a very visual way, very cinematic. I thought that was fine, but I had to meet this lady and see whether we had any possibility of actually doing the movie. So I met her at a restaurant, I think it was Quo Vadis, for a lunch or a tea, in early 1981.

What was your first impression?

She was much more elderly than I expected, and she had rather thick glasses, but she had a lot of presence. She was quite grand in her demeanor and deportment, and I liked her immediately, because she reminded me of all the grand dames in my past that I had always loved, the great divas of the stage: the Judith Andersons, the Joan Crawfords.

She was a lot of fun to meet. She seemed to have a sense of humor, a twinkle and a vitality. She was clearly not very well when I saw her. She walked very slowly. I thought, "This is a shame, because she's in her winter years, and it's very difficult for her."

What did you discuss?

I spoke to her about how excited I was by her writing and how inspirational I thought she was, and that she had such passion and commitment. I also said these were the kinds of things that I had in my character, and I wish there were more people who felt that way and could be inspired; that it just seemed like people didn't want to be inspired, that they wanted to water everything down and do everything in a convenient way, not to offend anybody, or not to be too much this way or that. I think she realized that I felt some kind of kindred spirit with her and her writing and that I was trying to say

I salute the same kind of flag as you.

She then proceeded to tell me that she was not sure whether this *Atlas Shrugged* could be done as a movie. She didn't want it to be done piecemeal—she wanted to do the whole story. She felt it was more for television than film, but she didn't think that the television people were going to let her do the whole book, and so she was not going to turn it over to them.

So she pretty much squelched my ideas. I don't think she necessarily meant to do that. She was just telling me that she was not willing to compromise an iota, and that pretty much went along with what she'd said in the book, that compromise is failure. So I thought, "I'm meeting an all-time great human being, who is certainly one of the extraordinary people of the century and certainly has a specific philosophy, but it's a real tough one to get this project done. It looks as though there's not going to be anybody around who would convince her otherwise, and I don't think I'm going to be the one. I'm just the actress. I would have to take on so many people that it would be a whole career in itself. I could spend the rest of my life trying to get this project done, and it might never happen."

She probably thought that if they were going to do a film or TV miniseries of the major work in her life, she wasn't going to let it be bastardized. So that was the end.

It was discouraging from the point of having put something up and seeing it rejected, but exhilarating to have had the privilege of meeting somebody who is that much of an individual. My attitude is that I don't mind if I disagree with somebody as long as I know who the hell they are. Most people are not going to show you who they really are; they're going to hide it behind some social behavior and answers and ideas they know will be socially acceptable. I didn't find that in her.

What happened to the Atlas *project or your involvement?*

Nothing happened. She pretty much said there was not much chance that it was going to be made the way she wanted it, so I didn't follow through afterwards with anything except to write a thank you letter. I just kept an eye out for her. Whenever I would read something about the project, I would take note of it, because I was curious, but there was nothing happening with it. There was no momentum.

I hope that somebody down the road will do it. It would be interesting to see it done, but I'm too old for it now, so I wouldn't be able to play the Dagny role.

Did Miss Rand seem positive about you playing Dagny?

Yes, she was.

What else did you talk about?

I must say I was rather shocked to find out that she had spent all her girlhood in Russia. It made sense to me how she had come to the point of view that there was not going to be any compromise from her individualistic philosophy, because she came from a country which was anti-individualistic—it was collectivist—and for her that was the anti-Christ. That was the first time I knew that was her background. I had read her books, but I hadn't read about her.

What did she say specifically?

She told me that it was a great privilege to live in this country. That she came here and it was like heaven, that this was the place where the future was being formed. She thought Russia was the worst, the lowest.

She was pretty much like her book. She still seemed very passionate to me. I was surprised that her conversation was as passionate as any of her books, that she was still charged up with energy about this: that people don't understand what a gift it is to live with freedom of thought and to be able to design your own life; and people don't realize it because Americans have never experienced being suppressed and being told that they just have to follow along for the good of the whole. She was still saying things like that.

Did her books influence you?

They encouraged me a lot to continue being strong-minded and courageous. I felt like I was a loner and somebody who did have a vision of the kind of woman that I wanted to portray. In many cases, people would want me for a role, physically, but they wouldn't want my persona. They would want to water the role down and make it cute. I never liked cute women. I always thought that women should be extraordinary and magnificent.

Steven Jolivette

Steven Jolivette was a history student when he met Ayn Rand. He later gained a PhD in American history.

Interview date: May 27, 2003

Scott McConnell: *You spent an evening asking Miss Rand questions about history. Tell me how that came about.*

Steven Jolivette: I had met Miss Rand very briefly on two occasions. I introduced myself to her when she came to Leonard Peikoff's apartment to hear one of his grammar lectures. I should mention that I was friends with Cynthia and Leonard; Cynthia was Miss Rand's secretary. Cynthia later told me that Miss Rand had asked about me. I mentioned to Cynthia that I had been tempted to ask Miss Rand a question about history. Cynthia mentioned that to Miss Rand, and Miss Rand invited me for a discussion of history. The discussion was in August 1981. Leonard and Cynthia accompanied me.

The brief notes I now have—and which I must rely on and sometimes quote—were taken either then or some time after.

Tell me what progressed.

She was pleasant to me, or at least not unpleasant, all evening, in spite of the fact that she was not pleased with my questions. In fact, she was appalled at many of them. Sort of flabbergasted or shocked—speechless for a while—and her eyes would get big and would go back and forth as if for awhile she did not know what to do with this nonsense. But the interesting thing about this is that she regarded my ideas—in this case, my mistakes—as personally important enough to be shocked about. She really took me seriously. And I understand that this is a famous trait of hers: always taking ideas—and you—seriously.

What were some of the questions you asked?

One of the questions that I asked was her view of the cause of the fall of the Roman Empire. And she was shocked. Her first response to a lot my questions was, "How would I know, I'm not a historian." Now to me, she had written the introductory essay of *For the New Intellectual*, and she often makes sweeping comments about history, and she's studied history; yes, she's not a historian, but I would think she would have some idea. But she also said, "What gives rise to these questions? What would you take for an answer?" But at the end, she did say, off-handedly, "I think it was the welfare state."

I also asked her about the reason for France and England developing so differently through the centuries. Again, she protested that she was not an historian. She asked me if I had any ideas on this difference, and I said, "No, not really," but did posit that Alfred the Great was a great king, and there were several other very good ones after him. She said that a few good kings would not be enough to make the kind of difference between England and France that there was.

Perhaps in this connection, one thing that she said that has helped me a great deal is that in considering this kind of question, you have to consider the ideas of the culture and then the external factors, for example, outside political influences, and you have to evaluate what is operative in a given case—that is, to paraphrase—you have to determine, is this culture or nation or civilization growing by its own devices, or are there external, say political factors, which are influencing it?

I asked her a question about the nature of feudalism and whether it had anything to do with the dynamic quality of European civilization. She just took it as if, what's the big deal about feudalism, it's just the result of caste tradition from early days when peasants needed military protection, and it's simply handed on by tradition. She did say that the crusades were crucial in awakening Europe, and in breaking down feudalism.

She said that she had studied the Middle Ages because she had thought that there was individualism there but that she had learned differently. Here she said anecdotally that she had thought of writing a small science fiction novel dealing with individualism. I found the idea of the story to be ingenious and delightful, but unfortunately I can no longer remember the idea precisely enough to really convey it. It had to do with traveling to other planets and somehow thereby discovering individualism.

What other questions did you ask?

I asked a few about the French Revolution. She said the French Revolution was very much needed, but that it made France worse. It was a turning point, but she thinks that the resulting bureaucracy stifled intellectual life, and they were more free under the *ancien régime*.

I mentioned that I was impressed by how collectivist the French Revolution was; I cited the fact that the first revolutionary French assembly had taken over the Church and made it a state institution. She replied that you cannot look at any isolated thing like that to judge whether they're basically collectivist or not, you have to look at their ideas.

Did you discuss famous historians or history texts?

I asked whether she knew any good history books, and she flatly said no. She asked if I knew any, and I said I was somewhat impressed by Tocqueville's *The Old Regime and the French Revolution*, and she asked what was his philosophical framework. I answered that as best I could tell he was a kind of aristocrat, and she dismissed it, saying, in effect, that if that were relevant to his frame of reference, he couldn't be too good.

Was there any discussion of ancient history?

She said, if I remember the wording correctly, that the classical civilization did not have any real respect for the individual. It was Christianity that introduced the sanctity of the individual. And she used infanticide as an example of this disrespect in the ancient world.

Did you ask her questions she liked?

I did have one question which she liked, or at least did not dislike: I said, now that you've done it, it seems easy to demolish altruism; why do you think men have not done it until you? She said, that's a good question. She gave an anecdote about Columbus. Somebody had defied him and others to make an egg stand upright, and he did it by crushing the end of it; she gave that as an example of the point that once it's done, then people think it's easy. She ended by saying something to the effect that she thought men were afraid. I do not think she intended that as a full answer.

Did she make any other significant points?

At a certain point, Leonard said that my questions seemed rationalistic, and she said, "Oh yes," in a way which I took to mean: rationalistic, plus more. Perhaps in this connection she said that what I needed was a "skeletal view of history." She also said that a historian's questions about history are the foundation for his theory of history.

Louis Rukeyser

Louis Rukeyser was an internationally recognized and influential economic analyst and commentator. In November 1981 he interviewed Ayn Rand in New Orleans on his show *Louis Rukeyser's Business Journal*. In 1968 he began hosting television shows as an economic commentator and for a number of years hosted the popular *Louis Rukeyser's Wall Street*. He wrote best-selling books on both economics and investing; edited the top-circulation monthly financial newsletters *Louis Rukeyser's Wall Street* and *Louis Rukeyser's Mutual Funds*; and ran heavily attended investment conferences and cruises, and the Web site *www.rukeyser.com*. Mr. Rukeyser died in 2006.

Interview date: May 6, 1998

Scott McConnell: *How did you become aware of Ayn Rand or her works?*

Louis Rukeyser: I was probably first exposed to them through *The Fountainhead* movie and then went to the novels. I was quite a young fellow when they came out. I thought she was on target, the minute I started reading her.

So I had known of her work for many years by the autumn of 1981, when I was making a speaking appearance at New Orleans, where she was also speaking, and I set up a television interview with her for a short commercial syndicated series that I was doing at the time called *Louis Rukeyser's Business Journal*.

It was most interesting because, before the interview, I was told by members of our production staff, "You have a groupie," that she was terribly excited about the prospect of talking with me and was spending a great deal of time in makeup and was like a teenage girl worrying about her appearance. I went in to see her to make sure she was relaxed and ready to go. She was just as sweet and as gentle as she could be and said what a great thrill this interview was going to be for her, and that she admired my own work on behalf of freedom and liberty, and other very flattering things.

We then sat down to do the interview and as soon as I asked the first question, she turned into the tigress the world knows, and any sign of deference was completely out the window. She was terrific—full of fire and excitement. And then when we finished taping the interview, she reverted to her initial persona and said, "Was that what you wanted?

I want you to have exactly what you want; would you like to do it again?" I told her it was just perfect.

Do you agree with Ayn Rand's social philosophy?

I believe that the same government that louses up the economy has no great capacity to rule in social issues either—to tell us which movies to see and what we should do in our bedrooms.

Has Ayn Rand influenced you?

Well, I don't know that she's influenced me, because I agreed with her. But she certainly was a seminal thinker, if one can say that about a woman in these gender-conscious days. She was a brilliant thinker, one of the leading thinkers of the twentieth century, no question about it. She was ahead of her time. I have a feeling that the future lies with those who believe in freedom; that the twentieth century has, among other things, been the testing ground and discrediting of government as the answer to everyone's problems, real and perceived. And I would hope that in the twenty-first century we proceed down the road that neither lets the government come in and screw up the economy, as it has shown great capacity to do all over the world, or, on the other hand, turn to government as the house nanny and censor. I think that the philosophy that she put forward is the way of the future. Whether I would dot every *i* or cross every *t* with her philosophy is irrelevant as compared with the fact that she was in a very early and incisive way pointing the way toward what I hope will be the future of the world.

Harry Binswanger

Harry Binswanger's first exposure to Ayn Rand came when he attended a lecture she gave in 1962 at the Massachusetts Institute of Technology, where he was then a freshman. He met her in 1964 and over the years progressed from being a student to a junior associate to a close friend. Dr. Binswanger, a PhD in philosophy, is the author of *The Biological Basis of Teleological Concepts*, the editor of *Introduction to Objectivist Epistemology* (expanded edition) and *The Ayn Rand Lexicon*, and for eight years published and edited *The Objectivist Forum* [*TOF*]. He is currently a professor at the Ayn Rand Institute's Objectivist Academic Center and is writing a book on the nature of consciousness.

Interview dates: The following extracts are from a 52-hour series of interviews conducted in August and September 1999 and July 2001.

Scott McConnell: *When you think of Ayn Rand, what comes to mind?*

Harry Binswanger: A fighter for values. An intense woman who took every moment of her life as precious and enjoyable and important.

In my speech "Ayn Rand's Life: Highlights and Sidelights," I said, "Right through her life, Ayn Rand's had this same violent passion for her values. I think of it as Ayn Rand's metaphysical outlook. As a mutual acquaintance once put it, she projected that every minute of her life was important to her. This sense of her intensity was palpable. When you talked with her, you knew you were in the presence of something totally out of the ordinary. A kind of power radiated out from her. High tension crackled in the air around her. It was a positive tension—unless you crossed her, of course. She once asked me, whether I thought she was the kind of person who was easy to talk to, and I was rather surprised that my honest answer was 'Yes.' She had an odd combination of formality and warmth. And, at the age at which I knew her, great dignity. At the same time, she had a spirit of gaiety and even playfulness. You can see it in the music she loved, and in *The Fountainhead* and *Atlas Shrugged*, for all their seriousness."

How was she unique?

Let me quote again from my speech: "The quality everyone recognized as characteristic of Ayn Rand was her phenomenal intelligence. Even her opponents marveled at her mental powers. I want to comment on one aspect of her mind: she possessed extraordinary self-consciousness: she was constantly aware of what her mind was doing; if you asked her about any of her ideas, values or emotional reactions, what they came from, she could tell you—and in detail. Her thinking was self-conscious, explicit, definite, decisive. She remembered her thinking because her thinking was so important to her."

Ayn was extremely introspective. She always knew what was going on in her mind, and as she said on several occasions, "I always could understand every emotion that I had." And this was not an idle boast. This is what she committed herself to, so she did work to understand her emotions. She could always tell you what she was feeling and why. Or you could ask her, for instance, "How did you arrive at your theory of concepts, what questions did you ask yourself?" and she could tell you. Boy, did Ayn ever know herself.

Someone told me that a psychologist in her circle used to say, "Ayn doesn't have a subconscious—it's all conscious." And he was half serious. What he meant was that everything in Ayn's brain was accessible to her. She didn't have any hidden material in there. It was all transparent. None of it was unavailable to her conscious mind. And it was all just logic. Except that it was logic with values. That's important—it wasn't cold logic, it was passionate logic.

Ayn's psychological perceptiveness was terrific. And she could understand you—but not by some kind of special vision into your soul. No, she didn't do it that way at all. She would ask you questions. If you read her article "Art and Moral Treason," for example, you see the way that she worked: somebody tells her he felt guilty over the intensity of his positive response to a certain movie, and she asks follow-up questions. She eventually identifies his basic premises and whole psychology.

Ayn used to say, "I don't understand psychology." But she did. She understood psychology much better than anybody else. The reason is that she introspected and she extrospected using that high-powered brain of hers. When she would say, "I don't understand psychology," she meant: "I don't understand how people can hold the contradictions that they do. I don't know how they function being as irrational as they are. I can't feel my way into them and make intuitive sense, from my framework, of what they do, because it's so messed up." That's what she meant—not that people baffled her intellectually.

During the nonfiction-writing course she gave in 1969, the thing that impressed me the most was the objectivity she had about her own consciousness. Time and time again, she would say about her own writing, "Now, at this point, I was stuck. So I asked myself the following questions. And I saw that I had given my subconscious a contradictory assignment, and that led me to the way out of it."

Or she would say, "I got the squirms."[201] And then she would say, "So I asked myself: 'What orders have I given myself that I can't fulfill?'" She took it diagnostically. It was a technical issue for her. It was not a self-esteem question: "Oh, what's wrong with me?"

Did she talk about how much she had learned over the years?

Also from my talk: "Near the end of her life, I asked Ayn, projecting my own experience onto her: 'Do you feel that you didn't become mature when you reached a certain age, but that you are always becoming more mature?' She said no, she didn't, and looked at me faintly questioningly. Trying to save my dignity, I rephrased the question: 'Well, do you feel that you are constantly learning more about life?' 'Oh yes,' she responded, 'and I wonder how I ever survived yesterday, not knowing what I know today.' That captures her attitude toward the urgent practical need for understanding. And understanding, for her, meant conceptual understanding, identifying abstract principles that she could apply in relation to her values."

Was Ayn Rand always Ayn Rand?

Oh yes. Absolutely. There was never a moment, never a blink of an eye where I wasn't totally aware that this was the author of *Atlas Shrugged* and originator of Objectivism. She never "let her hair down." She never became different from what I saw in public. I don't mean that she had "hair to let down" but didn't do it. I mean that she never "relaxed" in the way Peter Keating means when he says to Roark, "Can't you ever relax and be normal? Just be human?" She never relaxed in the sense that Keating wanted Roark to "relax." She was physically relaxed. In many of our late-night conversations, she would be lying on the couch, but she was never intellectually out of focus.

If she was making a snack for us or washing the dishes, she gave her full attention to that. She would talk with me while she was doing it, but I could see those eyes riveted on what she was doing. She would not do things with less than full concentration. She was always intense.

---

201 "Squirms" was Ayn Rand's term for a specific kind of writer's block. See Ayn Rand's *The Art of Fiction*, ed. Tore Boeckmann (New York: Plume, 2000), pp. 4–6.

I want to say some more about her personality or her manner as she came across. "Formality" doesn't quite cover it, because I want to also convey that she was not a regular Joe. She was like Kay Gonda in her play *Ideal*: she was different from anyone you would ever have met, and you would have seen that instantly. She was a larger-than-life figure, but the opposite of a grave or brooding genius. It wasn't any one emotional content. It could be anger, joy, depression, amusement, boredom, disgust, excitement, enthusiasm. It could be anything. But it was always riveting, because she was so intelligent and so value-focused.

So in giving a kind of rounded portrait—although what I usually stress is what a dynamo she was, what a forceful personality she had, and the in-focus, piercing way she looked at you and all that—I want to round it off by emphasizing that she was also amiable, warm, affectionate—much more affectionate than most repressed Americans.

Yet you called her "cautious."

In manners, she was. For instance, she wouldn't have any of the Manhattan-style of crossing the street. New York City is a pedestrian city where you weave between the cars because they're going slowly, and you don't wait on sidewalks, and you don't cross at lights, you just step out into the street where you feel like and then wait for an opening in the traffic, ignoring the lights. She wanted to cross at the green light, and she didn't want to step off the sidewalk until she looked both ways very cautiously.

And whenever I would leave the apartment at three or four in the morning, she would say, "Now, you know, it's late and it's dangerous" or something like that, in expressing concern about something that could happen to me on the way home. Just a slight apprehension. And I would say, "Don't worry, Ayn, I won't mug anyone." Her expression acknowledged that it was a humorous comment, but she remained a little concerned. You know, how the heroine says to the cowboy when he's going off to face the villain? A sincere "Be careful." Not a perfunctory "Take care."

She was consciously on the premise that you should do everything you can do to make sure that nothing bad happens in that way. Because if it does, and you had done everything you could, well, that's life. But you didn't want to have the regret, "Oh, if only I had looked before crossing the street" or whatever it might be. I should add that when I knew her best, she was in her seventies. But she wasn't creaky at all. She was spirited and vigorous and youthful.

Did she change over the time that you knew her?

Only physically, particularly after she had lung surgery in 1975. In the same period, Frank was declining, and there was an edge lost, a spring not in her walk. It's not that she became less intense, but there was a vigor and zest that was not as strongly there, afterwards. You got the idea that she could become tired if you overloaded her, whereas before that, you thought she couldn't become tired. It was a noticeable difference but not a pronounced one. I'm talking about going down from one hundred to ninety. I once asked her about the effects of that lung operation on her, and she acknowledged that it had some impact on her psychologically. I suggested it had to do with confronting her own mortality, and she agreed.

But in the intellectual, emotional, philosophical ways, she was always exactly the same. Her last question period, in New Orleans, after her "Sanction of the Victims" speech,[202] resonated exactly, in my mind, with the first question period I heard her give in 1962. I don't mean just that the content was consistent. I mean her style of answering—her feistiness, her delight, her quickness of mind—reminded me exactly of what so impressed me in how she handled questions in 1962.

For instance, after the New Orleans speech in 1981, there was one question I remember. Now, this was to an audience of three thousand "gold bugs," hard-money enthusiasts. Somebody in the audience asked her, "What is the basic reason for a gold standard?" Now imagine a typical answer: "A medium of exchange must have high unit-value and certain other physical attributes such as high density, homogeneity, easy divisibility, not spoil over time—and gold has these features more than any other commodity." That's what any good free-market economist or speaker would say in terms of why gold is needed. Ayn said, "To keep the looters' hands off your savings." The audience burst into applause. She was the same in 1981 as she was in 1962, in content, in approach and in spirit.

Changing the topic, what about how she dressed?

She had her own way of dressing, which was in a classical style, like her cape outfit, a fairly simple black dress with a black cape. Once she came out into the living room of her apartment wearing high red "wedgies"—platform shoes that were the latest fashion trend. The soles must have been three inches thick. She smiled and quipped, "Don't you

---

202 The speech was given on November 21, 1981.

think they add to my stature?"

She told me a story once related to clothes. She once went shopping with a friend, an eligible young woman, and Ayn found a brightly colored, slightly flamboyant dress and said, "Here, you'll really attract attention in this." The girl said, "I don't want to attract attention." Ayn said she grasped something about the difference between her and other people on the basis of that, because she couldn't imagine a woman wanting to be a wallflower. She wanted to be noticed, but this girl didn't, and she thought, "That's a failing. It's a lack of a certain ambitiousness on the part of the girl." That's typical of Ayn that she always took herself as the given—that is, she approached psychological issues using herself as her frame of reference. She didn't just feel her way into the psychology of other people, but she was very observant, and she was always trying to grasp a wider principle about anything, including about people and about psychology.

How was she when receiving public recognition?

She was pleased when she got recognition. Of course, she was the one who explicitly identified the crucial difference between the desire for recognition from worthy people versus the neurotic desire for social approval. She did have a desire for recognition, but only from people she could respect. When she got invited to go to the moon launch and to the President's dinner for Malcolm Fraser, I think she was really glad. It made her feel there was justice in the world.

She wanted recognition, on her own terms, and she did care about how her ideas were being received. One day, I guess it was after her second *Phil Donahue Show* appearance, she said to me, beaming, "You know what? I've got clout. That was the word my agent used. He said, 'You've got clout.'" Her agent had told her she could get invited on any TV show. And she liked that. She was speaking wryly, almost self-mockingly, with a kind of self-consciously smug and a little embarrassed look on her face, if you can picture those two being combined.

Did she feel she had earned a certain status?

She expected her due after *Atlas Shrugged*. She did have a view of her standing and what she had earned, and she didn't tolerate presumptuousness. Presumptuousness offended her. You can see it in how she handled questions, such as the question on the *Donahue* show by a woman in the audience who prefaced her question with a statement to the effect, "I used to believe in your ideas but then I became educated." Ayn wouldn't take any kind of implied insult like that.

She did think she'd earned her readership and her standing, and she held that if you had earned something objectively, it ought to be recognized. Ayn, lifelong, insisted on that, both as the giver and as the receiver. I point you towards those letters she wrote to Frank Lloyd Wright when she was the admiring, respectful petitioner.[203] When she reached the position that Frank Lloyd Wright had been in, vis-à-vis her, she expected to be treated by the same standard.

Was she always predictable?

No. She had such a fresh perspective on things. She would come out with statements like "*High Noon*? Oh, that doesn't have a plot." Or, she told Leonard that he could go ahead and buy a rare recording of an Emmerich Kálmán operetta, even though it had been produced in a communist country, on the grounds that it would fuel him in his work, which was fighting the same kind of enemy that Communism represents. That's not something she allowed to herself, and it's not what a dogmatic or doctrinaire Objectivist would think. So you'd never know what to expect.

Another example: she thought Muhammad Ali would be good to play a part in a movie version of *Atlas Shrugged*. I was surprised that she even liked a boxer. And you could be surprised by things that she didn't like too. For instance, she liked the music used in the TV commercial for Virginia Slims cigarettes: "You've come a long way, baby, to get where you've got to today . . ." But when a friend played it for her, she was very repulsed by the fact that the music didn't come to a proper ending, but just repeated a line while fading out in volume. That kind of fade-out, which is common in pop music, ruined the piece for her. So there were constantly intellectual and artistic things like that that came as a surprise to me. She did not check things off against the theories of Objectivism to see if they were right. She looked at things inductively, straight.

Was Ayn Rand a patient person?

With her work—incredibly patient. Remember, this is a woman

---

203 See *Letters of Ayn Rand*, p. 108–109.

who spent twelve years writing *Atlas*—and this was after initially thinking it would be a short project. Much shorter to do than *The Fountainhead*, which took her seven years. Patient with people? Yes. I think she was extremely patient, but if she thought something was wrong, she would flare up instantly. In that sense, I don't think you should call it impatient. She was decisive in her judgments, but she was extremely patient in trying to explain anything to you. For instance, I once asked her, "What exactly is wrong with sacrificing others to self? What's the error in that idea?" And she talked to me for about fifteen minutes on that. And then follow-up questions would be given the same careful, detailed discussion. She was very patient at explaining. She was always quite concerned to help anyone understand, because she was passionate about ideas and responded to anyone else's interest in ideas.

Ayn Rand and anger?

She once said to me, "If I ever become very polite and calm and mild, that's the time for you to worry, because then I've lost all respect for you. If I'm angry at you, it's because I expect better of you, and I still care about you, I still respect you. But when that's gone, without that, when I'm just bored and polite, that's when you know I've lost all interest in you."

One time later in our relationship, she asked, "You're not afraid of me, are you?" I had to be honest, so I said, "A little." And she said, "Well, let me give you Elizabeth's ring." She asked if I knew the story of Elizabeth's ring, and I said I didn't. She explained that Queen Elizabeth the First had been romantically involved with Lord Robert Essex.[204] And there was a certain problem because she was the queen, and if she lost her temper, she could order him to be executed; so Elizabeth gave him her ring and said, "If I ever threaten you, just send me the ring and you will be given immunity." So Ayn said to me, "I give you Elizabeth's ring." What she meant was—in my words—"If ever I start to denounce you or attack you, you just remind me that I said you have immunity. If I start to drop context by forgetting what you've earned in my eyes, you can remind me, by the device of Elizabeth's ring." That put me more at ease, reassured me.

Did you ever have to "send her the ring"?

---

204 This story was dramatized in the movie *The Private Lives of Elizabeth and Essex* (1939), starring Errol Flynn and Bette Davis.

No. In fact, I never even had to think about it again.

What about Ayn Rand and laughter?

I don't remember her having intense, prolonged laughter, but I told jokes and she laughed. You try not to laugh at your own jokes, but when she told jokes she would chuckle at them.

One amusing statement she liked—I think it was something she'd heard—was "I'm a great admirer of the American common man. But the common woman?" She was specifically a male-worshipper.

An example of humor she liked was the movie *Trouble in Paradise.*[205] We watched the video of it together. One line I remember was when the heroine says to the hero, as they are flirting with each other, "I have a confession to make to you. You're crazy about me." When I laughed, Ayn said, "Now isn't that benevolent humor?"

Once I was wrestling with some minor moral issue; it was an issue of sanctioning evil. I think it was about the morality of continuing to buy Coke after Coca-Cola had started trading with the Russians. Ayn said, "Let me be the Mahatma of morality for you and tell you it's okay." That's the kind of wry humor that she would often use.

How would you describe Miss Rand's character?

She was the most moral person I've ever interacted with. She was a heroine. Morality is rationality, and she was 100 percent rational. She lived her life according to her best understanding of what the right thing to do was.

Do you have any key examples of that integrity? Where she was in a challenging situation and did not buckle?

I don't think there were any challenging situations for her, at least not during her later years when I knew her. She clearly knew what was right and effortlessly did it. You know that she once said, "I'm not brave enough to be a coward: I see the consequences too clearly." That sums up her attitude.

What was the primary benefit you got from knowing Ayn Rand personally?

Seeing what life had to offer. Seeing a totally rational, passionate, heroic human being—the thrill and inspiration of talking with and

---

205 A 1932 Ernst Lubitsch film starring Herbert Marshall and Miriam Hopkins.

interacting with an Ayn Rand heroine, if I can put it that way.

What was the consequence of that?

It's just like what you get from reading *The Fountainhead* or *Atlas Shrugged*. It was the same consequence, in the sense of getting emotional fuel. Not just knowing that kind of person was in the world, but also interacting with her. It was life-altering. And second to that, there were the things I learned. But most of the major philosophical things I learned from Ayn Rand did not actually come from my personal discussions with her, but from her writings and lectures.

What do you miss most about her?

First, the inspiration. Then, I would say the sense of intellectual adventure, the excitement of discovery. At any moment she could say something that would open exciting new avenues of knowledge. And the encouragement, because she was positive about the work of people who were developing or fighting for rational ideas. She would definitely criticize specific things, but she tried to encourage young intellectuals. For instance, once I talked with her shortly after "putting to bed" an issue of my journal, *The Objectivist Forum*.[206] She said I probably felt as she had whenever she "put to bed" an issue of her magazine *The Objectivist*: "That's another small victory." That phrase stuck with me, because it named exactly the perspective I needed to keep in mind when I got immersed in the day-to-day struggles in meeting deadlines; it's still a small victory in the larger battle for my ideas and values.

How would you summarize your attitude toward Ayn Rand?

Awe. I enjoyed her personality, but I was in total awe of her. She was forty years older than me, and she towered so far above me in intellect and life-experience and achievement. So it was really difficult to have a normal, friendly relationship, although she was on that premise. I have an almost irrepressible personality, but if anything could repress it, it was being in the presence of Ayn Rand! It took a very long time before I felt at all free to be spontaneous, but I consciously tried to be as natural as I could.

Let's turn to your conversations with Miss Rand during your visits with her. How did she treat you?

---

206 *The Objectivist Forum* was a bimonthly Objectivist journal that Binswanger published and edited from 1980 through 1987.

Ayn was cordial and she was conversational. She acted to put people at ease.

How did she put you at ease?

She was skilled in holding your context. And in a social sense, she made an effort to put you at your ease and ask you about things that were of common interest.

In the last year or two of her life, we had phone conversations daily, and I came to visit her in her apartment once or twice a week. It wasn't that every time that I went there we would we have a philosophical conversation of any significance. The official reason for my visits was usually to play Scrabble. Sometimes we would talk about current events, and that was interesting too, but not necessarily of lasting historical importance. I tend to remember the philosophical discussions. The most interesting ones were the ones that were more speculative.

Can you give me an example?

Her speculation about "circular time." I never quite got it straight. She didn't have anything really worked out. She said that, taking the universe as a whole, all the motions "cancel out," and therefore there is no one time applicable to the universe as a whole.

We had a couple of conversations about it, but her idea was rather vague, at least for me. On the first occasion, she brought it up, kind of casually; and there was a second time when I followed up, and we explored it together a little more.

The idea was that there is not one time for the whole universe; the universe is not "in" time, time is "in" the universe. She said that time is local, using "local" in contrast to "across the whole universe." So there would be one time for our galaxy, maybe, but if you go out far enough, across hundreds of thousands of galaxies, they're not all in the same time. Now, I'm not saying that this made time relative to a single galaxy because she didn't say that specifically. She didn't know where to draw the line beyond which there stopped being a common time for the whole ensemble, but I gathered that she didn't think one time applied to the whole universe.

It was in that context that she said, "You know, I have this speculation about circular time." I said, "What do you mean?" She said two things that I can recall: The motions "cancel out." She agreed with Aristotle's idea that time is a measurement of motion. She said, "If you look at the whole universe, the motions cancel out." What that means specifically, I don't know, but I saw and was intrigued by the direction in which she was thinking.

Then she said, "A circle is the only form in which you can have a potential infinity without there being a limit." She didn't say the following, but I take it that what she meant was this: you can go on the surface of the earth around the earth forever. Around and around. But there's no infinity involved: it's 25,000 miles around. In some sense, she thought that space and time were circles in that way, which I guess means you eventually get back to the time where you are. I don't really know.

She also said that she had told this idea to someone years before our discussion, and that person had said, "Oh, that's what Einstein says." She said to me that she hadn't heard that before, and she didn't know if it was true. She didn't know if her theory was the same, in fact, as Einstein's theory, but it was intriguing to her that Einstein might have had the same idea.

Did she talk about a theory of propositions?

Not to me personally, but years earlier she had said to a mutual friend that she would write on the organization of concepts into propositions, just as she had written on the integration of percepts into concepts, and concepts into higher-order concepts. That would have been, in effect, volume two of *Introduction to Objectivist Epistemology*.

It wasn't on any list of projects to be done. When Frank died in 1979, she had no projects. She hadn't yet started to do *Atlas* as a miniseries.

The only other late project I can recall concerns politics. When some religious conservatives were launching a movement called "The Moral Majority," Ayn said that she was considering starting a movement called "The Immoral Minority." Her idea was to find people who were not Objectivists but who were horrified at the Moral Majority, the religious right, and would join in a common front to oppose these people.

Did you discuss modern philosophers?

Only a little. Here's an interesting story she told me after a Ford Hall Forum in about 1969. Years before, a professor she knew suggested that he introduce her to other philosophers he knew, so that she could get an entrée into discussing her ideas with contemporary philosophers. And she said, somewhat eagerly, "Oh, really? Would they be interested in meeting me?" And the professor she was talking to said, "Oh yes, after all, you've been to Hollywood and you know all those Hollywood celebrities. You're practically Hollywood yourself. They'd be thrilled to meet you."

Ayn's response to hearing that? She said, "I almost cried." To her, the thought that philosophers would want to meet her to say, "You actually met Gary Cooper?! What's he like?"—that philosophers would be reduced to that star-struck, movie-fan level was such a comedown from what she expected and wanted a philosopher to be that she almost cried.

Did you have conversations on ethics?

What first comes to mind is a minor remark that came up casually, but I think it's significant. She mentioned that her cat had scratched the furniture or done something destructive like that. I turned to the cat and said to it, "Bad cat!" Ayn immediately said, "No—good cat who took a bad action." She said it with a smile on her face—she knew it was cute to apply a philosophical distinction like that to an animal, but in fact that is an important philosophical distinction. A good person can take a bad action, and when you say, "That's immoral," you have to distinguish between: the action is immoral and the person who took it is immoral as a person.

That distinction was just something that came up casually that way. Of course, we also had real discussions on ethics, like the one I already mentioned about the immorality of sacrificing others to self.

One discussion that sticks in my mind was when I told her I was thinking of writing an article against egalitarianism. I was going to criticize it as being a version of "intrinsicism"—the "intrinsic" theory of the good, as she wrote about in "What Is Capitalism?" She told me sternly that if I didn't state that egalitarianism was hatred for the men of ability, it would be a betrayal. At the time, although I could see that egalitarianism did mean this, I didn't see how essential that point is, but over the years I've come to agree wholeheartedly with her on that. Epistemologically, egalitarianism does represent intrinsicism, but the real meaning and motive of it is just what she said.

Let's move to more personal topics. Did you talk with Ayn Rand about her family?

Only a little about her father. He was Victorian and strict. She told me how shocked he was at the sexy material that she had put into her drafts for fiction she was then writing in her teenage years.

She did have in her bedroom a framed montage of photos of her family—pictures that she brought from Russia. But generally, she was not family-oriented.

Anything else about her life in Russia?

She told me about the poverty and starvation after the communist revolution. When a sick horse would fall dead in the street, a crowd of people would descend on it, ripping off pieces for food. Meanwhile, party bosses would speed by in limousines. I asked, "How could the people put up with this?"—meaning the disparity between the communist theory and the daily sight of starving masses and rich bosses. She had an answer immediately. She said it was a combination of two things: cynicism and idealism. Cynicism because the Russians feel, "Well, somebody's always at the top and the masses are always under the boot. That's just the way life is. The poor get ground down." And then there was the idealism. She said people would think, about the Party bosses getting their limousines, "After all, it's for the good of the people, isn't it?"

Did she ever tell you her Russian name?

Not her last name. I understood that she didn't want to reveal her last name because of relatives who could be persecuted. She told me once, "I'm very proud that there's a death warrant out for me in Russia." She went on to explain that when people left Russia claiming they were going to return but didn't, a death warrant was automatically put out on them. So it wasn't anything specific to her ideas or her achievement that made her a particular enemy of the Soviet state in the Soviet state's eyes—at least not on this account— but she was proud anyway that there was a death warrant out on her because of her life-choices.

Did she discuss people's faces, or yours?

She said, "I'm not good at describing faces," literarily, in writing. She regarded that as one area in which she wasn't skilled.

She obviously liked strong, high cheekbones. Frank had that. Once, she showed me pictures of him from about 1930, three soft-focus, black-and-white portraits of him. And she said, "Now, isn't that benevolent? Isn't that the benevolent universe?" She took a lot of pleasure in that. A lot of her attraction to Frank was his benevolent-universe attitude.

I think, personally, that her conviction that the universe is benevolent was tested by events at several times in her life. It would have been easy for anyone in her situation to give in to despair. But she always fought against despair and against being paralyzed by revulsion. Being a highly Romantic artist, she had strong ups and strong downs. And in her writing, her heroes often have to struggle against being overwhelmed by disgust, revulsion at the world. She had to do that sometimes. And I think Frank was very important to her in maintaining her sense of the benevolent universe.

Did she ever talk about that?

After Frank died, she told me she couldn't have done what she had done without him. She said, "I'll write an article for you sometime called 'My Debt to Frank O'Connor.'" This would have been for *The Objectivist Forum*, the journal I was then publishing. So about a year later, I brought it up: "How about doing that article 'My Debt to Frank O'Connor?' You said you would write that for *TOF*." She looked at me grimly and said, "And if you really want to torture me, you'll hold me to that promise." Of course, it would have been terribly painful for her to write that article and relive all those experiences with Frank, who was now gone forever.

Did you talk to her about music?

We had some discussions about music. One was about "America the Beautiful," which she liked. I noted that it has a phrase "from sea to shining sea," which sounds like the line in *Atlas* about Taggart Transcontinental: "From ocean to ocean forever." And she said that line was in fact based on "from sea to shining sea." She also said "America the Beautiful" has a good structural feature: it has stopping points but only one final stopping point. She said she thought that when the ultimate esthetics of music was someday worked out, each song would be represented by an equation or a series of equations. The difficulty of the equation would be what made the complexity of the music.

Did you discuss classical composers?

I had two conversations about who was her favorite composer, and she gave me different answers. In the late 1960s I asked her if Rachmaninoff was her favorite composer, and she said, "No, that's not exactly my sense of life. It's more Chopin." Maybe she said Chopin's "Butterfly Etude." But the idea I came away with was that Rachmaninoff did not rank as high as Chopin for Ayn. I asked, "Too much struggle in the Rachmaninoff?" And she said, "Exactly." But thirteen years later, Chopin came up in a discussion and she said, "Oh, that's music for old ladies."

Did she explain why?

No, but I think in the later comment, she was thinking of Chopin's dreamy nocturnes, but I just can't recall if she said that or I assumed it. I can't believe her love of the "Butterfly Etude" ever changed. That was one of what she called her "top favorites."[207]

What about Mozart?

She was not a Mozart fan. I'm not either, but I happened once to play her the opening movement of his Piano Sonata no. 11 in A Major [Andante grazioso], and she remarked that that was one of his few good melodies.

And "tiddlywink" music?

She shocked me by saying that she thought popular music that you loved gave you a bigger emotional response than the best classical music. I take it that tiddlywink music was a bigger emotional experience for her than she got even from Rachmaninoff or Chopin.

Rock and roll?

She said to me in 1979 or 1980 that the last kind of rock that she could hear as music, as opposed to just noise, was The Beatles. I was surprised that she was that positive about The Beatles.

Did you talk with Miss Rand about investing money?

She was very conservative. She stayed in savings accounts until Alan Greenspan pried her out of them. Here's an interesting incident. Around the late 1960s, I was considering whether to take another investment gamble. I had already made something like fifteen highly risky option contracts, all of which I'd profited on handily. Now I had to decide whether to continue to pyramid or pull out. When I told Ayn, she said to me, "Protect your standard of living."

What did she mean?

Don't risk it. I didn't agree with that, and I thought, "Well, she

---

207 "The Butterfly Etude" was her entry for 1917 in her "musical biography."

knows philosophy but she doesn't know investing." I did pyramid it again, and I lost all of my previous gains. Years later, when I got to know her well, I told her, "You know, Ayn, the only time I didn't listen to you was the time when you told me, 'Protect your standard of living.' I ignored that and went ahead and lost all this money." She looked at me sort of concerned and said, "You should have asked me my reasons." That was a very characteristic "Ayn Rand statement." Her reaction wasn't, "Well, you paid for not listening to me, buddy." Nor, "Oh, I'm so sorry but that's the way life is. We don't learn until we're older." But her reaction was, "Why didn't you ask me my reasons?" She had reasons for everything she said, and had I asked her for her reasons, I might have chosen differently.

Did Miss Rand discuss the differences between the sexes?

She did. She talked about it in the context of the Women's Lib movement. She said that several times in her life, from college on, she had experienced discrimination or prejudice against her because she was a woman. Skepticism like "Well, she's a woman. What's she ever going to do?" She added that she never had the slightest difficulty proving herself, and that that is the attitude that a proper woman should have: "Okay. You don't think I can do the job. I'll show you I can."

Did she talk about the Solidarity movement in Poland in the early 1980s that was trying to overthrow the communist system?

She made an interesting and typically "Ayn Rand comment." She said that the fight against communism in Eastern Europe had to begin with Poland, because the Poles were the only people united by an ideology, namely Catholicism, an ideology opposed to Communism. This was in the context of Communism being on the retreat now. And she thought the strongest opposition to it in its retreat will be in the country with the most unifying ideology, that is, Poland.

I think she said that the only meaningful thing that would make it not a skirmish but an actual permanent change would be the end of censorship. And that came with glasnost—after she had died. After that, the communists couldn't control things.

You noted her turn-of-the-century and European background. Did you discuss etiquette with her?

She said etiquette is important, and that it is not about content—the way ethics is—but was about form, about the "how" of action. She regarded etiquette as a distinct field, something that would have principles, and in that way is on a par with ethics. Etiquette's not just a bunch of isolated "dos and don'ts," anymore than ethics is. It should be a system rationally developed concerning the form of behavior.

The content of etiquette I only know concrete by concrete. She didn't give any principles, but there were many times when she would insist on something that was a matter of etiquette, and it was over some concrete that our discussion of this topic came up. She was herself very polite, and, of course, she'd been raised in turn-of-the-century St. Petersburg, by a father she described as a Victorian, so she was very formal but not in any stiff or brittle way.

There are things that she would consider impertinent, such as a young person being argumentative with her. After one lecture, a small group had gathered around her at the podium to ask her questions. At one point, I heard her say angrily to a young woman in this group, "Are you arguing with me?" That might sound authoritarian if you don't understand that it came after her lecture, given to her audience, when she had no reason to believe that this maybe 23-year-old, who was obviously a victim of modern philosophy, had any standing to argue on an equal basis with her. But she wouldn't have that attitude if she were having a discussion with someone who had earned her respect. She would never, for instance, have said to Henry Hazlitt, "Are you arguing with me?" That would be ridiculous. But if a young person who was a fan of hers came to her lecture to learn her philosophy and was argumentative without knowing what he was talking about, she would consider that impertinent. Note that when she was researching *The Fountainhead*, she wrote to Frank Lloyd Wright, and she was highly respectful. And that's the way she expected her fans to act towards her after she had achieved something that made her world-famous.

Did you discuss beauty with Miss Rand?

No. I mean we talked about girls I thought were beautiful, and Ayn was always supportive of that. There was a blonde model who used to be in ads on the back cover of *TV Guide* who was just gorgeous. I told Ayn about it, and because she subscribed to *TV Guide* and I didn't, she started saving me photos of this model. She liked the idea of a man admiring feminine beauty. I think she was attractive in her youth, but she was not attractive when I knew her, and she knew that, but she never experienced any jealousy. She admired beautiful women. She liked Farrah Fawcett and Jaclyn Smith from *Charlie's Angels*. She was more directly interested in men who were good-looking, but she approved of men lusting after women.

She thought that beauty was a symmetry or harmony of proportions in the features. So she had a very sensory—"mechanical," you could almost call it—concept of beauty.

Did she ever tell you what masculinity is?

Yes, I asked her about just that. And this is so typical Ayn Rand, because there's this whole theory that she had, and it's covered in *The Objectivist,* yet when I asked her, "What is masculinity?" she thought about it and gave me a fresh answer. She gave me an answer that was nowhere in the literature or in the apocryphal stuff that was circulating. I was prepared for the following answers: strength, psycho-epistemological control or some synonym for self-esteem. But what she said was: "decisiveness in action."

Let's now turn to your magazine The Objectivist Forum, *for which Miss Rand was a philosophical consultant.*

Although the first issue of *TOF* came out in February 1980, the decision to start it was made in the summer of the preceding year. So in the summer of 1979 when I took that on, I got to meet with Ayn about it. I hoped she would supply her mailing list, and give her public approval of the venture.

Ayn knew me and was glad I was doing it. But before we finalized the arrangement, she said, "If there's anything in Objectivism that you have any questions about, doubts about, ask me about them and let's get them cleared up before you begin." It wasn't set as a condition of my beginning, but there had been a lot of people in Ayn's circle who had dropped away, who really didn't understand Objectivism. These people knew they were "supposed" to hold some particular Objectivist position, but didn't really believe that position themselves, because they didn't first-handedly understand the reasons behind it and didn't face the issue or even admit their non-understanding to themselves.

Ayn wanted to discuss any disagreements or questions that I might have. So I wrote a list of every topic in Objectivism that I could think of a question on. I listed about twelve things that I didn't fully understand, like the relation of volition to causality and the status of sensory qualities.

When she saw my list, she said something like "Well, this isn't the kind of thing I had in mind." But she said I'd been very diligent. She approved of my coming up with all these questions, but she could see that they were really advanced topics in Objectivism, not at all the kind of thing that she would worry about in my doing *The Objectivist Forum*, just hard questions in philosophy—hard for me, anyway, particularly with my coming from a training in contemporary "analytic" philosophy. Ayn said, "I'm glad that you erred on the side of asking too much. It shows a certain honesty." She gave me points for openness and diligence.

She wasn't worried about my having any of these questions and was happy to talk about them, which we did, leisurely, over the next several months.

What was the audience for TOF?

The audience was intended to be people who were advocates of Objectivism, and its purpose was to provide new knowledge, theoretical and applied, and "emotional fuel" from the Announcements section, which listed upcoming events, such things as the taped lecture courses, that were spreading Objectivism.

I named it "The Objectivist Forum," partly to indicate that it's a forum for students of Objectivism to exchange their ideas, rather than being an official representative of Ayn's views, as her own journal *The Objectivist* had been.

The way it turned out, I never knowingly published anything I disagreed with. Everything I published, I tried to ensure was absolutely true by my own judgment and didn't contradict Objectivism. It didn't turn out to be as much of a forum as I thought in the beginning, but she had been willing even to publish something arguing against an article she had written, taking the other side; but she did suggest it would be a good idea to have a rebuttal in the following issue.

What specific agreements did you have on what she would edit or approve?

Our agreement was that I would submit to her for her approval any article that I wrote, because I was the editor and publisher, so anything that I wrote would have more standing than something by somebody else, because it would have more claim to being really a presentation of Objectivism.

She did want me to tell her in advance the essential theme of the articles by others. And she wanted approval of the Announcements section, so that she wouldn't be indirectly giving her sanction to some event she didn't approve of. Both of us were so much more wary than there turned out to be cause to be. None of our worries ever came close to being materialized, neither in my articles, those of other contributors, nor in the Announcements section. We never disagreed on these things at all.

Tell me about being edited by Ayn Rand.

For the first issue, I decided to write my article "The Swing to the Right." Incidentally, Ayn always called it the "turn to the right," and I always called it the "swing to the right," adopting what was in the press. "Swing to the right" is not as good as "turn to the right" because "swing" suggests it's going to swing back. Of course, that was part of my thesis, that it would, but that's fatalistic, a kind of historical determinist perspective. I should have called it "The Turn to the Right."

I showed a first draft to a lawyer friend, who suggested that I should separate facts from conclusion as a lawyer does: marshal your evidence and then draw your evaluative conclusion. That sounded good to me, so I rewrote the piece and gave it to Ayn. Leonard came over with me to Ayn's apartment, and she read it through while I sat there. I'd see her pencil move every now and then. She was gentle but she wasn't enthusiastic, and she wanted a lot of cuts. So my article was getting rather low marks, and we were dragging ourselves through it, trying to fix it up. Then it occurred to me to say, "Maybe you would have liked the first draft better; it's got the evaluations and the facts together."

Soon afterwards, I brought her the first draft, and she thought it was infinitely better. She asked, "Why did you think you had to separate the facts and the values?" I said, "Well, this friend who's a lawyer told me that that's the way they do it in law and it's more logical." And she said, "No. Actually the reverse is true. It's a stronger integration if you include the values with the facts." We had a little discussion of slanting and why it was not non-objective to include value-judgments in with your presentation of the facts.

What I took away was this. If you write, "It's wonderful that government welfare programs are being rolled back," a person who is pro-welfare can read that, disagree with your evaluation but agree with your facts, so that isn't non-objective writing.

There was a lot of cutting of whole topics that were philosophically interesting but were simply digressions, rather than straight-line logical connections. I was on the premise of putting in every interesting idea that could be remotely related to the topic. Ayn told me subsequently, "Writing is like making a withdrawal from your savings account to make a purchase. You don't want to empty everything out of your savings account, only a small portion of the money. The savings account represents your knowledge. So you always need to know something like three times more, on the topic, than you put into an article." Which I thought was fascinating and was totally new and totally against my premises. This explains a lot about how she wrote—for instance, she got her idea of concepts as based on measurement-omission in the '40s but never said "boo" about it until the mid-60s.

After the first year of *TOF* was completed, she turned me over to Leonard. She said, "I don't need to see everything you write and go over everything with you, because you've got a good track record now, so why don't you work with Leonard in my place, and you can talk to me about things that you want to talk to me about." For instance, I talked extensively with her about my article "The Possible Dream,"[208] which came out in that second year. But basically it was Leonard who was her stand-in in my second year. After Ayn's death, from the third year on, I was on my own.

Did you edit Ayn Rand for TOF?

Yes, when I reprinted her 1981 Ford Hall Forum speech, "The Age of Mediocrity." That was her criticism of the Reagan administration, creationism and the religious right. I edited that speech for written publication. I made editorial suggestions, and we went over them. She had no problem with my doing that. She agreed with most of my suggested changes, which were small, but there were quite a few of them. Some of them she didn't agree with, and she said why.

If what you were saying was rational, she actively appreciated it. She was not touchy about getting my editorial suggestions, she was completely open to them and interested in them and thought them through.

Of course, in this case, it was mainly changes in connection

---

208 *The Objectivist Forum,* February and April 1981.

with preparing a speech for written publication. But I remember one substantive intellectual issue that came up. In this speech, the topic of abortion was covered. I asked her, "Don't you think that there is a right to abort in the eighth or ninth month of pregnancy?" because the way one sentence was worded, it sounded like there might not be a right to abort in the eighth or ninth month when the fetus could live outside the womb. She said, "It's fully formed then," which is true; it can live outside. I said, "Yes, but isn't your point here that there's a crucial difference between the potential and the actual? It hasn't lived yet." And she said, "Yes, but it would be wrong to kill it." I argued, "Well, are you saying it's morally wrong but within the woman's rights?" So we discussed these kind of issues for a minute or two. Then she reached for the pen and decisively and dramatically scratched out the previous phrase, and wrote, in one stroke, this unambiguous statement: "a human being's life begins at birth."

It must have been exciting working with her.

It was. Every interaction with Ayn, every chance to talk to her was a thrill. Even being edited by her—which was at first an intimidating prospect. But as it turned out, she was always considerate, even once when she thought that a draft of an article I gave her was hopeless and I needed to start over from the beginning. She was very considerate of my situation, knowing having to start over would be painful to me. She was affirmatively kind. And a better article did come out of it.

Were there any issues she wouldn't write on for any reason? Something she might just be bored or disgusted by, for example.

I think she considered the topic of anarchism to be so stupid that it was beneath her to write on it. After I wrote a polemic against anarchism for *TOF*, she asked, "So have you gotten that out of your system now?" I said, "Yes."

Her view was if you advocate anarchism, you're a child intellectually. It's virtually beneath discussion. She thought that libertarian anarchism is just the latest wrinkle on the Russian anarchists, whom she had read in Russia as a teenager. Once she had a run-in with someone when she was signing autographs in the Green Room after one of her Ford Hall Forum talks. This guy wanted her to read some piece by a libertarian anarchist, attacking her views; he had it with him and wanted her to take it. She refused, saying contemptuously, "I've read better than these modern anarchists; I read the original Russian anarchists." I think she mentioned Kropotkin. She regarded anarchism as subjectivist, whim-worshipping nonsense.

Let's now move to a new topic, Frank O'Connor. Did she tell you other stories about him?

Yes. Several stand out in my mind. When Frank was six, he started the first grade at a Catholic school. After a few weeks, the first grade teacher from the school contacted his parents and asked, "Where's Frank?" His parents said, "What do you mean? We've been sending him to school every day." The teacher said, "We haven't seen him for weeks." It turned out that Frank, at age six, did not like Catholic school, and so he had taken himself out and enrolled himself in a public school where he was going every day. His family acceded to that and let him stay in the public school. Frank was very anti-religion. Ayn said he was harder against religion than she was. If so, it was probably because Frank had come from a Catholic background and rebelled against it from the start.

She told me another story about when she and Frank were living in Hollywood, around the time that they got married, in 1929. Frank was driving alone and was stopped for speeding, and he thought he was innocent. The police took him before a judge, and he refused to plead guilty, so they made him spend the night in jail. Ayn didn't know what happened to him and was very worried because he didn't come home. But by the way she told the story, she admired his refusal to submit and that he would choose to spend the night in jail rather than give in to an unjust accusation.

Frank, she said, was always interested in which areas a city was expanding into—which suburban areas were growing and which were not. It was almost a hobby of his, she said. When they moved to Hollywood after selling *The Fountainhead* to Warner Brothers, Ayn wanted to buy a Frank Lloyd Wright house, the Storer House, in the Hollywood Hills. She wanted to buy it for esthetic reasons, but the house would have cost a lot to fix up, and that idea was rejected in favor of Frank's idea to buy a house with a lot of land in the San Fernando Valley, because Frank saw that was where Los Angeles was growing the fastest. They found a Richard Neutra house out in the Valley and bought it for $24,000 and sold it about twenty years later for about $200,000 (which in today's dollars would be over $2 million). So Frank was very important in their financial history.

She once told me that Frank was a very good driver. Sometimes she said things to me in the hope that I would pick up on them, which

I didn't always have enough sense to do. In this case, she waited a moment, and when I didn't respond, she said, "Do you know why I say he was a good driver, since I don't know how to drive?" I said, "Why?" She said, "For three thousand miles, I saw his face only in profile." They drove across the country several times, and on these trips he always looked at the road ahead; he never looked at her. This is not actually an achievement—naturally when you're driving, you look at the road—but it's more interesting about Ayn than it is about Frank. I think it's a cute story. She obviously had it set up and composed. I had the feeling I wasn't the first person who had heard it.

Another time, after a lecture, when she and Frank were near the door about to leave the room, some young kid from the audience was arguing with Ayn. She welcomed questions and discussion but she didn't permit arguing, at least not from people who had not proved themselves to her. She said that she wouldn't speak to him anymore, and he popped off with "You're censoring my ideas." Frank shot back, "You don't have any ideas," and they left. So he could put you down too. I never saw him be anything but friendly to Ayn or any of their friends, but he did put down this hostile kid.

She once told me that Ohio is her idea of the archetypical American state. She said that her idea of real America was Ohio, that Frank came from there, she had Roark and Galt come from there, and all her heroes would come from there. I don't mean that she went around praising Ohio, but she thought of it as the most standard American state. I didn't ask her why, but I think that Frank coming from there was a big factor.

I was walking with her once and going a little faster than she wanted to go, and she said she had that same problem with Frank and that she told him, "I can't keep up with those beautiful, long legs of yours." Then he would slow down. Later they shortened it: she would simply say, "Beautiful, long legs," and he would slow down. I thought that was interesting, because she didn't say, "Hey, Frank, come on. Slow down for me, will you?" She didn't say, "Frank, you're going too fast." She made a compliment out of it. That's the way she was with people she admired, and particularly with Frank. She was adoring. She would never boss him around. She would always ask him sweetly for any consideration that she'd want.

There was one notable exception. She said that one time during their early romance, Frank showed up with a moustache that he was growing for a movie part he had. Now Ayn detested facial hair, and when she saw it, she was horrified. She told me she literally screamed when she saw it on him, and said, "Frank, you must take that off!" She got him to shave it off. She said that she never had given him an order like that before or since. She just could not stand it. She told me it was a desecration of his beautiful face.

Was there any contrast in their senses of life?

She lived with him for fifty years, but in no way was Frank, sense of life-wise, the creature of Ayn Rand. I mean you might wonder, "Well, with that forceful personality in front of you, so to speak, maybe you would just take on the coloration of Ayn Rand's sense of life by force of her personality." You could see his sense of life in everything that he did and said and in his paintings. He had a very independent, firsthand attitude towards the world and life. It wasn't exactly the same as Ayn's, because his was more Francisco-ish, and she was the more Rearden-ish. He was more playful. She had a streak of playfulness in her, such as her coming into the living room wearing wedgies and asking, "Don't you think they add to my stature?" But Frank did it effortlessly. Ayn was generally aware when she made a quip. She would have a cat-that-swallowed-the-canary look, because she was pleased with herself for having made a cute quip. Frank would be amusing constantly, effortlessly and unself-consciously.

Were you with Miss Rand when she learned about his death?

No. When he died, she became very depressed. She didn't want to do anything. It took about a year for her to recover somewhat. She didn't have any motivation for any long-range action. She told me she dreamed about him every night. She told Phil Donahue on his show that if she believed there was an afterlife, she'd kill herself right then to go and defend Frank to St. Peter. About grieving for Frank, she said, "I'm like a lion. I go in private to lick my wounds."

Did you see her cry?

Never saw her cry. She also told me once that she didn't believe in suffering in public, that she wouldn't cry in public. She didn't like showing her feelings about Frank's loss. And when I say "public," I don't mean just on national television. I mean in front of other people. As I said, you wouldn't have known she was depressed, but when she was alone in her room it probably flattened her.

She loved Frank so much, and he was so central to her happiness— she knew him from 1926 to 1979, and I can only imagine the loss of someone so inextricably interwoven into your life. She shared everything with Frank. For instance, he was there at all those intellectual conversations. He was there at the epistemology workshops. He was there when she was writing *Atlas*. He was there to drive across country. Just everything.

Plus, there was her theory of femininity as looking up to man, and that a woman's femininity is a relationship to man, not a relationship to reality. So I actually thought she might commit suicide after Frank died. Fortunately that didn't happen, but it was a kind of death for her. But you didn't see it; she always had so much passion that if you had only just met her then you wouldn't have any clue about the dampening effect on her of Frank's death. If you look at her on the Donahue show after Frank had died, you don't see a subdued, passive person. You see the fiery Ayn Rand. I only know that she was depressed because of this faint dimming. Instead of a blast-furnace heat of intensity, it was a raging fire of intensity. After Frank's death, she took antidepressant medication. But Ayn Rand depressed was more intense than you and I, normal.

For about six months after Frank's death, she had no desire to do anything. She only reread Agatha Christie novels, watched TV and met with a few friends. It was nothing pathological, just an understandable loss of ambition, temporarily.

*Can you tell me about Ayn Rand's last writing project, the A*tlas Shrugged *teleplay?*

Someone once asked her, "What would be the value of bringing *Atlas* to the screen, rather than just leaving it as a novel?" Her answer was: concretization. I believe she said that it would make it visual, but it was definitely that it would make the story perceptually real.

And with that in mind, it would have tortured her to see someone, like, say, Spencer Tracy, who was a fine actor but didn't have her kind of looks, playing an Ayn Rand hero but not looking like one. On the other hand, it would also have tortured her to have someone with the right face who couldn't act, who was wooden or unintelligent.

Arline Mann once asked Ayn, "If you had to choose between an actor who could play a leading role for a hero in *Atlas*, but didn't look the part, or one who looked the part but couldn't play the role, which would you take?" Her reaction was that that was exactly the question that she often struggled with, and it was a terrible dilemma because she very much wanted visually to see her kind of man on the screen, but she also valued real acting. For instance, she had been troubled by Gary Cooper's inability to correctly portray Roark. She answered Arline that, unfortunately, she didn't know what to say and she would be tempted in both directions.

By the way, she wanted Vincent Price to play James Taggart at the time she wrote *Atlas*. She wrote it with his face in mind, I believe. He's elegant but with that slouch, that dissipated, creepy look. He oozes. He's so James Taggart. He's so slippery. And with a petty kind of vicious, malevolence.

Do you know anything about the movie deal she had with Henry and Michael Jaffe?[209]

The *Atlas* project was dropped by NBC because of an accidental timing issue: at the crucial moment, a big change occurred in who were the executives in charge of programming. Even though Ayn was not enthusiastic about Stirling Silliphant's script, something could have been done with it. Either she would have fixed it or a new writer would have been hired to do a new script or she would have worked with Silliphant to fix it. But this cancellation happened after they had gotten this far. So the Jaffes were already underway with a rather flat, plodding script. But the Jaffes had an agreement with Ayn, so they had to try to find another broadcaster.

All kinds of avenues were being explored to find money to do this. And Ayn was watching and keeping informed, but I think it was the Jaffes' game. They were the ones out knocking on doors, but she had script approval. They tried to be creative in their approach, but in the end nobody wanted to do it. That's why, when Ayn got excited about Hans Gudegast in the role of Francisco, she knew there were two things she had to do: write the screenplay herself and arrange for private financing through her fans.

Let's turn, then, to Hans Gudegast.

Okay. It started in 1981. She came back from her last Ford Hall Forum, which was April 26, 1981. This was her last year of life. She died on March 6, 1982, so it's eleven months before she died. It was around that time that she told me she had been watching a TV show in reruns, *The Rat Patrol*, which was holding her interest.[210]

Now, at this stage in her life, she's just recovering from Frank's death in November 1979, and she hasn't found anything that interests

---

209 See page 513 for Michael Jaffe's interview.
210 *The Rat Patrol* was a World War II adventure series set in the North African desert.

her. This is a year and a half after the loss of Frank.

She had mentioned a little earlier liking *The Rat Patrol*. She said the show had a premise that she liked, which is: friendly enemies in war. I argued with that to some extent: "If it's war, you should just try to kill the enemy as quickly as you can before you're killed. What do you mean 'friendly' enemies?" She didn't argue against that specifically, but she liked the idea, literarily. It was in that Victor Hugo-way of Gauvain and Lantenac in *Ninety-Three*, where they are father and son on opposing sides, but they respect each other. It makes for good literature. I also think she liked the underlying benevolence of the idea of friendly enemies.

When she got back from Ford Hall Forum, she told me, "I had the idea that one of the characters in *The Rat Patrol* could play Francisco." Now that interested me enormously because Francisco is my favorite character in all of literature. So I watched the show, and I said, "Boy, I see what you mean. This guy has got that Francisco flair." Within a month she had moved from real interest to passion. She was, quote, in love, unquote, with the actor. Now when I say "in love," what I mean is she had a crush on him. She knew that it was a crush—she had a fan's attitude toward a movie figure. There was nothing unrealistic or silly in her attitude. But he was her kind of hero. He looks like Cyrus, actually.[211] He was German. His real name was Hans Gudegast, which he changed to Eric Braeden after *The Rat Patrol* series. He spoke with a slight German accent, and he played a German character, so he had a European flair. Right around this time, she said, "I thought I would have to cast *Atlas* with one of those flat-footed Americans." Gudegast was very aristocratic.

Anybody who knows Eric Braeden from *The Young and the Restless* knows he is a romantic lead. But the way he is now has nothing to do with the dashing, sarcastic, mockingly superior, unmoustachioed German army commander that he played on *The Rat Patrol*. She really thought that he played her kind of man, and she said, "I don't think you can act that part unless you have something of that in you." True, you can be inconsistent, you can contradict it—now this is me adding in words and context, but I think this is what she means: if you don't know what it feels like to be at ease with yourself, have real self-esteem and love your ability to perceive the world, you wouldn't be able to project that in acting. You have to base your acting on what's within yourself, at least in part.

---

211 Cyrus Paltons, Ayn Rand's first literary hero, appeared in the 1914 novel *The Mysterious Valley* by Maurice Champagne. The story was illustrated with drawings, including some of Cyrus.

So it was like in her play *Ideal*, when her Greta Garbo-type character, Kay Gonda, goes around looking for someone who can perceive what she's trying to project, the kind of heroism she portrays. As you get from *Atlas Shrugged*, there's the ordinary kind of average person, then the good but unexceptional kind of person, like Eddie Willers, and then there are real heroes—passionate, independent individuals who live on a different plane. She says these are not superhuman people, but they are people who live with an intensity and an ability that is much beyond the ordinary. Life is supremely important to them. And it's those kind of people that Ayn created in her novels and wanted to find in reality, just as Kay Gonda wanted to.

She thought she found it in Hans. Now, I'm not saying in Captain Dietrich, who was the character he played. I'm saying in Hans the actor, for being able to portray that. She felt that he must be her kind of man himself, even if he's got problems and contradictions. She knew that this was a risky leap. She was never foolish about it. "Hope" would be the right word for it. Her mind knew, "Well, he's probably got this and that failing." But hope was what was dominant. "I hope that what I see in him is real." So she became dedicated. Hans became the focus of her life. She said that when she discovered him, when she made the connection of him and Francisco, it was like the sun came out again for her. She had admired him while she had watched the series in the previous months, but once she thought of him as Francisco, it all clicked. And that's when her infatuation or crush began. That was the first thing that brought her back to life after the loss of Frank. She was always a man-worshipper. When she didn't have Frank to look up to, she needed some man to look up to. Hans supplied that.

She began to research who he was. She probably wondered why wasn't he a world-famous actor. Because he really was an excellent actor. She found out he was on *The Young and the Restless*. Although soap operas are great steady work, and their stars achieve a certain fame and status, it's lame and pathetic compared to being a movie star. She thought maybe his talent couldn't break through in today's culture. She probably thought that here is a man of obvious ability and talent, my kind of man. And where does he end up? On a soap opera.

So she was motivated to "rescue" him professionally. She regarded him as a man of superlative ability who was being ignored by his profession—ignored because he was too good or because there weren't any roles being cast for the kind of hero he could play. He was a victim of his own virtue, like Steven Mallory in *The Fountainhead* or Richard

Halley in *Atlas Shrugged*. Probably Ayn felt that way herself at times, particularly in the '30s—tremendous talent, not being perceived, limping along. So she decided he would be ideal to cast as Francisco in a movie of *Atlas*.

By the way, let me set the record straight here: there was never, to my knowledge, anyone else that she was really enthusiastic about casting for one of the heroes for *Atlas,* except casting Hans Gudegast for Francisco. Her strongest motivation, the thing that really set her on fire, was that by having him as Francisco in a movie or miniseries of *Atlas Shrugged,* she would be giving him the audience he deserved, helping his career and saving him from the world. In her eyes, he was the neglected hero, ignored by the world, whom she was going to vindicate. That was why she sat down to write the screenplay for *Atlas Shrugged*. And that's why it was easy, as long as she thought that about him.

During this early period of infatuation, she said Eloise asked her, "When you die and go to heaven and Frank is there and Hans is there, who are you going to choose?" Ayn told me this with some incredulity. She said, "And I told Eloise, 'Frank! Of course.'" She thought it was bizarre that Eloise even asked the question.

So she started to see herself as Hans's defender. And, like her heroes, Ayn took action. She didn't just moon over her values or her men. In this case, she began finding out more about him. First, she bought a VCR—and this was 1981, when they were pretty new. She started researching Hans through her agents, getting a list of everything Hans had ever been in. She arranged to take pictures of him off the TV. It's technically hard to do, or so she was told, so she had a lab make some pictures. She read interviews of him. She rented the movies he was in. She tracked down all the information she could.

She made a videotape of every episode of *The Rat Patrol*. I think it was originally on the air for two years, from 1966 to '68, almost sixty episodes. She had five six-hour tapes. I have several of those tapes, where she recorded the episodes and then graded them. She would write down the episode's name, and then she would put a letter grade next to it. The basis for grading them was how much Hans was in it, and how well the episode showcased him. Occasionally there would be an episode where Hans didn't even appear because he was the German captain, and not every story involved him. Those episodes would get an F. So it was a Hans-relative system.

Do you remember her favorite episode?

Well, there were several. The "B Negative Raid," where Hitch, the American patrol's second-in-command, needs a blood transfusion. He's got a rare blood type. So the hero of the series, who is the American sergeant, Sam Troy, played by Christopher George, sneaks into the German camp, puts a gun to the head of Captain Dietrich and orders him to search for anyone with B negative blood. It turns out there's only one person who has it, and it's an American deserter. The series had interesting plots like that. Ayn loved any of them with this face-to-face confrontation between Dietrich and Sergeant Troy.

Any others?

One she didn't like was "The Fatal Reunion Raid." Reading from her notes, I see she wrote: "Gabrielle and her husband. Lousy B.S. No Hans Gudegast."

Now let me read you her notes on one she liked. "5/28. 'The Street Urchins Raid.' A." And there's a check mark next to the "A." Then, in parentheses: "Little Arab boy in aerial photographs." That was to remind herself what it was about. "Some magnificent shots of HG's face. But not enough of him in story. Marked M-R and U.A." I think the "M-R" denoted "Mirisch-Rich," the production company, and "U.A." was United Artists. She was even interested in the business angle of who did this show, as someone possibly to be used in a movie production of *Atlas*.

Here's an A+. "'The Decoy Raid.' 6-1-81. A+. HG kills a vicious German S.S. officer and helps the Rat Patrol. HG is excellent. There are wonderful close-ups and the story is built around him." Marked "M-R and U.A."

Sometimes I went to her apartment to watch the show with her. When it came on, she would give a little military salute. It was half in jest and half serious. I think she liked an occasional hand gesture, appropriate to the meaning of events.

A sense of drama, in a way, isn't it?

Yes, but it's also symbolizing the meaning of things in some sort of physical form, like at the end of *Atlas* when Galt moves his hand in the air to make a dollar sign.

Did she have any other purpose in supporting Hans Gudegast?

When she made *The Fountainhead* movie, it brought her into conflict with a lot of people involved in making it. She said she wouldn't go through that again with *Atlas* and that she wouldn't have done it with *The Fountainhead* movie if she had known how hard it was going to be and how painful. I don't know if she absolutely meant that, but she had totally underestimated the problem in dismembering your baby, your novel, for another medium, and in dealing with all those people wanting to make changes over months and months. She said she would only undertake *Atlas* as a movie if she could have at least one artistic ally, such as a director, or a star actor or a producer or a writer who shared her sense of life. Now she thought that Hans would be that ally.

Tell me more about your interactions with her concerning Hans.

She would talk to me about Hans in a particular show—what he looked like and how he came across—and ask what I thought. I was her confidante, and that strengthened our friendship. I also responded to Hans, and I shared her interest in Hans as Francisco. She loved being able to talk about Hans. I would help her tape the shows. I would go over her grades with her, and I would say, "That was a great scene there. Look at his profile." That kind of thing.

Hans had this characteristic way of talking. It was a little different from other people, and I was able to pick it up and imitate it with a little German accent that I can put on. She said it would give her a thrill just to hear me do that. That's how totally wrapped up and worshipful she was of Hans.

Later, when Ayn was writing the screenplay for the miniseries of *Atlas*, one evening she let me and my then girlfriend read part of it aloud for her, with me doing Francisco's lines in Hans's voice. I didn't feel up to that task. To play Francisco in front of Ayn Rand in somebody else's voice was a little intimidating, but I gave it a shot. She had my girlfriend read Dagny's lines. It was a Dagny and Francisco scene.

So I tried to do it, but I can't act. I read these lines and I just went up in pitch on the ends, as Hans characteristically did, adding a bit of a German accent. And she loved it. My girlfriend did an uninspired straight reading of the words that Dagny had in this dialogue, and Ayn praised us both. She was delighted in hearing it, picturing Hans delivering it. I knew my reading stank to high heaven, but Ayn got out of it what she wanted, and I was glad to be able to please her.

At her New Orleans talk in November 1981, did anything happen regarding the Atlas *movie?*

What I'll always remember is that at one point during the question period, she said something like "I have some ideas for casting." I was seated in the front row—and she looked right at me and asked, "Should I tell them?"—because I was her confidante about Hans. So I shook my head back and forth, "No. No." And she didn't.

I remember her telling me on the train coming back from New Orleans that maybe *Atlas Shrugged* should be shown in the theaters, in two parts, two three-and-a-half-hour movies. She pointed to some precedent where this had already been done a long time ago.[212] She told me that she had come up with the idea of putting *Atlas* on TV as a multi-part series before there were what later came to be called "miniseries"—long before the first miniseries, which was *Rich Man, Poor Man* [1976]. So she was active in thinking of different ways to bring *Atlas* to the screen and had different creative ideas.

Did her "crush" subside?

As she got more information about him, certain negatives started turning up. There was an interview in *TV Guide* or *Soap Opera Digest* in which he said a couple of things that were pretty deflating. One was that he had been glad in *Rat Patrol* to be able to play a sympathetic German, because the Germans got a bad deal in Hollywood. Germans, he said, were treated as stereotypical sadists in all stories about World War II, and he was glad to be able to redeem the German army or something like that. It wasn't pro-Nazi, but it was not anti-dictatorship either. It was not a good sentiment, and Ayn was very disappointed in him for that.

The interview listed his interests. They were physical, outdoorsy things. That was a disappointment to her, because she wanted him to be like her heroes—maybe, "His only hobby is reading Victor Hugo in the original French." At least something a little bit intellectual. But he seemed to be interested in the physical, not the intellectual. That was maybe a bigger turn-off for Ayn even than the pro-German sentiment, which she also didn't like. And there were a couple of other touches like that. So now she didn't know quite what to make of him. Obviously, she couldn't say he's not what she thought he was on the basis of just a couple of indications like that—which might have been cooked up by his press agent anyway.

Then we saw some of his other movies. She didn't want to watch

---

212 Ayn Rand might have been referring to one of her favorite films, *Das Indische Grabmal* (*The Indian Tomb*), a two-part, three-and-a-half-hour film, which she first saw in Petrograd in 1923.

him on *The Young and the Restless*, because he wore a moustache
and she loathed moustaches. Not only did she loathe moustaches, but
when it was a beautiful face, like Frank's or like she thought Hans's
was, she regarded it as a vilification of that beauty, a blasphemy of a
beautiful face as well as something ugly on any face. Sometimes she
would see pictures of him in soap opera magazines, and she would put
her finger over the moustache and try to imagine how he would look
if it weren't there.

But we rented some of his other movies. One of them was *Escape
from the Planet of the Apes* [1971], where he's a villain. He always
seemed to be cast as a bad character. And in *Escape from the Planet
of the Apes*, he's defeated by the apes, who are good characters, and
there's one scene at the end where he's not only defeated but he's
humiliated. It isn't this, but it's something like: he's thrown face down
into the mud and people walk over his back. When Ayn saw that, she
said, "I want to die." And she meant it for that moment.

Then there was *Colossus: The Forbin Project* [1970], with Hans in
it. She liked looking at him, but again he loses in the end; he's put in his
place in the end. It wasn't a good movie.

I watched with her a rerun of an episode of the *Mary Tyler Moore
Show* (1977) that had Hans in it. The climax was a pie being shoved
in his face by the Ted Baxter character. And she said after seeing it, "It
seems like they have to drag him down." She didn't enjoy it. After the
Mary show, she said, "I know it's good that he was on the show, that
it gave him exposure, and probably the person who cast him in that
role was doing him a favor professionally by using him, but to see
him, this ideal character with a pie shoved in his face and humiliated
at the climax is hideous."

In everything she saw, maybe four different roles, he was always
the villain, and in the end his face would be slapped, he would be
defeated and humiliated. So she didn't enjoy any of the things she saw
him in other than *The Rat Patrol*. Actually, on *Mary*, which was the last
in these series of things, he played a hostile, supercilious critic, which
in a way was a parody of his own aristocratic arrogance. They used
the mocking arrogance that Ayn always associated with her heroes and
turned it into something supercilious and negative.

After that he seemed to go downhill in many ways. He also started
to lose his accent, and his roles seemed to be cardboard characters, and
the whole thing began to be more and more discouraging to Ayn.

By November, when she went down to give her New Orleans

speech, she had concluded, I think, that he wasn't her kind of hero, but he might have an element of greatness within him, and on the chance that he did, she had to go ahead with her *Atlas* project. She became progressively disillusioned with him over about two or three months, but still held out hope. Even after November, she said she was going to move to Hollywood to do the movie. She was quite serious. She said that she might have to spend two years in Hollywood, a place which she loathed. But she was ready to move. So, as old as she was, once she had found a man to look up to, she was ready to do anything. I told her I wanted to go out to Hollywood with her. She said: "Fine. I'll make you my guru so you can go on the set and see the filming." So it was really getting exciting.

What happened after her talk in New Orleans?

She continued writing the teleplay for *Atlas*.[213] At first, it looked like she could raise the necessary money.

When I would come over at 8 o'clock, I would ask if there was any news. Like, "Any word on channel so and so running this?" It seemed like there was going to be no problem raising the money. Then people who had promised the money kind of disappeared, and there was a problem raising the money. Meanwhile, the more important thing was that she was getting discouraged with Hans Gudegast and therefore losing her motivation. She did write the whole first miniseries episode, the first two hours.

What happened next?

Nothing was going well. Her health was declining. She got sick on the train coming back from New Orleans, and she never was in full health again. She had to go into the hospital for a little while. And the financing was not developing. Hans, her inspiration, was looking more and more like someone she wouldn't particularly admire as a person. So the writing slowed down. Actually, it began to slow down before November. She worked maybe two or three days in December. She certainly was not progressing and not happy with her own situation. The last writing she did was on January 1, 1982, the first page of the second part of the proposed miniseries. She did that writing to continue her tradition of doing on the first day of the year what she planned to do throughout the year.

---

213 She began writing on June 10, 1981.

Did she ever communicate with Hans Gudegast?

No. She considered writing to him, but decided against it. She didn't want to get his hopes up prematurely. She wanted to be further along in the *Atlas* project before she contacted him.

So Hans doesn't know the story to this day. He doesn't know how tremendously she admired his looks, his bearing, his ability to project greatness in his acting. In that Captain Dietrich role, he embodied for her the special kind of confident and proud hero that she created in her novels.

That's what her life was about, actually. The dramatization of the human ideal and the formulation of the philosophy that underlies it, the system of principles that explains and defends the heroic in man.

What comes to mind here is what she said in "The Goal of My Writing": "The motive and purpose of my writing can best be summed up by saying that if a dedication page were to precede the total of my work, it would read: 'To the glory of Man.'"

Index

Note: A bold-face number indicates an interview with that person.

K

L